Kenya: Into The Second Decade

KENYA: INTO THE SECOND DECADE

Report of a mission sent to Kenya
by
The World Bank

Chief of Mission and Coordinating Author
JOHN BURROWS

Published for
THE WORLD BANK
by
THE JOHNS HOPKINS UNIVERSITY PRESS
Baltimore and London

Copyright © 1975 by the International Bank for
Reconstruction and Development

All rights reserved
Manufactured in the United States of America

Library of Congress Cataloging in Publication Data:

International Bank for Reconstruction and Development.

    Kenya, into the second decade.
    Bibliography: p.
    Includes index.
    1. Kenya—Economic conditions. I. Burrows, John R.
II. Title
HC517.K415   1975   330.9′676′204   75-10895

ISBN 0-8018-1754-4 (clothbound)
ISBN 0-8018-1755-2 (paperbound)

Foreword

This is the tenth in the current series of World Bank country economic reports, all of which are listed on the following page. They are published, in response to a desire expressed by scholars and practitioners in the field of economic and social development, to aid and encourage research and the interchange of knowledge.

Economic reports on borrowing countries are prepared regularly by the Bank in support of its own operations. These surveys provide a basis for discussions with the governments and for decisions on Bank policy and operations. Many of these reports are also used by the governments themselves as an aid to their economic planning and by consortia and consultative groups of governments and institutions providing assistance in development. All Bank country reports are subject to the agreement of—and several have been published by—the governments concerned.

The present study is the result of the work of a mission to Kenya under the leadership of John Burrows. Although certain of the quantitative projections may have been affected by such recent events as increases in petroleum prices, the basic analysis remains valid.

HOLLIS CHENERY
Vice President for Development Policy
The World Bank

Washington, D. C.
June 1975

WORLD BANK COUNTRY ECONOMIC REPORTS

Published for the Bank by The Johns Hopkins University Press

Kenya: Into the Second Decade
Yugoslavia: Development with Decentralization
Nigeria: Options for Long-Term Development
Economic Growth of Colombia

Published by the World Bank

Turkey: Prospects and Problems of an Expanding Economy
Senegal: Tradition, Diversification, and Economic Development
Chad: Development Potential and Constraints (also published in French as *Le Développement du Tchad: Possibilités et Limites*)
Current Economic Position and Prospects of Peru
Current Economic Position and Prospects of Ecuador
Employment in Trinidad and Tobago

NOTES

KENYA'S AREA: 582,647 sq.km.
POPULATION: 12.1 million (1972)
DENSITY: 20 per sq.km. (overall)
122 per sq.km. (arable land)

UNITS OF VALUATION

The official unit of currency in Kenya is the Kenya Shilling (Sh.). However, in accordance with the practice of the Kenya Government, most large values in the report are expressed in Kenya Pounds (£).

£1 = Sh.20
Sh.1 = 100 cents

Some values have been expressed in terms of constant US dollars for purposes of international comparison.

CURRENCY EQUIVALENTS

For most of the period since Independence, Kenya, together with Uganda and Tanzania, has maintained a par value of 7.14286 shillings per US dollar. This is the exchange rate used throughout the report. Kenya has adopted a central rate of 8.61675 shillings per SDR.

US dollar = Sh. 7.14286
SDR = Sh. 8.61675
Kenya Pound = $2.80

FISCAL YEAR
July 1 through June 30

TABLE OF CONTENTS

Foreword v

Preface ix

Summary xi

Maps 243–250

PART I EMERGING ISSUES AND POLICY OPTIONS

Chapter 1 Major Goals and Achievements 3
        2 Resources Available for Development 7
        3 Efficiency of Resource Use 13
        4 A Strategy for Increasing Growth and Employment 24
        5 Feasibility, Constraints, and Tactics 33
        6 Implications for Management 45

          Statistical Tables 51
          Select Bibliography 76
          Postscript 81

PART II THE ANALYTICAL ANNEXES

Annex One The Macro-Economic Model and Projections 85
Chapter 1 The Nature and Uses of the Model 87
        2 The Structure of the Model 89
        3 Analysis of the Past and Hypotheses for the Future 93
        4 Projections and Policy Analysis 104
        5 Some Development Policy Issues 111

          Appendices 114
          Statistical Tables 134
          Charts 157

Annex Two Fiscal Policy for Development 161
Chapter 1 Introduction 163
        2 Development Finance 168
        3 Fiscal Policy and Income Distribution 184
        4 Employment and Rural Development 194
        5 A Fiscal Strategy for Development 201

          Appendix 206
          Statistical Tables 208

Annex Three Key Issues in the Private Sector 255
Chapter 1 Introduction 257

	2 The Role and Performance of the Private Sector	260
	3 Price Signals and Performance	264
	4 Controls on Trade and Foreign Exchange	294
	5 Foreign Private Investment	307
	6 Conclusions	316
	Appendices	318
	Statistical Tables	329
Annex Four	Domestic Savings and Financial Intermediation	351
Chapter 1	The Role of Saving Propensity in Growth	353
	2 Domestic Savings in Kenya	355
	3 Development in Financial Intermediation	360
	4 Some Policy Implications	362
	Appendix	367
	Statistical Tables	372
Annex Five	Priorities for Planning and Project Design	385
Chapter 1	Priorities for Planning	387
	2 Plan Organization	391
	3 Expanding Planning Capacity	394
	4 Implications for Project Design and Appraisal	403
	Appendix	410
Annex Six	Priorities for External Assistance	415
Chapter 1	Aid Requirements and Terms of Aid	417
	2 Sectoral Composition of External Assistance	421
	3 Conditions of Financial Assistance	424
	4 Conditions of Technical Assistance	431
	5 Aid Coordination	434
	Statistical Tables	438

PART III   AGRICULTURAL SECTOR SURVEY

	Preface	447
Chapter 1	The Role of Agriculture in the Kenya Economy	448
	2 The Land and Its People	453
	3 A Proposed Development Strategy	458
	4 Policy and Program Improvement	461
	5 Public Services Organization	492
	Appendices	494
	Statistical Tables	505
	Chart	526
	Index	527

Preface

In 1973 Kenya was nearing the end of its first decade of independence, and the Government was drawing up the Third National Development Plan in preparation for the second decade of economic management. The World Bank sent out an economic mission in March/April of that year to determine how far Kenya had come during the past ten years, to review its major successes and failures, to assess prospects and pinpoint future dangers, and to identify major policy issues. This report represents the views and judgements of that mission.

This is not the first World Bank report on Kenya, but the latest in a series. In 1963 a major Bank report on the Kenya economy reviewed the development prospects of the colony as it moved toward Independence.[1] Since that time the Bank has prepared a series of unpublished economic reports on Kenya. In 1967 a major Bank mission reviewed the revised development plan (1966–70), and in 1969 another mission reviewed the second plan (1970–74). Each of these missions and the subsequent reports differed in composition and scope, but each represented a critical review of Kenya's national plans and offered constructive comments. At the request of the Government, both the 1969 mission and the recent 1973 mission visited Kenya while the new plan was still in draft form, so that the mission's comments could be taken into account before the plans were published.

A report of this nature must essentially represent a compromise between comprehensiveness and brevity. The Kenya economy is much too broad and its operations much too complex to allow for complete coverage. We have therefore deliberately circumscribed the scope of the report in a number of ways.

First, the report is intended to be a review of the operations of the Kenya economy only. It makes no attempt to review progress or prospects of the wider geographical region to which that economy belongs, or even to assess in any comprehensive way how Kenya's development prospects are affected by its membership in the East African Community (EAC). Some of these relationships are referred to when they are of particular relevance, but the report does not try to review the Kenya economy from an integrated regional perspective. This limitation does not in any sense mean that either the mission or the World Bank feels that regional economic considerations are unimportant. On the contrary, it is clear from its major financial commitment to the EAC corporations and institutions that the Bank fully supports this experiment in regional cooperation that Kenya, Tanzania, and Uganda have pioneered.

To remain manageable in scope, the report focuses on Kenya and ignores the wider community. This narrow focus becomes seriously myopic only in those areas (on trade policies, for instance) in which Kenya clearly must act in concert with its partners in the community. Again, although we try to suggest what options might be best for Kenya, viewed in isolation, we are conscious that these options will have to be reviewed by all three partner states, and that the decisions will ultimately be taken with the interests of the whole region in mind.

Second, the scope of the mission is circumscribed in another respect. Even in its focus on Kenya, the report does not undertake a detailed review of all sectors of the economy and of all economic problems. The economic literature on Kenya is prolific, and we have drawn heavily on this. In particular the recent report on employment, incomes, and equality in Kenya published under the combined aegis of the International Labour Organisation and the United Nations Development Programme has presented a very comprehensive and innovative analysis of unemployment and poverty.[2] We make no

---

1. Edmond H. Leavey et al., *The Economic Development of Kenya.* Baltimore: The Johns Hopkins Press, 1963.
2. *Employment, Incomes and Equality—A Strategy for Increasing Productive Employment in Kenya* (Geneva: ILO, 1972), hereafter referred to as the ILO/UNDP report.

attempt to repeat this. Rather, we see this report, with its sharper macro-economic focus, as being essentially complementary to the ILO/UNDP report. We do not attempt to add in any significant way to the existing knowledge on the various sectors; instead, we try to consolidate and integrate this knowledge into our overall understanding of the operation of the economy. However, because of the importance ascribed to agriculture in its macro-economic strategy, the report incorporates the principal findings of the previously unpublished 1973 World Bank agricultural sector survey report on Kenya.

Third, we do not place great emphasis on reviewing progress under previous plans or on describing the objectives of the 1974–78 plan, because these tasks have been done very well by the Government itself in the 1974–78 plan document.

Our report therefore does not try to deal with everything in depth. On the contrary, it draws heavily from the wide range of studies already available and tries to use this information to provide a synoptic view of the way in which the economy as a whole functions and perhaps some new insights into important relationships among variables. Thus, although the report tries to be as informative as possible and to present sufficient background data on most aspects of the economy for the general reader, the detailed analysis is highly selective and focuses mainly on a number of key issues which we see as critical to the future development of Kenya and the well-being of its people.

A further limitation of the report is that it was prepared before the recent increase in oil prices and the upsurge of world inflation in commodities. These events will profoundly affect Kenya, as they have other countries, and we refer briefly to some of the implications in the postscript to Part I. In general, we believe that recent events serve mainly to reinforce the conclusions of the report and add urgency to most of its prescriptions. But we do not attempt to incorporate these developments into the analysis of the report, mainly because their full dimensions and implications are still far from clear.

The report is divided into three parts. Part I traces the major developments in Kenya's first decade of independence, identifies the emerging issues, and examines the major options open to the Government in the future, as the mission sees them. Part II contains six analytical annexes, which discuss the major issues in detail and extend the technical arguments. Part III comprises the abbreviated main report of the 1973 Kenya agricultural sector survey. The analysis is assisted by tables appended to each section of the report and by a number of maps and charts. A select bibliography of references and some major sources of information on Kenya are given at the end of Part I.

Parts I and II are based on the findings of the main economic mission, consisting of Bank staff members Ramgopal Agarwala, macro-economist; George Beier, general economist, project planning and external assistance; Ved Gandhi, fiscal economist; Randolph Harris, general economist, public services; and Martin Wolf, general economist, private sector. Also participating in the mission's work were Sven Burmester, education; Andrew Hayman, tourism; and Frank Stubenitsky, health. Lyle Hansen was adviser to the mission. The abbreviated agricultural sector survey is based on the findings of a mission which visited Kenya in October/November 1972 under the leadership of L. T. Sonley. Other members of the survey mission are listed on page 447. Brian Svikhart coordinated all editorial and production activities for the report, Sadie Gold edited the manuscript, and Barbara Spies prepared the index. The main mission and survey mission reports were discussed with the Government of Kenya during the course of 1973 and the Government's comments have been incorporated whenever possible. The present volume, however, does not necessarily reflect the view of the Government of Kenya or any of its officers, and the overall conclusions remain my responsibility as chief of mission and coordinating author.

JOHN R. BURROWS

Summary

Kenya gained independence twelve years ago, and in reviewing the economy's past development we acknowledge the excellent progress which Kenya has achieved in terms of growth during this period. In many respects, the performance of the Kenya economy has been quite remarkable by comparison to most other countries faced with similar problems. Only with respect to the growth of employment and its impact on the poverty of the lowest income groups has Kenya's performance been rather disappointing. But the difficulties of distributing the benefits of development equitably over as diverse a community as Kenya's are immense. In particular, there is no easy way to ensure that any development program will reach the really needy. Thus, while pointing out Kenya's shortcomings in distribution and employment, we are well aware that this is a field of development in which problems are far easier to identify than to solve.

The purpose of this report, however, is not to pick holes in past performance. Rather we try to analyze the processes which determine the growth of the economy and to identify the emerging problems and constraints. A recurring hypothesis is that the Kenya economy has reached a turning point in its development, and that the job of mobilizing resources and using them efficiently is likely to become increasingly complex over the second decade. A fast pace of development may be harder to sustain as a result, and the problems of widespread poverty and growing unemployment could grow even more serious unless there is a pronounced shift in the nature of the development process.

There are essentially three arguments to support this general thesis. The first is that, as Kenya has expanded her investment program, the economy has come much nearer to the limits of the resources available for development, and that this emerging resource constraint will inevitably force a harsher discipline on the economic choices facing Kenya. We show that the resource constraint is an amalgam of several factors. One part of the problem is that Kenya's potential for mobilizing additional resources is already limited by the very success of its past performance. Domestic savings, for example, are already very high by comparison with other countries. Another part of the problem concerns those factors—such as the terms of trade or the availability of external assistance—which critically affect the resources available for development, but over which Kenya has little or no control.

The second thesis is a familiar argument about the end of the "easy" stage of growth, and applies particularly to our analysis of investment and growth. Much of past investment has been in the simpler forms of import substitution in manufacturing, in high potential land in agriculture, and in infrastructure sectors, such as roads, where absorptive capacity could be most easily expanded. But the argument also applies to other parts of our review. For example, Kenya has already instituted most of the "easy" taxes and, while additional sources of revenue can be tapped, the necessary fiscal measures may be much more difficult to implement, both politically and administratively.

The third argument occurring throughout our analysis contends that Kenya has not benefited as much as it might have from the very creditable savings and investment record of the past. We show, for example, that Kenya not only had a poor payoff to its investment program in terms of employment and distribution, but that even growth might have been higher under different conditions. We apply this argument first to the private sector, to show that rapid growth of the urban formal sector has not always been to the benefit of society as whole, and then to the allocation of public expenditure, to show that the efficiency of resource use by the public sector has been falling.

The thesis underlying much of the report, that Kenya is at a turning point, should not be overstated. Kenya has not yet reached a point of crisis, and its achievements over the first decade generate confidence in its ability to cope with the changing circumstances and new challenges of the future. Our report does not recommend any dramatic or revolutionary change in the Kenyan way of life or in the management of the economy.

But we do emphasize that a significant change in the pattern and process of growth is needed if Kenya is to achieve rapid growth in incomes and employment within the resources likely to be available, and that a more intensive and rather different style of economic management may well be necessary.

Extending the analysis, we identify what might be an appropriate strategy for the second decade. Within the framework of a macro-economic model, which is described at length in Annex One, we project the development of the economy during the 1974–78 plan period, and to 1985, on varying assumptions about the rate and structure of growth and the use of various policy instruments. In making these projections we are conscious of the inadequacy of our data and of the limitations of the economic model used in our analysis. In particular, we stress that the projections do not purport to predict the future, but merely seek to indicate the likely direction of the economy in response to alternative policy measures. The initial set of projections reflects the kind of development which would result from a continuation of the pattern of growth which Kenya has experienced in the past. The resulting "basic scenario" is found to be unacceptable for two main reasons. First, it suggests that Kenya would eventually face an unmanageable balance of payments deficit, even with fairly optimistic assumptions about Kenya's foreign exchange earnings and the likely level of external assistance. Second, and perhaps more serious, the basic projections suggest that this pattern of development would not succeed in relieving unemployment or in making a substantial impact on widespread poverty. In fact, even if the resources could be found to maintain a high overall rate of growth, the poorest levels of society might end up even poorer in real terms.

The mission is forced to conclude, therefore, that there must be a significant change in the pattern of growth if Kenya is to achieve the dual goals of rapid growth and increasing employment and incomes within its resource constraints. What is required, quite simply, is to induce the economy to operate more efficiently: to utilize fewer inputs of scarce resources (particularly capital and skilled manpower) and generate greater benefits (particularly new employment and incomes). To achieve this, the mission proposes a progressive change in the *structure* of growth, with greater emphasis on agriculture and other domestic resource-based industries, and a reform in the *process* of growth in all sectors, particularly through factor price changes. When these changes in the pattern of growth are combined and fed into the model as the "preferred strategy," the results are encouraging. Moreover, these two general areas of reform are shown to be complementary, so that while a change in key factor prices (particularly the cost of capital and the exchange rate) are most useful in alleviating the resource constraint, a shift in the structure of growth (and particularly a faster development of agriculture) is the most powerful instrument for increasing employment and attacking poverty.

We emphasize both in the main report and in the annexes that the "preferred strategy" is not intended to be a package of specific policy proposals, nor are the projections in the model supposed to be forecasts. However, we do suggest that the various components of the "preferred strategy" might indicate the general directions in which the economy could move over the next decade, to ensure that the goals which Kenya has set itself can be achieved.

The report examines the feasibility of all these changes as practical alternatives. In particular, in view of its importance, Part III reviews both the potential of the agricultural sector and the constraints to its further development. We conclude that, given continued good management and political commitment to development, Kenya can go a long way in the directions indicated. But the task will not be easy, and many of the changes will take time to implement and then take effect. We stress that the restructuring of growth will be hampered by the absorptive capacity of agriculture, by the momentum of development built up in the infrastructure sectors, and by the need for growing expenditure on social services. These call for an intensification of planning in the public sector: not only accelerated project preparation and implementation in agriculture, but also a closer identification of priorities and probably some curb on expenditure on infrastructure and services.

The report gives considerable attention to the operation of private enterprise, which has been the mainspring of development in the past and can be expected to continue in this role in the future. The mission is concerned that the private sector, or more precisely the urban formal sector, has not always operated to the maximum advantage of the country; its past development has often been detrimental to the health of other sectors of the economy, particularly agriculture, industries, and the informal sector.

We suggest that a vigorous formal sector will be necessary to maintain a fast rate of growth, which is in turn a vital precondition for any determined attack on poverty and employment. We therefore examine ways in which private enterprise activity can be induced to operate to the greater benefit of the economy as a whole, and suggest that the urban formal sector can be made not only more compatible with the development of the informal sector, but largely complementary to a thriving, export-oriented agricultural industry.

The report strongly favors incentives, particularly price signals, as the appropriate means for regulating the behavior of the private sector. The most important of these are factor prices and the cost of foreign exchange, and we assert that, while private entrepreneurs have responded quite accurately to price signals in the past, these signals were not always the appropriate ones. Moreover, there has been a marked trend toward the use of direct controls over private sector activity. Such control is generally inefficient, is often ineffective, and has a genetic capacity for breeding further controls. We suggest that direct controls are not an appropriate way of manipulating private sector behavior in Kenya, and that they should be eliminated before the psychology of direct government intervention becomes entrenched, as has happened in other countries.

We also examine some of the wider implications of the proposed strategy. Some of the conflicts between goals which are feared in development—notably the possible trade-off between employment and growth—need not arise in Kenya. On the contrary, the structural changes we advocate could accelerate the growth of both incomes and employment. But other inherent conflicts, including the conflict between rising wages and employment, do lie under the surface, and will need careful scrutiny by the Government.

The mission is impressed by Kenya's potential and its scope for utilizing both domestic and foreign resources for the future development of the economy and the welfare of its people. The changes in economic management we have advocated would, among other things, move Kenya towards self-reliance in the longer term, by increasing the efficiency of domestic resource use and curbing the demand for imports. But even under the most optimistic assumptions, Kenya faces a worrying, and possibly critical, balance of payments constraint. The Government of Kenya has accepted the general strategy of the report. If the management of the economy moves along the directions indicated, Kenya will have an exceptionally good case for external assistance. It was suggested at the recent meeting of the Consultative Group that, apart from supplying the additional resources which Kenya so clearly warrants, the donors themselves can play a constructive role in helping to promote the changes in the structure and processes of growth which their report advocates.

Part I

Emerging Issues and Policy Options

Chapter 1

Major Goals and Achievements

The Inherited Challenge

On taking over power at the end of 1963, the newly elected Kenya Government inherited a formidable challenge. The essential ingredient of the challenge was, as elsewhere in the developing world, poverty. In 1963, per capita income in Kenya was around £30 or US$85 a year. But, allowing for the fact that much of the wealth was held within the European and Asian communities, per capita income among the African population was probably no more than £20 or $50 a year, much of it concentrated in the urban areas. Thus, the problem of poverty in the rural areas, where 90 percent of the population lived, was as distressing in Kenya as in most African countries.

The dualistic nature of the economy was both a help and a hindrance in tackling this problem of poverty. On the positive side, the existence of a modern and relatively opulent segment of the society provided some impetus to the economy which it would not otherwise have had. The European and Asian populations not only supplied the entrepreneurship, managerial talent, and skilled labor for modern sector operation, but also created an expanding market for its products. Partly because of this local market, Kenya had a head start in manufacturing and services, and built up an early export market with neighboring countries, which helped to offset her external trade deficit. In agriculture, the long established European large farm sector had laid the foundation for the rapid development of African farming by successfully pioneering commercial crops, establishing Kenya in world markets, and creating—by virtue of their political power—the infrastructure and services in the high potential farm areas which have always been the economic heart of Kenya.

On the other hand, this situation which Kenya inherited from the past presented an explosive political problem, and in some respects made it harder to tackle the fundamental tasks of development. The modern sector was run largely by Europeans and Asians, and the public service was heavily dependent on expatriate personnel—circumstances which called for an urgent program of Africanization in the more conspicuous areas of the modern sector. But the very existence of a modern, relatively sophisticated economy demanded a disproportionate amount of the scarce management capacity of Government and tended to distract attention from the wider problem of mass poverty. As we shall argue later, the civil service has become very involved in running the modern (or formal) sector, not always to the benefit of society as a whole. Moreover, the rapid growth of the urban formal sector has led to the formulation of policies and standards—for wages, education, and housing, for example—which were irrelevant to Kenya at her stage of development and have worked sometimes against the interests of the majority of the population.

Added to these economic problems, the Kenya Government was faced with a difficult political situation. Kenya's struggle for Independence had been bitter and divisive, even between the African people, and, on the eve of Independence, the resident noncitizen populations were apprehensive about their future. The new Government had the seemingly impossible job of reestablishing the confidence of the noncitizen population (on whom so much of the vitality of the economy depended), while at the same time satisfying the African population (in whom lay the political power) that they would truly control their own destiny.

Initial Goals

The first priority of Government was clearly to build the new nation. Initial problems were not lacking. Internally, the Government had to redesign the administration, following the rejection of the unpopular regional constitution, and the new nation faced early calls for secession from both the Somali and Coast people. Kenya also had much to do externally. There were border disputes with Somalia and sporadic outbreaks of fighting along both the Somali and Ethiopian borders which had to be prevented from escalating into more serious conflict. On the more positive side, there was an urgent need to renegotiate the range of common services and cooperative arrangements which had existed between Kenya, Tanganyika, and Uganda before they gained independence. This renegotiation led, in the 1967 Treaty for East African Cooperation, to the establishment of the East African Common Market, and the first formal step towards possible closer political cooperation in the future. Finally, in the external field, Kenya was anxious to take her proper place in the community of nations and particularly in Africa, where the Organization of African Unity had just been created.

The economic objectives of the new Government were clearly defined, first in the original 1963 Election Manifesto of the Kenya African National Union, and subsequently in Sessional Paper No. 10 of 1963/65.[1] These two documents, together with the Constitution and Laws of Kenya, have formed a consistent economic and political philosophy, which has guided subsequent policy and has been incorporated into successive development plans.

The economic objectives of Government have been orthodox enough: "to achieve high and growing per capita incomes, equitably distributed, so that all are free from want, disease and exploitation," while at the same time guaranteeing political equality, social justice, human dignity and equal opportunities.[2] The particular blend of policies put forward to secure these objectives, however, was seen to be uniquely Kenyan, in the sense that the Government wished to draw upon the best of African tribal traditions (particularly individual political equality and the concept of mutual social responsibility inherent in the extended family system) in forging a new approach to African socialism. While eschewing any particular foreign ideology or culture, the architects of Kenya's development philosophy were willing to adopt the best of foreign technology, culture, and law, and to borrow capital and manpower from abroad, whenever this seemed to be to Kenya's advantage and was consistent with national sovereignty and Kenyan cultural identity. This philosophy of economic nonalignment manifested itself in a pragmatic blend of laissez faire capitalism and African socialism which has characterized Kenyan economic policy during the first decade.

Major Achievements and Failures

We do not intend to provide a systematic assessment of the progress that Kenya has made during the first decade.[3] Rather, we shall set out the major themes of our analysis in this section and develop them at later stages.

In devising a strategy for development, Kenya concentrated on three major economic goals:

---

1. *African Socialism and its Application to Planning in Kenya*, Sessional Paper No. 10 of 1963/65, Republic of Kenya.
2. *Development Plan, 1966–70*, Republic of Kenya, 1966, Preface by the Minister for Economic Planning and Development, para. 3.
3. For a review of past progress, see Chapter 2 of the *Development Plan, 1974–78*, Republic of Kenya, 1974.

- to achieve a fast overall growth rate;
- to ensure that the benefits of development are distributed equitably; and
- to undertake the Kenyanization of the economy.

During the first decade of Independence, Kenya has been remarkably successful in the first objective of achieving rapid economic growth. Virtually every indicator of performance in this field is well above average for a country at Kenya's stage of development. The Gross Domestic Product (GDP) grew at an average rate of about 7 percent a year between 1964 and 1972, and few developing countries can better this kind of performance over an eight-year period. Such a rapid rate of growth has meant that real per capita incomes have increased significantly since Independence, despite one of the highest rates of population growth in the world.

This success has been due to many factors which are discussed at various points of the report. But there is little doubt that the chief credit must go to the Government, which has on the one hand created the politically stable atmosphere necessary for a high level of private investment, and on the other hand has exercised consistent and generally sound management of the economy. Again, the indicators are impressive. National savings mobilization has been remarkably high for a country as poor as Kenya, even when account is taken of the non-African population and the uneven distribution of income. Government and the Central Bank have generally followed a cautious financial policy and, as a result, inflation has been until recently a factor of minor importance and Kenya has kept her external debt well within manageable proportions. In its fiscal policies, the Government's record has been particularly praiseworthy. During the first eight years of independent fiscal management, the Central Government turned a budget deficit into a sizable surplus, increased its development expenditure sevenfold, and reduced its relative dependence on foreign aid. At the same time, the Government greatly expanded the provision of basic social services. There is no doubt that Kenya's performance in mobilizing resources for growth has been impressive by any standard. Since we shall be critical of other aspects of Kenya's development, there is no harm in giving praise where it is richly deserved.

On the debit side, two facets of Kenya's past performance are less satisfactory and will have to receive careful attention in devising a strategy for the second decade. The first is that Kenya has not really reaped as many benefits as she should have from her impressive performance in resource mobilization and investment. The most generally recognized aspect of this problem has been her failure to distribute the benefits of development as widely as the Government would like and, in particular, the twin problems of growing unemployment and the continuing poverty of what the ILO/UNDP mission has called the "working poor." As explained in the preface to this report, we do not intend to go over this ground again since it was the major theme of the ILO/UNDP report[4] and has been actively debated within Kenya. But a major objective of the strategy underlying this report is to launch a much more effective attack on what we regard as the core of the distribution problem—the low productivity and continuing poverty of the mass of Kenyan people.

But, while growing unemployment and poverty may be conspicuous manifestations of a maldistribution of benefits, we are also concerned that efficiency of investment could have been higher in both the private and public sectors of the economy, given a different policy package. In other words, the benefits themselves might have been greater, with favorable consequences for both growth and equity. We hope to be able to draw from an analysis of Kenya's past experience to suggest how her scarce resources of capital and skilled manpower could be used more advantageously in the future.

---

4. *Employment, Incomes and Equality. A Strategy for Increasing Productive Employment in Kenya* (the ILO/UNDP report), International Labour Organisation, 1972.

The second worrying aspect of past development is harder to define but will be a recurring theme of much of this report. This is that in recent years a variety of factors have started to emerge in the economy which will almost surely cause increasing problems for Kenya unless they are removed very soon. Some are obvious dangers, such as the temptation to resort to inflationary financing tactics or desperate measures to combat unemployment, which we are sure that Kenya can and will avoid. But other dangers are more insidious, such as the incentive effects of Kenya's trade policy or the indirect consequences of some Kenyanization programs. Sometimes, we shall argue that policies may run counter to the objectives for which they were framed, or that they conflict with other policies of Government. For example, it appears that the policy of protecting import substitution industries may, in fact, increase Kenya's reliance on imports, and conflict with the goal of promoting agriculture and rural development. Other times, there may be easier or less costly ways of achieving the same objectives, as for instance in the use of price incentives, instead of direct controls, as a method of affecting private sector behavior. In nearly every instance, however, we shall attempt to show that these factors may well lead to greater problems in the future if they are not removed now, and that in many cases they may become irreversible before too long.

The Challenge Ahead

We therefore conclude that Kenya's performance since Independence has not been quite as good as first appears, and that some policy changes are called for in the second decade if she is to achieve her goals. Moreover, we shall put forward the hypothesis that it might also be harder for Kenya to sustain as high a rate of growth in the future as in the past, without significant change. We feel that in many respects, Kenya has now reached a turning point in her development where she is at the end of the first "easy" stage of growth and is facing a growing resource constraint, as indicated by the tighter fiscal position, balance of payments pressure, and the first serious impact of inflation.

Our contention, therefore, is that the path ahead will not be easy, and that the Government and people of Kenya will be faced with a number of difficult choices. But the potential for development is impressive, and we shall try to indicate the kind of strategy Kenya might follow during the second decade of Independence and the nature of some of the decisions which need to be taken.

Chapter 2

Resources Available for Development

The business of development is very largely concerned with resources: on the one hand, what volume of resources can be mobilized for development, and on the other hand, how efficiently these resources are used to achieve society's goals. This chapter will examine how far Kenya has succeeded in mobilizing resources since Independence, and will concentrate on the four major resources which have proved to be the most restrictive constraints to development—domestic savings, government revenue, foreign exchange, and skilled manpower. In Chapter 3 we will assess how well these resources have been used.

Domestic Savings

In aggregate terms, Kenya's savings performance in the first decade has been excellent. Gross domestic savings, as a proportion of GDP, have been around 19-20 percent in most years since 1964 and, as pointed out later, this is a level of achievement few countries have matched. The major item in the high level of domestic savings has been household savings (including unincorporated business savings), which have amounted to about 10 percent of personal disposable incomes during the period. Corporate savings have accounted for an increasing part of total savings as the Kenyan economy has expanded. In particular, depreciation allowances alone have contributed about 30 percent of domestic savings. On the other hand, undistributed profits have been a rather small component, and the public sector has generally generated more savings that corporate profits, even though Kenya has remained a predominantly private sector economy. As a result of the successful fiscal policies of Government described below, public sector savings have been particularly important in recent years, rising to over 23 percent of total savings in 1971.

In looking at the trend in savings there is some reason to believe that the increasing rate of savings in the past is now levelling off, and there is little scope for further increase since savings are already high. On the contrary, there is cause for concern that savings performance may decline somewhat in the future. Both in 1970 and 1971, there was already a slight decline in overall savings owing to a fall in household savings. We do not suggest that the fall between 1969 and 1971 (from 20.5 percent to 19.2 percent) is necessarily significant: Kenya has recovered from random dips in the savings rate before.[1] But, taken together with the processes which are operating in the economy, it could be a sign of a structural move towards a lower propensity to save.

Below, we suggest that it will be difficult to maintain the impressive rate of public savings in the future, and in Annex 4 it is suggested that the stagnation of business profits in the past must also throw some uncertainty on prospects for greater corporate savings in the future. The absolute decline in household savings during 1970/71 gives most cause for concern, however, because it could indicate a tendency for households' average propensity to save to fall. Unfortunately, we have virtually no detailed empirical evidence of household savings behavior in Kenya. It is frequently asserted that household savings have been high in the non-African population, and particularly in the Asian business community, and that African households and businesses have a lower propensity to save. There are no data to support this hypothesis, although it is consistent with what is known of the redistributive processes which operate within the extended

---

1. The savings rate in 1972 did, in fact, return to about 1970 level.

family system, and the effects of urbanization. If this hypothesis is true, then household savings are likely to decline as the economy is progressively Kenyanized.

In looking at the future, later in the report, we shall make the assumption that Kenya's savings performance continues at about the same high level as in the past. We consider this to be an optimistic assumption because there are many reasons why any or all of the components of domestic savings could level off or fall back in the coming years. We shall therefore stress the need for more effective mobilization and deployment of domestic savings, through both interest rate policy and a more efficient intermediation process. At this stage we are merely concerned to sound a warning that the domestic economy will not necessarily provide as generous a proportion of investable funds as it has in the past, without a great deal more vigilance and inducement.

Public Savings and Fiscal Policy

Government's fiscal policy influences the domestic resource position both directly, through the generation of public savings, and indirectly, through its effects on household and business savings. The Central Government's efforts in mobilizing public savings has been one of the most impressive aspects of Kenya's development since Independence. In 1963/64, the Government had a sizable recurrent budget deficit and had to rely on foreign aid and borrowing to fill the gap and meet the whole of its slender development budget. Over the next eight years, however, the position changed dramatically.

As a result of a most creditable tax effect by Government, recurrent revenue was boosted from less than £50 million in 1963/64 to about £144 million in 1972/73, or an average increase of more than 14 percent a year. By 1970, Government revenue accounted for almost 23 percent of GDP, which is an exceptionally high ratio in the developing world. Recurrent expenditure also increased quickly by 11 percent a year, in line with the growth of the economy and the Government development program. But the revenue effort was sufficient to meet increasing demands made on the recurrent budget and to convert the initial budget deficit into a substantial surplus. The marginal savings rate over this period was a very high 20 percent, which pushed Central Government savings to more than 20 percent of total national savings, or to about 5 percent of monetary GDP.

This good revenue performance permitted Government to meet its expanding recurrent budget and make a substantial contribution—an average of 28 percent over the period—to development expenditure, which was boosted nearly sevenfold in this time. It also meant that, at least until the last two years, Government was able to finance the balance of its overall deficit very largely by noninflationary borrowing on the domestic market and by borrowing on concessional terms from abroad.[2] Thus, in a very direct way, the Government's success in generating public savings allowed it to undertake a rapidly increasing investment program without the dangers of inflationary financing or commercial borrowing from abroad which have beset many other developing countries.

Over the last two years (since 1970/71), the Government's performance in mobilizing resources has noticeably slackened. This is due to a slowing down of revenue growth as well as an acceleration of recurrent expenditure. As a result, public savings have fallen, and the Government has been obliged to depend upon Central Bank financing to a significant extent for the first time. It has also had to rely on foreign borrowing, including some borrowing at commercial rates, to a relatively greater degree.

---

2. Over the whole eight-year period, the Government financed 80 percent of its total (recurrent and development) budget out of recurrent revenue, 10 percent from net domestic borrowing, and another 10 percent from net foreign borrowing.

This recent sharp deterioration in government savings performance is due partly to purely temporary causes, and the mission feels that the revenue position should improve following a relaxation of import controls and the recent introduction of a sales tax and other fiscal measures. However, a large part of Kenya's excellent performance in the past has been due more to a progressive extension of fiscal instruments than to the built-in elasticity of the fiscal system. There is some hope, as described in Annex 2, that the buoyancy of the tax system can be improved, and there is still room for tightening tax administration and scope for introducing new taxes. But it is unlikely that Kenya can sustain the rapid growth of government expenditure (16.9 percent recurrent and 21 percent capital since 1970/71) without increasing reliance on less prudent methods of financing. Until recently, government finances were barely a constraint to Kenya's development. However, in the future, public finance is likely to be a much more constraining factor in the development scene. This implies that, while new ways of mobilizing revenue should continue to be explored, government resources will have to be more carefully husbanded, and possibly redirected to more productive uses.

In theory, one of the ways to mobilize additional resources would be through other components of the public sector, such as local authorities and public enterprises and agencies. In the past, these agencies have not been important savers in Kenya, even though they comprise an important segment of the public sector in all other respects. The local authorities, in particular, are going to need an increasing level of support from Central Government, even if their revenue base is broadened, and this will increase the strain on Government's budget still further. The mission feels that even though potential savings are probably not large, it will be necessary to examine the role of the public sector as a whole in resource mobilization to see what additional revenue could be raised by other agencies. In particular, some of the public utilities might aim to produce greater surpluses, either to finance their own development or other programs. The power sector is one example of an urban utility which is generating surpluses for the development of rural areas.

Foreign Exchange

Until recently, Kenya has not been particularly worried by a foreign exchange constraint. The growing domestic resource gap has certainly been reflected in a widening deficit in the balance of payments. But, although Kenya has been increasingly dependent on a free flow of imported goods and services, the economy has not experienced any great difficulty in obtaining the foreign exchange necessary to finance these imports through her own exports and a large inflow of foreign capital.

Kenya traditionally has had a deficit in her merchandise trade account, and this his gradually widened as domestic resources have come under pressure. The trade deficit grew quite slowly during the 1960s, when imports increased a little faster than GDP and exports a little more slowly. Most of the deficit was covered by Kenya's net receipts from "invisibles," particularly the sale of services to Uganda and Tanzania, and expanded earnings from the tourist industry. Thus, until the end of the 1960s, Kenya's balance on current account either was favorable or reflected a deficit which could easily be met by foreign private investment and increased foreign aid.

Since 1969, the balance of payments position has changed rather dramatically. By 1971, the value of imports had increased 62 percent, largely due to higher world prices, and exports had increased only about 34 percent, again mainly because of changing prices. Thus, at the start of the seventies, Kenya had already experienced the first major impact of world inflation. At the same time, as the trade deficit widened, her net earnings from "invisibles" also levelled off due to a disruption in her service trade with her Partner States, some slackening in tourist expansion, and an increasing repatriation of dividends. This deficit on the current account grew rather alarmingly from an insignificant amount in 1969, to £16 million in 1970, and £54 million in 1971.

Net flows of foreign capital were not sufficient to cover a deficit growing at this rate. Private foreign investment, while still high, was not increasing very quickly, and the inflow of official capital to the public sector did not rise as fast as the Government had hoped. As a result, foreign exchange reserves fell rather sharply towards the end of 1971, and the Government felt obliged to take abrupt measures to improve the balance of payments position.

Measures taken, which are described in more detail elsewhere, included the introduction of a range of import controls, the restriction of domestic credit, and the curtailment of government expenditures. There is no doubt that these measures dampened down imports, and, assisted by good export performance and an increased flow of external capital, helped to make the balance of payments position in 1972 much stronger. However, these temporary measures were imposed at considerable cost to the economy and at great risk of becoming entrenched as more permanent management tools, and the Kenya Government has recognized that a longer term and more satisfactory solution must be found to maintaining equilibrium.

It is difficult to judge whether the 1971/72 deterioration in Kenya's balance of payments position was a temporary phenomenon or the first sign of a more permanent disequilibrium. During the course of 1973, the position has improved far enough to allow the relaxation of import control and credit restrictions, but it is still too early to assess whether the lifting of controls will again result in an unmanageable increase in imports in the short term. In the long term, the prospects are very uncertain since the balance of payments depends upon so many variables.

On balance, the mission feels that foreign exchange is likely to be a greater constraint to Kenya's development in the future than it has been in the past. The country's very success in pushing beyond the limits of her own resources is bound to be reflected in a growing external resource gap. But there are a number of factors which will exacerbate the foreign exchange constraint, many of which are largely beyond Kenya's ability to control. Thus, as we show in Annex One, the balance of payments position is most sensitive to changes in terms of trade, and we assume that the balance of payments will continue to move against Kenya in the foreseeable future. Similarly, while we have forecast a considerable increase in external aid disbursements over the next five years, foreign aid is only partly responsive to changes in demand, and cannot be relied on to fill a continually growing gap of the kind thrown up by the basic projections given in Annex One.

In the general strategy of the mission, the way to avoid increasing balance of payments crises is not by imposing controls on imports or curtailing growth, since these are costly to the economy and often self-defeating. Instead, we shall argue that our strategy for restructuring the pattern of growth will lead the Kenyan economy towards self-reliance, by promoting growth in sectors, such as agriculture and resource-based industry, which utilize domestic resources and make the most efficient use of foreign resources. Given this kind of policy reform, the mission is optimistic that Kenya can maintain a fast pace of development without encountering structural problems in her balance of payments. It is most encouraging to see that the Government is already moving towards the kind of policy reforms we feel are indicated by the developments of the past.

Skill, Experience, and Management

The last and possibly the most critical resource required for development has been Kenya's small cadre of skilled manpower. The country has gone a long way since Independence in overcoming her initial manpower shortages, a tremendous effort having been made by the Government and the people to overcome deficiencies in education and to boost the training of qualified men and women. Great initiative, responsibility, and imagination have been displayed by young people who have found themselves thrust into positions of power without having had much experience. In overall quantitative terms, manpower shortages are now concentrated in a few categories of skilled workers and highly specialized occupations. Some of the occupations in which Kenya is still heavily dependent on expatriate manpower, secondary school teachers for example, are expected to be fully Kenyanized by the end of the 1970s; but shortages in other occupations will continue to constrain development for much longer. On the other hand, overproduction is now apparent in many areas, particularly in general arts, resulting in considerable wastage in Kenya's limited education and training capacity.

The real constraint in manpower is a qualitative one. All too many of the young people who leave schools and training institutions are not provided with the right skills to fill available jobs, nor does the education system prepare the new generation of workers—either technically or emotionally—for employment in rural occupations. Clearly, the problem of equating supply and demand will not be solved just by implanting a rural orientation to primary education and adding a few vocational courses to the secondary school curriculum—at least not as long as the economy continues to offer the greatest rewards to those who have climbed the highest rungs of the academic ladder.

Another aspect of quality is experience, which is inevitably scarce in a young country such as Kenya, since experience is mainly a function of time. The progressive Kenyanization of the labor force has undoubtedly led to inefficiencies in the use of manpower, especially in the public sector where Kenyanization has been most rapid. The problem takes a number of forms, as pointed out by the recent commission of inquiry into the public sector.[3] Young entrants to the civil service are often well qualified academically but lack experience. High positions in the ministries are filled by the first generation of trained African officials who, because they are young, seem to stand in the way of promotion prospects. Moreover, top officials overburdened with work, much of which could be delegated, have little time to devote to training and supervising younger persons. As a result, the younger civil servants become frustrated and fail to gain the responsibility which might attract delegation.

Perhaps the most serious manpower constraint is the general scarcity of entrepreneurial and managerial ability. These qualifications—particularly in their emphasis on utilizing resources efficiently and the willingness to take risk—are vital to the development of the economy both in the private and public sectors. Yet, while Kenya's development philosophy is favorable to the full development of entrepreneurship and managerial talent, the vast potential energies and enterprise of the population has so far been scarcely tapped. For example, in the private sector, the majority of small scale independent farmers are still operating at low levels of productivity; and for many the challenge of mere survival under harsh conditions leaves little time or energy for entrepreneurial initiative to emerge. In some respects, the economy has operated in ways which discourage entrepreneurial ability. As pointed out later, the industrial protection system and domestic prices have tended to favor the urban formal sector, at the expense of both agriculture and small scale "informal" activities, and thus to discriminate against the very sectors in which potential small businessmen have the best chance to establish themselves. In the public sector, neither the civil service structure nor the financial regulations has encouraged entrepreneurial risktaking, and there is a serious scarcity of management capacity in some key ministries and agencies.

The mission's conclusions, therefore, go a little further than the now common plea for education and training to be more relevant to the country's social and economic

---

3. *Report of the Commission of Enquiry (Public Service Structure and Remuneration Commission), May, 1971,* Republic of Kenya (the *Ndegwa Report*).

needs. We feel it necessary for the whole economic environment to be manipulated, by both direct and indirect means, so that it offers suitable rewards to the individual to acquire and use skills that are appropriate to the needs of the society as a whole. In other words, the people of Kenya will demand "relevant" education and training when—and only when—the incentives system makes it individually profitable for them to do so. The central problem is to provide the incentives and the means to the more than one million rural households to use Kenya's vast resources of land and labor to best advantage. We feel that the small scale entrepreneurs, both farmers and businessmen, can probably do the job better than anyone else. But they need the right incentives and a great deal of help.

Much of the emphasis in manpower development since Independence has gone into programs of Kenyanization—in the civil service, in private sector employment, and in business. Necessary for both political and economic reasons, it is desirable that the process should be continued at the fastest rate compatible with efficiency and rapid development. In the public sector, government administration is almost fully localized, and the teaching service will be largely Kenyanized in the coming years. Yet the Government is still heavily dependent on a small cadre of expatriate personnel, particularly experienced professionals and workers in the technical grades, and still receives a very large amount of technical assistance from the bilateral, multilateral, and private sources. Much of Kenya's development capability—especially in the technological field—will depend on expatriate manpower for some years to come. The Government realizes that many of these positions cannot be Kenyanized in the short term without serious harm to the economy. The position in the private sector is rather different and Kenyanization has gone much more slowly—partly because it is more difficult to replace experienced personnel in business and partly because businessmen are typically reluctant to be told whom they can (or cannot) employ.

One unfortunate consequence of the Kenyanization program, however valuable it has been, is that it has centered around a relatively small and elite group of Africans, who were fortunate to be in a position, by virtue of their age, or education, or political commitment, to inherit the jobs or farms or businesses of the expatriate community who held the reins of power before Independence. This process, which might be termed the "Kenyanization of the formal sector," is inevitably running out of steam. Politically imperative and economically desirable, the process cloaked two inherent dangers which could cause damage to the economy unless the concept of Kenyanization can be broadened. The first is that, by Kenyanizing the formal sector, the country has entrenched many of the standards of the previous colonial regime, sometimes to the detriment of the rest of society. The second danger is related to the diminishing scope for further Kenyanization. Most of the "easy" types of Kenyanization have already been undertaken, and it will certainly prove increasingly difficult to bring about further gains as the process of localization reaches up to the higher levels of skill and experience. Yet there is likely to be mounting political pressure on the Government to push ahead with Kenyanization, particularly as the burden of unemployment grows; and this could result in increasing cost to the economy, combined with meager and diminishing returns to African employment.

If these dangers are to be avoided, it may be necessary for Kenya to reassess the goals of Kenyanization. Most of her people might feel that the real purpose of a policy of Kenyanization is to provide expanding incomes and employment opportunities for all of them. If this is so, it may be incompatible with a short term political resistance to the continued purchase of foreign skills in the key sectors of development. This possible conflict of interest is referred to again in the final chapter of this report.

CHAPTER 3

EFFICIENCY OF RESOURCE USE

It has already been shown that Kenya's performance in mobilizing resources has been very good, but that in recent years the rapid development of the economy has brought increasing pressure on domestic resources and public finances and that this resource constraint has been reflected in a sharp deterioration in the balance of payments. It was concluded that these trends made it more important than ever that Kenya's resources should be used to maximum advantage. We shall now go on to look at the efficiency with which Kenya's resources have been used in the past in the economy as a whole, not only in generating additional growth but also in expanding employment and overcoming poverty. We shall then look at resource use in the private and public sectors and try to explain what factors have affected their efficiency.

Investment and Growth

If we use movements in the incremental capital output ratio (ICOR) as an indicator, the efficiency of resource use in Kenya has been high by international standards. Using a three-year moving average to smooth out annual fluctuations, we have calculated that the overall ICOR in Kenya was 2.4 in 1966. This compares very favorably with all but the most efficient developing countries. For example, during the late sixties, countries like Egypt, Ghana, Zambia, and the Philippines had ICORs of more than five, and many, like India, Colombia, and several African countries, had ICORs of between three and four (see Annex 1, Table 1).

Such estimates of ICOR need to be interpreted with care, particularly when the series covers a short period of time. However, the tendency for total ICOR to increase since 1964 does provide some evidence that the efficiency of investment has been falling in Kenya. By 1970, we estimate that ICOR had risen to 3.2 and, while this is still good by international norms, the rising trend must be of concern to a country which wants to maximize growth and is facing an increasing resource constraint.

The rise in overall ICOR is apparently due to two factors. First, the structure of investment and growth in Kenya has tended to shift towards those sectors in which ICOR is either high or rising. Second, ICORs have increased within a number of important sectors, thus pushing up ICOR as a whole. For example, ICORs have increased significantly in five sectors (including transport and communications, construction and mining) which together accounted for 32 percent of GDP in 1971, while ICORs have noticeably fallen in only three sectors (manufacturing, trade, and electricity and water) accounting for 23 percent of GDP.

Without a great deal more study of individual sectors, it is difficult to know what the real reasons are behind the changes in sectoral ICORs. We suggest some plausible arguments in Annexes One and Three. These include the existence of excess capacity in the earlier years, the encouragement of capital intensive production by distorted factor pricing, and the possibility that the efficiency of investment has fallen as some of the "easier" opportunities have been taken up. Whatever the reasons behind the increasing ICORs in the past, the significant conclusion is that Kenya cannot really afford to let ICORs continue rising indefinitely. If Kenya wants to get the most out of her resources, she will have to seek new ways of simply getting more growth out of the very considerable investment effort she is making.

The comparison of investment cost and incremental output which ICORs provide, however, is not a very good indicator of the efficiency of resource use under Kenyan conditions. This is because price distortions give a false value of the real cost of resources used in investment, while product price distortions mean that the real value of production may be higher or lower than it appears. Thus, many of the sectoral ICORs we have used probably give a misleading impression of the efficiency of resource use. In particular, as argued later, resource use in manufacturing may sometimes be considerably less efficient than it appears to be from the calculated ICORs.

As a general principle, resources will always be used less efficiently in an economic sense, when market prices deviate from economic prices. In Kenya, we feel that price distortions have had an important, and generally unfavorable, influence on both the choice of factors used in production and the allocation of resources between competing uses. The most serious *factor price* distortions in Kenya are those which have provided an incentive to use capital-intensive techniques in production, by overvaluing labor and undervaluing capital. Wages in the formal sector severely overvalue labor as a factor of production (particularly for middle and lower grades of worker), partly because of union action and wage legislation, and partly because urban formal sector activity has been protected to a level where it can afford to pay high wages. On the other hand, capital is undervalued both through an overvalued exchange rate[1] (which makes all imports seem less costly than they really are) and a liberal interest rate policy (which makes the cost of capital seem less than it is). The effect of these two distortions is therefore to encourage the entrepreneur to use more of the resource Kenya lacks (capital) and less of the plentiful resource (labor) than he might do if he had to pay their real costs.

Although the factor substitutability argument is well known, there is no conclusive evidence that it has been of great importance in Kenya. A much more worrying aspect of factor price distortions is not the effect they have on the factor mix within a particular sector, but their indirect effects on other sectors and the economy as a whole. The best example of this more indirect effect is the central role played by urban wage rates in the economy. This relationship has been lucidly described in the ILO/UNDP report and is examined at length in Annex Three. Overvalued wage rates in the modern sector—both private and public—disrupt the labor market as a whole, raising the cost of labor far above the supply price. But the effects are far more pervasive. The relationship between high urban wage rates, rural-urban migration, and the demand for the formal education which is seen as a passport to a well rewarded job in the city, is now recognized. Along with the high wage rates come inflated standards of living, consumption, housing, and other services, which encourage resources to flow into relatively costly, and often capital-intensive uses. Other externalities of factor price distortions, such as the effects of a cheap money policy on savings and the allocation of credit, are important, but these will be discussed elsewhere.

The effects of *product price* distortions are also important in Kenya and tend to reinforce and interact with factor price distortions. In this report, we are essentially concerned with the major distortion in product pricing which arises from the protection afforded to the manufacturing sector against competition from imports. By overvaluing the real benefits of industrial output, the protective system encourages resources of all kinds, especially foreign capital, managerial talent, and skilled manpower, which are the scarcest resources, to flow into forms of investment which give society a poor return for its money and sometimes no return at all. Again, the external effects are important, particularly on the agricultural sector in Kenya. Thus, some of the less efficient industries preempt resources which might be better used elsewhere, and tax the rest of the

---

1. In the mission's view, the Kenya shilling is probably overvalued—not in the sense of short-run balance of payments equilibrium, but in the sense that the value of the Kenya shilling (in terms of foreign exchange) is higher than it would be, were the exchange rate used as a more flexible tool of development policy.

economy, especially agriculture, through the inflated cost of their products consumed in rural areas and the taxation of exports which is implicit in the protective system.

When we take account of both the direct and indirect effects of price distortions in Kenya, it is probable that resource use has not been very efficient. Kenya's growing unemployment problem is one conspicuous indicator of failure in proper domestic resource use. In addition, the economy has not yet learned to conserve its scarce resources very well. Much of Kenya's most valuable asset, land, is still worked at low levels of productivity. Some of the land is being eroded or exploited by individuals at high social cost, and some high potential land is kept idle for reasons of tribal exclusiveness or individual financial speculation.[2] Some of the scarce foreign capital flowing into Kenya is being used to establish industries which increase rather than decrease her dependence on foreign exchange, and are sheltered by protective tariffs which tax the exports of other sectors. The skills of scarce experienced Kenyan manpower are increasingly being used to control the economy when they could be more profitably used in promoting development.

Thus Kenya may not have made as much progress as she could have in the priority task of applying the scarcest factors of capital and skill to the potentially most productive factors of land and labor. Price distortions have worked against this allocative process, and the task has been made harder because in many cases the country does not yet know how the process should be undertaken. Much of the emphasis of this report is therefore on the need to induce resources to flow into the more productive uses and on the implications which this has for economic policy and management.

The efficiency of resource use is, of course, not measured only in terms of growth. There are other, often more important, benefits to be taken into account. In the following section, we shall examine the efficiency of investment in generating employment and incomes and in attacking the central problems of poverty and low productivity. In a much broader sense, Kenya and her people want to know whether their resources are generally being used to achieve the objectives they seek: not only expanding incomes and employment but continuing social and political development which is an inherent part of a country's overall economic strategy. Some of these goals of development, such as the Kenyanization of personnel, the local ownership of property and the means of production, and the exercise of economic sovereignty are very difficult to quantify; and only the Government and the people of Kenya can decide on their priorities. We shall, however, point out from time to time that the economy has not always achieved these wider objectives very efficiently, and that some of the objectives themselves may be in conflict with one another.

Employment and the Attack on Poverty

The Continuing Problem of Distribution

As briefly described in Chapter 1, Kenya inherited an economy at Independence which was poor in average per capita terms and in which incomes and wealth were very unevenly distributed. There were wide disparities in income, some of which were conspicuous and politically unacceptable, and which held potential dangers. Other conspicuous problems were the concentration of economic power and wealth in the hands of noncitizens; large scale European farms and estates; the predominance of Asian traders in rural areas; and the overwhelming dependence of the civil service administration on expatriate officers. It is understandable, therefore, that the main thrust of

2. See Part III, pages 454–56, 478.

Government's attack on distribution was the rectification of the more obvious racial imbalances.

But other manifestations of skewed distribution were to be found everywhere. The urban areas had already drawn far ahead of the rural areas in their standard of living and amenities, and even within the rural areas themselves there were marked differences in living conditions. Some of the people, in the high potential areas of the highlands, were starting to enjoy reasonable living standards, while, at the other extreme, those in the northern provinces of Kenya were still fighting a harsh environment, at a bare subsistence level, with very primitive and far-flung services.

Within the towns, again, Kenya had inherited one of the most skewed wage structures in the world, which obliged employers to pay skilled workers perhaps ten to fifteen times what they paid unskilled workers. Yet even the unskilled wage earner was starting to emerge as a privileged member of society in the distribution of benefits, when compared with the majority of the rural population.

The Government of Kenya, in its policy statements, undertook to launch a determined attack on this inequitable distribution of income, and to ensure that the benefits of independent development would be more fairly allocated. Yet after the first decade of Independence, the problems of distribution are still there, and some indications suggest that the imbalances are growing, not lessening. The assessment of the first decade would therefore not be complete without some comment on the measures which Government took to achieve more equal distribution and the problems it encountered.

The Inadequate Remedies

In tackling the problems of poverty and distribution, the Government has in general relied heavily on creating the conditions for rapid economic growth. As we have seen, this policy was successful in achieving a fast rate of growth in GDP and in average per capita income. But it has been recognized within Kenya that this policy, while undoubtedly a precondition for any determined attack on poverty, has not been adequate to make any great impact on distribution problems. In particular, the country has become increasingly worried about the disappointing failure of employment to expand in line with production. However, as the ILO/UNDP report shows, the sluggish growth of employment is only one manifestation of the much wider problem: that the rapid growth in production and incomes has not been as widely distributed as the country would have liked.

What other remedies have been taken, therefore, to redistribute the benefits of development more widely? In its statements of policy, the Government has given considerable emphasis to fiscal policy as an instrument of redistribution, and the nominal tax rates now operating in Kenya appear to go some way in this direction. But, after examining the fiscal system at some length, the mission has concluded that Kenya's fiscal policy has not been a significant instrument for the redistribution of incomes and wealth, or for reducing rural, urban and regional inequalities. Nor is there any evidence that the expenditure pattern of Government has gone very far in offsetting income inequalities.

Built-in Concentrators of Income and Wealth

Part of the problem has been that, while Government has wished to correct inequalities in income, the economy has been operating in such a way as inevitably to concentrate incomes and wealth even further, partly as a result of Government's own, if unwitting, management decisions. These processes have been well described by the ILO/UNDP report, and we do not intend to go over the same field again here. However, there are three closely related built-in concentrators of income and wealth which shall be mentioned briefly because they are central to the theme of this report.

The first, referred to elsewhere in this chapter, is the effect of modern sector wage rates on the rest of the economy. We have already mentioned that high wages, by encouraging similarly high standards of housing and other services, suck resources into the urban areas to support a standard of living far above what the majority of Kenya's population can aspire to. But much more serious is the effect of the formal sector on the rest of the economy, particularly the insidious relationship between urban wage rates, rural-urban migration, and the demand for ever-higher levels of academic education. As we show in Annex Three, increasing formal sector wages discourage employment in the urban formal sector while at the same time breeding open unemployment in the informal sector. The same concept of unrealistic income standards even percolates into the rural areas and threatens to start a whole new cycle of rural unemployment by the same process.[3] This kind of lottery, in which the few succeed and the majority fail, can never contribute to a more equitable distribution of income.

The second closely related factor is the built-in tendency for the urban areas (where most of the rich live) to go ahead faster than the rural areas (where most of the poor live). This is partly due to the high wages of urban workers and the high standards that go along with them. But the process is far more general than this. As we point out later, neither external trade policy nor domestic agricultural pricing policy have generally been determined with the interest of the majority of the rural population in mind. Thus, it is not surprising that the terms of trade between the rural and urban areas have moved in favor of the urban areas (and therefore towards a greater, not lesser, concentration of income) in most years since Independence.

Finally, the emphasis on Kenyanization has been a mixed blessing. It has, as noted above, achieved its major aims of increasing African control of the administration and the economy and removing the politically more embarrassing vestiges of colonial rule. But the preoccupation with racial inequalities, while understandable, sometimes diverted attention from the underlying economic causes of poverty and tended to entrench income inequalities and inappropriate standards of the past. To this extent only, some Kenyanization programs may prove to have been a disservice to the country.

The Remaining Problem of Poverty

Thus, the problem of inequitable distribution remains, and there is growing concern that a more effective attack should be launched. The problem does not have to be approached in terms of narrowing "gaps" or redistributing incomes from the rich to the poor, although the mission has stressed the importance of restraining the growth of real wages. The real problem is one of poverty, and the real challenge is to raise the level of the majority of the population who have as yet benefited little from past progress. This will be the emphasis of the strategy we outline towards the end of the report.

Resource Use by the Private Sector

An essential aim of Kenya's development philosophy since Independence has been to foster the rapid growth of the private enterprise sector, subject only to the degree of control necessary to ensure the wider interests of society. This policy has led to the particular brand of controlled capitalism which differentiates the Kenyan economic climate from most of her neighbors in Africa. Encouraged by this policy, the private

---

3. For example, there is some pressure to raise the "target incomes" of new irrigation schemes, which would reduce the number of beneficiaries, create a new class of rural elite, and further widen income disparities. The greatest danger is that minimum wage legislation will be extended to small scale agriculture, as trade unions have threatened. This would almost certainly extinguish the last hope for absorbing Kenya's growing labor force into productive employment.

sector has expanded rapidly and private investment, both domestic and foreign, has been substantial. Although the relative role of the public sector has increased since Independence, the private sector continues to dominate the economy and has provided the thrust of development in most of the major sectors. It is, therefore, particularly important to examine how well the private sector has used the resources which have been entrusted to it.

Although the Kenya Government has made clear its desire to encourage private enterprise, particularly African business enterprise, some of the policies put into practice have been ambivalent. For example, the urban formal sector has had most favored treatment within the private sector, yet the Government is not always willing to accept the degree of foreign control or the free use of expatriate manpower which are part of the costs of unrestrained free enterprise. Similarly, while emphasizing the importance of encouraging small entrepreneurs and self-reliance, both Central Government and the local authorities have applied policies which are detrimental to the "informal" sector, although this is believed to be the most important breeding ground of indigenous entrepreneurial ability.[4] We shall therefore look at the effective policy environment which Government has created for the private sector to see how this policy package has affected the performance of the private sector, what effects private enterprise has had on the rest of the economy, and what problems seem to be emerging. In so doing, we shall find it convenient to divide the private sector into three components: the urban formal sector, the urban informal sector, and agriculture.

The Urban Formal Sector

We have examined the policy environment of the urban formal sector at length in Annex Three. Apart from the limited influence that Government exerts on the private sector through its direct participation in ownership and management of a few jointly owned firms, the Government manipulates the behavior of the private sector in two main ways. The first is through controlling or influencing the prices of its factors of production or its outputs; the second is through the use of direct controls. Both facets have profoundly affected the behavior of the urban formal sector and other sectors of the economy.

For much of the period since Independence, the most powerful single influence on the behavior of the formal sector was the pricing system. The wage rate structure of the modern sector has, as mentioned earlier in this chapter, had a dominant influence on development of the urban formal sector and the economy as a whole. The high wage rates which have resulted from labor legislation and union pressure, together with other benefits such as social security payments and housing allowances, have discouraged employers from using labor intensive methods. On the other hand, the relative attractions of capital have been increased by tax investment allowances, readily available credit at low interest rates, and low or zero import duties. These distortions in prices, which operate in direct opposition to Kenya's natural resource endowment, may help explain the disappointing past growth of employment in the private sector.

Another major influence on the formal sector has been the trade protective system. This system was originally enforced through the medium of the external tariff, but has been supplemented by an increasing range of direct import controls. The combined effect of these interventions has been very successful in taking Kenya virtually through the first stage of import substitution—the production of the simple types of consumer goods. However, the high and arbitrary rates of effective protection afforded to local

---

4. The impediments which have been put in the way of informal sector activity have been discussed at length in the ILO/UNDP report.

industries have all too frequently resulted in inefficient resource use and severe penalties to the rest of the economy. Some of the industries Kenya has established, although financially profitable to their owners, are not profitable at world prices and sometimes use up more foreign exchange than they earn.

A more recent method of controlling private sector behavior has been the use of a wide range of controls, principally controls on imports. These controls have been introduced both to provide additional protection to local industries and to contain a worsening balance of payments position. Fortunately, some of these controls have now been relaxed, and Kenya will hopefully avoid the dangers implicit in the use of controls of this kind: particularly the effect of the high and sometimes infinite level of protection which controls imply; the risk that one form of intervention will lead to another and result in recurring balance of payments crises; and that a disproportionate amount of Kenya's critically scarce skilled manpower will be tied up in manipulating wide areas of private sector behavior, which could be much more efficiently left to regulation by the price system. The mission has no doubt that, as a general rule, the private sector can be regulated much more efficiently, safely, and at less cost by providing the right price signals than by direct intervention.

Thus, as we show in Annex Three, Kenya's benign attitude to the urban formal sector has all too often backfired since, although entrepreneurs have responded efficiently to the price signals given them, these price signals have not generally induced the urban formal sector to perform to the maximum benefit of society. Moreover, these same price signals have also induced the urban sector, and particularly the manufacturing sector, to operate to the detriment of the rest of the economy, and particularly agriculture.

Our criticism of the operation of the urban formal sector, which closely parallels the analysis by the ILO/UNDP report, in no sense implies that we feel the formal private sector is unimportant, or that it should be repressed in some fashion. On the contrary, the continued dynamism of this sector is vital to the continued prosperity of Kenya, and its continued vigor is both consistent with and necessary for the full development of Kenya. But its past development has not given the payoff it should have, particularly in increasing employment and in generating foreign exchange, and much of its past apparent prosperity has been illusory and won only at the expense of the rest of the economy. Later we try to suggest the kind of policies, starting with a reform of trade policy, which would provide the right package of incentives to the private sector to grow and prosper, not only to the profit of the investor, but to the much greater benefit of the whole country.

The Urban Informal Sector

In contrast to the benign, if sometimes misguided support that the formal sector has received in Kenya, the urban informal sector has at best been neglected, usually ignored, and sometimes actively persecuted—as in the demolition of substandard housing, the prosecution of unlicensed businesses, and so on. The whole subject has been discussed in previous, unpublished World Bank reports and subsequently analyzed at great length in the ILO/UNDP report, where the "informal sector" and the "working poor" were made major themes of the analysis. Since the nature and the importance of the informal sector is, we believe, now generally recognized (if still not documented by empirical evidence), we will not discuss this subject at any length here. However, it is necessary to assess briefly where, in our opinion, the informal sector fits into the total economy.

We believe that in Kenya the urban informal sector has, to a very large extent, been a byproduct of the growth of the formal sector. In the later extensions of the Harris-Todaro type of models which attempt to explain the phenomena of rural-urban migration and unemployment, the urban informal sector serves as a sort of residual employer of those who have failed to win the prize of formal sector employment in the rural-urban migration lottery.[5] This is not to say that the informal sector does not have a valuable and lasting economic function, particularly in offering employment and income opportunities to many of the working poor. We strongly support previous Bank reports and the ILO/UNDP report in advocating that the impediments to the informal sector be lifted and later in the report we suggest some ways by which the small-scale businessmen in the informal sector can be helped. But we do have some doubts whether a generalized policy can be framed for the urban informal sector. Not only the size of the informal sector, but the level of incomes within it, are largely a function of policies designed for other sectors: in particular, the urban formal sector and the agricultural sector. In the last analysis, the role of the informal sector and the welfare of its working poor will depend upon the whole range of macro-economic policies which are the subject of this report.

Agriculture

Finally, in Part III we look at the agricultural sector and the environment which has been created for it. It should be noted that the agricultural sector subsumes the largest proportion of the "informal" sector, but we have chosen to look at the agricultural sector as a single entity since the environmental influences on its behavior are quite different from those operating on the urban informal sector.

The agricultural sector is by far the most important part of the private sector from all points of view. It contributes the largest proportions of GDP and exports, it employs the overwhelming proportion of the labor force, and contains the vast majority of all self-employed entrepreneurs in Kenya. It is therefore of crucial importance that the right environment should exist for agriculture, that price signals should equate private profit with social benefits, and that the sector should receive an appropriate flow of domestic and foreign resources.

On the whole, the environment has not been as conductive to agricultural development as the importance of the sector requires. There are several facets to the problem. First, as we explained earlier in this chapter, the concentration of emphasis on the urban formal sector has generally been at the expense of the rest of the economy, particularly agriculture. Thus, the farmer, and especially the small-scale farmer, gets less than he might for his export commodities and pays more than he should for his imported inputs, because of the trade protective system. He sells his produce to the urban consumers at prices which are usually less than c.i.f. import prices (and sometimes even less than f.o.b. export prices) while he buys the local manufactures at far above their world market values. Similarly, the banking system diverts rural savings to the towns, to be lent to foreign-owned companies (who find it cheaper to borrow in Kenya than abroad), while the majority of small farmers have access to no credit at all. Thus cheap capital and protection against competition have allowed both the urban worker and the foreign investor to prosper, partly at the expense of the rural poor.

It is important neither to overstate nor to understate this argument. Full recognition needs to be given to the tremendous advances made in agriculture since the late fifties, particularly in opening up the previous Scheduled Areas to African settlement and the introduction of export commodities, like coffee, tea, and pyrethrum, to many thousands of small scale farmers. Nor do we underestimate the magnitude of the task involved in introducing more than a million peasant farmers to the market economy. However, the mission is convinced that Kenya's agricultural sector will typically make better use of resources than most other sectors, provided the right environment for investment and entrepreneurial development is created, and provided the Government reinforces this favorable environment with sound development programs and adequate supporting services. Some of the constraints to this intensification of development effort are

---

5. See Annex Three, Chapter 3, for an analysis of this subject and for reference sources.

discussed later, and we shall suggest that these constraints must be overcome if Kenya is to realize her full potential in the future.

Resource Use by the Public Sector

The direct contribution of the public sector to the economy has not been as high in Kenya as in many African countries, since Kenya's development philosophy has been oriented towards the private sector. However, the public sector has been playing a steadily increasing role since 1964. By 1972, the total public sector accounted for more than 30 percent of GDP, of which about 16 percent was contributed by the Kenya Government itself, 7 percent by the EAC (principally the common service organizations), 5 percent by Kenya parastatal bodies, and only 2 percent by local authorities. The public sector has also been increasingly important in capital formation: whereas only 25 percent of capital formation was generated in the public sector in 1964, the proportion had risen to more than 30 percent by 1972.

In line with this increasing participation in the economy, the public sector has been preempting an increasing share of the total resources available to the economy to carry out its development program. As a consequence of the commendable fiscal effort referred to earlier, government revenue has mounted to over 30 percent of monetary GDP, and by 1971 government savings accounted for over 20 percent of total domestic savings. Supplementing the available domestic resources, the public sector has also absorbed an increasing (though still small) proportion of total imports, and now attracts about the same volume of long-term capital from abroad as the private sector. It has also resorted to an increased scale of borrowing on the domestic market.

Thus the public sector, though still overshadowed by the private sector, is utilizing an increasing share of the economy's total resources. It is therefore important to see how well these resources are being used. It should be borne in mind, too, that apart from the financial resources with which we are mainly concerned, the public sector has also attracted a high proportion[6] of Kenya's skilled citizens, who are probably her most valuable single resource at present.

We have not calculated incremental capital-output ratios for the private and public sectors separately. However, the calculations of sectoral ICORs made by the mission (see Table 2, Annex One) do indicate that ICORs have been rising rapidly in most sectors in which public participation is highest. In "general government," where the concept of ICOR is admittedly rather confusing, ICOR has risen from 1.4 in 1964 to 2.6 by 1971. More relevant, perhaps, are the rising ICORs in the enterprise sectors in which the public sector has a substantial or dominant role. In transport and communications, for example, ICOR has risen from less than three to more than eight between 1964 and 1971, while ICOR in construction and works has increased from two to more than seven. Only in electricity and water, in which ICORs were very high to begin with, has the ratio shown any tendency to fall over this period.

There is therefore some evidence of falling efficiency in the use of investment resources in the Kenya public sector. In fact, as described in Annex Three, the whole of the rising trend in total ICOR seems to be attributable to the public sector, and ICORs in the private sector have generally been stable or, in some critical sectors like manufacturing, actually falling. However, the use of ICORs as a measure of efficiency in resource use is, as pointed out earlier, of limited reliability, and is perhaps particularly inadequate in examining general government activities which, by their very nature, have an indirect rather than a direct effect on development. We shall therefore briefly look at

---

6. In 1971, the public sector employed 46 percent of middle and high level citizen manpower.

the public sector's contribution to employment and income distribution and then examine the broader impact of public sector activity on the economy as a whole.

The public sector's direct contribution to employment has been very limited if its total resource use is taken into account. Although the public sector employs about 38 percent of wage earners in the "modern" sector and about 25 percent of all wage earners, when we look at *total* employment, the public sector's contribution is insignificant. It employs only 5 percent of the estimated labor force, even though it contributes over 30 percent to total GDP.

If the public sector's direct contribution to employment has apparently been limited, its direct impact on the problems of income distribution has certainly been negative. Public services at all levels, including teaching, fall wholly within the "modern" sector as described in the previous paragraph, and enjoy an average income far in excess of the income of all but the most successful farmer or self-employed businessman, and has now almost caught up with average earnings in the nonagricultural private sector. Given this structure of earnings, any increase in the relative share of public sector employment will widen the income gap between wage earners and the rest of the economy. And, of course, any increase in salaries, such as that proposed by the Ndegwa Commission and recently implemented, further establishes public servants among the elite in the labor force.

The public sector has not generally been a price setter in wages and salaries; that role has been played by the private urban sector. But public sector salary policy has reinforced the detrimental effect urban formal sector wages have had on the rest of the economy, as described above, and it has been accepted that the private sector lead should be followed rather than resisted.[7] The public sector has not provided the leadership it might have in setting standards for housing and other conditions of service which are appropriate to Kenya's stage of development.

We can examine Government's indirect role in development in three ways: first, a look at the overall management of the economy and the general economic program which results; then, a look at the environment provided to steer the private sector along the right lines; and finally an examination of the pattern of resource use by the public sector itself. Both direct participation in production and the expenditure incurred on behalf of the whole economy will be considered.

The mission has scrutinized trends in government expenditure over past Plan periods in previous Bank reports. It is only necessary therefore to state briefly, by way of summary, that the allocation of expenditure between the various categories of services has been reasonable, and the Government has succeeded very well in holding down the total outlay on administration, defense, and other general services, as well as the servicing of its financial obligations, to enable the bulk of available resources to be channeled into economic, community, and social services which can directly benefit her people.

However, within the resources devoted to development, there has been a very pronounced trend towards an increasing emphasis on social services and infrastructure, and a corresponding fall in the proportion of resources available for directly productive investments.[8] We do not wish to offer fine judgments on intersectoral allocations, since, in the final analysis, these can be made only by the country in the light of its own

---

7. This was, for example, the prime argument for a general increase in civil service salaries accepted by the Ndegwa Commission.

8. For example, between 1968/69 (the last year of the previous Plan) and 1972/73, total government expenditure more than doubled. Of the £107 million increase in expenditure over this period, £41 million went for additional social services, £21 million for transport and highways, and £23 million for increased administrative and financial expenditures. If transfer payments are excluded, expenditures for agriculture showed only a small increase in current terms, and no increase in real terms (see Table 10.3, *Economic Survey*, 1973.).

complex economic and political goals. However, it is clear that the change in the pattern of government expenditure over the years has been one contributing factor to increasing ICOR and the slow rate of growth of employment. Nor, as far as we can tell, does the increasing expenditure on social services seem to have gone very far towards redressing the previous imbalances in the distribution of benefits in Kenya. Later, we shall be arguing that there will need to be a greater emphasis on the more productive sectors of the economy—particularly agriculture—if Kenya is to achieve her goals of rapidly expanding and widely distributing incomes and employment within the resources available to her.

CHAPTER 4

A STRATEGY FOR INCREASING GROWTH AND EMPLOYMENT

Analysis of the first decade leads us to conclude that Kenya will not be able to achieve her development goals simply by continuing past policies. A significant redirection of policy will be required in the future. The emerging resource constraint obliges Kenya to look for other ways to mobilize resources, but more important, to make better use of presently available resources, such as scarce skills and managerial talent. Since it may not be possible to increase average savings rate any further it becomes even more necessary to ensure that investment funds are used efficiently. Wide disparities in incomes, growing unemployment, and widespread poverty mean that Kenya must find better ways of sharing the benefits of development if rapid growth and equitable distribution are both to be achieved. But budgetary constraints will impede the rate at which the Government can extend services to the poor, so the use and nature of such expenditure have to be reexamined. Finally, Kenya is likely to face a severe constraint in the foreign exchange she can earn. This will almost certainly prove the effective brake on development until she can become more self-reliant in the way she orients production towards exports and utilizes more of her own resources, particularly land and labor, and fewer foreign inputs, in the production process.

The challenge which faces Kenya as she enters the second decade is to sustain or accelerate the past high rate of growth, within the resources likely to be available, and at the same time to increase employment opportunities and provide rising incomes to all her people. The problems are simply expressed and the Government is all too well aware of them. Solutions are not always obvious or easy and often they are unpalatable. We shall now examine the direction in which Kenya might move in confronting her problems. We shall look at some of the alternative policy instruments and changes which might be open to her, and suggest which could be of most value in striving towards accelerated growth and a wider distribution of income. In so doing, the mission is conscious of the limitations of its own knowledge and very much aware that only the Government and the people of Kenya can decide what course is best for the future development of the country. However, we hope that some of the suggestions offered may be of value to the Government in arriving at the difficult decisions which it faces.

The Need for Change in Development Strategy

To assess the prospects for future development the mission projected the development of the economy up to 1978 (the end of the Third Plan period) under varying assumptions about the rate and structure of growth and the policy instruments which might be applied. Since this report is concerned with basic strategic choices which face the economy, some of which can only have effect over the longer term, the projections were also extended on to 1985. The analysis was undertaken within the framework of a macro-economic model of the economy which is explained in detail in Annex One. It should be emphasized that these projections are intended not to predict the future, but to suggest the directions of movements within the economy and to provide a framework for testing the sensitivity of key economic variables and policy instruments.

As a starting point, we calculated a basic set of projections (the "basic scenario") based on assumptions very similar to those which were being discussed within Government at the time of the mission's visit to Kenya as a base for the forthcoming plan.[1] We

---

1. The major difference between the two sets of assumptions is that our basic scenario builds in a deterioration in Kenya's terms of trade with the rest of the world, considerably increasing the external gap to be financed.

were thus able to use the basic projections to test whether the underlying strategy of the 1974–78 Plan is likely to be feasible in terms of the resources which might be available, and acceptable in terms of the probable impact on growth, employment, and the attack on poverty.

On the whole, the basic projections assume that Kenya seeks to follow a pattern of growth similar to that followed in the past. They assume that the average growth rate of GDP over the Plan period would be significantly higher (7½ percent) than in the past, allowing average per capita income to grow by about 4 percent a year in real terms. Assuming stable ICORs, this expansion in production would require a total investment of £1,150 million (1970 prices) over the Plan period, or about 25 percent of GDP. On the whole, in testing the feasibility of such a growth target, the basic projections are based on optimistic assumptions, especially in regard to ICORs, domestic savings, and movements in the terms of trade.

If the increased foreign resources could be found to fill the growing external resource gap generated by the rapid rate of development we have assumed, domestic savings would be adequate—based on the optimistic assumptions made in the model. But, in the opinion of the mission, it is most unlikely that foreign resources could be found on the scale implied by the projections, at least not on any sort of reasonable terms, and it appears that the balance of payments will emerge as the binding constraint during the new Plan period, if the pattern of development approximates that assumed in the basic scenario.

Looking at the balance of payments a little more closely, it was estimated that imports will need to expand at about 11 percent a year (in current prices) to support the projected rate of growth, which would mean that Kenya might face a resource deficit of over £96 million by 1978, even after allowing for an optimistic 9½ percent annual growth in exports. Over the whole period 1974–78, the projections indicate that the total deficit on current account might be about £521 million. Against this, the mission estimated that net disbursements of external assistance (including private investment) might amount to £270 million over the period, which would leave nearly half of the external gap unfilled. If we extend this pattern of growth to 1985, the resource position rapidly gets out of hand: by 1985 the external gap increases to over £400 million a year, which appears to be out of all proportion to the inflow of foreign capital which could be attracted to Kenya on any kinds of terms. We therefore consider that the pattern of development projected in the basic scenario could not be long supported by the resources likely to be available.

But the basic scenario is unacceptable for another reason. Even if the resources could be mobilized to attain the target growth rates, the pattern of growth would continue the past less than adequate attack on employment and poverty. On the rather optimistic assumption that the historical rise in labor productivity slows down, wage employment in the modern sector would increase by 171,000 by 1978, absorbing only about 18 percent of the increased labor force. Even if we include the employment offered by a vigorously growing urban informal sector, the position is not materially changed, and more than 75 percent of the young people who will have entered the labor force during the Plan period would have to be absorbed into agriculture or remain unemployed.

Of course, it is widely accepted that the bulk of the labor force will continue to be occupied in agriculture and related activities. The really important variable in the employment equation is the average level of incomes in the agricultural sector, where most of Kenya's "working poor" are to be found. We have calculated the average income per worker in agriculture on the assumption that all adults in the rural areas are workers and that agriculture absorbs all the residential labor not employed elsewhere. The resulting "poverty index" becomes, in our view, an important and perhaps over-riding criterion by which to judge development strategies. In our basic scenario, the poverty index creeps up from £43.4 in 1973 to only £47.2 in 1978, or at an annual rate of only about ½ percent in real terms. In contrast, average per capita incomes in the economy as a whole would be expected to grow at about 4 percent each year and average personal consumption at 3½ percent. Then, even if the ambitious growth targets were attained, the poor would get relatively poorer during the Plan period, and even by 1985, the average income per worker in agriculture would be only £53.8 in 1970 prices.[2] We are sure that such meager progress in spreading the benefits of development is no longer acceptable in Kenya.

Thus the basic projections we have made—not substantially different from the preliminary projections which were being considered as a framework for the Third Plan—fail to meet the basic criteria outlined above, since the high target growth rates are neither feasible within the resources likely to be available, nor adequate in terms of their impact on employment and poverty. Therefore, we feel that substantial reorientation in the pattern of development will have to take place if the objectives of rapid growth and widely dispersed incomes are to be achieved. In the next section, we shall examine how this might be done.

An Examination of Alternatives

In examining the kind of policy changes which could help to increase growth, expand employment, or conserve resources, and thus to bring about an accelerated flow of benefits to the people of Kenya, we have relied heavily on the conceptual framework of the macro-economic model developed by the mission. We feel it necessary to stress the limitations of such a model, particularly in view of the inadequacies of the data. The model is used not to try to predict the future but as a device for computation and as an aid to systematic analysis of the likely effect of alternative policies. We are conscious that some of the parameters of the model are derived a priori, and that many of the assumptions built into the model are based on inadequate historical data or reasonable guesses about the future. For example, the ICORs used are average and not marginal coefficients, and knowledge of household consumption or saving behavior is very scanty. Again, because Kenya's experience in using such policy instruments as the rate of interest or the exchange rate is limited, we have looked to the experience of other countries for guidance about what might happen in Kenya, at the same time recognizing the dangers of relying too heavily on such reasoning. Finally, estimates have had to be made about the future in areas of considerable uncertainty. For example, projections of the future resource gap are particularly sensitive to changes in terms of trade, although future import and export prices are very difficult to estimate at the present time.

Thus, conscious as we are of the limitations of our model and of projecting the effect of alternative policy decisions on the basis of inadequate data, we have tried whenever possible to err on the side of caution, and, if anything, may well have overcompensated for data inadequacies in predicting the magnitude of Kenya's future resource gap. For instance, assumptions about import and export prices are probably on the optimistic side, implying that Kenya's resource gap may well increase faster than projected. Similarly, assuming that household savings income ratio will return to its previously high level may also be optimistic. In estimating the possible effect of changes in factor prices we have also been conservative. While not claiming, therefore, that any of the individual assumptions are necessarily highly accurate, we do believe that our

---

2. We have not tried to estimate the value of remittances in calculating residual rural incomes, although the ILO/UNDP report concluded that these were an important supplement to rural income. The index may therefore exaggerate the poverty of the rural poor. Moreover, the value-added in agriculture is assumed to be unaffected by the size of the agriculture labor force.

general diagnosis of Kenya's development problem is correct and that the changes in policy which will be suggested in our "preferred strategy" lead in the right direction.

Some Nonsolutions

First of all, we have examined a range of alternatives which may appear to offer a solution to the problem of sustaining a fast rate of well distributed growth, but which we think are at best inadequate, and perhaps even directly harmful or counterproductive. On the one hand are measures which might be taken to help supplement or conserve resources. Faced with a sharp deterioration in the balance of payments, Kenya recently resorted to the imposition of *import controls* as a means of containing the position. The Government recognizes that this is not a solution to a long term disequilibrium in the balance of payments, and we have used the model in Annex One to demonstrate that controls are less than fully effective in curtailing imports, and can cause serious problems of domestic inflation. In Annex Three, we emphasize that such controls tend to be self-defeating in the long run, since they may actually increase Kenya's relative dependence on imports (by shifting import demand towards intermediate goods), discourage exports by implicit taxation, and thus perpetuate balance of payments crises which in turn call for increased controls.

On the other hand, an alternative solution might seem to be a much greater degree of *foreign borrowing* to meet the increasing resource requirements generated by high growth rates. As noted above, the basic projections already allow for the increased flow of private capital and official aid which we think Kenya is likely to attract over the next Plan period. We believe that this supply is somewhat responsive, both up and down, to the attractiveness of her development strategy, and we refer to this flexibility later. However, there is little prospect of borrowing on the rapidly expanding scale implied by the basic projections, without a major shift towards commercial sources of finance. Kenya has already taken on some suppliers' credits, and has floated one moderate loan on the Eurodollar market. Clearly, some borrowing on conventional terms is justified, depending upon the nature of the case; but a growing reliance on commercial borrowing to fill a major part of the resource gap would be very difficult to defend. As indicated in Annex One, an undue reliance on suppliers' credits would result in a rapid increase in the cost of servicing external debt which may or may not be acceptable to the Kenya Government. But, even more serious, the cost of servicing commercial credits would soon overtake the new disbursements, so that the net transfer could well become negative within a few years. Only a remarkably productive use of loans, combined with a package of really sound domestic policies, could justify such a course of action.

As a last resort, it might be decided that the high target rates of growth would have to be reduced, and that Kenya must settle for a rather more modest development goal. We therefore examined the consequences of *reducing the rate of growth* to about 5 percent a year, which is still a reasonable rate of growth in the developing world as a whole. However, in the view of the mission, this is not a solution for a country with Kenya's potential and past performance. In particular, such a growth would slow down the rate of employment and have an even more serious effect on the poverty index: the effect of lower overall growth would mean that the poor would not only become *relatively* poorer, as projected in the basic scenario, but could even become worse off in *absolute* terms. Thus, we do not see a lower rate of growth, on the same pattern of development as in the past, as an acceptable policy option for Kenya.

Finally, it could be argued that a lower rate of growth might be acceptable if it were combined with direct programs to *increase employment*. Unfortunately, some of the most misguided nonsolutions in development economics are motivated by a genuine desire to increase employment and benefit the poor. The developing world is replete with "make-work" programs, national youth brigades, and other similar nonsolutions, and as we caution in Annex Two, it is sometimes difficult for a democratic government to avoid costly, but ineffective political gestures once the pressures of unemployment and poverty become too great. Kenya, in its tripartite agreements, has its own experience of temporary palliatives. There is, we believe, some room for promoting labor-intensive methods of production and thus lowering labor productivity in the modern sector. But even if labor productivity is held constant in our projections, the prospects for employment and poverty are not materially improved, since the modern or formal sector accounts for such a small proportion of the labor force.

Perhaps the most dangerous form of nonsolution is a policy to *increase wages*, in the mistaken belief that this will help "income distribution." By contrast, the likely effects, as we discuss elsewhere, are to widen the most worrying "gap"—that between wage employees and the rest—to increase unemployment, and to throw an increased burden on the informal sector.

We do not mean to dismiss out-of-hand the alternatives discussed above. In the proper circumstances, any of these alternatives might be employed in conjunction with other policy instruments. But we believe none of them get to the heart of the problem, and all of them contain dangers. What, then, are the realistic methods of tackling the problem?

Some Feasible Alternatives

Having identified some of the less useful alternatives facing Kenya in considering her future development, we examined the sensitivity of the basic projections to two major areas of policy: changes in factor prices and changes in the structure of growth. The methodology employed was first to examine the sensitivity of each variable separately to see how important it might be for development policy, and then to combine the various elements into a single policy package which might be the basis for a development strategy.

We first of all examined the likely effects of changes in the exchange rate, as a policy variable, and the effective cost of capital. In Annex One we examined the effects on the economy of a 20 percent increase in the price of foreign exchange, on generally conservative assumptions about elasticities.[3] In our model, a devaluation of this magnitude, without other changes of policy, would reduce the resource gap quite substantially over a period of time, though it accentuates domestic inflation. It would also have favorable, though limited, effects on wage employment and rural poverty, primarily through its stimulating effects on agriculture. We then examined the possible effects of increasing the cost of capital by raising interest rates from 9 to 12 percent and abolishing capital investment allowances (which would be equivalent to an 8 percent increase in the cost of capital). On the assumption of unit elasticity of factor substitution, these measures would also reduce the resource gap, by reducing the demand for capital goods inputs, and would have a greater effect on employment and rural poverty than a change in the exchange rate.

When we combine these changes in factor prices, on the assumptions made in the model, the mission believes that they can have a significant impact on Kenya's development prospects. Taking the changes together as one policy package, we calculate that the resource gap projected in our "basic scenario" could be roughly halved; although at the expense of some additional domestic inflation. However, it is important to note that while these policies help in alleviating Kenya's resource constraint, they are by no means a complete solution, and in particular, are inadequate as a weapon against unemployment and poverty. Thus, even under the combined package of changes, the residual resource gap over the Plan period would still be sizable, and wage employment would

3. See Annex One, page 102.

only increase by 120,000 by 1985, or 23 percent of the increase in the labor force. Moreover, improvement in the standard of living of the rural poor would still be painfully slow. The mission has therefore concluded that factor price adjustments are a useful but insufficient instrument of change, and that it must look to additional measures to do the job.

We suspected that the most significant variable in our projections would be the pattern of growth, or the different growth rates of the major sectors. This is because the efficiency of investment varies substantially between sectors, not only in the productivity of investment (ICOR), but in the contribution each sector makes to employment and incomes, and the demand each sector makes on Kenya's scarce resources.[4] More specifically, we can single out investment in agriculture as Kenya's most efficient use of resources. Pound for pound, investment in agriculture contributes more to development, at less cost, than any other kind of investment. This holds good for every test of efficiency. In resource use, past data on investment and output imply that sector ICORs in agriculture are low, Kenya's input-output table shows that the sector generates little demand for imported machinery or inputs, and manpower survey data demonstrate that very modest calls are made on scarce local or expatriate skilled manpower. Yet the benefits of agricultural growth are very considerable, producing more growth per unit of investment than most sectors, are primarily export-oriented, and are instrumental in generating employment and attacking poverty among the rural poor.

We therefore examined the effects of increasing the rate of growth in the agricultural sector by one percentage point, while reducing growth rates in the principal infrastructure sectors—construction, transport and power—in which resource use (in the widest sense of the term) is presently less efficient. The effects of changing the composition of growth in this way, while maintaining the same overall growth of the economy, are encouraging. In particular, the accelerated growth of agricultural production results in a real improvement in rural incomes, and the standard of living of the rural poor rises by 2.6 percent a year, which is close to the growth in average per capita income in the country as a whole. Yet changes in the structure of growth taken by themselves, are not sufficient to achieve Kenya's economic objectives; in particular, the resource gap arising in the future is still considerable. As a final step, therefore, we have examined the combination of factor price changes and restructured growth into a single policy package, which we henceforth refer to as our "preferred strategy."

Towards a Strategy for the Second Decade

The combination of factor price changes[5] and restructured growth has a marked influence on development in Kenya, according to our projections. Assuming about the same overall growth rate as in our "basic scenario," the combined effect of these policy changes would be to reduce the external resource gap to near manageable proportions, while making a valuable additional contribution to employment. Compared with the

---

4. From Annex One, we quote the following indicators of the wide variations in the efficiency of resource use:

	ICOR (1970)	Skilled Manpower as % of Total Labor	Imported Raw Materials as % of Domestic Value-Added
Agriculture	2.6	3.5	8.8
Manufacturing	2.2	20.6	76.9
Construction	6.9	13.8	45.2
Electricity and Water	6.6	25.0	13.1
Transport	8.5	17.0	16.2

5. In the "preferred strategy," we have assumed only a 10 percent exchange rate adjustment, instead of the 20 percent referred to previously.

results of the "basic scenario," this "preferred scenario" would increase the rate of growth of wage employment from about 5.3 percent to 6 percent (leading to an additional 135,000 jobs in 1985), but, more significantly, would increase the average income of the poor by an additional 13 percent by 1985. Under the preferred strategy, the poverty index would increase by about 2.8 percent a year which would mean that the average level of the poor would be about $170 (at 1970 prices) by 1985.

The value of this combination of policy measures lies in their complementary nature. Thus, while factor price adjustments (particularly a change in exchange rate) have most impact on reducing the resource constraint, the attack on unemployment and poverty is assisted mainly by changes in the pattern of growth. Of course, the projections made are not intended to forecast the precise effect of policy changes. But we do feel that the direction and magnitude of their effects are sufficiently reliable for us to go on, in the coming section, to suggest the general outline of a development strategy for the coming decade.

Elements of a Development Strategy

The general objective of a development strategy is to induce the Kenyan economy to operate more efficiently so that the people of Kenya get more growth, more employment, and a wider distribution of benefits per unit of resources invested. But in recommending that the efficiency of resource use must be increased, we would like to ensure that increased efficiency should not simply be another planning goal or management slogan, but should be *built in* to the fabric of the economy, so that the process of growth will automatically produce greater benefits from the resources that are fed in. This is no easy task, and there is no minimum package of policy reform, no magic formula, which can be offered as a solution. Rather, we see a number of desirable directions of policy change, many of them complementary, and any of which could promote faster or better development. The further and faster the economy can move in these directions, the faster the incremental benefits will be achieved; but the mission does not try to suggest either a minimum requirement or an optimum target.

However, while we are concerned with a combination of many policy changes, we believe that there are two principal means by which the efficiency of resource use can be increased: by *restructuring* the *pattern* growth and by *reforming* the *process* of growth. Through these two processes Kenya can, in our opinion, get the most out of her development efforts.

Restructuring the Pattern of Growth

By this term we mean a change in the sectoral composition of growth, so that a larger proportion of Kenya's resources, and the resources she gets from abroad, are channeled into those sectors which can use them most efficiently. Essentially, this means allocating a larger proportion of investment, foreign exchange, and skilled manpower to the directly productive sectors, particularly agriculture, which are the most efficient sectors in Kenya. This policy does not mean, of course, that other sectors should be starved of resources. Demands for infrastructure, public utilities, and social services will continue to preempt a large share of resources. What we propose is a large quantum increase in the flow of resources into productive uses, and a significant shift in relative sector allocations. With limited resources, this would mean that a lower proportion of resources—and perhaps even fewer resources in absolute terms—would be channeled into infrastructural investments, and that there would be a tighter curb on the growth of social services. Some implications of this are discussed later.

In our macro-economic model, the restructuring of the pattern of growth is affected by manipulating sectoral growth rates, or in other words, by altering the sectoral composition of Kenya's growth. But there is another aspect of restructuring which might prove to be equally powerful in the longer term. This is to alter the structure of growth *within* sectors, so that preference is given in resource allocation to those subsectors which make the most efficient use of resources, in terms of ICOR, labor intensity, or their demand on foreign exchange. There would appear to be much scope for this kind of intrasectoral reallocation of resources, particularly in the infrastructural and construction sectors where ICORs are presently high. For example, a relative shift in the emphasis of road construction towards rural roads should lower overall ICOR within the construction sector, as well as increasing the employment and distributional impact of highway expenditure. Similar improvements in the efficiency of sectoral investment programs might be expected to result from a relative shift towards small scale enterprise in the industrial sector, or a significant diversion of resources from large office blocks to low cost housing in the construction industry. Another important application might be in the social services, where we argue that the means must be found to widen the benefits which flow from social expenditures by changing the intrasectoral pattern of resource use.

As with any other change in economic management, restructured growth can be achieved partly through the Government's own investment program directly, and partly through the manipulation of the private sector. We would put major emphasis on direct government action for two reasons: first, the majority of investment decisions in infrastructure, economic services, and social services are made within the public sector; and, second, an improvement in public sector planning and services is an essential precondition for any acceleration in the productive sectors, particularly agriculture. But in many cases, direct action will be rendered less effective, or even futile, unless an appropriate set of incentives is provided to the private sector to move in the right direction. We see the major policy instrument for steering private enterprise in the right direction as being the price mechanism, and this theme recurs in the following chapter.

Reforming the Process of Growth

This calls for improving the efficiency of resource use within every sector and subsector, down to the project level, so that *all* investments contribute more to development. This requires a set of policies which will induce the entrepreneur and manager to employ resources to the greater advantage of society as well as himself. Society's needs are to make greater use of its own abundant resources, particularly labor, and to conserve scarce resources, particularly foreign exchange and skilled manpower. Thus, at all levels of the economy, down to the smallest investment decision, the objective of reform is to combine resources in a proportion which more closely reflects their real scarcity value.

Again we believe that the Government can use both direct and indirect means to reform the process of growth, but in contrast to the restructuring of growth it is better for the emphasis to be on the indirect but powerful influence of price signals on economic behavior. The public sector program can contribute directly to some extent to more efficient growth, through better project design and appraisal, but the major task lies with the private sector which must be induced to use the country's resources well. In the past, the private sector has responded efficiently to price signals, which unfortunately, as indicated in Annex Three, have not always been the most appropriate ones. There is good reason to suppose that a more appropriate set of signals will induce the private sector to perform more effectively.

The exchange rate has been stable in Kenya for most of the period since Independence, although the Kenya shilling was revalued against sterling in 1967 and has since 1973 been devalued along with the US dollar. The mission feels that it is appropriate that Kenya, together with her Partners in the East African Community, might now consider the *exchange rate* as a positive and flexible instrument of policy—not simply because it is becoming fashionable to think of the exchange rate as just another price signal which the Government can influence, but also because the price of foreign exchange, in conjunction with other policy changes, could be a most powerful instrument in stimulating growth and benefiting the poor.

The *interest rate* structure in Kenya has been virtually static for the last ten years and is now well below the level in most of the countries from which Kenya borrows. Apart from the discouragement given to savings (the real interest rate is now negative in Kenya for the first time), low interest rates encourage foreign investors to raise money in Kenya (thus preempting her scarce resources) instead of borrowing abroad. Low interest rates also encourage excessive capital intensity by reducing the effective cost of capital, and may lead to less efficient allocation among sectors. The investment allowance provided under the income tax law has the same result. The effect of abolishing the investment allowance and raising typical lending rates from 9 to 12 percent, according to the assumptions made in our projections, is again significant.

We have already indicated that increasing *wage rates* can in no way be considered a means towards a better income distribution in Kenya and would on the contrary be likely to make matters worse. On the other hand, the mission did not consider a reduction in wage rates, even though present levels do lead to substantial distortions in resource use. This is not because we underestimate the significance of the relative level of formal sector wages: on the contrary, we believe wage rates are very important and have discussed them at some length in Annex Three. Rather, it is felt that an immediate and direct reduction in nominal wages rates would be neither politically feasible nor sociallly desirable.

Chapter 5

Feasibility, Constraints, and Tactics

In this chapter we shall attempt to test the feasibility of the general strategy outlined in the previous chapter, first by explaining in more detail what is meant by restructuring of growth as it affects the major sectors of the economy; second, by describing the instruments to be used in reforming the process of growth. Finally, since a more efficient use of resources presupposes the availability of resources, we shall conclude the chapter by examining prospects for mobilization of domestic savings and external capital for development.

Restructuring the Pattern of Growth

The general strategy outlined in the previous chapter calls for an increased flow of resources into directly productive sectors and a curb on the growth of infrastructure and social services. But is such a policy feasible in terms of the absorptive capacity of the productive sectors, and what would be the implications of a deliberate policy of constraining resource use in sectors such as construction, transport, or education? Clearly, we cannot attempt a systematic sector-by-sector review of feasibility, but we shall briefly examine the possibilities in the principal sectors and identify what seem to be the major constraints to implementing a strategy of this kind.

The Priorities

The significance of the productive sectors springs from the need to ensure the more efficient use of resources, not only in the growth of domestic value-added but also in terms of employment, the distribution pattern of incomes, and the expansion of exports. Without underestimating the valuable contribution which can be made by other sectors, including the small but rapidly growing mining sector, we are primarily concerned with the two largest productive sectors, agriculture and manufacturing. This report unreservedly allocates the most immediate priority to agriculture for two reasons. First, since agriculture is already a very efficient user of resources, an increase in agricultural investment can safely be relied upon to produce substantial benefits without any fundamental reforms to policy or the structure of production. Second, since the overwhelming proportion of the people of Kenya presently depend upon agriculture for their livelihood, an improvement in agricultural productivity is the *only* way a major attack can be launched on rural poverty in the immediate future.

However, an emphasis on agriculture does not mean a corresponding neglect of industry. On the contrary, as indicated at the end of the report, we believe that manufacturing will become increasingly important as a growth sector, particularly as the pressure of population on the limited supply of good land continues to grow. We see the two major sectors becoming increasingly complementary, rather than competitive, since agriculture will provide both the raw materials for industrial exports and an expanding domestic market for manufactures. But the manufacturing industry is not likely to play this crucial complementary role without a significant change in direction; this is why we have put so much emphasis on the need for its reform.

Agriculture

Since 1967, the monetary agriculture sector has grown at an average rate of about 6½ percent a year in real terms, a very commendable performance. However, investment has not increased in real terms in recent years, which suggests that the momentum of development may be difficult to sustain for much longer.[1] The sluggish pace of investment is due in some measure to the completion or slowing down of some of the large land reform measures of the late fifties and early sixties, and also reflects the fact that much of the development expenditure on agricultural ministries has been going into buildings and transport equipment for supporting staff, rather than productive investments in the land.

The mission's first concern, therefore, is for a resurgence of investment in agriculture, by both the private sector and by Government, to ensure that the momentum of development is maintained at its past high level. But further than this, the preferred strategy of this report calls for a *higher* rate of growth of agricultural production as well. It may be useful first to make explicit the magnitude of the shift towards agriculture which might be necessary. The acceleration in agricultural development which is built into the preferred scenario means that the average growth rate of the agriculture sector would have to increase by about one percentage point—or from the 6½ percent rate assumed in the basic projections to about 7½ percent a year. In investment terms, this acceleration in growth would call for investment in agriculture to grow at about 6½ percent a year, in real terms, rather than 5½ percent, assuming no change in ICOR.[2]

We regard such an acceleration in growth perfectly feasible. The recent Agricultural Sector Survey[3] has suggested a strategy for the further development of agriculture, and we need do no more than indicate the general outlines of this strategy. The report draws attention to the pressure of population which already exists on the land, with present techniques, particularly west of the Rift Valley, and the importance of providing measures to increase incomes and employment *in situ* by intensifying land use in heavily populated localities, mainly through integrated area based programs. The report lays particular stress on the development of the areas of medium ecological potential, containing dense concentrations of population at totally unsatisfactory income levels, often at bare subsistence. The need for an integrated approach to smallholders is stressed, which will combine results of research with effective farmer training, and design an integrated delivery service for credit and farm inputs. Much more research is needed to establish the technical basis for increasing production in the context of practicable smallholder farming systems.

The technical constraint is least serious in the case of maize, and the survey mission placed top priority on maize expansion as a basis for future rural development. A fair amount of evidence is also available on improved production practices for such crops as wheat, coffee and tea, and, to a lesser extent, sugar. Modest investments in technical research and design of farming systems, together with improvement in the organization of promotion programs, would enable a rapid expansion in other crops, such as oilseeds, pulses, small grains, and horticultural crops. Over the medium term, livestock can also be significantly expanded, particularly in high potential areas. The survey noted that the demand prospects, both domestically and for exports, are generally strong, although some export commodities may face market difficulties.

Nearly all these programs which have been identified by the sector survey mission would have a major impact on a large number of smallholders; and it is for this reason that we put so much emphasis on the distribution advantages of agricultural growth. Any program to diversify agriculture and increase productivity automatically increases the

1. In constant (1964) prices, capital formation in agriculture has remained virtually static, at about £10 million a year since 1968. In relative terms, agriculture's share of total capital formation in the monetary economy has fallen from around 17 percent in the mid-sixties to 8 to 10 percent in the last three years.
2. Assuming this accelerated rate of investment could be achieved immediately, it would mean that the total investment program in agriculture over the 1974–78 Plan period would be increased by only about 7 percent above the Plan target.
3. See Part III.

demand for labor, and much of this spills over into a demand for wage labor.[4] Thus whether new development takes place among emerging subsistence farmers, through increased production on commercial smallholdings, or even on large farms or estates, the increment in output will mainly benefit people who are at the lower end of the income scale.

It appears, therefore, that the potential is there. The major constraints are also clearly definable—in tribal and cultural barriers to improved land use, in particular areas of research, in the organization of the public support services, in the delivery system for smallholders and, as we suggest in Annex Five, in the capacity of the operating ministries to define sector strategy and identify and implement development programs. We take up the question of absorptive capacity again later, as it is crucial to the feasibility of the mission's strategy. At this point, however, it is only relevant to emphasize that we see no inherent obstacle—in ecological potential, technology, or the availability of markets—to the growth rate envisaged by our strategy. We might, in fact, state the position even more directly—the mission can see no option, at least during the seventies, but to accelerate agricultural development if Kenya's goals are to be achieved.

Industry

We have not, in our general strategy, suggested a faster rate of growth in industry. Instead, we have put emphasis on reforming the manufacturing sector (and the rest of the urban formal sector) to eliminate some of the obviously inefficient firms and to reduce the extent to which manufacturing operates at the expense of agriculture and other sectors of the economy. The range of policies we have suggested in this report for the manipulation of the private sector might discourage the growth of manufacturing in Kenya. However, the main discouragement would be to the kind of firm which, in the past, has earned good profits in a highly protected market at the expense of the majority of the population. The loss of these investments could only be of benefit to Kenya. On the other hand, it is important that she should get an increasing flow of foreign investment of the right kind, and we would hope that the range of policy reforms advocated here would induce profit-oriented private capital of the right kind to flow into Kenya's manufacturing industry. However, we would go further, and suggest that the Government might play a much more active role in identifying new opportunities for overseas investment and in seeking out potential investors.

We have also suggested two changes of emphasis within industry. The major change would be a relative switch from import substitution to resource-based export industries. The scope for further import substitution in final consumption goods is limited; and past experience has shown that these industries tend to have a low value-added, are relatively capital-intensive, and are able to demand high levels of protection to the detriment of the rest of the economy. Of course there will still be some scope for efficient import substitution, especially in capital and intermediate goods (which have hitherto received negative tariff protection), but it seems reasonable to presume that Kenya's comparative advantage in manufacturing lies not in providing skilled cheap labor to process imported materials, but in processing her own resources derived from the rich diversity of her soil.[5] It is, of course, impossible to demonstrate this comparative advantage, except on a

---

4. The African smallholder sector is already the largest single employer of wage labor in Kenya. In 1971, smallholders employed some 342,000 workers compared with less than 190,000 on large farms, 72,000 in private industry, and 42,000 in commerce. We would see the smallholder sector, spurred by increased productivity, the major source of employment for the expanding labor force in the years ahead.

5. Thus the sort of international subcontracting in footloose industry which has been the driving force of industrial development in countries such as South Korea is not likely to be appropriate for Kenya because of the scarcity of skilled labor and the generally high level of wages, in relation to efficiency.

case-by-case analysis of costs and markets, but a general move in this direction should make good sense.

Kenyan policy is already moving in the suggested direction. The recently announced export subsidy should be a useful incentive for export-oriented production, and a number of export-based investments have been made in Kenya in the last year or so.[6] However, even though industrial promotion is now more closely related to export industries, it will still be necessary to exercise great care in evaluating individual projects and in reviewing the level of protection-affected industry.

The second suggested shift in emphasis in our strategy is for an acceleration in small scale industry and other types of small scale economic activity. It has been indicated (in Annex Three) that we do not look to the informal sector as a major growth point of the economy. But there is impressive scope, nevertheless, for expanding opportunities for entrepreneurship and employment in small scale activities. The major constraints, referred to at greater length in Annex Three and Annex Five, are the present restrictions imposed on informal sector activity, on the one hand, and the inadequacy of public services and promotional programs, on the other. The Government has now indicated its intention of working to ease both of these constraints.[7] There is little point in pretending that the development of small scale activity will be easy, and in some respects it will depend upon reform of the urban formal sector. However, the longer term prospects for a thriving labor-intensive, low cost indigenous entrepreneurial sector must be regarded as favorable.

Infrastructure and Economic Services

It is not the contention of this report that expenditure on infrastructure or economic services is in any way unimportant. On the contrary, it is obvious that many investments in these sectors will be necessary to support Kenya's general development over the coming years, and some of them will be of high priority. In particular, public investment in infrastructure and public utilities is a necessary condition for the private sector to thrive. Thus, clearly, a large proportion of Kenya's total investment resources and government budget will continue to be channeled into power and water supplies, into highways, bridges and airports, and into a large variety of buildings. However, compared with many developing countries, Kenya is already relatively well served with infrastructure. For example, a fairly well developed road network serves the major concentrations of population, the basic rail link and power transmission lines have been established, and urban infrastructure is far ahead of that provided in the rural areas. There would therefore appear to be scope for curbing the *relative* share of the nation's resources which go into infrastructure, and thus freeing a larger share for directly productive investments.

It may not be necessary to think in terms of reduced value-added in these sectors, since there may well be scope for increasing efficiency of resource use within these sectors, as indicated in the previous chapter. These are typically the sectors with the highest ICORs (see Chapter 4, footnote 4) and a restructuring of the pattern of investment could have a significant impact on the capital-output ratio. This is also an area in which direct government action can be most effective, because much of the investment takes place within the public sector expenditure program. Thus, many of the possibilities for restructuring investment mentioned before, such as moving from trunk highways to rural access roads, or a shift in favor of low cost housing, are decisions

---

6. For example, fruit canning, vegetable dehydration, bean processing, coffee and tea processing, and tanning.

7. See, for example, *Sessional Paper on Employment*, No. 10 of 1973, Republic of Kenya, May 1973, particularly pp. 18–19 and 44–46.

which can be made by Government in determining the national plan, and all could succeed in reaping greater benefits from a given amount of capital expenditure.

There are, however, two related constraints which will affect the rate at which it can be feasible to taper off the flow of resources into infrastructure and economic services. The first is that some of these sectors, particularly road construction, have built up a momentum which will be difficult to slow down in the short term.[8] Another more serious constraint is that there is often not the means—either in terms of technology or the institutional basis—for reorienting an investment program. For example, the Ministry of Works is only now trying to identify a labor-intensive program for rural access road construction, and there is as yet no national program for shifting the emphasis of house construction to the lowest cost brackets, even though such a shift has now been accepted in principle. Thus, although there is no overall deficiency in planning in these sectors as there is in the productive sectors, the technology required for a reorientation towards rural services or towards labor-intensive technology will take time to develop. There is typically some change required in the attitude of planners and other professional staff to reexamine the uses to which resources can best be applied.[9]

Social Services

A rather similar situation can be seen within the social services. Again, the strategy proposed in this report calls not for a reduction in social expenditure but for a deceleration in the rate of growth of expenditure. No one can deny that a rapid growth is justified in education, health, and other services on both economic and humanitarian grounds, especially if social expenditure can be made a more effective instrument for achieving greater equitable distribution of benefits. But the past rate of increase in expenditure on social services—particularly education—is such that some curb is essential if it is not to run away with the budget. Since social services have great political support and can absorb very large increments of expenditure, it is certain that any denial will hurt, and thus the pressing need is to redefine priorities and ensure that the resources which can be spared for social services are used to the maximum benefit of the people for whom they are intended.

This may sound like a trite recommendation, but it does seem that resource use is not presently very efficient in the social services. We can illustrate what room there is for improvement by reference to the education sector, which has increased its expenditure faster than any other sector since Independence. But we feel that similar principles apply to the other social services, including health. In the case of education, government expenditures are expected to rise by 13 percent a year, in real terms, over the next five years, compared with an average growth of 7 percent GDP and 9 percent in total government expenditure. Yet the link between the education system and the labor market is obviously not functioning, and the country urgently needs to question the usefulness of turning out expensively educated young people who cannot be employed. A more disciplined control of secondary and university education, in line with the needs of the labor market, is perhaps the most obvious potential source of savings in education expenditure.

But other sources of savings are also evident—especially in the cost effectiveness of the education system. The mission has estimated that over £20 million could be saved over the next five-year plan period by increasing the average class size to forty in

---

8. For example, in trying to follow this principle in the new 1970–74 Plan, the Ministry of Finance and Planning has allocated a reduced share of investment to highway construction in the public expenditure program. But at the time of writing, the Ministry of Works appeared to have existing commitments (for roads under construction or committed under various aid agreements) amounting to the whole sum allocated.

9. One excellent example of the restructuring of sectoral growth patterns is the development of a rural water supply program.

primary schools and twenty-five in secondary schools, and there are other more radical and cost saving reforms, such as a shorter basic education than the nine years envisaged in the forthcoming plan, which might be considered. No changes of this kind can be introduced overnight, and nearly all of them involve very sensitive policy issues. But one of the implications of the tighter resource position we see Kenya facing is that policymakers will have to give a much closer scrutiny to the priorities within rapidly expanding areas such as education. The Government intends to establish a National Commission on Education Objectives and Policies which will, it is hoped, examine these priorities.

Planning and Implementation

The major constraint to any rapid restructuring of growth in the economy is the planning and implementation capacity of the public sector. The most serious deficiency, as mentioned earlier, is the absorptive capacity of the productive sectors, particularly in agriculture, but also in other productive sectors such as tourism, fisheries, and small scale business. We have given attention to this problem in Annex Five, which puts the highest priority on the need to identify and implement integrated agricultural production programs which can have a significant impact on agricultural growth and which affect a large number of rural households.

The absorptive capacity constraint in the productive sectors is the larger part of the problem. But, as indicated previously, the other part of the problem is the need to examine the priorities within those sectors, such as infrastructure and social services, where absorptive capacity is running ahead of available resources. Planners may have to learn to stretch their resource allocations to benefit more people.

The situation really calls for intensified management, as pointed out later, with perhaps more experienced manpower than Kenya can presently lay her hands on.[10] Moreover, many of these restructuring tasks take time, and the mission has no illusions that a significant change in direction of the kind proposed in the preferred strategy can be accomplished overnight. Some of the programs in infrastructure and social services have built up considerable momentum which should probably be allowed to run down only slowly; strong political support goes hand-in-hand with rising aspirations to demand continually improved services, and some of the most urgent innovations in the productive sectors can be expected only at the end of a long day's work. But to concede that the task is a long and difficult one only adds to the urgency of starting it. The longer the task is left, the more difficult and painful it certainly will become.

Reforming the Process of Growth

Manipulating Private Sector Behavior

Objectives. Since private enterprise is the preferred method of production in Kenya, most of the reforms suggested must take place within it, and this may need some revision in the country's management methods. The major goal is to manipulate private enterprise activities in such a way that the private sector will function more efficiently to the benefit of the country as a whole. This translates into the efficient use of resources in generating incomes and employment. This in turn means, as shown above, redirecting resources to the most productive sectors of private enterprise and increasing the

---

10. We have also pointed out, however, that Kenya's skilled manpower could frequently be deployed more productively than at present. For example, we have suggested (in Annex Five) that some diversion of planning staff from macro-economic planning could be productive, and (in Annex Three) that some of the competent civil servants now employed in operating various control measures might be better used to administer and monitor new production programs.

efficiency of resource use within each sector. But it also means seeking ways for the private sector to contribute to other major goals of society, such as more widely distributed income and progressive Kenyanization of personnel and property.

Means. We believe the most effective way to improve the economic performance of the private sector—as well as control its behavior in other ways—is to establish an appropriate set of price signals. The mission suggests in Annex Three that the entrepreneurs in Kenya, who make most of the important decisions affecting the economic health of the nation, have been given a false set of signals. They have followed them fairly faithfully, usually to their own advantage, but not always to the maximum benefit of society. Therefore, the first priority is to move towards more appropriate prices for the value of output and the factors of production. The most serious price distortion is probably the external tariff, which encourages the uneconomic use of resources in manufacturing and effectively taxes the productive use of resources in other sectors. The Kenya Government is already moving in the direction of reforming trade policy. But factor price distortions also induce resources to flow into sectors which do not use them very efficiently and encourage entrepreneurs to use capital, rather than labor. We have therefore suggested a further set of price adjustments effected through interest rate policy, taxation policy and a more flexible use of the cost of foreign exchange as a tool of development, and have indicated the dangers of rising urban wages.

The price system can also be used to manipulate the private sector performance in other ways as well, and the mission believes that as a general rule, prices are a more effective form of persuasion than direct controls and regulations. Thus, we feel there is merit in the suggestion put forward by the ILO/UNDP employment mission that expatriate labor can be more efficiently rationed by a foreign labor tax than through administrative fiat, and that this would give more incentive for genuine Kenyanization than moral persuasion and political rhetoric. While the Government has not agreed to this suggestion in its entirety, it is considering the introduction of a system of work permit fees which would vary with the length of training required for the job. This would be an encouraging move towards a more flexible use of the price system.[11]

Priorities. The most effective single way of improving performance in the private sector is, in our view, by inducing more resources to flow into agriculture and resource-based industry. The agricultural sector is already "reformed" in the sense that it is efficient at converting plentiful resources (particularly labor) into scarce resources (particularly foreign exchange). Thus, it provides the most direct means of increasing incomes and employment for the nation as a whole, and of generating exports with the minimum use of scarce resources. However, we believe that agriculture could make an even larger contribution to the economy if some of the handicaps under which it now operates were removed.

If agriculture is to realize its full potential, the right set of price signals must be provided so that farmers have an incentive to work, to invest, to produce and export, and to employ more labor. To accomplish this, it will be necessary to reduce agricultural taxation which is now implicit in the trade protective system, and prevent a further deterioration in terms of trade between agriculture and the rest of the economy, as has occurred in recent years. Indeed, the importance of agriculture to Kenya, particularly in the attack on poverty and unemployment, implies that both trade policy and domestic pricing policy should be formulated with the interests of farmers in mind. But this does not seem to have been the dominant consideration in the past.

There is ample evidence, we believe, to support the hypothesis that the hundreds of thousands of small scale farmers who have entered the monetary economy respond very effectively to price incentives.[12] This report has also suggested (see Annex Five) that an

---

11. *Sessional Paper on Employment,* para. 94.
12. In Kenya, some recent examples of marked responses to price changes—among smallholders—are to be found in dairying and pyrethrum.

attractive price environment should attract new large scale investments into agriculture and agro-industry, providing the political constraints to foreign use of land can be overcome. However, a favorable set of price signals will not be sufficient to achieve the kind of accelerated growth envisaged in this report, because a great many—perhaps the majority—of rural households still lack the entrepreneurial ability to take advantage of expanding markets and new technologies. It is primarily for this reason, scarcity of entrepreneurial ability, that we have stressed the need for a quantum increase in the level of public sector involvement in the agricultural sector—in planning, the provision of integrated services, and the overall management of the industry.

The mission feels that a similar approach needs to be followed in regard to the urban informal sector, and does not see the urban informal sector as a dynamic growth point in the Kenyan economy in spite of its valuable contribution to employment. It is difficult to suggest a "strategy" for this sector, since its size and economic health depends largely upon the policies followed in regard to agriculture and the urban formal sector. What characterizes the informal sector rather is not any inherent features which are peculiar to it, but the fact that the informal sector workers have "failed" to reach the threshold of the formal sector. Therefore, we believe the most effective way to help the informal sector is to provide several graduated levels of activity, recognized by law and by the Government's assistance programs, to help small scale business and the self-employed to progress up the scale. These "stepping stones to formality" can be devised to coincide with the markets which the informal sector serves.[13]

While the urban informal sector, like its counterpart in the rural areas, is already "reformed," the urban formal sector frequently uses resources poorly and sometimes operates against the interests of other sectors. The priorities here are therefore to induce the urban formal sector to reform, through appropriate price signals, and thus to divert resources from those activities which cannot use them efficiently. We see this process to be urgently required in manufacturing, where the need is to replace the past emphasis on protection and import substitution with an increasing emphasis on productivity and export promotion. In particular, it is most desirable for Kenya to avoid going through the second stage of import substitution (protection of intermediate goods) with the additional taxation of the rest of the economy which this brings in train.

A Development-oriented Public Sector

While the private sector will carry the burden of Kenya's future development, the public sector will be critical, not only in the sense of Government as overall manager of the economy, but in directly using resources efficiently in its own development program and in supporting private enterprise. The overall strategy called for in this report would demand a significant shift in the pattern of public sector expenditures, and we have already referred to the difficulties this would create. But there is also scope for the public sector to improve the economic performance within the sectors for which it is responsible by striving towards improved project design and appraisal methods. In this area, the public sector has an advantage over the private sector inasmuch as it has the freedom to employ economic rather than financial measures of efficiency, and thus to implement projects which will bring enhanced benefits to the country.

The use of shadow pricing and other social costing methodology is undoubtedly a second-best technique, and it would be much more useful and efficient to bring *actual* prices more into line with the real economic scarcity value of domestic and foreign resources. There is also an inherent risk that complex social costing can be spuriously

---

13. The nature of the informal sector is discussed at greater length in Annex Three, Appendix C, and in Annex Five we suggest the possible outline of a project designed to reach small businessmen who are characteristic of informal activity.

used to justify unsound projects and thus to mislead the policymaker. However, it is possible to make more accurate appraisals of investments by introducing quite simple techniques, and it is hoped that Kenya can soon move in this direction. We believe that there will be mounting social and political pressures to override financial prudence: to increase the labor content of public sector work or set up "make work" programs; to establish large import substitution industries; or to redirect expenditure indiscriminately to the poorer regions of the country. It would be highly desirable to have a methodology which can take account of social benefits, as well as financial profitability, on a consistent basis, so that these pressures can be accommodated. Many proposals might then be found to be economically justifiable and desirable, while the obviously foolish suggestions could be revealed as such.

Mobilization of Resources for Development

Although we foresee an implementation constraint in key sectors, if Kenya is to move towards a more efficient pattern of growth, it does seem that the economy as a whole is now facing a resource position which may well constrain the possibilities for growth in the future. Many of the aspects of the strategy proposed in this report would have the effect of relieving the resource constraint: by increasing the efficiency of investment; by reducing the reliance upon imports; by orienting production towards exports; and even by reducing Kenya's dependence on skilled manpower. But despite all this, are the necessary resources likely to be available?

The report's general conclusions have been that it will not be easy for Kenya to improve her performance in the mobilization of resources for development, partly because her past performance has been so good and partly because of some indications that the economy may have reached a turning point, particularly in the generation of domestic savings. Thus, although there is obviously scope for some improvements, we place the priority more in terms of maintaining the level of achievement in the past, and learning to use the available resources more efficiently.

Domestic Savings

Kenya's past savings-income ratio has been so high that it is difficult to suggest that it should be higher. However, there is some evidence in the last few years that domestic savings propensity may be falling, particularly in the household sector. This could be merely a temporary phenomenon, but there are some a priori reasons to think that it may be a more permanent change in behavior. If so, it might seriously aggravate Kenya's already widening resource gap, and the mission would suggest that it is time for Kenya to consider a more dynamic approach to the mobilization of savings.

There are, in our view, two lines of approach: a general increase in interest rates, and a reform of the structure and operations of financial intermediaries. We have earlier suggested generally higher interest rates, as a means of rationing scarce capital resources more efficiently, and encouraging foreign investors to borrow abroad, rather than in Kenya. Interest rates in Kenya have been stable for a number of years, while rates in other countries have increased very considerably, and the *real* rate of interest in Kenya (after taking account of inflation) is now negative for the first time. It is difficult to be certain about the effects of higher interest rates on the propensity to save. However, as we point out in Annex Four, the experience of other countries which have increased interest rates in recent years is encouraging, and there is good reason to suppose that a higher structure of interest rates in Kenya might help growth, through stimulating savings, encouraging better allocation, or inducing a more prudent use of capital.

If interest rates are raised, they should of course be raised on both borrowing and lending. Higher lending rates should not exclude small-scale farmers and African businessmen, even though these are the priority areas for allocating credit supplies. It seems to us that the real problem for the small entrepreneur is access, not cost, and that it is much better for small scale farmers to have access to credit at an economic rate, than not to get it at all. In fact, the cost of credit should not be a major item in a well designed farm budget.

It is something of an enigma that, although Kenya's overall savings (and investment) performance has been so good, the country has so far not succeeded in finding a means for either mobilizing savings from, or channeling funds to, the majority of the population. The commercial banks, which are the most important financial intermediaries, are still oriented mainly to the formal sector, both in their borrowing and their lending, and few public sector financial institutions have reached many of the *wananchi*. Thus many households in the rural areas have no convenient way of holding their savings, while most of the entrepreneurs on whom the future development of Kenya depends have no access to development finance. We believe that the latter problem (channeling resources to the entrepreneur) is the more urgent, and some suggestions have been made in the Agriculture Sector Survey (Part III) and in Annex Five on how the problem might be tackled.

However, looking at the matter from a resource mobilization point of view, we are concerned about the intermediation process by which household savings can be mobilized for development. Experience in most countries tends to show that small businessmen and farmers generally have a high propensity to save, and there is no reason to believe that such behavior should not also be found in Kenya. In fact, the more widely distributed the benefits of development become, the more emphasis there will need to be on mobilizing savings from the little man. The key to a solution is institutional reform and Kenya has already made some progress along those lines, through the outreach of the Kenya Commercial Bank, the introduction of deposits in the cooperative movement, and the first steps towards streamlining procedures in the Post Office Savings Bank. There is clearly need to do much more, however, to provide effective intermediation.

Fiscal Policy

The excellent fiscal effort of the Central Government has shown some indications of slackening in recent years, and it appears that public finance could be a much more constraining factor in the future than it has been in the past. There are also potential dangers (in expanding social services expenditure and salary increases) that the position could deteriorate further.

However, the mission feels that the budgetary position need not get out of hand. The Central Government has never had any serious problem in controlling recurrent expenditures, and there is, in our opinion, substantial scope for improving the tax revenue base in as yet untapped instruments of indirect taxation, as well as tightening tax administration. The recent introduction of a sales tax on manufactures should go a long way to improve the built-in elasticity of indirect taxation, although the immediate net gain, after the abolition of the graduated personal tax and most of the previous consumption taxes, will not be that great. We see the new sales tax being used in concert with a progressive move towards a uniform tariff on imports and a complementary excise duty on domestic substitutes. The Kenya Government has recognized the need for tariff reform, and has started moving in this direction in conjunction with the other two Partner States. The primary benefit of such a move is, of course, to encourage a better pattern of development, but a uniform tariff will also avoid the self-eliminating fiscal features of protective tariffs.

The mission feels that there is also scope for mobilizing more resources through direct taxation. Even after the lower allowances introduced with the 1973/74 budget, we have estimated that probably no more than 3 to 5 percent of Kenya's households are eligible for direct taxation, and many of these escape assessment. Without any increase in tax rates, there is certainly scope for increasing revenues through more efficient administration. The potential revenue from income taxation is limited, however, not only by widespread poverty, but by family allowances which are still relatively high, and by other various factors. Moreover, as we show in Annex Three, Kenya's policies are presently encouraging foreign firms operating there to evade company taxation.

Finally, the mission feels that the whole area of wealth taxes (inheritance, capital gains, land) has been neglected in the past and might be more seriously considered. In the foreseeable future, these taxes would not be great sources of revenue, but they would help to make fiscal policy more redistributive. This may be important in view of the fact that Kenya's total structure at present is not very progressive in nature. The mission is impressed with the scope for increasing urban property taxes, and, in the long run, introducing land taxes in rural areas. These two forms of taxation could go a long way towards providing a more secure financial base for the local authorities.

External Capital

We have already indicated, and in more detail in the technical annexes, some of the ways in which Kenya can mobilize more domestic resources for development. We have also suggested a range of policy changes which would help to reduce external resource constraints on Kenya's future development. But even with all these instruments of policy and optimistic assumptions about savings and exports, there seems no way in which Kenya can maintain a fast rate of growth or, perhaps what is more important, intensify the war against poverty, without an expanding inflow of foreign capital. We need, therefore, to examine whether these flows of aid are likely to arise.

In our projections we have estimated the volume of official aid which we feel may be available to Kenya over the next few years, and have made a guess at future levels of private investment. Flows of aid are notoriously difficult to predict, and we make no claim for accuracy in these rather crude forecasts. The projections of official aid are based on known commitments of the major donors, supplemented by estimates of future commitments. The projections of private capital are much more crude extrapolations of past levels of investment in Kenya. Neither of these resources are within Kenya's power to control, but we feel that ensuring the flow of foreign capital and using it to best advantage, have implications for policy in Kenya.

We have put forward the view that, although some of the past investments in Kenya have not really benefited the country, she will continue to need a steady flow of private investment, both to supply the capital and to provide entrepreneurial ability and technical know-how. The issue we see is not whether foreign investment is desirable; rather whether Kenya can continue to attract foreign private investment and whether she can learn to use foreign investment more efficiently for the benefit of the country.

The mission gathered from its contacts with the private sector that investment in Kenya is not as attractive as it used to be. In part, this may be due to economic factors already discussed—dwindling opportunities for simple import substitution, reduced access to markets in East Africa, and so on. But it is also partly due to the increasing range of controls and regulations which irritate businessmen (including Kenyan businessmen) and may, if they become too onerous, persuade potential investors that entrepreneurial life is less tedious elsewhere.

As suggested earlier, it would be desirable for Government to be more active in identifying new opportunities for overseas investment and in seeking out potential investors. We feel it is of the utmost priority for industry to encourage overseas companies to invest in export industries, particularly where they have established outlets and export experience. We also feel that the Kenya Government should reexamine the scope of greater foreign investment in agriculture. There are, of course, emotional and political problems in regard to the use of land, which do not arise in industrial estates. But the country has shown in several recent projects that these problems can be overcome to the benefit of a great number of people, and there seems to be much wider scope for this kind of investment. We can think of no better use, in fact, for foreign private investment than to bring the scarce capital, managerial abilities and technical know-how which Kenya lacks to combine with the rich potential of the land and its people.[14]

Is there some way in which Kenya can ensure that private investment will really benefit the country, and will not ransom Kenya's resources to foreign control? The degree to which Kenya will accept the costs which come together with large scale foreign investment is, of course, a political choice in which the expected benefits can be weighed against the costs. We have tried in this report to suggest, however, that the benefits to Kenya of private foreign investment can be substantially increased, mainly by giving investors the right set of signals. We also believe that many of the social costs of foreign investment can be avoided or minimized once they are more clearly identified. As a first step, we have suggested a more vigorous weeding of the many obviously dubious investment propositions which are received by the Government.

Finally, we have suggested that the Government steer the private sector in desirable directions by indirect means, principally through the pricing system, rather than through direct controls which bring unforeseen problems along with them, cause frustration and inefficiency to the firms involved, and needlessly tie up a disproportionate amount of Kenya's skilled manpower.

There is a similar need, in our opinion, to increase both the volume and effectiveness of official aid. Kenya has now moved out of the postcolonial period of major reliance on one or two donors, and is receiving a large flow of aid from a growing number of donors, which include international agencies, bilateral sources, and a wide range of private and religious organizations. In addition, Kenya, on a per capita basis, is one of the largest recipients of technical assistance in the world.

An aid program of this magnitude is big business by any standard, and Kenya urgently needs to improve her aid management. In particular, we feel that she will need to do much more to coordinate technical assistance and capital aid among donors and to ration aid among competing users within the country. There has been a significant improvement in aid management in recent years, following the reorganization of the Ministry of Finance and Planning. However we maintain, in Annex Five, that a further strengthening will be necessary if Kenya is to reap the full potential of available aid. We believe that aid flows from donors who are responsive to need, and we also think that donors are rather more flexible than the Government gives them credit for. Since external capital is likely to be a more severe constraint in the future, it would be to Kenya's advantage to give greater priority to the identification, packaging, and presentation of projects for external assistance. In Annex Six, we describe some of the priorities for change on the part of donors.

14. This suggestion is discussed at greater length in Annex Five. We feel that there is much more scope than generally realized for the foreign investor to be associated with smallholder production, particularly if the Government acts as intermediary.

CHAPTER 6

IMPLICATIONS FOR MANAGEMENT

The suggestions for structural change and economic reform mentioned in earlier chapters and in more detail in the technical annexes have important implications for management. Many of the more direct implications have already been discussed at length and need not be referred to again. In this concluding section, however, we shall take up some of the more general implications of our strategy for the domestic policymakers and for external donors, and shall examine some of the apparent conflicts which might arise. Finally, we shall take a quick look at some of the adjustments to strategy which might be required in the longer term.

Some Possible Trade-Offs

It is currently popular to refer to the "trade-offs" in economic development, particularly the trade-off between growth and employment or income distribution. In our analysis of Kenya's past development, we have pointed out that other conflicts of interest have started to appear: between agriculture and the rest of the economy, between the formal and informal sectors, between foreign investment and the development of Kenyan entrepreneurship, and even between Kenyanization and growth. Conflicts between goals will, of course, always arise in development policy, and their resolution will require bold political choices to be made. But we believe that some of the most feared trade-offs can be reduced or even eliminated provided they are recognized and accounted for in drawing up an appropriate development strategy.

Growth, Employment, and Income Distribution

The most dreaded trade-off is between growth and employment, since it may appear that in order to achieve an acceptable increase in employment and the incomes of the poor, it will be necessary to adopt less efficient methods of production which will lower the growth rate. We do not accept that this hypothesis need be true in Kenya; on the contrary, our projections suggest that a high rate of growth is the first and most important condition for expanding employment and launching an attack on poverty. It is certainly true that rapid growth in capital intensive forms of production will not solve Kenya's unemployment problems, and this is one important reason why we have advocated a shift in emphasis in the pattern of production. In particular, a shift towards agriculture and other productive sectors would accelerate *both* growth *and* employment, with less demand upon Kenya's scarcest resources, and would allow development to reach more of the poorest people. Under our preferred strategy, therefore, there need be no trade-off between employment and growth, or between growth and increasing incomes for the poor, because all these goals can be achieved by the same means.[1]

As with the ILO/UNDP report, this report is concerned with increasing incomes as well as employment, and we have particularly stressed that Kenya must look to the agricultural sector for the primary source of expanding incomes. The stress on incomes, rather than employment, is important, if only because a preoccupation with employment all too often translates into measures aimed at the modern sector, most of which are either nonsolutions (like the Tripartite Agreements) or positively harmful to the nation

---

1. There is inadequate evidence to determine whether there is likely to be any trade-off between the preferred strategy and the generation of savings. The mission suspects not.

as a whole (like wage increases in the formal sector). The implications for policy of an orientation towards self-employment and informal sector employment are quite profound.

It may also be noted that this report has not been concerned with equitable income distribution as an end in itself, and there is only limited discussion of the size of "gaps," or which gaps are most important, or whether or not they can or should be narrowed. The mission feels that the distribution of incomes and wealth within Kenya is a matter for her own people to decide, and we have concluded that a continuing uneven distribution of income need not be a major obstacle to future growth. We have made clear, however, our concern for an attack on poverty, because we believe that Kenya is unwilling to continue a process of development which runs the risk of passing over the heads of the poorest segments of the community. We have therefore given considerable weight, in considering alternative strategies, to the impact on the rural poor, and we believe that a substantial improvement in their standard of living is possible, given the kind of strategy which we discuss. But even with a new optimum package of policies, we have no solution to narrowing the gap between the rural poor and the urban proletariat; in fact, the gap will continue to grow in both absolute and relative terms for the foreseeable future. In our view, this conclusion simply makes it even more urgent to undertake the reforms outlined.

Intersectoral Conflicts

Another potential conflict is between continued growth in the urban formal sector and the accelerated development of agriculture and rural areas as a whole. This report has laid great stress on agriculture as the preferred sector, and has called for the removal of present policies which discriminate against it. But the mission does not wish to suggest any diminution in the role of the urban formal sector in general, or the manufacturing industry in particular. In fact, it is clear from our projections of the future that a rapid pace of development in the nonagricultural sectors is essential over the long haul to absorb labor from the rural areas. Good land is already scarce in Kenya, and the faster the population can be *productively* absorbed in nonagriculture activities, the faster average per capita incomes in agriculture can rise.

With the right combination of policies, therefore, we think that there need be no conflict between agriculture and industry. Industry depends upon growing rural incomes for its domestic market, and will have to rely on agricultural products much more heavily if it is to become oriented towards resource-based exports as we hope it will; while agriculture looks to the urban areas for its own domestic markets. There is, we believe, a real conflict of interest under existing policies, and without policy change, continued expansion of the manufacturing sector may well proceed at the expense of agricultural production, exports, and incomes. But this conflict is not necessary, and our proposals suggest how Kenya's manufacturing industries could be made to grow to the general benefit of the economy.

There is also no inherent conflict between the urban informal sector and the formal sector. The real trade-off, we believe, is between the growth of real wages in the formal sector, on the one hand, and the level of employment and incomes in the rest of the economy. This is a real conflict of aims which the Government and people of Kenya will have to resolve. Given the kind of strategy outlined in this report, Kenya could achieve steadily rising incomes and employment among the rural poor, and this process could help to stem the migration of people to the cities. But if real wages in the urban formal sector continue to increase so much faster than rural incomes, the incentive for young people to gamble on the move to town will remain, and the mounting pressure of job seekers in the towns will tend to lower average incomes in the urban informal sector and increase the scale of open unemployment. Thus, what we fear is a trade-off not between urban growth and rural development, so much as between rising urban wages and increasing employment.

Kenyanization and Growth

One trade-off which we think might face Kenya in the future is a possible conflict between accelerated Kenyanization, as now visualized, and the growth of employment. Whether there is a serious cost associated with Kenyanization policies depends largely upon the definition and application of these policies. It should be clear from the general strategy of this report that the mission is firmly convinced that Kenyanization, in the widest sense of the term, should proceed as fast as possible. It is also consistent with the general approach of the report that, in looking for ways to accelerate Kenyanization of the economy, we should have turned first to the macro-economic instruments of policy and, in particular, the great power which could be exerted by restructuring the pattern of overall growth. The "preferred strategy" advocated in this report would, we believe, make the greatest contribution to economizing skilled manpower, as well as maximizing employment, by shifting the emphasis of investment and growth to those sectors, such as agriculture, which make the least demand on skilled manpower.[2] At the same time, such a change in the pattern of growth could be the most effective way of promoting African entrepreneurship, by favoring those kinds of economic activity in which the mass of potential entrepreneurs can most readily establish themselves and thrive.

Thus, the thrust of all our proposals is aimed at increasing participation of the Kenyan people in the total process of development—in management and planning, in production, and in employment. If "Kenyanization" is defined in this sense, we feel that there is no conflict, since Kenyanization becomes an essential ingredient of a reformed structure of growth. However, while a reformed structure would be relatively less dependent on skilled manpower for its efficient operation, Kenya will still be critically dependent upon a few key expatriate personnel in both the public and private sectors—as technicians, managers and contractors. If Kenyanization policies should prevent their employment, or result in less experienced Kenyans being appointed in their place, a real conflict will arise.

Some Wider Implications

The various policy changes advocated here are all designed to induce the economy to perform more efficiently than in the past: to get more growth, more employment, and more widely distributed benefits from every pound invested in the economy. This is no easy task: many of the reforms suggested will be politically difficult to undertake, and some may prove impossible. Only a few of the components of the preferred scenario can be implemented quickly, and some of the most sensitive variables in the future of the economy, such as terms of trade, are neither easily predictable nor readily controllable.

We have stressed more than once that there is no single solution, no minimum package of reform, which can be offered to ensure Kenya's continued development. On the contrary, we have emphasized that no one policy on its own will be sufficient, and that a whole range of policy adjustments and actions will be required. Moreover, the regulation of the economy is becoming more difficult as Kenya moves out of the first phase of development, as many of the more obvious priorities have been attended to, and the economy itself has become more complex. Yet the potential for development in Kenya is very considerable, and the means for ensuring it are, we believe, in her grasp. What is really called for is a more intensive and sophisticated style of management—a

---

2. See Chapter 4, footnote 4.

more precisely directed supervision of the economy to achieve the goals which the country has set itself.

This is true of every sphere of national economic policy, whether it is the need to sharpen the tools of fiscal and monetary policy, to increase the development impact of public expenditure, to manipulate private sector behavior more skilfully, or even to negotiate a better deal from foreign investors. The need for more intensive management is so great, at all levels of the public sector, that the second decade might almost be referred to as "the management decade." But we have suggested that the highest priority should be given to reinforcing the management functions of the major development ministries, who must shoulder the main responsibility for translating the generalized goals of development strategy into implementable action programs.

Financing the Residual Gap

Kenya will have to push available resources to the limit if the pace of development is to be maintained. Even under the preferred strategy proposed, the economy would still have a residual external resource gap which would not be filled by the inflow of official aid which we have assumed in our projections. Of course, these projections are not forecasts, but indications of the results of a whole range of assumptions, and any or all of them may prove to be wrong. However, we believe that most of our assumptions are on the optimistic side so that the resource gap would, if anything, be larger than that revealed by the projections.

We do not think that Kenya should be frightened by resource constraints into lowering the ambitious targets of growth, provided the growth is making a maximum contribution to all aspects of development. If the economy should find itself with this kind of residual gap, Kenya would have an exceptionally good case for attracting more aid on concessional terms from official donors. Moreover, since the total burden of servicing external debt on the Kenyan economy would still be quite light (probably less than 10 percent), Kenya could also afford to make some use of commercial credits to fill a part of the gap. A resort to commercial credit, as we have shown, is no *first* solution to a foreign exchange constraint, but if taken together with structural reform, increased access to concessionary finance, and a supply of sound projects, some degree of commercial finance could certainly be justified as an alternative to reduced growth.

Since the scarcity of foreign exchange is likely to prove the most critical constraint to Kenya's development over the next decade, management will need to be particularly sensitive to the relationship between internal domestic policies and the balance of payments. Our general strategy is designed, among other things, to move Kenya towards self-reliance. But such key variables as changes in import and export prices, the future of tourism, or the likely flow of external assistance, are all subject to wide and often unpredictable movements, and probably at no time in the past have these factors been harder to predict than they are now. Kenya, like other countries, will have to learn to live with these changing circumstances, most of which are beyond her control. The implication, once again, is for more skilful management, and particularly for a more flexible and speedy response to changes in Kenya's external relationships. We have not openly advocated a devaluation of the Kenya shilling in the report, partly because the exchange rate policy is not wholly within Kenya's control. But we have suggested that the exchange rate could be a powerful development instrument, and that she should be willing to use it, in conjunction with her Partners in the Community, if the development effects were favorable.

Implications for Donors

The past performance of the Kenyan economy in mobilizing resources and using them in pushing ahead with development has warranted—and attracted—increasing support from the outside world. We have assumed in this report that the flow of aid on concessional terms will continue to grow, and our assumptions in this regard are given in Annex Six. In particular, we have assumed a large increase in disbursements from the Bank Group, a resurgence in aid from the United States, continuing British aid, and a growth of new donors, particularly from Scandinavia.

The continued good performance of the Kenya economy will merit still higher levels of aid and, as mentioned above, if Kenya succeeds in moving towards the preferred strategy suggested here, the case for maximum support will be unquestionable. However, she will need a lot more help to move towards such a strategy, both in terms of the amount of aid and technical assistance she requires and, perhaps even more important, in terms of the nature of the aid she receives. We shall be reviewing, in Annex Six, some of the implications of the mission's preferred strategy for the donors. In essence, these are that the donors will need to be much more flexible in their aid programs, and more willing to initiate and experiment and join with Kenya in risky ventures when the stakes are high enough. Sometimes this will mean being willing to work through new forms of institutions, learning to cooperate much more effectively with other donors, and perhaps being less concerned with donor identity and prestige.

Longer Term Considerations

We wish to conclude with a quick glance to the more distant future, not because we claim to know what lies ahead, but to put our strategy into a rather longer term context. In so doing, we are well aware of the limited time span of our review in this report. Kenya has been in control of its own affairs for only ten years, which is a very short time indeed in the history of a country. In looking at the strategic choices facing Kenya, we have been mainly concerned with the range of policies which might be appropriate over the next decade—or at least which might start to bite during the course of the seventies. We are conscious, on the one hand, that many of the policy changes and structural transformations discussed here would have little effect on events during the forthcoming Five-Year Plan. On the other hand, if we could see into the future a longer term perspective might well indicate other issues and different priorities.

One perspective which will change over time is the role of agriculture in development. We have put stress on this sector in our strategy for the second decade because we are convinced that this emphasis is essential if Kenya is to achieve the twin goals of growth and employment within the resources likely to be available. But this does not mean that the emphasis should continue indefinitely, and certainly does not mean that we believe Kenya is doomed to be a perpetual peasant economy.

Good land in Kenya is very limited and the pressure of population on the land is growing at an alarming rate. Greater land use in high potential areas, and accelerated research and development in medium potential areas, could absorb a large proportion of the increasing labor force over the next decade, and provide a tremendous impetus to the development of the whole economy. But Kenya will ultimately have to look to the urban sector, when it has really grown up, to take on a much larger share of the responsibility for growth. It may be noted, even in our preferred strategy, that manufacturing and other sectors will still grow faster than agriculture, and we foresee that as Kenya moves into the 1980s, what we have called the urban formal sector may well take over as the driving force of the economy. This is another important reason for reforming the urban formal sector now, so that it will be able to assume this responsibility and carry it out efficiently.

The final word must be reserved for population growth. In this report, which looks ahead a decade, population growth rate is not an important variable, since all the labor force we are trying to provide for during this decade is already in the homes and shambas of Kenya. No conceivable thrust in population control would significantly affect our major conclusions. But as we look ahead to the eighties, we are moving into a period where effective curbs on population growth instituted now, could start to have a real impact. More than anything else, a slower population growth getting under way in the seventies could relieve the burden on rural land and would allow an acceleration in rural household incomes towards the end of the century.

STATISTICAL TABLES
Part I—The Main Report
Index

Population, Employment and Earnings

1.	Estimates of Population, 1960–72	52
2.	Average Annual Growth of African Population in the Main Towns, 1948–62 and 1962–69	52
3.	Population by Age and Sex, 1969	53
4.	Distribution of the Population by Education, 1969–70	53
5.	Estimates of Employment by Sector, 1969 and 1971	54
6.	Wage Employment in the Modern Sector, 1968–71	54
7.	Average Annual Wage Earnings in the Modern Sector, 1968–71	55

National Accounts

8.	Resources and Use of Resources in Current Prices, 1964–72	56
9.	Resources and Use of Resources in Constant 1964 Prices, 1964–72	57
10.	Gross Domestic Product by Industrial Origin in Current Prices, 1964–72	58
11.	Gross Domestic Product by Industrial Origin in Constant 1964 Prices, 1964–72	59
12	Subsistence Production by Sector, 1964–72	60
13.	Gross National Product in Current and Constant 1964 Prices, 1964–72	61
14.	Capital Formation by Industry, 1964–72	62
15.	Capital Formation by Type of Asset, 1964–72	63

External Trade and Balance of Payments

16.	Balance of Payments, 1964–72	64
17.	Main Export Commodities Overseas, 1964–72	65
18.	Main Exports to Uganda and Tanzania, 1964–72	66
19.	Imports by Major SITC Classification, 1964–71	67
20.	Percentage Distribution of Major Exports, 1964–72	68
21.	Percentage Value Distribution of Imports by SITC Classification, 1964–71	69
22.	Trade Price Indices, 1964–72	70

Public Debt and External Assistance

23.	External Public Debt Outstanding as of December 31, 1972	71
24.	Projected Disbursements and Service Payments on External Public Debt Outstanding, December 31, 1972	72

Monetary Statistics

25.	Summary Accounts of the Kenya Banking System, 1968–72	73
26.	Principal Interest Rates, 1967–73	74

Table 1: Estimates of Population, 1960–72

Year	Population (thousand)	Year	Population (thousand)
1960	8,300	1967	10,210
1961	8,540	1968	10,540
1962	8,790	1969	10,880
1963	9,050	1970	11,220
1964	9,310	1971	11,670
1965	9,600	1972	12,070
1966	9,890		

SOURCE: United Nations *Monthly Bulletin of Statistics*.

Table 2: Average Annual Growth of African Population in the Main Towns, 1948–62 and 1962–69

Town	1948–62	1962–69[1]
	(percentage)	
Nairobi	6.5	15.2
Kisumu	7.2	8.7
Mombasa	7.1	7.6
Thika	10.5	5.6
Nyeri	9.1	5.2
Nakuru	6.3	4.9
Nanyuki	8.0	3.0
Eldoret	7.6	0.4

[1] Boundary changes artificially inflated some figures, particularly for Nairobi, which after adjustment for annexations is reduced to about 10.5%, and for Mombasa and Kisumu, to about 5%.

SOURCE: *Population Census, 1969*, Vol. II, from the ILO/UNDP report, Table 10, p. 48.

STATISTICAL TABLES

Table 3: Population by Age and Sex, 1969

Age Group	Total	Male	Female
All Ages	10,942,710	5,482,381	5,460,329
Under 1	361,786	181,280	180,506
1–4	1,742,696	876,822	865,874
5–9	1,809,958	916,599	893,359
10–14	1,378,515	714,707	663,808
15–19	1,104,999	560,152	544,847
20–24	878,111	428,015	450,096
25–29	760,839	349,594	411,245
30–34	580,189	280,948	299,241
35–39	516,955	252,136	264,819
40–44	395,872	193,936	201,936
45–49	336,360	172,508	163,852
50–54	271,538	132,466	139,072
55–59	216,904	114,669	102,235
60–64	196,974	102,466	94,508
65 and over	391,014	206,083	184,931

SOURCE: United Nations *Demographic Yearbook*, 1971.

Table 4: Distribution of the Population by Education, 1969–70

Category of Persons	None	1–4	5–8	9 or more	Total
	(percentage)				
Male Migrants					
Nairobi only	10.8	13.5	41.7	34.0	100.0
8 major towns	12.7	14.8	47.1	25.4	100.0
Total population					
Urban and rural	67.9	19.7	11.4	1.0	100.0

Column heading: NUMBER OF YEARS SCHOOLING

SOURCE: *Population Census*, 1969, Vol. III; and University of Nairobi, Institute for Development Studies: *Rural to Urban Labor Migration*, a tabulation of responses to the migration survey questionnaire, by H. Rempel, J. Harris and M. Todaro, Discussion Paper No. 92 (1970). From ILO/UNDP report, Table 11, p. 49.

Table 5: Estimates of Employment by Sector, 1969 and 1971

	1969				1971			
	Formal Wage Employment	INFORMAL EMPLOYMENT			Formal Wage Employment	INFORMAL EMPLOYMENT		
Sector		Rural	Urban	Total		Rural	Urban	Total
	(thousand)							
Agriculture, forestry and fishing	196	4,168	—	4,364	211	4,436	—	4,647
Mining and quarrying	3	1	—	4	3	1	—	4
Manufacturing	75	30	15	120	93	32	16	141
Building and construction	29	1	11	41	35	1	12	48
Electricity and water	5	—	—	5	5	—	—	5
Transport, storage and communications	48	3	1	52	46	3	1	50
Wholesale and retail trade	44	96	30	170	47	102	32	181
Services	227	19	39	285	240	20	41	301
	627	4,318	96	5,041	680	4,595	102	5,377

SOURCE: Mission estimates.

Table 6: Wage Employment in the Modern Sector, 1968–71

Sector	1968	1969	1970	1971	Average Compound Growth Rate
	(thousand)				(percentage)
Agriculture and forestry	190.2	195.0	204.5	211.1	3.5
Mining and quarrying	2.9	2.6	2.9	3.0	1.1
Manufacturing and repairs	70.7	72.7	82.3	92.8	7.0
Building and construction	31.9	28.9	30.8	34.8	3.0
Electricity and water	5.7	5.2	4.8	5.2	−0.3
Commerce	42.4	44.2	42.5	46.7	3.4
Transport and communications	51.3	51.8	44.9	45.6	−0.4
Services	211.3	226.8	231.8	240.6	4.4
TOTAL	606.4	627.2	644.8	679.7	3.9
Private sector	384.5	390.1	397.3	424.0	3.3
Public sector[1]	221.9	287.1	247.5	255.7	3.6

[1] Includes Government, parastatal and local government employees and Kenyans employed in the various EAC Corporations and General Fund.

SOURCE: *Statistical Abstract*, 1972.

Table 7: Average Annual Wage Earnings in the Modern Sector, 1968-71

Sector	1968	1969	1970	1971	Average Compound Growth Rate
		(£)			(percentage)
Agriculture and forestry	71.33	73.05	77.48	83.95	5.6
Mining and quarrying	234.31	320.26	332.93	348.33	14.1
Manufacturing and repairs	331.75	343.20	383.74	372.43	4.0
Building and construction	—	257.88	333.37	323.62	12.0
Electricity and water	339.98	434.20	439.89	446.50	9.5
Commerce	524.29	494.36	542.41	558.30	2.1
Transport and communications	452.82	426.84	462.18	442.44	−0.7
Services	252.94	259.98	273.79	295.85	5.4
TOTAL	241.12	244.89	261.28	271.21	4.0
Private sector	205.77	209.92	224.46	230.28	3.9
Public sector[1]	302.38	302.40	320.40	339.06	3.9

[1] Includes Government, parastatal and local government employees and Kenyans employed in the various EAC Corporations and General Fund.

SOURCE: *Statistical Abstract*, 1972.

Table 8: Resources and Uses of Resources in Current Prices, 1964–72

Resources/Uses	1964	1965	1966	1967	1968	1969	1970	1971	1972
					(£ million)				
Resources									
GDP at factor cost	328.4	327.5	381.1	403.1	493.3	475.7	521.9	575.8	646.9
Monetary	239.6	247.0	279.6	296.1	330.3	361.0	402.3	448.9	504.1
Nonmonetary	88.9	80.5	101.5	107.0	109.0	114.7	119.5	126.9	142.8
+ Net indirect taxes	+26.6	+28.9	+34.8	+34.4	+40.4	+44.6	+53.4	+67.2	+64.3
GDP at market prices	355.0	356.4	415.9	437.5	479.7	520.3	575.3	643.0	711.2
+ Imports of goods and NFS	+102.0	+114.5	+133.7	+133.5	+142.3	+144.9	+178.1	+218.7	+214.9
− Exports of goods and NFS	−120.4	−117.1	−139.0	−131.5	−137.4	−149.2	−167.4	−177.3	−196.6
TOTAL	336.6	353.8	410.6	439.5	484.6	516.0	586.0	684.4	729.5
Uses of resources									
Private consumption	240.6	250.2	276.1	288.4	319.0	328.1	365.6	407.2	431.8
General government consumption	49.4	52.3	57.1	62.2	73.5	85.6	94.3	115.0	128.7
Gross domestic investment	46.6	51.3	77.4	88.9	92.1	102.3	126.1	162.2	169.0
TOTAL	336.6	353.8	410.6	439.5	484.6	516.0	586.0	684.4	729.5

SOURCE: *Panorama of National Accounts* (unpublished) and *Economic Surveys*, Ministry of Finance and Planning; mission estimates.

STATISTICAL TABLES

Table 9: Resources and Uses of Resources in Constant 1964 Prices, 1964–72

Resources/Uses	1964	1965	1966	1967	1968	1969	1970	1971	1972
					(£ million)				
Resources									
GDP at factor cost	328.4	330.9	379.2	396.5	427.1	454.3	485.1	517.8	553.8
Monetary	239.6	251.2	281.6	295.1	322.0	345.3	372.5	401.8	433.8
Nonmonetary	88.9	79.7	97.6	101.4	105.1	109.0	112.6	116.0	119.9
+ Net indirect taxes	+26.6	+31.0	+37.7	+36.4	+39.6	+42.8	+51.5	+58.2	+53.5
GDP at market prices	355.0	361.9	416.9	432.9	466.7	497.1	536.6	576.0	607.3
+ Imports of goods and NFS	+102.0	+112.2	+131.1	+130.9	+136.8	+138.0	+166.4	+186.9	+170.6
− Exports of goods and NFS	−120.4	−114.8	−136.3	−128.9	−132.1	−142.1	−156.4	−151.5	−156.8
TOTAL	336.6	359.3	411.7	434.9	471.4	493.0	546.6	611.4	621.1
Uses of resources									
Private consumption	240.6	263.8	289.5	306.1	333.8	337.2	358.1	393.7	396.5
General Government consumption	49.4	45.4	47.5	50.7	57.7	68.0	80.5	88.5	100.2
Gross domestic investment	46.6	50.1	74.7	78.1	79.9	87.8	108.0	129.2	124.4
TOTAL	336.6	359.3	411.7	434.9	471.4	493.0	546.6	611.4	621.1

SOURCE: Panorama of *National Accounts and Economic Surveys*, Ministry of Finance and Planning; mission estimates.

Table 10: Gross Domestic Product by Industrial Origin at Factor Cost and Current Prices, 1964–72

Category	1964	1965	1966	1967	1968	1969	1970	1971	1972
					(£ million)				
Agriculture	125.3	110.3	138.5	139.7	142.7	152.8	164.6	170.2	202.2
Forestry	3.9	4.1	4.5	5.5	6.1	6.3	7.2	8.3	8.2
Fishing	0.9	1.1	1.4	1.3	1.3	1.3	1.3	1.4	1.4
Mining and quarrying	1.5	1.4	1.6	2.0	2.3	2.0	2.4	2.9	3.0
Manufacturing	34.2	37.4	41.6	44.7	50.0	56.8	62.2	71.7	78.3
Construction	12.6	13.4	16.7	20.3	23.4	24.3	26.4	28.9	32.5
Transportation, storage, and communications	24.5	27.0	30.8	32.7	36.2	37.8	40.8	43.5	46.7
Trade	32.5	35.0	39.2	40.2	44.2	46.9	55.8	61.6	64.8
Banking, insurance, and real estate	9.9	11.0	12.1	13.1	15.5	17.6	21.1	23.6	26.7
Ownership of dwellings	18.9	19.6	20.9	22.5	24.1	25.8	27.4	29.3	31.3
Government services	42.5	43.2	48.1	53.0	63.9	71.0	76.5	95.2	108.6
Other services	14.8	16.7	17.9	19.1	20.1	22.3	24.2	26.5	29.7
Electricity and water	6.9	7.3	7.8	9.0	9.5	10.8	12.0	12.7	13.5
GDP at factor cost	328.4	327.5	381.1	403.1	439.3	475.7	521.9	575.8	646.9

SOURCE: Panorama of *National Accounts and Economic Surveys*, Ministry of Finance and Planning; mission estimates.

STATISTICAL TABLES

Table 11: Gross Domestic Product by Industrial Origin in Constant 1964 Prices, 1964–72

Category	1964	1965	1966	1967	1968	1969	1970	1971	1972
					(£ million)				
Agriculture	125.3	112.7	139.5	141.6	149.0	159.0	165.6	168.9	184.4
Forestry	3.9	4.0	4.0	4.5	4.8	5.1	5.5	5.9	5.9
Fishing	0.9	1.0	1.3	1.2	1.4	1.3	1.2	1.1	1.2
Mining and quarrying	1.5	1.4	1.7	2.1	2.2	2.0	2.6	2.7	2.4
Manufacturing	34.2	36.2	38.2	40.9	44.5	48.6	52.5	59.3	63.6
Building and construction	12.6	13.0	14.9	16.2	18.4	18.6	19.0	20.2	21.5
Transport, storage, and communication	24.5	28.0	32.0	35.4	38.1	38.6	41.2	43.1	42.2
Trade	32.5	34.6	38.4	38.4	41.2	43.9	48.6	53.1	52.5
Banking, insurance, and real estate	9.9	11.2	12.1	13.0	15.1	16.9	19.4	21.1	24.5
Ownership of dwellings	18.9	19.2	19.6	19.9	20.7	21.1	22.0	22.8	23.3
Government services	42.5	46.4	52.0	56.1	62.6	68.2	73.8	82.5	90.4
Other services	14.8	16.1	18.1	19.4	20.9	21.9	23.9	26.5	30.3
Electricity and water	6.9	7.1	7.4	7.7	8.2	9.1	9.8	10.6	11.6
GDP at factor cost	328.4	330.9	379.2	396.4	427.1	454.3	485.1	517.8	553.8

SOURCE: Panorama of *National Accounts and Economic Surveys*, Ministry of Finance and Planning; mission estimates.

Table 12: Subsistence Production by Sector, 1964–72

Category	1964	1965	1966	1967	1968	1969	1970	1971	1972
				(percentage of total value added)					
Agriculture	58.5	57.6	59.3	60.9	59.5	58.2	55.8	57.1	55.0
Forestry	51.0	52.1	53.7	51.6	50.9	49.5	46.8	46.2	50.6
Fishing	12.2	10.9	10.7	10.7	10.7	10.7	11.5	10.7	10.7
Construction	46.1	47.3	43.7	39.1	36.9	36.9	36.2	34.4	32.0
Electricity and water	30.2	30.2	31.6	29.8	32.7	36.2	34.5	35.1	34.5
Ownership of dwellings	29.2	31.0	33.4	36.2	37.2	37.1	37.9	38.0	38.0
Value added at factor cost	27.0	24.0	25.7	26.5	24.8	24.1	22.9	22.0	22.0

SOURCE: Panorama of *National Accounts and Economic Surveys*, Ministry of Finance and Planning; mission estimates.

Table 13: Gross National Product in Current and Constant 1964 Prices, 1964–72

Item	1964	1965	1966	1967	1968	1969	1970	1971	1972
					(£ million)				
1 a. GDP at current prices	355.0	356.4	415.9	437.5	479.7	520.3	575.3	643.0	711.2
1 b. − Net factor payments	−8.7	−9.3	−12.3	−13.6	−14.1	−9.8	−11.5	−9.4	−9.9
1 c. = GNP at current prices	346.3	347.1	403.6	423.9	465.6	510.5	563.8	633.6	701.3
2 a. GDP at constant 1964 prices	355.0	361.9	416.9	432.9	466.7	497.1	536.6	576.0	607.3
2 b. − Net factor payments	−8.7	−9.1	−12.1	−13.3	−13.6	−9.3	−10.7	−8.0	−7.9
2 c. = GNP at constant 1964 prices	346.3	352.8	404.8	419.6	453.1	487.8	525.9	568.0	599.4

SOURCE: Panorama of *National Accounts and Economic Surveys*, Ministry of Finance and Planning; mission estimates.

Table 14: Capital Formation by Industry, 1964–72

Category	1964	1965	1966	1967	1968	1969	1970	1971	1972
					(£ million)				
Nonmonetary	5.2	5.7	6.5	7.5	8.4	8.7	9.2	9.9	10.5
Agriculture and forestry	7.0	7.0	9.3	9.7	10.9	11.0	12.6	12.6	15.8
Mining and quarrying	0.3	0.3	0.7	0.6	0.5	0.6	1.3	1.9	2.2
Manufacturing	5.8	6.6	8.1	10.0	12.2	9.5	12.9	18.5	28.7
Construction	1.9	2.4	2.8	4.0	3.8	4.2	7.0	7.8	7.3
Electricity and water	1.3	1.9	2.6	6.4	3.6	3.8	3.7	6.9	11.3
Transport, storage, and communications	10.3	7.4	13.0	16.3	16.6	16.7	19.9	27.2	20.9
Trade	3.0	2.4	2.9	3.7	4.3	4.1	4.4	5.7	5.6
Banking, insurance, and real estate	0.7	0.4	0.3	0.8	1.0	0.7	1.8	2.9	2.1
Ownership of dwellings	2.1	2.2	3.0	5.3	7.0	7.8	9.8	14.3	14.9
Other services	2.3	2.3	3.2	5.1	5.9	8.6	8.3	8.5	8.9
Government services	4.3	7.0	8.9	12.8	15.4	18.0	21.9	28.0	31.7
TOTAL CAPITAL FORMATION	44.3	45.7	61.2	82.2	89.5	93.7	112.7	144.2	159.9

SOURCE: Panorama of *National Accounts and Economic Surveys*, Ministry of Finance and Planning; mission estimates.

STATISTICAL TABLES

Table 15: Capital Formation by Type of Asset, 1964–72

Asset	1964	1965	1966	1967	1968	1969	1970	1971	1972
					(£ million)				
Buildings	12.2	12.9	15.3	22.8	28.6	30.4	32.8	40.7	45.6
Other construction	7.0	8.1	11.6	15.9	17.8	17.8	20.4	30.1	37.1
Land improvement	1.6	1.2	1.4	1.6	7.1	2.4	2.4	2.4	2.7
Transport equipment	9.7	8.9	12.6	17.5	15.4	17.1	20.2	26.4	21.3
Machinery and other equipment	14.2	14.4	19.0	23.1	24.4	24.8	34.9	44.2	51.1
Other	0.4	0.2	1.3	1.3	1.2	1.2	2.0	0.4	2.1
TOTAL	44.3	45.7	61.2	82.2	89.5	93.7	112.7	144.2	159.9

SOURCE: Panorama of *National Accounts and Economic Surveys*, Ministry of Finance and Planning; mission estimates.

Table 16: Balance of Payments, 1964–72

Category	1964 Dr	1964 Cr	1965 Dr	1965 Cr	1966 Dr	1966 Cr	1967 Dr	1967 Cr	1968 Dr	1968 Cr	1969 Dr	1969 Cr	1970 Dr	1970 Cr	1971 Dr	1971 Cr	1972 Dr	1972 Cr
									(£ million)									
Merchandise	84.5	79.0	97.6	79.7	115.2	90.7	113.6	82.4	121.7	87.2	121.3	93.8	152.7	106.1	196.8	109.5	185.7	125.5
Nonmonetary gold	0.1	0.1	0.1	0.2	0.1	0.1	0.1	0.3	0.1	0.3	0.1	0.2	0.1	—	0.2	—	0.4	—
Freight and insurance	0.5	7.7	0.5	8.2	0.5	9.8	0.2	9.6	0.2	9.1	0.1	10.3	0.1	11.1	0.1	11.4	0.2	11.7
Other transportation	5.4	9.4	5.5	11.1	7.1	12.2	7.7	14.5	8.5	15.1	8.7	17.1	9.3	18.7	8.8	20.2	9.1	21.5
Travel	6.8	9.4	6.4	8.2	5.6	14.4	7.0	14.7	7.7	17.3	8.0	16.7	7.4	18.5	9.1	23.9	9.7	26.5
Investment income	14.8	5.0	14.8	5.8	18.7	6.3	19.5	5.8	22.6	8.4	21.9	12.4	28.4	16.9	21.6	12.2	24.3	14.4
Government services	1.5	9.1	0.8	3.9	0.5	4.9	1.1	5.2	1.2	4.3	1.0	4.3	1.2	4.8	1.8	5.0	1.4	5.0
Other services	3.2	5.7	3.6	5.8	4.7	6.9	3.8	4.8	2.9	4.1	5.7	6.8	7.3	8.2	7.8	7.3	8.4	6.4
Private transfers	7.7	4.8	6.1	4.8	6.0	5.7	6.4	5.4	8.0	6.4	7.9	7.1	8.8	7.3	11.8	7.4	11.6	7.7
Public transfers	5.1	20.7	6.2	13.5	7.6	10.8	6.7	8.4	4.4	13.3	4.0	11.2	3.7	12.4	3.6	11.7	4.1	13.8
Current account balance	—	21.3	0.4	—	4.2	—	15.0	—	11.8	—	—	1.2	15.0	—	53.0	—	22.4	—
Private long term capital	26.3	10.9	7.3	8.8	1.1	2.1	—	8.9	1.0	10.0	1.9	14.9	0.5	15.4	0.3	17.3	0.3	16.8
Private short term	—	—	1.7	1.1	2.0	—	4.8	—	—	1.1	0.1	0.3	—	0.8	0.6	—	0.5	—
Government long term	2.9	3.1	3.0	9.6	1.0	14.6	1.9	9.1	1.0	8.1	1.1	8.7	0.9	16.9	1.2	12.6	0.1	16.0
Monetary institutions	—	3.6	1.8	—	13.7	3.9	10.9	3.5	12.4	1.1	23.5	0.5	13.7	1.3	0.1	28.5	10.5	1.5
IMF	0.8	—	—	—	0.6	—	—	—	—	—	—	—	4.9	2.1	2.3	2.3	—	—
Errors and omissions	8.9	—	5.3	—	—	2.0	—	11.1	—	5.9	—	1.4	1.5	—	3.2	—	0.5	—

SOURCE: Panorama of *National Accounts*; *Economic Surveys*, Ministry of Finance and Planning.

Table 17: Main Export Commodities Overseas, 1964–72

Commodity	1964	1965	1966	1967	1968	1969	1970	1971	1972
					(£ million)				
Coffee, unroasted	15.4	14.1	18.8	15.7	12.8	16.8	22.3	19.7	24.8
Tea	6.1	6.1	8.7	7.4	10.0	11.3	12.7	11.2	16.4
Petroleum products	2.1	4.5	5.7	7.2	6.1	7.6	8.2	9.2	8.9
Meat products	2.2	2.5	3.0	2.9	3.0	2.6	2.9	3.4	4.9
Petroleum extract	2.5	2.2	2.4	2.4	2.5	2.2	1.8	2.5	3.8
Sisal	6.0	3.9	3.3	2.1	1.8	1.7	1.9	1.4	2.1
Hides and skins	1.3	1.8	2.6	1.7	1.7	1.9	1.7	2.2	3.8
Wattle extract	0.9	0.7	1.5	0.9	1.1	1.1	1.1	1.3	1.7
Soda ash	0.7	0.8	1.1	1.0	1.1	0.9	1.7	2.1	1.9
Cement	0.8	0.9	0.8	1.0	1.2	1.4	1.6	1.6	2.0
Cashew nuts	0.3	0.5	0.5	0.5	0.6	0.7	1.6	1.1	1.1
Cotton	0.7	0.8	0.9	0.6	0.4	0.8	1.2	1.1	1.2
Pineapple	0.9	0.8	0.5	0.5	0.4	0.7	0.7	1.0	0.9
Other	7.2	7.6	8.3	9.4	15.1	13.6	12.2	15.4	17.1
TOTAL	47.1	47.2	58.1	53.3	57.8	63.3	71.6	73.2	90.6

SOURCE: *Statistical Abstracts*; *Economic Surveys*, Ministry of Finance and Planning.

Table 18: Major Exports to Uganda and Tanzania, 1964–72

Export	1964	1965	1966	1967	1968	1969	1970	1971	1972
					(£ thousand)				
Dairy products	1,194	1,670	1,618	1,740	686	2,187	1,657	1,974	2,994
Cereals and cereal preparations	2,645	2,137	1,398	1,996	1,947	2,157	1,646	760	2,446
Fruits and vegetables	477	519	650	763	722	686	854	1,047	1,151
Petroleum products	2,512	4,905	4,431	4,070	4,409	4,890	5,600	6,190	6,405
Soap and soap preparations	1,389	1,133	1,163	1,338	1,420	1,682	1,413	1,569	1,353
Paper, paperboard, and related products	866	1,085	1,418	1,354	1,537	1,434	1,485	1,421	1,491
Cement	883	948	884	688	999	927	1,419	1,181	773
Metal manufactures	1,616	1,740	1,750	1,492	1,372	1,418	1,686	1,800	1,272
Furniture and fixtures	397	537	661	202	558	589	724	677	n.a.
Clothing	1,943	2,367	1,655	1,390	975	775	615	764	336
Other	11,958	12,375	13,273	11,145	11,709	12,052	14,346	16,510	12,600
TOTAL	25,880	29,426	28,901	26,178	26,334	28,797	31,450	33,893	32,793

SOURCE: *Statistical Abstracts; Economic Surveys*, Ministry of Finance and Planning.

Table 19: Imports by Major SITC Classification, 1964–71

Import	1964	1965	1966	1967	1968	1969	1970	1971
				(£ million)				
Food and live animals	9.8	13.0	14.4	8.5	8.6	6.8	9.7	14.6
Beverage and tobacco	2.3	2.3	1.8	2.1	1.7	1.2	2.4	2.9
Crude materials	1.8	2.1	2.5	2.7	3.4	3.8	4.0	6.0
Mineral fuels	9.7	10.7	12.2	12.7	13.8	13.4	15.0	17.3
Animal and vegetable oils	2.0	3.3	2.6	2.0	2.4	2.9	3.2	4.6
Chemicals	7.1	9.0	9.7	8.8	11.9	12.7	15.6	19.1
Manufactured goods	22.4	26.7	30.7	30.8	33.6	34.6	42.2	51.3
Machinery and transport equipment	23.2	23.0	36.4	41.6	37.2	41.1	49.1	65.2
Miscellaneous manufactures	6.1	6.6	8.3	7.3	9.3	9.1	12.0	17.8
Other commodities	3.6	4.0	4.6	4.5	5.1	3.2	4.8	1.3
TOTAL	88.0	100.7	123.2	121.0	127.0	128.8	158.0	200.1

SOURCE: United Nations *Yearbook of International Trade Statistics*; *Economic Surveys*, Ministry of Finance and Planning.

Table 20: Percentage Distribution of Major Exports, 1964–72

Category	1964	1965	1966	1967	1968	1969	1970	1971	1972
					(percentage)				
Coffee	21.9	18.4	21.6	19.7	15.2	18.2	21.6	18.3	20.0
Tea	8.3	7.9	10.0	9.3	11.8	12.2	12.3	10.4	13.2
Petroleum products	6.3	12.2	11.6	14.2	12.4	13.5	13.3	14.3	12.3
Meat products	3.0	3.2	3.4	3.6	3.5	2.8	2.8	3.1	3.9
Petroleum extract	3.4	2.8	2.7	3.0	2.9	2.3	1.7	2.3	3.0
Sisal	8.2	5.0	3.7	2.6	2.1	1.8	1.8	1.3	1.7
Hides and skins	1.7	2.3	2.9	2.1	2.0	2.0	1.6	2.0	3.0
Cement	2.3	2.3	1.9	2.1	2.6	2.4	2.9	2.6	2.2
Dairy products	1.6	2.2	1.8	2.1	0.8	2.3	1.6	1.8	2.4
Cereals	3.6	2.7	1.6	2.5	2.3	2.3	1.6	0.7	2.0
Soap and soap preparations	1.9	1.4	1.3	1.6	1.6	1.8	1.3	1.5	1.1
Paper and paperboard	1.2	1.4	1.6	1.7	1.7	1.5	1.4	1.3	1.2
Metal manufactures	2.1	2.2	2.0	1.8	1.6	1.5	1.6	1.6	1.0
Other	35.4	36.0	33.9	33.7	39.5	35.4	34.5	38.8	33.0
TOTAL	100.0	100.0	100.0	100.0	100.0	100.0	100.0	100.0	100.0

SOURCE: Tables 17 and 18.

Table 21: Percentage Value Distribution of Imports by SITC Classification, 1964–71

Import	1964	1965	1966	1967	1968	1969	1970	1971
				(percentage)				
Food and live animals	11.1	12.9	11.7	7.0	6.8	5.1	6.1	7.3
Beverage and tobacco	2.6	2.3	1.5	1.7	1.3	1.0	1.5	1.4
Crude materials	2.0	2.1	2.0	2.2	2.7	3.0	2.5	3.0
Mineral fuels	11.0	10.6	9.9	10.5	10.9	10.4	9.5	8.5
Animal and vegetable oils	2.3	3.3	2.1	1.7	1.9	2.3	2.0	2.3
Chemicals	8.1	8.9	7.9	7.3	9.4	9.9	9.9	9.5
Manufactured goods	25.5	26.5	24.9	25.5	26.5	26.8	26.7	25.6
Machinery and transport equipment	26.4	22.8	29.6	34.4	29.2	32.0	31.2	32.5
Miscellaneous manufactures	6.9	6.6	6.7	6.0	7.3	7.0	7.6	8.9
Other commodities	4.1	4.0	3.7	3.7	4.0	2.5	3.0	1.0
TOTAL	100.0	100.0	100.0	100.0	100.0	100.0	100.0	100.0

SOURCE: Table 19.

Table 22: Trade Price Indices, 1964–72

Index	1964	1965	1966	1967	1968	1969	1970	1971	1972
Import price index	100	103	103	102	104	105	107	117	126
Overseas imports	100	102	102	102	104	105	107	117	125
East African imports	100	109	106	103	109	109	111	113	133
Export price index	100	101	101	99	100	99	107	109	118
Overseas exports	100	99	99	93	94	94	103	99	105
East African exports	100	102	105	114	114	111	113	126	141
Terms of trade	100	98	98	97	96	94	100	93	94

SOURCE: *Statistical Abstracts*; *Economic Surveys*, Ministry of Finance and Planning.

Table 23: External Public Debt[1] Outstanding as of December 31, 1972

	DEBT OUTSTANDING[2] DECEMBER 31, 1972		
Creditor	Disbursed	Undisbursed	Total
	(US$ thousand)		
Suppliers Credits	13,348	—	13,348
Germany, Federal Republic of	8,458	—	8,458
United Kingdom	3,465	—	3,465
United States	1,425	—	1,425
Private banks	20,662	2,479	23,141
Bahamas	620	—	620
Netherlands	532	577	1,109
United Kingdom	2,510	—	2,510
United States	17,000	1,902	18,902
Bond Issues (United Kingdom)	38,792	—	38,792
Publicly issued	37,927	—	37,927
Privately issued	865	—	865
Loans from International Organizations	78,228	109,156	187,384
African Development Bank	1,757	4,815	6,572
World Bank	32,590	55,978	88,568
IDA	43,829	47,955	91,784
International Coffee Organization	52	408	460
Loans from Governments	200,380	44,879	245,259
Canada	158	4,068	4,226
Denmark	2,179	687	2,866
Germany, Federal Republic of	15,746	2,509	18,255
Israel	1,179	—	1,179
Italy	5,503	2,580	8,083
Japan	2,013	166	2,179
Netherlands	857	7,772	8,629
Norway	1,505	—	1,505
Sweden	5,786	20,293	26,079
United Kingdom	140,175	4,151	144,326
United States	24,933	2,653	27,586
USSR	346	—	346
Unknown and unclassified	1,935	107	2,042
TOTAL DEBT OUTSTANDING	353,345	156,621	509,966

[1] The data cover debts with a maturity of one year or more, repayable in foreign currency.
[2] The figure for total debt outstanding excludes the uncommitted parts of the frame agreement with Japan ($4.36 million at the end of 1972) and is net of accumulated sinking funds of $29,786,000 in respect of bonds issued in the United Kingdom.
SOURCE: Economic Analysis and Projections Department, World Bank.

Table 24: Projected Disbursements and Service Payments on External Public Debt Outstanding, December 31, 1972[1]

Year	Debt Outstanding Beginning of Period — Disbursed Only	Including Undisbursed	Commitments	Disbursements	Service Payments — Principal	Interest	Total	Cancellations or Adjustments
				(US$ thousand)				
1968	219,637	326,928	25,795	37,027	6,967	10,927	17,894	−2,463
1969	247,236	343,293	31,646	26,747	7,522	11,783	19,305	−2,376
1970	267,303	365,041	41,596	30,260	7,340	11,480	18,820	−5,658
1971	283,733	393,639	55,035	42,878	7,803	12,269	20,072	−10,086
1972	306,209	430,785	104,253	59,163	10,553	13,415	23,968	−14,519
1973	353,653	509,966	—	51,998	17,659	15,320	32,979	−5,219
1974	380,536	487,089	—	43,522	15,970	16,310	32,280	−1,267
1975	406,821	469,851	—	23,954	15,835	16,843	32,678	−1,350
1976	413,590	452,665	—	17,922	22,423	17,043	39,466	−1,437
1977	407,585	428,738	—	9,533	21,270	16,567	37,837	−1,436
1978	394,412	406,033	—	6,192	34,484	14,940	49,424	−1,757
1979	364,364	369,792	—	3,219	19,976	13,154	33,130	−307
1980	347,300	349,509	—	1,663	18,115	12,355	30,470	−329
1981	330,520	331,066	—	469	16,842	11,611	28,453	−352
1982	313,795	313,872	—	72	20,153	10,481	30,634	−425
1983	293,290	293,294	—	3	17,346	9,411	26,757	—
1984	275,947	275,948	—	—	17,799	8,624	26,423	—
1985	258,148	258,149	—	—	17,714	7,806	25,520	—
1986	240,434	240,435	—	—	17,271	6,993	24,264	—
1987	222,942	222,943	—	—	16,448	6,208	22,656	—
1988	206,493	206,495	—	—	15,622	5,458	21,080	—
1989	190,871	190,872	—	—	16,009	4,781	20,790	—
1990	174,863	174,864	—	—	17,959	4,119	22,078	—
1991	156,904	156,905	—	—	15,758	3,285	19,043	—
1992	141,146	141,147	—	—	14,296	2,628	16,924	—

[1] Includes service on all debt listed in Table 23 with the exception of unclassified debts amounting to £2,042,000. Projected amounts reflect currency realignment in March 1973.

STATISTICAL TABLES

Table 25: Summary Accounts of the Kenya Banking System, 1968–72

Item	Dec. 1968	Dec. 1969	Dec. 1970	Dec. 1971	Dec. 1972
			(Sh million)		
Net foreign assets	824.3	1,255.5	1,616.9	1,200.5	1,381.3
Foreign assets	936.2	1,381.8	1,765.8	1,386.9	1,583.4
Fund reserve position	28.9	29.0	85.8	93.2	93.3
SDR holdings	—	—	41.6	92.9	132.4
Correspondents	410.5	832.5	942.7	608.5	695.8
EAC position	60.8	20.2	19.9	16.8	35.0
Government foreign exchange holdings	8.0	9.0	6.8	10.1	27.9
Other	428.0	491.1	669.0	565.4	599.0
Liabilities	106.9	126.2	148.9	186.4	202.0
Domestic credit	1,251.5	1,343.3	1,813.4	2,511.9	2,900.2
Claims on Government (net)	67.5	99.2	128.0	239.2	456.5
Advances	31.5	0.5	101.7	203.9	201.8
Treasury bills	—	59.9	200.0	76.0	315.3
Government securities	105.0	195.9	219.9	217.0	239.1
Treasury deposits	69.0	157.1	393.6	257.8	299.6
Claims on official entities (net)[1]	−69.7	−104.5	−110.7	−65.9	−158.6
Loans and advances	46.8	18.3	42.8	56.9	69.2
Securities	7.2	3.1	0.8	0.8	0.8
Deposits	123.7	125.9	154.4	123.6	228.6
Claims on private sector[2]	1,253.7	1,348.7	1,796.2	2,338.6	2,602.2
Capital participation	—	11.5	157.1	64.2	302.5
Loans and advances	—	1,330.1	1,631.8	2,267.1	2,291.8
Securities	7.7	7.0	7.3	7.3	7.9
Net unclassified assets or liabilities	−153.4	35.1	−24.9	23.9	−85.3
Liabilities to private sector[2]	2,229.2	2,633.9	3,367.0	3,654.8	4,075.2
Money	1,554.2	1,830.5	2,326.7	2,496.1	2,838.6
Currency in circulation	528.3	582.1	713.3	749.3	903.0
Demand deposits	1,025.9	1,248.4	1,613.5	1,746.8	1,935.6
Quasi-money	675.0	803.4	1,040.2	1,158.7	1,236.5
Time and savings deposits	675.0	803.4	1,040.2	1,158.7	1,236.5
SDR allocations	—	—	38.4	81.5	121.0

[1] Includes local governments and statutory boards.
[2] Includes public enterprises and EAC corporations.
SOURCE: International Monetary Fund.

Table 26: Principal Interest Rates, 1967-72

Item	1967	1968	1969	1970	1971	1972	As of March 31 1973
				As of June 30			
				(percentage rates)			
Central Bank of Kenya							
Rediscount rate for treasury bills			4.50	4.00[1]	2.00	4.00	3.79
Advances against treasury bills			5.00	4.50[1]	2.50	4.50	4.29
Bills and notes under crop finance scheme							
Discounts	5.00	5.00	5.00	5.00	5.00	5.00	5.00
Advances	6.00	6.00	6.00	6.00	6.00	6.00	6.00
Other bills and notes							
Discounts	5.50	5.50	5.50	5.50	5.50	5.50	5.50
Advances	6.50	6.50	6.50	6.50	6.50	6.50	6.50
Advances against Government securities	6.50	6.50	6.50	6.50	6.50	6.50	6.50
Kenya commercial banks[2]							
Deposits							
Time							
Minimum 30 days (7 days' notice)							
Sh 200,000 up to Sh 500,000	3.00	3.00	3.00	3.00	3.00	3.00	3.00
Sh 500,000 and over	3.25	3.25	3.25	3.25	3.25	3.25	3.13
3 to less than 6 months	3.50	3.50	3.50	3.50	3.50	3.50	3.50
6 to less than 9 months	3.75	3.75	3.75	3.75	3.75	3.75	3.75
9 to less than 18 months—w.e.f. 1/9/68	4.00	4.00	4.00	4.00	4.00	4.00	4.00
18 to less than 24 months (minimum Sh 500,000)—w.e.f. 1/9/68	n.a.	n.a.	4.50	4.50	4.50	4.50	4.50
Longer periods (minimum Sh 500,000)	n.a.	n.a.	n.a.	n.a.	n.a.	[3]	[3]
Savings	3.00	3.00	3.00	3.00	3.00	3.00	3.00
Loans and advances (minimum)	7.00	7.00	7.00	7.00	7.00	7.00	7.00

STATISTICAL TABLES

Other financial institutions:							
Kenya Post Office Savings Bank							
Deposits	2.50	3.00[4]	3.00	3.00	3.00	3.00	3.00
Agricultural Finance Corporation							
Loans	7.50[5]	7.50[5]	7.50	7.50	7.50	7.50	7.50
Hire purchase companies							
Deposits (various periods)	n.a.	3.00– 6.00	3.00– 6.00	3.00– 6.00	3.00– 6.00	3.00– 6.00	3.00– 7.50
Loans	n.a.	10.00–12.00	10.00–12.00	10.00–12.00	10.00–12.00	10.00–12.00	7.00–12.00
Building societies[6]							
Deposits (various periods)	n.a.	4.00– 6.50	4.00– 6.50	4.00– 6.50	4.50– 7.00	4.50– 7.00	5.50– 6.50
Loans	n.a.	7.50–10.00	7.50–10.00	7.50–10.00	7.50–10.00	7.50–10.00	7.50–10.00

[1] Valid until April 1970, when the balance of treasury bills outstanding was redeemed by the treasury.
[2] In Kenya, banks collectively agree on the rates they grant or charge on deposits and loans, respectively.
[3] Individual banks free to determine rate.
[4] W.e.f. July 1, 1968.
[5] Includes Land and Agricultural Bank of Kenya.
[6] Includes institutions not registered under the Building Societies Act, but whose primary function is to finance the purchase of property.

SOURCE: Central Bank of Kenya annual report for the years ending 30th June, and *Economic and Financial Review Quarterly*, Vol. V, No. 3, January–March 1973.

Select Bibliography

The literature on Kenya is considerable, and some of it is referred to at various places in the report. This bibliography lists the sources referred to and some of the more important official publications.

Sources for official publications listed are the following:

- Government Printer, P. O. Box 30128, Nairobi, Kenya. For a full list of available documents, see *Catalogue of Government Publications,* issued by Government Printer. Some earlier publications are out of print.
- Central Bank of Kenya, Box 30463, Nairobi, Kenya.
- Commissioner General of East Africa Customs and Excise, P. O. Box 90601, Mombasa, Kenya.
- East African Statistical Department, P. O. Box 30462, Nairobi, Kenya.

Other important addresses are:

The Director of Statistics, Central Bureau of Statistics, P. O. Box 30266, Nairobi, Kenya.

East African Community, P. O. Box 1001, Arusha, Tanzania.

Map Office, P. O. Box 30089, Nairobi, Kenya.

Institute for Development Studies, University of Nairobi, P. O. Box 30197, Nairobi, Kenya.

East African Publications

Republic of Kenya

>Development Plan, 1964–70.
>Revised Development Plan, 1966–70.
>Development Plan, 1970–74.
>Development Plan, 1974–78.
>Sessional Paper No. 10 of 1963/65, "African Socialism and its Application to Planning in Kenya."
>Report of the Select Committee on Unemployment, December 1970.
>Report of the Fiscal Commission, 1973.
>Sessional Paper on Employment, No. 10 of 1973, May 1973.
>Report of the Commission of Inquiry (Public Service Structure and Remuneration Commission), May 1971. (The Ndegwa Report)
>Report of the Training Review Committee, 1971–72. (The Wamalwa Report)
>Report of the Working Party on Agricultural Inputs, 1971. (The Havelock Report)
>Budget Speeches (1966/67 – 1972/73).
>Economic Surveys (published annually, 1962–73).
>Kenya Statistical Digest (published quarterly, since September 1963).
>Statistical Abstracts (published annually, 1968–72).
>Estimates of Recurrent and Development Expenditure and Revenue (published annually, 1958/59 – 1972/73).

SELECT BIBLIOGRAPHY

Reports by the Controller and Auditor-General on the Appropriation Accounts (published annually).

Ministry of Commerce and Industry, *Index to Manufacturers and Products,* 1972.

Ministry of Commerce and Industry, *A Guide to Industrial Investment in Kenya,* 2nd Edition, 1972

Central Bureau of Statistics, *Input/Output Table for Kenya, 1967,* December, 1972

Reports of International Agencies

International Bank for Reconstruction and Development

The Economic Development of Kenya. Baltimore: The Johns Hopkins University Press, 1963.

"Prospects for Economic Development in East Africa." Report No. AF-58b (in seven volumes), August 31, 1967 (unpublished).

"Economic Development Prospects in Kenya." Report No. AE-6a (in two volumes), October 22, 1969 (unpublished).

"Industrial Development in East Africa: Progress, Policies, Problems and Prospects." Report No. AE-12 (in four volumes), April 16, 1971 (unpublished).

"Economic Developments in East Africa." Report No. AE-16a, (in five volumes, including a Program of Pre-investment Studies), July 30, 1971 (unpublished).

"Economic Progress and Prospects in Kenya." Report No. AE-22, (in two volumes), March 3, 1972 (unpublished).

"Agriculture Sector Survey—Kenya." Report No. 254-KE (in two volumes), December 1973 (unpublished).

International Monetary Fund

Balance of Payments Yearbook.
International Finance Statistics.

United Nations

A Proposed Five Year Programme of Technical Assistance to Kenya, 1968–73, February, 1969.

Country and Inter-Country Programming, Kenya (AP/GC/KEN/R.I.) December 1, 1971.

International Labour Organisation, *Employment, Incomes and Equality— A Strategy for Increasing Productive Employment in Kenya,* 1972. (The "ILO/UNDP report")

Private Publications

Institute for Development Studies, Nairobi, Working Papers

No. 37. Phelps, M. G. and D. Wasow. "Measuring Protection and its Effects in Kenya." n.d.

No. 61. Dillon, B. "Financial Institutions in Kenya, 1964–71: A Preliminary Analysis." September 1972.

No. 66. Baily, Mary Ann. "Capital Utilization Rates in Kenya Manufacturing: an Interim Report." October 1972.

No. 75. Mureithi, L. P. "A Framework for Analysing Labor Absorption Capability for Different Firm Sizes in Kenyan Manufacturing." December 1972.

No. 79. Colebatch, H. K. "Some Political Implications of Service Provision: Roads and Schools and Health Services." n.d.

No. 90. Macrae, D. S. "Import Licensing in Kenya." n.d.

No. 157. King, J. "Wages, Efficiency and Labour Market Disequilibrium." August 1972.

IDS Discussion Papers

No. 29. Massell, Benton F. "Expenditure Patterns in the Central Province of Kenya: A Preliminary Analysis." September 1966.

No. 49. Massell, Benton F. "Determinants of Household Expenditure in Rural Kenya." April 1967.

No. 66. Ghai, D. P. "Incomes Policy in Kenya: Need, Criteria, and Machinery." June 1968. Mimeo.

No. 68. Diamond, P. A. "Effective Protection in the East African Transfer Taxes." n.d.

No. 69. Harris, J. R. and M. P. Todaro. "A Two Sector Model of Migration with Urban Development in Developing Economies." September 1968.

No. 71. Harris, J. R. and M. P. Todaro. "Urban Unemployment in East Africa: An Economic Analysis of Policy Alternatives." September 1968.

No. 96. Diejomach, V. P. "Financing Local Government Authorities in Kenya." September 1970.

No. 112. Hermann, B. "Some Basic Data for Analyzing the Political Economy of Foreign Investment in Kenya." 1971.

No. 148. Vinnai, V. "The System of Exchange Control in Kenya." September 1972.

No. 149. Pack, H. "Employment and Productivity in Kenyan Manufacturing." August 1972.

Other IDS

Wasow, B. "A Simple General Equilibrium Model of Wage/Exchange Rate Policy in an Open Undeveloped Economy." September 1970.

Reimer, R. "Effective Rates of Protection in East Africa." Staff Paper No. 78. July 1970.

Westlake, M. J. "Kenya's Indirect Tax Structure and the Distribution of Income." Staff Paper No. 102. June 1971.

"An Overall Evaluation of the Special Rural Development Programme." 1972

Other Publications

Bhagwati, J. N. and A. O. Krueger. "Exchange Control, Liberalization, and Economic Development." Papers and Proceedings of the Eighty-Fifth Annual Meeting of the American Economic Association. *American Economic Review,* May 1973, pp. 420–22.

Bhagwati, J. N. "Fiscal Policies, the Faking of Foreign Trade Declarations, and the Balance of Payments." *Bulletin of the Oxford University Institute of Economics and Statistics.* February 1967.

Bruton, Henry J. *The Elasticity of Substitution in Developing Countries.* Research Memorandum No. 45. Williamstown, Mass.: Center for Development Economics, Williams College, April 1972.

Chenery, H. B. and N. G. Carter. "Foreign Assistance and Development Plans Performance, 1960–1970." *American Economic Review,* Vol. 63, No. 2 (May 1973), pp. 459–68.

Chenery, H. B. and Peter Eckstein. "Development Alternatives for Latin America." *The Journal of Political Economy,* July/August 1970.

Corden, M. *The Theory of Protection.* London: Oxford University Press, 1971.

Donaldson, G. F. and J. D. Von Pischke. "A Survey of Farm Credit in Kenya." *USAID Spring Review of Small Farmer Credit,* Vol. 7, February 1973.

Dwyer, G. D. "Employment Opportunities in Kenya Agriculture." *East Africa Journal,* Vol. 9, No. 3 (March 1972), pp. 23–27.

Griffin, K. B. and J. L. Enos. "Foreign Assistance: Objectives and Consequences." *Economic Development and Cultural Change.* April 1970.

Guisinger, D. S. *Tariff and Trade Policies for the Ethiopian Manufacturing Sector.*

Harris, J. R. and M. P. Todaro. "Migration, Unemployment and Development: a Two-Sector Analysis." *American Economic Review,* March 1970.

Heller, Peter S. "The Dynamics of Project Expenditures and the Planning Process: With Reference to Kenya." Ph.D. dissertation, Harvard University, November 1971.

Kuznets, S. "Long-Term Changes in the National Income of the United States of America since 1870." In *Income and Wealth of the U.S.* edited by S. Kuznets, Cambridge: Bowes and Bowes, 1952.

Lewis, S. R., Jr. *The Effects of Protection on the Growth Rate and the Need for External Assistance.* Research Memorandum No. 49. Williamstown, Mass.: Center for Development Economics, Williams College.

Little, I. M. D., T. Scitovsky, and M. Scott. *Industry and Trade in Some Developing Countries,* p. 45, Table 2.2. Paris: OECD, 1970.

Marris, P. and A. Somerset. *African Businessmen: A Study of Entrepreneurship and Development in Kenya.* London: Routledge, Kegan, Paul, 1971.

Mikesell, Raymond F. and James E. Zinser. "The Nature of the Savings Function in Developing Countries: A Survey of the Theoretical and Empirical Literature." *The Journal of Economic Literature,* March 1973.

Needleman, L., Sanjaya Lall, R. Lacey, and J. Seagrave. *Balance of Payments Effects on Foreign Investment Case Studies of Jamaica and Kenya.* UNCTAD Document TD/B/C.3/79/Add.2/Corr. 1, June 30, 1970. Mimeo.

Papanek, G. F. "The Effect of Aid and other Resources Transfers on Savings and Growth in Less Developed Countries." *The Economic Journal,* September 1972.

Power, J. H. "The Role of Protection in Industrialization Policy with particular reference to Kenya," *Eastern Africa Economic Review,* June 1972.

Rahman, M. A. "Foreign Capital and Domestic Savings: A Test of Haarelmo's Hypothesis with Cross-Country Data." *Review of Economics and Statistics,* February 1968.

Rasmusson, R. *Kenyan Rural Development and Aid.* Stockholm: SIDA, 1972.

Rempel, H. "Labour Migration into Urban Centres and Urban Unemployment in Kenya." D. Phil. thesis, University of Wisconsin, 1970.

The Review, February 1973.

Scott, M. FG. "Estimates of Shadow Wages in Kenya." Unpublished mimeo, Nuffield College, Oxford, February 1973.

Stiglitz, J. E. *Alternative Theories of Wage Determination and Unemployment in LDCs: The Labour Turnover Model.* Cowles Foundation Discussion Paper No. 335, April 1972. Cited in M. FG. Scott, *op. cit.,* pp. 82–88.

Streeten, Paul. *The Frontiers of Development Studies,* Chap. 6. New York: John Wiley and Sons, 1972.

Todaro, M. P. "A Model of Labour Migration and Urban Unemployment in Less Developed Countries." *The Review of Economics and Statistics,* February 1972.

Weisskopf, T. E. "An Econometric Test of Alternative Constraints on the Growth of Underdeveloped Countries." *The Review of Economics and Statistics,* February 1972.

Winston, Gordon C. *On the Inevitability of Factor Substitution.* Research Memorandum No. 46. Williamstown, Mass.: Center for Development Economics, Williams College, April 1972.

Zarembka, Paul. "On the Empirical Relevance of the CES Production Function," *The Review of Economics and Statistics,* 1970.

Postscript

This report was designed to provide a timely review of Kenya's past successes and failures in development, and to assess the priorities for future economic management as the country prepared to enter the second decade of independent government. However, in the weeks before and after the celebrations of the tenth anniversary of Independence, the landed cost of crude oil on which Kenya depends for most of her energy needs increased over threefold. Together with all other oil-consuming countries, Kenya had to embark upon an urgent assessment of the implications of this development. But the problem was more than an increase in oil prices, since it was already clear by late 1973 that the unprecedented rate of inflation in industrial import prices would make it difficult for Kenya to finance the level of imports necessary to sustain the target growth rates of the new plan. Thus, the combined effect of oil price increases and world inflation has lead to a further and much more rapid deterioration in the relative terms on which Kenya trades with the rest of the world. This represents a real fall in resources which Kenya has available for consumption and investment.

We have not tried to incorporate these changed circumstances in our analysis or to reassess the future prospects of the Kenya economy. This would have involved a major revision of the report, and in any case it is by no means clear what the consequences of recent dramatic events will be on either the Kenya economy or the world as a whole. What is clear is that this loss of real income (which must be assumed to be permanent) has thrust Kenya much more quickly into the resource disequilibrium we had foreseen arising over the next few years. It is also possible that even with the best possible management and a great deal of external assistance, Kenya may have to settle for less ambitious targets than those which have been set, and achieved, in the past. On the whole, however, we believe that the deterioration in Kenya's resource position does not alter the general thrust of the report's prescriptions. On the contrary, we believe the serious position Kenya now finds herself in serves to underline the urgency for even more drastic and speedy reforms to the structure and process of growth. It may also provide a more conducive political environment for the difficult decisions which lie ahead.

Part II

The Analytical Annexes

ANNEX ONE

THE MACRO-ECONOMIC MODEL AND PROJECTIONS

AUTHOR'S REMARKS ON A MACRO-ECONOMIC MODEL

In designing a macro-economic model of the economy of Kenya, the mission's purpose was twofold: first, to assist in a systematic analysis of the economy and its development potential; second, to demonstrate that a macro-economic model can be a useful management tool to the development planner once the model's capabilities and limitations are understood.

Unfortunately, the general reader usually finds it difficult to understand a technical discussion of the structure and equations of a model, and may fail to see its relevance to real life. There is a real danger, therefore, that a macro-economic model may end up as no more than a mathematical toy with which econometricians play. The mission has tried as far as possible to avoid this pitfall by presenting the model and analyzing the results of their projections in nontechnical language, and relegating the technical description of the methodology employed to the appendices.

Chapter 1

The Nature and Uses of the Model

In recent years, computerized econometric models have become an important tool of economic management to put at the disposal of national economic managers as well as corporate management. However, there is still a widespread misunderstanding of the nature and use of these models (leading to either abuse or neglect of the tool), and therefore it seems worthwhile to begin by clarifying our approach.

We regard a computerized model primarily as a *computational device*. In other words, given the best guesses about the basic relationships in an economy and working hypotheses about the magnitudes of various critical parameters, the model works out their implications for different sectors of the economy and over a given time horizon. In formulating the "best guesses" and "working hypotheses," econometric techniques play only a subsidiary role. Apart from statistical regressions, they are based on economic theory, on the study of economic history of the country and, above all, on the judgments of the persons involved with the management of the economy. For example, the model presented here makes some working hypotheses about the effects of relative prices of capital and labor on employment prospects and capital requirements within different sectors. It also makes some assumptions about the elasticity of imports with respect to import prices. These assumptions are not made by rigorous econometric investigatons in the Kenyan economy (because relevant data are not available) but are presented as working hypotheses on the basis of experience in other countries and scattered evidence in Kenya. Quite often, parameters are put not at "most likely" levels, but at "optimistic" or "pessimistic" levels, in order to work out the implications of alternative sets of conditions. Thus, the projections in the model are not to be regarded as "predicting the future," but to influence it in the desired directions by applying appropriate policy changes now.

It may be asked, "What is the use of a model, if it does not foresee future and does not, on its own, test alternative hypotheses about the effects of policies?" Admittedly, this leaves for a model only a humble role, but, we believe, a correct and useful one. For example, it is obvious that if a country is running balance of payments deficits and borrowing abroad to fill the gap, it is accumulating a burden of debt servicing for the future. No model is necessary to tell us that. However, it is not intuitively obvious, but important to know, when the burden of debt will become intolerable (however defined) and how this could be ameliorated by changing the terms of borrowing. This is extremely laborious to work out by hand, and a computerized model can be helpful.

Similarly, if one accepts that abolition of "investment allowances" will improve employment prospects (as we in fact suggest in this report), it is useful to know how much difference it would make to the overall prospects of employment, say, over the next ten years. Again, if one suggests a list of policies for tackling, say, the unemployment problem, the question arises how serious the problem will remain if only parts of the package are accepted. By trying to quantify the broad orders of magnitudes, the model helps in getting a feel for these figures.[1]

---

1. A model, of course, does no more than work out the implications of the assumptions made by the user. However, quite often the process leads to some surprising conclusions. In this particular exercise, for example, we started with a supposition that factor price changes would prove to be a powerful instrument for influencing employment and poverty. Yet, on the assumptions used in the model, we found that the impact of factor price changes alone on employment and poverty was only marginal. Similarly, while we found that changes in the exchange rate could be a useful tool of policy for certain purposes, we were surprised by the inflationary implications

Another important use of an econometric model is to provide a framework, a skeleton, on which to hang the assumptions about different sectors of a development plan and ensure their consistency. Even the purely clerical job of keeping track of different sets of data of past and expected future—on national accounts, imports, exports, taxes, public expenditures, domestic credit, wages and prices—can be immensely simplified by computerized models. However, as emphasized before, these useful purposes can be served by the model only when it is used in an alert and flexible manner responding quickly to the changing environment and changing policy issues, and the limitations of the data used in the model must always be kept in mind.

---

shown in the model, and had to reduce the role of exchange rate policy in the final strategy. While some of these results were surprising at first sight, a closer examination of the interrelationships involved showed them to be creditable and helped to throw further light on the operations of the economy. For example, since factor price changes will primarily affect employment in the modern sector (which is a small proportion of the total labor force), it is not difficult to believe that their overall impact on employment will be relatively small. Similarly, it could be expected that devaluation would be a very appropriate policy tool when the foreign exchange gap is much larger than the domestic resource gap. But in our projections, the difference between the two "gaps" was not very large, so that the usefulness of exchange rate manipulation in reducing the external gap was limited by the scarcity of domestic resources and the consequent inflationary pressure on prices.

Chapter 2

The Structure of the Model

The prime purpose of our model is to assess whether the past rate and pattern of growth in Kenya can be sustained in the future, within the resources which are likely to be available, and if not, whether a different set of policies could help in attaining the targets. Another important objective is to analyze the employment prospects over the next decade and to examine policies that might be helpful in tackling unemployment. We hope that this kind of analysis can be of value in identifying the nature and sensitivity of the policy decisions which have to be made in Kenya durng the Third Five-Year Plan and afterwards and in assessing Kenya's external aid requirements.

For assessing the resources required to achieve the target growth rates, we use a modified version of the well known "two-gap" approach which has become a standard tool of analysis in country plans as well as in international aid agencies. Broadly speaking, the approach accepts that at an early stage of technological development, growth may depend critically on importing goods and services from abroad, and that domestic resources may not always be freely convertible into foreign resources due to the limited potential for expanding exports. In this situation, foreign capital inflows have to fill up the bigger of the two gaps—trade gap and saving gap. The problem of what happens to the nonbinding gap (the smaller of the two gaps) and how the two gaps are equalized at the end of the day (as they must be) are not resolved in the classical two-gap approach.

Because of this analytical problem in the usual two-gap model, we have tried to introduce a modification to it. We assume that the ex post equalization of the two gaps is brought about by changes in prices of consumer goods relative to the general price level.[1] If this increase in price is unacceptable, additional imports would be required to meet the increased propensity to consume. In fact, in this procedure, there are not two gaps but two parts of the trade gap—one part due to basic imports requirements, another part to prevent an excessive rise in consumer prices. With this distinction, one could examine various policy alternatives such as increasing foreign capital inflow, changes in exchange rate, relative prices of consumer goods, or change in pattern of growth, instead of being forced into the assumption that foreign capital inflow is always available to fill the bigger of the two gaps. This becomes particularly useful if part of the domestic consumption goods gap is for nontradables, for in this case, foreign capital inflow cannot fill the domestic goods gap in the current period.

The above gap analysis could, of course, be done in two ways: either through the "requirements approach" or the "availability approach." In a "requirements approach," we start with a target growth rate and try to compute the foreign resources required to achieve this growth rate. In the "availability approach," the model is run in reverse gear, and starting with the available resources, the model works out the growth rate that can be expected with these resources. The model presented in this annex may be termed a "modified requirements approach." In this approach, we start with the target growth rates and work out the net resource transfers required. However, instead of stopping at that point, we bring in our best guesses about the availability of resources from the usual sources and, after taking into account the pattern of disbursements expected to flow from these commitments and the debt servicing requirements of past debts, try to estimate the additional resource requirements over and above those likely to be available. Moreover, even the residual resource gap is not taken as given; instead, internal policy options are also examined to see if the resource gap could be reduced without diminishing the

---

1. For further discussion, see the section on "Money and Prices" in the following chapter.

objectives of growth, employment, and the attack on poverty. In this fashion, the residual gap we are left with represents the minimum of extra effort required on the part of the external donors.

Given the target growth rate, the first step in the analysis is to estimate the investment required. This implies that we assume that output is determined by the supply of factors of production and not by demand. This is a reasonable assumption for medium and long term analysis, but cannot be used to analyze year-to-year variations in output. The problem of demand becomes even more important when one is considering a disaggregated approach, as the Plan does (and as we are doing in this annex). In this context, it is important to ask whether the structure of output implied by different sectoral growth rates is consistent with the demand pattern likely to be generated by the structure of production. This is obviously a very difficult question, requiring assumptions about input/output structure, final expenditure patterns and the influence of fiscal, monetary and other policies on demand pattern. In our analysis, we do not tackle this problem, beyond making some spot checks on consistency for some important sectors such as agriculture and manufacturing.

In estimating investment requirements for a given rate of growth, the parameter that we use is the incremental capital output ratio (ICOR). This does not imply that we assume capital as the only factor of production. We treat ICOR not as a technological parameter, but as an economic parameter influenced by the rate of growth, pattern of growth, technical change, and relative factor prices. Gross ICOR in each sector is inversely related to its rate of growth, because with higher rates of growth, the depreciation component of gross investment becomes a smaller part of total investment. Aggregate ICOR is also a function of the pattern of growth. For the same level of aggrevate growth rate, ICOR (and thus investment) could be reduced if the pattern of investment is oriented towards sectors in which ICOR is lower than in others. Even in a particular sector, ICOR could be changing (as it is in Kenya), due to changes in degree of utilization and other sources of efficiency of resource use. In our model, we try to take into account the overall trends in ICORs in different sectors. Similarly, one could change factor proportions (and thus ICORs) even in a given sector for a given degree of efficiency, by changing factor prices.

The next stage in the analysis is to compute the amount of foreign resources (imports of goods and services) required for target growth rates. Here again we try to take into account the effect of the pattern of growth and prices on import requirements. Imports are divided into five categories: consumer goods, raw materials, capital goods, government imports, and imports of nonfactor services. Imports of raw materials are obviously dependent on the pattern of growth; because a unit of value-added in, say, manufacturing, requires more imported raw materials than does a unit in agriculture. Imports of raw materials were therefore related to value-added in different sectors, weighted by the ratios of imports of raw materials to gross value-added obtained from the 1967 Input/Output Table.[2] For imports of consumer goods, the sectoral weights were derived from the ratio of taxable income to GDP in each sector, on the assumption that those whose incomes fall below the taxable minimum are not by and large rich enough to consume imported consumer goods. Lastly, for import of capital goods, it was assumed that machines and vehicles are imported, but not structures or animal stocks, so that the weights used for investment in different sectors were derived from the ratio of machines and vehicles to total investment. Government imports have been taken as a function of GDP in the government sector and imports of nonfactor services as a

---

2. See *Input/Output Table for Kenya, 1967*, Central Bureau of Statistics, Nairobi, December 1972. It is possible that in the light of structural changes going on in the economy, the 1967 table is a little dated. However, there was no other more recent source of information on Input/Output structure.

function of time. Imports in different categories are also influenced by the ratio between domestic prices and import prices (adjusted by rate of exchange).

In order to assess the net foreign capital required to meet import requirements, we need to estimate exports. In the model, exports are largely exogenous. However, we introduce two influences to make them quasiendogenous. In the first place, exports are sensitive (although to a limited extent) to the exchange rate. Second, they are sensitive to variation in the rate of growth of the agricultural sector. Import and exports as discussed above are in constant prices. However, in order to assess the foreign capital requirements, we have to transform them into current prices in foreign currency (in our case US dollars) because this is how foreign capital inflows will be denominated. The model therefore uses import and export price indices to compute the net resource balance in current US dollars. This gives the external imbalance expected from target growth rates.

To compute the internal resource gap, we have to estimate saving potential. This has been done at a disaggregated level: savings by households, Government, and the business sector, the latter separated into depreciation allowances and undistributed profits.

Household savings are computed as a residual after deducting consumption from disposable income. In computing household disposable income, account is taken of wages, property incomes, net transfers from abroad, income tax, and other taxes, etc. Government savings are calculated from figures of tax and other receipts computed in the model and the government consumption expenditure is a function of GDP in government. In estimating business savings, we compute depreciation allowances as a function of past investment rates, and undistributed profits are then a residual. The ex ante consumption of the *households* sector is compared with the supply of consumer goods available after deducting investment and government consumption from total resources available. The gap between ex ante consumption and the supply of consumer goods shows the degree of inflationary pressure—or internal imbalance—associated with the target growth rates. Depending on whether such inflationary pressure is acceptable or not, an increase in foreign resources may be required.

If the domestic resource gap is filled through additional imports, the ex post imports will be higher than the ex ante imports. If, on the other hand, import controls are imposed, the ex post imports might be lower than ex ante imports. After adjusting for import prices and deducting export earnings, we get the current trade balance at current prices. In order to obtain the gross foreign capital inflows required, we have to make a number of other adjustments. First of all, net factor income payments and net unrequited transfers have to be added. By adding in the debt servicing payments from old loans, and deducting the disbursements from old commitments, we get the new gross transfers required. In order to estimate the transfers generated by new commitments, we have to assume the pattern of disbursement of aid from different sources (such as international agencies, governments, or private sources) and on different terms of lending (relating to maturity, grace period, and rates of interest). After deducting the disbursements from new loans, and adding the future debt servicing from new disbursements and additional foreign reserve requirements, we get the size of the unfilled "gap" for which new resources will have to be found. In making these calculations about debt servicing, we have used a detailed computer program developed for the purpose in the World Bank.

In addition to gap calculations, our model is geared to making estimates of employment in different sectors. Calculations are made for three types of employment: wage employment in the modern sector, high and middle level manpower requirements, and total employment, including wage employment in the informal sector, self-employed and family workers. The broad approach is to estimate the incremental employment in each sector, which depends upon the rate of growth of value-added and of labor productivity in each sector. High and middle level manpower requirements in each sector are assumed to be fixed proportions of wage employment, the proportions varying for different sectors, as indicated by the 1972 Manpower Survey.[3]

Assumptions about labor productivity are made on the basis of past trends, but the model itself uses different assumptions about this parameter in order to analyze employment prospects under different assumptions. The incremental labor-output ratios are also influenced by factor price policies that change ICORs.

The above analysis is so far in terms of constant internal prices. However, to analyze government revenues and balance of payments, one needs an estimate of prices. The model does not, however, integrate internal prices into the system, except for estimating the influence of internal prices on imports. Ideally, it would be desirable to link the domestic saving-investment gap to prices—either through its effects on money creation, or directly. However, at present, the model assumes the rate of domestic credit creation as a policy instrument. Domestic credit, plus foreign reserves, give money supply. The total nominal value of resources (GDP, plus imports, minus exports) depends on current and lagged money supply. The price level is then determined by dividing total resources at current prices by resources at constant prices. The consumption goods gap, however, determines the relationship between the prices of consumer goods and the general price level.

The above section has given a brief nontechnical description of the structure of the model. Further technical details are presented in the technical appendices, and a flow diagram of the main lines of causation is shown in Chart I as a further aid to understanding the structure of the model.

How do we use the model? We start the model with the sectoral growth rates, which were the rates being used in the provisional plan projections provided to the mission. We also make somewhat optimistic assumptions about export prospects, terms of trade, ICORs, and saving propensities. Under these assumptions, we use the model to project the basic economic scene up to 1985. We then examine whether the gap in resources is manageable over the next few years, and how the employment situation looks around 1985.

If there is a gap, the next question is how to fill it. One possibility is increased borrowing on hard terms such as suppliers' credit. The model then examines the consequences of this on the debt servicing capacity of the country around 1985. It also examines whether a softening of terms of lending by lending agencies can make a substantial difference to debt servicing position. A second possibility is to impose import controls to reduce the foreign resources gap. The model works out some of the consequences of this on domestic prices and the balance of payments situation. A third possibility is to reduce the gap by lowering growth targets. However, this is found to have unacceptable effects on employment and poverty prospects. Finally, we go on to examine more interesting possibilities of reducing the gap, by changing the pattern of growth and by changes in policy.

The model examines the effects of changes in the pattern of growth on the size of the gap and on employment and poverty. More specifically, it examines the effects of increasing growth rate in agriculture and reducing that in infrastructure investment. The second set of alternatives is examined by changing successively the rate of exchange, investment allowances, and interest rates; and we examine how much difference is made by each strategy.

Finally, the results of the above analysis are utilized to obtain an illustrative "preferred policy" package, and the model works out the scenario up to 1985 under these conditions. As emphasized in the preceding chapter, these results are to be regarded mainly as suggestions of the orders of magnitudes involved, and these have to be supplemented by various judgmental analyses before a policy package could be decided.

3. See "A Preliminary Report on the Kenya High and Middle Level Manpower Survey, 1972," *Kenya Statistical Digest,* December 1972.

CHAPTER 3

ANALYSIS OF THE PAST AND HYPOTHESES FOR THE FUTURE

In this chapter, we present the main quantitative results of our analysis. As already mentioned, we shall give only broad results, and the methodological and analytical procedures are left aside for discussion in the technical appendices.

Developments over the Period 1964-71

Our analysis is based on the developments in the Kenyan economy since Independence, because of the limitations of data before that period. More specifically, the years covered are from 1964 to 1971, with the 1971 figures still provisional.[1] Even for the conventional econometric analysis, this is a small number of observations, and the problem is further complicated by indications that during the last two years, 1970 and 1971, the economy may have been going through a turning point. Because of these reasons, we have to exercise caution in using the equations estimated over this period for projections through the next decade.

Productivity of Investment

We begin our analysis with movements in incremental capital output ratios. In a very broad sense, ICORs can be regarded as indicators of efficiency in resource use.[2] In this respect, there are three observations to be made about the level and movements in ICORs in Kenya: First, the overall ICOR in Kenya was low by international standards at the beginning of the period; second, the overall ICOR (and some sectoral ICORs) have been rising rapidly over the years; and third, by the end of the period, the overall ICOR was higher than the good performers among developing countries, but still better than poor performers, and not significantly out of line with the average for all developing countries.

Using three-year moving averages for smoothing out investment and output figures, we get an ICOR (for fixed capital) of 2.1 for the total GDP and 2.34 for monetary GDP in Kenya in 1966. Adding 0.3 for inventories, we get an overall ICOR of 2.4. The estimates of ICORs computed by the Bank for a number of other developing countries are presented in Table 1. We notice that even for countries that have experienced good growth recently, ICORs were not significantly lower than 2.4. For example, it was 2.46 for South Korea, 2.45 for Brazil, and 2.11 for Indonesia. Kenya's performance, of course, was most creditable in comparison with ICORs of countries such as Philippines (where it was 6.45), Colombia (3.93), Egypt (5.05), and India (3.64).

However, over the period since 1964, overall ICOR increased rapidly, and by 1970 it had increased by almost 50 percent to 3.2. Since an analysis of the causes for this rise in ICORs would be useful for projections as well as policy analysis, we analyzed the disaggregated sectoral ICORs for twelve sectors. To obtain a better measure of efficiency of new capital, we subtracted depreciation allowances from gross investments and computed net ICORs, the results of regressions on which are presented in Table 6. From these sectoral net ICORs, we notice that there was a significant increase in net ICORs in five sectors: mining and quarrying, building and construction, transport, storage and communication, other services, and general government. However, there was a significant

---

1. Provisional data for 1972 have since become available, but it has not been possible to take them into account in our analysis.
2. Although one very significant aspect of efficiency that ICORs ignore is the longevity of capital.

decline in net ICORs of manufacturing and repairs, so much so that by 1970, ICOR in manufacturing and repairs was lower than that in agriculture, forestry, and fishing.

The explanation for these varying trends requires more intensive study by sectors than we have been able to provide. However, we may suggest some plausible lines of argument. One possible explanation is that Kenya inherited some excess capacity from the previous period, so that output could be increased without much input of capital in the earlier years. As the slack in the economy was taken up, additional capital was required for increases in output. Another possible explanation is that during this period, factor prices have been distorted, so that capital was made excessively cheap, and this distortion encouraged an excessively capital intensive structure. This was perhaps particularly likely in building and construction, as well as in transport, storage and communications.

The declining trend in manufacturing and repairs is more puzzling. One possible explanation is that the system of protection introduced over this period gave artificially high values to output in the manufacturing sector. Ideally, this price rise should have been captured in the price deflator used to estimate constant prices in manufacturing; but typically, these price indices use base-year weights, in which the new items of production are underrepresented. Since capital goods are typically exempt from duties, and new manufacturing items were developed under protection, ICORs tended to have a downward bias. Moreover, as more new manufacturing activities were started, the effective average rate of overvaluation of manufacturing output increased, so that ICORs were not only low but falling over time. Another possible line of explanation may be the lumpiness of investment in particular sectors such as petroleum and cement. Investment undertaken in these sectors did not lead to output until the later years, so that ICORs tended to decline as gestation lags in these investments were over. A similar reason may be that in the early period, a considerable amount of industrial capacity was *created* (in contrast to the *inherited* excess capacity mentioned above) as a means of preempting a wider East Africa market, and ICORs therefore declined over time as capacity utilization was increased.

A more intensive study, industry by industry, would, of course, be required to understand the forces behind the efficiency of resource use. But even our preliminary analysis suggests some policy implications. As shown in Table 1, ICOR in Kenya was significantly higher by 1970 than that of good performers such as Brazil, South Korea, or Indonesia. Kenya's ICOR is still better than poor performers, although no longer significantly better than the average in developing countries. If she wants to be in the league of good performers, therefore, Kenya must try to improve her efficiency, or at least prevent further deterioration.

In our policy package analysis, we suggest two lines of action. In the first place, we consider a number of policy instruments, such as exchange rate, interest rate, and investment allowances, which could change the price of capital relative to labor, and thus might influence ICORs. Second, we note that ICORs differ significantly from sector to sector, and that by changing the pattern of growth, therefore, the overall ICOR could be lowered. In particular, we examine the benefits to be derived from a relative shift towards agriculture. Some extra output (and value-added) will be required in other sectors to supply the raw materials required by agriculture. But, even after these indirect resource requirements are considered, we find that overall ICOR can be reduced significantly by changing the sectoral pattern of growth.

Import Requirements

Except for the last two years of the period, namely, 1970 and 1971, imports have grown at about the same rate as GDP. While this does not imply any significant reduction in import dependence (as might have been expected from the so-called import substituting protectionist strategy), this was better than the experience of some developing countries which have seen an increasing degree of import dependence while carrying out import substitution. The last two years have, however, witnessed a surge in imports (in constant prices), in spite of a rise in import prices. In part, this rise in imports can be explained by the high level of economic activity and especially investment, and possibly a build up in inventories in the expectation that import controls would be introduced. Whether in the future import requirements will increase more in line with GDP or not will probably depend on what kind of policies are followed regarding the expatriate business community and whether encouragement is given to agro-based manufacturing.

In our analysis, we break down total imports into five categories: consumer goods, raw materials, capital goods, government imports, and imports of nonfactor services. As shown in Table 7, imports of nonfactor services have been almost static, while the percentage share of raw materials has been increasing fast. In our analysis of the demand for imports, we try to take into account the differences in import requirements arising from growth in different sectors. For example, the Input/Output Table for 1967 suggests that the requirements of imported raw materials and intermediates in manufacturing were as much as 77 percent of value-added, while those in agriculture were only about 9 percent. One could also expect similar differences in the demand for imported consumer goods in different sectors. For example, it seems reasonable to assume that "poor" people do not consume any significant amount of imported consumer goods, and sectors such as the "nonmonetary" and agricultural sectors are likely to generate a higher proportion of income going to the poor than are sectors such as manufacturing or banking. It is, of course, difficult to get any reliable set of data on patterns of income distribution generated by different sectors. One approximation may be wage versus nonwage income. But for sectors such as "nonmonetary" or agricultural, where poorer people predominate, wage income is small because most of the people belong to the category of self-employed poor.

We therefore decided to use another set of data. The income tax data show the amount of income generated in different sectors which is assessed for income tax purposes. Assuming that those people whose income is not high enough to be assessed for income tax purposes are not importers of consumer goods, we used the ratio of assessed income to GDP in each sector as a weight to apply to sectoral value-added in obtaining an equation for consumer goods imports. The highest weight was shown by banking, insurance, and real estate sectors, where 83 percent of the value-added was assessed for tax. The smallest weight (except for the nonmonetary sector) was in agriculture, where it was 13.7 percent. The weights are, of course, not ideal but it seems to us that these differences might be closer to reality than the assumption of equal weights implied in a purely aggregative approach.

A similar approach was taken for imports of investment goods. It seems reasonable to argue that capital goods in mining or manufacturing are likely to be more import-intensive than in agriculture. Again we could not get any systematic information on this and had to rely on a crude assumption that machinery and transport equipment are imported while breeding stock and structures are not, and we used the information on type of capital goods required by different sectors for formulating weights in the equation for import of capital goods.

The weighting procedure described above enabled us to form some judgment as to how much of the increase in imports over the period was due to the increase in GDP and how much due to changes in the composition of GDP. On the basis of our analysis, we have estimated that 25 percent of the increase in imported consumer goods, and 28 percent of the increase in raw materials, have been due to the change in sectoral composition. Only 3 percent of the increase in investment goods imports was due to sectoral changes. For the analysis of imports by government and imports of nonfactor services, we employed a fairly simple approach. Government imports were regressed on value-added in government, and the marginal propensity to import was found to be 7 percent. Imports of nonfactor services were growing at an annual rate of 2.3 percent, or distinctly lower than that of imports of goods or of GDP.

Analysis of Savings and Exports

In order to assess the domestic resources and foreign resources required for target growth rates, we have to deduct savings from investments requirements, and exports from import requirements. Our analysis for domestic savings will be presented in Annex Four, and we do not propose to repeat it here. Broadly speaking, our conclusion is that Kenya's savings performance, until recently, has been very good. In 1970 and 1971, the savings rate, particularly of the household sector, has declined and there is some question in our minds whether the previously high savings propensity can be maintained. However, for our model, we made the optimistic assumption that the savings performance during the period 1964–71 will prevail in the future. The savings functions in different sectors—household, business, and government—have been estimated in unpublished work undertaken by the Ministry of Finance and Planning, and in our model we utilized their equations. Household savings are assumed to be 10 percent of personal disposable income; depreciation allowances are made a function of past investments, with weights obtained from tax laws. The undistributed profits of businesses are treated as residuals. Government consumption is assumed to grow as a function of value-added in general government, and savings are estimated as the residual, after deducting tax receipts. The equations used in the model are presented in Appendix D.

Movements in Employment

The growing rate of unemployment in the economy is widely regarded as an important shortcoming in Kenya's otherwise good performance. However, while the problem is regarded as crucial, adequate data are not available to make a proper analysis. Data on wage employment in the modern sector are available for the period 1964–71, but there are no GDP figures to correspond to the modern wage employment only. On the basis of the results of the population census of 1969 and other related information, a set of data for total employment by sectors for 1969 and 1971 was prepared by the mission and this is presented in Table 15. The formal wage employment in 1969 (627,000) accounted for only 12.4 percent of total employment (5 million). The urban informal sector, accounting for 96,000 (2 percent of total), is certainly a significant sector, but could hardly be regarded as a likely mainspring of growth in employment. Similarly, the rural nonagricultural informal sector, although much bigger than the urban informal sector (3 percent of the total), is insignificant when compared with informal employment in agriculture, which accounts for some 83 percent of the total. The agricultural sector is assumed in the model to be the residual employer, and thus it is by increasing productivity in this sector that the conditions of the "working poor," as ILO/UNDP report on Kenya calls them, can be really improved.

On the basis of these inadequate data, we could not estimate any meaningful employment equations. The simplified approach that we used was to make different assumptions about changes in labor productivity over time in different sectors and deduce their employment implications. On an overall basis, over the period 1964–71, the rate of growth of GDP has been about 7 percent, and that of wage employment between 3 and 4 percent, thus implying (for sectors where the ratio of formal to informal employment did not change significantly) a productivity growth of 3 to 4 percent a year. As regards sectoral employment growth rates, we note that the figures in agriculture and trade are significantly influenced by settlement schemes and Kenyanization programs, so that wage employment figures may be misleading. Employment figures in electricity and water and transport, storage and communications, also showed some irregular patterns of movement at a generally low level of employment. We could not therefore infer any consistent sectoral differences in rates of growth in labor productivity. For projection purposes, we had to make judgmental estimates about the rates of growth in labor productivity in different sectors. We note, however, that the rate of growth in labor productivity is connected with the rate of growth of capital output ratios and, since we are assuming no further increase in ICORs, the rate of growth of labor productivity may be expected to be lower in the future than in the past.

For projections of total employment, we have used a weighted average of the rate of growth of labor productivity in the formal and informal sectors, and have assumed that the agricultural sector absorbs the residual labor force.[3] The income generated in the agricultural sector, divided by the labor force it has to absorb, determines the level of income of the "working poor" in agriculture. Thus, while the *ceteris paribus* gains in labor, productivity in other sectors tends to reduce employment in these sectors and lower the standard of living of agriculturists; whereas an increase in labor productivity in agriculture does not result in unemployment but in a higher standard of living of the "poor."

In the Kenyan economy, skilled manpower may be regarded as a scarce factor of production, and in our model we make some rough projections for its future requirements. Here again, it is important to note the significant differences in high and middle level manpower required by different sectors. Table 16 presents the figures of high and middle level manpower as a ratio of wage employment in different sectors: while agriculture requires less than 4 percent of its wage employment as skilled labor, the electricity and water sector requires 25 percent, and trade 30 percent. Since the supply of skilled manpower will continue to be limited in Kenya for some years, changes in sectoral patterns of growth may become one of the most useful ways of reducing that constraint.

Money and Prices

In the usual two-gap analysis, money and prices are absent. This creates problems of estimation as well as analysis. Some of the functions, such as tax functions, should really be analyzed in terms of current prices. Similarly, the general rate of inflation as well as relative prices may have important implications for such variables as the capital-labor ratio, import requirements, or income distribution, and these should ideally be analyzed within the model. Even the question of ex post equalization of the two ex ante gaps—the saving gap and the trade gap—can be tackled only by bringing in price changes. However, while we have not been able to analyze the influence of prices at all adequately, we have attempted to bring prices into the model. In our system, price changes equate the two gaps, and also influence the level of imports.

Until recently, Kenya has experienced a remarkable degree of price stability. The average annual rate of increase in the GDP deflator was less than 2 percent, and this degree of price stability, associated with rapid growth, must be regarded as good performance in comparison with other developing countries. The reasons for this price stability over most of the period, and the recent increase in prices, should be interesting to analyze. On the one hand, Kenya's experience could be regarded as a text book justification of the monetarist view of inflation. During this period, monetary policy was very conservative, and the rate of expansion of money supply was low. As shown in Annex Two, the deficits in government budget were not financed by borrowing from the

---

3. Therefore, in this model, there is no unemployment. The actual scale of unemployment in the future will largely depend upon the "gap" between rural incomes and wages in the urban formal sector.

Central Bank. In fact, until recently such borrowing was limited by legislation to £12 million. However, in 1972 there was a change in legislation and the ceiling on government borrowing was raised to 25 percent of gross current revenues, or the equivalent of about £30 million in 1972/73. The Government has, in fact, borrowed more heavily from the Central Bank, money supply has expanded rapidly, and the rate of inflation has picked up.

On the other hand, one could also make a plausible case for the nonmonetarist view. There was probably some excess capacity in the economy in the early part of the period. The import prices increased significantly in 1970 and 1971, and some agricultural prices were also increased by the Government in these years. One might therefore argue that the past price stability and recent inflation could be explained with reference to "cost push" prices. In fact, the recent price rise in Kenya may only be a part of the present worldwide wave of inflation.[4]

It is, of course, difficult to sort out the relative influences of these factors. However, it seems to us that for a long term analysis of inflation a monetarist approach may have statistical as well as analytical advantages. Using current and lagged money supply as independent variables, we found excellent fit for monetary expenditure. The elasticity of money expenditure with respect to money supply was about 0.65, thus implying a declining velocity of money as has been found to be the case in many other countries. The fall in velocity could have been due partly to the declining proportion of the nonmonetary sector in total GDP, and partly to the increasing demand for cash balances which is generally associated with growth. However, we could not separate these influences.

Policy Variables in the Model

As mentioned before, we have tried to design our model so that we could make illustrative calculations about the effects of changes in policy instruments, such as exchange rate, interest rate, wage rate, or investment allowances. In general, it is difficult to estimate the effects of these policy instruments by using them directly in regression equations; it is even more difficult to do this in Kenya, because these policy instruments have not been changed significantly over the period. The general approach we have followed therefore is to analyze the effects of these instruments in a nonquantitative way outside the model and then use the model to get some quantitative feel by using different plausible assumptions about the critical parameters. Whenever appropriate, we have drawn upon the experience of other countries which have chosen to employ these policy instruments in the management of their economies.

Effects of Change in Exchange Rate

In Kenya, the exchange rate in terms of US dollars has been stable since Independence.[5] Over this period, however, it has been revalued in terms of sterling, the currency of Kenya's main overseas trading partner. Now that Kenya seems to be entering a phase of foreign exchange constraint, it may become desirable to consider the exchange rate as a positive and flexible instrument of policy. At present, when the old dogma of fixed and inflexible exchange rates seems to be coming to an end, the rate of exchange should not be treated as a symbol of national prestige but as just another price.[6] When

---

4. Subsequent events show this to be true.
5. We ignore the small, temporary revaluation against the dollar in 1973.
6. Brazil's recent experience is yet another vindication of this point of view. Similarly, Pakistan's massive devaluation in May 1972 was followed by a dramatic improvement in her balance of payments. For the eleven months July 1972 to May 1973, exports increased by 39 percent (in US dollars) over the same period in 1972. Apart from merchandise exports, there was a considerable increase in recorded "invisible" receipts, especially remittances.

viewed as a positive instrument of policy, a reduction in the exchange rate might well be expected to confer significant benefits in terms of export promotion, import displacement, employment promotion, stimulation of agriculture and agro-based manufacturing, and some redistribution of real income from the urban rich to the rural poor. In the light of these effects, one could in fact argue that it is preferable to err in the direction of an *undervaluation* rather than an *overvaluation* of the exchange rate.

In the usual analysis of the effects of devaluation, the impact effect is an immediate deterioration in terms of trade of the devaluing country. If the increase in real exports and the decrease in real imports more than counterbalance the adverse terms of trade effect, its foreign exchange position will improve over a period (of say two to three years). However, in Kenya (as in most other developing countries), the prices of nearly all major exports are determined in foreign markets in terms of foreign currency. Thus, the most noticeable effect of a devaluation is not a worsening of terms of trade, but increased domestic profitability of export industries, and increased cost of imports.

The long term effects of changes in exchange rates will, of course, depend on elasticities of supply of different commodities with respect to their domestic prices, and demand elasticities in foreign markets in terms of foreign prices. It would be desirable to make a commodity-by-commodity study of elasticities to assess the effects of devaluation. However, our preliminary explorations suggest that the statistical data are not adequate for this purpose. The scattered evidence[7] that does exist suggests that Kenyan farmers who grow export commodities (such as tea, coffee, or sisal) are responsive to price changes. Moreover, since Kenya occupies a small share of world markets, world prices are unlikely to be affected to any significant extent by changes in the level of her exports.

The import displacement effects work through a number of channels. Imports of capital goods may be reduced partly because of the increased cost of foreign capital goods compared with domestic capital goods and partly because of the increased cost of capital vis-à-vis labor. Similarly, imports of consumer goods may be reduced partly because of redistribution of *real* income from the urban rich to the rural poor, and partly because of higher prices of imports. The effects on imports of raw materials are uncertain. Imports will increase to the extent that they are required for the production of consumer goods formerly imported but now domestically produced. However, to the extent that import-intensive luxury consumer goods are priced out of the market, the demand for imported raw materials will decline. The important point is that a higher price of foreign exchange would affect both the direct and indirect content of imported goods, and would bring about the desired effects on the domestic production system much more efficiently than the present ad hoc and arbitrary system of protection has done.

We have discussed at length in Annex Three how the exchange rate and a tariff subsidy scheme could be used as complementary instruments in obtaining intersectoral efficiency as well as balance of payments equilibrium. In our model we have not been able to tackle the effects of exchange rate changes on intersectoral allocations. We have considered only its effects on exports, imports and capital-labor substitution. In general, we have taken conservative estimates of elasticities.

Effects of exchange rate on income distribution—both interpersonal and intersectoral—can be quite significant. An overvalued exchange rate results in the taxation of exports and the subsidization of imports. Since poorer people consume a smaller part of imports than do the rich, an increase in the price of imports will reduce the real income of the rich more than that of the poor. Similarly, poorer people may derive a greater

---

7. See for example, G. D. Gwyer, "Long and Short-Run Elasticities of Sisal Supply," *Eastern Africa Economic Review*, December 1971; D. J. Ford, "Long-Run Elasticities in the Supply of Kenyan Coffee: A Methodological Note," *Eastern Africa Economic Review*, June 1971; and J. K. Maitha, "A Supply Function for Kenyan Coffee," *Eastern Africa Economic Review*, June 1969.

share of income from export oriented growth (based on agriculture[8] and agro-industries) than they do from import substituting manufacturing.

A reduction in the exchange rate by benefiting the agricultural sector will also benefit the rural areas, and thus reduce the pull of urban centers which is complicating the urban unemployment problem. Similarly, by increasing the price of capital relative to labor, it may be expected to improve employment prospects for the rural as well as the urban labor force.

Apart from the above mentioned longer run effects of adjusting the exchange rate, one should also note the expectational factors in the situation. Once a currency is generally regarded as overvalued (one indication is the rate prevailing on the open market), private capital inflow is discouraged, capital outflow is encouraged, the building up of imported capital goods capacity ahead of demand appears attractive leading to wastage in the form of excess capacity), and the situation becomes progressively more difficult.

Devaluation essentially means increasing the cost of foreign exchange, but the main problem created by such an increase is the possibility of a faster rate of inflation. If increased inflation could be used to reduce the real wages of the urban labor force, it might not be unwelcome. However, if it leads to pressures for money wage increases which cannot be resisted, it may accentuate the inflationary process.

Interest Rate Policy

The interest rate structure in Kenya has been almost static for the last ten years. In the meantime, world money market rates have risen to unprecedented levels, and inflation in Kenya seems to be gathering strength. This has had the serious effect of reducing the incentive of foreign private companies to borrow abroad, and has thus aggravated the resource situation. The increased rate of inflation is encouraging excessive capital intensity, by reducing the effective real cost of capital, and discouraging domestic savings, by reducing the effective real return from savings. Moreover, in Kenya there is no significant rentier class, so that low interest rates do not seem to have any significant benefits for income distribution. In general, it may now be appropriate for Kenya to reconsider its interest rate policy; on balance, a higher interest rate policy would seem to be desirable.[9]

Wage Rate Policy

Wage earners are generally identified with the poorer sections of a country, and higher wages may therefore seem desirable on income redistribution grounds. However, in Kenya, wage earners, especially in the urban formal sector, represent a privileged minority of the labor force. Higher wage rates for this sector have distortionary effects on capital intensity, urban-rural migration, the education system, and urban social services. As the ILO/UNDP report has emphasized, the real problem of poverty and unemployment lies with the "working poor," and a curb on the rate of wage increases in the formal sector may well help these poorer sections of the community.

As discussed above, all these policy instruments have far reaching effects on the economy, and our model does not pretend to capture all of them. In particular, it is unfortunate that income distribution effects which we regard as significant cannot be quantified. The model does try to capture the direct effects of exchange rate changes on imports and exports, and the indirect effects (via capital-labor substitution) on internal

---

8. Even in commercial crops such as tea, coffee, and pyrethrum, the share of production originating in small farms is quite significant. For example, smallholders produce 90 percent of Kenya's pyrethrum exports, nearly half the coffee, and a growing proportion of the tea.

9. For further details, see Annex Four.

and external imbalances, employment prospects, and the prospects of the working poor in agriculture.

One critical element in our analysis is the assumption that possibilities of capital-labor substitution are significant. A priori, it seems to us that the influence of factor prices on the capital-labor ratio works through so many channels—for example, changes in product mix, techniques, and the rate of utilization—that the total effect should be significant. On an empirical level, it is worth noting that Henry Bruton, after an extensive survey of the statistical results on elasticities of substitution in the United States, Philippines, Argentina, Chile, El Salvador, Korea, Paraguay, Peru, Portugal, Spain, and Mexico, found that elasticity varies from 0.5 to 1.6, and is generally significantly different from zero.[10] In the Kenyan economy, data on output, labor and capital by industry are not available for fitting an explicit production function. However, empirical analysis of the figures of labor productivity and wage earnings gives estimates of elasticity of substitution which are not significantly different from unity (see Appendix Five).

Thus, in the light of empirical evidence on production functions in developed as well as developing countries, it seems reasonable to assume unitary elasticity of substitution in factor proportions with respect to factor prices. We also use the share of wages in gross output as an approximation to the elasticity of output with respect to labor.

Lastly, we have conservatively assumed that existing factor proportions are not malleable, and that these substitution effects apply to incremental capital and labor only. Under these assumptions, alteration in relative factor prices will change ICORs and the incremental labor-output ratio in the model. As an illustration, it might be noted that an investment allowance of 20 percent may reduce the effective cost of capital by, say 8 percent (assuming a marginal tax rate of 40 percent), and this could increase ICOR by about 4 percent (assuming the wage share to be 50 percent). Similarly, an increase in the cost of foreign exchange by 20 percent may increase capital cost by 6 percent (assuming imported capital goods to be about 30 percent of total investment) and this may reduce ICOR by about 3 percent. These measures will also change the employment content of growth, pari passu.

Basic Hypotheses Used in the Model

The projections in our model require a large number of assumptions about exogenous variables, and even about the future movements in parameters. Our approach to the assumptions made in the model has been as follows:

- We have used as far as possible exogenous assumptions close to those of the Ministry of Finance and Planning. These could be regarded as proxies for the assumptions of the forthcoming 1974–78 Development Plan.

- In general, we have taken optimistic assumptions with regard to the future. This affects our assumptions about the terms of trade, ICORs, and foreign capital inflows. When we have introduced parameters, such as elasticities of exports or imports with respect to exchange rate, we have taken conservative assumptions.

- Although there are indications that the Kenyan economy may be going through a turning point, and behavioral equations are shifting, we have made optimistic assumptions that the past behavior pattern will hold for the future.

The starting point of our analysis, therefore, is the set of target growth rates, for different sectors, which form the preliminary targets of the Plan. We had to adjust them

10. See Appendix Five.

slightly because of the differences in sectoral breakdown; we also use the same rates of growth up to 1985, whereas the Government assumptions go up to only 1978. The actual figures are presented in Table 3. The targets imply a healthy overall growth rate of 7.5 percent (which is even higher than the growth rate in the past decade) and a considerable acceleration in the manufacturing sector.

As regards ICORs, we make the optimistic assumption that, in spite of the past tendency to increase, they would stabilize at the levels reached in 1972. These values are shown in Table 3. However, they are sensitive to changes in sectoral growth rates as well as to changes in relative factor prices.

For imports, we use the equations estimated from the past data, but we assume them to be sensitive to relative prices (defined as the overall domestic price, divided by the import price index adjusted for the price of foreign exchange). The elasticity is assumed to be somewhat low (0.25) for all imports except for imports of consumer goods, where it is assumed to be 0.50. Exports in constant prices are taken from Government projections (see Table 11). These appear to be optimistic, especially with regard to exports of manufactures to other countries in the East African Community. Similarly, tea projections appear optimistic especially in light of general trends in the world tea market. In the absence of any better assumptions, we decided to use Government projections. However, since these extend to only 1978, we had to make some judgmental forecasts of our own to continue the series up to 1985. The elasticity of exports with respect to exchange rate adjustments is assumed to be 0.5 for agricultural products and minerals and 0.2 for other exports.

One important change we do introduce is to make projections of agricultural exports sensitive to changes in value-added in agriculture, from the level obtained in the basic projections. More specifically, we assume that if there is any increase in agricultural output over and above that assumed in the basic projections, the whole of this increase will be exported.

As discussed before, the resource requirements for growth can be altered dramatically by changes in terms of trade. In general, since both capital inflows and debt servicing are denominated in current foreign currency prices, it is desirable to estimate the resource gap in current prices (i.e., in US dollars). For this purpose, we start with projections of import prices. Import prices in Kenya increased very rapidly (at the rate of about 10 percent) over the years 1970 and 1971. Part of this rise was due to inflation in developed countries (particularly the UK) and exchange rate realignments (affecting particularly import prices from Japan and Germany, expressed in US dollars). However, as Table 8 indicates, import prices rose much more sharply in Kenya than in other countries in a comparable situation—Tanzania, Ethiopia, Nigeria, and Malaysia for instance. The other factor that might have contributed to the recorded rise in import prices is overinvoicing of imports connected with the flight of capital. In recent years, the Government has taken severe measures to check overinvoicing. However, it is difficult to be sure of its effects on import prices, which seem to have increased by about 8 percent in 1972. For 1973, we assume a price rise of 5 percent, and thereafter 3 percent per annum.

As regards export prices, we have used the information on projections provided by the Commodities and Export Projections Division of the World Bank (see Table 12). According to the projections, the immediate outlook for primary product prices was generally bright, but the weighted average of commodity prices (excluding petroleum) in the seventies was expected to rise by less than half the projected rate of inflation in the developed countries. More specifically, coffee prices were expected to remain relatively strong throughout the seventies; tea prices were expected to remain on their secular decline; and sisal prices were thought likely to remain buoyant for a year or two, and then decline to the trend values by 1980.

Coffee prices have gone through some well defined cycles in the past. The recent experience of surplus and deficit phases is portrayed in Chart 2. The typical reaction to high prices leading to overproduction seems to have been modified by the restraint on investment imposed under the International Coffee Agreement and greater coordination of national policies among the producing countries. It is expected that heavy surpluses would not occur in the eighties. The outlook for tea prices continues to be unfavorable. World consumption is expected to grow at about 3 percent per annum, and world production at 3.1 percent. The London average price for all teas is projected to continue its downward trend to a 1980 level of about 38 new pence per kilogram. As shown in Chart 3, Kenyan tea has improved in price relative to other teas in recent years. We assume that in future, Kenya's tea prices will move in line with the prices of other teas. For sisal, the present spurt in prices is expected to be short lived. Our assumption implies that by 1980, prices will return to a level about 20 percent higher than those in 1970. For other exports—agricultural and nonagricultural—we assume a rate of inflation in terms of foreign currency at 3 percent per annum, which seems to be on the optimistic side. The export projections in current prices are presented in Table 3.

The next set of assumptions relates to the capital inflows that could be expected to fill the gap in foreign exchange resources. In the first place, we already know the likely disbursements from existing loan commitments. These are prepared by the Debtor Reporting System in the Bank and the projections are presented in Table 13. Next we have to add to these the disbursements from new commitments. This involves two sets of assumptions: one relating to the levels of commitments by different foreign agencies, and the second relating to the disbursement pattern of commitments. They are also presented in Table 13. On the whole, we are expecting a substantial increase in commitment levels of foreign aid agencies over the next five years.

From disbursement of old and new commitments, we have to deduct the debt servicing outflow. For old loans, the interest and amortization outflows are given from past agreements. For new commitments, the debt servicing burden depends on terms of lending. In general, we have assumed that new commitments conform to the same terms as in the past. However, in our sensitivity analysis, we also change these terms and analyze the effect of such changes on debt servicing problems. The levels of foreign private investment and factor income payments from these investments also play an important role in an open economy like Kenya's. We have made rather optimistic projections of net foreign investment on the assumption that the climate for foreign private investment will continue to be favorable (see Table 14).

In determining prices in our system, the exogenous variable is domestic credit creation. The assumptions of monetary policy in the Plan period have not been stated in the Plan documents we have received. However, the Central Bank has used 15 percent per annum expansion of domestic credit as a guideline to the banking sector. For our model, we assume that this direction is adhered to and domestic credit grows at 15 percent per annum over the period 1973–85.

For employment projections, the critical assumption is about the rate of growth of labor productivity in different sectors. Our basic assumptions about this are in Table 17. In general, we have assumed a slowdown in the rate of growth of labor productivity in the future compared with the past.

CHAPTER 4

PROJECTIONS AND POLICY ANALYSIS

On the basis of the parameters and assumptions discussed in the preceding chapter, we work out our initial set of projections of macrovariables over the period 1973–85. Since these assumptions are a close approximation to those of the Third Plan, the projections for 1974–78 could be regarded as approximations to the development in the Plan period.[1] The projections up to 1985 are obviously on shakier ground, but these are useful to analyze the long term consequences of foreign capital inflow on debt servicing capacity and the long run outlook on employment and poverty. As emphasized before, our interest is not in forecasting the future, but in anticipating the consequences of present policies so that the future could be changed, if necessary, by change in present policies.

The Basic Scenario

External and Internal Imbalances

The basic scenario projected under the assumptions of the Plan is given in Table 19. We note that over the Plan period the annual target rate of growth of GDP at factor cost is about 7.7 percent, which is higher than the Second Plan target (6.7 percent) as well as the actual growth rate over 1967–72 (which was 7.0 percent). This rate of growth will require gross investment over the period of £1,150 million, which is 26 percent of GDP at market price over this period. The ratio of investment to GDP at market price is not significantly higher than it was in the past.

However, over the past few years, import prices have been increasing at a rapid rate, and the import requirements in current prices expand at 11 percent per annum. Since exports even at the optimistic assumptions are expanding only at 10 percent per annum, this gives rise to a sizable trade gap which increases from less than £20 million in 1972 to nearly £97 million in 1978. After allowing for disbursements from old and new commitments, debt servicing and other payments, we are still left with a large residual gap in the balance of payments in 1978. Since Kenya had, until recently, a comfortable balance of payments situation, this would mark a turning point in her development, and she may be moving from an "absorptive capacity" constraint phase to a "resource constraint" phase.[2]

If the required amount of foreign resources could be obtained from abroad, domestic savings would be adequate on the optimistic assumption that the household savings propensity increases from its low level in 1971 (when it was 7 percent) to its average rate of 10 percent. In this situation, there will be no significant consumption goods gap so that consumer goods prices will rise *pari passu* with the general price index. If, however, the household savings propensity remains at 7 percent, there will be pressure on consumer goods, even after foreign resources are found to fill the trade gap. Nevertheless, the trade gap is a serious problem. Looking ahead to 1985, we find (subject to the limitations of long range forecasting) that the trade gap widens to about £275 million. This, however, is only the implication of assuming that the target growth

---

1. Without making any formal consistency check on sectoral composition, we made some spot checks on output of agriculture and manufacturing. By using the 1967 Input/Output Table, we found agricultural output marginally below and manufacturing output marginally above the "consistent" output.

2. Although, as we point out, Kenya has absorptive capacity problems in specific sectors.

THE MACRO-ECONOMIC MODEL AND PROJECTIONS

rates for the Third Plan period are maintained up to 1985, which it may not be realistic to do.

Employment

Even if external and internal resources are mobilized to attain the target growth rates, the employment problem looks disturbing. Formal wage employment increases to 958,000 by 1978, thus absorbing about 171,000 over the Plan period. However, during this time, the labor force is likely to increase by 908,000. Thus, the formal sector can absorb only about 20 percent of the increase in the labor force. Even if we include employment in the informal sector (outside agriculture), the situation is not materially different. The total labor force employed outside agriculture increases from an estimated 862,000 in 1974 to 1.08 million in 1978, thus absorbing 24 percent of the increase in labor force. The remaining labor force, therefore, has to be absorbed by agriculture, where employment increases from about 4.8 million in 1972 to 5.8 million in 1978, the implications of which for the standard of living of the agriculturalists are discussed below.

The model also works out the high and middle level manpower requirements. These increase from 120,000 in 1974 to 149,000 in 1978, thus implying an increase of skilled manpower requirements of 5,800 per year. It is worth examining (though we have not done so) whether these requirements could be met from indigenous sources or through increased dependence on expatriate staff.

The Poverty Index

As discussed before, we take the average income of agriculturalists as an index of the standard of living of the poor, on the assumption that the majority of the poor live and work in the field of agriculture. Taking the whole of nonmonetary GDP and 86 percent of monetary agriculture as accruing to the "poor," we find that average income per worker in agriculture was £42.9 in 1972 (at 1970 prices), £44 in 1974 and would rise to £47.2 by 1978. The rate of increase in their standard of living would therefore be only 1.7 percent over the Plan period, which is significantly lower than the overall per capita increase of about 4 percent for total GDP and about 3.5 percent for household disposable income. Thus, even if the growth targets are attained, the poor would get relatively poorer over the Plan period and even by 1985, the average income per worker would be only £53.8 in 1970 prices.

Sensitivity of the Basic Scenario to the Critical Assumptions

As already emphasized, the model is only working out the implications of our various assumptions and it is worth examining how far prospects could change if our critical assumptions are changed. We have therefore made a sensitivity analysis of our projections.

In the first place, it is obvious that our gap projections are critically dependent on assumptions about import and export prices. If, for example, import prices increase at 8 percent in 1973 (as they did in 1972) instead of at 5 percent (as assumed in the projections) the trade gap over the Plan period could increase by an additional £45 million, and by £60 million by the year 1985 (see Table 20). Similarly, if export prices or export earnings increase by one extra percentage point, the resource picture can change significantly. While noting sensitivity of the trade gap to our assumptions about terms of trade, however, we have to emphasize that assumptions are on the optimistic side.

Similarly, as regards the internal resource gap, we note that there is considerable uncertainty about the saving-income ratio of households. If this ratio were to remain at the 1971 level (7 percent), rather than increase to 10 percent (the average for 1964–71) as assumed in the projection, there could emerge a significant internal imbalance, reflected in higher consumer prices.[3]

Our employment projections are dependent on assumptions about the growth in labor productivity. However, even on the extreme assumption that productivity growth rate is zero, modern wage employment would rise to only 1.2 million by 1978 (see Table 21). By 1985, modern wage employment absorbs about 43 percent of the increase in labor force, but since productivity is assumed to remain constant, this increase in employment would probably imply no improvement in the standard of living of workers in the modern sector. Another possibility is to allow for a rate of growth of labor productivity in the informal sector at a lower level (say 50 percent) of that in the formal sector which again improves the employment prospect. However, in both cases, agriculture still has to absorb the major portion of the increase in labor force, and in neither case does the standard of living of the poor grow as fast as average per capita income.[4]

Some Apparent Policy Alternatives

On the whole, it seems that our assumptions are quite optimistic and the problem of resource gap, employment, and poverty has to be tackled by changing policy assumptions. Before we discuss some real policy options open to Kenya, however, it may be useful to consider some policies which look attractive but are mere palliatives in the short run and may be harmful in the long run.

Increase Commercial Borrowing

Faced with an increasing balance of payments gap, the first reaction may be to increase foreign borrowing. This may indeed be the unavoidable alternative in the short run when the country is threatened by a balance of payments crisis. However, external borrowing on hard terms is no solution to the basic problem of external disequilibrium, and if resorted to year after year, would soon exhaust its potential and create a creditworthiness problem for the future.

In order to get a quantitative feel of the problem, we have analyzed a hypothetical situation in which the gap is closed by suppliers' credits, which are on relatively hard terms: 9 percent interest and amortization over six years. The amount borrowed is assumed to be $50 million in 1973, increasing by $10 million every year, to $180 million in 1985. Thus, the debt service ratio (defined as the ratio of debt servicing payments to export earnings) would rise to 16 percent by 1979, or more than double its present level. It is doubtful whether this increase in the external debt burden would be acceptable to the Kenya authorities.

It is, of course, difficult to define a precise point at which increasing external debt creates a creditworthiness problem. However, in this case, there are other ways of looking at the problem which suggest its seriousness. On the terms under discussion, the

---

3. See Annex Four for details.

4. In this connection, it is important to note the consequences of different ways of reducing productivity in the formal sector, which, if brought about by "labor wasting" techniques, does not reduce the capital resource requirements for growth. As discussed below, an improvement in growth prospect (through reduced external and internal balance) could be brought about together with better employment prospects if changes in labor productivity are achieved by an active factor pricing policy. See Appendix Five.

extra cost of debt servicing catches up with the new inflows of suppliers credit by 1981, so that the extra net transfer is negative after that point (see Table 22). Another way of looking at this problem may be to compare the current account resource balance, plus debt servicing payments, with the imports of investment goods. It seems reasonable to assume that except for some temporary short term loans, regular foreign capital inflows are by and large used to finance imports of *investment* goods. Thus, the import of investment goods imposes an upper limit on the gross receipts of foreign capital. When borrowing requirements exceed this limit, it could be regarded as a danger signal. Thus, whatever temporary respite it affords, increased foreign borrowing on hard terms cannot solve the kind of external disequilibrium which may be starting to appear in Kenya.

Impose Import Controls

Another apparently attractive palliative is to impose controls to reduce the demand for imports. However, while this may sometimes prove necessary in the short run, it should not be regarded as the solution of the problem. In our model, we work out the scenario under the assumption that import controls are used to reduce imports from the ex ante level by $50 million in 1973 (at 1970 prices) and then increasing by $10 million every year up to 1985. The results of this exercise are given in Table 23. Before examining the table, it is useful to analyze how import controls work in our model. To begin with, import controls reduce the external resource gap by reducing imports. However, this also reduces the total availability of resources, and thus accentuates the internal resource gap. This leads to higher prices and thus increases ex ante import demand again. The extent to which prices rise depends, of course, on the associated monetary and fiscal policies. If foreign borrowing is curtailed, and investment is financed through credit creation (rather than tax increases), the inflationary pressure is even higher. However, even if we ignore the problem of domestic inflation, it is worth noting that part of the effect of import controls is nullified through the rise in internal prices, leading to a further increase in import demand.[5]

It seems from Table 23 that, even with a high level of import controls, the problem of the resource gap is not resolved. In fact, in this situation, the restriction imposed upon foreign trade and domestic inflation (open or suppressed) can follow each other in an unhealthy sequence. This is obviously an undesirable situation, but this phenomenon is not altogether unknown in the developing countries. While Kenya has so far avoided serious problems in either internal or external balance, the unfortunate experience of other countries does point to the possible dangers which lie ahead.

Lower Growth Rates of GDP

If the resource gap cannot thus be reduced by foreign borrowing or import controls, is it desirable to reduce the growth targets? To examine the consequences of such an alternative, we calculated the effects of reducing all sectoral growth rates by 3 percentage points. The results are also presented in Table 23, where they can be compared with the

---

5. In order to measure this "slippage" effect, we define an import control slippage coefficient (SC) as:

$$SC = (1 - \frac{\Delta X}{\Delta X_x})$$

where: ΔX = change in imports
ΔX_x = change in import controls

As we notice from Table 23, about 16 percent of the effects of import controls are nullified by an increase in the internal imbalance.

previous alternative. One result is that the GDP growth rate is reduced to about 5 percent. This is still a reasonable growth rate, by comparison with many developing countries, and also reduces the resource gap to about £66 million by the end of the Plan period. However, for a country with Kenya's potential and past performance, this is not an acceptable alternative. In particular, it means that the rate of growth of employment is slowed down, and it has an even more serious effect on the poverty index. Whereas in the basic scenario, the poor were getting *relatively* poorer, in this alternative even their *absolute* level of living declines by about 1.5 percent per year.

Lower Growth Rate of Labor Productivity

It may seem that if lower growth rates of GDP are combined with labor-using policies (leading to lower productivity growth), the problem of external imbalance could be tackled without serious consequences for employment. In Table 23, we examine the effects of this for the alternative, and have taken what is probably an extreme assumption —that average labor productivity remains constant at its present level. We notice that with slower overall growth, in spite of labor absorbing techniques, the prospects of employment and poverty are not materially improved (the income of the poor *declines* by 1 percent a year). In fact, it is reasonable to assume that with labor-hoarding techniques, the propensity to save of the household sector would decline. If we assume a saving-income ratio of 7 percent (the level in 1971) the present policy package may give rise to internal imbalance reflected in higher prices. Moreover, if labor-intensive policies mean inefficient techniques (i.e., where more labor is used without any less capital), they do not tackle the problem.

It seems, therefore, that it is desirable to think of policy alternatives which will increase labor requirements by reducing capital, and especially foreign capital requirements, so that a high GDP growth rate can be combined with steadily improving employment prospects and increases in the poverty index.

Some Real Policy Alternatives

The results discussed in the preceding section show the dilemmas and trade-offs involved in development policy. The resource gap can be reduced by foreign borrowing in the short term, but that increases the debt servicing burden and thus reduces prospects for continued growth in the future: a trade-off between present and future growth. Import controls can reduce the external imbalance but only at the cost of internal imbalance. A slower growth rate reduces the internal and external imbalance, but complicates the employment and poverty problem. Labor-absorbing techniques could alleviate the unemployment problem, but they would merely accentuate the internal imbalance and poverty problem. We therefore consider whether these dilemmas could be avoided if factor prices were used as positive instruments of development policy and the pattern of growth changed. Such a combination, we feel, could help in reducing the resource gap while also helping employment and poverty.

Change in Factor Prices

To test the possible consequences of a more flexible exchange rate policy, we have assumed a 20 percent devaluation. In our model this increases exports, reduces imports, and, by changing factor prices, reduces the amount of investment required for growth. The detailed results following from this change are presented in Table 24. We notice that an increase in the price of foreign exchange of this magnitude would reduce the resource gap over the Plan period very considerably. Moreover, it will provide extra wage employment to 28,000 persons by 1985 and also slightly improve the poverty index. On the negative side, however, it increases the internal imbalance, and thus prices, by reducing the resources available.

A second policy alternative is to vary the *rate of interest*. More specifically, we consider the effects of increasing typical lending rates by about one-third, or from 9 to 12 percent. The effects of such a policy on the economic situation are also shown in Table 24. Unlike a change in the exchange rate, this does not influence the external imbalance directly, but only through a reduced demand for imported capital goods, owing to changes in factor proportions. As a result, the effects of higher interest rates on the resource gap, while significant, are far less than those of devaluation. However, its effects on employment are more powerful: wage employment in 1985 is increased by 60,000 persons, and the income of the poor in agriculture rises by slightly more than 1 percent.

A third policy affecting factor prices could be to abolish the present accelerated *depreciation allowances*. As discussed before, this would be the equivalent of an 8 percent increase in the cost of capital, and the effects of this measure are therefore similar to those of a change in interest rate (see Table 24). For the same growth rate, it reduces investment and import of capital goods, relaxes pressure on the balance of payments, and slightly reduces the resource gap. Wage employment in 1985 is increased by 32,000 persons, and the income of the poor in agriculture by 1 percent.

A fourth possibility is to *combine* the above three instruments as we have done in the final column of Table 24 (where the exchange rate is increased by only 10 percent). The resource gap in 1978 is reduced by about one-third and by 1985, wage employment is expanded by 120,000 persons, and the average income of poor in agriculture increases by about 2 percent. The internal imbalance is accentuated slightly, giving rise to an additional 2 percent increase in consumer prices by the end of the Plan period. However, it is important to note that while these policies would relax Kenya's resource constraint and help employment and poverty, they do not solve these problems completely. Even under the combined package, the resource gap over the Plan period is sizable and wage employment by 1985 absorbs only 23 percent of the increase in labor force. Moreover, the improvement in the standard of living of the "working poor" in agriculture is still painfully slow. Clearly, there is need for additional policy changes.

Change in Pattern of Growth

The next important set of policy changes that we consider, therefore, are those relating to changes in the pattern of growth. More specifically, we are concerned with the implications of an increase in the growth rate of the monetary agriculture sector as well as the nonmonetary sector, associated with a decrease in growth rate of the principal infrastructure sectors, namely, building and construction, transport, storage and communication, and electricity and water.

To begin with, we consider the separate effects of changes in growth rates in each of the sectors mentioned above. The results are given in the various columns of Table 25 where it can be seen that dollar for dollar, the benefits of extra growth taking place in agriculture are higher, in terms of employment and the poverty index, and the costs lower in terms of internal and external resource imbalance, than an equivalent growth in other sectors.

The next exercise is to consider the effects of changing the pattern of growth as a whole. The results given in the final column of Table 25 are encouraging: although the resource gap arising over the Plan period is still considerable, wage employment in 1985 is increased by 10,000 persons, and the poverty index improves by 11 percent. This increases the standard of living of the "working poor" by 2.6 percent a year, which is close to the growth in per capita income for the country as a whole.

Preferred Strategy

On the basis of these results, it seems that factor price changes and structural changes are complementary policy instruments: changes in factor prices (particularly the exchange rate) are more valuable in reducing external imbalance, while employment and the income of the working poor are influenced more by structural changes. We therefore combine the two packages and the results of this exercise are given in Table 26. Under the combined effect of all these policy changes, the external resource gap in 1978 is reduced to £45 million, and additional wage employment is provided for 135,000 persons by 1985. The income of the poor in 1985 is 13 percent higher than under the basic scenario. The annual rate of increase in their income is now about 2.8 percent a year over the Plan period. This would mean that the average level of the poor would be more than £60 (at 1970 prices) per worker by 1985, or $170.

Summing up, therefore, the combination of policy changes we have assumed in our "preferred" strategy looks very encouraging, except for the remaining resource gap which would not be filled under our assumptions. However, in the opinion of the mission, Kenya would have good prospects of attracting additional external aid (above that assumed in our projections), if she succeeded in achieving this high level of performance. We realize that due to administrative as well as technological time lags involved, it may not be possible to change growth rate in different sectors by 1974 as assumed in the model. Our results are only illustrative of the effects of reformed strategy over a given five-year period.

Chapter 5

Some Development Policy Issues

In this chapter, we comment briefly on the implications of the results of our model for some important issues in development policy, such as the role of foreign capital, the trade-off between employment and growth, the nature of poverty-focused growth, the role of factor prices in development, and the possible trade-off between Kenyanization and growth. Needless to say, each of these issues has many complicated aspects—economic as well as socio-political—and our model is not geared to an intensive analysis of them. As emphasized before, models specifically redesigned for these problems would be necessary, even to discuss the purely economic aspects. However, in spite of these shortcomings, our model does have some implications for the above issues and especially may help to clarify a few misconceptions.

Foreign Capital

In recent years, the role of foreign capital in economic development has come under increasing scrutiny. In particular, it has been argued recently,[1] that foreign capital inflow reduces domestic savings, and thus reduces the growth prospects of a country. The conclusion is generally based on a single equation regression analysis of domestic savings on GDP growth (or GDP level) and foreign capital inflow. Our analysis of the Kenyan economy suggests that, in the context of systems analysis, this approach could be misleading, because both savings and GDP growth rates are jointly determined within the system, with the exogenous variables such as foreign capital inflow and others given. In this context, if foreign capital inflow changes, savings, investment, and income all change, and the single equation regression, which examines the effects of foreign capital inflow on savings, given the income level, is therefore misleading.

For a more satisfactory analysis, one has to see how the system as a whole moves under alternative levels of foreign capital inflow. This is done in a heuristic fashion in our model and the results are contrasted in Table 15 of Annex Four. We note that with a lower level of foreign capital inflow and a given policy package, the level of savings, investment, and income would have been lower, even though the partial effect of foreign capital on saving-income *ratio* were negative.

However, the above analysis does not take the effects of repayment of foreign capital on future growth into account. In order to examine this aspect, we have to compare two macro-economic scenarios over the period during which a loan is disbursed and repaid, to see if the discounted present value of the target variables is higher with an increased flow of foreign capital. However, this requires some redesigning of our model and we have not been able to do this so far, although we hope to analyze this later on.

The above discussion does not suggest that foreign capital inflow is always good. In fact, the results of our model suggest strongly that if foreign borrowing on hard terms is used freely to fill the resource gap, problems of creditworthiness could be created in the future and thus reduce growth. Similarly, if the availability of foreign capital acts as a soft option and diverts attention from rectifying fundamental problems of price distortions and structural distortions, the country could be harmed. However, these kinds of effects have to be discussed country-by-country by considering institutional and political elements, and cannot be estimated by a single equation regression approach.[2]

---

1. For details, see the Appendix to Annex Four.
2. For a more detailed discussion, see the Appendix to Annex Four.

Employment

The results of our model suggest that the formulation of a two-dimensional trade-off relationship between employment and growth is misleading. This relationship may be valid in some idealized "production possibility frontier." However, most developing countries are well within this frontier, and it all depends on the type of policies followed as to whether employment and growth have trade-offs, or are neutral to each other, or could both increase at the same time. As discussed in Chapter 4, if growth is constrained by foreign exchange, and employment-creating techniques are introduced which do not affect the foreign exchange gap, growth is neutral with respect to employment. If, on the other hand, the internal resource gap is the binding constraint, and employment-creating techniques reduce the savings propensity, the effort to increase employment could reduce growth. However, if employment-oriented policies work through factor price changes, which increase the demand for labor and reduce capital and import requirements, it may be possible to increase both employment and growth at the same time. Similarly, if the employment problem is tackled through changing the pattern of growth, to the extent that it reduces the demand for capital and imports, it is again possible to have more of both employment and growth. As Tables 19 and 26 suggest, and according to our analysis, Kenya's case fits into this category where, with correct policies, employment and growth can both be helped.

Poverty

Our conclusions on poverty and growth are rather similar to those on employment and growth. If incomes oriented growth means transferring resources from the urban rich to the urban poor, there may be a conflict between growth and redistribution. However, the majority of the poor in Kenya (as in most other developing countries) live in rural areas and make their living from agriculture. In general, the propensity to save of the agriculturalists—rich and poor—tends to be high and an increased emphasis on increasing the productivity and incomes of the rural poor (particularly the agriculturalists) should not reduce overall saving propensity. Equally important is the point that income generation in agriculture requires less capital and less imports, and thus reduces the foreign exchange gap for the same rate of growth. As Tables 19 and 24 show, it is possible to improve conditions of the poor *and* have a higher growth if structural changes in patterns of growth are achieved. Table 23 strongly suggests that a lower growth rate would undoubtedly hurt the poor. However, a higher growth rate, while necessary for any attack on poverty, is not a *sufficient* condition for helping the poor. The answer lies in restructuring growth. The theme of our "preferred" strategy is therefore not to benefit the poor at the expense of development as a whole, but to attack poverty through restructuring growth.

Factor Prices

The role of prices—both product prices and factor prices—has been very much neglected in postwar planning discussions. However, the experience of many developing countries, as well as socialist economies, is beginning to emphasize the need for a "rehabilitation of the invisible hand" as a useful allocative instrument, though not as a kingpin of economic policy. Our results suggest that, if used as positive instruments of economic policy, factor price changes could relax the constraints on economic growth. Thus, instead of assuming that developing countries are in a straitjacket and that the whole of the resource gap has to be filled by foreign aid, one could also look at internal policy instruments to see how far the gap can be narrowed before asking for more foreign aid. As Table 26 indicates, these instruments may not solve the problem of resource gap or employment; but they are steps in the right direction.

Kenyanization

We have suggested elsewhere that there may be some trade-off between a rigid application of Kenyanization and an uninterrupted rate of growth, particularly in some segments of the private sector. It is, of course, primarily a political choice how much Kenya wishes to depend on foreign skills in the future, even if they can help to ensure a faster rate of development. However, from the viewpoint of economic analysis, it is useful to know how the possible conflict between Kenyanization and growth could be minimized. Our results suggest (see Table 25) that restructuring growth, along the lines discussed, should reduce the need for high middle level manpower and thus help the process of Kenyanization.

Appendix A: A Simplified Algebraic Description of the Model

A simplified algebraic description of the model highlights its structure and the method in which we use it for policy discussion. The details of each of the subsectors are presented in the subsequent appendices.

I. The Equations

Output and Investment

$$g_i = \bar{g}_i$$

$$k_i = \left(\alpha_i + \frac{\beta_i}{g_i}\right)(1 + xp)^{-\alpha_i}$$

$$I_i = g_i \cdot k_i \cdot Y_i$$

where g_i = target growth rate of GDP for sector i
k_i = ICOR for sector i
xp = policy package affecting factor prices
I_i = investment
Y_i = GDP in sector i

Imports, Exports, and Balance of Payments

$$MR = \left[\alpha_1 + \beta_1\left(\sum_i W_i Y_i\right)\right]\left(\frac{p}{p_m f}\right)\lambda_1$$

$$MC = \left[\alpha_2 + \beta_2\left(\sum_i W_i^1 Y_i\right)\right]\left(\frac{p_c}{p_m f}\right)\lambda_2$$

$$MI = \left[\alpha_3 + \beta_3\left(\sum_i W_i^* I_i\right)\right]\left(\frac{p}{p_m f}\right)\lambda_3$$

$$MG = \alpha_4 + \beta_4 G$$

$$MO = Ae^{\lambda t}$$

$$M = MR + MC + MI + MG + MO + MX$$

$$p_x X = (X^o)(f)^\eta$$

$$GAP = p_m m - p_x X - F$$

where MR = import demand of raw materials
MC = import demand of consumer goods
MI = import demand of investment goods
MG = import demand by government
MO = import demand of other goods and nonfactor services
MX = exogenous change in imports reflecting import controls (when MX is $-ve$) or imports to take care of local shortages (when MX is $+ve$). The latter is equivalent to the saving constrained case in the usual two-gap approach.

M = total imports ex post
p_m = import price index
p = domestic price index
p_c = domestic consumer price index
G = GDP in government
t = time
$p_x X$ = exports in current US$
f = exchange rate
X^o = exogenously given exports
F = capital inflows reflecting gross foreign lending minus debt servicing payments, etc.

Credit, Money, Consumption, and Prices

$$MS = DC^o + FA$$
$$E = f(MS)$$
$$p = E/(Y + M - X)$$
$$HC = f(YD)$$
$$YD = f(Y)$$
$$GC = f(G)$$
$$C = Y + M - X - I - GC$$
$$\frac{pc}{p} = \frac{HC}{C}$$

where MS = money supply
DC^o = exogenously determined domestic credit
FA = foreign assets
E = total expenditure in nominal terms
p = price level
HC = ex ante household consumption
YD = disposable personal income
GC = government consumption
C = ex post household consumption
pc = consumer prices

Employment and Poverty

$$\Delta WE_i = WE_{i_{-1}}(g_i - PR_i)(1 + xp)^{1-\alpha_i}$$
$$SE_i = \lambda_i WE_i$$
$$\Delta TE_i = TE_{i_{-1}}(g_i - PR'_i)(1 + xp)^{1-\alpha_i}$$
$$LF = L_0(1 + 0.036)^t$$

$$EMAG = LF - \Sigma TE_i$$

$$pov = \frac{YA}{EMAG}$$

WE_i = wage employment in sector i

SE_i = skilled manpower required in sector i

TE_i = total employment (including informal) in sector i (except agriculture)

PR, PR' = rate of growth of labor productivity in formal sector and total economy, respectively

LF = labor force

$EMAG$ = residual employment in agriculture

YA = GDP in agriculture

pov = per worker value-added in agriculture taken as an index of poverty

II. The Process of Adjustment of Internal and External Imbalances

In the general equilibrium system, both these imbalances are rectified by price changes—the external through exchange rate and the internal through domestic price. In the two-gap model, neither of these balances is rectified, but foreign resources are brought in to fill the larger of the two gaps, thus presumably creating excess supply for the market with the smaller gap. In our system, the situation is in between the above two extremes. The internal imbalance is cured by price rises—although the price rise may prove to be too high in the light of social objectives. If so, foreign resources are brought in (positive MX) to relieve the pressure. However, the extent to which domestic inflation and MX are acceptable is a policy decision, explicitly considered (in contrast to the general equilibrium approach, where MX is zero, or the two-gap approach, where acceptable price rise is zero). If there is an external imbalance, it could be cured by an inflow of foreign capital, import controls, a change in the exchange rate, or other policies, each of which has different implications for the future. The choice is made outside the model, rather than hidden inside, as in the general equilibrium approach, where the exchange rate rises or falls to bring about equilibrium, or in the two-gap model where foreign capital inflow increases to fill the gap.

By bringing the instruments out into the open, our procedure helps in discussions of various policy alternatives and their consequences. This is elaborated in the following section.

III. The Method of Operation of the Model

In this sytem the instruments are:

g_i, xp, f, MX, DC

The arguments in the objective function are:

GAP, pc, p, pov, TE_i

Given a set of values of the instruments, the model works out the values of gap, inflationary potential, and poverty levels for different years.

If gap is big, there are several policy options with associated consequences:

A. *Increase Foreign Borrowing*

This solves the gap in the present but causes creditworthiness problems for the future.

B. *Impose Import Controls* (thus reduce MX)

This, however, increases inflationary pressure and also increases MC so that the net effect on the gap is less than the reduction of MX.

C. *Change Factor Prices Through xp and f*

This reduces gap and improves employment prospects but is associated with higher prices.

D. *Reduce Growth Rates*

This reduces gap, but also reduces employment prospects and worsens the poverty situation.

E. *Change the Structure of Growth Rates*

This also can reduce gap depending on the type of structural change. Employment and poverty implications could also be good depending on the pattern of change.

Similarly, if the rate of increase in employment and in the income of the poor is slow, various policy options could be examined, along the lines just discussed. It is important to note that in our scheme, the various problems and policy alternatives are discussed and the desired policy package is chosen in a judgmental fashion, rather than formal optimization through mathematical programming.

However, this procedure ignores the fact that part of gross investment is for replacement purposes and therefore does not produce any increased output. If this fact is taken into account, it becomes clear, as Chenery and Eckstein point out, why ICORs are almost always lower at high rates of growth.

Appendix B: An Analysis of ICORs in Kenya

In spite of the numerous conceptual and statistical problems,[1] the use of incremental capital output ratios (ICORs) remains popular in models depicting growth in developing countries. Among the reasons for ICOR popularity are: limited data requirement (ICORs do not require figures on capital or its structure, for example); simple interpretation; and ease of use in discussions of resource requirements for growth. In our model, we have used the ICORs but tried to refine them so as to take care of their more obvious weaknesses. More specifically, while using ICORs we have tried to assess the impact of depreciation allowances, sectoral composition, and factor prices on ICORs.

It is usual to compute ICORs by comparing *changes* in GDP with lagged gross investment figures. Following Chenery's and Eckstein's procedure, we can write the equation for ICOR as:

$$(1) \quad k = k^1 + \frac{Z}{r}$$

where k = gross ICOR

k^1 = net ICOR showing the effect of new investment on output

Z = share of current income devoted to replacement[3]

r = rate of growth of GDP.

This form of equation was also adopted in the model for Kenya presented in an earlier Bank economic report.[4]

As Chenery and Eckstein found, an unconstrained regression of equation (i), often leads to implausible results for the parameters (e.g., negative values of k^1). The procedure adopted by Chenery and Eckstein was to constrain k^1 to 2.0 and obtain estimate of Z from regression. However, since we have some figures on depreciation allowances, we decided to use these estimates of Z. It seems to us that in most of the cases, Z/r would account for a smaller part of k than does k^1 and it is desirable to predetermine the smaller component. The values of Z for different sectors were computed from the *Input/Output Table for Kenya, 1967* and these estimates are presented in Table 5.

Apart from the allowance for depreciation, we have a problem with changes in net ICORs over time. It is suggested that, in Kenya, productivity of investment has been declining over the years, and our formulation of the problem should be able to test this hypothesis. In order to test this we obtained k^1 as $k - (Z/r)$ and then ran regressions of k^1 on time.

As noted by Chenery and Eckstein, annual incremental capital-output ratios cannot always be used as the units of observation in a time series. Year-to-year movements reflect the effects of changes in degree of utilization of capital as well as in its amount. In order to tackle this problem, Chenery and Eckstein "identified... cycles and obtained single incremental ratios for each one by aggregating the total investment and change of GNP over the period." In the absence of any identified cycles, we used three-year

---

1. See, for example, Paul Streeten, *The Frontiers of Development Studies,* Chapter 6 (New York: John Wiley and Sons, 1972).

2. H. B. Chenery and Peter Eckstein, "Development Alternatives for Latin America," *The Journal of Political Economy,* July/August 1970.

3. In the Chenery-Eckstein formulation this also includes investment on social overhead investment.

4. *Economic Development Prospects in Kenya,* World Bank Report No. AE-6a, October 22, 1969 (unpublished).

moving averages as a smoothing device for obtaining smoothed values of GDP and investment. The equations thus obtained for different sectors are given in Table 6. The actual and estimated values of ICORs are presented in Table 2. The interpretation of the trends in ICORs and the analysis of their possible reasons are given in Chapter 3.

The analysis of sectoral ICORs is useful for studying the trends in ICORs and for analyzing the impact of patterns of growth on overall ICOR. However, in using the sectoral ICORs for sensitivity analysis with respect to sectoral growth rates, a problem is created by the interdependence of different sectors. Output in one particular sector uses the services of other sectors, so that an increase in output in one sector will also require an increase in output of other sectors. For example, an increase in value-added in the agricultural sector requires increases in output and investment in transport, construction, government services, and so on. In order to take this factor into account, we had to utilize the input-output table. Let b_{ij} be the value-added required in sector i for a unit of final value-added to sector i. Then G_i percent of extra growth in sector j will also require G_j percent rate of growth in i sector where G_i is given by

$$G_i = G_j b_{ij} \frac{Y_j}{Y_i} \frac{(i = 1, \ldots, n)}{(i \neq j)}$$

For computation of b_{ij} we used the total input coefficient matrix given in *Input/Output Table for 1967,* and adjusted these coefficients for the ratio of value-added to output in each sector.

In Part I we have emphasized the effects of an accelerated rate of growth of agricultural output, and a decrease in the rate of building construction and of the transport communications sector. Some illustrative calculations of GDP and investment required in each sector to raise GDP by one percentage point are given in Table 4.

ICORs are generally treated as purely technological parameters. Actually, they reflect the effects of various economic decisions relating to degree of utilization, factor proportions, rate of technical progress, and efficiency of allocation. With the limited amount of data available, we could not estimate the separate effects of each factor. However, on the basis of certain assumptions about elasticity of substitution, we do obtain a link between ICORs and factors influencing relative factor prices, such as wage rate, exchange rate, interest rate, and investment allowances. Since this link involves changes in employment generation also, it is discussed later in Appendix E.

The above analysis relates to fixed investment only. The rate of inventory accumulation is assumed to be 28.8 percent of the increase in monetary GDP.[5] In practice, there have been two inventory cycles in Kenya (the first one peaking around 1967, and the second around 1971). However, for long-run forecasting we did not try to analyze them. The total investment required is given by the sum of fixed investment and inventory investment.

---

5. Based on estimates of the Ministry of Finance and Planning.

Appendix C: An Analysis of Import Requirements Incorporating the Effects of GDP Composition

In most developing countries, growth is probably constrained by the availability of foreign exchange; analysis of import requirements thus becomes a critical element in assessing growth prospects. However, it is difficult to define a simple parameter like ICOR for measuring import intensity of growth. The elasticity of imports with respect to GDP is sometimes used as such a simple parameter. However, it fails to capture the important point that, in developing countries, investment may have a higher import content than noninvestment items in GDP, and an acceleration of growth through an increased investment-income ratio may increase the elasticity of imports with respect to income. It is therefore necessary to analyze import data in a more disaggregated fashion. Fortunately, some disaggregated data on various types of imports are available in Kenya, and we estimated separate import equations for consumer goods, raw materials, investment goods, government imports, and imports of nonfactor services.

In our macro model, we are particularly interested in working out the effects of changes in sectoral patterns of growth. Therefore, we tried to incorporate the differential import requirements for imported capital goods, raw materials, and so on for growth in different sectors. The main source of information for imported raw material requirements was the *Input/Output Table for Kenya, 1967*. However, instead of using input/output (I/O) information as representative of the entire sample period, we tried to use both I/O information and the aggregate time series information.

In a straightforward use of the I/O table, the imports would be estimated by equations such as

(1) $M = \Sigma M_i Y_i$

where M = imports

M_i = import of content of sector i

Y_i = output of sector i

On the other hand, purely aggregated analysis uses equations such as:

(2) $M_t = \alpha + \beta Y + \delta p_m$

where Y = aggregate output

p_m = price variable

It is obvious, however, that equation (1) misses out on the effects of overall factors, such as price changes or technological changes over time, and equation (2) misses out on the effects of sectoral changes.

The equations we used are of the following type:

(3) $M_t = \alpha' + \beta' (\Sigma_i M_i Y_i)_t + \delta' p_{m_t}$

The time-series for $\Sigma_i M_i Y_i$ was constructed by using I/O values of M_i and GDP time-series relating to sectoral Y_is. Instead of assuming that there is no change over time in I/O coefficients, we allow the regression to capture any overall changes in these coefficients (though not in relative changes), as well as the influence of factors such as prices. Depending on data and regression results, equations (1) and (2) could be "particular cases" of equation (3). If $\beta' = 1$ and $\alpha' = \delta' = 0$, we have the I/O case; if $M_i = MO$ for all i's, we have the aggregate time-series case.

Apart from being more general, equation (3) also enables us to separate the effects of changes in sectoral composition from that of change in overall GDP. Thus, if the equation (3) shows x percent increase in imports due to the variable $\Sigma M_i Y_i$, the contribution of sectoral change in GDP is

$$k = x\left(1 - \frac{Y}{z}\right)$$

where y is the percentage change in aggregate GDP and z is the percentage change in $\Sigma_i M_i Y_i$.

In order to use the above procedure, we had to compute, from various sources, some method of estimating the impact of different sectors on the various categories of imports. In the case of import of raw materials, we obtained the ratio of imported raw materials to GDP in each sector from the 1967 I/O table. For capital goods, there was no breakdown by sector of imported and nonimported capital goods. However, the official series of *Economic Surveys* give the figures of investment by type (construction, transport equipment machinery, breeding stock, etc.) for each sector separately. We assumed that transport equipment and machinery is mostly imported and used the ratio of these items to total investment as the indicator of import content of investment by different sectors. For imports of consumer goods, the problem of data was even more serious. However, the income tax department publishes figures of income assessed by sectors. We assumed that those whose income is not assessed for income tax purposes are not significant users of directly imported consumer goods, and we therefore used the ratio of income assessed for tax purposes to GDP in each sector to estimate consumer imports. These ratios are given in Table 10.

In estimating import requirements, we hoped to capture the effects of prices of imported goods (and thus the exchange rate) on imports of different categories. Unfortunately, in our regression equation, we failed to capture any such effect. The main problem was that prices—both imported goods and domestic—have been stable for the major part of the sample period. The estimated equations are given below.

Import Functions

(1) Import of Consumer Goods
$$MC = 31.34 + 0.155 \Sigma W_i Y_i$$
$$(2.17) \quad (3.4)$$

$\bar{R}^2 = 0.66$, D.W. $= 2.0$, SEE $= 6.88$
W_i's are the weights as given in column 2 of Table 10
Y_i = GDP in sector i

(2) Import of Raw Material
$$MR = 13.58 + 0.958 \Sigma W_i^1 Y_i$$
$$(0.66) \quad (9.18)$$

$\bar{R}^2 = 0.93$, D.W. $= 1.50$, SEE $= 10.3$
W_i^1's are the weights as given in column 3 of Table 10

(3) Import of Capital Goods
$$MK = -3.61 + 0.62 \Sigma W_i^* I_i$$
$$(-0.4) \quad (8.29)$$

$\bar{R}^2 = 0.92$, D.W. $= 1.90$, SEE $= 6.25$
W_i^*'s are the weights as given in column 4 of Table 10
I^i = Investment in sector i.

(4) Import of Government
$$MG = 3.79 + 0.07\, GG$$
(0.54) (1.80)

$\bar{R}^2 = 0.35$, D.W. = 1.55, SEE = 3.99

(5) Import of Nonfactor Services
$$\log MO = 4.23 + 0.023t$$
(101.0) (2.7)

$\bar{R}^2 = 0.55$, D.W. = 1.76, SEE = 0.05

The estimated values of $\Sigma M_i Y_i$ for different categories, as well as the actual and regression estimates of different categories, are presented in Table 9. The level of imports at constant prices in 1970 and 1971 was higher than estimated, even when we ignore the effect of prices, and this indicates a shift in the import equation. Whether this is temporary or lasting has to be decided on the basis of one's judgment.

In spite of our inability to capture price effects from the data due to random influences, it seems inadvisable to ignore the price effects completely in making projections. We have therefore introduced some purely subjective (probably conservative) estimates of elasticities of imports with respect to relative prices defined as (import price × exchange rate index)/domestic GDP deflator. These estimates are 0.5 for consumer goods and 0.25 for other categories.

Appendix D: Analysis of Savings of Households, Business, and the Government Sector

In the usual growth models for developing countries estimates of savings are based on an overall marginal propensity to save with respect to income. We disagree with this approach. In most countries—developed as well as developing—a significant part of gross savings comes from depreciation allowances, and these cannot be assumed to be simple functions of income but are dependent on durability, age structure of capital, and tax laws. This part of savings should therefore be estimated separately. Similarly, for the rest of the economy, government saving behavior cannot be analyzed in terms of the usual consumption function theories—relative income hypothesis, permanent income hypothesis or life cycle hypothesis. Government's recurrent expenditure is influenced by its past capital expenditure in ways that cannot be measured by household type consumption functions.

Fortunately, we found that the Ministry of Finance and Planning in Kenya has been following the disaggregated approach and has already developed equations for savings of households, government, and business. For most of these equations published data do not exist, and we therefore decided to use the equations developed by the Ministry as a starting point. These equations do not incorporate any effects of sectoral composition on savings behavior and this type of effect is important for our analysis. However, we could not get any data for this purpose, and we had to ignore this effect in our analysis.

Aggregate savings are divided into four parts: household savings, undistributed profits of businesses, depreciation allowances, and government savings:

(1) $SAV = HS + SD + UP + GS$

where SAV = total savings

HS = household savings

SD = depreciation allowances

UP = undistributed profits

GS = government savings

Household Sector—disposable income of the household sector is defined as follows:

(2) $YS = N + WB + WG + WH + FH - TPE - VHR + VRH + VGH$

where YD = disposable personal income

N = nonmonetary value-added

WB = wages paid by business

WG = wages by government

WH = wages paid by households

FH = interest, dividends, and other residuals received by households

TPE = personal taxes

VHR = transfer payments by households to rest of the world

VRH = transfer payments by rest of the world to households

VGH = transfer payments by government to households

The equations for each of the above elements are given below:

(3) $WB = 1.42 * (FB + SD)$

(4) $WG = (1 + YGGR)WG_{t-1}$

(5) $WH = 5.71 + 0.005 MGDP$

(6) $FH = 27.27 + 0.18 MGDP + 1.96t$

(7) $TPE = THO + TG$

(8) $THO = 31.25 + 0.086(MGDP - SD)$

(9) $TG = 8.4 + 0.005 MGDP$

(10) $VHR = 24.64 + 1.4t$

(11) $VRH = 20.44 + 0.84t$

(12) $VGH = 24.14$

where FB = other factor incomes paid by businesses
$MGDP$ = monetary GDP
t = time trend
THO = income tax other than companies
TG = graduated income tax
SD = depreciation allowance
$YGGR$ = growth rate in GDP in government sector

Household consumption is expressed as a fixed proportion of disposable income in the light of the secular constancy of consumption-income ratio in the developed countries, for which data over long historical periods exist.

(13) $HC = 0.90 YD$

Household savings are then a residual:

(14) $HS = YD - HC$

Business Sector—The undistributed profits of the business sector are determined by the following identity:

(15) $UP = MGDP - WB - WG - WH - FB - SD - TD - PG - YG$

where UP = undistributed profits
$MGDP$ = monetary GDP
WB = wages paid by business
WG = wages paid by government
WH = wages paid by households
FB = other factor incomes paid by business
SD = depreciation allowances
TD = direct taxes on businesses
PG = profits of public corporations and sales of government services
YG = imputed government income

Direct taxes on businesses are further broken down into three categories:

(16) $TD = TBY + TCD + TQD$

where *TBY* = income tax on companies

TCD = other direct taxes of Central Government

TQD = other direct taxes of municipal and county councils

Profits of public corporations and sales of services are divided into two parts.

(17) $PG = SF + PGO$

where *SF* = school fees

PGO = other incomes of public corporations.

The equations for *WB*, *WG* and *WH* are given in the household sector as equations (3)–(5). Other equations are as follows:

(18) $FB = 31.61 + 0.19MGDP$

(19) $TBY = 0.0583 YE$

(20) $TCD = 0.98 + 0.56t$

(21) $TQD = 1.18 + 0.008MGDP$

(22) $SF = 7.6SEN$

(23) $PGO = 0.84 + 0.049MGDP$

(24) $YG = 0.859GDPG$

where *YE* = net domestic product of enterprises defined as (monetary GDP) minus (value-added by government) minus (depreciation allowances).

SEN = school enrollment

GDPG = GDP in general government

Figures for depreciation allowances do not exist in the published national accounts of Kenya. Estimates prepared by the Ministry of Finance and Planning are based on tax rates applied to published investment figures (with some heroic assumptions of depreciation before 1964). For forecasting the depreciation element due to investment before 1972, $C(t)$ is estimated exogenously and for other subsequent years an equation is postulated on the basis of tax laws and past investment levels (*I*). The equation is:

(25) $SD(t) = C(t) + 0.038I_t$

$+ 0.077(I_{t-1} + I_{t-2} + I_{t-3})$

$+ 0.061I_{t-4}$

$+ 0.042I_{t-5}$

$+ 0.039I_{t-6}$

Government Sector—Government savings (*GS*) are given by the following identity:

(26) $GS = TD + TH + PG + TI + VRG - FG - U - VGR - VGH - GC$

where *TD* = direct taxes on business

TH = taxes on households

PG = profits of public corporations and sales of government services

TI = indirect taxes on business

VRG = transfer receipts, rest of world payments to government

FG = government interest payments
U = business subsidies
VGR = transfer payments, government to rest of the world
VGH = transfer payments, government to households
GC = government consumption

Indirect taxes (TI) are broken down in seven categories:

(27) $TI = TS + TM + TE + TP + TOI + TQF + TAO$

where TS = sales tax
TM = import taxes
TE = excise taxes
TP = petrol and diesel taxes
TOI = other indirect taxes and fees
TQF = licenses, cesses, fees, property income and interest of municipal and county councils
TAO = other revenues (retentions by EAC common services)

The equations for each of these are given below.

(28) $TS = 38$ for 1973
$= 48$ for 1974
$= 1.125 TS(t-1)$ for 1975 on

(29) $TM = 33.49 + 0.129(M - MR)$

(30) $TE = -8.9 + 0.049 MGDP$

(31) $TP = -2.8 + 0.008 MGDP$

(32) $TOI = -0.48 = 0.011 MGDP$

(33) $TQF = 0.009 MGDP$

(34) $TAO = 1.68 + 0.168t$

(35) $VGR = 10.61 - 1.288t$

(36) $FG = 19.6 + 1.96t$

(37) $VRG = 33.74$

(38) $GC = -0.98 + 1.19 GDPG$

Appendix E: Factor Prices, Employment, and Growth

In most growth models for developing countries, the factor proportions are taken as technological parameters, and it is implicitly assumed that factor prices are not important for determining employment and growth prospects. What is often not realized is that, apart from affecting choice of techniques at a micro level, factor prices are also important in influencing overall capital-labor ratio through change in product mix, change in degree of utilization, and change in type of labor and capital.[1] As Gordon C. Winston[2] has demonstrated:

> "In order for this to be true that there be no response in factor use to changes in factor prices—it is clearly necessary that *simultaneously*—
>
> 1. *Factor use is not affected by product mix*, either because there is only one product in the economy or because the consumption of output is fixed and immutable so its use of factors is not variable by variations in product mix—this is effectively one composite product, *and*
> 2. *Factor use is not affected by choice of techniques*, because there is only a single kind of ex post plant, that can produce for each of the industries that make up the sector or economy, *and*
> 3. *Utilization is not affected by factor prices*, because ex post all capital is utilized at its engineering maximum though that maximum is much greater than optimum—desired levels of utilization suggested by all empirical studies of capital utilization, *and*
> 4. *The crew required to operate each piece of capital is everywhere inflexibly set* so increasing the number of workers will never increase the rate of production and decreasing the number will always idle capital."

These conditions are clearly too stringent to be satisfied even by developing countries.

On an empirical level, the statistical studies in developed as well as developing countries give significantly positive values of the elasticities of substitution in factor proportions with respect to factor prices. Henry Bruton[3] after an extensive survey of the statistical results on elasticities of substitution states, "The most general conclusion is the most important: Factor substitutability is alive and well in developing countries. Policies and models that assume otherwise mislead." More specifically, his review of the results of statistical studies in the United States, Philippines, Argentina, Chile, El Salvador, Korea, Paraguay, Peru, Portugal, Spain, and Mexico found that the elasticity varies between 0.5 and 1.6 and is generally significantly different from zero. Similarly, after examining United States data on an industry level, P. Zarembka[4] concludes "... there is no significant evidence that the elasticity of substitution at the two-digit level departs from unity using either behavioral equation or direct estimation ... the estimates presented here lie on both sides of unity."

In Kenya, data on output, labor, and capital are not available by industry for fitting an explicit production function. However, empirical analysis by the mission of the figures

---

1. The variation in type of labor and capital may be due to differences in degrees of "human capital" in labor and in degrees of "foreign exchange" in different types of capital.

2. Gordon C. Winston, *On the Inevitability of Factor Substitution*, Research Memorandum No. 46 (Williamstown, Mass.: Center for Development Economics, Williams College, April 1972), mimeo.

3. Henry J. Bruton, *The Elasticity of Substitution in Developing Countries*, Research Memorandum No. 45 (Williamstown, Mass.: Center for Development Economics, Williams College, April 1972), mimeo.

4. Paul Zarembka, "On the Empirical Relevance of the CES Production Function," *The Review of Economics and Statistics*, 1970.

of labor productivity and wage earnings gives estimates of elasticity of substitution which are not significantly different from unity. As shown in Table 18, the elasticity of substitution (as measured by the elasticity of value-added per employer to wages) was 0.988 (± 0.19) for commerce, and 0.905 (± 0.14) for other services. For the private modern sector as a whole, the elasticity was 1.19 (± 0.12).

Thus, in the light of empirical evidence on production function in developed countries as well as in developing countries, it seems reasonable to assume unitary elasticity of substitution i factor proportions with respect to factor prices. We also use the share of wages in gross output as an approximation to the elasticity of output with respect to labor (α). Lastly, we assume that existing factor proportions are not malleable and these effects apply to *new* capital and labor only. Then if a policy package changes the cost of capital (r) relative to wage (w) by $100X$ percent, new ICORs and incremental employment-output ratios (e) will be:

(1) $ICOR_i = ICOR_i^o * (1 + xp_i)^{-\alpha_i}$

(2) $e_i = e_i^o * (1 + xp_i)^{1-\alpha_i}$

Where: subscript i's indicate sectors

Superscript indicates trend values in the absence of policy changes as discussed earlier.

The calculation of xp_is will be done outside the model and our broad scheme is explained below:

xp is defined as

(3) $xp = \dfrac{\dot{r}}{r} - \dfrac{\dot{w}}{w}$

where: $\dfrac{\dot{r}}{r}$ = proportional change in cost of capital

$\dfrac{\dot{w}}{w}$ = proportional change in cost of labor

capital cost (r) is defined as follows:

(4) $r = p_{inv}(1 - t)(\delta + i - p^e)$

where: p_{inv} = price of investment goods

t = present value of tax benefits through accelerated depreciation allowances as a proportion of price of investment goods.

δ = depreciation rate

i = nominal rate of interest

p^e = expected rate of inflation

The influence of exchange rate change will be felt to the extent that imported capital goods enter into the price of investment goods. Assuming no change in prices of domestic investment goods and rate of depreciation, xp can be written as:

(5) $xp = -\dfrac{\dot{w}}{w} + \dfrac{\dot{f}}{f}\lambda_1 + \dfrac{\dot{i}}{i}\dfrac{i}{D} - \dfrac{\dot{p^e}}{p^e} \cdot \dfrac{p^e}{D} - \dfrac{i}{1-t}$

where λ_1 = proportion of imported goods in total investment

$D = \delta + i - p^e$

f = exchange rate

Ideally, it will be desirable to calculate Xs for different sectors, allowing for differences with respect to interest rates λ_1s, depreciation rates, tax allowances, etc. However, in the present exercise, we have made an aggregative analysis, applying the same Xs to all the sectors.

In the Kenyan case, we find that the imported investment goods are about 30 percent of total investment (i.e., $\lambda_1 = 0.3$). Interest rates, of course, vary for different customers, but as an approximation 9 percent seems reasonable (i.e., $i = 0.09$). For depreciation rate, we assume an average annual rate of depreciation of 15 percent (i.e., $\delta = 0.15$). The increase in prices has been slow historically but is gathering momentum now. It seems reasonable to assume that about 4 percent rate of inflation may be expected over the near future. As regards depreciation allowances, a 20 percent extra write-off is allowed for tax purposes and at the present company tax rate, this returns about 8 percent of capital value as a tax benefit (i.e., $t = 0.08$).

With the help of the above formulae, we try to get in our model some quantitative feel of the effects of changes in factor prices. The a's in equations (1) and (2) were obtained from the I/O table. The values used were: 0.3 for agriculture, 0.5 for mining, 0.4 for manufacturing and repairs, 0.8 for building and construction, 0.3 for electricity and water, 0.6 for transport and communication, 0.4 for trade, 0.4 for banking and 0.7 for other services. The effects of changes in exchange rates, interest rates, and investment allowances are considered separately and jointly by computing their impact on X as defined in equation (5). For example, if the price of foreign exchange is increased by 20 percent, it increases cost of capital by 6 percent [$(f/f) \lambda_1 = 0.20 \times 0.3 = 0.06$]. Similarly, if the interest rate is increased by 33 percent, it increases cost of capital by 15 percent. The abolition of investment allowances increases the effective capital cost by 8 percent. If these three measures are adopted simultaneously, the capital cost increases by about 34 percent due to the interdependence of these effects.

The effects of each of these policies on the foreign exchange gap and on employment in our model are shown in Table 24. As emphasized before, these projections are only indicative of the orders of magnitude, and do not imply that the problems of unemployment on the foreign exchange gap could be solved by these instruments alone. All that we argue is that some of these distortions are accentuating these problems and it is desirable to remove them while also thinking of more direct policy measures such as those discussed elsewhere in this report.

Appendix F: Money, Prices, and the Equalization of the Two Gaps

We regard the absence of equations for prices an important weakness of the usual gap models. We also feel that it is only by introducing price equations that we can hope to explain how the ex post equalization of the two gaps is brought about. We do not pretend to have tackled these problems fully. However, as a tentative beginning we do introduce some simple equations for absolute price levels in our model, and also use relative prices to equate ex ante and ex post consumption.

The equation for the general price level is given by total expenditure in current prices divided by total available resources at constant prices.

(1) $\quad p = \dfrac{E}{Y + M - X}$

where p = general price level

E = total money expenditure at current prices

Y = GDP at constant prices

M = imports at constant prices

X = exports at constant prices

The total expenditure is a function of current and lagged money supply (the weighted being estimated by Almon distributed lag technique).

(2) $\quad \log E = 3.453 + 0.434 \log M + 0.217 \log M_{-1}$
$\qquad\quad\ \ (21.4) \quad\ \ (23.3) \qquad\quad\ (23.3)$
$\quad\ \ \bar{R}^2 = 0.99;\ DW = 2.56;\ SEE = 0.023$

Money supply is partly endogenous and partly exogenous. The endogenous element refers to changes in foreign reserves and the exogenous element to changes in domestic credit. Ideally, we should link changes in domestic credit to saving-investment deficits in different sectors, particularly to the deficit in the government sector. However, it has not been possible to incorporate this refinement. Our equations are:

(3) $\quad MS = FA + DC$

(4) $\quad FA = FA_{-1} + CR_{-1}$

where MS = money supply

FA = foreign reserves

DC = domestic credit

CR = change in reserves

Changes in reserves are a function of changes in imports and any exogenous movements specified from outside the model.

As regards the process of equalizing ex ante and ex post savings, we assume that it is the change in household consumption, in real terms, that brings about the equalization, and this in turn is brought about by changes in prices of consumer goods relative to the general price level.[1] The ex post consumption of households is given by:

(5) $\quad HCX = Y + M - X - I - GC$

---

1. It should be reemphasized that we do not imply that this is what will happen *in reality*. All that we imply is that, under the assumptions of the model, with output, investment exports and imports, and government consumption given, household consumption has to give way to close the domestic goods gap, and the relative price change required for closing the gap is one indicator of the severity of the cut in domestic consumption.

where *HCX* = ex post consumption of households
Y = GDP
M = imports
X = exports
I = total investment
GC = government consumption

The relative prices of household consumer goods are then

(6) $\quad p_c = \dfrac{HC * p}{HCX}$

where *HC* = ex ante household consumption

p_c = price level of household consumer goods

The ex post saving of the household sector is:

(7) $\quad HS_{xp} = HS - (HCX - HC)$

where *HS* = ex ante saving of households

HS_{xp} = ex post saving of households

The rise in consumer price index defined above will indicate the inflationary pressure due to inadequate ex ante saving.

Appendix G: Miscellaneous Equations in the Model

In this appendix we present some miscellaneous equations required in the model for computing disbursements from old loans, debt servicing burden of old and new loans, foreign exchange reserve requirements, employment in modern sector, skilled manpower requirements, and total employment prospects.

Treatment of Foreign Capital and its Debt Servicing Implications

The model treats separately the various sources of foreign capital, such as international institutions, bilateral governments, suppliers' credit, banking institutions and other financial institutions, and public and private bond issues. The model starts with the estimates of disbursements from each of these agencies arising from loans already committed but not completely disbursed. The source of data is the Debtor Reporting System (DRS) of the World Bank Group. From the same source, we also take figures of amortization and interest payments on old loans.

The next stage is to make assumptions about the levels of commitments from each of these sources, their disbursement pattern and terms of lending with regard to interest rate, grace period, and maturity. The computer then works out the disbursement pattern and debt servicing implications of these new commitments. Also specified exogenously are the expected inflows of private foreign investment and the expected outflow of factor payments. All these figures are in current US dollars in order to reflect the fact that loan obligations are in current prices. The effect of possible exchange rate realignment has not, however, been taken into account.

The additional resources required to maintain foreign exchange reserves are assumed to be equal to one-third of change in imports, in order to maintain resources at the equivalent of four months' imports. This is an assumption based on the Government's plan projections.

After deducting the expected resources from resources required for imports, debt servicing, and reserve changes, the model computes the residual gap. The exogenous assumptions and policy instruments have to be changed until this residual gap becomes negligible.

Employment Equations

As discussed in Chapter 3, detailed data are not available to make statistical estimates for employment equations. Our equations are mere computational devices for working out the implications of various assumptions about the rate of growth of labor productivity. The incremental labor output ratios are, however, further modified by factor price changes as discussed in Appendix E. The equations are of the form:

(1) $\Delta EM_i = E_{i_{-1}}(G_i - PR_i)(1 + xp)^{1-\alpha_i}$

where EM_i = employment in sector i

G_i = rate of growth of GDP in sector i

PR_i = rate of growth of productivity in sector i

xp = policy instrument changing relative factor prices as discussed in Appendix Five

α_i = wage share in sector i as discussed in Appendix Five

For estimating total employment a similar procedure is employed, with the difference that the rate of growth of labor productivity is a weighted average of productivity growth in formal and informal sectors. Thus we have,

(2) $PR_i = p_i(w_1 + Qw_2)$

where PR = rate of growth of total labor productivity (including informal sector)

w_1 = ratio of employment in formal sector to total multiplied by the ratio of labor productivity in formal to average labor productivity.

Q = ratio of the rate of growth of labor productivity in the informal sector to that in the formal sector

w_2 = same for informal sector as w_1 is for the formal sector

The weights w_1 and w_2 were obtained from data on employment and earnings presented by M. FG. Scott.[1] In our projections, we have used $Q = 1$ so that $PR_i = p_i$.

The equation for total employment does not apply to agriculture, which is assumed to be a residual sector for employment. The labor force is assumed to grow at 3.6 percent per annum. Thus employment in agriculture is:

(3) $EMAG = L_0(1 + 0.036)^t - TNAG$

where $EMAG$ = employment in agriculture

L_0 = labor force in the base year

$TNAG$ = total nonagricultural employment

The amount of labor absorbed in agriculture determines the standard of living of the agriculturists. Assuming that the whole of the nonmonetary income and 86 percent[2] of that in agricultural sector go to this residual population (who account for the majority of the poor), we define poverty level as:

(4) $pov = \dfrac{GDNM + 0.86\, GDAG}{EA}$

where $GDNM$ = GDP in nonmonetary sector

$GDAG$ = GDP in agricultural sector

Thus, the effects of a low rate of wage employment generation are felt not in open unemployment but in increasing the residual labor in agriculture and thus lowering the average standard of living of the agriculturists. It may also be noted that, whereas an increase in the productivity of labor among wage employees will, all relevant factors being equal, reduce wage employment, increasing productivity in agriculture will improve the living conditions of the "residual" sector.

---

1. See M. FG. Scott, *Estimates of Shadow Wages in Kenya,* Table 7.
2. Based on Table 10, as indicating the proportion of GDP not belonging to those whose income is assessed for tax purposes.

STATISTICAL TABLES
Annex One
Index
BASIC ASSUMPTIONS AND PROJECTIONS

Table No.

ICORs, Investment and Growth Rates

1.	ICORs and Growth Rates in Some Selected Countries	135
2.	Actual and Estimated Values of ICORs, 1966–70	136
3.	Sector Growth Rates and ICORs Assumed in the Basic Projections	137
4.	Total Investment Required for Increase in GDP in Different Sectors	137
5.	Ratio of Depreciation to Gross Value-added in Different Sectors	138
6.	Estimated Equations for Net ICORs in Different Sectors	139

Imports, Exports, and Capital Flows

7.	Imports by End Use, 1964–71	140
8.	Import Price Indices in Various African Countries	140
9.	Data Used for Import Equations	141
10.	Sector Weights Used for Estimating Import Component of Value-added and Investment in Different Sectors	142
11.	Export Projections	142
12.	Export Price Projections for Tea, Coffee, and Sisal	143
13.	Projections of Aid Flows and External Debt	144
14.	Projections of Private Foreign Investment and Net Payments on Direct Investment Income	146

Employment and Labor Productivity

15.	Estimates of Employment by Sector, 1969 and 1971	146
16.	High and Middle Level Manpower, by Sectors, 1972	147
17.	Past and Projected Growth in Labor Productivity	147
18.	Labor Productivity in the Modern Private Sector, 1964–70	148

Basic Projections

19.	Projections under the Basic Scenario, 1972–85	149

SENSITIVITY ANALYSIS OF THE BASIC ASSUMPTIONS

Terms of Trade and Labor Productivity

20.	Effects of Higher Import Prices	150
21.	Effects on Employment of Constant Labor Productivity	151

Apparent Policy Alternatives

22.	Debt Servicing Costs of Incremental Borrowing on Hard Terms	152
23.	Effects of Some Apparent Solutions on Future Development	153

Some Real Policy Alternatives

24.	Effects of Factor Price Changes on Future Development	154
25.	Effects of Structural Changes in the Pattern of Growth on Future Development	155
26.	Projections under the Preferred Scenario	156

Table 1: ICORs and Growth Rates in Some Selected Countries

	FIVE-YEAR AVERAGE ENDING 1970	
Country	ICOR[1]	GDP Growth Rates (% Annual)
Brazil	2.45	7.3
Colombia	3.93	5.6
Egypt	5.05	2.9
Ethiopia	3.22	4.5
Ghana	6.09	2.1
India	3.64	4.1
Indonesia	2.11	4.9
Korea	2.46	11.8
Malaysia	2.79	6.2
Philippines	6.45	3.3
Sri Lanka	4.17	4.4
Tanzania	3.27	6.0
Zambia	7.55	3.6

[1] Including capital in "stocks."

SOURCE: World Bank estimates.

Table 2: Actual[1] and Estimated Values of ICORs, 1966-70

Sector	1966	1967	1968	1969	1970
Nonmonetary					
Actual	1.33	0.68	1.62	1.74	1.83
Estimated	1.03	1.23	1.44	1.64	1.85
Agriculture, forestry, and fishing					
Actual	3.90	1.87	2.54	1.78	2.84
Estimated	3.58	2.22	2.53	2.03	2.57
Mining and quarrying					
Actual	1.82	1.63	4.00	2.67	4.40
Estimated	1.72	1.97	3.34	3.33	4.15
Manufacturing and repair					
Actual	3.05	2.64	2.63	2.44	2.12
Estimated	3.08	2.68	2.53	2.42	2.18
Building and construction					
Actual	2.10	1.69	2.97	5.00	7.72
Estimated	1.14	2.31	3.78	5.37	6.88
Electricity and water					
Actual	7.73	9.00	9.82	7.67	5.17
Estimated	9.26	8.37	7.93	7.20	6.62
Transport, storage, and communication					
Actual	2.81	3.75	6.35	7.61	8.22
Estimated	2.87	4.12	5.95	7.38	8.50
Wholesale and retail trade					
Actual	1.28	1.16	1.73	1.04	1.13
Estimated	1.30	1.25	1.57	1.05	1.19
Banking, insurance, and real estate					
Actual	0.37	0.57	0.38	0.35	0.48
Estimated	0.18	0.93	0.25	0.28	0.50
Ownership of dwellings					
Actual	46.70	18.00	20.80	15.90	18.80
Estimated	35.60	29.80	24.00	18.30	12.50
Other services					
Actual	1.54	1.94	3.29	3.71	3.69
Estimated	1.57	2.18	2.98	3.46	3.97
Government					
Actual	1.41	1.63	1.94	2.08	2.56
Estimated	1.38	1.65	1.92	2.20	2.48
Monetary GDP					
Actual	2.34	2.28	2.94	2.68	3.10
Estimated	2.34	2.40	2.73	2.79	3.10
Total GDP					
Actual	2.16	1.85	2.74	2.56	2.93
Estimated	2.07	2.09	2.52	2.64	2.92

[1] Actual values are obtained from three-year moving averages of investment and GDP in each sector.

SOURCE: Mission estimates.

Table 3: Sector Growth Rates and ICORs Assumed in the Basic Projections

Sector	Annual Growth Rate	ICOR
Nonmonetary sector	4.000	2.105
Agriculture	6.500	2.207
Mining and quarrying	7.800	5.021
Manufacturing and repairing	12.470	1.897
Building and construction	7.500	7.693
Electricity and water	8.000	6.727
Transport, storage, and communications	8.000	9.869
Wholesale and retail trade	8.000	1.113
Banking, insurance, and real estate	8.000	0.500
Ownership of dwellings	8.000	12.500
Other services	8.000	5.361
General Government	9.000	3.221

SOURCE: Mission estimates.

Table 4: Total Investment Required for Increase in GDP in Different Sectors[1]

Item	Investment Required for Agriculture-Oriented Growth	Investment Saved by Reduction in Growth Rate in Building and Construction	Investment Saved by Reduction in Growth Rate in Electricity and Water	Investment Saved by Reduction in Growth Rate in Transport, Storage, and Communications
	(1970 US$ million)			
Sector				
Nonmonetary	0	0	0	0
Agriculture, forestry, and fishing	2.400	−0.030	−0.003	−0.032
Mining and quarrying	0.197	−0.223	−0.019	−0.176
Manufacturing and repairs	0.158	−0.454	−0.029	−0.446
Building and construction	0.005	−4.195	—	−0.029
Electricity and water	0.012	−0.194	−1.716	−0.267
Transport, communication, and storage	0.431	−0.526	−0.047	−10.010
Trade	0.032	−0.043	−0.003	−0.039
Banking	0.010	−0.020	−0.002	−0.026
Ownership of Dwellings	0	—	—	—
Other services	0.237	−0.173	−0.023	−0.162
Central Government	0.022	−0.003	—	−0.025
Total investment required	3.506	−5.862	−1.844	−11.215
Change in GDP[2]	3.607	−1.997	−0.460	−3.028
Total ICOR[2]	0.970	2.940	4.010	3.700

[1] The figures in the table represent the sectoral investments required to achieve a 1% increase (or decrease) in sector growth rates. In every case, the investment required comprises the investment within that particular sector together with the necessary supporting investments in other sectors.
[2] The effect of a 1% change in sector growth rates on GDP and the overall ICOR.

SOURCE: Mission estimates.

Table 5: Ratio of Depreciation to Gross Value-added in Different Sectors

Sector	Ratio
Nonmonetary	0.0000
Agriculture and forestry	0.0858
Mining and quarrying	0.1116
Manufacturing and repairing	0.0994
Building and construction	0.0520
Electricity and water	0.0673
Transport, storage, and communication	0.1543
Wholesale and retail trade	0.0631
Banking, insurance, and real estate	0.0822
Ownership of dwellings	0.0000
Other services	0.0601
Central Government	0.0064
Total monetary	0.0711
TOTAL	0.0530

SOURCE: Calculated from Input/Output Table for Kenya, 1967.

Table 6: Estimated Equations for Net ICORs in Different Sectors

Sector	Constant Term	Coefficient of Time	$\bar{R}^2$	DW	SEE
Nonmonetary	0.823 (2.06)[1]	0.2057 (1.70)	0.320	2.90	0.3800
Agriculture, forestry, and fishing	1.281 (3.49)	−0.0790 (−0.71)	0.140	2.55	0.3500
Mining and quarrying	0.368 (0.589)	0.4500 (2.40)	0.540	3.55	0.6000
Manufacturing and repairing	1.560 (19.9)	−0.0710 (−3.0)	0.670	2.10	0.0700
Building and construction	−0.506 (0.50)	1.2720 (4.16)	0.800	1.49	0.9700
Electricity and water	8.420 (4.74)	−0.5060 (−0.9)	−0.030	1.38	1.6900
Transport, storage, and communication	0.603 (1.53)	0.9620 (8.11)	0.940	2.42	0.3800
Wholesale and retail trade	0.118 (1.03)	0.0412 (1.19)	0.093	2.65	0.1097
Banking, insurance, and real estate	−0.830 (−3.2)	0.1300 (1.71)	0.320	2.94	0.2450
Ownership of dwellings	41.390	−5.7800	0.350	2.12	10.3000
Other services	0.354 (1.08)	0.5690 (5.76)	0.890	2.14	0.3100
Central Government	1.040 (11.58)	0.2730 (10.11)	0.960	2.72	0.0850
Total monetary GDP	1.155 (7.26)	0.1890 (3.95)	0.785	3.39	0.1520
Total GDP	1.050 (5.04)	0.2070 (3.29)	0.710	3.45	0.1990

[1] Figures in parentheses are *t* values.

SOURCE: Mission estimates.

Table 7: Imports by End Use, 1964–71

Year	Imports of Raw Materials	Imports of Capital Goods	Imports of Consumer Goods	Government Imports	Imports of Nonfactor Services
	(US$ million, constant 1970 prices)				
1964	141.3	36.9	69.6	7.5	72.9
1965	172.9	35.9	71.8	13.4	67.4
1966	189.3	54.1	84.1	21.6	73.0
1967	189.0	72.4	70.4	16.2	73.4
1968	199.8	60.0	80.0	17.6	83.3
1969	209.4	62.0	75.1	14.9	83.0
1970	231.9	77.3	87.8	16.3	79.6
1971	263.9	96.9	101.7	21.8	78.8

SOURCE: Ministry of Finance and Planning, Kenya.

Table 8: Import Price Indices in Various African Countries

Country	1968	1969	1970	1971
	(Average 1967–69 = 100)			
Ethiopia	100.41	101.20	102.38	108.27
Ghana	97.77	101.54	107.17	97.88
Ivory Coast	98.37	101.75	103.51	n.a.
Malawi	97.45	101.01	106.37	n.a.
Morocco	99.60	101.60	102.70	108.23
Nigeria	97.96	100.86	108.06	115.52
Tanzania	98.96	102.00	100.00	106.71
Tunisia	100.78	98.16	101.81	104.99
Zambia	102.27	105.32	109.54	113.94

SOURCE: World Bank estimates.

Table 9: Data Used for Import Equations

IMPORT OF RAW MATERIALS

Year	GDP (Excluding Government)	GDP Weighted ($YW1$)	Imports (Constant Prices) Actual	Imports (Constant Prices) Estimated
1964	869.2	148.7	141.3	155.4
1965	870.6	155.2	173.0	161.6
1966	994.8	171.3	189.3	177.0
1967	1,034.9	183.3	189.0	188.3
1968	1,108.7	200.8	199.8	205.1
1969	1,174.6	215.1	209.4	218.6
1970	1,251.7	231.1	231.9	234.0
1971	1,319.7	255.9	263.9	257.6
% Increase 1964–71	52.0	72.0		

IMPORT OF CONSUMER GOODS

Year	GDP	GDP Weighted ($YW2$)	Imports (Constant Prices) Actual	Imports (Constant Prices) Estimated
1964	869.2	237.9	69.6	68.3
1965	870.6	256.1	71.8	71.1
1966	994.8	281.9	84.1	75.1
1967	1,034.9	294.3	70.4	77.0
1968	1,108.7	320.2	80.0	81.0
1969	1,174.6	343.0	75.1	84.6
1970	1,251.7	375.1	87.8	89.5
1971	1,319.7	402.7	101.7	93.8
% Increase 1964–71	52.0	69.0		

IMPORT OF CAPITAL GOODS

Year	Investment (Excluding Government)	Weighted Investment	Imports (Constant Prices) Actual	Imports (Constant Prices) Estimated
1964	130.6	70.2	36.9	39.7
1965	125.0	65.3	35.9	36.7
1966	157.9	86.0	54.1	49.4
1967	196.9	107.6	72.4	62.8
1968	209.1	112.5	60.0	65.8
1969	210.7	111.6	62.0	65.3
1970	254.2	141.8	77.3	83.9
1971	284.3	154.8	96.9	91.9
% Increase 1964–71	118.0	121.0		

SOURCE: Mission estimates.

Table 10: Sector Weights Used for Estimating Relative Import Component of Value-added and Investment in Different Sectors

Sector	Consumer Goods	Raw Materials	Capital Goods
Nonmonetary	0.000	0.0045	0.000
Agriculture, forestry, and fishing	0.137	0.0875	0.497
Mining and quarrying	0.406	0.1516	1.000
Manufacturing and repairing	0.334	0.7690	0.819
Building and construction	0.146	0.4517	0.828
Electricity and water	0.329	0.1310	0.437
Transport, storage, and communication	0.329	0.1617	0.838
Wholesale and retail trade	0.258	0.0787	0.623
Banking, insurance, and real estate	0.828	0.0199	0.639
Ownership of dwellings	0.518	0.0136	0.036
Other services	0.745	0.2018	0.514
Government	0.140	0.0000	0.000

SOURCES: Input/Output Table for 1967; economic surveys and report of East African Income Tax Department.

Table 11: Export Projections

Exported Commodity or Service	1972	1978	1985	Average Annual Growth Rate 1972–85
	(£ million)			(percentage)
Tea	16.4	32.2	56.1	9.9
Coffee	24.8	26.6	28.7	1.1
Sisal	2.2	1.8	1.8	−1.5
Other agricultural products	10.6	12.7	25.0	6.8
Minerals	0.4	0.4	0.4	0.0
Manufactures to EAC	33.8	65.6	100.0	8.7
Manufactures abroad	35.7	77.0	194.3	13.9
Tourism	25.9	71.9	89.3	10.0
Other goods and NFS	50.7	62.9	195.5	10.9
TOTAL	200.5	351.1	691.1	10.0

SOURCE: Based on Government projections for the 1974–78 plan period.

Table 12: Export Price Projections for Tea, Coffee, and Sisal

Year	Tea	Coffee	Sisal
	(Index 1970 = 100)		
1972	92.3	100.5	147.0
1973	91.0	103.0	200.0
1974	90.0	104.0	140.0
1975	89.0	105.0	130.0
1976	88.0	106.0	120.0
1977	87.0	107.0	120.0
1978	86.0	108.0	120.0
1979	85.0	109.0	120.0
1980	83.0	110.0	120.0

SOURCE: Based on price forecasts by Commodities and Export Projections Division, World Bank.

Table 13: Projections of Aid Flows and External Debt

Lending Agency	1972	1973	1974	1975	1976	1977	1978	1979	1980	1981	1982	1983	1984	1985
Projections of existing debt														
						Disbursements (US$ million)								
International organizations	24.0	25.3	21.0	17.1	10.7	6.2	4.4	2.3	0.5	0.1	—	—	—	—
Governments	19.0	4.2	2.3	1.3	0.8	0.6	0.3	0.1	—	—	—	—	—	—
Private banks	0.0	0.3	—	—	—	—	—	—	—	—	—	—	—	—
Public debt not elsewhere included	13.4	—	—	—	—	—	—	—	—	—	—	—	—	—
						Amortization Payments (US$ million)								
International organizations	1.2	1.3	1.7	3.6	4.1	4.4	4.6	5.2	6.1	6.3	6.3	7.6	7.9	8.3
Governments	7.9	8.9	9.8	10.4	12.3	12.3	12.2	12.3	13.1	11.6	11.9	11.4	11.7	11.4
Suppliers' credit	3.9	3.2	2.3	1.3	1.3	—	—	—	—	—	—	—	—	—
Private banks	1.3	1.3	1.3	1.0	0.7	0.3	0.1	0.1	0.1	0.1	0.1	0.1	0.0	0.1
Publicly placed bonds	0.0	0.1	0.0	0.1	0.0	0.1	0.0	0.1	0.0	0.1	0.5	—	—	—
Privately issued bonds	4.1	1.3	3.4	4.6	5.2	0.8	20.5	0.3	0.3	0.3	4.3	—	—	—
						Interest Payments (US$ million)								
International organizations	3.1	4.4	5.7	6.6	7.3	7.4	7.5	7.4	7.1	6.7	6.3	6.0	5.4	4.9
Governments	8.2	8.3	8.0	7.7	7.2	6.8	6.2	5.8	5.3	4.7	4.3	3.8	3.3	2.8
Suppliers' credit	0.8	0.6	0.4	0.2	0.1	—	—	—	—	—	—	—	—	—
Private banks	0.4	0.3	0.2	0.1	0.1	0.1	0.0	0.1	0.0	0.0	0.1	—	—	—
Publicly placed bonds	0.1	0.1	0.1	0.1	0.1	0.1	0.1	0.0	0.1	0.0	0.1	—	—	—
Privately issued bonds	4.5	4.5	4.3	4.3	3.8	3.5	2.5	1.5	1.5	1.5	1.5	—	—	—

THE MACRO-ECONOMIC MODEL AND PROJECTIONS 145

Projections of new debt (1971) Commitments (US$ million)

International organizations	26.5	70.3	121.0	87.0	68.7	71.9	75.3	78.7	82.4	86.3	90.4	94.6	99.2	103.8	108.7
Government	17.0	20.0	47.3	57.3	58.3	61.6	64.7	67.9	71.4	74.9	78.7	82.6	86.7	91.1	95.6
Suppliers' credit	7.3	10.0	10.0	10.0	10.0	10.0	10.0	10.0	10.0	10.0	10.0	10.0	10.0	10.0	10.0
Private banks	3.5	3.4	3.5	3.5	3.5	3.5	3.5	3.5	3.5	3.5	3.5	3.5	3.5	3.5	3.5

Assumed terms of lending

	Rate of Interest (%)	Maturity Period (Years)	Grace Period (Years)	Annual Payments (No.)	Disbursement Schedule (% Disbursed Each Year)										
					1	2	3	4	5	6	7	8	9	10
World Bank	7.25	20	5	2	3	13	20	20	17	12	6	4	3	2
IDA	0.75	50	10	2	2	12	19	16	15	13	10	7	4	2
Other international organizations (soft terms)	2.50	30	8	2	10	30	20	15	10	10	5	—	—	—
Other international organizations (medium terms)	7.00	20	5	2	10	30	20	15	10	10	5	—	—	—
Governments (soft terms)	2.50	30	6	2	15	25	20	15	15	10	—	—	—	—
Governments (medium terms)	6.50	20	5	2	15	25	20	15	15	10	—	—	—	—
Governments (hard terms)	6.50	10	3	2	15	25	20	15	15	10	—	—	—	—
Suppliers' credit (soft terms)	7.00	15	4	1	40	40	15	5	—	—	—	—	—	—
Suppliers' credit (medium terms)	7.00	10	3	1	40	40	15	5	—	—	—	—	—	—
Suppliers' credit (hard terms)	9.00	6	2	1	100	—	—	—	—	—	—	—	—	—
Private banks	8.00	5	2	1	100	—	—	—	—	—	—	—	—	—
Other financial institutions (private)	8.00	10	3	1	100	—	—	—	—	—	—	—	—	—
Publicly placed bonds	8.00	5	2	1	100	—	—	—	—	—	—	—	—	—
Privately issued bonds	8.00	10	3	1	100	—	—	—	—	—	—	—	—	—
Public debt not elsewhere included	10.00	10	1	1	100	—	—	—	—	—	—	—	—	—

SOURCE: World Bank debt reporting system, mission estimates.

Table 14: Projections of Private Foreign Investment and Net Payments on Direct Investment Income

Year	Private Foreign Investment	Net Payments on Direct Investment Income
	(US$ million)	
1973	41.8	38.0
1974	45.1	40.0
1975	48.7	42.0
1976	52.6	45.0
1977	56.8	48.0
1978	61.4	51.0
1979	66.3	54.0
1980	71.6	58.0
1981	77.3	62.0
1982	83.5	66.0
1983	90.2	70.0
1984	97.4	74.0
1985	105.1	78.0

SOURCE: Mission estimates.

Table 15: Estimates of Employment by Sector, 1969 and 1971

Sector	1969 Formal Wage Employment	1969 Informal Rural	1969 Informal Urban	1969 Total	1971 Formal Wage Employment	1971 Informal Rural	1971 Informal Urban	1971 Total
				(thousand)				
Agriculture, forestry, and fishing	196	4,168	—	4,364	211	4,436	—	4,647
Mining and quarrying	3	1	—	4	3	1	—	4
Manufacturing	75	30	15	120	93	32	16	141
Building and construction	29	1	11	41	35	1	12	48
Electricity and water	5	—	—	5	5	—	—	5
Transport, storage, and communication	48	3	1	52	46	3	1	50
Wholesale and retail trade	44	96	30	170	47	102	32	181
Services	227	19	39	285	240	20	41	301
TOTAL	627	4,318	96	5,041	680	4,595	102	5,377

SOURCE: Mission estimates.

Table 16: High and Middle Level Manpower by Sectors, 1972

Sector	Wage Employment	Skilled Manpower	Skilled Manpower as % of Wage Employment
	(thousand)		
Agriculture	216.2	7.5	3.48
Mining and quarrying	3.1	0.3	9.66
Manufacturing	97.4	20.0	20.58
Building and construction	35.3	4.9	13.76
Electricity and water	5.2	1.3	24.96
Transport, storage, and communication	58.4	17.5	17.0
Trade	46.2	7.9	29.91
Services	207.8	40.5	19.49
TOTAL	669.5	99.8	14.91

SOURCE: Kenya Statistical Digest, December 1972, Central Bureau of Statistics, Kenya.

Table 17: Past and Projected Growth in Labor Productivity

Sector	Rate of Growth of Wage Employment (1967–71)	Rate of Growth of GDP (1967–71)	Implicit Rate of Growth in Labor Productivity	Projected Growth in Labor Productivity
Agriculture	2.9	6.4	3.5	3.5
Mining and quarrying	4.6	8.0	3.4	3.5
Manufacturing	7.7	9.6	1.9	2.5
Building and construction	2.2	6.8	4.6	4.5
Electricity and water	−4.2	8.7	12.9	6.0
Transport, storage, and communication	−4.9	5.3	10.2	3.5
Trade	0.4	7.6	7.2	3.5
Services	4.4	8.2	3.8	3.5

SOURCE: Economic surveys and mission estimates.

Table 18: Labor Productivity in the Modern Private Sector, 1964–70[1]

Industry	Constant	Log Wages	$\bar{R}^2$	DW
Manufacturing	7.766	0.988	0.93	1.51
(*t* ratio)	(57.17)	(8.90)		
Commerce	8.060	1.627	0.92	1.36
(*t* ratio)	(55.27)	(8.65)		
Other services	6.888	0.905	0.86	1.27
(*t* ratio)	(27.78)	(6.25)		
Total private modern sector	8.286	1.191	0.94	2.82
(*t* ratio)	(38.58)	(9.66)		

[1] The ordinary least squares method has been used to estimate the relationship between labor productivity and wages. The equation takes the following form:

$$\log \frac{V}{E} = a + b \log w;$$

where V = gross value-added (£ thousand); E = employment; W = average wages per year.

SOURCE: Mission estimates.

Table 19: Projections under the Basic Scenario, 1972–85

Category	1972	1974	1975	1976	1977	1978	1980	1985
Total use of resources				(1970 £ million)				
GDP at factor cost	596.0	684.4	737.2	794.5	856.8	924.3	1,077.7	1,597.2
Major areas								
Nonmonetary	127.6	136.8	142.2	147.9	153.8	160.0	173.0	210.5
Monetary	468.6	547.6	595.0	646.6	702.9	764.3	904.6	1,386.7
+ Indirect taxes	60.5	88.4	96.0	104.2	113.3	123.4	146.7	229.6
− Subsidies	5.0	5.7	6.1	6.6	7.2	7.8	9.2	14.1
= GDP at market prices	651.5	767.1	827.1	892.1	962.9	1,039.9	1,215.2	1,812.7
+ Imports of goods and nonfactor services	186.9	230.8	248.8	267.9	288.7	312.3	365.5	547.8
− Exports of goods and nonfactor services	181.8	207.4	221.6	237.0	252.3	276.2	321.0	442.1
= Import surplus	5.1	23.4	27.2	30.9	36.4	36.1	44.5	105.7
Total resources available	656.6	790.5	854.3	923.0	999.3	1,076.0	1,259.7	1,918.4
Gross fixed capital formation	145.4	182.1	197.3	213.7	231.5	251.0	295.1	445.2
Increase in stocks	9.8	11.8	13.6	14.8	16.2	17.7	21.1	33.0
Gross investment	155.2	193.9	210.9	228.5	247.7	268.7	316.2	478.2
Public consumption	111.2	132.2	144.2	157.1	171.3	186.7	221.8	341.7
Private consumption	425.9	464.5	499.2	537.4	580.3	620.6	721.5	1,098.6
TOTAL CONSUMPTION	537.1	596.7	643.4	694.5	751.6	807.3	943.4	1,440.3
Balance of payments				(£ million)				
Exports of goods and nonfactor services	200.5	239.8	260.9	283.9	311.3	351.1	432.8	691.0
Imports of goods and nonfactor services	220.2	294.1	326.4	362.1	401.9	447.8	556.0	966.1
Resource balance	19.7	54.3	65.5	78.2	90.6	96.7	123.2	275.0
Gap, after allowing for new disbursements from foreign capital inflow and debt servicing	−3.2	37.8	46.1	60.4	73.9	92.9	133.8	377.1
Employment and poverty				(thousand)				
Wage employment	718	787	826	867	911	958	1,059	1,373
High and middle level manpower requirement	108	120	126	134	141	149	167	224
Labor force	5,570	5,979	6,194	6,417	6,648	6,887	7,392	8,822
Total nonagricultural employment (including nonformal sector)	776	862	911	963	1,019	1,078	1,209	1,620
Labor in agriculture	4,794	5,117	5,283	5,454	5,629	5,809	6,183	7,202
				(in 1970 k£)				
Average income, agricultural workers	42.9	44.0	44.8	45.5	46.3	47.2	48.9	53.8

SOURCE: Mission estimates.

Table 20: Effects of Higher Import Prices[1]

Category	1972	1978	1985
Use of resources	(£ million, constant 1970 prices)		
GDP at market prices	651.5	1,039.7	1,812.3
Imports	186.9	310.4	544.6
Exports	−181.8	−276.2	−442.1
Total fixed investment	145.4	251.0	445.2
Gross domestic investment	155.2	268.6	478.2
Government consumption	111.2	186.7	341.7
Ex post household consumption	390.2	618.6	1,095.0
Ex ante household consumption	413.3	613.5	1,033.9
Balance of payments	(£ million, current prices)		
Exports	200.5	351.1	691.0
Imports	220.2	457.9	987.8
Resource balance	−19.6	−106.8	−296.7
Residual balance of payments gap	−3.2	106.9	415.6
Employment	(thousand persons)		
High and middle level manpower	107.8	149.3	223.9
Total modern sector wage employment	717.8	957.5	1,373.4
All employment	776.5	1,078.2	1,620.4
Average income, agricultural worker (poverty index)	42.9	47.2	53.8

[1] Table shows effects of 8% increase in import prices in 1973 instead of the 5% assumed in the basic projections.

Table 21: Effects on Employment of Constant Labor Productivity

	\multicolumn{3}{c}{Employment under Basic Scenario}	\multicolumn{2}{c}{Employment Assuming Constant Productivity}
	1972	1978	1985	1978	1985
Wage employment, modern sector			(thousand)		
Agriculture	217	260	319	328	510
Mining	3	4	6	5	9
Manufacturing	100	167	315	201	458
Building and construction	36	44	54	59	98
Electricity and water	5	6	7	9	15
Transport, storage, and communication	49	63	86	79	136
Trade	48	63	89	78	133
Services	260	350	497	440	786
TOTAL	718	958	1,373	1,200	2,145
High and middle level employment					
Agriculture	8	9	11	11	18
Mining	0	0	1	1	1
Manufacturing	20	34	65	41	94
Building and construction	5	6	7	8	13
Electricity and water	1	1	2	2	4
Transport, storage, and communication	8	11	15	13	23
Trade	14	19	27	23	40
Services	51	68	97	86	153
TOTAL	108	149	224	185	346
Total employment, all sectors					
Mining	4	5	8	6	11
Manufacturing	151	254	478	306	696
Building and construction	50	60	74	82	135
Electricity and water	5	6	7	9	15
Transport, storage, and communication	189	245	333	308	529
Trade	52	70	98	85	146
Services	325	438	622	550	983
NONAGRICULTURE SUBTOTAL	776	1,078	1,620	1,346	2,515
Agriculture	4,794	5,809	7,201	5,541	6,306
TOTAL LABOR FORCE	5,570	6,887	8,821	6,887	8,821
Average income per agriculture worker (£)	42.9	47.1	53.8	49.4	61.5

SOURCE: Mission estimates.

Table 22: Debt Servicing Costs of Incremental Borrowing on Hard Terms[1]

	1973	1974	1975	1976	1977	1978	1979	1980	1981	1982	1983	1984	1985
						(US$ million)							
Debt Position I[2]													
Amortization	16	19	24	29	27	50	36	42	46	57	58	64	70
Interest	19	21	24	28	32	35	39	43	47	51	53	57	60
Net transfer	31	53	69	75	86	67	82	74	72	63	65	63	62
Debt Position II[3]													
Additional suppliers' credit on hard terms	50	60	70	80	90	100	110	120	130	140	150	160	170
Amortization	16	19	34	51	63	102	106	122	136	157	168	184	200
Interest	19	26	34	43	52	61	69	76	84	92	97	104	112
Net transfer	81	108	119	118	119	90	92	81	75	62	61	55	50

[1] Hard terms defined as interest rate of 9%, grace period of two years, and repayable in six years.
[2] Showing the effect of the pattern of borrowing assumed in the basic projections.
[3] Showing the effect of additional borrowing on hard terms.

SOURCE: Mission estimates.

THE MACRO-ECONOMIC MODEL AND PROJECTIONS 153

Table 23: Effects of Some Apparent Solutions on Future Development

Category	Basic Scenario 1972	1978	1985	Effects of Import Controls 1972	1978	1985	Effects of Lower GDP Growth Rate 1972	1978	1985	Effects of Lower GDP Growth Rate and Constant Labor Productivity 1972	1978	1985
	(£ million, constant 1970 prices)											
Use of resources												
GDP at market prices	651.5	1,039.9	1,812.7	651.5	1,035.4	1,804.9	651.5	906.2	1,312.7	651.5	906.2	1,312.7
Imports	186.9	312.3	547.8	816.9	276.8	487.2	186.9	270.7	420.7	186.9	270.7	420.7
Exports	−181.8	−276.2	−442.1	−181.8	−276.2	−442.1	−181.8	−253.3	−382.2	−181.8	−253.3	−382.2
Total fixed investment	145.4	251.0	445.2	145.4	251.0	445.2	145.4	150.9	224.0	145.4	150.9	224.0
Gross domestic investment	155.2	268.6	478.2	155.2	268.6	478.2	155.2	161.3	240.2	155.2	161.3	240.2
Government consumption	111.2	186.7	341.7	111.2	186.7	341.7	111.2	162.4	244.3	111.2	162.4	244.3
Ex post household consumption	390.2	620.6	1,098.6	390.2	580.6	1,030.2	390.2	599.9	866.7	390.2	599.9	866.7
	(£ million, current prices)											
Balance of payments												
Exports	200.5	351.1	691.0	200.5	351.1	691.0	200.5	321.9	597.4	200.5	321.9	597.4
Imports	220.2	447.8	966.1	220.2	408.2	883.8	220.2	388.1	741.9	220.2	388.1	741.9
Resource balance	−19.6	−96.7	−275.0	−19.6	−57.2	−192.8	−19.6	−66.2	−144.5	−19.6	−66.2	−144.5
Residual balance of payments gap	−3.2	92.9	377.1	−3.2	42.6	237.1	−3.2	48.5	177.4	−3.2	48.5	177.4
	(thousand persons)											
Employment												
High and middle level manpower	107.8	149.3	223.9	107.8	186.2	346.4	107.8	127.3	156.1	107.8	159.6	244.3
Total modern sector wage employment	717.8	957.5	1,373.4	717.8	1,199.7	2,145.4	717.8	813.3	953.5	717.8	1,024.4	1,506.8
All employment	776.5	1,078.2	1,620.4	776.5	1,346.8	2,515.5	776.5	918.0	1,128.5	776.5	1,152.6	1,771.7
	(£)											
Average income, agricultural worker (poverty index)	42.9	47.2	53.8	42.9	49.5	61.5	42.9	39.7	35.6	42.9	41.3	38.8

SOURCE: Mission estimates.

Table 24: Effects of Factor Price Changes on Future Development

	Basic Scenario			Effect of 20% Devaluation			Effect of Higher Interest Rates			Effect of Lower Depreciation Allowances			Combined Effects of Factor Price Changes[1]		
	1972	1978	1985	1972	1978	1985	1972	1978	1985	1972	1978	1985	1972	1978	1985
							(£ million, constant 1970 prices)								
Use of resources															
GDP at market prices	651.5	1,039.9	1,812.7	651.5	1,037.9	1,808.9	651.5	1,039.3	1,811.6	651.5	1,039.6	1,812.1	651.5	1,037.8	1,809.0
Imports	186.9	312.3	547.8	186.9	296.5	520.4	186.9	307.2	539.1	186.9	309.4	542.9	186.9	296.2	520.0
Exports	−181.8	−276.2	−442.1	−181.8	−290.8	−465.2	−181.8	−276.2	−442.1	−181.8	−276.2	−442.1	−181.8	−283.7	−453.9
Total fixed investment	145.4	251.0	445.2	145.4	245.2	435.0	145.4	239.3	424.4	145.4	244.4	433.6	145.4	229.8	407.5
Gross domestic investment	155.2	268.6	478.2	155.2	262.9	467.9	155.2	257.0	457.4	155.2	262.1	466.5	155.2	247.5	440.5
Government consumption	111.2	186.7	341.7	111.2	186.7	341.7	111.2	186.7	341.7	111.2	186.7	341.7	111.2	186.7	341.7
Ex post household consumption	390.2	620.6	1,098.6	390.2	593.9	1,054.6	390.2	626.5	1,109.6	390.2	623.9	1,104.7	390.2	616.0	1,093.0
Ex ante household consumption	413.3	613.4	1,033.9	413.3	614.3	1,035.3	413.3	615.0	1,036.8	413.3	614.4	1,035.5	413.3	616.2	1,039.1
Balance of payments							(£ million, current prices)								
Exports	200.5	351.1	691.0	200.5	369.6	727.2	200.5	351.1	691.0	200.5	351.1	691.0	200.5	360.6	709.6
Imports	220.2	447.8	966.1	220.2	425.2	917.7	220.2	440.4	950.7	220.2	443.7	957.5	220.2	424.7	917.1
Resource balance	−19.7	−96.7	−275.0	−19.6	−55.5	−190.6	−19.6	−89.4	−259.7	−19.6	−92.6	−266.4	−19.6	−64.1	−207.5
Residual balance of payments gap	−3.2	92.9	377.1	−3.2	36.3	225.8	−3.2	82.8	349.7	−3.2	87.3	361.7	−3.2	48.0	256.3
							(thousand persons)								
Employment															
High and middle level manpower	107.8	149.3	223.9	107.8	150.6	228.7	107.8	152.1	234.2	107.8	150.8	229.4	107.8	154.8	244.7
Total modern sector wage employment	717.8	957.5	1,373.4	717.8	965.6	1,401.3	717.8	974.7	1,433.2	717.8	966.8	1,405.3	717.8	991.2	1,493.2
All employment	776.5	1,078.2	1,620.4	776.5	1,087.6	1,655.1	776.5	1,098.0	1,694.6	776.5	1,088.9	1,660.0	776.5	1,117.0	1,769.0
							(£)								
Average income per agricultural worker (poverty level)	42.9	47.2	53.8	42.9	47.2	54.1	42.9	47.3	54.4	42.9	47.3	54.1	42.9	47.5	55.0

[1] Assumes only 10% devaluation.

SOURCE: Mission estimates.

THE MACRO-ECONOMIC MODEL AND PROJECTIONS 155

Table 25: Effects of Structural Changes in the Pattern of Growth on Future Development

	Basic Scenario 1972	Basic Scenario 1978	Basic Scenario 1985	Effects of Higher Growth Rate of Nonmonetary Agriculture 1972	Effects of Higher Growth Rate of Nonmonetary Agriculture 1978	Effects of Higher Growth Rate of Nonmonetary Agriculture 1985	Effects of Higher Growth Rate of Monetary Agriculture 1972	Effects of Higher Growth Rate of Monetary Agriculture 1978	Effects of Higher Growth Rate of Monetary Agriculture 1985	Effects of Lower Growth Rate of Building and Construction 1972	Effects of Lower Growth Rate of Building and Construction 1978	Effects of Lower Growth Rate of Building and Construction 1985	Effects of Lower Growth Rate of Transport and Communications 1972	Effects of Lower Growth Rate of Transport and Communications 1978	Effects of Lower Growth Rate of Transport and Communications 1985	Effects of Lower Growth Rate of Electricity and Water 1972	Effects of Lower Growth Rate of Electricity and Water 1978	Effects of Lower Growth Rate of Electricity and Water 1985	Combined Effects of Structural Changes 1972	Combined Effects of Structural Changes 1978	Combined Effects of Structural Changes 1985
									(£ million, constant 1970 prices)												
Use of resources																					
GDP at market prices	651.5	1,039.9	1,812.7	651.5	1,047.7	1,838.1	651.5	1,048.2	1,845.0	651.5	1,035.7	1,794.7	651.5	1,034.0	1,787.9	651.5	1,039.0	1,808.8	651.5	1,044.8	1,823.7
Imports	186.9	312.3	547.8	186.9	311.7	545.9	186.9	314.5	554.2	186.9	309.0	537.5	186.9	307.2	533.6	186.9	311.8	546.5	186.9	305.2	526.5
Exports	−181.8	−276.2	−442.1	−181.8	−276.2	−442.1	−181.8	−284.5	−465.3	−181.8	−276.1	−441.8	−181.8	−276.1	−441.8	−181.8	−276.2	−442.1	−181.8	−284.2	−464.6
Total fixed investment	145.4	251.0	445.2	145.4	255.1	452.4	145.4	254.0	453.4	145.4	246.6	434.4	145.4	242.5	424.2	145.4	249.6	442.0	145.4	244.0	425.6
Gross domestic investment	155.2	268.6	478.2	155.2	272.8	485.3	155.2	272.3	487.6	155.2	264.0	466.6	155.2	259.8	456.2	155.2	267.2	474.8	155.2	261.5	458.0
Government consumption	111.2	186.7	341.7	111.2	186.7	341.7	111.2	186.8	341.8	111.2	186.7	341.7	111.2	186.7	341.6	111.2	186.7	341.7	111.2	186.7	341.6
Ex post household consumption	390.2	620.6	1,098.6	390.2	623.6	1,114.9	390.2	619.1	1,104.6	390.2	617.9	1,082.1	390.2	618.6	1,081.9	390.2	620.6	1,096.8	390.2	617.5	1,086.1
Ex ante household consumption	413.3	613.4	1,033.9	413.3	620.0	1,056.0	413.3	717.3	1,049.2	413.3	612.1	1,026.6	413.3	611.7	1,024.7	413.3	613.2	1,032.4	413.3	620.2	1,053.2
Balance of payments									(£ million, current prices)												
Exports	200.5	351.1	691.0	200.5	351.1	691.0	200.5	361.6	727.3	200.5	350.9	691.0	200.5	350.9	690.5	200.5	351.1	691.0	200.5	361.3	726.2
Imports	220.2	447.8	966.1	220.2	447.0	962.7	220.2	450.9	977.3	220.2	443.1	948.0	220.2	440.5	940.9	220.2	447.1	963.8	220.2	437.6	928.5
Resource balance	−19.7	−96.7	−275.0	−19.6	−95.9	−271.6	−19.6	−89.4	−250.0	−19.6	−92.2	−257.0	−19.6	−89.6	−250.4	−19.6	−96.0	−272.9	−19.6	−76.3	−202.3
Residual balance of payments gap	−3.2	92.9	377.1	−3.2	92.0	372.2	−3.2	85.0	340.4	−3.2	87.0	350.4	−3.2	83.5	338.9	−3.2	92.0	373.7	−3.2	67.9	267.5
Employment									(thousand persons)												
High and middle level manpower	107.8	149.3	223.9	107.8	149.3	223.9	107.8	150.1	226.3	107.8	148.4	221.0	107.8	148.2	220.3	107.8	149.2	223.5	107.8	148.0	219.5
Total modern sector wage employment	717.8	957.5	1,373.4	717.8	957.5	1,373.4	717.8	974.4	1,421.0	717.8	952.2	1,356.8	717.8	951.4	1,353.7	717.8	957.0	1,371.0	717.8	962.4	1,383.2
All employment	776.5	1,078.2	1,620.4	776.5	1,078.2	1,620.4	776.5	1,080.5	1,628.4	776.5	1,070.6	1,596.5	776.5	1,061.1	1,568.4	776.5	1,077.6	1,618.5	776.5	1,055.2	1,550.5
									(£)												
Average income, agricultural worker (poverty index)	42.9	47.2	53.8	42.9	58.5	57.4	42.9	48.1	56.8	42.9	47.1	53.6	42.9	47.0	53.4	42.9	47.2	53.8	42.9	49.2	59.6

SOURCE: Mission estimates.

Table 26: Projections under the Preferred Scenario

	1972	1974	1975	1976	1977	1978	1980	1985
Total use of resources				(£ million, 1970 prices)				
GDP at factor cost	596.0	685.5	739.4	797.9	861.4	930.2	1,086.2	1,611.6
Major areas:								
Monetary	127.4	547.4	594.5	645.7	701.6	762.4	901.2	1,375.6
Nonmonetary	468.6	138.1	144.9	152.2	159.8	167.8	185.0	236.0
+ Indirect taxes	60.5	86.6	93.9	101.9	110.7	120.5	143.1	223.0
− Subsidies	5.0	5.8	6.2	6.7	7.3	7.9	9.3	14.4
= GDP at market prices	651.5	766.3	827.1	893.1	964.8	1,042.8	1,220.0	1,820.2
+ Import of goods and NFS	186.9	216.5	232.5	249.9	268.7	290.1	338.2	501.2
− Export of goods and NFS	181.8	214.9	230.9	248.1	265.5	292.1	343.1	477.6
= Import surplus	5.1	1.6	1.6	1.8	3.2	−2.0	−4.9	23.6
Total resources available	656.6	767.9	828.7	894.9	968.0	1,040.8	1,215.1	1,843.8
Gross fixed capital formation	145.4	164.5	177.7	192.1	207.7	224.6	262.9	392.0
Increase in stocks	9.8	11.8	13.6	14.8	16.1	17.5	20.9	32.3
Gross investment	155.2	176.3	191.3	206.9	223.8	242.1	283.8	424.3
Public consumption	111.2	132.2	144.1	157.1	171.3	186.7	221.9	341.6
Private consumption	425.9	459.4	493.3	530.9	572.9	611.9	709.4	1,077.9
Total consumption	537.1	591.6	637.4	688.0	744.2	798.6	931.3	1,419.5
Balance of payments				(£ million)				
Exports of goods and NFS	200.5	248.4	271.7	297.3	327.6	371.3	462.6	746.5
Import of goods and NFS	220.2	275.8	305.1	337.7	374.0	415.9	514.5	883.8
Resource balance	19.7	27.4	33.4	40.4	46.4	44.6	−51.9	−137.3
Gap (after allowing for new disbursements from foreign capital inflow and debt servicing)	−3.2	7.9	8.6	14.4	17.7	24.3	33.5	151.0
Employment and poverty				(thousand persons)				
Wage employment	718	797	843	891	943	998	1,120	1,508
High and middle level manpower requirement	108	120	128	136	144	153	174	239
Labor force	5,570	5,979	6,194	6,417	6,648	6,888	7,392	8,822
Total nonagricultural employment (including nonformal sector)	776	864	914	969	1,028	1,091	1,230	1,684
Labor in agriculture	4,794	5,155	5,280	5,448	5,620	5,797	6,162	7,138
				(in 1970 £)				
Average income, agricultural worker	42.9	44.5	45.7	46.9	48.2	49.5	52.4	60.8

SOURCE: Mission estimates.

THE MACRO-ECONOMIC MODEL AND PROJECTIONS

CHART I
A Simplified Flow Diagram of the Model

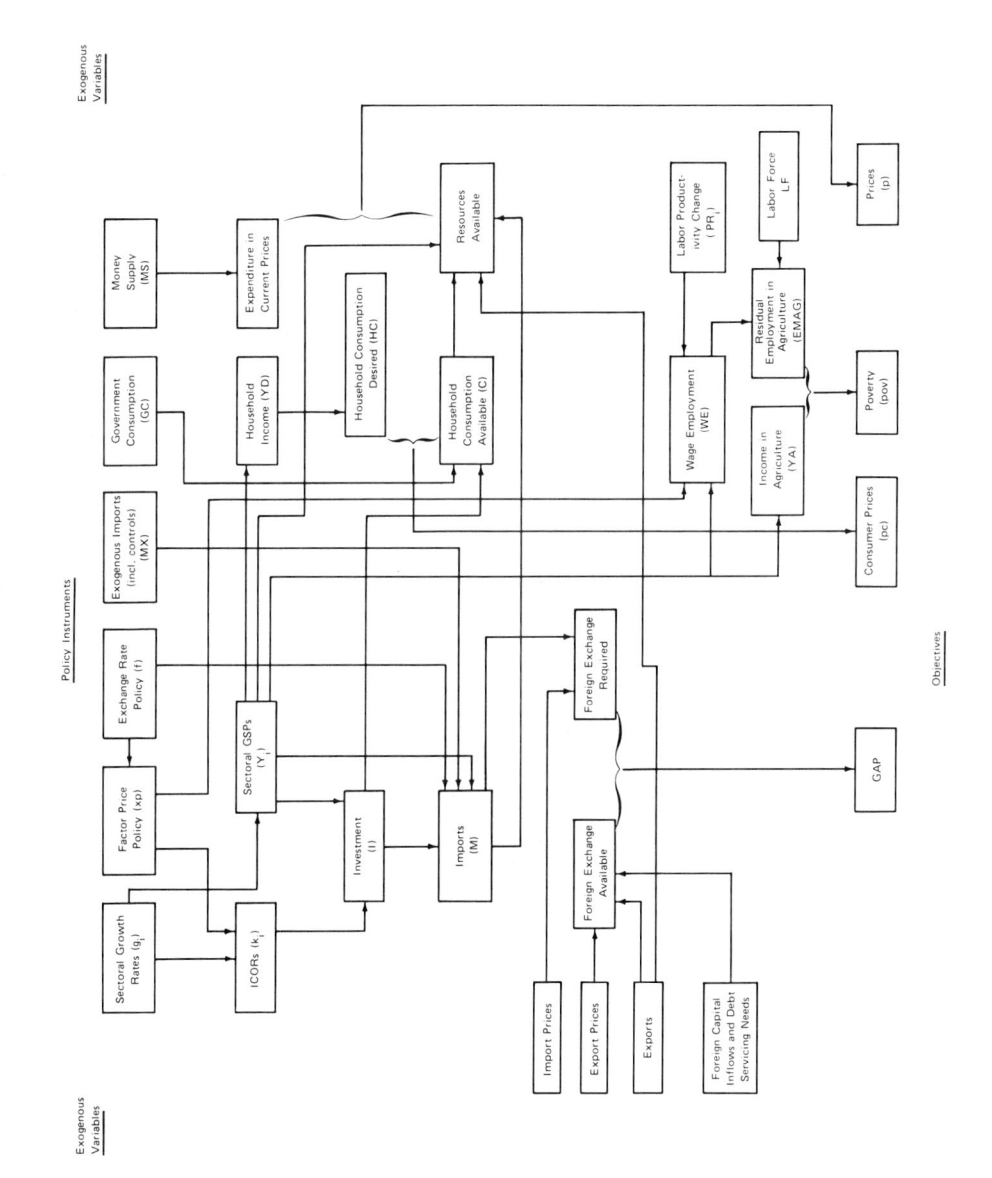

CHART II
WORLD SUPPLY AND DEMAND FOR COFFEE

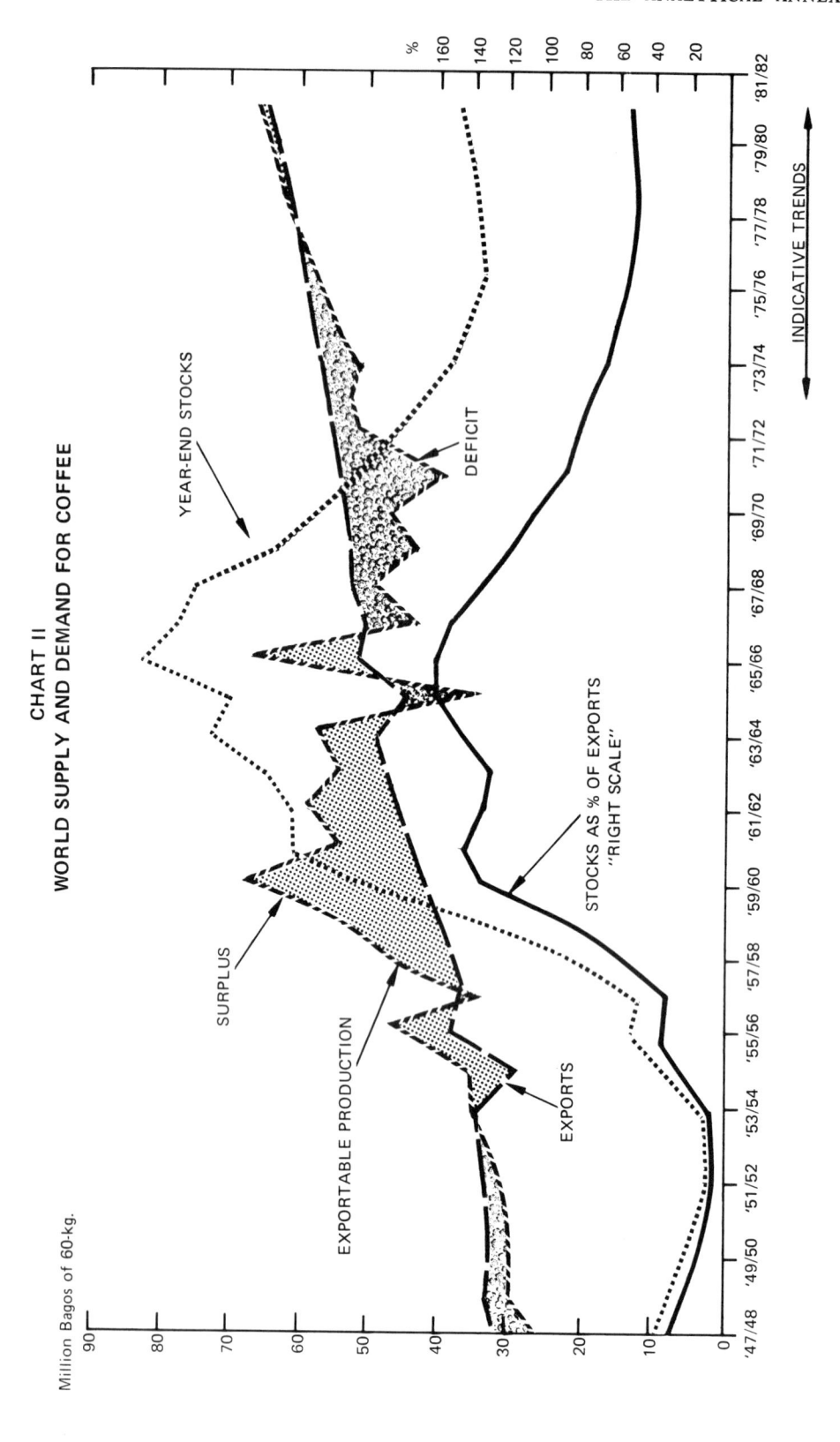

CHART III
ANNUAL AVERAGE TEA PRICES FOR SELECTED COUNTRIES AT LONDON AUCTIONS, 1955–1973
(NEW PENCE PER KILOGRAM)

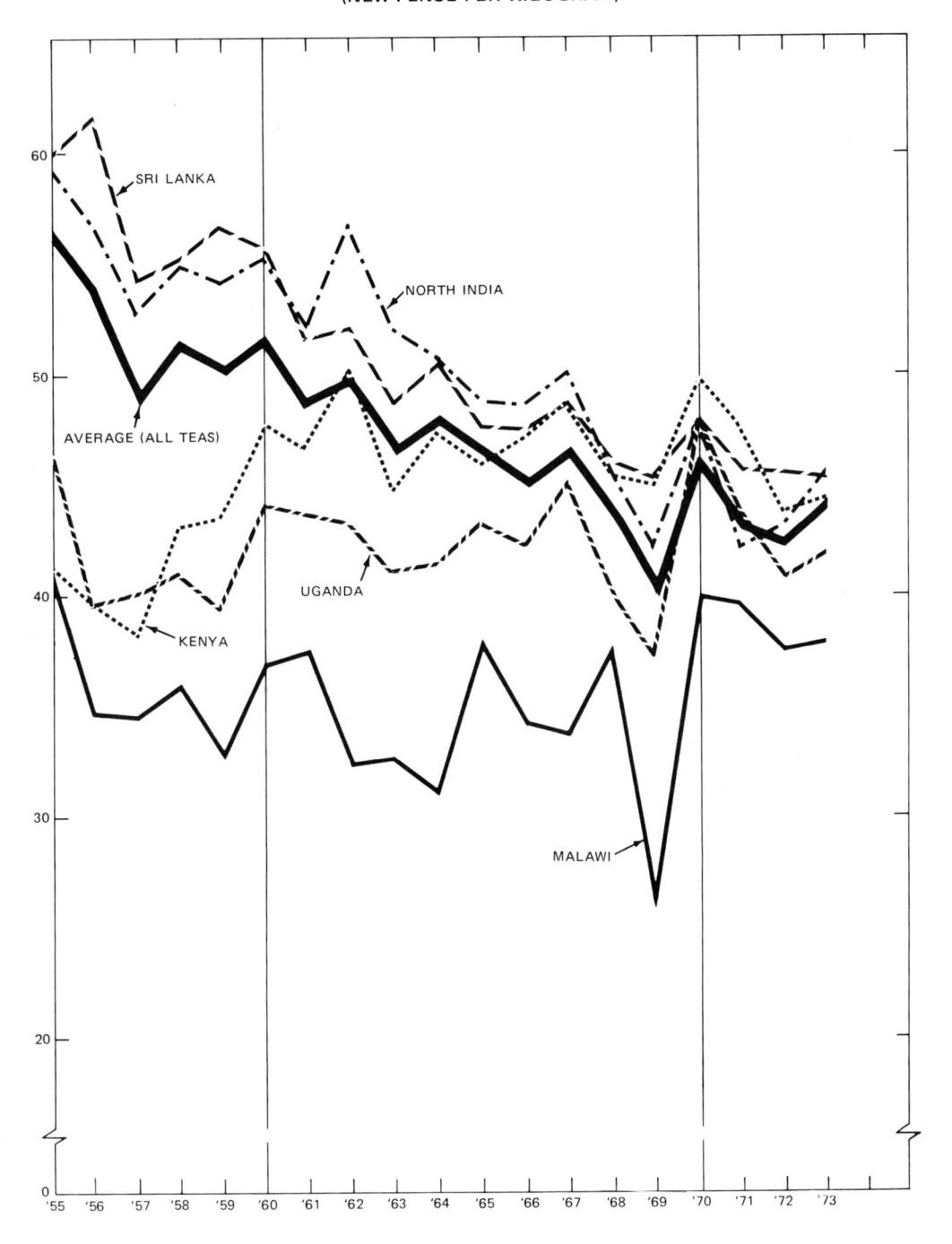

Annex Two

Fiscal Policy for Development

CHAPTER 1

INTRODUCTION

The Public Sector in the Kenyan Economy

The public sector in Kenya consists of the Central Government, various levels of local government, and a wide range of parastatal organizations, including the statutory agricultural boards. In addition, the East African Community (EAC) plays a significant role in the Kenyan economy, particularly through the operations of the common service corporations. It is not intended in this annex to provide a lengthy analysis of the role of the public sector in the total economy. However, we shall try to put the subsequent discussion into context in this introduction by referring to some of the major macro-economic indicators and summarizing the primary underlying economic relationships.

Macro-economic Indicators

While the public sector has not been as dominant in Kenya as in many African countries, its role and influence on the economy has been growing since Independence. Moreover, *within* the public sector, the importance of the Central Government has tended to increase relative to the other parts of the public sector. Most of the available indicators bear evidence of these two trends.

The public sector's contribution to *value-added* has increased from less than 25 percent in 1964 to over 30 percent by 1972 (Table 1). The fastest rate of growth was in Central Government, while the role of local government fell sharply after 1970, when the Central Government took over the most important functions of the rural county councils. The relative importance of the public enterprises has not changed since Independence, although they now account for over 22 percent of the total value-added in the enterprise sector of the economy.

The increasing importance of the public sector is also shown by the statistics of *capital formation*, where the public sector's share has risen from about 25 percent to over 38 percent between 1964 and 1972 (Table 2). Again, the Central Government was the principal agent of growth, having expanded its share of public sector investment from 35 percent to 60 percent.

The growth of the public sector, in terms of both consumption and capital formation, has generated an increasing demand for *imports*, as shown in Table 3. The absolute level of public sector imports has more than doubled between 1964/65 and 1971/72, while "general government" imports have nearly tripled. However, while the overall growth of public sector activity has led to a rapid expansion in the absolute level of government imports, the public sector's share of imports has not increased. In fact, after rising quite sharply soon after Independence, the public sector's share of imports has fallen every year since 1966/67 and, by 1971/72, has returned to about the same level (10 to 11 percent) as in 1964/65. A similar trend is found in the relationship between public sector imports and value-added in the public sector, which indicates that the average import intensity of the public sector has not increased over the period.[1]

---

1. "General Government" imports constituted only 4 to 5 percent of total imports during the period, and there were also no significant changes in the import intensity of either general Government value-added or Central Government expenditure. It should be noted that this information relates only to direct government imports and excludes public sector purchases of imported goods from domestic suppliers. The actual import content of public sector activity will therefore be greater than these figures imply.

Finally, in view of the public sector's increasing role, it is clearly important to indicate its contribution to *employment*. The public sector has traditionally been an important employer in the "modern sector", and its share of employment has been increasing since 1964, roughly in proportion to its share of value-added. Nearly all of the employment increase was in the Central Government, particularly since the transfer of functions from the local authorities in 1970. By 1972, the Central Government employed one out of every four wage earners in the modern economy (Table 4).

It follows that a substantial proportion of the *wage bill* in the economy is borne by public budgets. About 22 percent of the wage bill in the modern sector is paid by central and local government, and another 12 percent by the parastatals and the EAC institutions in Kenya (Table 5). While average government earnings still lag behind those in the formal urban sector (Table 6), they are generous when compared with wages in agriculture and the average per capita income in the economy as a whole.[2] Moreover, government salaries have tended to catch up with those in private industry and trade (the real wage setters) in recent years. Thus, average government earnings have increased by 50 percent in nine years, or at an average rate of about 5 percent a year.[3]

In summing up the macro-economic indicators, in Kenya central and local government alone accounted for about 16 percent of value-added in 1972, about 28 percent of investment, 28 percent of wage employment, 25 percent of the wage bill in the economy, and about 5 percent of the country's imports. To these findings must be added the role of the statutory boards and parastatal enterprises which, in 1972, accounted for another 15 percent of value-added, 8 percent of investment, 10 percent of wage employment as well as the wage bill in the economy—altogether far from an insignificant sector in the Kenyan economy.[4]

Financial Indicators

Certain other indicators may now be emphasized to highlight further the importance of the general government and parastatals in the economy. The *revenues mobilized* by the central and local governments were about 33 percent of the monetary GDP in 1971/72, and *total government expenditure* about 32 percent. Both proportions have increased significantly in recent years (Table 7). In particular, Central Government investment expenditure[5] has increased from 18 percent of total spending in the midsixties to 32 percent in the early seventies. Table 15, which gives the cross-section data on revenue and expenditures of various governments in other developing countries, confirms that the relative role of Central Government in Kenya is, indeed, significant.

The parastatal sector has always been an important instrument of government investment effort in Kenya. In 1965/66, the Central Government invested almost half of its development outlay through the parastatals. Although this proportion has declined

---

2. The average wage of the government employee in 1972 was about six times the per capita income of about £50. Besides, the civil servants in Kenya also received medical benefits and housing provided by the Government. The input value of these benefits has been estimated by the Ministry of Finance and Planning to be about 9 percent of total government consumption.

3. Wages in private industry and commerce have always been somewhat higher than in government. This gap has narrowed over time however, from more than 30 percent in 1963, when the average wage in private industry was £266, to about 25 percent in 1972, when the average wage was £377 (Table 6).

4. No mention is made here of the control and regulation of the rest of the economy which the Government exercises in the interest of various national objectives. An analysis and appraisal of these form the subject matter of Annex Three.

5. The term "investment expenditure" is used in this report as synonymous with the national accounting concept of capital expenditures. The estimates of capital expenditure, made by the Central Bureau of Statistics, are quite distinct from the development expenditure estimates given in the budget documents.

since, it still was close to 35 percent in 1970/71 (Table 28). In contrast, the parastatals have contributed no more than between 5 and 6 percent of the total government revenues. Therefore, the parastatals have played a limited role in resource mobilization, largely because generally they have not been operated as profit-making enterprises. Moreover, a large part of government investment in parastatals, at least up until recently, has taken the form of loans rather than equity.

Central Government Finances

Tables 8 and 9 set out the overall financial position of the Central Government since 1964/65 and suggest two distinct periods in terms of budgetary performance—one between 1964/65 and 1970/71 and the other since 1971/72.

1964/65 to 1970/71

This period was marked by very rapid growth of revenues and the generation of substantial government savings. Table 9 shows that during the period 1964/65 and 1970/71, recurrent revenues of the Government grew at over 16 percent a year, while recurrent expenditures grew at only 10 percent. Therefore, at the margin, Government saved about 39 percent of its growing income, and its average savings rate turned from −5 percent in 1964/65 to +45 percent in 1970/71. This was a remarkable performance.

Government also expanded its investment effort substantially—with the result that even rapidly growing government savings proved inadequate. Government savings could finance only about one-quarter of capital expenditures over the whole period, and another 43 percent had to be financed by net foreign capital. Thus, while the Kenya Government was unable to mobilize sufficient savings to finance its burgeoning investment program, it did make impressive efforts in this direction. Recurrent savings as percent of capital expenditure increased from −24 percent in 1965/66 to +53 percent in 1970/71. Correspondingly, dependence on foreign aid was reduced from 95 percent to 22 percent.

During the whole of this period, the Kenya Government did not borrow anything from the Central Bank (Table 10); instead the Government had a positive outstanding balance with the Central Bank. The Government's deposits increased from £3 million in December 1967, to £16 million in June 1970, to £22 million in June 1971. Against these deposits, the Central Bank's holdings of Kenya Government securities and treasury bills (as well as advances) were only £3 million in December 1967, £8 million in June 1970, and £15 million in June 1971.[6] Thus, as an overall policy, the Kenya Government built up a large cash balance with the Central Bank, while financing a significant proportion of its own expenditures from net foreign borrowings.

The rapid growth of revenues, the accelerating investment effort, and the sustained high level of domestic savings during these early years of Independence are all creditworthy achievements. The fact that Kenya was able to do this without recourse to deficit financing and without increasing her relative dependence on foreign savings is a remarkable achievement.

1971/72 and 1972/73

Since 1970/71, however, the high momentum of the Central Government budget has been lost. Annual growth of recurrent revenues has been less than 9 percent, while

---

6. Central Bank of Kenya, *Economic and Financial Review,* Vol. V, No. 1 (July-September 1972), p. 11.

recurrent expenditures have grown at about 17 percent per annum. The average savings rate (savings as percent of revenues) of the Government has come down from a high of 19 percent in 1970/71 to 6 percent in 1972/73, and marginal savings have been negative.

While the growth of government investment has been maintained at the past rate of about 27 percent a year, the role of budgetary savings in financing government capital expenditure has declined—from 53 percent in 1970/71 to 16 percent in 1972/73. Consequently, the dependence of the budget on foreign capital and deficit financing has increased. In 1972/73, about one-third of capital expenditure by the Government was financed through net foreign borrowings and another 17 percent through the Central Bank.

The financing of capital expenditure through the Central Bank is a new phenomenon in Kenya's budgetary history. Whereas before 1970/71, the Central Government was a net creditor to the Central Bank, in the last two fiscal years, the Government has financed almost one-fifth of its capital expenditure by drawing upon its cash reserves.[7] A detailed analysis of the Central Government finances is presented in Chapter 2; the brief and sketchy overview given here only highlights certain policy issues which will be indicated before the end of this chapter.

Local Government Finances

As suggested by Table 7, local authorities played an important role in Kenya up until 1968/69. They spent about 20 percent of the total expenditures of central and local governments combined. However, from the very beginning the financial position of the local authorities, particularly the county councils, was weak. Between 1966 and 1968, while revenues of the local authorities remained constant, their recurrent expenditures increased by approximately 25 percent. As a result, local authorities' recurrent deficits doubled in two years, and a very large part of these deficits had to be financed through Central Government grants (Table 24). But in 1968, almost 50 percent of the overall budget deficit of the local authorities was financed through overdrafts and drawing down of reserves.

Such a financial position could clearly not be sustained for long. Besides, it was not clear whether the county (nonmunicipal) councils in particular had the necessary capability and discipline to manage such large funds. In these circumstances, the Central Government considered it advisable to take over some of the major expenditure and revenue functions of the county councils. In 1970, the expenditure functions of primary education, health services, and road maintenance, as well as the levy of the graduated personal tax (GPT), was transferred from county councils to the Central Government. As a result, the local authorities altogether earned a marginal (current) surplus and their overall budget deficit was reduced sharply. In 1972, the local authorities still show a positive current surplus although their overall deficit has now grown once more. In 1973/74 the GPT was abolished. The implications of this for local authorities will be discussed later.

Major Policy Issues

The Central Government budget has, in more recent years, started showing the strains of rapid development. The growth rate of recurrent expenditure has accelerated,

---

7. This was in addition to short term borrowings made possible by the recent amendment to the Central Bank of Kenya Act, which increased the limit on Central Bank's advances to the Government from £12 million set in 1966 to 25 percent of its gross recurrent revenues. For 1972/73, the new limit would permit a borrowing level close to £30 million, compared with actual net borrowing of £6.6 million in 1970/71 and £17.4 million in 1971/72.

while the pace of capital expenditure has continued unabated. This situation raises certain crucial policy questions, particularly in the context of the Third Plan. Why have the trends of 1964/65–1970/71 been reversed? Has the buoyancy of the existing tax structure been exhausted? What reforms in the tax structure can be undertaken to revitalize revenue elasticity? Have the recurrent expenditures got out of control in any structural fashion? Can the Government investment program be sustained without generating additional savings? Can the parastatals play a role in mobilizing resources, as well as in development? What role can be assigned to the local authorities in the development process? How can these levels of government be made financially viable?

All of these questions, which relate to development finance, must be answered if a feasible role for the public sector as an agent of economic development is to be defined over the next plan period. But development expenditure on economic growth is only one, albeit major, national objective. The 1974–78 Plan, and the period beyond, must also aim at other major goals—social justice, income redistribution, employment generation, rural development, and export promotion to mention some. Government's fiscal policy can and should play an important role in the achievement of these objectives as well.

Therefore, we shall pose a further set of questions. What role has the Government tax policy played in the past in income redistribution? What has been the role of the allocation of important public services in reducing inequalities? How far have local authorities, which up until recently were responsible for the education and health services at the grass root level, been able to spread the benefits of public services? What is the likely effect of the recent centralization of these services in terms of their effectiveness and distribution among areas and regions? How far does the existing fiscal structure of Kenya have the potential of being redistributive?

More recently, growing unemployment, particularly in the urban areas, has become a major concern of the Kenya Government. What role can fiscal policy play in generating employment and increasing incomes among the poor? What tax reforms seem to be particularly suitable for this purpose? What role needs to be assigned to rural development in the allocation of plan resources? How do agricultural marketing boards and other parastatal bodies fit into the aims of rural development and agricultural-based exports?

These are some of the major policy issues which the Government would have to attend to in planning for the future. What follows only lays down a framework for the analysis of these issues rather than provides answers for them. The next three chapters will consider the questions of Development Finance, Income Distribution, and Employment and Rural Development, while the last chapter will suggest the need for the scope of fiscal reforms and strategy.

Chapter 2

Development Finance

The preceding chapter noted that in the two years immediately after Independence, net foreign borrowings were the only means by which the Government could finance its capital budget. The domestic capital market was just about absent then and the Government on its own was a net dissaver. Of course, its development effort at that time was also relatively small—capital expenditure was approximately 15 percent of the total budget and 3 percent of the GDP at factor cost.

Since then, the Kenya Government has consistently reduced its dependence on net foreign borrowings by consciously developing the domestic capital market and making increasingly larger use of the banking system, and improving its own savings effort. Various sources of development finance are therefore available to the Government in financing further development. Now, we shall first look at the savings performance of the Central Government and other parts of the public sector; we shall then go on to review other sources of funds which might be tapped to finance the development program.

Public Sector Savings

Central Government as a Saver

Tables 9 and 11 highlight the savings performance of the Central Government. Starting with a dissaving of significant amount after Independence, the Kenya Government has built up an impressive savings rate. Over the period 1964/65 to 1970/71, the marginal savings rate of the Central Government was close to 40 percent, and the average savings rate about 6 percent (Table 9). Central Government savings consistently increased during the sixties, and in 1970/71 they accounted for 22 percent of national savings and about 5 percent of GDP (Table 15). Between 1964/65–1970/71, government savings financed an average of about 24 percent of capital expenditures, which themselves were growing at a rate of about 27 percent a year.

This tremendous savings performance was obviously the result of an impressive tax effort by the Government. During 1964/65 and 1970/71, government revenues grew at over 16 percent a year, while recurrent expenditures grew at only 10 percent. As noted in Chapter 1, Kenya's budgetary performance during this period was remarkable. Since 1970/71, however, the budgetary situation has changed. The growth rate of revenues has recently slowed down[1]—from a peak of around 25 percent in 1970/71 to about 4 percent in 1972/73—while the growth rate of recurrent expenditure has increased. Against the average revenue growth of around 9 percent in the last two years, the average recurrent expenditure growth has been about 17 percent. As a result, the marginal savings rate has declined significantly. Government capital expenditure has tended to grow, as in the past, at about 20 percent a year, but is now increasingly financed by net foreign capital inflows and by borrowing from the Central Bank. Government's own savings are expected to finance only 13 percent of capital expenditures in 1972/73 against about 53 percent in 1970/71.

Thus, there has been a sharp turn in government savings performance since 1970/71. An explanation of this turnaround can be sought within the framework of Government's revenue efforts and expenditure pattern.

---

1. Recent restrictions on imports, particularly consumer durables carrying higher customer duties, plus the general slowdown of the manufacturing sector due to credit restrictions, have seriously affected the receipts from custom duties.

Revenue Performance. Tables 12 and 13 reflect the impressive revenue performance of the Government. In 1964/65, the Central Government raised about 20 percent of monetary GDP in the form of revenues, and this was gradually increased to over 30 percent in 1971/72. Even as a proportion of total (monetary and nonmonetary) GDP, government revenues increased from 15 percent in 1964/65 to about 24 percent in 1971/72.[2]

Government's tax effort since Independence has been directed towards first, increasing the proportion of tax revenues in monetary GDP; and second, bringing about structural changes in the tax structure. Table 13 highlights both these trends.

The Kenya Government increased its tax revenues significantly between 1964/65 and 1971/72, and tax revenues as a proportion of monetary GDP grew from 16 to 23 percent. This increase was achieved by progressively raising the average burden of all taxes, except for import duties. The nominal rates of East African import duties were also raised within the Community, but the increases were just about enough to offset the shift in the composition of imports towards lower duty items, so that the average burden of import duties hardly changed.

The average rate of taxes on (factor) incomes increased from around 6 percent in 1964/65 to 10 percent in 1971/72. The chief elements in income tax reform were the reduction of personal allowances and the revisions in child allowances in 1965/66, introduction of "Pay-as-you-Earn" in 1966/67, and changes in the timing of income tax payments, as well as revisions in the rate structure, in 1970/71 and again in 1971/72 and 1973/74.

The effective rate of personal income tax was more than doubled—from about 4 percent in 1964/65 to about 9 percent in 1971/72. In addition, although less significant, company tax rates were raised from 35 to 40 percent and, more recently, withholding taxes have been levied on dividends, interest, and rent of nonresident companies. Thus, income tax in general, and personal income tax in particular, has been the major source of additional revenue to the Central Government and the public sector as a whole.

The burden of indirect taxes on domestic output was also consistently raised over time. The average burden of taxes on (private) consumption was raised from 3 percent to more than 5 percent between 1964/65 and 1971/72,[3] largely through the upward revisions of excise duty rates and the widening of the excise duty net to include new commodities. Consumption taxes were levied for the first time in 1971/72, and further extended in 1972/73. For the most part, these consumption taxes have now been replaced by a sales tax on manufactures, to which we refer later. This consumption will now be taxed on an ad valorem basis, rather than a specific one, and the sales tax will be more broadly based. It may be expected that this broader base will improve the built-in elasticity of expenditure taxation.[4]

As a result of these efforts, there took place a structural shift in government revenues: the share of direct taxes increased significantly, while the share of indirect taxes fell. Today, Kenya's reliance on indirect taxes is one of the lowest in the developing world. A major element in the increase in direct taxation was the income tax whose share increased from roughly 34 to 44 percent,[5] while there was a decline in the share of import duties. The structural shift towards an increased reliance on direct taxes (partic-

---

2. A cross-section regression suggests a "norm" of revenue effort of 16 percent for a country with ten million population and GNP per capita of US$100. Thus it would appear that Kenya's performance surpasses this cross-section "norm".

3. Annex One has found the following equation for the period since Independence:
Excise Duty Revenues $= -3.18 + 0.046$ (Monetary GDP).

4. However, the revenue effect of this change may at first be negative, since the sales tax revenues will have to be shared with local authorities. (see p. 176).

5. This is the highest proportion among all African countries, excluding Liberia, as well as Asian countries, excluding Burma. Only some countries in Latin America have achieved such a degree of income taxation.

ularly personal income tax) had significant implications for the built-in elasticity of tax revenues.

Built-in Elasticity of Taxation. Table 14 emphasizes how successful the Government's tax efforts were in producing buoyant revenue sources. At the margin, Government taxed about 30 percent of the monetary GDP (and 25 percent of total GDP) every year between 1963/65 and 1971/72. Consequently, the *buoyancy* of tax revenues was 2.0 with respect to monetary GDP and 2.2 with respect to total GDP (Table 14)—a very impressive achievement, indeed, in the light of the experience of other developing countries.[6]

However, a substantial part of this buoyancy was the product of structural changes, such as revisions in tax rates, tax base, exemptions, and deductions, referred to earlier. An estimate made in the Ministry of Finance and Planning suggests that of the £105 million of tax revenues raised in 1971/72, about £31 million (or 30 percent) were the result of tax revisions undertaken by the Government since Independence. (This estimate is probably on the low side, since it is based on anticipated revenue, rather than actual revenue, which, as Table 16 suggests, has usually been higher.) But even allowing for the revenue effects of these tax revisions, the built-in elasticity of tax revenues is estimated to be 1.2 with respect to monetary GDP[7] and 1.3 with respect to total GDP for the period since Independence. There are very few developing countries which can boast of a built-in elasticity of more than unity.

Recurrent Expenditures. In practice, even an elastic tax structure would not remain an instrument of government savings for long if government consumption grows at a rate equal to or more than the growth rate of revenues; consequently, keeping a watch on the recurrent budget is absolutely essential. In many African countries, recurrent expenditure on administration and defense has been claiming an increasingly larger share of government resources in recent years. In Kenya, fortunately, this has not occurred. Tables 17 and 18, which give the data on the functional classification of recurrent expenditures, suggest that allocation of the Government's recurrent budget has changed little since Independence—except for a large increase in the share going to education. The recent upsurge in education expenditure is due to the Central Government's takeover of primary education from the county councils, but the budget data indicates that education has always had priority over all other allocations, including that for agriculture.

It is, of course, possible, under certain conditions, for Government to lose control over its own rate of consumption. Some of those conditions are now starting to appear in Kenya for the first time. The first condition arises when the major components of

---

6. The following figures of tax buoyancy in twenty developing countries in 1971 shows that very few equalled Kenya's performance:

Argentina	1.6	Indonesia	1.1	Peru	1.3
Brazil	1.3	Israel	1.7	Sri Lanka	1.1 (1970)
Cameroon	1.7 (1970)	Jamaica	2.1	Thailand	0.8
Costa Rica	1.4	Korea	1.2	Uganda	1.7
Ethiopia	0.5	Mexico	2.2	Venezuela	2.2
Gabon	1.8 (1970)	Pakistan	1.5 (1970)	Zaire	0.8 (1970)
Guatemala	1.2	Panama	1.4		

7. This is composed of the following built-in elasticities of major individual taxes with respect to monetary GDP:

Personal income tax	1.6 − 1.7
Company tax	0.8
Excise duties	1.3 − 1.4
Import duties (elasticity with respect to net commercial imports)	0.5
Other indirect taxes	1.1
GPT	0.4

recurrent expenditure have an income elasticity of demand greater than unity. In Kenya, education is the outstanding example of a service which has claimed an ever increasing proportion of the recurrent budget, and which now appears to absorb a disproportionate share of national resources.[8] Clearly, the past rate of increase in education expenditure is unsustainable in the long run. And yet the fact is that, given the present wage differentials, the return on, and consequently, the demand for, education is so great[9] that the Government will find it extremely difficult to control the continued demand for schooling. Therefore, unless the Government takes firm action in this regard, income elasticity of demand for education might force the Government recurrent budget completely out-of-gear.

The second dangerous condition could arise if the Government (as the largest single employer of labor force in the economy) is forced to expand its payroll under political pressure. This could be a real risk if the private sector fails to absorb the growing labor force, and open unemployment becomes more prevalent. So far, the Government has not resorted to public sector employment creation, except during the Tripartite Agreements and for specific purposes, such as famine relief. But there has been mounting concern, in Government and among the people, as unemployment in Kenya has grown. Unless better solutions can be found, there will be an increasing danger of the public sector being obliged to take on the role of employer of last resort (especially for school leavers). Unfortunately, such an expedient, while having little impact on employment or output, would have serious consequences for the budget.

A somewhat related risk is that wages will continue to increase in the private sector in the absence of policy reform, and that government salaries will be drawn up after them, with further adverse effects both for budget and income distribution. This question is discussed in Annex Three. We have assumed a 4 percent annual rate of "creep" in civil service salaries (see Appendix), but the rate could be much faster if wages and incomes in the economy as a whole are not controlled. In the past, government employees were able to get their salary structure reviewed twice (in 1967 and in 1971) and their average earnings have increased by about 50 percent since Independence (Table 5).

Third, if capital expenditures grow very rapidly, particularly in those sectors for which the recurrent expenditure commitments are heavy, this could significantly affect the growth rate of recurrent expenditures and consequently government savings.[10] The rapid growth of capital expenditure in Kenya—about 25 percent per annum since Independence—has already been mentioned. It may be pointed out that capital expenditures in the current plan period have far exceeded the targets. The Second Plan proposed a capital outlay of £180 million (in constant prices) between 1969/70 and 1973/74. Against this, the actual capital expenditure (in current prices) has already been £195 million during the first four years of the Plan.[11] The annual capital expenditure thus more than doubled during the three years 1969/70 and 1972/73.

8. The following data for 1971 compare the share of education in the Kenya recurrent budget with that in other countries:

Burma	16.3	Malagasy Republic	19.1
Cameroon	11.1 (1970)	Malaysia	20.7 (1970)
Gabon	7.8	Rwanda	28.0
Iran	7.2	Sierra Leone	19.1
Iraq	16.6	Sri Lanka	15.1
Kenya	26.9	Sudan	7.9

As a proportion of GDP, Kenya's expenditure on education is among the highest in the world (see Table 15).

9. For further discussion, see Annex Three.

10. Rapid growth of capital expenditures also has serious implications for the balance of payments.

11. A part of this expansion must be illusory in view of the rapid rise in the import prices.

Tables 19 and 20 suggest that in Kenya there has been a heavy bias towards general, community, and social services, at the expense of economic services. The former three services, which accounted for about 35 percent of total capital expenditures in 1964/65, accounted for over 70 percent in 1971/72. Given the fact that general, community, and social services normally involve a large recurrent expenditure commitment,[12] the rapidity with which these services are growing could have serious implications for government savings.

The Kenya Government thus faces a potential situation where its recurrent expenditures could grow faster than its revenues, particularly if the buoyancy of revenues is seriously reduced for one reason or another. Perhaps the fiscal situation of the last two years is symptomatic of all factors at work in an embryonic stage. While the salary increase of 1971 and 1972 is the visible factor in the high growth rate of recurrent expenditures (estimated to have increased the government wage bill by about £10 million), rapid increases in recurrent expenditure on education (which grew almost 50 percent over the last two years) and in capital expenditures, are also relevant. The effect of rapidly growing capital expenditures on recurrent expenditures must have been large from the beginning, and it is likely to become even greater in the next few years if inflation continues. As mentioned earlier, the slowdown in revenue growth, caused by the adverse impact of import restrictions, was yet another contributory factor to the recent fiscal situation.

It may be worthwhile, therefore, to estimate what the built-in growth rate of recurrent expenditures might be under normal conditions. This should in no circumstances be considered as minimum or desirable. An estimate of the "normal" or "built-in" growth rate of recurrent expenditure for the Kenya Government can be developed using the economic classification of recurrent expenditures in Table 21. It appears that presently some 50 percent of Central Government recurrent spending is on wages and salaries, about 25 percent on purchases of "other" goods and services, and another 25 percent on transfers of various kinds (including interest). In estimating the future built-in growth rate, the mission assumed that the government wage bill increases by 9 percent a year (5 percent employment growth, plus 4 percent salary "creep"); that government consumption on goods and services grows by 12 percent a year (7 percent real growth, plus 5 percent price inflation); and that transfer payments grow by 2 percent a year.[13]

All told, it is estimated that the growth rate of recurrent expenditures could be about 8 percent a year on reasonable assumptions about future trends. This growth rate could go to 10 percent per annum if some increase in real wages is allowed to compensate for an increase in productivity. This compares reasonably well with the average growth rate of about 9 percent per annum realized during the 1964/65 to 1969/70 period. However, the annual increase in recurrent expenditure of about 17 percent experienced in recent years has been far above the built-in increase, and the most recent data suggest that this fast growth rate may continue,[14] possibly indicating that a structural shift has taken place in the level and growth rate of recurrent expenditures.

Projections of Central Government Savings. The preceding analysis provides the necessary information to make an *illustrative* set of projections (Table 23) of govern-

---

12. For example, education and health sectors have been found to cause 33 percent and 25 percent respectively of recurrent expenditure for every pound of government investment in these sectors, against 10 percent in agriculture and electricity. See Peter S. Heller, "The Dynamics of Project Expenditures and the Planning Process: With Reference to Kenya," (Harvard University, Ph.D. thesis, November 1971), p. 6, Tables 1–2. This finding is fairly consistent with the official position given in *African Socialism,* p. 34.

13. For a detailed description of these assumptions, see the appendix to this annex.

14. For 1973/74, recurrent expenditure is budgeted at £154 million, which is about 12 percent higher than the outcome of 1972/73. If the past is any indicator (Table 16), the actual recurrent expenditure in 1973/74 would exceed £154 million by at least £5 million if not more.

ment savings and investment at an aggregative level. For these projections it is assumed that GDP will grow at 12 percent per annum at current prices (or at 7 percent at constant prices). For the purposes of the analysis, we compare the likely consequences of two alternative fiscal policies.

One extreme is that the Government may decide to continue its past fiscal policy, in which case the overall budget deficit is likely to grow from about £60 million in 1972/73 to about £200 million in 1977/78, intensifying the current budgetary problems to unmanageable proportions. Annex One, which projects the trends in government revenues and expenditures in a much more disaggregated fashion than has been done here, also suggests a similar conclusion.

The other extreme is that if the Government takes early action to improve the fiscal situation, there is no reason why a rapid pace of development could not be maintained. One "package" of reforms, for example, might comprise the following government actions:

- improve the overall elasticity of the existing tax structure from 1.3 to 1.9 (instead of continuously proposing tax revisions similar to those of the period 1967/68 to 1971/72);
- limit the growth rate of recurrent expenditures to the built-in level of 8 percent per annum; and
- slow down the growth rate of capital expenditure from 25 percent per annum to about 15 percent per annum over the next five years,[15] either simultaneously improve the efficiency of government investments and change the investment pattern from more capital intensive projects like those of roads, or to less capital intensive projects like those of rural development.[16]

In theory, if all these policy changes were brought about simultaneously, the Kenya Government could finance all its investment from its own savings by 1976/77, which, of course, does not necessarily mean that this would be its wisest course.

Reality lies somewhere in between these two extremes. The sensitivity analysis done on the foregoing assumptions suggests that an effort to improve revenue elasticity is the most crucial of all the suggested measures. Should the Government simply focus on improving the revenue elasticity and nothing else, it would be able to increase the financing of its capital expenditures from the present 12 percent to more than 50 percent in 1977/78.

The 1973/74 budget has made substantial moves in this direction. Introduction of the general sales tax and lowering of income tax exemption limits will have important effects on revenue generation. The sales tax should have a built-in elasticity of close to unity (see Chapter 5) while the reform in income tax, which accounts for some 40 percent of tax revenues should improve the built-in elasticity of personal income tax greatly. The mission expects that in the long run the impact of these two reforms on the overall built-in elasticity of taxation, which is presently a little over unity, should be more than marginal.

Local Authorities as Savers

Local authorities in Kenya have never been important savers; in fact many of them, particularly the county councils, have been dissavers. The financial position of the local authorities has always been vulnerable because, while their responsibilties have grown in

15. The Government may already have initiated this policy. The development expenditure proposed for 1973/74 is similar to the capital expenditure which was achieved in 1972/73.
16. The interrelationship between the changes in the composition of government investment and growth rate of recurrent expenditure must be stressed here. A shift to rural development would probably imply a higher level of recurrent expenditure in future.

line with population and standards of living, they have never had an elastic source of revenue. Moreover, some of the service fees that they can charge are dictated by political rather than economic considerations.

In Kenya there are two categories of local authorities—municipal or urban councils (eleven of them), and county or rural councils (thirty-eight of them). Both categories are required to provide local services such as housing, water supplies and sewerage, fire protection, welfare services, public libraries, public transport, markets and inspection centers for grading and storing of produce. Local authorities are also responsible for land conservation and wildlife.[17] In addition, municipal councils provide primary education, health clinics, dispensaries and other medical services, and road construction and maintenance. Local authorities, as already mentioned, have only a limited revenue base to finance these very important public services and these funds are inadequate for the purpose. Local authorities can levy rates (or property taxes) and cesses, and impose license fees, but none of these sources of revenue is very elastic.[18] They can also charge for the provision of water and sewerage, public markets, slaughter houses, and other services. In addition, municipal councils charge school fees,[19] which have been predetermined by the Central Government. Similarly, health facilities are provided free of charge following the policy decision of the Central Government.[20]

County Councils. Until 1969, there was no distinction between municipalities and county councils in terms of the services they provided, nor in the taxes and charges they levied. But, by 1969 almost all the county councils had got themselves into grave financial difficulties. Tax administration was lax,[21] arrears were growing, and financial and expenditure control had become wholly inadequate.[22] As a result, recurrent budget deficits of the county councils were growing very rapidly, from £3 million in 1966 to about £6 million in 1968, or 70 percent of their own revenues. If fully provided from out of the central government budget, the 1968 deficit would have absorbed about 8 percent of central government revenue.[23]

Such a situation clearly could not be tolerated for long. The Central Government could have helped the local authorities to improve their tax administration and expenditure control, but instead the Government decided to take over their more important functions.[24] On January 1, 1970, therefore, the Government took over education, health,

---

17. In the *Local Government Regulations,* some fifty public services are listed as coming under the jurisdiction of the local authorities.

18. The marginal rate of direct and indirect taxes of local governments, with respect to monetary GDP, is extremely small. Annex One found the following relationships: (a) direct taxes of municipal and county councils = 1.18 + 0.008 (Monetary GDP); (b) other receipts of municipal and county councils = 0.009 (Monetary GDP).

19. Until 1973, local authorities levied a Graduated Personal Tax (GPT) as well. This tax was abolished January 1, 1974, thus reducing the elasticity of municipal taxation still further.

20. This is not strictly true because the Central Government does charge a "hospital contribution" of £6 from taxpayers whose taxable incomes exceed £1,000, and £12 from those whose taxable incomes exceed £2,000. These revenues are earmarked.

21. Despite the powers given to the Minister of Local Government (under the *Graduated Personal Tax (Imposition of Sanctions) Regulations, 1965)* to withhold grants from those local authorities that do not take adequate steps to improve GPT collections, the situation apparently did not improve.

22. Republic of Kenya, *Report of the Controller and Auditor General on County Councils and Municipal Councils (1972).* The county councils are said to be overstaffed even now. See the *Ndegwa Report,* p. 219.

23. Of course, the Central Government did not meet the whole of the deficit and the local authorities had to resort to bank overdrafts and the use of their provident funds and capital renewal funds. Over time, the local authorities have built up a bank overdraft of £4 million.

24. In centralizing the functions of county councils, the Finance Minister in his 1970/71 budget speech accused them of "mismanagement, dereliction of duty, incompetence, failure to collect revenue, failure to keep accounts, failure to maintain financial control, misuse of funds, and decisions based on local political expediencies" and the minister hoped that centralization would improve the quality and continuity of the services taken over.

and road maintenance from the county councils which had accounted for about 80 percent of their total expenditures (Table 27), and at the same time the Central Government also took away county council authority to levy Graduated Personal Tax[25] and charge school fees, and stopped their road maintenance grants.[26] Consequently, from 1970, the total expenditure of county councils was cut down to one-quarter of its previous level. But, since their revenues had also been cut by one-third, county councils were, for a while, financially viable, though at an extremely truncated level. But the situation has once again started deteriorating, and in 1972 the county councils' administration expenditures alone exceeded the whole of their tax revenues.

It is difficult to know whether centralization of the functions previously undertaken by county councils has made a significant impact on the quantity or quality of local services. Certainly, there is evidence that the Central Government ministries charged with taking over local services have all experienced difficulty absorbing them. For example, while the construction and maintenance of classified roads have undoubtedly improved since they were centralized under the Ministry of Works, neither the Roads Department nor local authorities have any effective program for rural access roads. The transfer of education is difficult to evaluate, since the Central Government's efforts in primary education are focused not on building schools, but on staffing and equipping the schools built by self-help efforts. Here again, it seems that the quality of primary schools is still very low, although the average cost of primary education has increased sharply under the Central Government, mainly because of higher salaries.[27] The takeover of health services from the county councils does seem to have improved the facilities as well as the quality of staff, but at the same time has created serious organizational and coordination problems. Supply of staff and drugs from Nairobi often takes time, provision of many services has to wait for Central Government's approval, and in the meantime it is the local populations that suffers.[28]

It is clearly premature to assess the effectiveness of the centralizing local services. In many county council areas, the services were either nonexistent or deteriorating before 1970, and it is still too early to judge whether Central Government can carry out local services more efficiently than a strengthened and reformed local government structure. Kenya still has a number of critical decisions to make as regards local participation in the provision of services, before the role of local authorities can be adequately defined.

Municipal Councils. Since county councils operate principally in rural areas, where it is their responsibility to bring many services to Kenya's poor, it is hardly surprising that county councils have traditionally operated at a deficit, and have therefore been "dissavers" in the economic sense. Rather more surprising, however, is the fact that municipal councils (which operate in the richest areas of Kenya) have, as a whole, managed to save very little (although in the past they have never depended on Central Government to any great extent).

The combined current surpluses of municipal councils have rarely exceeded £1 million in any given year, and they have often amounted to only £0.5 million. Yet

---

25. *The Local Government (Transfer of Functions) Act, 1969.*
26. Besides the road maintenance grants, the county councils used to receive public health grants, which were also abolished.
27. H. K. Colebatch, "Some Political Implications of Service Provision: Roads and Schools and Health Services." Working Paper No. 79 (Nairobi: Institute for Development Studies, February 1973), p. 8.
28. "Standards seem to have fallen in health centers where drugs are increasingly difficult to obtain and the already deficient manpower situation is being worsened with low morale and resignation among former county council staff who have been transferred to Central Government service in many cases at lower rates of pay." See V. P. Diejomach, "Financing Local Government Authorities in Kenya," Discussion Paper No. 96 (Nairobi: Institute for Development Studies, September 1970), p. 9.

municipal councils have been an important channel for investment in the public sector. In 1966, for example, their combined capital expenditure was almost 10 percent of that of Central Government, and by 1972 this proportion had increased to about 20 percent. With this level of expenditure, and little savings of their own, the municipalities have been obliged to rely on borrowing to an increasing extent. Thus, in 1966 they borrowed about one-third of their capital expenditure, and by 1972 this proportion had increased to about 70 percent.

The Financial Viability of Local Authorities. The Government's attitude towards the future role of local authorities is not yet clear. As mentioned already, difficult decisions have yet to be reached. In particular, it is uncertain whether the past trend towards centralization of services will continue and be entrenched, or whether the Central Government will wish to return some or all local services to a strengthened local government structure at some future time. It is clear, however, that the financial position of local authorities is not adequate even under the present allocation of responsibilities, and that a more satisfactory financial system will have to be sought. Fortunately, there does exist some scope for improving the financial position of local authorities and, provided the Central Government can exert enough control over their expenditures, it appears that the local authorities (at all levels) could be made financially viable.[29]

The Graduated Personal Tax (GPT) formerly levied by the municipal councils was theoretically a good tax[30] except that its rate structure was never really progressive.[31] (In fact, it was regressive beyond £600 per annum.) Its administrative requirements, in terms of continuously assessing the incomes of the small wage earners and self-employed, were also disproportionately large. It is no surprise then that there were serious tax evasions as well as collection problems.[32] These problems were found to be more serious in county council areas, where a greater proportion of income earners are self-employed, than in cities where most urban formal sector wage earners are employed.

It was clear to the Government that if the GPT were to be retained its administration in municipal council areas would have to be tightened. As an alternative solution, the Government has chosen to abolish the tax, and share part of its sales tax revenues with municipal councils. Some form of revenue sharing may help to alleviate the position, although no formula has yet been announced, but would obviously be only a partial solution. The financial autonomy of the municipal councils will still be severely

---

29. "Financial viability" is used here to mean the ability of local authorities to cover their recurrent expenditures through their own sources of revenue, perhaps with some contribution to their capital budgets.

30. It was a hybrid between pool tax and income tax and therefore could have been an elastic source of revenue. As an example, between 1967 and 1971, while the GDP at current prices grew at 10.7 percent per annum, Nairobi's GPT collections grew at about 12.7 percent per annum.

31. The rates of Graduated Personal Tax were as follows:

Income Bracket (£)	Annual Tax (Sh.)	Average Tax Rates (percentage)	Average Tax Rate at Mid-point of Bracket (percentage)
Less than 48	Nil	Nil	Nil
48–96	48	5.00–2.50	3.3
96–144	72	3.75–2.50	3.0
144–204	108	3.75–2.64	3.1
204–312	156	3.82–2.50	3.0
312–420	240	3.85–2.85	3.2
420–516	360	4.29–3.48	3.8
516–600	480	4.65–4.00	4.3
600 and over	600	5% and lower	—

32. An exercise carried out by the Government indicated a collection rate of 50 percent even when an extremely conservative estimate of potential revenue was made. As a matter of fact, the revenues from GPT had always been stable around £6 million since Independence.

limited. In the long run, municipal councils must have their own (elastic) revenue instruments, if they are to exercise a responsible role in the country's development.

One of the most obvious underutilized revenue sources is the rates or property assessments in urban areas.[33] The valuation base for rating purposes in most areas has not been revised since 1959, although property was supposed to be revalued every five years. The increase in market values during this period must be very considerable. What is more, the rates are only levied on *unimproved* values of properties at flat rates ranging between 3 and 7 percent in different areas, although some municipalities have been revising their rates upwards to get more revenues. The scope for raising additional revenue from property rating is enormous, particularly in major urban areas. It would be well worth while for municipalities to put a major emphasis on property revaluation, and for them to move towards the improved value basis of rating which is permissible under the Rating Act.

Then, there is the whole area of service pricing. In most areas where public housing is provided by local authorities, often for political reasons, rents charged are substantially lower than the economic rents and far lower than the market rents. (The municipal councils of Nairobi, Mombasa, and Kisumu have substantial deficits in their housing accounts.)[34] Local health services are provided free, as a national policy, while education is greatly subsidized at present, with the political promise that it will be made free in due course. These services absorb a significant and growing proportion of local budgets[35] (Table 27); yet their pricing does not lie within the jurisdiction of local authorities.[36] Local authorities could also explore the possibilities of local sales taxation, as well as licensing of professions, although it is not clear whether or not they can legally levy these taxes at this stage.

In the past, local authorities, particularly municipal councils, had to rely heavily on loans for financing their capital programs. While the National Housing Corporation provided funds for housing, the Local Government Loans Authority was the source for all other purposes. Lately, both these authorities are finding it difficult to cope with the growing demands of the local authorities.[37] The local authorities are consequently being advised to raise loans from the market but, given their weak financial position, even the commercial banks, are unwilling to lend them the money. Therefore, it may be desirable for the Central Government to strengthen the lending capabilities of the two organizations just mentioned, and impart guarantee and tax exemption status to local authority bonds.

A tax with a more identifiable base will have to be found for county councils. The commodity cesses which are presently the mainstay of county councils—they account for about one-quarter of their revenues—are unsatisfactory in many respects. First, they are discriminatory among the counties. Counties which are predominant in commercial agriculture, particularly coffee—those for instance, in the Central Province—are able to sustain a higher level of public services than other counties. Second, to the extent

---

33. Nairobi is in a unique position here—it gets about one-half of its revenues from rates or property assessments of government and commercial properties. Other areas of the country are less fortunate.
34. V. P. Diejomoah, "Financing Local Government Authorities in Kenya," Discussion Paper No. 96 (Nairobi: Institute for Development Studies, September 1970), p. 18.
35. Population in urban areas is growing at annual rates far exceeding 3 percent, which is the national average. In Nairobi and Mombasa, population is growing at rates of 7 percent and 5.5 percent respectively.
36. Similarly, the Central Government has not increased road grants to the municipal authorities even though the latter's expenditure on roads has risen steadily over a number of years. See *Ndegwa Report*.
37. This is partly because central government loans to the Local Government Loans Authority for further on lending to local authorities have significantly shrunk from £1 million in 1960 to £8,000 in 1967 and £107,000 in 1969. See *Ndegwa Report*, p. 220.

commodity cesses are levied at flat rates, specific or ad valorem, and are unrelated to price and marketed quantities, they are inequitable.[38] And lastly, cesses discriminate among crops and thereby distort the allocation of land and other resources. While some cesses might be justified in view of the market and nonmarket conditions pertaining to particular crops (e.g., coffee), it is advisable to move towards a more uniform system of taxation, such as a land tax.[39] But, then, land tax must be simple to be within the present administrative capabilities of various local authorities. This would require that a tax should generally be levied on the basis of land area with as few complications as possible associated with the productivity of land or income from land.[40] For the larger farms, some concept of "potential income" could become the basis. Idle lands could probably be taxed at a higher rate than lands under farming.

The possible advantages of a land tax—both as a source of revenue and as an instrument of land use policy—have been fully discussed elsewhere.[41] In the short run, there are administrative impediments to the introduction of a general land tax, particularly in the absence of any capable administrative machinery. There are also dangers and inequities in applying land tax to only registered farms. But in the longer run, a land tax might well become a major instrument of taxation for a reformed local government system.

To sum up, there definitely exists some potential to improve the financial position of local authorities and to make them move in the direction of financial viability. But this will call for a bigger tax effort, including a tightening of tax administration, as well as serious attempts to control expenditure. Even when these aims are attained, local authorities probably will not become an important instrument of savings; a large part of their capital formation will still have to be financed with loans from the Central Government, borrowing from the capital market, and even foreign aid.

Parastatal Sector as Saver

Very little information in any consolidated form is available on the parastatal sector in Kenya, even though this sector is responsible for about 15 percent of GDP,[42] absorbs one-third of government investment and one-tenth of the country's imports, and contributes more than 5 percent of government revenues. There are about fifty-five parastatal bodies (including fourteen commodity boards) which have primarily regulatory and administrative functions, and whose budgets are a part and parcel of government budget. Then, there are more than twenty-five organizations (in the fields of agriculture, livestock, tourism, construction, trade, financial institutions, transport, etc.) which have mainly enterprise functions. Lastly, there are more than thirty enterprises in which government has a minority interest, either directly or indirectly through its financial institutions, such as the Development Finance Company of Kenya, Kenya Tourist Development Corporation, Agricultural Development Corporation, and Kenya Tea Development Authority. Therefore, altogether there are over 150 organizations

---

38. It has been found that the smallholder coffee sector pays an estimated 0.3 percent more in gross revenues to local authorities than does the estate sector.

39. It must be noted that while the cesses are collected through cooperative societies, with hardly any cost of collection to the county councils, land taxation will certainly involve some staffing and tax administration.

40. However, once all lands have been fully registered and classified, which may well be the case by the end of the seventies, land tax should be levied on the basis of "potential" productivity of land.

41. See ILO/UNDP Report, Technical Paper No. 15. The 1972 World Bank Agriculture Sector Survey also examined the possibility of introducing land taxes (see Part III of the report).

42. This and the following figures include the East African Community and associated corporations.

belonging to the parastatal sector (excluding the East African Community corporations) which have government budgetary involvement, either in the form of recurrent budgetary grants, long term loans, or equity participation.[43]

Public Corporations. Fortunately for the Kenya Government, the public corporations need few subsidies. As Table 29 shows, it is only in 1969/70 that a small subsidy was given to a few of them. A major explanation for this seems to be that, in the past, the Central Government mainly gave them long term loans (at interest rates ranging between 5 and 6 percent) rather than participate in their equity. And, as long as the public corporations were not making losses, the Central Government usually received the interest due to it. It is only recently that equity participation of the Government in parastatal enterprises has grown (Table 22).

Nevertheless, the profitability of many public corporations is extremely low and sometimes negative. Table 30, which gives the profitability of certain selected large public corporations, substantiates this generalization. The Kenya Tourist Development Corporation, which is not covered in this table, is another organization which often makes net losses if the administration expenditure grant it receives from the Government is excluded. In 1971, the KTDC had a net loss of £1.7 million on total assets of £32.5 million.

General Government Agencies. The general government agencies have received a net transfer from the government budget practically every year since Independence (Table 31). The agencies' financial dependence on the central government budget has been large and increasing—in 1970/71, grants made to them were about 5 percent of the Government's recurrent budget. A very large part of the income of the Government from its agencies has taken the form of "interest, dividends, and profits" which has been growing.[44] But, most of this income represents the dividends of the Central Bank of Kenya and its predecessor, the Currency Board.

This brief review of the performance of the parastatal sector clearly suggests that both public corporations and general government agencies (with the exception of the Central Bank of Kenya) have not been of any significance in making profits or generating savings. Considering that the Government has invested over £36 million in public corporations and another £24 million in government agencies since 1964/65. the financial returns from these investments have not been very impressive. Perhaps the Government was able to receive a return of about 5 to 6 percent (which is the interest it charged on its loans) but, then, it is not clear if this should be considered adequate in terms of the "social cost" of capital. An answer to this question would, of course, depend upon the perceived role of the parastatal sector by the Central Government and others.

Domestic Borrowing

Table 10 reveals that the indebtedness of the Kenya Government has been going up consistently since Independence,[45] and this is also the case for the share of domestic debt in total debt. Domestic debt, which was less than 20 percent of the total debt in 1965, exceeded 45 percent of the total debt in 1972.

43. According to the data of the Central Bureau of Statistics, the bulk of long term loans and equity of the Central Government in recent years has gone to the National Housing Corporation (something like 40 to 50 percent), and the Industrial and Commercial Development Corporation (another 20 to 25 percent). Local authorities have absorbed about 10 to 15 percent of central government loans.

44. Annex One finds the following statistical relationship: rents, royalties, interest, and profits of the Government $= 0.60 + 0.02$ (Monetary GDP).

45. This is only in absolute terms. Relative to the GDP, Kenya Government debt has been constantly low at around 30 percent.

National Social Security Fund

The National Social Security Fund (NSSF), created in 1966, has played a major role in providing long term credit to the Government. The NSSF has been funded since 1966 largely by social security contributions.[46] So far benefit payments by the NSSF have been negligible,[47] with the result that, since inception, the NSSF has been able to invest more than £26 million in government securities, representing almost one-third of the domestic borrowing of the Central Government since 1965.

In appraising the prospective role of the NSSF in financing future development, note must be made of the following: first, the NSSF is likely to improve its registration of private employers in the years ahead,[48] particularly in rural areas, which should lead to an increase in contributions and in the NSSF's loanable resources; second, as the wage bill grows over the years, the Fund's annual receipts will also increase. Assuming that the wage bill in the economy grows at the rate of 10 percent per annum (5 percent for employment growth and another 5 percent for wage increases),[49] contributions received by the NSSF should grow from the present level of £7 million by about £0.7 million per annum. Consequently, the Fund's investment income would also grow by £1–1.5 million per annum from the present level of £7 million.

However, a third factor must be mentioned here. The NSSF is not bound to invest all its resources in central government securities. In fact, lately the Fund has been investing in local authority (particularly Nairobi) stocks, as well as EAC corporations stocks. The Fund has also invested in private equities (with the concurrence of the Treasury, of course), and in nongovernment and equity stocks in recent years.[50] As a result, the Central Government has been able to mobilize a sum of only £5 million annually through the NSSF.

Thus, it seems that the Kenya Government can look to the NSSF for no more than £6 to 7 million a year to finance its future development expenditure.

Other Nonbank Lenders

Other nonbank lenders to the Central Government include the Kenya Post Office Savings Bank, insurance companies, and other private (largely nonbanking finance)

---

46. Contributions are at the rate of 10 percent of the wage bill, and paid for equally by the employer and the employee, although the maximum amount payable by an employee is £20 per month.

47. They totalled £2 million between 1966 and 1971, against £39 million in contributions. *Economic Survey*, 1973, p. 199.

48. The degree of underregistration can be gauged from the fact that in 1971 the NSSF received contributions of about £7 million; whereas it should have received contributions of £18 million from "modern" sector employees alone (whose wage bill amounted to £184 million in 1971).

49. Between 1968 and 1971, the wage bill in the economy grew from £146 million to £184 million, an increase of about 26 percent, in three years.

50.

Investment Pattern of the NSSF (in £ Millions)

Year	Total Investments at cost	Local Authority and EAC Stocks	Private Equities	(3) + (4) as percent of (2)
(1)	(2)	(3)	(4)	
1966	1.2	—	—	—
1967	4.8	0.5	0.1	12.5
1968	10.3	0.5	0.6	10.7
1969	17.5	0.7	1.0	9.7
1970	22.8	1.9	1.6	15.4
1971	29.7	2.7	4.8	25.2

SOURCE: *Annual Reports* of the National Social Security Fund

companies.[51] It would be difficult to expect any major increase in contribution from the Post Office Savings Bank under present circumstances as its net deposits (after withdrawals) have remained static around £6 million since Independence.[52] Table 10 confirms that insurance companies have contributed little to domestic public debt, and this is largely because they have found housing loans and real estate investment more profitable. Insurance companies can perhaps be expected to lend no more than £1–2 million a year to the Government in the future.

Some of these nonbank institutions have been investing in government securities to fulfill their statutory obligations. But, others, particularly private companies and commercial banks, have been lending larger sums over a period of time. This would seem to suggest that existing interest rates on government securities have not proved a disincentive. However, as the rate of inflation accelerates, private support to public securities would shrink unless interest rates are raised.

Bank Borrowings

Nonbank domestic debt, of course, is only one of the means of financing the development effort. In Kenya's case, as Table 8 suggests, only about one-quarter to one-third of capital expenditure has been financed through nonbank domestic loans. In more recent years, as the growth rate of capital expenditures accelerated,[53] the nonbank borrowings proved inadequate, and the Government had to borrow increasingly from commercial banks and foreign sources, as well as draw down accumulated cash reserves at the Central Bank. In 1971/72, this net reduction of cash balances with the Central Bank financed about 35 percent of the budget deficit, and borrowings from the commercial banks another 25 percent. This was the largest amount the Central Government ever borrowed from the banking system, and is in sharp contrast to the policies followed during the early years after Independence. A similar picture seems to emerge, too, in 1972/73.

While some people have queried the propriety of the deficit financing of the last two years, others have seen it as a policy of pump priming, justified by the agricultural drought of 1971, and the recent slowdown of the manufacturing sector of the economy. But, for the economy to benefit from such a policy without serious inflation, it is essential that such bank monies must be used directly in production activities, or in activities which help supply the private needs of the bulk of the population. When about two-thirds of government expenditure is on social, community, and general services which meet the social, rather than the private, needs of the population, a large degree of deficit financing could carry serious inflationary potential. Obviously, then, the acceptable size of the noninflationary budget deficit in the short run would be determined by the extent to which the employable resources in the economy can be made to produce and expand the supply of private goods.[54] Otherwise, the inflationary effects of the budget deficit can be moderated only by further pressure on the balance of payments.

From the analysis presented thus far, it is clear that there are limitations to local borrowing—both bank and nonbank—to finance the next Plan. Much will depend upon the policy which the Government adopts regarding interest on government securities, for this is the relevant factor for attracting capital from the noncaptive markets. As

---

51. Cereals and Sugar Finance Corporation, an apex organization of the marketing boards, has lately been providing some short term credit to the Government.

52. Central Bank of Kenya, *Annual Report*, June 30, 1972, p. 49. The deposits of the POSB have increased lately but only marginally.

53. The average annual growth of capital expenditures during the last three years was 28 percent compared to 19 percent in the three years prior to that (Table 9).

54. The extent to which the Kenyan economy is monetized in any particular period would also be relevant here.

Table 10 suggests, neither the size of the domestic debt nor the debt service cost to the budget is very high, thus still permitting the Government to examine the question with an open mind.

Interest on Loans to Government

The Government pays 3.6 percent to 4.25 percent interest on treasury bills and other short term advances, 6.1 percent on under five year loans, 6.8 percent on five-to-ten-year loans, and 7.2 percent on long term (ten years and over) loans. If the captive market for government securities proves inadequate in future, which might well be the case, interest rates on public debt will have to be reexamined. The capacity of the NSSF seems to be limited to £6–7 million, and that of the insurance companies to £1–2 million, and both might consider the relative return on other forms of investments more attractive than the interest rate on government stocks.

The two principal, and somewhat related, issues that the Government will have to face are how to maximize borrowing from local sources, given its plan requirements, *and* how to minimize the cost of borrowing. The Central Government will face a serious resource gap over the next five years, as already mentioned, if nothing is done on the tax and expenditure fronts. Therefore, the two questions raised here are not irrelevant.

Depending upon the liquidity of the banking system, and the probability that it will stay that way, the Kenya Government might be able to borrow substantially, while reducing the overall maturity of its debt structure and simultaneously lowering its cost of borrowing. However, should the Government not find itself in such a fortunate situation, it would be able to borrow more only by offering higher interest rates on government securities. This would certainly imply an increase, rather than a reduction, in its total costs. Should such a need arise, it would also be advisable to increase the maturity structure of domestic debt over time.

No attention has been paid in this annex to the availability of foreign capital to finance the government budget, as the whole question of external assistance to Kenya is dealt with in Annex Six. The general conclusion of Annex Six is that the gross (and even the net) foreign capital available to the Government during the next three to five years is likely to increase gradually, but that the supply will depend, in part, upon the direction of government investment efforts. Should these efforts be directed to the productive development of the rural areas, the mission feels that net foreign resources available to the Government could grow at a faster rate.

Conclusions

If past experience is to be the guide for the future, local authorities certainly, and parastatal bodies probably, will not provide any significant savings to finance future development. The burden of public investment will have to be borne by the Central Government, partly because it is the largest single entity in the public sector, and partly because it has the necessary potential.

The Central Government, on its part, might find it difficult to generate substantial savings largely due to the slowdown of revenue growth. It will need to undertake certain elasticity oriented tax reforms, and simultaneously it will need to look into the growth rates of certain recurrent as well as development expenditures. As already indicated, these fiscal reforms, to some extent, have been incorporated into the 1973/74 budget and this is most welcome. However, without the continued emphasis of fiscal reforms during the coming years, the Government will have a difficult task in financing its development programs.

The Central Government can certainly mobilize additional resources by borrowing in the domestic money and capital markets. The capacity of the NSSF and insurance companies is likely to increase over time, and the Government should make every effort to tap these latter sources. The Government can also tap short term funds from commercial banks and the Central Bank and use them for productive purposes without too great a danger of causing serious inflation. However, if the rate of inflation picks up in Kenya, and alternative assets start yielding a higher return, Government will be compelled to restructure its own interest rates to encourage a larger flow of developmental resources to meet its planned outlays.

Most of Kenya's local authorities, even with the best of efforts, are liable to become financially viable only in terms of their recurrent budgets, and will continue to depend on outside help to finance a greater part of their capital formation. This makes the Central Government's task of generating savings and mobilizing other resources doubly important, and urgently calls for an exploration of revenue sharing possibilities with local authorities.

Certain parastatal bodies, particularly government agencies and public corporations, could generate increased resources, but to make specific recommendations in this regard would require a much more detailed study than has been possible for this mission to undertake.

Chapter 3

Fiscal Policy and Income Distribution

Data on income distribution in most developing countries are hard to collect, and Kenya is no exception. However, most indicators show that income disparities in Kenya are wide. In this report the mission does not intend to undertake any detailed review of the nature and extent of the problem, in view of the now extensive literature on the subject, particularly the ILO/UNDP report.[1] However, some of the indicators of inequality might be referred to briefly to demonstrate the extent of the problem.

There are several dimensions to the problem of inequality of income. The best known is the income differential between urban and rural areas. In Nairobi, average income per household in 1970 was £1,035 a year, which for a family of five, would yield a per capita income of about £200. This is about four times the per capita income of the country as a whole. On the other hand, most rural households have an income of less than £60 a year, and many have less than £20.[2]

But, comparisons of central tendency are misleading, and it is recognized that another dimension of the problem is the wide disparity of incomes *within* the urban and rural areas. According to an estimate made in Nairobi City Council, for example, while the top 20 percent of income earners in Nairobi receive 59 percent of the total income, the lowest 20 percent earn only 3 percent, and the lower 40 percent only 10 percent of the income.[3] Similarly, there is growing evidence that income is very unevenly spread in rural areas, where the real problem is not the conspicuous continued existence of large farms but the growing number of rural poor, who have not significantly benefited from past agricultural development programs, particularly in less favored regions.[4]

In Kenya's case, there is the additional problem of racial inequalities. In 1971, whereas about 63 percent of the European employees and 27 percent of the Asian employees earned wages exceeding £1,200 per annum, the proportion of African employees earning such high wages was only a little more than 1 percent.[5] While the average wage of a European employee was £2,500 per annum, that of an Asian was £370, and of an African only £190.[6] Even as late as 1971, the average earning of a European was more than thirteen times that of an African employee.

It is no surprise, then, that achieving social justice and reducing inequalities have always been the goals of the Kenya Government since Independence. The previous (1970–74) development plan stresses that, "A fundamental objective of the Government ... is to secure a just distribution of the national income, both between different sectors and areas of the country and between individuals,"[7] and this emphasis is even stronger in the new 1974–78 plan. The Government has always considered fiscal policy generally, and tax policy in particular, major instruments to achieve its goals. "The tax system should in fact be a major weapon for implementing African Socialism," the Government

---

1. See especially Chapters 1 and 16 and Technical Paper No. 4. The subject was also discussed in the *Ndegwa Report* and the Report of the Select Committee on Unemployment to the National Assembly, December 1972.
2. See the ILO/UNDP mission's estimates quoted in Annex Three.
3. Data provided by the Nairobi Urban Study Group. Not only are the inequalities large, they appear to have been growing over time. Cf. the findings of the *Ndegwa Report*, "that there are growing inequalities in remuneration among employees" (p. 34). The data for Nairobi are fairly consistent with the data for the whole urban sector given in the ILO/UNDP report, Table 26, p. 75.
4. This is an important theme of both the ILO/UNDP report, and the World Bank Agricultural Sector Survey (see Part III).
5. *Statistical Abstract*, 1972, Table 233.
6. Ibid., Tables 219 and 228.
7. *Development Plan, 1970–1974*, para. 1.8, p. 2.

stated in Sessional Paper No. 10, stressing that, among other things, it must "be a major means for effecting a more equitable distribution of income and wealth."[8]

In this chapter, we shall indicate the role Kenya's tax structure can have played in the past in reducing the inequalities in incomes and wealth. Although there is little relevant information concerning the impact of fiscal policy on income distribution and equity, we hope that the analysis will serve to highlight some of the limitations of the existing tax system of Kenya in respect to equity, and to point to some possible implications for policy. The limitations of the present government expenditure pattern as a redistributive device will also be indicated, though somewhat briefly.

Equity in Taxation

The most important instrument of reducing inequalities, short of direct expropriation of wealth, is often to impose taxes on wealth. At the second level are taxes on personal incomes and, only at the last level can taxes on consumption be expected to be an effective means of bringing about any major redistribution. In discussing the role of Kenya's tax structure as an equity measure, an attempt is made later in this chapter to examine the direct taxes which influence the concentration of wealth and then the taxes which reduce the inequalities in personal incomes and consumption.

Taxes on Wealth

Theoretically, taxes on wealth can take various forms. They may be levied on individual items of wealth, for example, land or urban property, or they may be annually levied on the total wealth. Then, instead of levying a tax on wealth annually, the Government may levy it only once at the time of the death—in the form of an estate duty on the total estate or an inheritance tax on the estate. Instead of levying the tax at the time of the death, the Government can also decide to tax the increments in wealth, rather than the total wealth, particularly as and when they are realized, in the form of capital gains.

Thus, the Government has a wide array of wealth taxes at its disposal, and the rate structure, breadth of the tax base, as well as the frequency of the tax, will determine how heavy the equity orientation of the tax structure will be. A highly progressive tax on wealth, with as few exemptions and deductions (or loopholes) as possible, levied and collected annually, could be the most equitable single tax in this respect, but, then, there is nothing that prohibits the Government from levying more than one tax on wealth simultaneously and, in fact, many governments do precisely that.

In Kenya, the Government has so far chosen to be somewhat lenient in matters of wealth taxation. It only levies once-in-a-lifetime estate duty and an annual urban property tax,[9] the base for which, as will be shown later, is further narrowed by granting generous exemptions and deductions. Kenya does not have an annual wealth tax or a land tax or a capital gains tax at the moment. The need for a capital gains tax, at least has been admitted by the Minister of Finance in the 1973/74 budget. However, the introduction of a capital gains tax has been postponed for the time being because of the administrative complexities which would be involved.

The estate duty, which is levied on the estates of the deceased, is on the face of it a highly progressive tax. It is levied at rates varying between 1 percent on estates between

---

8. *African Socialism*, pp. 33, 35.
9. There is also a 2 percent stamp duty on the conveyancing of property which has now been raised to 3 percent for urban property in the 1973/74 budget.

£2,500 to £5,000, and 50 percent on estates over £1 million. But, for purposes of taxation, the following items, among others, are exempt:
- immovable property situated outside Kenya;
- any disposition or gift made by the deceased more than three years before his death;
- any disposition or gift made in consideration of marriage; and,
- a gift which does not, together with all other gifts to the same donee, exceed £500.

It is obvious that the exemption of gifts from taxation is a major loophole in the estate duty. This almost reduces the tax into a noninstrument of equity as well as revenue. In 1972/73, collections under this tax were no more than £0.6 million.

The urban property tax is an even less effective instrument of equity. First, it is levied at flat rates and not at progressive rates. Second, being an instrument of local taxation, it suffers from the problem that the urban properties owned by a person are taxed independently by the local authorities, and not combined for taxation purposes with income or wealth subject to central government taxation. (Of course, given the fact that the tax is not levied on progressive rates, this hardly matters.) Worse still, the tax is levied on an unimproved value basis, therefore excluding those improvements, which, over time, become a substantial part of an individual's wealth. To top it all, even reassessments of unimproved values, which are supposed to be made every five years, have seldom been undertaken. In certain urban areas, property reassessments have not been made since 1951. Therefore, is it surprising that municipal councils earned no more than £3 million from this source in 1971?

In Kenya, since there is probably more wealth in rural than in urban areas, any form of wealth taxation which excludes rural wealth will remain a relatively unimportant instrument of redistribution. Of course, it must be admitted that the land reforms of the sixties, including the break up of large farms and the initiation of the smallholder settlement schemes, must have reduced inequality in land holdings, but much inequality still remains.

Although there is now no data to support or refute the contention, it is possible that income and consumption distribution is more skewed than distribution of wealth. If this is so, and when evidence becomes available to show it, the Government would clearly have to focus greater attention on personal income taxation and consumption taxation in order to achieve greater equity.

Taxes on Personal Incomes

In theory, progressive taxation of personal incomes can be viewed as an alternative to control of incomes, particularly where political and other factors act as serious obstacles to adopting an "effective" incomes and wages policy.

Kenya's income tax is a fairly progressive tax in structure. The marginal tax rates graduate from a minimum of 10 percent to a maximum of 70 percent[10] and, as Table 32

10. The income tax rates, which have been revised with effect from January 1, 1974, are as follows:

Total Income	Tax Rates	Total Income	Tax Rates
On the first £1,200	10.0	On the next £600	45.0
On the next £600	15.0	On the next £600	50.0
On the next £600	20.0	On the next £600	55.0
On the next £600	25.0	On the next £600	60.0
On the next £600	30.0	On the next £1,800	65.0
On the next £600	35.0	On income in excess of £9,000	70.0
On the next £600	40.0		

Every income taxpayer in Kenya also pays a fixed hospital contribution of £6 (if his taxable income is £2,000 or less) or £12 (if his total income exceeds £2,000).

suggests, this implies an average tax rate of 4 percent for income around £1,000, and 55 percent for incomes around £20,000 per annum. An interesting feature of Kenya's income tax structure from the equity point of view—and this was introduced in the 1973/74 budget only—is that the income taxpayers are given personal tax reliefs instead of personal income allowances. Before the 1973/74 budget, single persons used to be able to deduct a personal allowance of £216 from their income for tax assessment purposes. For married persons, the personal allowance was £480, plus an allowance of £120 for every child (up to a maximum of four children). This meant that a family of six would pay no income tax at all if its income was less than £960 per year. Under the new system, a single person receives £18 as personal relief from his tax liability, while married individuals receive double this amount for themselves (and £9 for each child up to a maximum of four children). This reform is certainly most welcome because the previous system of deducting a given amount as personal allowance from the total income to arrive at taxable income benefited the richer taxpayers more than the poorer ones, and hence was inequitable.

Although the redistributive effect of income taxation is apparently high, there are certain factors which could mitigate this, and which must be pointed out in any assessment of the income tax's potentialities in this respect.

First, it should be noted that the income tax rates given in Table 32 do not reflect the "effective" rates of taxation on the middle and higher income groups. This is because these taxpayers enjoy certain allowances and exemptions which further reduce their taxable incomes and therefore tax liabilities. There are three important tax benefits which the relatively better off taxpayers enjoy under the personal income tax:

- The imputed income from owner occupied housing, which was taxable up until 1960, is now exempt. As a matter of fact, the self-employed professionals have now been allowed a deduction of £700 per annum from their income as housing allowance.
- Only income earned in the Partner States, and not world income, is subject to taxation in Kenya.
- Various benefits provided by employers in kind are not adequately taxed: for example, the value of free medical service is not taxable, and the value of furnished housing provided by the employer is calculated at 15 percent of the employee salary, which, in most cases, is much less than the true market rental.

It is clear that most, if not all, of these allowances benefit the richer taxpayers more than the poorer ones so that, at the upper ends of the income scale, income tax in Kenya is not as progressive as would appear from Table 32. Until 1973/74, there were many other deductions benefiting the richer taxpayers as well, such as full or partial deductions for contributions to pension funds, provident funds, retirement funds, and insurance premiums, but many of these deductions have now been abolished or greatly modified. While this is a welcome step in improving the equity of the income tax, there is still room for further change to be made.

A second factor which determines the potency of income tax in Kenya is the scope of taxation which is determined by the exemption limits which are allowed. Presently, a married individual whose income is less than £360 does not pay income tax and earns a further exemption of £90 for each child up to a maximum of four children. Considering that the definition of a "child" is extremely liberal in the income tax legislation (it includes an adopted child, stepchild, or any child who is in the custody and maintenance of the taxpayer by virtue of any custom of the community to which he belongs) and that the extended family system is prevalent in Kenya, it should be quite common for married individuals to avoid income tax altogether.

Although exemption limits have been reduced in 1973/74 (from £960 to £720 for a married individual with four children), they are still very high in the Kenya context, where per capita income is around £50 and the minimum urban wage less than

£150 a year. The validity of this can be seen from the fact that in 1971 only 40,000 or so employees forming about 7 percent of wage earners in the modern sector of the Kenyan economy earned more than £750 per annum.[11] A tax which only just touches the fringes of the modern sector will always have limited potential for redistribution, even though its rate structure is adequately progressive.

Another limitation to the redistributive effects of taxation are the weaknesses in the tax administration, particularly in respect of the self-employed and taxpayers with multiple sources of incomes, who often belong to higher income groups. There is some evidence that income tax avoidance by individuals not subject to "PAYE" (and that means practically all nonwage earners) is large. While the average tax assessment on wage incomes of employees increased from 12 percent in 1966/67 to 20 percent in 1970/71, there was no increase whatsoever in the tax burden for the self-employed.[12] There was also hardly any increase in the total income of the latter which was subjected to income tax.

There may also be some tax evasion in agriculture—particularly among large scale farms. For instance, while the gross marketed production of large farms increased by about 14 percent between 1965 and 1969,[13] tax revenue from agriculture has remained constant, and has declined significantly as a percentage of total income tax revenue.

It is possible that the relatively generous capital allowances given to commercial farmers is one of the factors responsible for reducing taxable income in agriculture, but it cannot be the major one. Certain capital expenditures in agriculture, particularly clearing of agricultural lands, planting of permanent and semi-permanent crops, prevention of soil erosion, etc., can be completely written off in the year in which they are incurred. Capital expenditures on farm works can be written off in five years, which is substantially more favorable than investment in agricultural or industrial machinery. There has certainly been some growth of tax exempt capital expenditure on fencing and plantations on large farms—from £0.7 million in 1964 to £1.3 million in 1971—even though the total number of large farms as well as their area have been almost constant. It is more likely, though, that the major explanation for tax evasion by farmers lies with the laxity of the administration of income tax in respect of agricultural incomes, particularly as most farmers do not keep proper accounts and records.

It is true, of course, that the nature of the agricultural sector has changed significantly since Independence, and the progressive settlement of the previous Scheduled Areas has also reduced the taxable income of the sector. Even the nature of the "large" farm sector has changed, and many of these farms are now under some form of communal settlement, and hence largely outside the scope of personal income tax. The

---

11. *Statistical Abstract*, 1972, Table 232 (d). This statement, of course, is valid for the wage earners only. A similar statement can also be made for the self-employed and other individuals paying income tax in Kenya.

12. Average Tax Assessments on Categories of Individual Taxpayers.

	Employees			Individuals		
	Aggregate Income	Net Tax Assessed	Average Assessment (% per £)	Aggregate Income	Net Tax Assessed	Average Assessment (% per £)
	(£ million)			(£ million)		
1966/67	39.8	4.6	11.6	22.3	3.7	16.6
1967/68	41.0	6.9	16.8	21.1	3.2	15.2
1968/69	44.1	7.8	17.7	23.5	3.7	15.7
1969/70	51.7	9.8	18.9	26.6	4.5	17.2
1970/71	50.9	9.9	19.5	24.4	3.9	16.0

SOURCE: Income Tax Department (*Annual Reports*).

13. From £33.3 to £37.9 million, see *Economic Survey*, 1972, Table 44.

task of taxing agricultural incomes is always difficult, however, and there is reason to believe that some genuine and profitable large farms are evading income tax, particularly among the newly established African farms, many of whom do not yet have adequate accounting systems.

It is time now to sum up the redistributive powers of present income taxes in Kenya. The bulk of income earners, even in the modern sector, pay no income tax whatsoever. Taxation of very high incomes is surely progressive, but then the nominal degree of progressivity in income taxation is substantially reduced due to the various tax deductions and allowances high income taxpayers enjoy in Kenya. Tax avoidance and evasion are probably greater among richer members of the community, including many self-employed, than among taxpayers as a whole;[14] this further limits the scope of utilizing income tax as a primary redistributive device in Kenya. The recent levy of a 12.5 percent withholding tax on dividend and interest incomes[15] should, however, help tighten the tax administration and contribute to greater equity.

Taxes on Personal Consumption

Indirect taxes in general and taxes on consumption in particular are seldom considered a means of affecting equity, in any significant sense, largely because these taxes are often regressive in their incidence. Some progressivity can definitely be introduced in their burden by exempting food and other basic necessities, and by taxing more heavily those goods and services consumed mainly by the rich. It would, indeed, be surprising if the overall progressivity thus introduced will ever be adequate for equity purposes.

At present, personal consumption in Kenya is taxed in three ways: First, excise duties are levied on the domestic output of selected items, for example, sugar, matches, cigarettes and tobacco, soap, mineral waters, fabric, beer, wines, and paints. Second, a 10 percent general sales tax is levied on all domestic as well as imported manufactures[16] with the exception of petroleum, beer, and electricity, which are subject to specific sales tax rates. Third, taxes are levied on selected personal services including foreign travel, betting and gaming, hotel accommodation, and entertainment. There is also a special tax on the purchase of second hand motor vehicles and impost of a special license fee on them.

In analyzing the distributive impact of these taxes, it must be mentioned that, up until recently, most consumption taxes in Kenya were specific, which meant that their effective burden tended to fall with rising prices, and this required the Government to increase tax rates from time to time. The levy of a general sales tax in 1973 is a welcome step towards strengthening the revenue elasticity of consumption taxes as well as introducing a greater degree of progressivity in the tax burden—at least in respect of consumption, but possibly in respect of income as well. There are certain factors which lead the mission to the last judgment. The fact that the general sales tax is levied on manufactures, both domestic and imports, would suggest that its incidence might be progressive with respect to income. Exempting sales tax of traditional food items and of very small manufactures would seem to further reinforce possible progressivity. However, while the new Kenya sales tax has many of the attributes of a relevant and desirable tax, we do not believe that indirect taxes in general can be as powerful tools of redistribution as progressive taxation of income or wealth.

14. See Annex Three, Chapter 3, for a discussion of tax evasion by firms in the urban formal sector.
15. A withholding tax also exists on the payments of royalties, management fees, etc., to non-residents. In the 1973/74 budget, a withholding tax has also been levied on the payments of pensions.
16. This tax, levied in April 1973, replaced the then existing specific consumption taxes. For the details of this tax see Chapter 5.

Several considerations lead to this conclusion. First, the Government depends heavily on the excise taxation of certain items of basic necessities, for example, sugar, matches, clothing, and footwear, which generally have low income elasticities. Even beer and cigarettes, which account for the bulk of excise duties,[17] do not have an income elasticity much higher than unity, so that the redistributive impact of excise duties is limited.[18] In fact, excise duties may perhaps be considered the least redistributive element in Kenya's indirect tax structure.

Some progressivity seems to have been imparted to Kenya's indirect tax structure by introducing taxes on certain luxury items—electricity, second hand cars, tires, transistor batteries for example, plus various personal services in recent years. All the same, this list of luxury items is not as large, nor are the rates sufficient, to make a serious impression on income distribution. The specific tax rate of one Kenya cent per kilowatt hour of electricity, Sh. 5 per automobile tire, £10 per second hand car, or even 10 percent on entertainment could hardly be considered high. The only luxury items on which indirect taxes of any significance are levied are automobiles and road vehicles (which pay duties when imported), gasoline taxes,[19] and annual licenses when used. The average import duty on passenger cars has increased by 50 percent since 1964, to £70 in 1971 (Table 33). Consequently, government revenues from road taxation have increased from £7 million in 1964 to £18 million in 1971.

A word about the burden of import duties on the consumer is in order here. Table 13, which gives the data on tax ratios for various years since Independence, suggests that the share of import duties in tax revenues has declined over time, and that the average rate of import duties has remained constant at around 20 percent since 1964/65.[20] The breakdown given in Table 34 suggests that the average rates of duties on manufactured articles have also remained constant. The average duty rate on beverages and tobacco has declined, while that on food and live animals has increased. All this would seem to suggest that, at least at the margin, import duties have not become significantly redistributive. There is, however, no denying the fact that import duties affect the rich as well as urban income earners more than the poor and rural income earners. The precise effect, however, is hard to quantify.

Summing up, while most important excise duties are not a progressive burden on the richer income earners in Kenya, this anomaly is partially corrected by taxing luxury imports and levies on personal services. On the whole, it would be difficult to conclude that there will be much overall progressivity in indirect taxes. In fact, a recent study, utilizing the consumption expenditure data collected in certain urban surveys, concluded that the burden of indirect taxation was in the past regressive, and there is no reason to believe that the recent levy of a sales tax in place of consumption taxes would substantially alter this conclusion.[21]

17. In 1972, for example, out of a total of £17.6 million of excise duties, £7.6 and £5.2 came from beer and cigarettes respectively. See *Economic Survey*, 1973, p. 164.

18. Household surveys conducted by the Institute for Development Studies, Nairobi, found the income elasticity of these items to be close to 1.1. See Benton F. Massell, "Expenditure Patterns in the Central Province of Kenya: A Preliminary Analysis," IDS Discussion Paper No. 29, (September 1966). Also see by the same author, "Determinants of Household Expenditure in Rural Kenya," IDS Discussion Paper No. 49 (April 1967).

19. As Annex One reveals, the built-in elasticity of gasoline and diesel taxes is extremely small. Gasoline and Diesel Taxes = −2.8 + 0.008 (Monetary GDP).

20. The (built-in) marginal rate of import duties has been even smaller according to Annex One. Import Duties = 11.96 + 0.129 (Value of Imports *minus* Residual Imports). This means that import duties would have had a marginal rate of 13 percent if no revisions were made over a number of years.

21. M. J. Westlake, "Kenya's Indirect Tax Structure and the Distribution of Income," Staff Paper No. 102 (Nairobi: Institute for Development Studies, June 1971). Also note the following, "It is apparent, from the date given in the note, that the distribution of income (in the urban areas) was not affected by taxation in 1968–69." ILO/UNDP report, p. 346.

Redistributive Role of Kenya's Tax System

Although the Kenya Government expected that it would rely heavily on the tax system to bring about income redistribution, the present structure of taxation does not seem to be very progressive. Admittedly, some elements of progression exist, particularly the heavier taxation of very high incomes and some degree of taxation of personal services. But the taxation of wealth and consumption leaves much to be desired. In 1965, the Government itself designed a taxation package aimed at a more equitable distribution of income and wealth.[22] It included progressive capital gains and inheritance taxes, a plan to lower personal exemptions and make income taxes more progressive, and a proposal to tax luxury items heavily. The package also provided for the elimination of taxes on extremely poor people, and the strengthening of property taxes. For the benefit of poor people, basic necessities were proposed to be exempt from excise duties.

The present tax structure, though moving consistently in this direction since Independence, still has a long way to go. Over the next plan period, depending upon how seriously the Government takes the problem of income distribution and whether or not it wishes to use the tax instrument to remedy the structure, the present system of taxation will have to be reviewed and revised.[23] Some possible reforms towards this end are indicated in Chapter 5.

Admittedly, the inequality problem in Kenya is multifaceted; nevertheless, her tax system can primarily affect inequality of personal incomes. Other facets of the problem —regional or rural-urban inequalities, for instance—can be influenced only indirectly by the tax structure, through tax incentives or disincentives, which, in practice, often prove to be rather ineffective.

Regional or rural-urban inequalities can, however, be directly affected through patterns of public expenditure and distribution of public services. A pattern of public expenditure which distributes public services more evenly, or favors backward over advanced regions, or rural over urban areas, is a useful tool in the hands of a government which is worried about the problem of regional or sector inequalities. It may now be interesting to see how far the Kenya Government has succeeded in this respect.

Patterns of Public Expenditure

Lack of data does not permit an analysis of the direct effects of government expenditures on personal inequalities; however, the little data which are readily available suggest that public expenditure has not been used as a major device to reduce rural-urban and regional inequalities in any significant manner, nor has it generally been used to favor the poorest section of the community.

Any systematic analysis of expenditure by region is precluded by the fact that budgetary expenditures in Kenya are generally not classified on a geographical basis,[24] and there is little information about the distribution of services. The few indicators which do exist all tend to show that the distribution of services in Kenya at the time of Independence were heavily in favor of the more prosperous areas, especially the urban areas. This pattern still exists today, although the absolute level of services has been increased in all areas. Some data on the availability of public services have been

---

22. *African Socialism*, p. 35.
23. Cf. ". . . the tax system in Kenya . . . does not have any significant redistributive effect . . . There is therefore a need for a major overhaul of the tax system to improve its equity. . ." ILO/UNDP report, pp. 271–72.
24. The disaggregation of national plans and budgets into district programs now being undertaken by the Ministry of Finance and Planning will throw much more light on the progress being made to distribute government expenditure more equitably.

compiled in Table 36 which, though fragmentary, do suggest that the distribution of services in Kenya (in 1970) was still very uneven. Nairobi, for example, has 4.4 percent of the total population of the country but 18.7 percent of secondary school enrollments. Similarly, Central Province has 15.3 percent of the total population but 24.9 percent of primary school enrollments. Both also have very high proportion of school age children in the schools—Nairobi with 72 percent. On the other extreme is North-Eastern Province with only 4 percent of its school age population going to schools.

A similar picture emerges with respect to health facilities. While the exceptionally dense services in Nairobi are not really comparable with other areas (partly due to the concentration of services in the Kenyatta Hospital, which serves the whole nation), clearly, there are tendencies for the distribution of health services to be correlated with prosperity.

Of course, to assess the effects of fiscal policy on equity, we need to know how expenditures on public services have been distributed. In other words, granted that services were unevenly distributed at the time of Independence, has the pattern of expenditure done anything to redress these inherited imbalances since? Unfortunately, there are no conclusive data on this question, although, again, the few indicators available do not suggest that inequalities have been reduced.

The most comprehensive indicator of the geographical distribution of expenditure comes from the expenditure pattern of local authorities. Before centralization of county council functions in 1970, local authorities used to provide primary education, health facilities, water supplies and sewerage, maintenance of minor and unclassified roads, and housing.[25] Altogether, local authorities spent something on the order of 20 to 25 percent of total (both central and local) government expenditures. An examination of their expenditures on social and community services per capita given in Table 35 suggests that the impact of local government expenditure was, in fact, to widen rather than reduce the inherited discrepancies among provinces.

In 1968, one of the latest years before centralization took place, the average expenditure per head by municipal councils was about ten times that incurred by county councils. But there were wide variations even within the county councils: for example, the two county councils in the North-Eastern province were able to spend only £0.6 per capita on all services while, on the other hand, average per capita expenditure by the more prosperous councils in Central Province was £2.2 in the same year.

It can be argued that a given amount of public expenditure does not necessarily signify the same amount of service; and it is questionable whether the quality and even the quantity of public services should be the same in densely populated urban areas like Nairobi as in sparsely populated rural areas. But the extremes of the availability of services indicated by Table 35 suggest that local government expenditures in the past were certainly not redistributive. We suggest elsewhere in this annex that, sooner or later, the Government will have to consider some form of revenue sharing if local authorities are to be made financially viable again. It is certainly clear that local authorities can never be an instrument for reducing regional inequalities as long as weaker councils in poorer areas have to rely mainly on their own financial resources.

Evidence on the pattern of central government expenditure is much harder to find and when available, is fragmentary and not very conclusive. The few indicators which do exist do not reveal any redistributive tendency. For example, Table 36 shows that 65 percent of expenditure on housing in 1970 was in Nairobi, and (as pointed out later) this was mostly spent on middle and upper income housing. More significant, perhaps, is progress made with education, not only because of the great social demand for education, but also because education is one obvious way in which income disparities can be reduced, by providing access to improved employment opportunities. Therefore, data

---

25. For details, see Chapter 2.

presented in Table 37 are of considerable interest. They show that those provinces which in 1968 had more than their "share" of school places had either retained or increased their share by 1972. On the other hand, those provinces which had less than their share in 1968 have (with one main exception) lost further ground during these four years. Again, it should be emphasized that this is only fragmentary evidence and that other factors in the past have compensated for the continuing emphasis on the more developed areas.[26] But it is a further indication towards the conclusion that the pattern of public expenditure has not been effective as a major tool for narrowing regional differences.

There is even less evidence of the extent to which public expenditures have been used to redress imbalance between rich and poor, wherever they live. All we can do is to make a qualitative assessment from what we know of the general pattern of expenditure in some of the major sectors. Here, again we have to be selective, but on balance it is difficult to conclude that the net impact of government expenditure has been redistributive. A substantial proportion of the capital expenditure program since 1964 has been directed towards the urban formal sector, including most of the power, water, and other relatively costly services. Virtually all public sector expenditure on housing (including civil service housing) has gone to the upper 30 percent of the urban population—meaning the upper 3 percent of the total population. In rural areas, the Government has made great strides to develop agriculture and the quality of life in general, and a large amount of resources has been invested in land transfer and registration, settlement, and the provision of infrastructure services.

Expenditure on agricultural development, as we emphasize in this report, is generally favorable from an income distribution point of view, particularly in reducing (or controlling the increase in) the gap between the farmer and the urban wage earner. However, much of the past expenditure in the agricultural sector has gone into the more developed areas of Kenya. It is also typically the more progressive farmers within any particular area who are best able to take advantage of new developments. Thus, it is not clear how effective even agricultural expenditure has been to reduce income differentials in an overall sense.

Conclusion

The existing fiscal policy of Kenya has not been a significant instrument to redistribute incomes and wealth, or to reduce rural, urban, and regional inequalities. Taxation policy is obviously only one—though perhaps an important—instrument in this respect and, as already indicated, there is scope for sharpening the present fiscal policies in this respect.

The Government is clearly concerned that its expenditure program should have a more redistributive effect, and some of the measures now being taken or contemplated (for example in housing, rural electrification, and rural water supplies) are discussed elsewhere in the report. The mission feels, however, that there is an urgent need for a much more profound reorientation, not only of government expenditure but of the whole structure of economic growth in Kenya, if an effective attack on the problem of poverty is to be launched. It is clear that this is a central theme of the report.

---

26. For example, the remission of school fees in some of the poorest areas of the country.

CHAPTER 4

EMPLOYMENT AND RURAL DEVELOPMENT

In view of the growing concern over employment in Kenya, it is appropriate to assess the extent to which fiscal policy can help to promote employment and increase the incomes of the poor. Kenya's unemployment problem can be looked at in two quite distinct ways. First, it can be viewed as a problem of frustrated job seekers, including the presently unemployed, particularly in the urban areas, as well as the school leavers. On the basis of urban surveys conducted recently, the average urban unemployment rate alone is around 11 percent. The rate of unemployment among school leavers and new entrants to the job market is much higher—probably about 21 percent.[1]

Second, the problem of unemployment can be viewed as a more general problem of the "working poor," that is, the majority of the population in both the urban as well as the rural areas of Kenya who have very low incomes and poor services. The poverty of this category which includes most of the very small landowners, the landless, and much of the urban informal sector, is as much symptomatic of the unemployment problem as the more conspicuous form of poverty brought about by open unemployment.[2]

Before examining the role of fiscal policy in alleviating unemployment, it must be explicitly stated that no single policy instrument will ever be sufficient to remedy the serious unemployment problem which the Kenya Government is facing at the present time. Fiscal policy, in particular, is often an inadequate remedy, especially in the context of dualistic and pluralistic economies with weak economic links. Therefore, tackling unemployment in Kenya requires a wide frontal attack, as is now well recognized.

The emphasis of the strategy underlying this report is a restructuring of growth towards more productive sectors, and a reform in the process of growth particularly through factor price changes. These two measures could go a long way towards alleviating Kenya's poverty and towards achieving both rapid growth and more equitable distribution. The purpose of this annex is to suggest what kind of fiscal policy would be consistent with such a strategy, and the emphasis in this chapter will be on measures to affect employment, rather than poverty, although in the final section, we shall briefly discuss fiscal policy in relation to rural development, which is so central to the strategy of reformed structural growth.

On a very general level of argument, it can be said that the level of employment in Kenya should be influenced by:

- the growth performance of the economy;
- the factor proportions which back this growth performance; and,
- the structure of growth.

In Kenya, the growth rate has been impressive—the economy has grown at an annual rate of about 7 percent since Independence—so that attention must be focused on factor proportions which have supported the growth of the Kenyan economy as well as the structure of growth. Indeed, factor proportions also throw much light on the inequalities in income distribution which were referred to earlier.

In Kenya's particular circumstances, two important factors have a bearing on the factor proportions. First, foreign investment in Kenya is important and this implies that

---

1. Kenya's population is growing at an annual rate of about 3.5 percent while the urban population (including migration) is growing at about 7 percent. It is estimated that employment in the modern sector will increase by about 4.5 percent per annum over the next plan period, which would mean that urban unemployment is likely to grow even further in the future.

2. This second and more pervasive aspect of distribution—the problem of the working poor—formed the main theme of the ILO/UNDP report.

often, if not always, foreign technology and factors proportions appropriate to the developed countries are transplanted in Kenya. Second, the existence of a strong trade union movement in Kenya suggests that the efforts of the Government to encourage employment through policies which might induce wage reduction are likely to meet strong resistance.[3]

Factor proportions can be influenced by changing relative factor prices (provided that a variety of techniques of production are available) and here government policies, fiscal as well as all others, become highly relevant. In an extreme sense, it can be argued that, as the Government itself does not need to be motivated by profit maximization, it can alter the factor proportions utilized in the production of public services without reference to relative factor prices. But if this expedient is taken too far the Government can all too easily take upon itself the role of a direct employer of the unemployed, and in some countries governments have done precisely this.

Direct Employment by the Public Sector

Government employment (including the Kenya Government and the local governments) has increased by 44 percent between 1964 and 1972 (Table 4) and the share of government sector in modern employment has increased from 24 to 28 percent. Thus, government employment has increased significantly faster than employment in non-government sectors.[4] Since 1964, the Government has negotiated two Tripartite Agreements with labor and management to increase employment. Under the first agreement of 1964, the Government contracted to expand its employment by 15 percent while other employers were to increase their employment by 10 percent. In return, labor unions agreed not only to abide by a wage freeze but to refrain from work stoppages. Under the second Tripartite Agreement, signed in 1969, both the Government and other employers undertook to expand employment by 10 percent each.

It is now generally agreed that such agreements cannot be expected to provide the answer to the unemployment problem. However, as the problem of unemployment grows, it can be expected that increasing political pressure will be put on Government to expand its role as employer. But the public sector in general, and the government sector in particular, cannot take upon itself the responsibility of providing jobs without regard to efficiency criteria or cost considerations. Providing employment for employment's sake would affect the costs of providing public services and would severely impinge on limited government resources. The net effect might well be adverse on total output and even on income distribution in the remainder of the economy. Besides, if the Government becomes too big an employer (the public sector already employs close to two-fifths of employees in the modern sector), heavy union pressures could threaten the government budget.

The government sector's own employment strategy might be guided by two principles. One, to replace capital intensive *techniques* by labor intensive techniques, wherever economically feasible; and two, to put more resources into labor intensive *sectors*, whenever this is consistent with overall national policy. A good example of the first principle in action is the Government's continuing experiment with labor intensive road schemes. If found successful, such methods might be expanded to cover other fields of government activity as well. The second principle is consistent with the general theme of this report. In particular, we show elsewhere in the report that incremental investment in developing small scale agriculture might be expected to give maximum returns in terms of both output and employment.

3. See Annex Three.
4. Also see *Ndegwa Report*, pp. 28–29.

Government investment in training, which would enhance the productivity and employability of labor, is yet another avenue, particularly in programs designed to build up levels of entrepreneurial ability.[5] Government investment in the development of technology appropriate to Kenya's factor availabilities is also essential. A pattern of government expenditure to narrow the gap which exists between rural and urban public services, noted earlier, must accompany expanded efforts to enhance agricultural productivity and incomes.

While the government as well as the public sector generally would certainly absorb some of the rapidly increasing labor force directly, most of the additions will have to be absorbed in the economy's private sector. Fiscal policy can, and must, play a role in making it profitable for the nongovernment sector to employ more labor.

Fiscal Distortions and Private Employment

As it stands now, the tax structure works in favor of capital intensity artificially lowering the price of capital and this is in addition to the subsidy enjoyed by capital through the protected exchange rate and generally low interest rates. Three features of existing tax policy need particular mention here. First is the investment allowance of 20 percent (over and above the normal depreciation of 12.5 percent per annum on reducing balance value) which all new industrial buildings, machinery, and equipment, are entitled to under the present company tax.[6] Second, imports of most capital goods and many intermediate goods are either exempt from custom duty or pay low rates of duty. Finally, as pointed out earlier in this annex, all capital gains are exempt from tax.

What the incentive effect of these features of tax policy is on in the economy or the growth rate achieved by Kenya in the past would be hard to say; the price of capital certainly has been reduced below true cost and therefore may have encouraged capital intensity. This is particularly disturbing when the price of labor has been taxed through social security contributions,[7] in addition to higher costs imposed by minimum wage legislation and union action.

From a theoretical point of view, it would appear desirable to abolish the concessions given to capital. Even though the additional revenue generated would be small,[8] some alternative use could be found for this revenue which would have a favorable effect on employment. Another cheaper way to increase the number of jobs will be to use the tax system to encourage a fuller utilization of existing industrial capacity. In theory, there could be many reasons for capacity underutilization. They include faulty design of plants, purchase of equipment for larger markets and larger scale of production, and high levels of protection which enable firms to establish themselves in markets prematurely with less than optimum levels of output.[9] The proposed export subsidy is a step in the right direction. The abolition of the investment incentive and a reduction in the level of protection, by lowering the custom duties on consumer goods, would also help.

There are, however, certain crucial questions on which more research will need to be conducted before correcting the price distortions which have been implicit in tax

---

5. See, for example, Annex Five.

6. New hotels and the machinery installed in them are also entitled to investment allowance.

7. Social security contributions are fixed at 10 percent of gross wages to be shared equally between the employers and employees, subject to a maximum contribution by an employee of £20 per month.

8. About 135 enterprises investing some £4.5 million during 1966–1968 claimed £0.9 million in investment allowance costing the exchequer about £0.4 million in lost revenues.

9. See Annex Three. It may be mentioned in passing that many of the suggestions contained in the preceding paragraphs have also been made by the ILO/UNDP report, largely on the ground that capital should be valued at its social cost and should not be subsidized.

incentives given to capital so far. First, it is probable that valuing capital at its shadow price would raise the labor-capital ratio and therefore improve employment prospects. But effects on the labor-output ratio are not so certain. Should the two ratios move in the same direction (and there may be some sectors where this might happen), the trade-off between employment and labor productivity could be avoided. Otherwise, the trade-off will have to be assessed, and a political decision made.

A second effect of the employment oriented development strategy could be its effect on savings and capital formation. Once again, very little is known about the saving propensity of profit (particularly when they are likely to be repatriated abroad) vis-à-vis wages, and it would be unwise to make a judgment on these relationships without better information.

Finally, an employment strategy oriented towards the modern sector alone would be both inadequate and self-defeating: inadequate, because the scope for generating new jobs in a relatively small modern sector of the economy, simply by correcting price distortions, will always be limited;[10] self-defeating, because the wage differential between the urban formal sector and the rest of the economy might widen still further, leading to accelerated urban migration and even greater unemployment. An employment strategy which ignores the remedies for generating employment and incomes on the farm, as well as encouraging the labor force to stay in rural areas, is bound to be partial at best and fail at worst.

Tax Policies Toward Agricultural Employment

Adopting fiscal policies to raise farm incomes and improve public services in the rural areas must be the twin principles underlying the strategy of generation of agricultural employment. Despite progress made in both these fields in the past, much more vigorous action will be required if any real impact is to be made on rural poverty and unemployment. The wide gap between rural and urban areas in matters of community and social services was pointed out in the last chapter. What needs to be stressed now is that closing this gap is essential not only on equity grounds but on employment grounds as well.

The level of farm incomes clearly depends, among other things, upon the prices that farm products fetch, the intensity with which farm land is utilized, and the level of farm costs. Elsewhere in the report, we have emphasized the importance of correcting distortions in agricultural prices, which are strongly influenced by pricing policies laid down by the Government, often in the interest of urban consumers.[11] Besides this, some marketing boards are operating at a low level of efficiency, which further penalizes the producer. The Government has promised to remove the local authority cesses on agricultural commodities at the earliest possible opportunity, and this should be welcome. But price distortions are far more pervasive, and the whole question of agricultural prices and terms of trade between agriculture and industry must be urgently reviewed.

Incomes from agricultural exports face the handicap of an overvalued exchange rate,[12] and until recently coffee and sisal also were subjected to an export duty. Fortunately for Kenya, the Government never depended heavily on export duty revenues for financing the budget so that the revenue aspect of export duty could be ignored. The

---

10. As Annex Three finds, the elasticity of private modern sector employment with respect to output has been as low as 0.1 in the past. Price distortions may also have had some positive effects on investment (and therefore employment) which would be lost.

11. Terms of trade between the agricultural sector and the rest of the economy moved from 100 in 1964 to 87 in 1970. See *Ndegwa Report,* Table 22.

12. The exchange rate is maintained at its present level in part by import tariffs and controls. Implicit in this system is a significant taxation of agricultural exports. See Annex Three.

retention or otherwise of the export duty was therefore examined on the basis of nonfiscal considerations such as their allocative and distributional effects. The case for removing export duties was always strong, and the mission welcomes its abolition in the 1973/74 budget. But if taxation on agriculture, now inherent in the Kenya economy, is to be removed, the agricultural exporters should also be partially compensated for overvaluation of the exchange rate. This would require a generalized export subsidy with as few exceptions as possible. The export incentive announced in the 1973/74 budget would apply only to manufactured exports outside the Community.

The whole package of taxation and subsidies affecting the agricultural sector needs to be looked into with a view to encouraging agricultural employment. The Kenya Government has never received any substantial budgetary revenues from the agricultural sector and this should make the task of revision easier. In general, it would appear that the Government might work towards imposing a general land tax and tightening the administration of agricultural income taxation. At the same time, specific taxes (and subsidies) on individual commodities, which distort land use and create problems of equity, should be progressively removed, and the Government has made a good start in this direction. The mission concurs with the recommendation of the Agricultural Sector Survey (see Part III) that input subsidies should be scrapped unless they can be administered to benefit the uninitiated small farmers, and be made self-eliminating, whenever possible.

How much of a dent all this makes on farmers' productivity and incomes is hard to say. We feel that tax policy alone can have little effect. But tax measures, coupled with a reorientation of government investment and recurrent budgets to assist agricultural and rural development, would certainly reinforce the effects of the more general strategy which we propose in this report.

Government Expenditure on Agriculture and Rural Development

Soon after Independence, the Kenya Government made major efforts in rural areas in the form of resettlement schemes, land registration and consolidation, introduction of cash crops and crop intensification schemes, and encouragement of self-help efforts. Attempts were also made to improve rural water supplies, electrification, and rural transportation. All these measures helped greatly to increase the employment capacity of small scale agriculture.[13] Government expenditure on agriculture and rural development has not grown in line with other sectors, however. As a matter of fact, it has been almost static since Independence (Table 37).

The Second Development Plan stressed the role of agriculture and rural development and explicitly stated: "The key strategy of this Plan is to direct an increasing share of the total resources available to the nation towards the rural areas."[14] Apart from agriculture, the emphasis in rural areas during the Plan period was to be on roads, water supplies, and housing. Another major ingredient of the Plan was to be the government experiment with an integrated Special Rural Development Program (SRDP), which sought to coordinate the provision of services, such as credit, marketing, and agricultural inputs, to smallholder farms, to be carried out initially in six divisions of the country, and to be extended later to other areas.

The Second Plan allocated £40 million for agriculture, £2.5 million for integrated rural development, £7 million for rural water supplies and sewerage, £11 million for

13. G. D. Gwyer, "Employment Opportunities in Kenya Agriculture," *East Africa Journal*, Vol. 9, No. 3 (March 1972), pp. 23–27.
14. *Development Plan 1970–1974*, p. 2. Nevertheless, the Second Plan allocated only 24 percent of total expenditure to agriculture (excluding rural development against 42 percent during the First Plan).

rural roads, £1.5 million for rural housing, and another £0.5 million on self-help and social welfare schemes. Excluding rural education and rural health, which would obviously absorb large recurrent expenditures, the Government proposed to spend about £63 million, or about one-third of the total Plan investment, on agricultural and rural projects. This allocation of resources towards rural sector projects was obviously consistent with the stated key strategy of the Plan and would have made significant impact on the country's rural and urban unemployment problem.

Unfortunately, achievements have not matched the planned targets. From the very start, the integrated SRDP faced severe difficulties of formulation, coordination, and implementation. The SRDP also experienced financial problems.[15] Moreover, while expenditure targets of the Plan as a whole have generally been exceeded (see Chapter 2), expenditure on agriculture and other rural services lagged behind the levels proposed in the Plan.[16] Excluding expenditure on land adjudication, expenditure on agriculture during the 1970–74 Plan period has amounted to some £24 million, or about the same level as allowed for in the Plan (Table 38). However, the actual expenditure figures are at current prices, while the Plan targets were in constant prices, and a substantial proportion of actual expenditures were for transfers, particularly the purchase of state equity in the sugar industry. Thus, in real terms, development expenditure on agriculture has not been as high as hoped for.

Table 38 also shows that the share of government capital expenditure going to agriculture has consistently declined since Independence—from almost 80 percent in 1964/65 to less than 10 percent in 1972/73. Most of this dramatic fall is due to the sharp decline in costs of the settlement program after the mid-sixties. But even if these costs are excluded, expenditure on agriculture does not appear to have grown very substantially. A similar picture emerges with respect to recurrent expenditures on agriculture (Table 17). Rural water supply and rural roads have, however, been absorbing a gradually increasing share of government investment from the very low level in 1964/65.

While the absorptive capacity problems in agriculture are admittedly serious, the fact remains that government investment expenditures in agriculture and rural development match neither the large needs of the rural population nor the goals the Government laid down in the last Plan.

Conclusion

The Kenya Government can partially remedy open unemployment by directly employing the job seekers in the public sector itself. However, such a solution must not ignore the cost and efficiency considerations, which, not being easily quantifiable, can easily fall prey to political pressures. It must be stressed that there would always be a resource constraint on the capacity of the Government to employ a growing proportion of the labor force.

A more useful role that the fiscal policy itself can play in solving the unemployment problem would be:

- to remove price distortions favoring capital as a factor of production, such as the investment allowance, the import duty exemption given to capital goods, and the nontaxation of capital gains;
- to remove, or at least reduce, price distortions against labor; and
- to drop the cesses levied on individual agricultural commodities.

15. The World Bank Agricultural Sector Survey reviewed the achievements of the SRDP, and its views are incorporated in Part III.
16. These levels themselves were considered to be too low by past World Bank economic missions.

All that this would mean is that fiscal policy would be neutral to factor prices and agricultural prices. This is probably the least that Kenya's fiscal policy can do.

On the positive side, while various instruments such as wage subsidies or employment allowances have been suggested in the past, the mission believes that a more useful purpose could be served by redirecting the pattern of government expenditure towards the employment and income-generating activities in agriculture. Among other things, this would require breaking the barrier of limited absorptive capacity in the rural sector, as discussed in Annex Five.

CHAPTER 5

A FISCAL STRATEGY FOR DEVELOPMENT

Avoiding a Resource Problem

Any fiscal strategy for the future must, at the very least, avoid a serious resource constraint on continued development. Some recent tendencies suggest a possibility that, unless certain policy measures are undertaken, the Government might not be in a position to have at its disposal adequate resources to finance its expanding investment during the coming years.[1]

It is true that, to some extent, the Kenya Government can reduce the seriousness of this problem by reorienting its investment pattern more towards directly productive and less capital intensive activities like agriculture. The Government can also do more to stimulate an increased flow of foreign aid to Kenya. But, even with these measures, a budgetary constraint is likely to arise during the next plan period, unless the Government undertakes some reform of fiscal policy.

Nevertheless, the mission feels that the budgetary position, given such reform, need not get out of hand. For example, if the Kenya Government improves its tax effort (by raising the present built-in elasticity of 1.3 to 1.9) and keeps an eye on the overall growth of its recurrent expenditures, the government sector resource gap would be easily manageable.

Recurrent Expenditures

Keeping an eye on recurrent expenditures in Kenya's particular circumstances would involve first, decelerating the rate of growth of recurrent expenditure on social services, particularly education. In a sense this process has already been initiated—the share of recurrent expenditure going to education in the 1973/74 budget has declined slightly over the last year. Review of education policy and instituting revisions in the educational structure could provide further scope for trimming expenditures, and at the same time should also help reduce the degree of open unemployment in the economy in the long run.

Second, many governments, in Africa and elsewhere, have tended, under political pressures, to solve the problem of school leaver unemployment through public employment. Often, this has meant that efficiency and cost considerations are ignored, and the government wage bill tends to expand without regard to government resources. While Kenya has not resorted to "make-work" of this kind in the past, increased vigilance will be called for in the future, as political pressures of increasing unemployment build up.

Third, in an economy such as Kenya's, there are likely to be strong pressures on government salaries to catch up with salaries offered in the modern private sector. Despite political pressures, salary levels need to be determined with reference to supply conditions and other economic considerations. If the Government can control its own salary levels, it will be easier for it to bring about a more appropriate wage and incomes structure in the economy as a whole. The Government recognizes the urgency of this matter.

---

1. Already in 1973/74, the level of development expenditure is being reduced from £73 million to £62 million, as the Finance Minister has said, "not due to slackness on the part of Ministries, but as a result of deliberate action by the Treasury in controlling development spending *in accordance with the estimates of the financial resources available*" [italics added]. Budget Speech, 1973/74.

While these are points to be watched, it should be noted that Kenya has never had any serious problem in controlling recurrent expenditures in the past. In fact, as mentioned earlier, the Government was fairly disciplined in this respect, perhaps a little conservative, up until 1970/71. Only in very recent years has the growth in recurrent expenditure accelerated and exceeded the growth in revenues, leading to some worry. The Kenya Government itself is very conscious of the changed environment and is attempting to remedy the position. The growth rate of recurrent expenditure proposed for 1973/74 is about 12 percent, which is significantly lower than achieved in the last few years. It remains to be seen to what extent this reduction can be absorbed without a loss in momentum.

Scope for Tax Reform

There is scope for improving the tax revenue base in the yet untapped instruments of indirect taxation, as well as for tightening administration of direct taxes. The Kenya Government has already taken some steps to exploit these as will be indicated later. The main instruments of *commodity taxation* until now have been the excise duties (and consumption taxes) which were specific[2] and limited to less than ten major items, and the import duties, which exempt very many rapidly growing commodities. In addition, the imports of the Kenya Government and the EAC institutions were until recently also exempt from duty. This kind of indirect tax structure consequently had very limited elasticity indeed.

To improve upon the elasticity of these taxes, as well as to use them as development tools, it is essential to:

- broaden the base as much as possible;
- make the rates ad valorem;
- have discriminating tax burdens on domestic output and imports to provide the necessary protection; and,
- make the tax rates as nonselective as possible, except for luxuries and other commodities, where the need for discouraging conspicuous consumption is clearly felt.

The Kenya Government has very recently started moving in this direction by imposing a broad-based *sales tax*, and by repealing the limited consumption taxes. In mid-1973, a 10 percent sales tax was levied on all manufactured goods, locally produced as well as imported, except for petrol, beer, and electricity, on which the previous high specific tax rates have been retained. Most food products (e.g., maize and wheat flour, sugar, meat, milk), certain basic necessities (e.g., medicines and pharmaceutical goods, newsprint, and books) and some of the agricultural inputs like fertilizers and diesel fuel have, also been exempted from sales tax. The tax also does not apply to the output of small manufacturers, with a turnover of less than £5,000. Although exports will be exempt from sales tax, government departments, like other consumers, will have to pay this tax. These exemptions are not very important, and the introduction of the sales tax should go a long way to improve the built-in elasticity of indirect taxation.

The immediate net gain to the Government from sales tax will not be very large, however, because of the abolition of the GPT and most of the previous consumption taxes. Sales tax is expected to yield about £22 million in 1973/74[3] against which must

---

2. The 1973/74 budget has changed the excise duties on cigarettes and pipe tobacco to an ad valorem basis.

3. The value of domestic output plus the imports (including import duties) net of exports was was £290 million in 1970. Of this the sales tax exempt items were about £57 million (grain mill products, £15 million; sugar, £11 million; meat products, £4 million; dairy products, £8 million; printing and publishing, £9 million; miscellaneous chemical products, £10 million).

be written off the loss of £8 million, due to the repeal of consumption taxes, and the grants-in-aid which the Government will need to give to municipal councils to offset the loss of £8 million of revenues from GPT. On a net basis therefore the addition to present government revenues will be small, but in the long run, as consumption in the economy grows, sales tax can be expected to become a powerful revenue tool. Assuming that the GDP (at current prices) will continue to grow at about 12 percent per annum and that aggregate consumption grows at the same rate, sales tax revenues can be expected to grow at least as fast.

The Kenya Government has recognized the need for a tariff reform and has started to move in this direction in the 1973/74 budget in concert with the other two Partner States. Some previous exemptions to import duty have been abolished and dutiable items are now taxed on an ad valorem basis. The old structure giving very high protection to consumer goods industries and almost no protection to domestic production of capital goods, is beginning to change.[4] Import duties on a list of very select raw material items have been lowered, and government departments, as well as EAC corporations, have lost their duty exempt status. It is quite possible that the immediate net revenue impact of these import duty reforms would not be very large, particularly as the Government has simultaneously agreed to adopt a scheme of export subsidies, the details of which have not yet been clearly worked out. But, then, the purpose of tariff reform would be largely to make custom duties a tool of development and not a major tool of additional revenues.

Specifically, the direction in which Kenya's indirect tax structure could move over the next Plan period would involve:

- a uniform tariff on imports determined by the needs of protection accompanied by selective additional sales taxes on luxury imports;
- a set of excise duties on domestic manufactures, the rates of which should be determined in comparison with the structure of import duties and in the light of crucial allocation and equity considerations; and,
- a broad based sales tax, levied on both domestic manufactures and imports, the rates of which could be determined by revenue considerations.

Some scope also exists to mobilize resources through *direct taxation*. In the area of personal income taxation, there has always been an urgent need to reduce the still high exemption limit resulting largely from generous child exemptions. The recent abolition of GPT has clearly added to this urgency and, recognizing it, the 1973/74 budget incorporated a number of important income tax reforms. Exemption levels granted under income tax have been reduced, so that married persons with four children earning incomes between £720 and £960 will also be subject to income tax. Taxpayers now get only fixed tax credits relevant to their family status, and income tax rates have also been slightly adjusted, with effect from 1973/74.

The Kenya Government might examine the possibilities of tightening the loopholes which exist in the present tax structure, such as deductions and allowances for life insurance,[5] employees' entertainment, and owner-occupied housing.[6] Various possibilities of tightening income tax administration, particularly in relation to the self-employed, might also be explored. It is hoped that the establishment of a national income tax department will significantly improve income tax administration.

It must be emphasized that some tax reforms need to be considered primarily on grounds of redistribution and equity, although these reforms would also have some revenue implications. A form of wealth taxation is one possibility. Another is the

---

4. See Annex Three.
5. The 1973/74 budget has restricted life insurance relief to a tax credit of £18.
6. Income tax deductions for contributions to pension funds and provident funds have been disallowed in the 1973/74 budget.

imposition of land taxation, coupled with an extension and improvement in urban property taxation, and levying a capital gains tax.

The Government of Kenya has invested a substantial amount of resources in *public enterprises*, many of which are, by their very nature, commercial enterprises. While most of them are performing useful regulatory and development functions, it is not at all clear as to how far they are acting as instruments of resource mobilization or capital formation. The relatively low (and often negative) profits that they are earning at present would seem to suggest that there is scope for improving their efficiency and generating higher profits. But, then, the Kenya Government would need to define their role in these terms and make conscious efforts in those directions.

It is extremely difficult to estimate the revenue impact of all these possibilities and therefore the resulting effect on the intensity of remaining resource constraint. To the extent that the resource constraint itself is a function of level and growth rate of capital expenditures, a reexamination of patterns of expenditures may also be in order.

Reviewing the Investment Pattern

A question that has to be faced by the Government is whether or not to slow down the rate of growth of expenditure, particularly of capital formation in infrastructure. Besides the fact that adequate domestic and perhaps foreign resources may not be available, the impact of a rapidly growing public investment program on the balance of payments, as well as the future recurrent expenditures, cannot be safely ignored. What impact a slowing down of the government's capital expenditure program will have on the overall rate of growth of the economy must also be considered. This would obviously depend upon the category of expenditure which is decelerated.

In the past (and this is true of 1973/74 budget as well) road construction and housing construction in the public sector have absorbed very significant proportions of government investment, and both of these factors have been capital intensive in Kenya's case. It has also meant that the country's physical infrastructure, particularly roads, has been relatively well developed. An underlying thesis of this report therefore is that Kenya might now divert expenditure from infrastructure, decelerate (and redirect) expenditure on education and reallocate expenditure, in a relative sense, to directly productive sectors like agriculture. This shift in emphasis seems to be justified, not only on grounds of employment and income generation, but on many equity grounds as well.

Focusing on Equity and Employment

While a fiscal strategy for the future must attempt to avoid a serious resource problem, it must do so in such a way as to serve the objectives of distributive justice and employment generation. As mentioned earlier, Kenya's tax structure seems to have had limited success in respect of both these objectives. Although personal income tax is progressive in Kenya, it affects a very small proportion of the population and will probably continue doing so even after the recent reforms. The existing property taxes are least progressive over most income ranges. A further lowering of personal allowance, the imposition of progressive capital gains taxes, (and, possibly, land taxes), and the tightening and extension of urban property taxation, could all become instruments of greater equity.

On the indirect taxes side, the excise duties are somewhat regressive, and the recently enacted sales tax can be expected to introduce only limited progressivity, since it exempts basic foods. A more progressive taxation of luxuries under excise duties, alone, could ensure further redistribution effects.

On the expenditure front—deemphasizing urban and higher education in favor of rural and vocational education; deemphasizing trunk primary roads in favor of feeder and rural roads; and reallocating public expenditure in favor of agriculture and rural development, generally should be welcome both on equity and employment grounds.

Tariff reforms, indicated earlier, should help to discourage capital intensity and, given the elasticity of factor substitution, encourage employment. Employment generation may also be helped, though admittedly marginally, by the abolition of investment allowances and the grant of positive tax incentives to employment.

Financial Viability of Local Authorities

If the Kenya Government wants to retain the local authorities and bestow a developmental role upon them, local government structure will have to be strengthened and made financially viable. (On the other hand, local authorities will also have to be provided with trained personnel and be taught financial responsibility.) The fiscal alternatives lie between an autonomous and elastic source of revenue, or else a revenue sharing formula, based on criteria of need and efficiency of revenue mobilization. The 1973/74 budget has already initiated the process of Central Government revenue sharing with the municipal councils following the abolition of the GPT.

But the regional inequality of natural, physical, and human resources in Kenya is such that sooner or later the Government will have to consider some formula for compensatory grants, even if the local authorities were provided with elastic revenue instruments of their own.[7] The scope for improving existing property ratings in municipal council areas and the assessment of land taxation in the county council areas could be the two most important instruments of local taxation. The possibility of an additional sales tax by local authorities (or a surcharge collected for them by the Central Government) could also be explored.

Integrating Self-Help Efforts

Self-help has been ignored in this annex on the ground that it is not really a fiscal instrument. However, to the extent voluntary contributions by the public towards development projects ease the strain on fiscal policy, a brief mention is in order. In Kenya, the Harambee, or self-help, movement has proved an extremely valuable way of mobilizing local resources and encouraging local people to participate in development. During the years 1965–1972, some £16 million[8] has been raised for capital projects in the fields of education, health, water supplies, agriculture, and other construction. While such efforts should certainly be encouraged, they must be integrated into the design and planning of the Government's fiscal policy. In particular, staffing, maintenance, and recurrent spending on such projects must be coordinated with overall national policies.

---

7. See the *Report of the Fiscal Commission* (1963), pp. 68–69.
8. Of this amount, over £5 million were contributed during 1971 and 1972 alone. See *Economic Survey*, 1973, p. 198.

Appendix: Estimating "Built-in Recurrent" Expenditure

In estimating the future "built-in" or "normal" growth rate of government recurrent expenditure, we have made separate assumptions about the rate of growth of the three major components of government expenditure—wages and salaries, consumption of goods and services, and transfers. The basis of these disaggregated assumptions are given below.

Wage Bill

We have assumed:

(a) *That government employment grows at 5 percent per year.* This was the rate of increase of central government employment between 1964 and 1969,[1] and implies that government investment grows at the same pace as in the past and that the labor-capital ratio in the government sector remains constant.
(b) *That government employees get only the "normal" salary increments of about 4 percent a year,*[2] *which implies that* there is no overall salary structure review or general cost of living adjustment during the period.

Under these assumptions, the total government wage bill would rise by about 9 percent a year, which, in itself, would result in a built-in rate of growth of 4.5 percent a year in total recurrent expenditure.[3]

Goods and Services

We have assumed:

(a) *That government "real" purchases of goods and services (other than salaries) increase by 7 percent a year.* Of this, 5 percent would be the result of the Government's increasing employment (assuming a constant ratio of "real" goods and services to employees), and the other 2 percent reflects an increase in the use of stocks and supplies.
(b) *That there is a price rise of 5 percent a year.* This rate is higher than experienced generally in the past, but is consistent with the rate of inflation in 1971 and 1972 and with our macro-economic projections.

On these assumptions, government expenditures on goods and services would increase by about 12 percent a year, leading to a further 3 percent increase in total recurrent expenditure.[4]

Transfers

There is likely to be some increase in transfer payments in the future (at least the interest payments are likely to grow), but there is little basis for estimating what the

---

1. See Table 4. The terminal year of 1969 has been chosen for this purpose, as after this year the civil service was expanded by the Central Government takeover of certain functions and employees of the local authorities.
2. The new 95-point single salary scale, which was proposed by the Ndegwa Commission, and implemented by the Government in 1971, yields such an annual salary "creep." In reality, the wage bill would rise by less than 4 percent if higher salaried staff retire and are replaced by lower salaried staff.
3. $0.50 \times 0.09 = 0.045$.
4. $0.25 \times 0.12 = 0.030$. During 1964/65–1968/69, government expenditure on other purchases of goods and services increased by about 10 percent per annum (Table 21) of which 3 percent could be estimated to be the effect of inflation.

rate of increase will be. We have assumed that transfer payments grow at the same rate as in the past, that is, by about 2 percent a year.[5] This would cause the overall recurrent expenditure to grow by another 0.5 percent a year.[6]

Total Built-in Growth Rate

These assumptions therefore give us the following estimate of the total "normal" (or "built-in") growth of recurrent expenditure:

	Annual Rate of Growth			% of Total Expenditures	% Increase in Total Expenditure
	In Real Terms	Price Increase	In Current Terms		
	(percentage)					
Wages and salaries	5	4	9	50	4.5
Goods and services	7	5	12	25	3.0
Transfers	—	—	2	25	0.5
Total recurrent expenditure				100	8.0

---

5. Since this rate was about equal to the average rate of inflation in the past, transfer payments have remained more or less constant in real terms. This is consistent with the assumptions made in Annex One.

6. $0.25 \times 0.02 = 0.005$.

STATISTICAL TABLES

Annex Two

Index

Table
No.

Public Sector in the Economy

1.	Contribution of the Public Sector to Gross Domestic Product at Factor Cost, 1964–72	210
2.	Contribution of the Public Sector to Capital Formation, 1964–72	211
3.	Public Sector Imports, 1964/65–1971/72	212
4.	Wage Employment in the Public Sector, 1964–72	213
5.	Wage Bill in the Public Sector, 1964–72	214
6.	Average Earnings of Government Employees, 1963–72	215
7.	Consolidated General (Central and Local) Government Finances, 1966/67–1971/72	215

Central Government Finances

8.	Central Government Finances, 1964/65–1972/73	216
9.	Fiscal Trends, 1965/66–1972/73	217
10.	Trends, Ownership, and Servicing of Public Debt, 1965–72	218
11.	Central Government Savings, 1964/65–1971/72	220
12.	Revenue Effort, 1964/65–1972/73	221
13.	Central Government Revenue Ratios, 1964/65–1971/72	222
14.	Central Government Tax Effort, 1963/64–1971/72	223
15.	Central Government Finances: Kenya in Comparison with Other Developing Countries, Around 1970	224
16.	Budget Performance, 1964/65–1972/73	225
17.	Functional Classification of Central Government Recurrent Expenditures, 1964/65–1972/73	226
18.	Functional Allocations of Central Government Recurrent Expenditures, 1964/65–1972/73	227
19.	Functional Classification of Central Government Capital Expenditures, 1964/65–1972/73	228
20.	Functional Allocations of Central Government Capital Expenditures, Selected Years, 1964/65–1972/73	229
21.	Economic Classification of Central Government Recurrent Expenditures, 1964/65–1971/72	230
22.	Economic Classification of Central Government Capital Expenditures, 1964/65–1971/72	231
23.	Budgetary Projections, 1973/74–1977/78	232

Local Government Finances

24.	Local Government Finances, 1966–72	233
25.	Local Government Revenues, 1966–72	234
26.	Economic Classification of Local Government Expenditures (Total), 1966–72	235

27.	Functional Classification of Local Government Expenditures (Total), 1966–72	236

Parastastals and Government Agencies

28.	Parastatal Enterprises in Relation to the Government Budget, 1965/66–1970/71	237
29.	Government Budget and Public Corporations, 1964/65–1970/71	237
30.	Profitability of Selected Public Corporations, 1964/65–1970/71	238
31.	Government Budget and General Government Agencies, 1964/65–1970/71	239

Impact of Fiscal Policy

32.	Income Tax Rates, 1973/74	240
33.	Burden of Road Taxation, 1964–71	240
34.	Average Burden of Import Duty, Selected Years (by SITC)	241
35.	Distribution of Local Government Services, 1968	242
36.	Distribution of Public Services by Province, Around 1970	251
37.	Primary School Enrollment by Province, 1968–72	252
38.	Government Development Expenditure on Agriculture and Selected Rural Services, 1964/65–1972/73	253

Table 1: Contribution of the Public Sector to Gross Domestic Product at Factor Cost, 1964–72

(percentage)

Sector	1964	1965	1966	1967	1968	1969	1970	1971	1972[1]
General Government Sector	12.9	13.3	13.0	13.1	14.5	15.1	14.8	16.5	16.8
Central Government	8.5	n.a.	n.a.	n.a.	n.a.	n.a.	n.a.	n.a.	14.3
EAC	0.8	n.a.	n.a.	n.a.	n.a.	n.a.	n.a.	n.a.	0.8
Statutory boards and parastatal bodies	0.2	n.a.	n.a.	n.a.	n.a.	n.a.	n.a.	n.a.	0.3
Local authorities	3.4	n.a.	n.a.	n.a.	n.a.	n.a.	n.a.	n.a.	1.4
Enterprise Sector	11.1	12.0	11.6	11.7	12.0	11.7	12.9	14.4	13.9
TOTAL PUBLIC SECTOR	24.0	25.3	24.6	24.8	26.5	26.8	27.7	30.9	30.7

[1] Provisional.

SOURCE: *Statistical Abstracts* (annual) and *Economic Survey*, 1973.

Table 2: Contribution of the Public Sector to Capital Formation, 1964–72

Sector	1964	1965	1966	1967	1968	1969	1970	1971	1972[1]
					(£ million)				
Public sector	11.1	11.9	19.4	28.5	32.9	30.6	34.2	55.6	61.6
Kenya Government	4.2	7.0	8.8	12.8	15.0	17.9	23.7	31.0	36.4
EAC	4.8	2.3	6.4	8.8	7.4	6.3	5.6	11.2	6.0
Statutory boards and parastatal bodies	0.6	1.2	2.4	3.3	5.2	2.3	2.0	7.7	10.8
Local government	1.4	1.4	1.9	3.7	5.3	4.1	3.0	5.7	8.5
Total public and private sectors	44.3	45.7	61.2	82.2	89.5	93.7	112.7	144.2	159.9
					(percentage)				
Share of public sector in capital formation	24.8	26.0	31.9	34.8	36.8	32.7	30.4	38.6	38.6

[1] Provisional.

SOURCE: *Statistical Abstracts* (annual) and *Economic Survey*, 1973.

Table 3: Public Sector Imports, 1964/65–1971/72

Sector	1964/65	1965/66	1966/67	1967/68	1968/69	1969/70	1970/71	1971/72[1]
	(£ million)							
Public sector[2] imports	8.5	14.2	19.1	17.5	16.6	15.9	18.4	19.3
General Government[3] (final consumption) imports	3.1	5.2	5.4	4.7	4.8	5.3	7.2	9.3
Total net imports	82.8	100.7	109.5	110.7	115.4	129.5	163.0	180.8
Total (recurrent and capital) expenditures of the Central Government	59.8	69.9	82.6	99.5	111.7	130.2	168.6	195.0
General Government GDP	42.9	45.6	50.6	58.5	67.5	74.2	83.7	101.9
Public sector GDP	81.2	88.1	96.4	108.3	122.5	136.7	151.9	188.5
	(percentage)							
Public sector imports as % of total net imports	10.3	14.1	17.4	15.8	14.4	12.3	11.3	10.7
Public sector imports as % of public sector GDP	10.5	16.1	19.8	16.2	13.6	11.6	12.1	10.2
General Government imports as % of total net imports	3.7	5.2	4.9	4.2	4.2	4.1	4.4	5.1
General Government imports as % of General Government GDP	7.2	11.3	10.7	8.0	7.1	7.1	8.6	9.1
General Government imports as % of Central Government expenditures	5.2	7.4	6.5	4.7	4.3	4.1	4.3	4.8

[1] Provisional.
[2] Public sector here consists of Kenya Government, East African Community (EAC), and East African Corporations.
[3] General Government here means Kenya Government and General Fund Services of EAC only.

SOURCE: *Statistical Abstract*, 1972.

Table 4: Wage Employment in the Public Sector, 1964–72

Sector	1964	1965	1966	1967	1968	1969	1970	1971	1972[1]
					(thousand)				
Public sector	182.0	188.2	200.4	212.1	221.9	237.1	247.5	256.0	275.5
Kenya Government	85.5	85.1	93.5	94.9	99.1	108.6	159.6[2]	164.3	177.0
EAC (general fund services)	3.1	3.3	3.1	3.0	2.9	2.8	3.1	3.2	3.7
East African railways and harbors	23.3	24.3	26.4	25.4	25.3	23.2	22.5	22.6	23.1
East African posts and telecommunications	4.5	4.5	4.8	4.7	4.8	4.8	5.5	5.8	5.8
East African Airways Corporation	1.7	2.0	2.1	2.5	3.0	3.3	3.8	3.7	3.9
East African cargo handling services	8.1	9.2	10.0	7.8	9.6	8.2	8.7	9.9	9.1
East African Harbors Corporation	n.a.	n.a.	n.a.	n.a.	n.a.	1.9	2.2	3.1	3.0
Other East African public bodies	n.a.	n.a.	n.a.	n.a.	n.a.	n.a.	n.a.	0.8	1.0
Parastatal bodies	n.a.	n.a.	n.a.	13.4	14.1	17.0	18.4	18.8	23.1
Local Government	55.5	59.4	60.2	59.8	63.1	67.3	23.7[2]	23.8	25.8
Total wage employment in the modern sector	575.4	582.0	585.4	597.5	606.4	627.2	644.5	679.7	709.4
					(percentage)				
Share of public sector in total wage employment	31.6	32.3	34.2	35.4	36.6	37.8	38.4	37.7	38.8

[1] Provisional.
[2] Reflects the major transfer of functions from the county councils to the Central Government which took place in 1970.

SOURCE: *Statistical Abstracts* (annual) and *Economic Survey*, 1973.

Table 5: Wage Bill in the Public Sector, 1964–72

Item	1964	1965	1966	1967	1968	1969	1970	1971	1972[1]
					(£ million)				
Public sector	45.1	51.4	58.0	62.9	67.1	71.7	79.3	86.8	96.2
Kenya Government	19.9	22.8	26.2	27.1	29.4	31.8	43.5[2]	49.7	52.9
EAC and Corporations	14.8	17.0	19.8	18.2	19.4	19.7	21.7	22.7	23.5
Parastatal bodies	—	—	—	3.4	3.9	4.3	6.6	6.8	11.1
Local Government	10.4	11.6	12.0	14.2	14.5	15.9	7.5[2]	7.6	8.7
Factor incomes in the monetary economy	240.0	250.0	283.5	296.2	330.4	359.9	404.9	448.9	504.1
Remuneration of employees in the monetary economy	131.6	137.6	153.2	167.7	189.6	203.4	224.7	257.3	285.4
					(percentage)				
Public sector share in factor incomes	18.8	20.6	20.5	21.2	20.3	19.9	19.6	19.6	19.1
Public sector share in the remuneration of employees	34.3	37.4	37.9	37.5	35.4	35.3	35.3	34.7	33.7

[1] Provisional.
[2] Reflects the major transfer of functions from the county councils to the Central Government which took place in 1970.

SOURCE: *Statistical Abstracts* (annual) and *Economic Survey*, 1973.

FISCAL POLICY FOR DEVELOPMENT

Table 6: Average Earnings of Government Employees, 1963–72

Year	General Government[1] Wage Bill	General Government[1] Employment	Average Earnings Government Employees	Average Earnings Private Sector[2] Employees	Average Earnings Private Industry and Commerce Employees
	(£ million)	(thousand)	(£)	(£)	(£)
1963	24.4	120.6	202.3	146.1	266.3
1964	30.3	141.0	214.9	153.7	250.4
1965	34.4	144.5	238.1	159.5	259.7
1966	38.2	153.7	248.5	179.5	285.4
1967	41.3	154.7	267.0[3]	191.8	292.4
1968	43.9	162.2	270.7	206.0	316.3
1969	47.9	176.4	217.5	210.0	325.9
1970	51.1	184.0	277.7	224.8	353.9
1971	57.2	187.8	304.6[4]	230.1	352.0
1972[5]	61.6	202.8	303.7	247.5	377.3

[1] General Government is defined to cover the central and local governments only.
[2] Includes agriculture, forestry, and fisheries.
[3] There was a salary review commission in 1967 (see Sessional Papers Nos. 10 and 11 of 1967).
[4] Across-the-board pay increases were announced in May 1971 following the Ndegwa Commission.
[5] Provisional.

SOURCE: *Statistical Abstract*, 1972, and *Economic Survey*, 1973.

Table 7: Consolidated General (Central and Local) Government Finances, 1966/67–1971/72

Category	1966/67	1967/68	1968/69	1969/70	1970/71	1971/72[1]
			(£ million)			
Recurrent revenues	83.1	95.0	102.1	115.2	139.9	158.1
Central Government	66.0	77.7	84.9	99.2	124.2	141.2
Local Governments	17.1	17.3	17.2	16.0	15.7	16.9
Recurrent expenditures[2]	84.8	92.3	95.1	102.2	115.9	134.2
Central Government	64.8	70.1	75.2	87.1	100.8	118.5
Local Governments	20.0	22.2	19.9	15.1	15.1	15.7
Capital expenditures[2]	19.2	25.7	30.8	34.4	51.4	63.3
Central Government	16.6	21.8	26.8	31.0	44.4	53.8
Local Governments	2.6	3.9	4.0	3.4	7.0	9.5
Total expenditures	104.0	118.0	125.9	136.6	167.3	197.5
Central Government	81.4	91.9	102.0	118.1	145.2	172.3
Local Governments	22.6	26.1	23.9	18.5	22.1	25.2
GDP at factor cost	394.1	421.3	459.6	502.2	548.8	611.4[1]
Monetary GDP at factor cost	288.0	313.0	345.0	383.0	425.6	476.5[1]
			(percentage)			
Recurrent revenues/monetary GDP	28.8	30.4	29.6	30.1	32.9	33.2
Total expenditures/GDP	26.4	28.0	27.4	27.2	30.5	32.3
Capital expenditures/total expenditures	18.4	21.8	24.4	25.2	30.7	32.1
Local Government expenditures/total expenditures	21.7	22.1	19.0	13.5	13.2	12.8

[1] Provisional.
[2] This is a national accounting concept somewhat different from the concept of the budget documents.

SOURCE: *Statistical Abstracts* (annual) and *Economic Survey*, 1973.

Table 8: Central Government Finances, 1964/65–1972/73

Item	1964/65 (A)[1]	1965/66 (A)	1966/67 (A)	1967/68 (A)	1968/69 (A)	1969/70 (A)	1970/71 (A)	1971/72 (B)[2]	1971/72 (A)	1972/73 (B)	1972/73 (R)[3]
					(£ million)						
Recurrent revenues[4]	49.3	57.8	66.0	77.7	84.9	99.2	124.2	130.4	141.2	140.0	146.3
Recurrent expenditures[5]	56.9	60.7	64.8	70.1	75.2	87.1	100.8	111.2	118.5	124.6	137.7
Recurrent surplus (+)/deficit (−)	−7.6	−2.9	+1.2	+7.6	+9.7	+12.1	+23.4	+19.2	+22.7	+15.4	+8.6
Capital expenditure[5]	10.5	12.1	16.6	21.8	26.8	31.0	44.4	56.6[6]	53.8[6]	69.3[6]	64.9[6]
Overall budget deficit	18.1	15.0	15.4	14.2	17.1	18.9	21.0	37.4	31.1	53.9	56.3
Financed by external sources (net)	18.6	11.5	8.3	7.8	6.2	10.1	9.6		9.4		26.4
Gross borrowings	20.5	14.6	11.3	9.8	8.1	12.3	11.7		12.9		30.0
Less contributions to sinking fund and redemptions	1.9	3.1	3.0	2.0	1.9	2.2	2.1		3.5		3.6
Financed by internal sources (net)	−0.5	3.5	7.1	6.4	10.9	8.8	11.4		21.7		29.9
Borrowings (net of use of cash balances)	0.6	5.1	7.6	7.0	11.0	10.7	19.6		27.6		33.7
Central Bank	—	—	—	−1.6	−1.8	−1.5	0.6		10.8		8.9
Commercial Banks	0.1	3.8	3.2	1.0	5.6	2.2	5.1		7.3		}24.8
Others[7]	0.5	1.3	4.4	7.6	7.2	10.0	13.9		9.5		
Less contributions to sinking fund redemptions	1.1	1.6	0.5	0.6	1.1	1.9	8.2		5.9		3.8

[1] A = Actual.
[2] B = Budget estimate.
[3] R = Revised estimate.
[4] Includes appropriations-in-aid or departmental revenues.
[5] Excludes repayment of public debt and sinking fund.
[6] These figures correspond to the budget concept of development expenditures.
[7] Borrowing from the National Social Security Fund, Cereal and Sugar Financing Corporation, etc.

SOURCE: *Economic Survey* and information supplied by the Ministry of Finance and Planning.

Table 9: Fiscal Trends, 1965/66–1972/73

Item	1965/66	1966/67	1967/68	1968/69	1969/70	1970/71	1971/72	1972/73	Average 1964/65–1966/67	Average 1967/68–1969/70	Average 1964/65–1970/71	Average 1970/71–1972/73	Average 1964/65–1972/73
								(percentage)					
Annual growth rates of Central Governments':													
Recurrent revenues	17.2	14.2	17.7	9.3	16.8	25.1	13.7	3.6	15.7	13.0	16.6	8.5	14.5
Recurrent expenditures	6.7	6.8	8.2	7.3	15.8	15.7	17.6	16.2	6.7	11.5	10.0	16.9	12.1
Capital expenditures	15.2	37.2	31.3	22.9	15.6	43.2	21.2	20.6	25.8	19.3	27.0	21.0	24.6
Recurrent savings as % of recurrent revenues	−5.0	+1.8	+9.8	+11.4	+12.2	+18.8	+16.1	+5.9	−3.2	11.1	8.1	13.6	8.9
Marginal Government savings as % of marginal revenues	55.3	50.0	36.2	29.2	17.5	45.2	−6.5	−276.5	62.0	27.6	38.9	neg.[1]	21.4
Recurrent savings as % of capital expenditure	−24.2	+7.2	+34.8	+36.2	+39.0	+52.7	+42.2	+13.3	−30.0	36.7	24.3	36.1	27.7
Contribution of net foreign capital to capital expenditures	95.0	50.0	35.8	23.1	32.6	21.6	17.8	40.7	96.5	30.5	43.0	26.7	39.4
Central bank financing of capital expenditure	—[2]	—	−7.3	−6.7	−4.8	1.4	20.0	13.7	—	−6.3	—	11.7	3.1

[1] Neg. = negative.
[2] — = negligible.

SOURCE: Table 8.

Table 10: Trends, Ownership, and Servicing of Public Debt, 1965–72

Category	1965	1966	1967	1968	1969	1970	1971	1972
(as of 30th June[1])				(£ million)				
Net public debt[2]	95.4	105.4	118.6	121.7	142.4	160.1	170.1	194.3
External (net)	76.9	86.1	91.1	85.5[3]	93.3	102.0	94.8[4]	105.8
Internal (net)	18.5	19.3	27.5	36.2	49.1	58.1	75.2	88.5
Major holders of internal debt								
National Social Security Fund	—	1.2	3.6	8.2	17.4	17.5	22.5	30.4
Central Government[5]	4.7	7.4	8.6	8.4	9.1	9.8	10.4	18.7
Kenya Post Office Savings Bank	1.2	2.1	2.1	2.1	2.1	2.6	2.6	3.5
Insurance companies	2.5	3.3	3.8	4.3	4.8	4.9	5.3	6.5
Other private companies	0.7	1.0	1.3	1.7	2.6	4.1	6.2	9.2
Commercial banks	1.0	1.1	1.7	1.7	2.3	8.0	8.5	8.1
Central Bank	3.5	3.5	3.5	3.5	3.5	3.5	3.5	5.7
Debt servicing charges (annual)	6.4	7.7	9.3	7.9	8.9	10.7	17.7	16.7
Interest	4.4	4.8	5.2	5.4	6.0	6.6	7.4	8.7
External	1.1	1.3	1.5	1.9	2.4	3.4	4.1	n.a.
Internal	3.3	3.5	3.7	3.5	3.6	3.2	3.3	n.a.
Repayments (excluding sinking fund)	2.0	2.9	4.1	2.5	2.9	4.1	10.3	8.0
External	1.5	1.9	3.9	2.3	2.4	1.6	7.4	n.a.
Internal	0.5	1.0	0.2	0.2	0.5	2.5	2.9	n.a.

FISCAL POLICY FOR DEVELOPMENT

(percentage)

Net public debt as % of GDP at factor cost[6]	28.9	29.4	30.0	28.9	30.9	31.9	29.5	30.0
Domestic debt as % of total debt	19.4	18.3	23.2	29.8	34.5	36.3	44.2	45.5
Interest payments as % of recurrent revenues[7]	8.9	8.3	7.9	7.0	7.1	6.7	6.0	5.8
Debt servicing charges as % of total expenditures[7]	9.5	10.6	11.4	8.6	8.7	9.1	12.2	10.0
External debt payments as % of value of domestic exports[8]	5.5	6.1	10.4	9.5	7.9	7.4	16.0	8.0

[1] Except for 1965 and 1966 where the figures pertain to the end of December.
[2] Figures here relate to net of sinking fund and exclude short-term borrowings. The amount of outstanding Treasury bills at the end of June, 1972 was £16 million.
[3] Reduction here reflects devaluation of sterling in 1967/68.
[4] Reduction here reflects the repayment of a major railway loan.
[5] This includes the nominal value of sinking funds along with other Treasury holdings.
[6] Data for GDP at factor cost are taken from *Statistical Abstract*, 1972.
[7] Data for recurrent revenues and total expenditures are taken from Table 10.
[8] Value of domestic exports taken from *Statistical Abstract*, 1972, and external debt payments assumed at £7 million for 1972.

SOURCE: *Economic Survey*, 1973.

Table 11: Central Government Savings, 1964/65–1971/72

Item	1964/65	1965/66	1966/67	1967/68	1968/69	1969/70	1970/71	1971/72[1]
	(£ million)							
Central Government savings	−7.6	−2.9	+1.2	+7.6	+9.7	+12.1	+23.4	+22.7
National savings	51.5	56.5	66.8	67.7	80.2	95.8	108.0	124.6
Monetary GDP at factor cost	243.0	263.0	288.0	313.0	345.0	383.0	425.6	476.5
GDP at factor cost	329.7	358.3	394.1	421.3	459.6	502.2	548.8	611.4
	(percentage)							
Central Government savings as % of national savings	−14.8	−5.1	1.8	11.2	12.1	12.6	21.7	18.2
Central Government savings as % of monetary GDP at factor cost	−3.1	−1.1	0.4	2.4	2.8	3.2	5.5	4.8
Central Government savings as % of GDP at factor cost	−2.3	−0.8	0.3	1.8	2.1	2.4	4.3	3.7

[1] Provisional.

SOURCE: Table 8, *Statistical Abstracts* (annual) and *Economic Survey*, 1973.

Table 12: Revenue Effort, 1964/65–1972/73

Revenue	1964/65	1965/66	1966/67	1967/68	1968/69	1969/70	1970/71	1971/72	1972/73[1]
					(£ million)				
Taxes on income and capital	14.0	16.9	20.1	24.4	25.9	32.5	41.4	47.0	48.9
Personal income tax	6.3	7.9	9.9	10.8	14.0	17.3	21.9	24.6	23.0
Company tax	7.2	8.0	8.9	12.2	9.6	11.9	15.9	19.7	22.0
Graduated personal tax	—[2]	—	—	0.4	1.5	2.4	2.7	1.8	2.8
Others[3]	0.5	1.0	1.3	1.0	0.8	0.9	0.9	0.9	1.1
Taxes on consumption and production	25.8	27.5	33.2	35.7	39.3	43.6	51.7	58.1	60.2
Import duties	15.9	17.2	20.1	20.0	21.8	24.4	28.7	31.1	26.8
Excise duties	6.2	6.3	8.5	10.4	11.8	13.2	15.3	16.0	16.5
Petrol and diesel tax	1.1	1.2	1.6	1.7	1.8	2.1	2.4	2.4	2.7
Others[4]	2.6	2.8	3.0	3.6	3.9	3.9	5.3	8.6	14.2
TOTAL TAX REVENUE	39.8	44.4	53.3	60.1	65.2	76.1	93.1	105.1	109.1
Sale of goods and services	5.1	5.2	6.2	7.3	7.7	11.0	12.8	17.5	18.7
Education department	0.3	0.1	0.2	0.2	0.3	2.6	4.0	4.3	5.4
Water charges	0.7	0.9	0.9	1.0	1.0	1.1	1.1	1.2	1.2
Others[5]	4.1	4.2	5.1	6.1	6.4	7.3	7.7	12.0	12.1
Investment revenues	4.4	8.2	6.5	10.3	12.0	12.1	18.3	18.6	18.5
Loan charges[6]	2.7	2.7	3.6	5.9	6.4	5.5	9.8	4.5	4.3
Reimbursements from other administrations[7]	0.9	0.6	1.2	1.4	1.5	1.2	1.0	1.4	1.1
Miscellaneous[8]	0.8	4.9	1.7	3.0	4.1	5.4	7.5	12.7	13.1
TOTAL REVENUES	49.3	57.8	66.0	77.7	84.9	99.2	124.2	141.2	146.3

[1] Revised estimates.
[2] Nil.
[3] Includes estate duties and export duty.
[4] Includes tax on motor vehicle purchase, beer, trade licenses and other fees, and stamp duties.
[5] Includes aviation landing fees and charges of Government departments.
[6] Includes interest repayment and sinking fund contributions.
[7] E.g., local authorities, East African corporations, etc.
[8] Includes Central Bank of Kenya dividends, extra exchequer receipts, etc.

SOURCE: *Statistical Abstracts, 1966–71, Economic Survey,* 1973, and Ministry of Finance and Planning.

Table 13: Central Government Revenue Ratios, 1964/65–1971/72

Revenue Ratio	1964/65	1965/66	1966/67	1967/68	1968/69	1969/70	1970/71	1971/72
				(percentage)				
Total revenues as % of monetary GDP	20.2	22.0	22.9	24.8	24.6	25.9	29.4	31.0
Total revenues as % of GDP at factor cost	15.0	16.1	16.7	18.4	18.5	19.8	22.7	24.2
Tax revenues as % of total revenues	80.7	76.8	80.8	77.3	76.8	76.7	75.0	74.4
Tax revenues as % of monetary GDP	16.3	16.9	18.5	19.2	18.9	19.9	22.1	23.1
Direct taxes as % of tax revenues	35.2	38.1	37.7	40.6	39.7	42.7	44.5	44.7
Indirect taxes as % of tax revenues	64.8	61.9	62.3	59.4	60.3	57.3	55.5	55.3
Income taxes as % of tax revenues	33.9	35.8	35.3	38.9	38.5	41.5	43.5	43.9
Import duties as % of tax revenues	40.0	38.7	37.7	33.3	33.4	32.1	30.8	29.6
Excise duties and consumption taxes[1] as % of tax revenues	18.6	18.2	18.6	20.0	20.7	20.1	19.2	21.2
Income (personal and company) taxes as % of factor incomes in monetary economy	5.6	6.0	6.5	7.4	7.3	8.3	9.6	10.0
Personal income tax as % of incomes from remuneration of employees and rental surplus	4.3	5.0	5.7	5.6	6.6	7.5	8.6	9.1
Company tax as % of monetary GDP from enterprises (including nonprofit institutions)	3.7	3.7	3.8	4.8	3.5	3.9	4.7	5.4
Import duties as % of value of net imports	19.2	17.9	18.3	18.0	18.8	18.9	17.3	17.2
Excise duties and consumption taxes as % of private consumption	3.0	3.1	3.5	3.9	4.2	4.4	4.7	5.3

[1] Includes tax on petrol, entertainment, second-hand motor vehicle purchase, airport passenger, traditional liquor, hotel accommodation, beer, and cigarettes and tobacco.

SOURCE: Table 12 and *Statistical Abstract*, 1972.

FISCAL POLICY FOR DEVELOPMENT   223

Table 14: Central Government Tax Effort, 1963/64–1971/72

Item	1963/64	1964/65	1965/66	1966/67	1967/68	1968/69	1969/70	1970/71	1971/72	Average 1963/64 1967/68	Average 1967/68– 1971/72	Average 1963/64– 1971/72
						(£ million)						
Tax revenues realized	36.8	39.8	44.4	53.3	60.1	65.2	76.1	93.1	105.1	46.9	79.9	63.8
Revenue estimates of budget proposals[1] in individual years	1.5	1.6	2.4	2.0	3.5	0.7	0.4	0.3	4.5	—	—	—
Estimated cumulative revenue effects of tax revisions[2]	1.5	2.6	6.2	8.6	12.5	14.6	17.7	24.2	30.8	—	—	—
Tax revenues adjusted for tax revisions: 1963/64 tax structure	35.3	37.2	38.2	44.7	47.6	50.6	58.4	69.9	74.3	40.6	60.2	50.7
Built-in tax revenues: 1971/72 tax structure[3]	49.8	52.6	54.0	63.2	66.8	71.6	82.6	98.9	105.1	57.3	85.0	71.6
Monetary GDP	234.0	243.0	263.0	288.0	313.0	345.0	383.0	423.0	455.0	268.0	384.0	327.0
GDP at factor cost	316.6	329.7	358.3	394.1	421.3	459.6	502.2	546.5	584.0	364.0	502.7	434.7
						(percentage)						
Buoyancy[4] of tax revenues with respect to monetary GDP	—	2.2	1.4	2.1	1.5	0.8	1.5	2.1	1.7	1.9	1.6	2.0
Buoyancy of tax revenues with respect to total GDP	—	2.0	1.3	2.0	1.9	0.9	1.8	2.5	1.9	1.9	1.9	2.2
Built-in elasticity[5] of tax revenues with respect to monetary GDP	—	1.4	0.3	1.8	0.7	0.6	1.4	1.9	0.8	1.0	1.2	1.2
Built-in elasticity[6] of tax revenues with respect to total GDP	—	1.3	0.3	1.7	0.9	0.7	1.7	2.2	0.9	1.1	1.5	1.3
Marginal tax revenues as % of marginal monetary GDP	—	33.3	23.0	35.6	27.2	15.9	28.7	67.5	37.5	29.5	31.7	30.9
Marginal tax revenues as % of marginal (monetary and nonmonetary) GDP	—	22.9	16.1	24.9	18.3	13.3	25.6	60.9	32.0	22.4	27.6	25.6

[1] Given in the budget speeches. Insofar as the Treasury often underestimates total revenues at the budget time (see Table 16), the figures given in this row in all probability will be somewhat underestimated.
[2] Estimated in the Ministry of Finance and Planning, using disaggregated tax revenues and assuming that the "percentage effect" of a revenue measure adopted in any particular year continues every year thereafter, e.g., if a change in the tax i results in an increase in the tax revenues T_{it} by x percent, the same percentage effect will continue in the years $t+1, t+2 \ldots$ as well, and will be measured by $(x \cdot T_{it} + 1), (x \cdot T_{it} + 2), (x \cdot T_{it} + 3), \ldots$ etc. The figures given in this row are the result of
$$\sum_{i+1}^{n} x \cdot T_{it} + m \text{ where } (m = 0, 1, 2, 3, \ldots) \text{ and } n \text{ is the number of taxes.}$$
[3] This is tax revenues adjusted for tax revisions multiplied by the ratio of realized tax revenues to adjusted tax revenues for year 1971/72 (which is 105.1/74.3).
[4] Buoyancy is defined as percentage change in realized revenues divided by percentage change in the monetary GDP or total GDP as the case may be.
[5] Built-in elasticity is defined as percentage change in built-in tax revenues divided by percentage change in monetary GDP or total GDP.

SOURCE: Ministry of Finance and Planning.

Table 15: Central Government Finances: Kenya in Comparison with Other Developing Countries, Around 1970

			INDIVIDUAL EXPENDITURES			
Country	Year	Total Revenues	Administration (including Defense)	Education	Health	Agriculture	Total Expenditures
		(as percentage of GDP or GNP)					
Burma	1970/71	15.1	8.1	2.8	1.1	1.1	23.9
Ethiopia	1969/70	9.7	5.6	2.1	1.0	0.4	12.4
Ghana	1968/69	14.9	4.7	3.7	1.2	0.7	12.7
Guatemala	1970	8.7	3.7	1.7	1.6	0.5	9.7
Honduras	1970	12.6	5.0	3.0	1.7	0.6	15.9
Ivory Coast	1970	20.7	4.0	3.3	1.6	0.8	24.8
Jamaica	1970/71	19.7	5.4	3.0	4.1	2.6	24.6
Kenya	*1970/71*	*22.6*	*1.9*	*5.0*	*1.9*	*2.3*	*30.6*
Korea	1970	16.5	6.2	3.1	0.2	1.9	19.6
Malawi	1969	13.8	4.7	3.8	1.3	3.6	25.2
Mali	1969	n.a.	4.4	3.5	1.9	1.0	15.4
Mexico	1969	7.8	4.8	2.9	1.1	2.1	24.0
Nigeria	1969/70	7.5	13.5	0.4	0.1	0.6	20.1
Panama	1970	15.3	4.3	4.0	2.2	0.7	23.8
Philippines	1970/71	10.5	2.5	2.8	0.6	0.9	10.4
Rwanda	1970	n.a.	4.1	2.5	0.8	0.5	9.5
Senegal	1968/69	19.2	8.5	3.8	1.8	1.9	21.0
Sierra Leone	1968/69	14.5	3.2	2.6	1.0	0.5	13.5
Thailand	1971	15.0	6.3	3.4	0.6	2.0	19.6
Zaire	1969	n.a.	9.6	5.1	0.9	0.2	29.1
Zambia	1971	36.9	12.7	6.4	3.0	6.7	43.6

SOURCE: World Bank economic reports.

Table 16: Budget Performance, 1964/65–1972/73

Budget Item	1964/65	1965/66	1966/67	1967/68	1968/69	1969/70	1970/71	1971/72	1972/73
					(£ million)				
Revenues[1]									
Budget estimates	49.2	55.5	59.3	72.2	76.5	87.4	110.2	130.0	135.4
Actual	49.3	57.8	66.0	77.7	84.9	99.2	124.2	141.2	146.3[5]
Ratio (%)	100.2	104.1	111.3	107.6	111.0	113.5	112.7	108.6	108.0
"Voted" recurrent expenditures[2]									
Budget estimates[3]	27.3	35.9	39.2	43.1	48.0	65.5	81.0	98.5	110.6[6]
Actual	41.7	47.4	49.8	57.5	63.1	72.9	84.5	106.0	117.3[5]
Amount spent without authority of Parliament	neg.	0.1	0.1	0.1	1.1	1.2	1.8	3.1	n.a.
Ratio (%)	152.7	132.0	127.0	133.4	131.5	111.3	104.3	107.6	106.1
Development expenditures[4]									
Budget estimates[3]	15.7	18.4	22.0	26.7	29.3	36.1	37.9	56.6	69.3[6]
Actual	14.7	15.7	17.7	21.1	25.9	32.3	47.6	53.8	64.9[5]
Ratio (%)	93.6	85.3	80.5	79.0	88.4	89.5	125.6	95.1	93.7

[1] Includes appropriations-in-aid or the revenues originating on current account from various ministry's service functions.
[2] "Voted" recurrent expenditures is a budget concept which includes only the expenditures of the ministries and excludes all public debt charges, pensions and gratuities, and other nonvoted expenditures like subscriptions to international organizations and salaries of the president, attorney general, judges and justices, exchequer and audit account, public service commission and electoral commissions, etc. This concept is entirely different from the one used in *Statistical Abstract* and *Economic Survey*.
[3] Budget estimates cover the original budget estimates only and exclude supplementaries.
[4] This is a budget concept different from the concept of capital expenditures given in *Statistical Abstract* and *Economic Surveys*.
[5] Revised estimate.
[6] These are the original budget estimates and exclude supplementaries of about £8 million on current account and £3 million on development account.

SOURCE: *Estimates* (annual) and *Appropriation Accounts* (annual).

Table 17: Functional Classification of Central Government Recurrent Expenditures,[1] 1964/65–1972/73

Category	1964/65	1965/66	1966/67	1967/68	1968/69	1969/70	1970/71	1971/72	1972/73[2]
					(£ million)				
General services	17.2	18.6	21.5	22.7	22.7	25.0	27.1	34.5	38.0
Major areas									
Administration	4.6	3.8	3.9	3.8	4.1	5.3	6.5	8.9	11.9
Law and order	8.0	8.6	9.5	10.5	10.4	11.1	11.9	14.2	13.9
Defense	2.9	3.9	5.1	5.8	5.3	5.4	6.1	8.4	8.9
Community services	2.4	3.0	3.5	3.4	3.9	4.3	5.2	6.7	9.9
Major areas									
Roads	1.3	1.8	1.9	2.0	2.4	2.9	3.5	4.5	5.1
Water works	1.1	1.2	1.6	1.3	1.4	1.4	1.7	2.1	2.2
Social services	11.0	11.3	13.4	14.6	16.3	25.1	36.6	44.0	49.1
Major areas									
Education	6.2	5.9	7.2	7.9	9.0	15.8	25.9	31.9	37.0
Health	3.0	3.6	3.8	4.3	4.7	6.1	7.5	8.3	7.9
Community development and others	1.8	1.8	2.4	2.4	2.6	3.2	3.2	3.8	4.2
Economic services	7.0	8.3	8.4	12.7	15.0	12.8	12.8	15.2	17.9
Major areas									
Agriculture, veterinary, and forestry	5.2	6.5	5.8	7.8	8.7	7.8	7.9	9.8	10.4
Commerce and industry	0.7	0.7	0.8	3.1	4.2	2.9	1.5	2.0	2.0
Financial obligations and others[1]	19.3	19.5	18.0	16.7	17.3	19.9	19.1	18.1	22.7
Major areas									
Public debt interest	4.4	4.8	5.2	5.4	6.0	6.6	7.4	8.7	9.6
Pensions and gratuities	3.9	3.8	3.9	3.6	3.8	3.8	3.6	3.6	5.4
Transfers to local authorities	2.0	3.4	2.9	3.9	5.6	4.8	0.5	0.7	0.7
TOTAL EXPENDITURES	56.9	60.7	64.8	70.1	75.2	87.1	100.8	118.5[3]	137.7

[1] Excludes public debt sinking fund and redemptions.
[2] Provisional.
[3] Excludes unallocable expenditure of some £5 million.

SOURCE: *Statistical Abstracts* (annual) and Ministry of Finance and Planning.

Table 18: Functional Allocations of Central Government Recurrent Expenditures, 1964/65–1972/73

Category	1964/65	1965/66	1966/67	1967/68	1968/69	1969/70	1970/71	1971/72	1972/73[1]
					(percentage)				
General services	30.2	30.6	33.2	32.4	30.2	28.7	26.9	29.1	27.6
Major areas									
Administration	8.1	6.3	6.0	5.4	5.5	6.1	6.4	7.5	8.6
Law and order	14.1	14.2	14.7	15.0	13.8	12.7	11.8	12.0	10.1
Defense	5.1	6.4	7.9	8.3	7.0	6.2	6.1	5.1	6.5
Community services	4.2	4.9	5.4	4.9	5.2	4.9	5.2	5.7	7.2
Major areas									
Roads	2.3	2.9	2.9	2.9	3.2	3.3	3.7	3.8	3.7
Water works	1.9	2.0	2.5	1.9	1.9	1.6	1.5	1.9	1.6
Social services	19.3	18.6	20.7	20.8	21.7	28.8	36.3	37.1	35.7
Major areas									
Education	10.9	9.7	11.1	11.3	12.0	18.1	25.8	26.9	26.9
Health	5.3	5.9	5.9	6.1	6.3	7.0	7.4	7.0	5.7
Community development and others	3.1	3.0	3.7	3.4	3.4	3.7	3.1	3.2	3.1
Economic services	12.3	13.7	13.0	18.1	19.9	14.7	12.7	12.8	13.0
Major areas									
Agriculture, veterinary, and forestry	9.1	10.7	9.0	11.1	11.6	9.0	7.8	8.3	7.6
Commerce and industry	1.2	1.2	1.2	4.4	5.6	3.3	1.5	1.7	1.5
Financial obligations and others	34.0	32.2	27.7	23.8	23.0	22.9	18.9	15.3	16.5
Major areas									
Public debt interest	7.7	7.9	8.0	7.7	8.0	7.6	7.4	6.8	3.0
Pensions and gratuities	6.9	6.3	6.0	5.1	5.1	4.4	3.5	3.0	3.9
Transfers to local authorities	3.5	5.6	4.5	5.6	7.4	5.5	0.5	0.6	0.5
TOTAL	100.0	100.0	100.0	100.0	100.0	100.0	100.0	100.0	100.0

[1] Provisional.

SOURCE: Table 17.

Table 19: Functional Classification of Central Government Capital Expenditures,[1] 1964/65–1972/73

Category	1964/65	1965/66	1966/67	1967/68	1968/69	1969/70	1970/71	1971/72[2]	1972/73[3]
					(£ million)				
General services	0.6	0.7	1.1	2.1	1.8	2.4	3.6	4.8	6.5
Major areas									
Administration	0.4	0.3	0.3	0.5	0.5	1.1	1.6	1.7	2.1
Law and order	0.1	0.3	0.7	1.3	1.1	1.3	2.0	3.0	2.2
Defense	—	0.1	0.1	0.2	0.2	—	—	0.1	2.2
Community services	1.8	3.9	5.3	5.9	6.9	9.6	14.9	20.3	22.3
Major areas									
Roads	1.6	3.4	4.4	5.2	6.5	9.3	14.3	18.9	19.8
Water works	0.2	0.5	0.9	0.2	0.4	0.3	0.6	1.4	2.5
Social services	1.3	1.4	2.9	3.7	6.2	6.7	7.3	9.6	14.0
Major areas									
Education	0.6	0.6	0.6	1.4	2.4	1.5	1.4	1.0	3.1
Health	0.1	0.2	0.5	1.1	1.4	2.4	2.7	2.9	3.9
Housing	0.5	0.4	1.4	0.8	2.1	2.5	2.7	3.2	4.8
Others	0.1	0.2	0.4	0.4	0.3	0.3	0.5	2.5	2.2
Economic services	6.4	6.1	6.7	9.0	10.8	11.1	17.5	12.7	27.6
Major areas									
Agriculture, veterinary, and forestry	6.1	5.7	5.6	4.9	5.8	4.0	4.4	5.4	11.3
Commerce and industry	neg.	neg.	0.5	2.8	4.1	3.0	4.4	5.2	4.7
Electricity and power	—	—	—	—	—	2.6	4.0	—	4.8
Transfers to local authorities	0.4	0.4	—	0.1	0.1	0.3	0.3	0.4	1.7
Unallocable	—	—	0.6	1.0	1.0	0.9	0.8	0.5	—
TOTAL	10.5	12.5	16.6	21.8	26.8	31.0	44.4	48.3	72.1

[1] This is a national accounting concept somewhat different from the concept of development expenditure of the budget documents.
[2] Estimated.
[3] Budget estimate.

SOURCE: *Statistical Abstracts* (annual).

Table 20: Functional Allocations of Central Government Capital Expenditures, Selected Years, 1964/65–1972/73

Category	1964/65	1967/68	1970/71	1971/72	1972/73
			(percentage)		
General services	5.7	9.6	8.1	9.9	11.0
Major areas					
Administration	3.8	2.3	3.6	3.5	5.0
Law and order	0.9	6.0	4.5	6.2	4.3
Defense	—	0.9	—	0.2	1.7
Community services	17.1	27.1	33.6	42.0	33.6
Major areas					
Roads	15.2	23.9	32.2	39.1	30.7
Water works	1.9	0.9	1.4	2.9	2.9
Social services	12.4	17.0	16.4	19.9	19.7
Major areas					
Education	5.7	6.4	3.2	2.1	5.2
Health	1.0	5.0	6.1	6.0	5.2
Housing	4.8	3.7	6.1	6.6	6.7
Others	0.9	1.8	1.0	5.2	2.6
Economic services	61.0	41.2	39.4	26.4	34.6
Major areas					
Agriculture, veterinary, and forestry	58.1	22.5	9.9	11.2	17.1
Commerce and industry	neg.	12.8	9.9	10.8	3.7
Electricity and power	—	—	9.0	—	—
Transfers to local authorities	3.8	0.5	0.7	0.8	1.1
Unallocable	—	4.6	1.8	1.0	—
TOTAL	100.0	100.0	100.0	100.0	100.0

SOURCE: Table 19.

Table 21: Economic Classification of Central Government Recurrent Expenditures, 1964/65–1971/72

(£ million)

Category	1964/65	1965/66	1966/67	1967/68	1968/69	1969/70	1970/71	1971/72
Wages and salaries (including benefits)	23.9	24.9	28.0	29.6	31.7	42.1	53.9	68.8
Major areas								
Civilian	21.9	22.4	24.8	26.3	28.4	38.4	49.2	64.7
Armed forces	2.0	2.5	3.2	3.3	3.3	3.7	3.7	4.1
Other purchases of goods and services	10.8	12.6	13.7	15.0	15.8	19.1	22.6	30.1
Major area								
Maintenance and repairs	1.7	2.1	1.8	2.4	2.5	3.1	3.7	5.2
Subsidies	0.3	0.8	0.6	2.5	2.8	1.4	1.2	0.8
Agriculture	0.3	0.8	0.5	2.4	2.8	1.4	1.2	0.8
Other sectors	neg.	neg.	0.1	0.1	neg.	neg.	neg.	neg.
Interest	4.4	4.8	5.2	5.4	6.0	6.6	7.4	8.7
Internal debt	1.1	1.3	1.5	1.9	2.4	3.4	4.1	4.8
External debt	3.3	3.5	3.7	3.5	3.6	3.2	3.3	3.9
Other transfers	17.5	17.6	17.3	17.6	18.9	17.1	16.6	15.6
Major areas								
Persons, including pensions	4.2	4.1	4.4	4.0	4.3	5.1	4.3	7.7
Private nonprofit institutions, primarily educational	4.1	4.6	3.6	4.7	5.5	3.1	2.7	3.1
Local authorities	2.0	3.4	2.9	3.9	5.6	4.8	0.5	0.8
TOTAL RECURRENT EXPENDITURES	56.9	60.7	64.8	70.1	75.2	86.3	101.7	124.0[1]

[1] See Footnote 3 to Table 17.

SOURCE: *Economic Surveys* (annual).

Table 22: Economic Classification of Central Government Capital Expenditures,[1] 1964/65–1971/72

Category	1964/65	1965/66	1966/67	1967/68	1968/69	1969/70	1970/71	1971/72
				(£ million)				
Gross capital formation								
Major area	4.4	6.4	10.0	14.4	16.6	20.0	28.6	36.2
Construction and works	2.1	3.1	5.4	6.8	7.8	10.5	15.8	19.1
Loans to other sectors	6.1	5.7	6.3	6.9	9.9	8.2	6.0	10.3
Public corporations	1.1	2.9	3.7	3.0	3.1	4.7	4.0	6.6
Other General Government agencies	4.8	2.8	2.6	3.5	6.2	2.7	1.6	2.2
Others	—	—	—	0.4	0.6	0.8	0.4	1.5
Investments in Government enterprises	—	—	0.3	0.5	0.3	2.8	9.8	1.8
TOTAL	10.5	12.1	16.6	21.8	26.8	31.0	44.4	48.3

[1] The concept of "capital expenditure" used here is not synonymous with "development expenditure" as used in the budget. Besides, it excludes debt repayments and sinking fund contributions.

SOURCE: *Economic Surveys* (annual).

Table 23: Budgetary Projections, 1973/74–1977/78

Category	1972/73	1973/74	1974/75	1975/76	1976/77	1977/78	Assumptions
	(£ million, rounded figures)						
Set I: Do nothing							
Recurrent revenues	146	169	195	226	261	301	Built-in elasticity of 1.3 and GDP growth rate of 12% per annum.
Recurrent expenditures	138	161	189	221	259	303	Growth rate of 17% per annum realized during 1970/71–1972/73.
Recurrent savings	8	8	6	5	2	neg.	
Capital expenditures	65	81	102	127	159	198	Growth rate of 25% per annum achieved during 1964/65–1972/73.
Ratio of recurrent savings to capital expenditures (%)	12	10	6	4	1	neg.	
Set II: Policy changes							
Recurrent revenues	146	179	220	270	332	408	Restore buoyancy of 1.9 given annual GDP growth of 12%.
Recurrent expenditures	138	149	161	174	188	203	Growth rate contained to 8% per annum.
Recurrent savings	8	30	59	96	144	205	
Capital expenditures	65	81	99	119	140	161	Growth rate of 25%, 22%, 20%, 18%, 15% respectively.
Ratio of recurrent savings to capital expenditures (%)	12	37	60	81	103	127	

SOURCE: Mission estimates.

Table 24: Local Government Finances, 1966-72

Category	1966	1967	1968	1969	1970	1971[1]	1972[2]
				(£ million)			
Recurrent (own) revenues	17.2	17.0	17.6	16.9	15.0	16.3	17.5
Recurrent expenditures	19.5	20.4	24.0	15.8	14.5	15.8	15.6
Recurrent surplus (+)/deficit (−)	−2.3	−3.4	−6.4	+1.1	+0.5	+0.5	+1.9
Capital expenditures	1.9	3.3	4.4	3.7	3.0	11.1	7.9
Overall budget deficit	4.2	6.7	10.8	2.6	2.5	10.6	6.8
Financed by:							
Central Government grants	3.4	3.7	3.9	2.6	0.2	1.1	n.a.
Borrowings	0.6	1.4	2.0	2.2	1.5	8.9	n.a.
Others[3]	0.2	1.6	4.9	−2.2	0.8	0.6	n.a.

[1] Provisional.
[2] Budget estimates provided by the Ministry of Finance and Planning.
[3] Largely drawing down of reserves.

SOURCE: *Statistical Abstracts* (annual).

Table 25: Local Government Revenues, 1966–72

(£ million)

Category	1966 Municipal Councils	1966 County Councils	1966 Total	1967 Municipal Councils	1967 County Councils	1967 Total	1968 Municipal Councils	1968 County Councils	1968 Total	1969 Municipal Councils	1969 County Councils	1969 Total	1970 Municipal Councils	1970 County Councils	1970 Total	1971[1] Municipal Councils	1971[1] County Councils	1971[1] Total	1972[1] Municipal Councils	1972[1] County Councils	1972[1] Total
Tax revenues	4.7	3.5	8.2	5.0	3.4	9.4	4.4	3.5	7.9	5.2	4.3	9.5	5.6	1.7	7.3	8.5	1.6	10.1	7.9	1.9	9.8
Graduated personal tax	2.6	2.8	5.4	2.7	2.7	5.4	1.9[a]	2.4	4.3	2.0[1]	3.3	5.3	2.3[2]	0.3	2.6	4.7	0.3	5.0	4.1	0.3	4.4
Licenses, cesses, and rates	2.1	0.7	2.8	2.3	0.7	3.0	2.5	1.0	3.5	3.2	1.0	4.2	3.3	1.4	4.7	3.8	1.3	5.1	3.8	1.6	5.4
Nontax revenues	5.0	4.0	9.0	4.8	3.8	8.6	5.2	4.6	9.8	5.2	2.1	7.3	6.1	1.6	7.7	6.6	1.6	8.2	6.9	1.7	8.6
Income from property (buildings and land rents)	1.1	0.2	1.3	1.1	0.2	1.3	1.3	0.4	1.7	1.4	0.3	1.7	1.5	0.5	2.0	1.7	0.5	2.2	1.9	0.6	2.5
Sale of goods and services	3.5	3.7	7.2	3.2	3.3	6.5	3.6	4.0	7.6	3.1	1.6	4.7	4.0	0.9	4.9	4.5	0.9	5.4	4.4	1.1	5.5
School fees	0.4	2.8	3.2	0.4	2.7	3.1	0.5	3.2	3.7	0.5	0.8	1.3	0.5	—	0.5	0.6	neg.	0.6	0.6	neg.	0.6
Sale of water				1.1			1.0			1.1			2.2			2.2			0.6		
Sale of beer				0.3			0.5			0.4			0.3			0.4			0.3		
Market and slaughter charges	3.1	0.9		neg.	0.6		0.1	0.8		neg.	0.8		neg.	0.9		0.1	0.9		0.1	1.1	
Sewerage and refuse removal charges				0.7			0.9			0.5			1.0			0.5			1.2		
Other sales				0.6			0.6			0.6			0.7			0.7			10.6		
Interest on investments	0.3	neg.	0.3	0.4	0.1	0.5	0.2	0.1	0.3	0.4	0.1	0.5	0.2	neg.	0.2	0.2	neg.	0.2	0.1	0.1	0.2
Court fines, Government grants, loan repayments, sale of capital assets, etc.	0.1	0.1	0.2	0.1	0.2	0.3	0.1	0.1	0.2	0.3	0.1	0.4	0.4	0.2	0.6	0.2	0.2	0.4	0.5	0.1	0.6
TOTAL REVENUES	9.7	7.5	17.2	9.8	7.2	17.0	9.5	4.1	13.6	10.4	6.4	16.8	11.7	3.3	15.0	15.3	3.2	18.5	14.8	3.7	18.5

[1] Provisional.
[2] The decline over previous years is due to the transfer of 50% of the GPT revenues of Nairobi and Mombasa to the Central Government. This was done away with in 1971.

SOURCE: *Statistical Abstract, 1972* and *Economic Survey*, 1973.

Table 26: Economic Classification of Local Government Expenditures (Total), 1966–72

Category	1966 Municipal Councils	1966 County Councils	1966 Total	1967 Municipal Councils	1967 County Councils	1967 Total	1968 Municipal Councils	1968 County Councils	1968 Total	1969 Municipal Councils	1969 County Councils	1969 Total	1970 Municipal Councils	1970 County Councils	1970 Total	1971[1] Municipal Councils	1971[1] County Councils	1971[1] Total	1972[1] Municipal Councils	1972[1] County Councils	1972[1] Total
									(£ million)												
Recurrent expenditures	8.9	10.6	19.5	8.6	11.7	20.3	9.7	14.2	23.9	9.9	5.9	15.8	11.2	3.2	14.4	12.5	3.3	15.8	14.4	4.2	18.6
Personal emoluments	4.0	7.7	11.7	4.2	8.7	12.9	4.6	10.7	15.3	5.1	3.9	9.0	5.6	1.8	7.4	6.4	1.8	8.2	7.8	2.4	10.2
Other goods and services	3.0	2.5	5.5	2.4	2.6	5.0	2.8	3.0	5.8	2.4	1.7	4.1	3.0	1.0	4.0	3.5	1.1	4.6	4.0	1.5	5.5
Loan charges	1.6	0.2	1.8	1.8	0.2	2.0	2.0	0.2	2.2	2.1	0.2	2.3	2.3	0.2	2.5	2.4	0.3	2.7	2.5	0.2	2.7
Transfers	0.3	0.2	0.5	0.2	0.2	0.4	0.3	0.2	0.5	0.3	0.1	0.4	0.3	0.2	0.5	0.3	0.1	0.4	0.1	0.1	0.2
Capital expenditures	1.6	0.3	1.9	0.3	0.3	0.6	4.0	0.5	4.5	3.5	0.2	3.7	2.5	0.5	3.0	5.0	0.6	5.6	8.3	2.1	10.4
Error in double counting	neg.[2]	neg.	—	0.1	neg.	0.1	0.1	−0.1	—	−0.2	−0.1	−0.3	−0.3	neg.	−0.3	−0.3	neg.	—	−3.2	−0.2	−3.4
TOTAL	10.5	10.9	21.4	9.0	12.0	21.0	13.8	14.6	28.4	13.2	6.0	19.2	13.4	3.7	17.1	17.2	3.9	21.2	19.6	6.1	25.7

[1] Provisional.
[2] Negligible.

SOURCE: *Statistical Abstract*, 1972 and *Economic Survey*, 1973.

Table 27: Functional Classification of Local Government Expenditures (Total), 1966–72

Category	1966 Municipal Councils	1966 County Councils	1966 Total	1967 Municipal Councils	1967 County Councils	1967 Total	1968 Municipal Councils	1968 County Councils	1968 Total	1969 Municipal Councils	1969 County Councils	1969 Total	1970 Municipal Councils	1970 County Councils	1970 Total	1971[1] Municipal Councils	1971[1] County Councils	1971[1] Total	1972[1] Municipal Councils	1972[1] County Councils	1972[1] Total
									(£ million)												
Administration	1.0	1.0	2.0	0.9	1.0	1.9	1.0	1.2	2.1	0.8	1.3	2.1	1.1	1.3	2.4	1.3	1.5	2.8	1.5	2.0	3.5
Community services																					
Roads	3.1	1.2	4.3	2.7	1.4	4.1	3.1	1.5	4.6	2.6	0.3	2.9	3.0	0.3	3.3	3.3	0.3	3.6	4.0	0.5	4.5
Sanitary services	1.5	1.2	2.7	1.2	1.3	2.5	1.6	1.4	3.0	1.4	0.2	1.6	1.3	0.2	1.5	1.6	neg.[2]	1.6	1.6	0.2	1.8
Others	1.1	neg.	1.1	1.3	0.1	1.4	1.3	0.1	1.4	1.0	0.1	1.1	1.4	0.1	1.5	1.1	0.3	1.4	2.0	0.3	2.3
	0.4	neg.	0.4	0.2	neg.	0.2	0.2	neg.	0.2	0.2	neg.	0.2	0.3	neg.	0.3	0.6	neg.	0.6	0.4	neg.	0.4
Social services																					
Health	2.8	7.7	10.5	3.6	8.6	12.2	4.4	10.7	15.1	4.0	2.9	6.9	4.2	0.5	4.7	5.0	0.5	5.5	5.6	0.6	6.2
Education	0.8	1.0	1.8	0.8	1.1	1.9	0.9	1.3	2.2	0.7	0.3	1.0	0.8	neg.	0.8	1.0	—	1.0	1.2	—	1.2
Others	1.5	6.5	8.0	1.8	7.3	9.1	2.4	9.1	11.5	2.2	2.3	4.5	2.3	neg.	2.3	2.8	neg.	2.8	3.0	neg.	3.0
	0.5	0.2	0.7	1.0	0.2	1.2	1.0	0.3	1.3	1.1	0.3	1.4	1.1	0.5	1.6	1.2	0.5	1.7	1.4	0.6	2.0
Economic services	—	0.3	0.3	—	0.2	0.2	—	0.3	0.3	—	0.3	0.3	—	0.4	0.4	—	0.4	0.4	—	0.5	0.5
Trading services																					
Water undertakings	3.4	0.4	3.8	4.2	0.5	4.7	5.2	0.7	5.9	5.8	0.6	6.4	5.0	0.9	5.9	7.5	0.9	8.4	8.4	2.0	10.4
Market and slaughter houses	1.4	0.2	1.6	1.5	0.2	1.7	1.5	0.2	1.7	1.7	0.2	1.9	1.3	0.2	1.5	1.8	0.3	2.1	3.4	0.3	3.7
Breweries and beer shops	0.1	0.1	0.2	0.2	0.1	0.3	0.2	0.2	0.4	0.2	0.2	0.4	0.2	0.3	0.5	0.3	0.3	0.6	0.3	0.5	0.8
Housing estates, including staff housing	0.3	neg.	0.3	0.2	0.1	0.3	0.3	0.1	0.4	0.3	0.1	0.4	0.3	0.1	0.4	0.4	0.1	0.5	0.3	0.2	0.5
Others	1.3	neg.	1.3	2.0	neg.	2.0	2.9	0.1	3.0	3.3	0.1	3.4	2.9	0.2	3.1	4.7	0.1	4.8	3.8	0.9	4.7
	0.3	0.1	0.4	0.3	0.1	0.4	0.3	0.1	0.4	0.3	neg.	0.3	0.3	0.1	0.4	0.3	0.1	0.4	0.5	0.1	0.6
Unallocable	0.2	0.3	0.5	0.3	0.2	0.5	neg.	0.2	0.2	neg.	0.5	0.5	0.3	0.3	0.3	0.1	0.3	0.4	0.1	0.5	0.6
TOTAL	10.5	10.9	21.4	11.7	12.0	23.7	13.7	14.6	28.3	13.2	5.9	19.1	13.4	3.7	17.1	17.3	3.9	21.2	19.5	6.1	25.6

[1] Provisional.
[2] Negligible.

SOURCE: *Statistical Abstract, 1972* and *Economic Survey, 1973*

Table 28: Parastatal Enterprises in Relation to the Government Budget, 1965/66–1970/71

Category	1965/66	1966/67	1967/68	1968/69	1969/70	1970/71
			(£ million)			
Revenues from parastatals	3.6	2.5	3.8	4.5	4.9	8.0
Public corporations	0.8	0.9	1.1	1.2	1.5	1.5
Government agencies	2.8	1.6	2.7	3.3	3.4	6.5
Total Government revenues	57.8	66.0	77.7	84.9	99.2	124.2
Contribution of parastatals to Government revenues (%)	6.2	3.8	4.9	5.3	4.9	6.4
Government loans to and equity in parastatals	5.7	6.6	7.0	9.6	10.3	15.4
Public corporations	2.9	4.0	3.5	3.4	7.6	13.8
Government agencies	2.8	2.6	3.5	6.2	2.7	1.6
Government capital expenditures[1]	12.1	16.6	21.8	26.8	31.0	44.4
Proportion of capital expenditure allocated to parastatals (%)	47.1	39.7	32.1	35.8	33.2	34.6

[1] This is a national accounting concept somewhat different from the concept of development expenditure of the budget documents.

SOURCE: *Statistical Abstract*, 1972.

Table 29: Government Budget and Public Corporations, 1964/65–1970/71

Budget Items	1964/65	1965/66	1966/67	1967/68	1968/69	1969/70	1970/71
				(£ million)			
Budget incomings							
Interest dividends and profits	0.7	0.8	0.9	1.1	1.2	1.5	1.4
Transfers from	neg.[1]	neg.	neg.	neg.	neg.	neg.	0.1
Loan repayments	0.4	0.3	0.3	2.5	3.3	2.0	4.4
TOTAL	1.1	1.1	1.2	3.6	4.5	3.5	5.9
Budget outgoings							
Transfers to	—	—	—	—	—	0.1	—
Loans	1.1	2.8	3.7	3.0	3.1	4.7	3.9
Purchase of equity	—	0.1	0.3	0.5	0.3	2.8	9.9
TOTAL	1.1	2.9	4.0	3.5	3.4	7.6	13.8
Balance of budget incomings and outgoings	+neg.	−1.8	−2.8	+0.1	+1.1	−4.1	−7.9

[1] Negligible.

SOURCE: *Statistical Abstracts*, 1970 and 1972.

Table 30: Profitability of Selected Public Corporations, 1964/65–1970/71

Item	1964/65	1965/66	1966/67	1967/68	1968/69	1969/70	1970/71
Industrial and Commercial Development Corporation				(£ thousand)			
Total assets	524	1,012	1,226	1,702	2,572	4,112	6,278
Income	76	91	83	117	152	277	478
Expenses	31	55	89	98	109	173	272
Profit/loss	+45	+36	−6	+19	+43	+104	+206
Rate of profit/loss (%)	8.6	3.6	−0.5	1.1	1.7	2.5	3.3
Development Finance Company of Kenya (calendar years)							
Total assets	821	1,533	2,194	2,199	2,597	2,766	3,311
Income	23	77	117	128	140	173	204
Expenses	21	26	33	200	34	58	97
Profit/loss	2	51	84	−72	106	115	107
Rate of profit/loss (%)	0.2	3.3	3.8	−3.3	4.1	4.2	3.2
Kenya Tea Development Authority (calendar years)							
Total assets	1,458	1,991	2,160	2,274	2,484	2,740	n.a.
Income	172	261	316	509	568	712	n.a.
Cess	93	143	135	324	407	600	n.a.
Expenses	448	544	454	504	745	626	n.a.
Profit/loss	−276	−283	−138	+5	−177	+86	n.a.
Rate of profit/loss (%)	−18.9	−14.2	−6.4	0.2	−7.1	3.1	n.a.
Agricultural Development Corporation							
Total assets	n.a.	2,422	3,862	n.a.	6,879	7,757	8,219
Income	n.a.	n.a.	n.a.	n.a.	n.a.	347	340
Expenses	n.a.	n.a.	n.a.	n.a.	n.a.	460	411
Profit/loss	n.a.	−146	−293	n.a.	−83	−113	−71
Rate of profit/loss (%)	n.a.	−6.0	−7.6	n.a.	−1.2	−1.5	−0.8
Agricultural Finance Corporation							
Total assets	9,003	10,056	9,922	n.a.	10,180	10,792	11,615
Income	553	621	644	n.a.	870	735	777
Expenses	511	687	682	n.a.	999	819	831
Profit/loss	+42	−66	−38	n.a.	−129	−84	−54
Rate of profit/loss (%)	0.5	−0.7	−0.4	n.a.	−1.3	−0.8	−0.5
National Irrigation Board							
Total assets	n.a.	n.a.	1,393	1,589	2,211	2,834	3,094
Income	n.a.	n.a.	144	160	192	255	316
Expenses	n.a.	n.a.	193	204	266	341	363
Profit/loss	n.a.	n.a.	−49	−44	−74	−86	−47
Rate of profit/loss (%)	n.a.	n.a.	−3.5	−2.8	−3.3	−3.0	−1.5
National Housing Corporation							
Total assets	n.a.	n.a.	n.a.	6,146	7,517	9,232	11,263
Income	n.a.	n.a.	n.a.	303	375	523	660
Expenses	n.a.	n.a.	n.a.	322	392	512	618
Profit/loss	n.a.	n.a.	n.a.	−19	−17	+11	+42
Rate of profit/loss (%)	n.a.	n.a.	n.a.	−0.3	−0.2	0.1	0.4

SOURCE: Ministry of Finance and Planning and Central Bank of Kenya.

Table 31: Government Budget and General Government Agencies,[1] 1964/65–1970/71

Budget Items	1964/65	1965/66	1966/67	1967/68	1968/69	1969/70	1970/71
Budget incomings				(£ million)			
Interest, dividends, and profits	0.9	2.1	1.2	2.3	3.3	3.2	6.5
Currency Board/Central Bank of Kenya dividends	—	1.4	—	1.1	2.3	2.4	4.9
Transfers from	1.0	0.8	0.4	0.4	—	0.2	—
Loan repayments	0.4	0.6	0.6	0.9	0.6	0.4	2.4
TOTAL	2.3	3.5	2.2	3.6	3.9	3.8	8.9
Budget outgoings							
Transfers to	2.8	1.1	2.4	1.7	1.9	2.6	4.8
Loans	4.8	2.8	2.6	3.5	6.2	2.7	1.6
TOTAL	7.6	3.9	5.0	5.2	8.1	5.3	6.4
Balance, budget incomings and outgoings	−5.3	−0.4	−2.8	−1.6	−4.2	−1.5	+2.5

[1] Excluding EAC and local governments.

SOURCE: *Statistical Abstracts*, 1970–1972.

Table 32: Income Tax Rates,[1] 1973/74

Income Level	Tax Payable[2] by a Family with Four Children	Average Tax Rate
(£ per annum)	(£)	(percentage)
720	—	—
1,200	48	4.00
1,800	138	7.67
2,400	258	10.75
3,000	408	13.60
3,600	588	16.33
4,200	798	19.00
4,800	1,038	21.63
5,400	1,308	24.22
6,000	1,608	26.80
6,600	1,938	29.36
7,200	2,298	31.92
7,800	2,688	34.46
8,400	3,078	36.64
9,000	3,468	38.53
10,000	4,168	41.68
15,000	7,668	51.12
20,000	11,168	55.84

[1] These rates are only illustrative. The legal rate schedule is in terms of marginal tax rates and not average rates.
[2] Calculated by deducting the personal tax relief granted under the Act from the tax liability calculated from the rate schedule.

SOURCE: *Budget*, 1973/74.

Table 33: Burden of Road Taxation, 1964–71

Year	Licenses	Petrol and Diesel Oil Taxes	'Other' Import Duties	Total	Petrol Taxes per Vehicle[1]	Import Duties per New Registered Road Vehicle[2]	Import Duty Passenger Car Imported[3]
	(£ million)				(£)		
1964	0.7	4.7	1.6	7.0	50.3	134.3	154.2
1965	0.9	5.1	2.1	8.1	51.6	157.3	161.4
1966	1.2	5.9	2.7	9.8	56.4	186.5	181.9
1967	1.3	6.6	3.3	11.2	61.1	197.2	188.0
1968	1.4	7.2	3.3	11.9	63.5	219.4	217.0
1969	1.3	8.0	4.0	13.3	64.5	238.9	226.1
1970	1.4	8.9	4.8	15.1	65.1	235.4	235.4
1971	2.0	10.4	5.9	18.3	69.1	279.1	235.7

[1] Petrol and diesel oil taxes collected divided by the total number of vehicles.
[2] 'Other' import duties divided by the new registration of road vehicles.
[3] Import duty collected on passenger cars divided by the number of cars imported.

SOURCE: *Statistical Abstract*, 1972.

Table 34: Average Burden of Import Duty, Selected Years (by SITC)

Category	1964 Duty Collected	1964 Net Imports	1964 Average Rate (%)	1970 Duty Collected	1970 Net Imports	1970 Average Rate (%)	1971 Duty Collected	1971 Net Imports	1971 Average Rate (%)
	(£ thousand)			(£ thousand)			(£ thousand)		
Food and live animals	1,031	5,867	17.6	1,610	5,552	29.0	2,925	11,010	26.6
Beverages and tobacco	1,415	867	163.2	1,469	900	163.2	1,706	1,512	112.8
Crude materials (except fuels)	49	2,265	2.2	554	2,812	19.7	708	4,488	15.9
Mineral fuels, lubricants, and related minerals	4,052	9,272	43.7	7,400	14,559	50.8	8,851	16,747	52.9
Animal and vegetable oils and fats	6	903	0.7	169	1,956	8.6	35	3,557	1.0
Chemicals	442	6,779	6.5	771	14,816	5.2	1,051	18,415	5.7
Manufactured goods, classified chiefly by materials	4,349	19,359	22.5	7,138	36,737	19.4	8,668	45,176	19.2
Machinery and transport equipment	2,045	23,152	8.8	5,925	48,570	12.2	7,551	64,787	11.7
Miscellaneous manufactured articles	1,401	5,524	25.4	2,725	11,328	24.1	4,260	17,114	24.9
Miscellaneous transactions and commodities	183	3,609	5.1	823	4,796	17.2	−526	1,299	—
TOTAL	14,971	76,595	19.5	28,585	142,026	20.1	35,229	184,105	19.1

SOURCE: *Statistical Abstracts*, 1966 and 1972.

Table 35: Distribution of Local Government Services, 1968[1]

Category	Population 1969 (thousand)	Total Receipts[2] (£ thousand)	Total Expenditures (£ thousand)	Community and Social Expenditures (£ thousand)	Receipts[2] per Head (£)	Expenditure per Head (£)	Community and Social Expenditure per Head (£)
Municipal Councils							
Nairobi	509.3	n.a.	8,850	4,585	n.a.	17.4	9.0
Mombasa	246.1	n.a.	2,728	1,987	n.a.	11.1	8.1
Nakuru	47.2	n.a.	853	338	n.a.	18.1	7.2
Kisumu	32.4	n.a.	605	295	n.a.	18.7	9.1
Thika	18.4	n.a.	236	99	n.a.	12.8	5.4
Eldoret	18.2	n.a.	318	141	n.a.	17.5	7.7
Kitale	11.6	n.a.	172	77	n.a.	14.9	6.7
SUBTOTAL	883.2	11,826	13,762	7,522	13.3	15.6	8.6
County Councils							
Nyanza Province (169)[3]	2,090.0	n.a.	2,169	1,942	n.a.	1.0	0.9
Western Province (162)	1,310.0	n.a.	1,706	1,443	n.a.	1.3	1.1
Central Province (127)	1,658.0	n.a.	3,653	3,156	n.a.	2.2	1.9
Rift Valley Province (13)	2,163.0	n.a.	3,481	2,754	n.a.	1.6	1.3
Eastern Province (12)	1,895.0	n.a.	2,725	2,409	n.a.	1.4	1.3
Coast Province (11)	697.0	n.a.	851	668	n.a.	1.2	1.0
North Eastern Province (2)	246.0	n.a.	141	101	n.a.	0.6	0.4
SUBTOTAL	10,059.0	11,751	14,726	12,471	1.2	1.5	1.2
ALL COUNTRY TOTAL	10,943.0	23,577	28,488	19,993	2.2	2.6	1.8

[Tabular matter resumes on page 251.]

[1] In 1968, local authority functions were not yet curtailed. Their expenditures were 22% of the total expenditures of central and local governments taken together.
[2] Includes both recurrent and capital receipts.
[3] Figures in parentheses are the number of councils.

SOURCE: *Statistical Abstract*, 1971.

MAPS

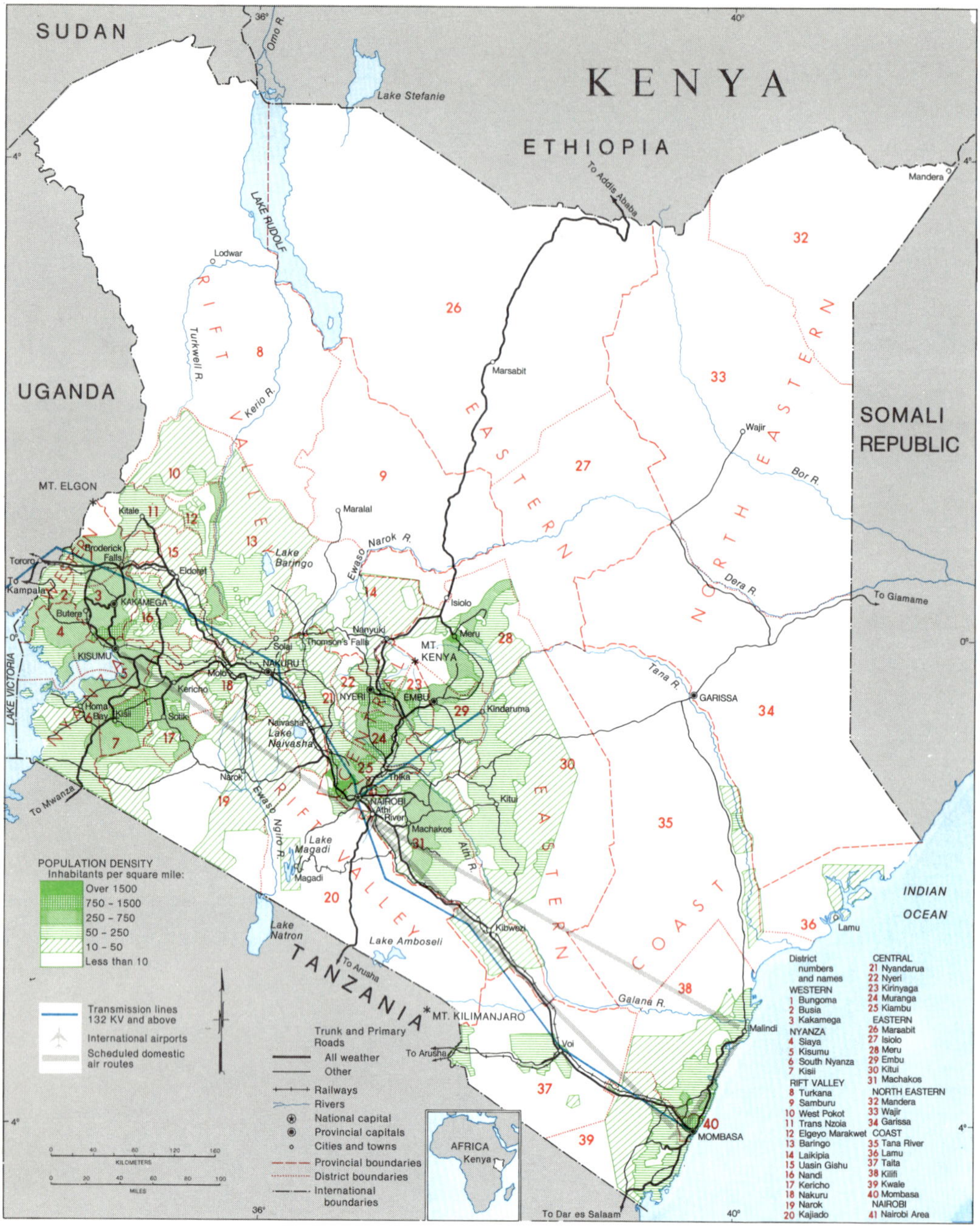
KENYA
SUDAN
ETHIOPIA
UGANDA
SOMALI REPUBLIC
TANZANIA
INDIAN OCEAN
Lake Stefanie
LAKE RUDOLF
Omo R.
Lodwar
Turkwell R.
Kerio R.
RIFT VALLEY
EASTERN
NORTH EASTERN
COAST
WESTERN
NYANZA
CENTRAL
To Addis Ababa
Mandera
Marsabit
Wajir
Bor R.
Dera R.
To Giamame
Maralal
Ewaso Narok R.
Lake Baringo
Isiolo
MT. ELGON
Kitale
Tororo
To Kampala
Broderick Falls
Eldoret
KAKAMEGA
Butere
KISUMU
Kericho
Molo
Solai
Thomson's Falls
Nanyuki
MT. KENYA
Meru
NAKURU
NYERI
EMBU
Kindaruma
Tana R.
GARISSA
Homa Bay
Kisii
Sotik
Naivasha
Lake Naivasha
Thika
Narok
Ewaso Ngiro R.
NAIROBI
Athi River
Kitui
Machakos
Athi R.
To Mwanza
Lake Magadi
Magadi
Lake Natron
Lake Amboseli
To Arusha
Kibwezi
MT. KILIMANJARO
Galana R.
Malindi
Lamu
Voi
MOMBASA
To Dar es Salaam
LAKE VICTORIA
36°
40°
4°
0°
POPULATION DENSITY
Inhabitants per square mile:
Over 1500
750 - 1500
250 - 750
50 - 250
10 - 50
Less than 10
Transmission lines 132 KV and above
International airports
Scheduled domestic air routes
Trunk and Primary Roads
All weather
Other
Railways
Rivers
National capital
Provincial capitals
Cities and towns
Provincial boundaries
District boundaries
International boundaries
KILOMETERS
MILES
AFRICA
Kenya
District numbers and names
WESTERN
1 Bungoma
2 Busia
3 Kakamega
NYANZA
4 Siaya
5 Kisumu
6 South Nyanza
7 Kisii
RIFT VALLEY
8 Turkana
9 Samburu
10 West Pokot
11 Trans Nzoia
12 Elgeyo Marakwet
13 Baringo
14 Laikipia
15 Uasin Gishu
16 Nandi
17 Kericho
18 Nakuru
19 Narok
20 Kajiado
CENTRAL
21 Nyandarua
22 Nyeri
23 Kirinyaga
24 Muranga
25 Kiambu
EASTERN
26 Marsabit
27 Isiolo
28 Meru
29 Embu
30 Kitui
31 Machakos
NORTH EASTERN
32 Mandera
33 Wajir
34 Garissa
COAST
35 Tana River
36 Lamu
37 Taita
38 Kilifi
39 Kwale
40 Mombasa
NAIROBI
41 Nairobi Area

MAPS

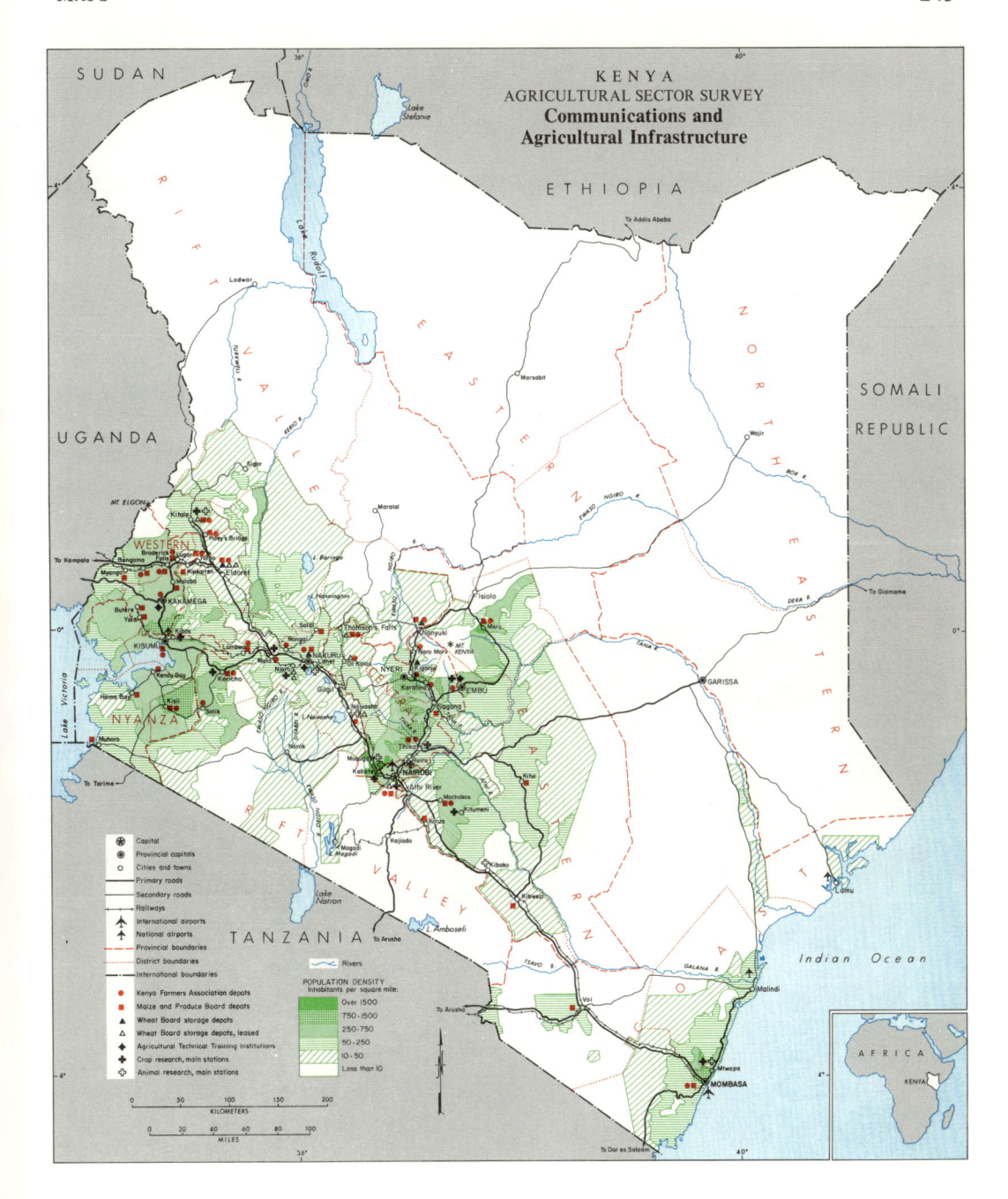

KENYA
AGRICULTURAL SECTOR SURVEY
Communications and Agricultural Infrastructure

246 MAPS

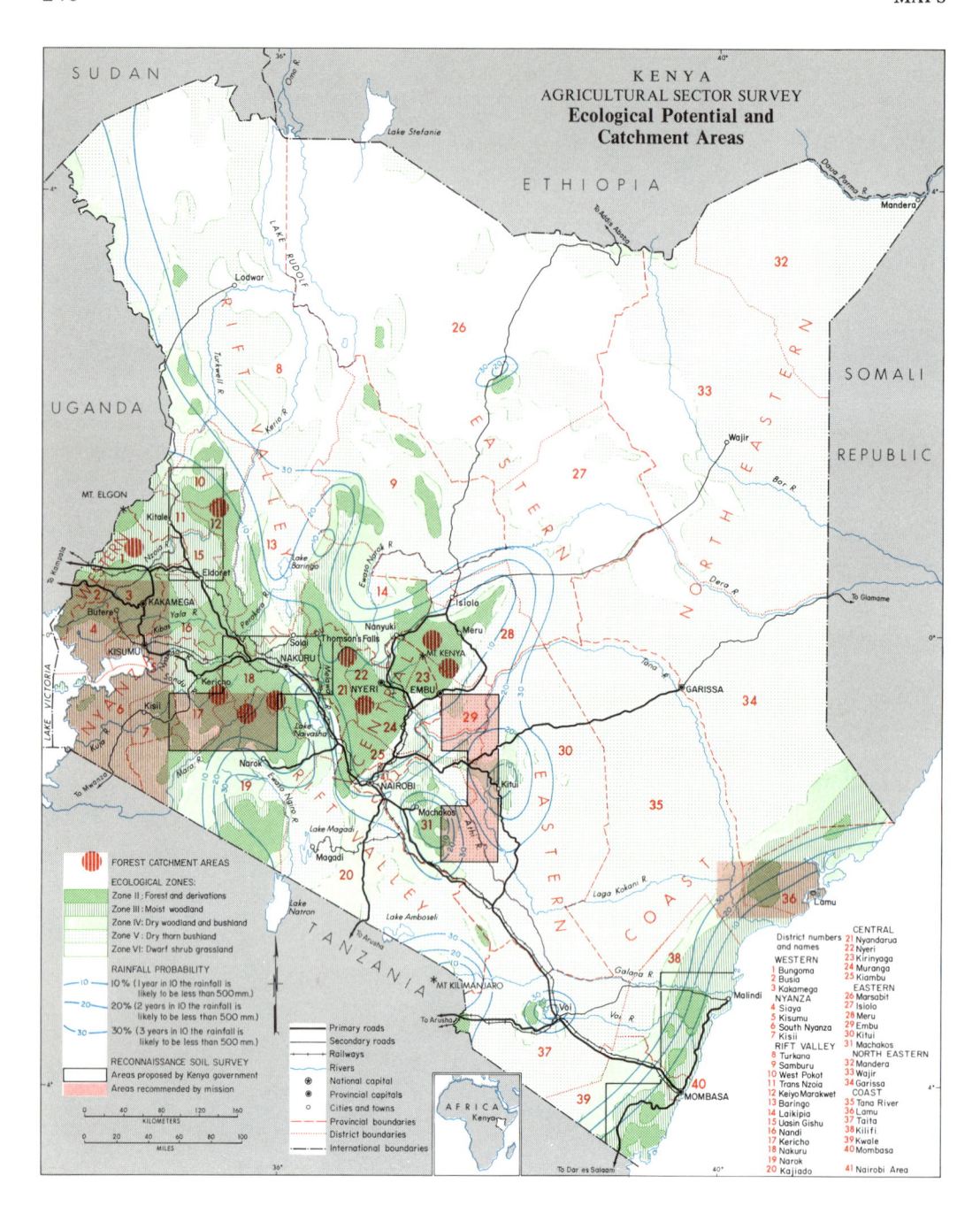

MAPS

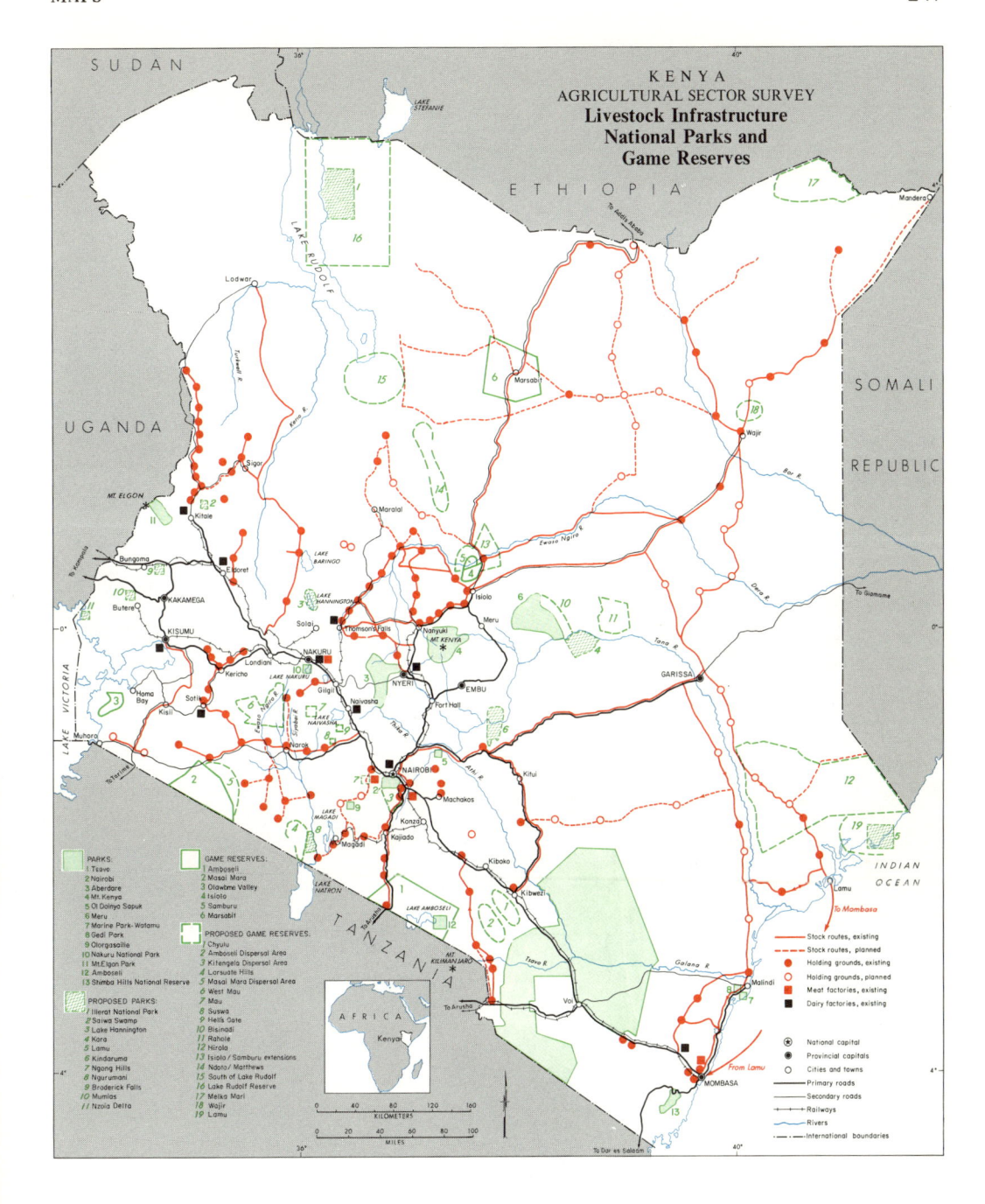

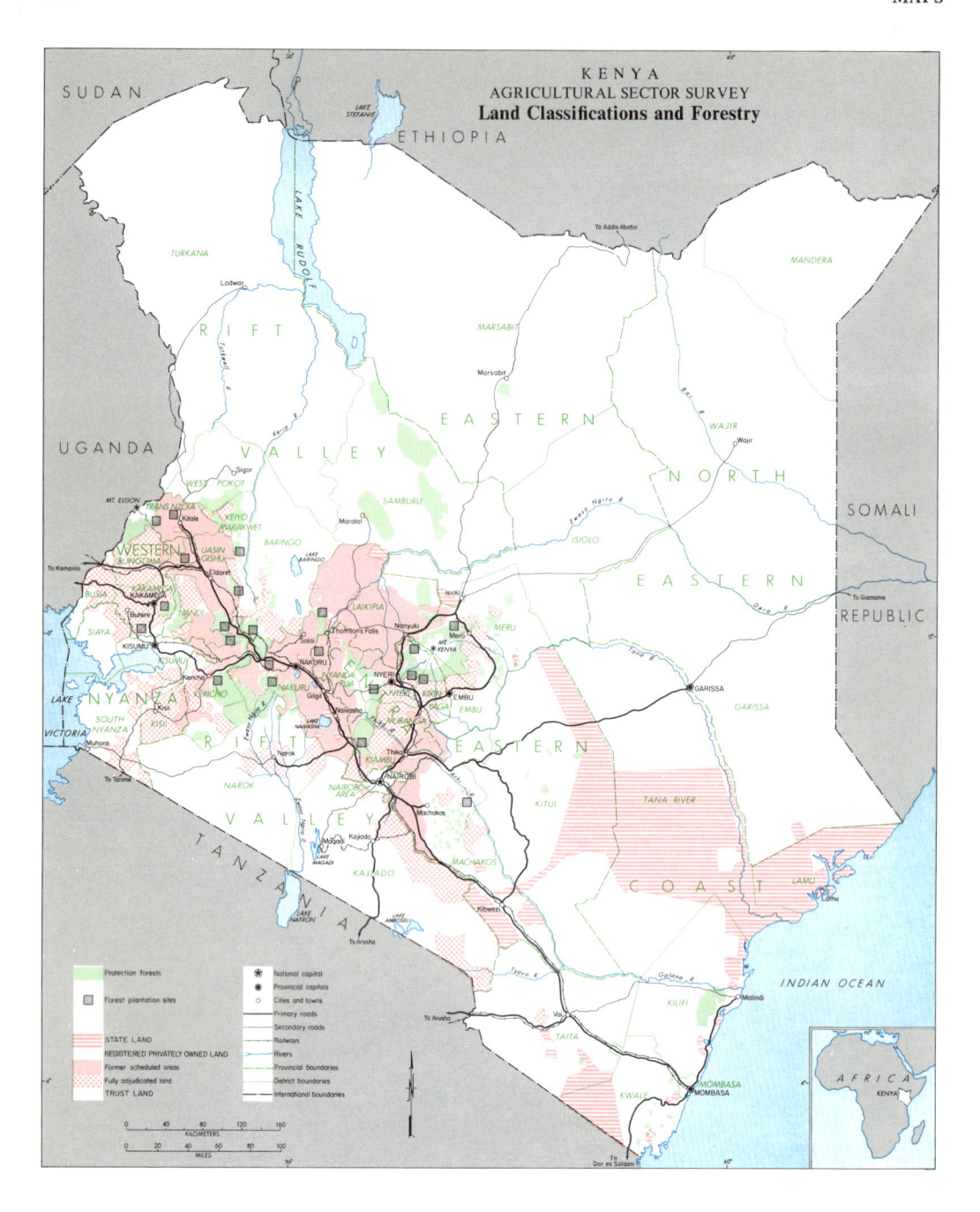

KENYA AGRICULTURAL SECTOR SURVEY
Land Classifications and Forestry

MAPS

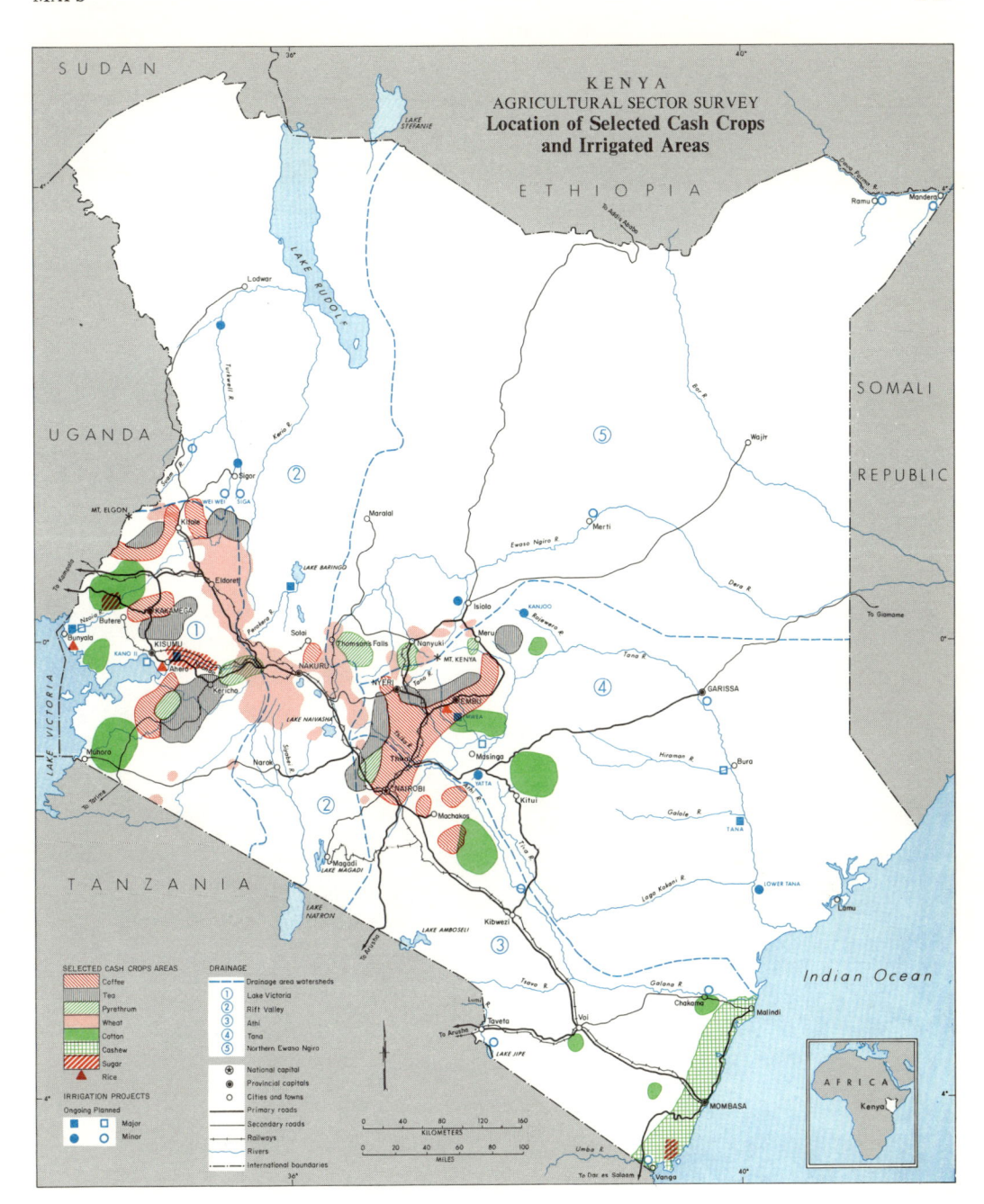

KENYA
AGRICULTURAL SECTOR SURVEY
Location of Selected Cash Crops and Irrigated Areas

FISCAL POLICY FOR DEVELOPMENT   251

Table 36: Distribution of Public Services by Province, Around 1970

		EDUCATION SERVICES			HEALTH SERVICES					HOUSING	ROADS
		% of School Enrollment		% of Primary School Enrollment to Age Group 0–9[1]	Number of People		Health Centers per Million Population[2]	Health Center Beds per Million Population[2]	Dispensaries per Million Population[2]	% of Housing Funds[3]	% of Secondary and Minor Roads[4]
Province	% of Total Population	Primary	Secondary		per Hospital Bed	per Medical Practitioner					
Rift Valley	20.4	14.7	12.1	24	820	1,755	29	152	58	6.0	28.8
Nyanza	19.4	16.1	13.1	27	1,269	2,219	9	76	30	1.2	8.0
Eastern	17.4	20.2	13.6	39	834	1,734	13	85	37	2.4	24.5
Central	15.3	24.9	22.9	47	766	1,287	20	141	39	15.1	11.3
Western	12.3	13.1	10.1	34	1,033	3,569	23	169	6	2.9	5.0
Coast	8.6	6.3	9.3	25	511	707	14	30	71	7.2	12.2
Nairobi	4.4	4.4	18.7	72	152	84	n.a.	n.a.	n.a.	65.2	n.a.
North Eastern	2.2	0.3	0.2	4	1,308	1,230	12	49	49	0.0	10.2
Whole Country	100.0	100.0	100.0	36	715	871	17	106	38	100.0	100.0

[1] *Statistical Abstract*, 1972.
[2] These have been computed from the 1972 data provided by the Ministry of Health and the population data for 1969.
[3] Expenditure of Native Housing Corporation.
[4] Ministry of Works, *Road Classification*, July 1972.

SOURCE: ILO/UNDP report, Chap. 18.

Table 37: **Primary School Enrollment by Province, 1968–72**

Province	% of Total Population 1969	% OF TOTAL PRIMARY SCHOOL ENROLLMENT				
		1968	1969	1970	1971	1972
Central	15.3	24.5	24.3	24.5	24.4	24.3
Coast	8.6	5.9	6.0	5.9	5.7	5.7
Eastern	17.5	20.1	21.0	21.3	20.7	20.3
Nairobi	4.7	4.5	4.7	4.3	4.4	4.3
North Eastern	2.2	0.2	0.3	0.2	0.3	0.3
Nyanza	19.4	18.3	16.1	15.5	16.3	16.1
Rift Valley	20.2	14.4	14.3	14.2	15.0	15.0
Western	12.1	12.1	13.3	14.1	13.2	14.0
TOTAL	100.0	100.0	100.0	100.0	100.0	100.0

SOURCE: *Statistical Abstract*, 1972, p. 170.

Table 38: Government Development Expenditure on Agriculture and Selected Rural Services, 1964/65–1972/73

Category	1964/65	1965/66	1966/67	1967/68	1968/69	1969/70	1970/71	1971/72	1972/73[1]
					(£ million)				
Agriculture[2]	8.3	5.3	5.5	4.7	5.4	4.9	5.1	6.9	6.4
Land settlements	6.6	3.1	2.5	1.8	2.4	1.5	1.8	2.7	1.3
Rural water supply[3]	0.1	—	0.1	0.2	0.4	0.4	0.5	0.8	1.0[5]
Rural roads[4]	0.1	0.2	0.7	1.3	1.5	1.8	4.9	3.8	5.0[5]
Total capital expenditure	10.5	12.1	16.6	21.8	26.8	31.0	44.4	48.3	64.9
Share of agriculture in capital expenditure (%)	79.0[6]	43.8	33.1	21.6	20.1	15.8	11.5	14.3	9.9
Share of rural water supply and rural roads in capital expenditure (%)	2.0	1.7	4.8	6.9	7.1	7.1	12.2	8.6	9.2

[1] Provisional.
[2] These figures exclude government expenditure on land adjudication.
[3] This represents the development expenditure of Water Development Division on rural water supplies plus the water development expenditures of the Ministries of Health, Land and Settlement, and Cooperatives and Social Services. Taken from *Economic Survey* (annual).
[4] This is the development expenditure of the government on settlement, feeder, tea, sugar, and similar roads. Taken from *Appropriation Accounts* (annual).
[5] Projection of the trend.
[6] A very large part of this reflects government expenditure on land purchases and resettlement.

SOURCE: *Statistical Abstracts* (annual).

ANNEX THREE

KEY ISSUES IN THE PRIVATE SECTOR

CHAPTER 1

INTRODUCTION

Scope

The major purposes of Annex Three are to examine the key structural features of the private sector and the policy environment in which it operates, to explain performance, and to consider the range of alternatives which appear to be open to the Government in influencing the future role of the private sector. Our main focus will be on the urban formal sector,[1] not only because of its prime importance within the private sector, but also because we believe that the performance of the urban formal sector has a profound effect on almost everything else in the economy.

In our examination, we shall be particularly concerned with the overall environment in which the urban formal sector operates. Three crucial areas will be reviewed. The first, which covers trade policy, wage policy, and access to credit, will concern the responsiveness of the private sector to prices. The second will range over the effect on the private sector of the increasing number of controls which Government has imposed on trade, factor use, and financial transfers. The third will focus on the role of foreign private investment and, in particular, on what this investment has given and might give to the Kenyan economy.

Limitations of Focus

This annex is not intended to be a full sector review in the normal sense of the term as used in the World Bank; therefore the discussion will not range over all the conceivable issues. For example, some important factors affecting the development of the private sector, such as the provision of infrastructure and services, will not be reviewed at all. Furthermore, some of the issues dealt with, while crucial to efficient operation of the private sector, may not be amenable to government influence or control. However, for the most part, the emphasis will be on policy and the policy choices which appear to be emerging in Kenya.

There are two conspicuous gaps in the coverage of the annex which call for explanation. By concentrating on the activities of the urban formal sector, the annex gives little direct attention to the *informal* sector. This has been done deliberately, because we feel we can add little to the analysis of the informal sector and the recommendations for its development contained in recent publications. In particular, the recent ILO/UNDP report, as the definitive work on the subject, needs no supplementation.[2] We are in broad sympathy with the view that the urban informal sector is economically productive and of particular value in providing opportunities for employment. It is also clear that much can be done—as indicated in both reports—to remove impediments operating against small businessmen and to assist the development of these businessmen.[3]

---

1. We define the "urban formal sector" in the same way as the ILO/UNDP report. The sector approximately equals nonagricultural activity in the "modern sector" as that term is used in official publications of the Government of Kenya. We shall use the term "modern sector," as interchangeable with "formal sector," whenever comparisons with official statistics are thereby facilitated. In Appendix C, we suggest, however, that the distinction between the formal and informal sectors is, at least in some respects, artificial.

2. See especially, Introduction, Summary, and Recommendations, pp. 21–22, Chapter 13, and Technical Paper No. 22.

3. Appendix C to this annex discusses the legal and other reforms required to assist this development, and in Annex Five we suggest a program for development of small scale business.

Such a change in policy would make a substantial contribution to the creation of labor intensive activities, the development of indigenous entrepreneurship, the use of local materials, and the provision of cheap goods and services to the poor. We endorse these recommendations. However, we do not believe that the development of the informal sector can be the basis of an entire development strategy for Kenya and, as indicated above, this annex will focus on the direct and indirect effects of the formal sector, which we feel will continue to be dominant in the economy. Thus, the annex will be complementary to the ILO/UNDP report and its innovative analysis of informal activity.

The informal sector is important to the following discussion in three ways. First, and most important, policies directed toward formal activities (and most policies are) have very important indirect effects upon the rest of the economy, not least on the informal sector. Wage policy in the formal sector, for instance, has ramifications throughout the entire economy. These external effects will be a major theme of the annex. Second, the informal sector is important in a technical sense in the analysis of the reservation price of labor and its effect on migration and wage levels. Finally, the informal sector will appear in the concluding discussion of basic trade-offs between targets.

Thus, this report will not deal with the informal sector's requirements as a sector in its own right, nor will it make any further attempt to quantify its role of the informal sector in the economy; nor will it attempt to add to the little that is now known about the demand and supply linkages of formal and informal urban activity. However, all the known important effects of the formal sector on the informal and the choices between the two will be considered.

An even more conspicuous gap in our discussion will be the exclusion of agriculture from major consideration, even though agriculture is the most important part of the private sector and has been singled out in the basic analysis of the report as the key sector in Kenya's future development strategy. A major review of the agricultural sector itself, the prospects for development, and the key issues and constraints facing it has recently been undertaken by the Bank, and the main findings of that review are included as Part III of this report. In this annex, our task is only to show that the urban formal sector has important indirect effects on agriculture—through trade policy, which taxes it, through the dominant influence of the urban formal sector on wage policy, and through the preemption of credit. As with the informal sector, questions of indirect effect, of relationship, and of options are considered; but the agricultural sector is not treated as a separate entity to any great extent.

The Basic Theses

Three basic theses underlie our discussion in this annex. The first is the fundamental hypothesis that not only is the urban formal sector a leading sector in the economy, but that its existence and operation have a profoundly important effect on all the other sectors of the economy—particularly agriculture and the informal sector. Given this thesis, it follows that we are concerned with both the direct effects of policy on the performance of the sector itself (important and not always understood) and with the indirect effects these policies have on the rest of the economy.

The second basic thesis is that the urban formal sector has not performed as effectively as it might and that, under present policies, it is even debatable whether formal sector activity is beneficial to the economy. The substantive argument here is that there are certain major distortions which have arisen from existing policy, and that these distortions have induced the private sector to develop in a less than optimum way. It follows from the first thesis that these policy distortions will also have an important effect on the rest of the economy, and it is contended that an insight into these interactions is crucial to an understanding of the economy and of the policy options open.

The last basic thesis is that there may be certain conflicts between basic objectives, some of which may only now be starting to emerge clearly. For example, some important goals—such as accelerated Kenyanization or the need to limit the extent of foreign participation—may conflict with the goal of maximum growth, while the successful development of the sector itself may have considerable side effects on the economy as a whole and particularly on the informal sector. Some of these conflicts between ends, it should be noted, would still exist even if the distortions in policy were removed, although many would disappear.

The Method of Approach

In considering the options open to Government in managing the private sector, we shall be concerned with means, not ends. Thus, much of the discussion will center around alternative methods of achieving given goals. For example, we shall not suggest whether or not foreign investment is desirable, since this is ultimately a political choice, but we shall suggest how foreign investment could contribute more to the Kenyan economy, and that there might be better (that is, less costly) ways of achieving a given aim. We shall also demonstrate that the basic goals of society may sometimes conflict with each other, and that these conflicts will have to be resolved before a sound policy package can be formulated.

The discussion will center around the issues referred to previously, namely the effect of price signals and controls on the private sector, and the policy towards foreign investment. Under each of these issues, the logical sequence of analysis will be first to look at the policy situation and assess its effects on performance, and then to examine the policy options which appear to be open, given the basic objectives and the major constraints.

Finally, we shall attempt to bring into focus the implications of these major issues for overall strategy. The emphasis here will be on the basic choices which face the Government: mainly the choice between incentives and controls, and the cost and benefits of unconstrained formal sector growth.

Chapter 2

The Role and Performance of the Private Sector

Since Independence, Kenya has looked to the private sector to provide the major impetus to development. The importance attached to private enterprise by the Government has been stressed in a series of official publications and statements[1] and has been borne out by the policies applied since Independence. In its reliance on private enterprise, Kenya's development policy differs significantly from that of most other black African countries, which have tended to put more emphasis on the role of the public sector in spearheading development. It is true that Kenya has made it clear that private investment—particularly foreign investment—is welcome only if it can be seen to benefit the economy; the Government has never advocated a complete laissez faire doctrine.[2] In recent years, the Government has also decided to increase its participation in the enterprise sector in order to achieve effective Kenyan control over key sectors of the economy. Yet it is apparent that the Kenya Government is still committed to a mixed economy in which the private sector will continue to play a dominant role.

In applying this philosophy, the Government has followed a pragmatic policy of encouraging both local and foreign entrepreneurship by providing a generally attractive environment and a broad range of direct and indirect assistance. Domestically, the social and political atmosphere has been favorable to the development of entrepreneurial ability and initiative, and the Government has been anxious to foster the growth of indigenous enterprise by regulating the activities of noncitizens (as in the Kenyanization of trade) and by taking direct measures to assist the African entrepreneurship in overcoming the initial problem of establishment. For the foreign firm, the natural economic attractions of investment in Kenya have been enhanced by the political stability of the country, liberal taxation and free repatriation of profits, and a ready availability of protective devices. As we argue later, these measures, while financially attractive to the individual entrepreneurs, have not necessarily been to the economic benefit of the country as a whole.

In overall terms, the private sector has indeed borne the major burden of development, even though the relative role of the public sector has grown rather more important over the years. Since 1964, in fact, the private sector has contributed more than 60 percent of the real growth in value-added, and still accounted for 70 percent of GDP at factor cost in 1972. At a more disaggregated level, private activity is particularly important in the two largest productive sectors, namely agriculture and manufacturing. In 1972, agriculture accounted for about one-third of GDP, and virtually all of this was in the private sector. In the same year, manufacturing accounted for 11.5 percent of GDP, of which 82 percent was private. In fact, private activity accounted for over half of value-added in all enterprise activities, except for electricity and water, transport, storage and communications, where the proportion of private activity was much smaller.[3]

More striking than the high proportions of private activity is the relative constancy of these proportions. There are two major economic sectors where the public sector has expanded at the expense of the private. These are the electricity and water sector, which is now almost completely under public ownership; and banking, insurance, and real

---

1. The basic development philosophy, first enunciated in the original KANU Manifesto before Independence, was incorporated in Sessional Paper No. 10 (*African Socialism*) and has formed the basis of successive national development plans.
2. "The Government expects the private sector to play a large role in development, subject, however, to firm guidance and explicit controls when necessary." *African Socialism,* Para. 120, has been prophetic of Government's role in controlling private sector development. The nature of firm guidance and explicit controls will become apparent in later chapters.
3. See Table 4.

estate, in which the private sector share has dwindled from 72 percent to 51 percent since Independence. In all other sectors the role of private activity has either remained roughly constant or grown, as in forestry, building, and construction.

The private sector is also the major source of employment in the Kenyan economy. In the modern sector, the private sector accounts for about 61 percent of wage employment or a little less than its share of GDP (see Table 1), but estimates of employment should include the self-employed and those employed outside the modern sector, if the true contribution is to be assessed. Such estimates are notoriously unreliable, but from calculations shown elsewhere, a figure of 5,000,000 for the total labor force in Kenya is not unreasonable, of whom 95 percent work in some form of private activity.[4]

Therefore, it is clear that Kenya has relied on private activity as the major development force in stimulating productive activity and in providing employment opportunities to the expanding population. This policy has changed little since 1964. Because of this emphasis, a close look at the policy environment is clearly desirable. For, although the strategy has paid off in terms of development, certain problems have arisen and will be discussed later.

Past Performance of the Private Sector

This is not a sector review but an analysis of policy. For this reason, the detailed performance of the various sectors will not be discussed. The overall performance of the economy is described elsewhere in the report, and at this point, it is only necessary to pick out those particular aspects of the performance of the private sector which are relevant to the present discussion. Subsequently, some detailed points will be made in discussion of each policy and its effects.

Assessment of performance can be done in two ways, namely by looking at levels achieved or by looking at relationships between variables. The first approach would consider levels of output, employment, or investment against some target, perhaps plan expectations. The second approach would concentrate on asking whether, given the investment, output growth is satisfactory, or whether, given the output growth, employment growth was reasonable. This second approach is adopted here for two reasons. First, a line of logic going from targets, to realization, to policy defects and requirements, is appropriate to the review of a plan, which this report is not. Second, the approach taken here is to consider how to get as much as possible out of an activity by analysis of its environment. Crucial defects in the environment will appear in the relationships among variables rather than from a statistic in isolation.

As is shown in Table 2, the compound real rate of growth of private sector gross value-added was 5.6 percent between 1964 and 1972.[5] Within the monetary sector, the fastest growing activity was a rather small one, namely building and construction, which grew at 12.3 percent per annum. Of the two major sectors, the fastest growing was manufacturing, which achieved an overall compound rate of growth of 7.6 percent per annum, compared with agriculture's 6.3 percent per annum. As a result, manufacturing's share of private monetary value-added grew from 18 percent in 1964 to 20 percent in 1972, while agriculture remained at 32 percent. The striking feature of these figures is that, while indicating change, they do not reveal any rapid transformation of the economy. It is important to note that one of the economy's most important activities, tourism, does not appear in these national accounts. However, the growth of several sectors, especially other services, is related to tourism. Direct value-added in tourism was estimated at £9 million in 1971.

4. See Annex One, Table 15.
5. Choice of 1972 as a terminal year is unfortunate in some respects, because it was an exceptionally good year for agriculture which grew 17 percent in constant prices. This raises total growth upwards.

The overall level of investment has grown in the 1964–72 period at a compound annual rate of 17.4 percent at current prices to nearly £160 million in 1972. The share of the private sector has fallen from 75 percent of investment in 1964 to 62 percent in 1972 (Table 5). In the enterprise economy, however, the private sector has remained responsible for a slowly falling but very large proportion of investment over the period. Since public investment in the enterprise economy has been largely in electricity and water, transport, storage and communications, and ownership of dwellings, investment in other enterprise sectors is almost entirely in the private sector.

If the allocation of private investment is considered, the most striking feature is the growth of manufacturing's share and the falling allocation to agriculture (Tables 5 and 7). As might be expected, the share of investment going to electricity and water has fallen sharply as public ownership has increased.

In looking at the efficiency of the investment in the private sector, we have drawn on the macro-economic work of the mission to calculate net incremental capital output ratios for individual sectors (Table 8). The methodology of the approach and the implications for economic policy are described at length in Annex One. Some of the results are of doubtful validity, owing to the nature of the data. But it is interesting to note that the regressions tend to show fairly low NICORs for those private sector activities (agriculture, commerce, and manufacturing) which together accounted for 70 percent of private monetary value-added in 1972. In particular, the net capital output ratio in manufacturing was estimated to be relatively low and falling. On the other hand, the time trends in some sectors, such as building and construction, have been disturbing and are the subject of discussion elsewhere.

Since the private sector is judged in large measure by its contribution to employment, it is particularly useful to examine this aspect of performance. Scrutiny of various sources of information on employment reveals two important phenomena. The first is the decline in the absolute number of employees in agriculture, described elsewhere in the report. The second—and much more disturbing feature of past performance—is the very slow growth of private wage employment. Since 1964, wage employment in the modern sector, for example, has grown at an average rate of only 1.2 percent a year, while since 1967 total private wage employment has grown at only 1.4 percent.

At first sight, these dismally low growth rates (which are much below the labor force growth rate) appear to be due to the diminished importance of employment in agriculture, which even in 1972 accounted for more than 60 percent of all private employment. It is true that other sectors of the modern sector achieved higher employment growth rates between 1964–72, for example manufacturing (5.1 percent), building and construction (12.3 percent), and transport and communications (6.3 percent). Tourism has also grown rapidly, with direct employment reaching 11,600 in 1971. Yet an analysis of the output-employment relationship within the individual sector shows rather disturbing evidence of a negative trend in all the six major sectors of the enterprise economy:

Private Modern Sector Employment Per £1,000 Value-Added

		Trend per Annum
Agriculture	3.73	−0.21
Mining	1.94	−0.15
Manufacturing	1.77	−0.06
Commerce	1.43	−0.09
Transport	1.75	−0.14
Services	3.30	−0.14
Total	2.57	−0.13

Source: Table 12

These trends were calculated from an equation of the employment-output ratio on time and of the elasticity of employment with respect to output. It is particularly significant that the trend toward declining rates of growth in employment are most noticeable in those sectors (agriculture and services) in which the ratio of employment to value-added is presently highest.[6]

The striking relationship between employment and growth is confirmed by the following figures, which show the elasticity of modern sector employment, with respect to output, for five major sectors:

Elasticity of Private Modern Sector Employment with Respect to Output

Mining	0.2
Manufacturing	0.5
Building	1.3
Transport	0.6
Services	0.3
Total	0.1

Source: Table 12

Agriculture and commerce are not shown because they have negative elasticities, that is, their employment has fallen with increasing output. Other activities, with the exception of building and construction, have elasticities of less than one; in view of its importance to the economy, manufacturing's elasticity of 0.5 is especially interesting. Thus, with only one exception, employment growth has lagged far behind output increases, or has declined absolutely in every section of the private sector. The overall elasticity of private sector employment, at 0.1, indicates the dimensions of the problem. These figures define a situation, which may be insoluble, but they also demonstrate rather starkly the growth requirements, on current trends, of a significant rise in modern sector employment.[7]

To sum up, the description of salient features of the Kenyan private sector indicates this sector's importance to the economy in terms of output, investment, and employment. Information provided on performance of the private sector indicates no startling transformation of the situation but a fairly steady advance. The one important problem which is highlighted is that of employment, where responsiveness to output changes is very low. More detailed understanding of the private sector's performance and operation will follow from the discussion of key policy issues.

---

6. These tables are purely descriptive. Quite different explanations can exist, such as increasing capacity utilization, capital-labor substitution, or costless improvements in labor productivity.

7. The current trends may not continue. If the low employment growth has been caused by increasing capacity utilization or costless productivity increases, it is at least probable that future performance will be better.

Chapter 3

Price Signals and Performance

In this chapter, we shall be concerned with the way in which the private sector responds to price policies which govern the costs of its inputs and the price of its products. Then we shall turn to the direct controls which have been imposed on the economy by the Government, and we shall analyze their consequences. These two areas —price signals and controls—are the major ways in which the Government can influence the environment in which the private sector operates and, through them, manipulate the behavior of the private sector. Much of our argument will show that both the price signals and the range of controls will require modification if the private sector is to perform better. We shall suggest that, over a wide range of action, manipulating prices and imposing controls can be alternative ways of achieving the same desired objective, one being an indirect means of using market forces and the other being a direct restriction of entrepreneurial freedom.

In general, the mission believes that the use of the price system is the most appropriate way of orienting the private sector in an efficient direction, for two reasons. The most general is simply that, as a long term policy, controls have proved to be a rather costly and inefficient way of influencing profit-oriented activities, not only in Kenya but in most countries that have tried controls. The attempt to make entrepreneurs do what is against their financial interest seldom works except in the most disciplined societies and is often counterproductive. The second reason relates more directly to Kenya. A system of controls requires a large, honest, sensitive, flexible bureaucracy. Kenya would have to commit a good proportion of its scarcest resource, skilled manpower, to achieve such an organization. This is not necessarily an appropriate way to use these skills. At the same time, it is clear from experience with the trade control system that the present bureaucratic machine is not able to cope satisfactorily.

Price signals embrace a very wide field indeed. The areas concentrated upon in this annex are trade policy, wages, and the pricing of credit. There are interrelations between all these areas, which, in combination create a set of distortions which impede the efficient operation of formal nonagricultural activity and impose indirect external costs on the rest of the economy. These three areas have been independently analyzed in several research studies, which are used as sources for this analysis. We do not attempt to add to these studies, but rather attempt to pull into a coherent whole what is known about the overall situation in order to identify the policy options which are open to the Government. Not only is this a fruitful way of discussing policy, but it is also a useful way of understanding what is happening in the private sector.

Current Policy and the Price Environment

Past Developments in Trade

The basic aim of trade policy has been import substitution. The Development Plan 1970–74, for instance, states that ". . . the Government believes that the country has not yet exhausted all opportunities for import substitution industries. In the last five years, there has been a considerable amount of import substitution and this trend will continue in the next five years."[1] At the same time, there is no mention of exports among the seven "targets" of manufacturing.

The policy has not been very different from those of many of Kenya's neighbors.

---

1. *Development Plan, 1970–74*, pp. 304–5.

There is the important difference, however, that on the establishment of the East African common market in 1967, Kenya had a head start in many industries, including those for which there is natural protection, such as brewing and cement, and those requiring high tariff protection. Because of the head start, Kenya's trade structure differs from that of many African countries in having quite a high proportion of manufactured exports, the greater part of which go to Uganda and Tanzania. However, although the proportion is rather high, the rate of growth has been low.

The Kenyan economy has now largely completed the first phase of import substitution, namely the replacement of consumer goods. The pattern and extent of import substitution is shown in Table 20.[2] By 1970, only 28.2 percent of domestic consumption was supplied by imports; nevertheless, Kenya still remains dependent on the outside world for most of her supplies of intermediate goods (61 percent) and capital goods (68 percent).[3] The table also indicates the classic tariff structure, with average nominal duties falling from 29.6 percent on consumer goods to 18.0 percent on intermediates, and 12.7 percent on capital goods.

The success of the policy of import substitution is also shown by the changing structure of imports (Table 21). The average rate of growth of imports has been 10.9 percent per annum from 1964 to 1972. Consumption goods for household use have grown least, by 6.4 percent per annum, and government imports and capital goods most, by 17 and 15.5 percent per annum, respectively. Intermediate goods imports have grown at virtually the same average rate as imports as a whole. The effect of this has been a reduction in the share of household consumption goods from more than 27 percent in 1964 to 20 percent in 1972, and an increase in the share of capital goods from 14.5 percent to 20 percent.

In 1970, Kenya exported a little more than 18 percent of her total domestic supply of processed goods. About half the exports went to Tanzania and Uganda. The structure of Kenyan exports to the rest of the world is fairly typical of a developing country. In 1970, more than 60 percent of exports were of nonprocessed raw materials and foodstuffs (mostly coffee and tea) and only 12.5 percent were of manufactured goods (Table 21). On the other hand, 30 percent of Kenya's total exports went to the Community, and more than half of these were manufactured goods. Thus, Kenya occupies an intermediate stage in development. It exports primary produce outside the Community, but exports various kinds of processed goods to its partners.

This pattern may appear at first sight not inappropriate to a developing country slightly more advanced than its neighbors. However, there are certain inherent weaknesses in the situation. Kenya is vulnerable because of its relative dependence on exports of consumer goods to Uganda and Tanzania, not only because these kinds of goods are the easiest to replace under Tanzania's and Uganda's own program of import substitution, but also because the Treaty itself provides mechanisms (through the transfer tax and the operations of the East African Development Bank) to assist this process.

The average rate of growth of exports from 1964 to 1972 has been 6.8 percent a year, which is almost identical with that of GDP. Within that total, however, the share of manufactured goods has *fallen* from 25 percent to 20 percent, and the growth of manufactured exports has been only 4.1 percent per annum. The largest contribution to increased export earnings has been tea, which has grown at an average rate of 12.5 percent. Only one major export has grown more rapidly, and that is the products of the Mombasa petroleum refinery; but export statistics overstate the real contribution of

---

2. The classification used in this table is not entirely satisfactory. In particular, the locations of ISIC Code Nos. 313, 319, and 383 may be incorrect. The table follows Dr. S. Guisinger's classification for Ethiopia in his *Tariff and Trade Policies for the Ethopian Manufacturing Sector* and thus preserves comparability.

3. By comparison, Guisinger showed that Ethiopia imports 30 percent of her domestic consumption, 50 percent of intermediate goods, and 87 percent of capital goods.

refined oil products, since the domestic value-added in oil refining is very low—only 16 percent in 1970. Thus, in terms of the "true" contribution to the balance of payments, Kenya's major success in commodity trade has been tea. Direct expenditures by tourists were £26.5 million in 1972, which makes tourism larger than any other single foreign exchange earner. The increase was 280 percent over 1965, or a compound average, annual growth rate of 21 percent. Thus, tourism has been Kenya's greatest postindependence success among foreign exchange earnings activities.

The share of the East African Community in total exports has been falling, from 36 percent in 1964, to 30 percent in 1970, and less than 27 percent in 1972. (The latter figure is perhaps not typical because of the exceptionally low level of exports to Uganda in that year.) Part of the reason for the poor performance of manufacturing is the fact that EAC trade has fallen in proportion to the whole, and well over half of all manufactured exports go to the Community. However, there are more disquieting features within the pattern of exports to the EAC.

Looking at the pattern of exports since 1964, it is clear that manufactured exports to the EAC have virtually stagnated (Table 21). There have been sharp falls in the export of the simple import substitutes—particularly processed foods, clothing, and footwear—which Tanzania and Uganda are increasingly producing themselves. Allowing for the effect of import substitution in these three categories, together with the falls in base metal exports, it is estimated that Kenya lost some £5.7 million in export revenues to Tanzania and Uganda between 1964 and 1972. This loss in export markets has been almost exactly offset by increases in chemicals, paper, and metal manufactures and, particularly, petroleum products. Thus, overall, Kenya has been running very hard to stand still in its trade with its Partners, which accounts for so much of its total trade in processed goods.

The picture in relation to trade with the rest of the world has been somewhat different. First of all, the overall growth rate has been very reasonable—over 8 percent a year. Second, manufactured exports have been growing much faster than the average, at nearly 12 percent a year, and therefore are a growing proportion of the total. Most export growth to the rest of the world has come from nonprocessed primary goods, mainly meat, fruit and vegetables, coffee, tea, hides and skins, and raw cotton. Nevertheless, processed goods have been important, especially the processing of local raw materials. Thus, some 43 percent of the increased exports have been canned meat, pyrethrum extract, petroleum products (21 percent of the increase on its own), chemicals, paper manufactures, textiles, cement, metal manufactures, and footwear. Of these, only a very few are really important, namely, petroleum, pyrethrum extract, canned meat, chemicals, and cement.[4] It appears therefore that although Kenya remains largely an exporter of nonprocessed primary commodities to non-EAC countries, it has done reasonably well in processing manufactured exports as a whole, and has had striking success in a few industries. This is so in spite of the fact that some of these industries are taxed by the protective system.

Therefore, the overall picture is that stagnant trade with the EAC, except in petroleum products, has not been fully offset by the higher growth rate of exports of manufactures to the rest of the world, and Kenya has remained largely dependent on a few primary commodities, plus tourism, for her foreign exchange earnings. It is clear that, based on current trends, a major change in Kenya's overall export pattern calls for an extremely high rate of growth of exports to the rest of the world just to offset Kenya's stagnation of trade with EAC Partners. A greater rate of growth will also be desirable

---

4. It is interesting to note that, according to Phelps and Wasow, chemicals, cement, and pyrethrum extract were all profitable at world prices; and cement and pyrethrum were negatively effectively protected, as were industrial chemicals. No data are given for petroleum. See M. G. Phelps and D. Wasow, "Measuring Protection and its Effects in Kenya," Working Paper No. 37 (Nairobi: Institute for Development Studies, n.d.).

if manufacturing is to grow much at all, given the already high level of import substitution.[5]

The Protective System

The principal conscious aim of trade policy being import substitution,[6] the main policy instrument has been the tariff, which is, of course, determined at a Community level. In addition, there has been an increasing use of import controls as protective devices.[7] Since import controls have exacerbated rather than conflicted with the effects of tariffs and have many aspects separate from tariffs, discussion of the controls is postponed. (However, discussion of effective protection does allow for the effects of the controls.) It should be stressed that one of the reasons for increased use of import controls is that they are under Kenya's independent control. Apart from the tariff protection granted by the Community, Kenya is able to grant duty rebates and remissions on imported inputs used by exporters. The procedure is slow, however, and not always effective for firms lacking influence. In 1972, duty rebates were 2.6 percent of gross collection of import duties for the EAC as a whole. These would include rebates granted as a special protective device to producers of goods sold domestically.

The efficiency of the protection granted by the EAC tariff has been closely evaluated by a number of studies in recent years.[8] While these studies differ in methodology and in detail, their conclusions about protection are basically the same, and we shall draw heavily upon these studies in this and subsequent sections of the report. For the sake of the nontechnical reader we refer only to the general conclusions in this chapter; the technical reader may refer to Appendix B, "Measures of Protection and Viability," for a description of the methodology used.[9]

All the studies agree that a considerable and varying degree of effective protection is granted to manufacturing. Such protection may do no more than enhance the profitability of already viable industries, and thus transfer income from the Government or consumers to producers. But effective protection can also have the effect of making nonviable industries profitable, and in terms of productive efficiency, it is the latter that counts. Only one of the studies referred to (namely that done by Phelps and Wasow) took up the question of viability and its relationship to protection. The study comes to three main conclusions: first, that the protective system favors "finishing touch" industries; second, that no relationship emerges between factor intensity and protection, so that there is no reason to believe the system is biased against employment; and third, that there is a significant negative correlation between profitability at world prices and the level of effective protection. This last conclusion would imply that there is a consistent bias against the most viable sectors.

---

5. A change in Kenya's trade pattern is attractive not only because of the classic export-led growth arguments for manufacturing, but because of the worsening of terms of trade which follows upon primary commodity concentration. Kenya's terms of trade index moved from 100 to 94 between 1964 and 1972. Although tourism has played an invaluable role, it cannot substitute for a high rate of growth of manufacturing exports in developing the economy.

6. A detailed analysis of the direction of Kenya's total industrial policy appears in the ILO/UNDP report, pp. 177–202. The subject was also dealt with in "Industrial Development in East Africa: Progress, Policies, Problems, and Prospects," Volume IV, Kenya, World Bank Report AE-12, (unpublished), pp. 15–28.

7. D. S. Macrae, *Import Licensing in Kenya*, Institute for Development Studies Working Paper No. 90, p. 32. "Today the system is such that wherever there is domestic production of a good its importation is almost invariably banned or severely restricted so that the local producer gets as much of the domestic market as possible."

8. See R. Reimer, "Effective Rates of Protection in East Africa," Staff Paper No. 78 (Nairobi: Institute for Development Studies, July 1970), and Phelps and Wasow.

9. See also Appendix A for a nontechnical explanation. As stated in Appendix B, since the Phelps and Wasow study uses direct price comparisons, the effect of import controls is included in the calculations.

The Phelps and Wasow study calculates rates of effective protection ranging from −77.5 percent to 172.9 percent, and profitability at world prices ranging from −55.9 percent to 208.4 percent. Of the twenty-three categories defined in Table 20 as consumer goods industries, ten are unprofitable at world prices, as are five of the fourteen intermediate goods industries, and two of the eleven capital goods industries. Thus, inefficient protection is fairly well scattered, although there is a concentration among consumer goods industries, as might be expected. From a policy point of view, an especially important conclusion of the study is that no simple formulae for industrialization are likely to be very efficient. Some industries processing raw materials are viable, and some are not; some consumer goods industries are viable and others are not. There seems to be no substitute for detailed case-by-case analysis. For instance, it appears that the following industries are acceptable: truck and bus body building (but not cars), canvas goods, timber products, printing, leather tanning, some (by no means all) chemicals and pharmaceuticals, some agricultural machinery, pyrethrum, wattle, cement, and beef. This is a very disparate group, which only detailed analysis could identify. Moreover, several viable export industries, which are potentially taxed by the tariff structure, may not even exist at present.

What confidence can be placed in these results? As is shown in Appendix B, no great trust can ever be placed in results for individual industries, especially when an industry is shown to be nonviable at world prices. This must always be borne in mind. However, these are problems peculiar to this study. Although it appears thorough, and is apparently based on more detailed production information, as well as more careful price comparisons, than other studies of effective protection, this study has one great anomaly, namely the reported inefficiency of much of agricultural processing industry. As this is unlikely, it suggests that little faith can be placed in individual results, and must also qualify the overall conclusion that average effective protection was 34.2 percent, and average world price return to capital zero, since the former may well be too high, and the latter too low. These question marks spill over to affect the three main conclusions reported in the Phelps and Wasow study.

As present, there can be no more than a prima facie assumption of inefficiency. There can be no question that the system is potentially capable of leading to inefficiency, and that no checks in the project approval process exist to prevent it. There can also be no doubt that, if not inefficient, the system does lead to a large transfer of income to manufacturers, many of whom are foreign. However, the precise conclusions concerning average protection and world price profitability can be used only illustratively, and the negative relationship between protection and viability is probably, but far from certain.

A further important aspect of this work has been to study the effective protection inherent in the East African transfer tax system. Table 19 shows that the effects of the tax are considerable. Tanzanian taxes against Kenyan manufactures produce effective rates of protection (EPZ), which rise to 379.3 percent, and eight are over 100 percent.[10] More striking still is the fact that ten out of the twenty industry groups which Kenya exports to its Partners are taxed relative to the outside world (using the "modified" method). This finding explains in part the export behavior observed above, and points out the difficult problem Kenyan manufactured exports face.

Conclusions on Trade Policy

The situation analyzed above indicates Kenya is at a turning point not only because the first stage of import substitution is completed, but because some of the costlier

10. $EPZ = \dfrac{DVA - WVA.100}{WVA}$ (See Appendix B.)

aspects of that policy (and especially the weapon of protection) are becoming evident. Apart from this is the fact that many of the industries established have no apparent comparative advantage, and, having dominated the domestic market, have nowhere to go. The problem is especially sharp, since further blanket import substitution will inevitably mean high cost intermediate and capital goods input for potentially viable industries, especially export industries.

There is potential for further import substitution. The ILO/UNDP report recommends several categories of activity for further consideration,[11] and the evidence of Phelps and Wasow shows the following import substitution industries to be profitable at world prices: sugar confectionery, soap, some miscellaneous chemical products, sawed timber, tanneries and leather products, some basic industrial chemicals, some metal products, some nonelectrical machinery, and truck body building. All but three of these industries have negative net effective protection at present according to the study if the exchange rate is assumed to be 15 percent overvalued.

These is also a potential and great need for more manufactured exports, because of Kenya's vulnerable position vis-à-vis its EAC Partners, and the inhibiting effects of their transfer taxes and controls. This is also necessary to avoid excessive dependence on primary commodities and tourism, as well as the danger of future balance of payments difficulties. However, many of Kenya's most important present exports seem to have negative net effective protection, and potential exports are also taxed, especially those using domestic materials.

The situation calls for a major policy review before Kenya finds herself in the middle of a high-cost across-the-board strategy of replacement of intermediates and capital goods, which will probably be a coup de grace to prospects for manufacturing exports, and, in the long run, manufacturing development. It must be remembered that, given Kenya's trade structure, she must do very well merely to maintain her momentum in this field.

The Structure of Wages

In no sense is it our purpose to rework the field covered by the ILO/UNDP report. Nevertheless, any discussion of price signals and performance in the private sector cannot avoid consideration of wages and their influence on factor utilization, incentives, and income distribution. In Kenya this is one of the most important aspects of the private sector's environment.

The earnings structure in Kenya is to be understood within the basic divisions of formal and informal, on the one hand, and rural and urban on the other. Thus, there are essentially four categories of earnings. Formal urban employment (and rural also, to some extent) should be seen as further split into unskilled, semiskilled, and highly skilled. As can be seen in the following table, differentials between the four basic categories are considerable. Average formal sector pay in the urban sector is twice average earnings in the urban informal sector for the self-employed. Formal sector urban pay for an unskilled worker is twice that of a marginal self-employed man in the informal sector and three times that paid in the informal sector. Within the rural sector, there is also a large differential between wage employment in large and small farms. Finally, within the formal sector, pay in the urban areas is substantially above that in rural areas.

These nominal differences exaggerate considerably the differences in real incomes between rural and urban earners. Scott estimates the ratio of the urban to rural price index to be approximately 1.69. Taking this, and various other factors, such as the cost

---

11. For example, refined sugar, baby foods, knitting mills, cotton fabrics of high quality, wool processing, footwear, clothing, make-up textiles, plywood, wooden furniture, paper products, leather goods, rubber products, vegetable oils and special paints and varnishes. ILO/UNDP report, p. 182.

Data on African Adult Earnings in Kenya, 1969

Category of Income Earners	£ per Year Males	£ per Year Females
Rural		
Average large farm regular employee[1]	73	46
Average small farm regular employee[1]	41	34
Average small scale nonagricultural enterprise regular employee[1]	67	49
Self-employment		
Smallholders[1]	113	—
Owners of nonagricultural enterprises[1]	130	—
Urban		
Average employee formal sector[2]	250	185
Statutory minimum wage in formal sector, Nairobi[1,3]	105	84
"Unskilled" employee formal sector[1]	120	90
Average self-employed informal sector[2]	120	100
Marginal self-employed informal sector[1,2]	60	50
Wage earner in informal sector[1]	40	36[4]

[1] Derived from ILO/UNDP report.
[2] Independent estimate by M. FG. Scott.
[3] The minimum wage was raised to £135 for men and £117 for women in Nairobi and Mombasa from September 1, 1973. In other urban areas and municipalities it is now £123 for men and £111 for women.
[4] Estimated using 19 percent discount found by G. E. Johnson, *The Determination of Individual Hourly Earnings in Urban Kenya*, Discussion Paper No. 115 (Nairobi: Institute for Development Studies, September 1971).

SOURCE: *Estimates of Shadow Wages*, ILO/UNDP report, p. 77.

of family separation, he estimates the benefits from the extra wages as shown in the table on page 271. It appears that substantial improvements in real income only occur when a small farm worker moves to a large farm or the urban formal sector, or when an urban informal sector worker moves to urban formal employment.[12]

It appears there is a large gap between the informal sector (including small scale agriculture) and the formal sector. Some evidence indicates this gap is growing. Thus, D. P. Ghai[13] showed that between 1960 and 1966, "the average total income of farmers has risen at half the rate of unskilled urban workers." No data are available for wages in small farms prior to 1969, but it is known that real incomes per head have risen at a compound annual rate of approximately one percent in the agricultural sector as a whole. Real wages in the private formal sector have risen by at least twice that much.

Within the modern sector the gap between agricultural and nonagricultural wages grew until 1970. By the end of that year the index of average earnings (which has 1964 as the base year) was only 122 in agriculture, compared with 130 in the public sector, 134 in services, 151 in manufacturing, and 172 in construction.[14] Since 1970, the situa-

12. The figures for the gain derived from moving to urban informal activity assume self-employment. On this assumption, the real reward of urban informal activity is lower than for any rural activity apart from wage earning in the small scale sector to which it is equivalent. However, assuming that the informal activity is wage earning (estimated at £40 per annum), the rewards are *less* than in any rural activity. This seems the most likely immediate destination for a migrant. Unless these rewards are lower, the standard wage gap models of migration would predict disequilibrium, since workers in small farms can unambiguously increase their expected real income by moving to the towns.

13. D. P. Ghai, *Incomes Policy in Kenya: Need, Criteria, and Machinery*, Discussion Paper No. 66 (Nairobi: Institute for Development Studies, June 1968) mimeo.

14. Indices of average earnings are very unreliable sources of information, because of possible changes in the proportions of various skill (and wage) categories. This is what is assumed

Benefits from Extra Wages Paid on Transfer of the Marginal African Male Adult Worker
(£ per annum)

Occupation to which Worker Goes	Increase in Disposable Income			Compensation for Change in Conditions of Work	Net Gain of Worker and Family
	Total	Relatives	Worker and Family		
Small farm worker to:					
Rural unemployed	−41	−10	−31	−11	−20
Urban unemployed[1]	−41	−16	−25	−5	−20
Urban informal[1]	19	0	19	19	0
Large farm	30	0	30	0	30
Urban formal[1]	75	0	75	45	30
Urban formal[2]	75	0	75	55	20
Urban informal worker to:[3]					
Urban unemployed	−60	−16	−44	−12	−32
Urban formal[3]	56	15	41	0	41

[1] Family left in rural area
[2] Family brought with worker in urban area
[3] Family in urban area

SOURCE: *Estimates of Shadow Wages.*

tion has changed. Union pressure and seasonal scarcity have pushed the wage index for commercial agriculture to 153, at the same time that other sectors have experienced stagnant average wages. In 1971, there was actually a fall in average wages in manufacturing, construction, and commerce, presumably due to the Tripartite Agreement (Table 15). As a result of these contrary movements, the growth of agricultural modern sector wages has virtually caught up with that of the modern private sector as a whole.[15]

Another important dimension of the wage gap situation in Kenya is the relationship between educational level and wage rates in the formal sector. It is generally recognized that a primary school education is now becoming the minimum standard required for employment, even for many unskilled jobs. Moreover, as the supply of school leavers increases, the minimum standard of entry to formal employment rises. It now frequently requires some years of secondary school. Incremental skill can bring vastly increased income, as is shown in Table 18 and Table 16. Highly skilled formal sector employees can expect incomes at par with European incomes, while an unskilled worker earning £120 per annum is receiving perhaps 10 percent of the European equivalent. Even some educationally qualified people with relatively low skills can earn large multiples of minimum formal sector incomes. The ILO/UNDP report[16] mentions several examples: a stenographer in government can earn £489 to £690 per annum. These incomes are not merely large multiples of minimum formal sector wages, but even larger multiples of incomes to be earned in nonformal activity. This is a society in which rewards for qualified people in employment exceed the returns of all but the most successful entrepreneurs.[17]

---

to have happened as a result of the Tripartite Agreement. The lack of detailed information on wages by skill categories through time creates great difficulties in analyzing the labor market in Kenya.

15. Since average earnings in manufacturing are approximately four times greater than in agriculture, the absolute "gap" will increase even if the proportionate growth of each is the same.

16. ILO/UNDP report, p. 254.

17. P. Marris and A. Somerset, *African Businessmen; A Study of Entrepreneurship and Development in Kenya* (London: Routledge and Kegan Paul, 1971), stress this point in explaining the development of African entrepreneurship.

The relationship between income and education can be summarized in the following way: first, average income is estimated to rise by Sh.36 per month for every additional year of schooling. Second, the public sector is paying much higher salaries than the private sector for those who completed secondary school; for example, the public sector pays an average of Sh.45 per month more than the private sector for a worker with nine years of education. Third, the greatest advantages come to those who complete primary school and have at least some secondary school education.

These differentials no longer make sense, if they ever did in terms of supply and demand in the labor market. The problem of school-leaver unemployment has become increasingly severe. At all but a few levels (usually very senior), supply exceeds demand at ruling wage rates. Skilled craftsmen and professionals are in the categories where excess demand still exists.

A final important feature of the Kenyan labor market is that, apparently, wages for similar skills are not equated across industries. Turnover in formal sector employment, not surprisingly, is fairly low, and wages are determined through industry negotiations and wage councils.[18] The typical wages of completely unskilled workers in the formal sector are between Sh.200[19] and Sh.400 a month, a fact of considerable importance since it indicates that wages are determined by industry conditions as much as by the labor market. This has important implications for wage policy, if changes in industry conditions are used as a means of altering wages or the rate of change of wages.

The Causes of the Wage Structure

What we have described above is an extreme form of a dualistic economy, wherein wages in the formal sector are well above those outside it and also rise with educational qualifications more than labor market conditions would seem to warrant. There are many competing, and overlapping, hypotheses to explain these phenomena. At this point, the issues cannot be completely resolved, but some causal relationships can be identified.

The first factor to explain is the basic dualism between formal and informal sector wages for similar skill levels, or why formal sector wages are above alternative opportunity costs. Four main types of explanation pertain to the situation. First, minimum wage legislation applies to the formal sector only and is determined by a generally inappropriate concept of a minimum reasonable reward. Second, trade unions in the formal sector not only force up formal sector wages but also can impose additional costs on employers—for example by the dislocation of production. Third, some employers may feel it is in their interests to pay more to ensure higher efficiency and lower turnover, and to achieve a reputation as "good" employers.[20] On the other hand, employers of nonunion labor feel the threat of labor unrest should nonunion wages get too far out of line with union wages. Finally, the Government may be the initiating factor in some categories because it is not bound by profitability considerations and "pays itself" as it wishes.

A basic requirement for testing any of these hypotheses is a household study in which education and skill levels can be isolated. The most complete is G. E. Johnson's,[21]

18. The ILO/UNDP report discusses the labor relations system in detail; see pp. 253–64, 545–66.

19. The current legal minimum wage in Nairobi is Sh.225.

20. This is probably especially true in Kenya, where employers in the modern private sector are predominantly noncitizens and employees are mainly African.

21. G. E. Johnson, *The Determination of Individual Hourly Earnings in Urban Kenya*. The extent of the benefit of education was derived econometrically. He showed that the marginal benefits of education increase with the level of education (i.e., increasing returns). Thus, moving from five years to seven years schooling increases incomes by 27 percent, but from nine to eleven by 68 percent. The income increase due to a move from zero to eleven years education was 366 percent in Nairobi.

which used the Nairobi study. He found that estimated hourly earnings varied by type of employment as shown below. Clearly, unionization is a factor, as is government employment for nonunion workers. The fact that nonunion wages in private employment were much above informal sector self-employed income, indicates that minimum wages, which impose a floor at £135 per annum in Nairobi, are very important. (Predicted hourly earnings for the average self-employed[22] in Nairobi are Sh.0.46, which implies an annual income of about £50.) Other factors, such as employer self-interest, paternalism, or fear of "threat effects" may affect nonunion wages, but these are impossible to separate out.

Indices of Estimated Hourly Earnings by Type of Employment

Employment Type	Index
Private nonunion	100
Private union[1]	130
Government nonunion	116
Government union[1]	129
Self-employed	48

[1] By 1972, 40 percent of formal sector wage earners were unionized.

SOURCE: G. E. Johnson, p. 23.

In explaining the gap between the incomes of educated and relatively uneducated people, the most important factor is probably Kenya's colonial past.[23] Most positions involving any high degree of skill were held by Europeans prior to Independence. Kenyans who filled these posts after Independence were, naturally enough, not willing to have the incomes to which they had aspired reduced. Thus, the higher positions remained at European pay levels. This pressure was also felt at lower strata of skills, since enormous differentials within the formal sector were not easy to justify.[24] It should also be remembered that all categories of skilled persons were very scarce in the past,[25] and that, for skills of the highest level, there is an international market.

Some of the factors such as unionization, which explain the formal-informal gap, may also explain the increase in the gap over time. An additional explanation may be that wage bargaining is oriented to profits *within* an industry. The disparate earnings for similar skills across industries imply that productivity increases are being shared by employer and employee rather than by employer and consumer, as would normally be expected in a labor surplus economy. A "high profits cause high wages" hypothesis of employer self-interest[26] would be that highly capital intensive industries will pay more because the benefits of doing so outweigh the small additional cost. There is some evidence of this in the brewing industry, for example. If these hypotheses are correct, trade policy which would, according to Phelps and Wasow, have raised the average rate of profit in manufacturing by 20.7 percent (if wages were not also raised), may have

22. Defined by having "mean" characteristics for the other independent variables, which are education (= 5 years), age (= 33 years), arrival (= 20 years before) and tribe.
23. The ILO/UNDP report, pp. 83–88, presents a fairly full discussion of the effects of colonialism.
24. Even minimum wage and standards of housing and other services have been influenced by what was regarded as "decent" in European eyes.
25. In the mid-fifties there was a shortage of *all* types of workers in the urban sector as a result of the emergency conditions. This was probably the factor that opened the formal-informal gap for the first time for the unskilled.
26. A model of employer interest in the effect of wages on worker efficiency is presented in J. King, *Wages, Efficiency and Labour Market Disequilibrium*, IDS Working Paper No. 157 (Nairobi: Institute for Development Studies, August 1972).

in fact been instrumental in raising wage rates. However, the existence of any naturally protected high profit sector would have the same effect.

A final issue in wage developments is whether the private or public sector is the leader in setting high wages levels, or a high rate of growth. The data for average earnings indicate a lower rate of growth of public sector earnings from 1964 to 1972. Therefore, the Government is not the leading sector; moreover, average earnings in Government in 1972 were lower than those in manufacturing, construction, commerce and transport, storage and communications.[27] In the recent past (1968–72), the average wage in the public sector has risen pari passu with that in the private sector. These data, taken with those of Johnson quoted above, would indicate that the Government simply follows the modern sector trend, although it does pay more to nonunion employees. The one exception may be pay to middle level employees with secondary education where the Government appears to set the pace.

In all, there are more questions than answers. The wage gaps between skill levels and between formal and informal employment probably started because of genuine labor shortages in the fifties, as well as the colonial system. They have been maintained by minimum wages, union pressure in the case of unskilled workers, and by convention and perhaps civil service self-interest for educated workers.[28] Some shortages for skilled workers remain, but not many—certainly not at middle clerical levels. The nature of bargaining in Kenyan industry probably leads to rapidly rising wages in industries with high capital intensity or high growth of productivity. The latter would be especially true if such productivity increases were costless.[29] This process would increase the gap between formal sector wages and earnings in the informal sector, since the latter absorbs most of the increases in the labor force and thus has difficulty in raising productivity per head. At the same time, another gap is opened between wages paid in highly profitable industries or industries with a high share of profits in value-added and the rest.

Credit Policy

The third of the major parameters affecting the private sector is credit and its price. Some aspects of the effects of interest rates on the economy as a whole are discussed in Annexes One and Two, which also refer briefly to financial institutions in Kenya.[30] In this annex, we are concerned mainly with the consequences of credit policy as it affects the private sector, and the direction of lending. Later in this chapter we shall discuss the extent to which credit is preempted by the urban formal sector.

The most important institutions in Kenya are the commercial banks which, in the British pattern, are largely oriented to financing trade. Their main lending rates have not changed in the past six years, from 7 percent up to perhaps 10 percent. In Kenyan circumstances this has amounted to a real interest rate of approximately 5 to 8 percent.

Although adequate statistics were not available, it appears that commercial banks direct their funds[31] from rural to urban areas and, above all, to foreign owned firms in the formal sector. An indication of this is that, by December 1971, loans to Africans,

---

27. See Table 14. The qualifications in interpreting average earnings data must be remembered.

28. Highly skilled workers are usually a small proportion of costs, which reduces any pressure to change their wages.

29. That such increases exist is argued by H. Pack, *Employment and Productivity in Kenyan Manufacturing*, IDS Discussion Paper No. 149 (Nairobi: Institute for Development Studies, August 1972).

30. For a more detailed review of financial institutions, see B. Dillon, *Financial Institutions in Kenya 1954–71, A Preliminary Analysis,* Working Paper No. 61 (Nairobi: Institute of Development Studies, September 1972). The subject was also covered in *Economic Progress and Prospects in Kenya*, World Bank report no. AE–22, March 3, 1973, Annex B. *Mobilization of Private Savings* (unpublished).

31. Commercial banks mobilize about 30 percent of GDS.

although rising rapidly, were only 13 percent of all loans. The authorities have attempted to restrict the access of foreign firms to domestic Kenyan finance, which is cheap by international standards. The present regulations limit the borrowing rights of foreign firms to 20 percent of equity. If the local equity participation is more than 50 percent, the borrowing limit may be increased to 40 percent. The development of factoring (now forbidden) and equipment leasing have been ways to evade these restrictions.[32]

To sum up, two important features of the system of credit mobilization and allocation are noteworthy. First, the real rates of interest charged are quite low and vary very little with risk. Whether the level and spread should be raised depends on the excess demand, actual or potential, for funds.[33] In spite of the apparent absence of any unorganized money market, it is the implicit view behind several development projects[34] that there is such excess demand. On the other hand, the nonexistence of such a market does raise questions about the desirability of higher rates. Whatever the situation, real rates should probably not go below those to be earned safely abroad. Second, the banking system, which is a major means of fund mobilization, channels funds away from the rural economy towards the urban formal expatriate sector. This question will be examined later.

The Effects of Current Policy

Reviewing the environment of the private sector highlights certain crucial distortions. Even with all the qualifications to be made in interpreting effective protective rate calculations, there seems to be a distorted trade policy environment which exacerbates an already difficult trade situation. Current wage policy has become out of line with demand-supply relationships in the labor market; and has led to possibly disproportionate differentials between skilled and unskilled, rural and urban, formal and informal sectors, high and low levels of education. Finally, the banking system offers what is probably excessively cheap credit to a selected few, largely expatriate urban customers. In what follows, the direct effects of this "package" on the urban formal sector is considered. Subsequently, we shall discuss the indirect effects of present policy on the rest of the economy.

Effects on the Formal Sector

Factor Intensities. The most celebrated consequence of an environment of the type considered above is on factor intensity. Low interest rates, cheap imports of capital goods because of low duties and an overvalued exchange rate, and finally the high wage rates in the formal sector create an environment which a priori might be expected to raise capital output and capital labor ratios. This could possibly be an explanation for the extremely disappointing employment effects of the growth of the formal sector so far recorded. It should be stressed, however, that the data available do not permit any

---

32. At present rates of interest, there is a considerable incentive for foreign firms to borrow domestically rather than abroad. This leads to problems in implementation of the controls.

33. The existence of actual excess demand would imply a resource gap problem, while potential excess demand would mean that good opportunities are being lost. Correction of the latter would require institutional reform. It can be argued that the domestic real rate of interest should never be lower than the real return available abroad, regardless of domestic demand conditions. For the past, the return abroad would have been lower than the 4 percent–5 percent available in Kenya. Now, as Kenya's inflation accelerates and rates of interest elsewhere are high, this argument probably implies that the domestic rate of interest should be raised. (Any excess savings can be invested abroad by the Government.)

34. In rural credit, for instance.

easy conclusions. In particular, there is no useful information on the capital stock which would be necessary for any careful work on the effects of factor prices on factor intensities.

From the analysis carried out in the last chapter, it appeared that a significantly rising incremental capital-output ratio is observed only in "other services" among major private activities (Tables 8 and 12). Agriculture, manufacturing, and wholesale and retail trade have either insignificant trends or, in the case of manufacturing, strongly negative trends. At the same time, all these sectors have falling employment-output ratios.[35] This combination appears to indicate an increasing efficiency of labor use, which can mean either a greater application of nonenumerated factors such as human capital, or a more efficient use of labor or capital, or both.[36]

Equations showing the relationship between changes in average wages in the private sector and changes in average productivity were estimated by Harris and Todaro[37] for 1955–66. The coefficient of 0.761 which they estimate is the wage elasticity of demand for labor, assumes no effect on output but merely on factor proportions.[38] This coefficient is, in their view, not significantly different from unity. Our own estimates would indicate a somewhat higher elasticity since the estimate of the elasticity of substitution between labor and capital is itself unity. In any case, a strongly significant positive relationship between rising wages and output per person is indicated.

Essentially, two main hypotheses can be advanced. Harris and Todaro argue that higher wages actually lead to increased labor productivity, since employers are encouraged to augment labor by training unskilled workers,[39] substituting skilled workers and improving organization. Because these improvements are not costless, their effects are seen to be related to the wage. Interestingly enough, Harris and Todaro support the view advanced above that there has so far been no significant increase in capital intensities as a result of rising wages.

An alternative thesis, advanced by Pack,[40] is that wage increases are a consequence, not a cause, of rising productivity. He argues, on the basis of detailed interviews, that

---

35. These sectors accounted for 90 percent of modern sector employment in 1971.

36. Falling capital-output and labor-output ratios indicate greater efficiency in the use of both capital and labor. Constant capital-output ratios, combined with falling labor-output ratios, would indicate greater efficiency in the use of labor. The evidence outlined above is consistent with the assumption of Harrod neutral labor-augmenting technical progress. The rough constancy of the share of wages in modern private sector value-added would support the assumption.

37. J. R. Harris and M. P. Todaro, *Wage Policy and Employment in a Developing Economy*, Discussion Paper No. 72 (Nairobi: Institute for Development Studies, November 1968). Their equation for African workers was:

$$P = 1.78 + 0.761W \qquad R^2 = 0.703$$
$$(SE = 1.60) \quad (SE = 0.17)$$

where P = rate of change of productivity per head
W = rate of change of wages per man

38. Assuming a C.E.S. production function—the elasticity of employment with respect to the wage $= \dfrac{-S}{1-W}$

where S = elasticity of substitution between labor and capital
W = share of wages

Our own estimates of the equation (see Table 19) $\log \dfrac{V}{L} = a + b \log (W)$

give an estimate of b ($=S$) not significantly different from unity. In this case the elasticity of employment with respect to the wage must be about two, since labor's share in modern private sector value-added is less than half.

39. "We believe that the most important source of productivity increase has arisen from training workers and upgrading skills," p. 18.

40. H. Pack, *Employment and Productivity in Kenyan Manufacturing*.

techniques in Kenya are fairly labor intensive[41] especially in ancilliary process (such as handling of goods). However, skilled managers are able to achieve productivity improvements almost costlessly. The rising productivity leads to pressure for high wages, which firms are prepared to grant, for reasons already considered. There is a limit to such disembodied productivity increases, however, beyond which wage pressure would require a greater input of capital. Since, as he argues, there exists a wide range of techniques in most industries (largely because all processes include some subactivities where choices exist), this would be possible. Alternatively, assuming reduced wage pressure, future output growth will generate more employment than has been the case in the past.[42]

On the basis of available evidence there is no possibility of making a final discrimination between these two hypotheses. Indeed, it is not difficult to imagine both processes acting at the same time, showing that rising real wages may be both a cause and a consequence of increasing productivity. In any case, the process of rising wage rates will not be sustainable without rising capital intensities or further labor augmentation and correspondingly a lower rate of growth of employment than might otherwise be achieved.

The great weakness of this analysis is that it is concerned with a process, namely, changes in techniques associated wih changes in wages. However, many of the most important questions concern the effects of a price and policy *structure*.[43] For example, what labor intensive industries or techniques have never been considered because of the relative price of labor and capital? Is there a relationship between trade policy and factor intensity because import substitution ties production to a certain demand pattern and imports from developed countries are likely to be capital intensive? Do quality requirements predetermine technique? Answering these questions is more difficult since they are hypothetical. However, comparative analysis indicates that ICORs themselves are not especially high.[44]

There does exist a little evidence on the relation between the protective system and factor intensities. Phelps and Wasow[45] correlated the level of effective protection with capital-unskilled labor ratios. They found no significant relationship. However, since their measures of the increase in the rate of return, due to protection, and of capital-labor ratios use very dubious capital stock data, they may underestimate the protective effects of cheap capital, as opposed to cheap intermediate inputs. In that case, the results are not trustworthy.

One possible effect of the policy system would be to encourage greater capital intensity in large firms that in small ones, mainly because large firms are likely to have privileged access to cheap finance. The 1967 Census of Industrial Production, which was the only survey to cover firms employing less than fifty people, provides some relevant information. First, the share of wages in value-added is approximately the same in all sizes (56 percent for firms employing more than fifty people, 58 percent for firms employing twenty to forty-nine people, and 56 percent for firms employing five to nineteen people). Second, the share of depreciation in value-added, which, under fairly strict assumptions, is a proxy for the capital intensity, fell from 13 percent in the largest category to 7 percent in the smallest firms. These data certainly indicate a higher rate of

---

41. H. Pack argues (pp. 2–3) that Kenyan techniques in paint production and cotton textiles, in particular, are labor intensive by international standards. His evidence does, of course, only apply to manufacturing.

42. He argues that improvements in capacity utilization have been important in lowering capital-output and labor-output ratios but that these will also reach a limit after a while. He presents no evidence for this assumption, which is further discussed later.

43. The concentration on wages in discussion of the effects of relative prices on techniques *over time* is made logical by the fact that, in Kenya, trade policy and the interest rate have been relatively static.

44. The ICOR for manufacturing was estimated at 2.5 and falling.

45. Phelps and Wasow, "Measuring Protection and its Effects in Kenya," p. 22.

profit in small rather than in large firms, which is consistent with the thesis that the cost of capital is higher. The labor-output ratio and the wage may be the same as in large firms, or the wage may be lower and the labor-output ratio higher.[46] In both cases the capital-labor ratio would be lower.[47]

To summarize, the data do not indicate much deepening of physical capital in the formal private sector. However, there does seem to have been a process of labor augmentation which caused or was caused by rising real wages. The result has been very slow labor absorption. However, continued rising real wages would almost certainly lead to rising physical capital intensity in the future. There is no evidence that trade policy has affected capital-intensity, although this is possible.[48] There is also no evidence that physical capital intensity[49] is very high in Kenya, although it is always possible that some labor-intensive industries and processes have been precluded. Finally, there is evidence of lower capital intensity in *small scale industry, without lower shares* of profit in value-added.[50]

Capacity Utilization. The evidence discussed above is consistent with rising capacity utilization over time, and rising capital output ratios in new investment, the two offsetting each other. There is no evidence on this trend. However, the World Bank Report on industrial prospects in East Africa,[51] and the ILO/UNDP[52] report do discuss some recently collected evidence. The World Bank report concluded that capacity utilization was not as serious a problem as in other developing countries. The ILO/UNDP report concurred with this overall judgment. Their conclusions were based on a recent study[53] which showed that total gross product would have been 11 percent higher if all firms had been operating at their own desired levels of capacity utilization and 100 percent higher if they had achieved 140 hours a week. Thus capacity utilization appears not to be optimal.[54] There is no reason to suppose levels have changed in any consistent way since.

Several hypotheses can be advanced, some of them supported by the preliminary results of the survey. The first is that labor costs more at certain times of day because of unwillingness to work or lower efficiency; a second is that indivisibilities exist in plants; a third is that a firm wishes to get a jump ahead of its competitors by exploiting potential monopolies guaranteed by protection. Evidence for all these factors does exist, although it was the view of the World Bank's mission that, "in general, machinery and equipment have been well selected to produce limited production runs economically." This indicates the second explanation may not be all that important.

46. The thesis that the wage is higher in small industry than large is extremely unlikely.
47. See on this L. P. Mureithi, *A Framework for Analysing Labor Absorption Capability for Different Firm Sizes in Kenyan Manufacturing,* Working Paper No. 75 (Nairobi: Institute for Development Studies, December 1972).
48. In a world of biased substitution between factors and intermediates, all evidence based on effective rates of protection calculations breaks down.
49. Average capital requirement per job in manufacturing has been estimated at £2,000 by the ILO/UNDP report, p. 446.
50. This situation is always possible with sufficiently fragmented labor markets (i.e., wages are not equated across industries) and production functions with elasticities of substitution less than or equal to unity. It implies that theories which assume highly capital intensive industries entail high profits, and high savings break down at the first step—i.e., they require constant wages for given skills, or $\sigma > 1$. A simple hypothesis which would nullify the theory is that wage rates are a function of profit shares.
51. World Bank report no. AE-12, p. 31.
52. ILO/UNDP report, pp. 182–4.
53. The major source is a study being carried out by the Statistics Division of the Ministry of Finance and Economic Planning in cooperation with the Institute for Development Studies, Nairobi. A preliminary report appears in Mary Ann Baily, *Capital Utilization Rates in Kenya Manufacturing: an Interim Report,* Working Paper No. 66 (Nairobi: Institute for Development Studies, October 1972).
54. The word "appears" is used advisedly.

KEY ISSUES IN THE PRIVATE SECTOR 279

According to the same study, capital utilization in Kenya is very sensitive to trade policy, for two reasons: first, trade policy alters factor price ratios in favor of capital, which makes it cheaper to leave capital idle; second, import substituting firms are constrained by market size. In addition, particular problems have occurred in the recent past because firms, whose production was oriented to the entire East African market, have found themselves restricted to Kenya.[55] Another difficulty has been the growth of restrictions on current transactions.[56] Thus, although there are no data on the trend, it does appear that the level of capacity utilization is not as high as it could be. The entire environment, trade policy in particular, seems to be responsible for this situation.

Taxation of Exports. Although this theme appears under the mission's discussion of trade policy, taxation of exports is particularly important to the operation of the formal sector. Exports of goods produced within the formal sector are taxed through the trade policy structure because of the raising of the price of inputs and *also* through the high wages. The dual wage structure may itself be the product of the trade policy system, but it taxes any activity separately. Since the share of wages in value-added in industry is over 50 percent[57] in Kenya, an excess wage (over opportunity cost) of 25 percent is an important factor in determining profitability.

Balance of Payments

A policy system of the kind discussed above has certain fairly well known consequences for the economy as a whole, some of which can be documented for Kenya and the others cannot be. The first is for the balance of payments. On the basis of the formula used by Phelps and Wasow and their average effective rate of protection, it is estimated that world value-added is about 66 percent of domestic value-added for manufacturing.[58] This has two major consequences. First, policy which continues on these lines saves very much less foreign exchange than appears to be the case.[59] For example, an increase in manufacturing value-added of £100 would have not US$280 in foreign exchange as the present exchange rate indicates, but only US$184. Thus, the balance of payments consequences of manufacturing growth with an import substitution bias are by no means as favorable as they appear.[60] On the other hand, £100 of value-added in an export commodity like tea generates the full US$280 (discounting the small demand elasticity effect). Second, the growth of manufacturing at world prices is substantially below that in domestic prices. Taking the growth of private sector agriculture and manufacture[61] between 1964 and 1971 in constant prices, we observe an increment of £20 million and £21 million, respectively. However, if it is assumed that agriculture's effective rate of protection is zero (which is probably an overestimate—its

55. One example observed by the mission was the manufacture of bicycle tires.
56. See Chapter 4, *Controls on Trade and Foreign Exchange,* for a more complete discussion.
57. It is interesting to note that this share is exceptionally high. See I. M. D. Little, T. Scitovsky, and M. Scott, *Industry and Trade in Some Developing Countries* (Paris: OECD, 1970), p. 45, Table 2.2.
58. Derived from:

$$\frac{DVA - WVA}{DVA} = 0.342$$

$WVA = 0.658\, DVA$

59. See S. R. Lewis, Jr., *The Effects of Protection on the Growth Rate and the Need for External Assistance,* Research Memorandum No. 49 (Williamstown, Mass.: Center for Development Economics, Williams College, n.d.), which discusses this problem exhaustively.
60. This ignores, of course, the problem addressed by cost-benefit methodologies such as Little-Mirrlees, namely the incremental consumption out of additional factor incomes and its balance of payments effect. However, one effect should be stressed, namely incremental profit expatriation. This reduces foreign exchange savings still further.
61. These are the major traded goods sectors.

EPZ is probably negative), and manufacturing's is 34 percent, the figures in terms of foreign exchange generation are £20 million and £14 million respectively.[62] Thus, manufacturing's contribution in terms of foreign exchange earnings or savings is substantially less than that of agriculture.

Apart from the obvious effects of encouraging inefficient import substitution and taxing viable exports, the system can reduce the use of domestic raw materials. The effect works in the following way: because the tariff system will lower the equilibrium price of foreign exchange (perhaps by about 15 percent in Kenya), any imported input whose nominal tariff is less than this will become cheaper in comparison with domestic goods. Thus, there is an incentive to use imported low duty inputs rather than domestically produced nontradable goods.[63] This will affect choice of both industry and technique. Domestically produced tradable inputs will not be penalized in use if there are low tariffs on imported substitutes, but their production will be less profitable, at least by the extent of the exchange adjustment.[64] Finally, goods using protected inputs will also be taxed and be less likely to expand. (Examples in Kenya are industries using pulp and paper products, or tires, or several other intermediates now produced under protection.)

This last effect of protection is what makes the "second stage" of import substitution so lethal, because it encourages the production of highly protected intermediates and capital goods,[65] which tax all industries using them. The costs of such development do not depend on activity being inefficient, but merely on the price of output being substantially raised above the world price. At the three digit level such industries already exist in Kenya. Thus, development is likely to involve fewer domestically produced input-linkages, either because they are nontradable and thus more expensive than low duty tradables, or because they are low duty tradables and thus unattractive to produce, or because they are high duty tradables and thus unattractive to use. These factors may explain, in part, the low value-added in Kenyan industry (an average of 29.8 percent in 1970) and the apparent lack of vertical integration.

Low vertical integration leads to the phenomenon of import dependency. As has been noted previously, the structure of Kenyan imports is shifting towards inputs, because of the increasing local production of consumer goods. (Table 24 shows how high the import intensity of production is.)[66] In balance of payments crises, such as occurred in 1971, the first impulse is to cut "inessential" imports of consumer goods—in that case by controls. This step further increases the weight of inputs in the import bill and thus the vulnerability of production levels (which depend on imported inputs) to remedial action in the face of subsequent balance of payments crises. Moreover, the import controls further increase the incentive to substitute for inessential consumer goods while making the inputs for their production "essential." In this way, a vicious cycle of balance of payments crises and controls is started. Each successive crisis is more difficult to control than the last because there is progressively less left to cut. Moreover, the further the protection system develops, the more heavily taxed export

---

62. This phenomenon is well documented in *Industry and Trade in Some Developing Countries—A Comparative Study*, by Ian Little, Tibor Scitovsky, and Maurice Scott (Paris: OECD, 1970), pp. 70–76.

63. If the nominal rate of tariff on a tradable good is less than the equilibrium exchange adjustment, that good becomes relatively cheaper than nontradables after the system is put into effect. In Kenya, this applies to most capital goods and intermediates.

64. At this point, the relevant concept is net effective protection or effective protection after allowing for the effect of the tariff system on the exchange rate.

65. From the user's viewpoint, the crucial rate of protection is nominal. This determines the extent of the difference between world and domestic prices. Table 20 shows how many industries in the intermediate and capital goods industries have high nominal rates of protection.

66. The section above shows how small the true foreign exchange saving of import substituting production can be.

earning power becomes. Kenya, after the 1971 crisis, is at the very beginning of this process.

Another important effect of the strategy is on revenue from tariffs. As imports shift from highly taxed consumer goods to low-duty intermediates and capital goods, tariff revenue becomes less elastic. Thus, in Kenya, the ratio of import duties to net imports shows a downward trend in spite of higher rates imposed from time to time. In 1964/65, the ratio was 19.2 percent, but it had fallen to 17.2 percent by 1971/72. The tariff structure at present in force will inevitably lead to declining revenue ratios as the more highly taxed consumer goods are all replaced.

The Taxation Effect on Agriculture

There are two main sectors producing traded goods, agriculture and manufacturing. Since manufacturing is protected (or subsidized) in the domestic market, agriculture is correspondingly antiprotected (or taxed);[67] and since most agricultural output is tradable, at a price determined in world markets, the antiprotection occurs through raising the price of protected inputs and of goods which farmers buy for consumption. In other words, terms of trade are shifted against farmers. The effect is exacerbated if nontradable goods used by farmers, or factors of production, labor, for example, become more expensive in relation to tradable goods, through maintaining an exchange rate at a higher level than would be sustainable under a free trade system. This effect would worsen profitability even if the relative prices of tradables in agriculture were unchanged.[68]

The effect on rural-urban terms of trade can be assessed in various ways. One of the simplest is to use factors to convert agricultural production and consumption into foreign exchange equivalents. M. Scott has estimated these for rural consumption as a whole, and for the marginal product of small and large farm workers.[69] The latter can be taken as estimates of the ratio of the value in foreign exchange to the value in domestic currency of a typical bundle of small and large farm production. These ratios are given as 1.02 and 1.10, respectively. They imply that for every £1 received by these farms £1.02 and £1.10 worth of foreign exchange are being earned at ruling exchange rates.[70] The ratio for consumption on the other hand is 0.9, which implies that the cost of £1 of consumption is only Sh18 at ruling exchange rates, or US$2.52. Thus, a farmer who earns £1 and spends £1 in domestic currency is, in fact, earning US$2.85 or US$3.08 and spending US$2.52. The deterioration of terms of trade from those obtaining in free trade (assuming identical production and consumption patterns, and world prices) is from 100 to 88, or from 100 to 82, respectively, where 100 is the world price terms of trade.[71]

Until recently, there was no sales tax in Kenya, so that the bulk of the differential is due to the fact that some agricultural exports are taxed (coffee, for example, pays

---

67. The "extra" income received by manufacturers has to come from someone else. A large country might tax foreigners (because of inelastic supply curves), but a small country can only tax exports in general and agriculture in particular.

68. Any such effect would, however, not worsen terms of trade for agriculture as a whole but merely shift the distribution of income in agriculture between labor and employers. For the smallholder who farms himself the effect is irrelevant, of course.

69. M. Scott, "Estimates of Shadow Wages in Kenya," p. iii.

70. An alternative way of putting it is that, if £1 = US$2.80 at the official exchange rate, the farmers are actually earning US$2.85 and US$3.08 for every £1 received.

71. This ratio is defined as $= \dfrac{Cf}{Cd} \cdot \dfrac{Pd}{Pf}$

where C = consumption
P = production
f = foreign prices
d = domestic prices

exports taxes).[72] Various other agricultural commodities have domestic prices fixed below the border price (meat is an important current example), and, at the same time, many manufactured goods are protected. The "revenue" generated by "taxation" of agricultural producers is divided between the government, urban consumers, and urban producers. The greater the proportion of rural consumption going to domestically produced goods, the greater the proportion of the "tax" going to urban producers. Similarly, the greater the proportion of output sold to urban consumers at below world prices, the greater the proportion of the "tax" going to them.

The magnitude of transfers between sectors can be calculated by taking the tax or subsidy per £1 of value-added, and multiplying by the total value-added in current prices. For agriculture, the weights of small and large farms in monetary value-added were assumed to be proportional to their respective shares in monetary output, which were 43.8 and 56.2 percent, respectively, in 1971. The tax rate was therefore US$0.45 per £1, and the total implicit tax on agriculture in 1972 is estimated at US$41 million.[73]

A similar calculation can be done for manufacturing where, as we have shown above, the conversion factor on the output side is 0.66, which is the average ratio of world to domestic value-added. In other words, for every Kenya pound received by a factor of production in manufacturing, only US$1.84 is earned. At the same time the conversion factor for urban consumption is estimated at 0.80, which means that US$2.24 is actually spent for every £1 received. Terms of trade have improved from 100 to 122, and the implicit rate of subsidy is 22 percent. The value in 1971 of the subsidy was US$31 million.[74]

These figures indicate a large income transfer generated by Kenya's pricing policies in agriculture and her protection of manufacturing. This transfer has three obvious effects which, considering the economic situation in Kenya, are particularly serious. First, since taxation of agriculture reduces the incomes of the poorest people, the process involves a transfer from the relatively poor to the rich, and leads to a further widening in income distribution between the urban and rural areas. Second, the taxation of agriculture inherent in the system has the effect of reducing the attractiveness of agriculture and rural life as a whole, and thereby exacerbates rural-urban migration and the pressure for formal education. Third, to the extent that the system taxes exports, it reduces the number of commodities that can be profitably produced for export, in domestic currency terms. This last factor may be very important indeed in view of the difficulty in expanding income-earning opportunities for the mass of the rural population.[75]

Since the manufacturing sector has large foreign ownership,[76] much of the transfer is expatriated as "profit." Indeed, this fact entails a qualification to the figure for the subsidy to manufacturing. Profits can be repatriated at US$2.80 to the Kenya pound, while consumption in urban areas has an implicit exchange rate of US$2.24 to the

---

72. However, the coffee tax appears to do no more than compensate for the difference between average and marginal revenue, some marginal coffee is sold in nonquota countries at a relatively low price.

73. The foreign exchange receipts are used as a base for computing the implicit tax rates.

74. These calculations are done by taking the dollar tax or subsidy per £1 of value-added, and multiplying by the total value-added in current prices. The tax per £1 in agriculture was US$0.45, and the subsidy in manufacturing was US$0.40.

75. The recent World Bank agricultural sector survey pointed out the pressing need to find new cash crops to intensify smallholder production. Since Kenya is already largely self-sufficient in agriculture products, new smallholder production has to be mainly export-oriented.

76. The ILO/UNDP report shows that 57 percent of manufacturing gross product is in foreign-owned firms, and that 42 percent of capital formation in manufacturing in 1968 was financed by private long term inflows. See pp. 441–46.

pound. Thus, the implicit rate of subsidy to expatriated profits is 52 percent of the average foreign exchange earning of US$1.84 per £1 in manufacturing. In other words, for every £1 repatriated, the profit earner is receiving a subsidy of US$0.96.

What is observed above is a system of multiple exchange rates the effects of which are to benefit the foreign capitalist most, then the local capitalist, then the wage earner in manufacturing, all at the expense of agricultural producers. This is the major effect of the protective system.

Migration, Unemployment, and the Demand for Education

The second major effect of the distorted urban formal sector is on the labor market in the economy as a whole. It is useful to consider two aspects: migration of unskilled workers from rural to urban areas and demand for education. Formal models have been developed for the first case, but the latter can be fitted in.

Discussion of the first problem can be conducted in terms of models associated with J. R. Harris and M. P. Todaro, and subsequently developed and used by others in the Kenyan context.[77] The basic components of the model are two: first, it is assumed —rightly in the case of Kenya—that there is a gap between wages in the urban formal sector and elsewhere in the economy;[78] and, secondly, it is also assumed that workers will equate the expected value of a job in the urban formal sector to the wage to be obtained elsewhere. In a very simple model, where the only choice in urban areas is between formal sector employment and open unemployment, formal sector jobs can be obtained only by those in the cities, and the probability of getting a job is the ratio of formal sector employment to employment plus unemployment. Unemployment will then be a function of the wage gap and the number employed in the urban formal sector.[79] In this kind of model, any increase in the numbers employed in the urban formal sector, or in their wage, will generate more unemployment.

---

77. See J. R. Harris and M. P. Todaro, *A Two-Sector Model of Migration with Urban Unemployment in Developing Economies*, Discussion Paper No. 69 (Nairobi: Institute for Development Studies, September 1968); idem, *Urban Unemployment in East Africa: An Economic Analysis of Policy Alternatives*, Discussion Paper No. 71 (Nairobi: Institute for Development Studies, September 1968); idem, "Migration, Unemployment, and Development: A Two-Sector Analysis," *American Economic Review*, March 1970. See also H. Rempel, *Labour Migration into Urban Centres and Urban Unemployment in Kenya* (D.Phil. diss., University of Wisconsin, 1970); B. Wasow, *A Simple General Equilibrium Model of Wage/Exchange Rate Policy in an Open Undeveloped Economy*, Staff Paper No. 83 (Nairobi: Institute for Development Studies, September 1970); J. E. Stiglitz, *Alternative Theories of Wage Determination and Unemployment in LDCs: I: The Labour Turnover Model*, Cowles Foundation Discussion Paper No. 335 (April 1972); and M. FG. Scott, "Estimates of Shadow Wages in Kenya," pp. 82–88.

78. This model does not do justice to the four sector division that is appropriate to Kenya. Such a situation complicates the model and modifies the conclusions. For instance, the existence of an urban informal sector reduces the extent of open unemployment and also costs of migration.

79. If Weu is the expected urban wage, Wr is the rural wage, p is the probability of getting an urban job, and Wu is the urban wage, then:

1) $Weu = pWu = Wr$

Moreover, if Nuf is urban employment and Nuu is unemployment, then:

2) $p = \dfrac{Nuf}{Nuu + Nuf}$

rearranging and substituting:

3) $Nuu = Nuf \dfrac{Wu - Wr}{Wr}$

which implies that urban unemployment will increase proportionately with urban employment or the wage gap.

A dynamic model of migration presented by Todaro[80] can be used to predict the required increase in the annual rate of job creation in the urban formal sector just to keep the unemployment *rate* from increasing, if there is a widening of the percentage wage gap. Figures for Kenya might be set at 4 percent for urban formal employment growth, 60 percent as the percentage rural-urban wage gap in real terms, and 2 percent for the natural rate of growth of urban population. If the increase in the wage gap were 10 percent, the required increase in the rate of growth of urban employment would be 1.9 percent. Under past experience this would require an increase in the rate of growth of output of at least 3.8 percent. Thus, a small increase in the wage gap (which requires a rise in the urban wage itself of only 3.8 percent) would entail an increased formal urban rate of growth of output of 3.8 percent. This would be a 50 percent increase over past experience.

Whatever the reliability of specific models, and the simplifications implicit in them, it is certain that the continuance of productivity-linked wage increases in a dual economy will lead to a steady worsening of the employment problem. Table 2, in Part I, shows the growth of the African population in the main towns. Taken against a population growth of 3.5 percent, the implicit migration is very considerable. As the ILO/UNDP report states, "An inflow of job seekers at roughly three times the rate of job opportunities in the formal sector has inevitably made it very difficult to absorb the migrants into production employment."[81] The result has been marginal informal sector activity, unemployment, and frustration.

The point should not be overstressed. The pull on rural workers may be less than the simple model predicts. Rempel's[82] econometric study indicated that the rural-urban wage gap was not a significant explanatory phenomenon for migration, and Scott[83] developed a model which predicts that unemployment may rise or fall in response to changes in formal sector employment. However, the basic result, especially with regard to the effects of changes in the wage gap on unemployment, can be accepted.

The most important part of migration induced by wage expectations is on educated people. It also determines the demand for education itself, which, given current wage differentials, is an understandable and perhaps rational choice on the part of the individual, if not for society as a whole. These effects are documented by the ILO/UNDP report, which notes the proportion of male migrants with more than four years of schooling was 75.7 percent in 1969/70, while only 12.4 percent in the population as a whole.

Income Distribution and Efficiency Implications

This area is so complex that little more than indications can be given. However, efficiency is easily dealt with. In an economy where marginal products are generally positive, any unemployment, or voluntary acceptance of a less productive job than is available, will reduce potential output. Kenya is therefore working inside the frontier.

The effects on income distribution between sectors and factors of production

---

80. M. P. Todaro, *A Model of Labour Migration and Urban Unemployment in Less Developed Countries*, mimeo, p. 11, cited in J. R. Harris and M. P. Todaro, *Urban Unemployment in East Africa: An Economic Analysis of Policy Alternatives*, p. 11.
The equation is:
$$dG = \frac{-G^2 dA}{GdA - GB - AB - BdA}$$
where
G = rate of urban employment growth
A = percentage urban-rural wage differential
B = natural rate of permanent urban labor force growth
81. ILO/UNDP report, p. 49.
82. Rempel, "Labour Migration."
83. M. Scott, "Estimates of Shadow Wages in Kenya," pp. 85–86.

depends, in the first place, on whether the economy is open or not.[84] Assuming an open economy, the high wages in the urban formal sector probably reduce labor's aggregate earnings in that sector, since, assuming a unit elasticity of substitution between labor and capital, the demand for labor will have greater than unit elasticity. Urban formal sector wage raises will increase urban unemployment somewhat, but this may improve wage incomes in the rural formal sector, as wages are raised in that activity because of labor migration.[85] The latter effect appears documented in Kenya by difficulty in obtaining labor for coffee and other estate crops, and recent wage raises. The unorganized sectors are more complex. However, if what happens is a transfer from small scale rural to informal urban because of rising wages in urban formal activity, the effect on aggregate income depends on marginal products in the two sectors. If it is higher in rural activities, total incomes fall.

Thus, it can be seen that this is a very complex issue, and any solution requires a precise model which takes into account distribution of ownership of assets as well as functioning of the labor market. However, it does appear that if elasticities of demand for labor are low, rising urban formal sector wages may increase aggregate labor incomes, as well as the consumption standards of rural smallholders. The standard of living of urban informal workers may go down through falling prices of informal sector services as supply increases.

It is probable therefore that the wage gap has important effects on the labor market. Since it is likely that the gap will grow, the problem will become progressively more severe. (The fast growth of population combined with wage increases in the formal sector related to industrial productivity will guarantee such a rising gap.) It is almost impossible to determine the effect on income distribution. It may go either way. However, we can be sure that the wage gap reduces aggregate output.

The Urban Informal Sector

The urban formal sector has an important, and largely negative, effect on the informal sector. So important is this, that it should be mentioned, in spite of lengthy discussions in the ILO/UNDP report. The most important effects are twofold—the imposition of controls, and the pressure of labor inflow. Many of the controls, restrictions, and harassments inflicted upon the informal sector arise from a government orientation towards formal activity, itself determined by developed country standards and attitudes. It is quite obvious that senior members of organizations such as the Federation of Kenya Employers do not regard the informal sector as providing anything more than make-work activity of a low standard. Several formal sector employers resent —understandably enough—the ability of the informal sector ("bamboo garages" as an example) to evade labor legislation and wage council regulations, and do what they can to prevent it. Moreover, it is very often newly established African businessmen in the formal sector who feel most threatened by the activities of the informal sector, and who frequently have the political power to step up the level of harassment.

A second important effect, already alluded to, is on labor supply. As the ILO/UNDP report states, far more people go to towns looking for work in the formal sector than can be absorbed by available jobs. Although many fail in their primary aim of

---

84. Harris and Todaro have usually assumed a closed economy, while Wasow, in his paper, assumed an open economy. For Kenya, the open economy assumption seems appropriate and has the great advantage that rural-urban terms of trade effect can be ignored (i.e., trade policy and world prices are taken as parameters). Thus, rural-urban commodity price relatives are given, and only factor prices can vary. Contrary to standard theorems in trade theory, factor price relatives can vary, even though commodity prices do not, because of unemployment.

85. The necessary condition for an increase in formal rural aggregate wages is an elasticity of demand for labor of less than unity.

finding formal sector wage employment, they can participate in informal sector activity fairly easily. The effect of this constant pressure on the informal sector is to increase competition and drive down returns. In this way, the gap between formal sector wages and incomes in the informal sector increases, the increasing gap continually drives down returns to informal activity, and the informal sector will probably never "take off" as long as this pressure persists.

Entrepreneurial Development

This is, undoubtedly, a most important theme but, as with so much in development, unquantifiable. Two factors need to be stressed. In Kenya, returns to paid employment in private formal industry far exceed those from all but the most profitable forms of self-employment. Indeed, businessmen are clearly not as prestigious as higher level employees in private industry or in the public service. Second, the greater part of private activity is run or owned by foreigners, most of whom are basically imitating techniques learned in their home countries.

In Kenya, there is at present little African entrepreneurship. The importance of its development cannot be overstated. Nevertheless, all the highest perceived rewards go to employment in a sector which is largely foreign-owned and not all that innovative itself. Nor need it be since profits are often guaranteed by tariff protection and controls. In the long run, this aspect of formal sector activity may be the most costly. It preempts many of the most capable men, but is not itself providing any major entrepreneurial dynamic, probably with the major exception of tourism.

Credit Preemption

Finally, the role of the formal sector in preempting cheap credit mobilized through the banking system should be considered. The most serious effect is to draw financial savings from rural areas and thus deprive the agricultural sector of one of the necessary conditions for accelerated growth. The point is not that there is an unsatisfied effective demand for credit in agriculture: rather, the reverse is true. But as long as financial intermediaries can make easy loans to large, creditworthy clients in the towns, they have no incentive to tackle the much harder job of getting credit to the small scale farms. In the urban areas, too, there is some evidence that small scale industry uses capital more efficiently than large firms do—certainly it seems to generate more employment. This may also be true of informal activity in the towns, which does not even appear in the statistics.

Annex Two has discussed the need for a more active and flexible interest rate policy, and concludes that generally higher interest rates might be expected to stimulate savings as well as lead to more effective utilization of scarce financial savings. Given a restricted domestic supply of funds, it is certainly peculiar to continue an arrangement whereby those firms which can borrow abroad have every incentive not to; while, for those firms which must borrow domestically, banks have no incentive to lend.

Conclusion

In the previous sections, the effects of the price environment of the formal sector on the economy have been discussed. It appears that trade, wage, and interest rate policy not only have much reduced efficient operation of the formal sector itself, but have created spillover effects onto agriculture, the labor market, the credit market, the informal sector, and the development of entrepreneurship. These effects may not have worsened income distribution in a static sense, although this is overwhelmingly likely, given the taxation of agriculture, but they have certainly impeded efficient growth.[86] Moreover, much *social* frustration is generated by the offer of glittering prizes through education, which are then snatched away. The key to more efficient and, in the long run, more equitable growth, is reform of these policies. Although many issues will remain, at least some consistency and efficiency in sectoral allocation will be encouraged, as well as a reduction in the conflict between the formal sector elite and the rest.

The Need for Policy Change

In the sections that follow, the concern is simply with how to get the most out of the formal sector, while at the same time minimizing its external costs. Because some such costs will almost certainly remain, the issue of how much formal sector to have, even in the best circumstances, will be addressed subsequently.

Trade Policy and the Exchange Rate

The basic proposals for reform of the trade policy environment are by now "stale, flat, but, we hope, profitable." Because of the staleness, this discussion will focus on the consequences of a move towards tariff uniformity and on alternative ways to get there. The areas to be considered are wage policy, taxation of the service sectors, problems of transition and infant industries, and effects on income distribution and government revenue. Apart from these indirect consequences, effects on imports and exports themselves will be briefly touched upon.

Uniform Tariffs. Previous discussion of trade policy and its effects leads logically to a proposal for greater uniformity of tariffs and some way to assist exports. This reform would reduce the variance of effective protective rates; reduce taxation on production of capital goods, intermediates, and exports; increase incentive to use domestic materials; reduce incentive to capital intensity; increase tax revenues; and, generally, achieve all sorts of beneficial results as promised by economists in many books and articles.[87] In spite of the fact that the results promised do seem a little too good to be true, and, indeed, that the precise effects cannot be predicted, nevertheless, evidence from other countries does indicate that this reform could be most productive.[88]

It should be remembered that any level of uniform tariffs and subsidies combined with an equilibrium exchange rate has identical economic effects to any other set of uniform tariffs and subsidies combined with an equilibrium exchange rate. The differences only arise for administrative costs, and for any payments or receipts which do not involve tariffs or subsidies. Capital outflows, or service payments abroad, if untaxed, will be cheaper under a uniform tariff and subsidy system than under free

---

86. For reasons outlined above and further considered below, it does not seem probable to us that capital intensive development leads to higher savings rates and, consequently, growth, in Kenya. First, the share of profits does not seem to be simply related to capital intensity, and, second, large foreign ownership of formal sector firms means that much of the profit is expatriated.

87. The *locus classicus* is I. M. D. Little, T. Scitovsky, M. Scott, *Industry and Trade*.

88. This has been accepted by the Government. In his budget speech of June 1973, the Minister of Finance stated, "I am drawn to the conclusion that our long-term objectives would be reached more easily with a more even tariff structure than we have at the present time." He also stated, "... our tariffs should not encourage the excessive use of imported raw materials and capital goods: the system should not discriminate against production to export; it should not discourage the use of labor." The Minister also emphasized that, in any case, the Kenya situation requires a major change, if the manufacturing sector is not to stagnate. Thus, the alternative is not simply more of the same, as most of the easy import substitution opportunities have been taken up already.

trade because foreign exchange will be cheaper and vice versa for inflows and receipts. It is, however, possible to devise a system of taxes and subsidies on these transactions which will make the system identical to free trade. However, administrative costs will inevitably be higher if tariffs and subsidies are used.

A second important point is that the effect of the trade policy reform is twofold. The major aim is to make the domestic *relative* prices for producers the same as international *relative* product prices.[89] This is the reason for tariff and subsidy *uniformity*. (It may, subsequently, be possible to choose—with care and discretion—exceptions to the rule, for infant industry reasons.) A second aim is to achieve equilibrium in the balance of payments. This can be done by adjusting the exchange rate or by raising or lowering the uniform tariff and subsidy system.[90]

Two considerations therefore determine the structure to be chosen. The first is that the higher the tariff subsidy structure, the greater the costs (in both administration and skilled manpower) of preventing evasion and fraud, and the greater the distortion between goods which are taxed or subsidized and those which are not, such as services or capital flows. The second and countervailing consideration is that the lower the structure chosen, the more probable becomes a devaluation. If, for political reasons, devaluation is ruled out, a lower bound to a tariff subsidy structure is determined, given a goal of balance of payments equilibrium.

It is not possible here to determine the desirable ultimate structure, except that it should be more nearly uniform.[91] Given existing tariff levels, movements towards a uniform 20 percent tariff would probably be compatible with equilibrium given the current exchange rate. Indeed, since this entails raising average tariffs for intermediates, capital goods, and government imports, which account for 80 percent of total imports, the Kenya pound might then become undervalued in relation to other currencies.

Export Subsidies. As long as export subsidies are less than tariffs, exports will remain taxed. Three arguments might be used to justify such a relationship. The first is that, unless export subsidies are lower than tariffs or limited in scope, the tariff system will generate no revenue. If net revenue is desired, export subsidy rates must be lower than the tariff[92] either by setting them at a lower level or limiting them to selected commodities. The second argument might be a desire to impose a general tax on exports because the Government wishes to discourage excessive reliance on them. The third, which is for limiting the scope of subsidies, is that some goods face inelastic demand, supply constraints, or both. These goods, such as coffee, tea, and possibly pyrethrum, might therefore not be subsidized. Taken together, these three arguments justify a level of export subsidy lower than the uniform tariff and a scope

---

89. In this discussion, given world prices for all traded goods are assumed. The alternative—that Kenya affects world prices—can almost certainly be ignored, except for a few crops.

90. Since relative domestic prices of traded goods are given by world prices and the tariff structure, exchange rate adjustments only affect relative prices between tradables and nontradables. Moreover, accepting the notion of decomposition of nontradables, amounts to alteration of the relative price of labor where its price is *not* fixed by a demand supply equilibrium in foreign exchange (e.g., in the formal urban sector) and all other goods. This shift can be produced by lowering of nominal wages or by raising the exchange rate or the entire tariff subsidy system. Thus, tariff reform and exchange rate adjustment are complementary, not substitutive. This point is developed in Wasow, op. cit. A devaluation lowers the real wage of labor if the wage is fixed in nominal terms. If the wage is equilibrated to demand and supply in foreign exchange (as in smallholder tea) a devaluation, as such, will not affect the real wage at all, since the marginal product in tea remains the same. If there were *no* labor market disequilibrium, a devaluation could only be used as a deflationary device, through cash hoarding.

91. The Government has taken tentative steps in the direction of uniformity by reducing the level of duty on some items to 40 percent from previously higher levels and imposing duty on almost all government imports.

92. This assumes balance of trade equilibrium. Kenya runs balance of trade deficits, so there will be revenue, even with a uniform tariff and subsidy.

limited to commodities with highly elastic supply and demand. In Kenya, this would imply a uniform subsidy of perhaps 10 percent on manufactured exports.[93]

If the administrative cost argument previously outlined is considered of importance, the whole system could be simplified by abolishing the export subsidy, lowering the uniform tariff to 9 percent, imposing a 9 percent export tax on the items to be exempted from the subsidy, and allowing a corresponding devaluation.

Sales and Value-Added Taxes. Since Kenya still wishes to discourage consumption of luxuries and is in favor of a sales tax, these elements should be included in the scheme. As J.H. Power[94] has shown, a value-added tax is a superb basis for a uniform tariff and subsidy system,[95] in addition to collecting plenty of revenue. A sales tax is a good second best. (It is second best because it encourages vertical integration and would therefore discourage subcontracting, an aspect which is minimized in Kenya, as small firms are exempt.)

A sales tax device can be used to penalize consumption of luxuries without providing incentives to their production as import duties do. A sales tax can also be used to generate more nearly uniform protection if the tariff structure cannot be changed because of EAC disagreement.[96] A system of sales and production taxes and subsidies can be devised which will have exactly the same effect as a uniform tariff and export subsidy. Thus, Kenya can achieve its aims without a tariff reform. However, such a system would have to be very complex since effective protection for the producer depends on the price he receives for his goods net of tax, while the effect of protection on the user depends on the price of goods after tax. In general, introduction of a sales tax will lower effective protective rates. The reason is that producers' prices net of tax are unchanged, but the cost to the user after tax is raised.[97]

Problems of Transition. There are several aspects of the problem of transition to a uniform tariff and subsidy system. First, the change will entail major alterations in relative prices and profitabilities. Second, some industries will become unprofitable. Finally, a squeeze on manufacturing factor incomes as a whole, including wages, will develop since the manufacturing sector on balance is highly protected. Needless to say, these aspects of reform will create major problems.

To cope with changes in relative prices and profitabilities, it will be necessary to announce tariff changes in advance, and to introduce such changes very slowly—perhaps

---

93. The Government has announced as a major step towards this aim a 10 percent subsidy on a range of exports valued at approximately £25 million per annum. At the same time, the export tax on coffee and sisal has been abolished.

94. J. H. Power, "The Role of Protection in Industrialization Policy with particular reference to Kenya," *East African Economic Review*, June 1972.

95. Some taxation of exports can be provided by raising the tariff above the value-added tax rate.

96. As the main report has explained, our basic analysis is not concerned with the implications for policy of Kenya's membership of the EAC. Of course, any change in trade policy, especially any change in the common external tariff, would require the agreement of all three partner states.

97. The effective rate of protection formula becomes:

$$g_j = \frac{t_j - a_{ij}[t_i + C_i(1 + t_i)]}{1 - a_{ij}}$$

where
  g_j = rate of effective protection on j
  t_j = tariff rate on j
  a_{ij} = input coefficient of i into j
  t_i = tariff rate on i
  C_i = sales tax on i

Thus, the effective rate of tax for exports and other low duty items will be higher as a result of Kenya's reform. The export subsidy becomes still more important. Since agricultural inputs, such as fertilizer are exempt, and farm gate prices of agricultural crops sold domestically will not be affected, agriculture will be relatively favored by the sales tax reform. On the other hand, prices of manufactured consumer goods will rise.

over a period of five years—which does appear to be the Government's intention. Thus, in the first phase of reform, perhaps only a 5 percent duty on zero duty items might be imposed, and so forth. If the Government's decision is to fix the level of tariffs and subsidies at about 20 percent and 10 percent respectively, the advantage to Kenya would be to raise the relative price of tradables on balance, and diminish the likelihood of a devaluation during the process.

The problem of inefficient industries would be more difficult to handle. Most of them will be profitable at world prices on a current basis, although unable to amortize their capital costs. Thus, they could be allowed to continue until machinery, for example, is worn out or unprofitable on a current basis. Perhaps the best procedure is, after identifying various industries, to provide the protection required for profitability, while refusing permission to make further investment. Alternatively, a precise *terminus ad quem* can be given for the protection, as with infant industries.

The most difficult problem of all is wages. If the newly unprotected manufacturing sector is not to be taxed by high wages, wages must be reduced in real terms. This will be accomplished if the prices of tradables in general are raised by devaluation, or if the tariff subsidy structure is raised. At the same time, a profit squeeze should lead to much greater resistance to further wage claims. Although there is evidence that the Government and employers are sufficiently strong to win such a battle, the situation would undoubtedly create enormous difficulties. Therefore, any transition to a less protected manufacturing sector must be done over a considerable period of time, and some form of wage subsidy might be an appropriate interim measure.

Government Revenue. A uniform tariff, export subsidy, and sales tax can considerably expand government revenues. Precise estimates require a precise scheme, but, as long as subsidy rates are lower than tariffs, and/or the scope is limited to a few goods, net revenue will be positive. Under most schemes, net revenue will be higher than at present, even leaving aside the effect of sales tax.

Policy Reform and Agriculture. The sort of reform just discussed will continue to entail taxation of agriculture. Since major crops will be exempt from export subsidies, while tariffs on manufactured goods will level at 20 percent, terms of trade will remain against agriculturalists. This effect can be reduced if the Government permits a rise in domestic prices of commodities sold at below f.o.b. prices, such as meat, and, at the moment, maize. Since several crops, though in theory tradable, are, in fact, largely sold domestically at officially determined prices, it is open to the authorities to adjust them. A simple procedure would be to provide a price rise of 20 percent, or the export subsidy, which would have the same effect. In this way, all crops except tea, coffee, and pyrethrum would be benefited, and the urban real wage would be further squeezed, as desired.

Policy Reform and Noncommunity Transactions. Since Kenya has important service transactions and capital inflows, the effects of a policy change upon them should be taken into account. As already stated, if the decision is for a tariff subsidy arrangement, rather than for flexible exchange rates, the exchange rate will be "overvalued." The effect is to tax service receipts and capital inflows and to lower the costs of service payments. There is no general reason why desirable levels of taxation of the two types of payment should be the same, since the taxation should be determined by the individual elasticities of supply of foreign exchange. For Kenya, the most important type of service receipt is tourism, whose elasticity of demand is apparently completely unknown. Because of this ignorance, a uniform tax on all noncommodity transactions may be the simplest compromise.

Infant Industries. A uniform tariff and subsidy system can permit some exceptions for infant industries. The number of these industries must be limited, since the greater the quantity that are protected, the smaller the protection of each one. Infant industry protection should be limited in time as well. There should be advance notice to industries being phased out during the transitional period, that an extra 20 percent tariff will be provided for five years and then will be reduced progressively. In this way, Kenya can avoid nourishing "infants" who never grow up.

Determination of infant industry protection would become the main responsibility of the Protection Committee. All applications will have to be scrutinized very carefully from an economic point to view, to ensure that the infant industry is likely to be viable when protection is reduced; otherwise pressures for permanent exceptions may become irresistible.

Investment. Reform already discussed and now proposed by the Government will reduce the incentive to invest in certain industries, while increasing the incentive to invest in others. There will not necessarily be overall reduction, just change, in a more efficient direction.

Conclusion. A precise scheme could have an extremely important effect and offer a way out of the important substitution blind alley. Exporting will provide potential for further rapid growth of manufacturing;[98] the pressure of competition that is necessary to improve efficiency; and will make it easier to resist wage pressure, since competitiveness must be retained. Kenya, at present, has really little choice if the well-documented effects of further import substitution, export taxation, and consequent exchange crises are to be avoided. Exports will grow only through incentives, and not because of any amount of moral persuasion. The Government has become aware of this, and has announced its desire to move towards greater tariff uniformity, to implement an export subsidy, and to take greater care in appraising projects, moves which are both appropriate and sensible.

Wage Policy

We have described the adverse impact of a growing rural-urban income gap, particularly on income distribution, migration, unemployment, and the demand for education. The reformed policy package we have outlined would go a long way towards alleviating these adverse effects. Reduction of protection to manufacturing and increased exports in competitive markets would certainly provide a substantial incentive for employers to resist wage increases. Failing an incomes policy, increased competition is probably the best way to restrain firms' willingness to grant wage increases, and also employees' desire for them, since as argued before, high and secure profits allow firms to be generous and encourage employees to be demanding. At the same time, the devaluation or raising of the general tariff subsidy level, combined with corresponding rises in the prices of domestically consumed agricultural commodities, will reduce the real wages of those whose incomes are fixed in nominal terms. The result will be to lower the rural-urban real wage gap, increase equilibrium wages in the urban informal sector because of reduced migration, and increase real incomes of smallholders because of improved terms of trade.[99] (Wages in the formal rural sector may fall, however, because of reduced migration.) Thus, the trade policy package fits naturally with the aim of formal sector wage control.

98. The greatest advantage is that demand elasticities being very high, exports of manufactures are, if competitive, only limited by supply constraints, and full advantage can be taken of economies of scale. This is very rarely so for import substituting firms in small markets. Moreover, import substitution in Kenya has, as might be expected, required the creation of many inefficient monopolies or tight oligopolies. The market is too small to support many firms in most industries. These competitive efficiency arguments are important. See J. N. Bhagwati and A. O. Krueger, "Exchange Control, Liberalization, and Economic Development," Papers and Proceedings of the Eighty-Fifth Annual Meeting of the American Economic Association, *American Economic Review,* May 1973, pp. 420–22.

99. The real incomes of smallholders may conceivably fall if returned migrants have marginal products below consumption, but this is most unlikely given the assumed terms of trade improvement.

For such a strategy to work, it is essential that Government can "win" in any confrontation with labor unions. If nominal wages in the formal sector are forced up again, and minimum wages are raised as well, little will have been gained, even after a devaluation. For this reason the adjustment must be slow. It should be stressed, however, that there are cases in which employers have won such battles. In Kenya, unions represent only 40 percent of the total number of wage earners in the formal sector, and 25 percent of all wage earners; therefore, their power is limited.

One important precondition of success is that productivity increases are not accepted as an argument for wage increases. This would mean, inevitably, that the wage gap will grow with consequences in terms of increased unemployment. In a dual economy, productivity related wage increases in the modern sector mean that benefits which might accrue in the form of faster growth[100] or lower prices, in fact go to labor. Since growth is a central aim in itself, this use of productivity changes is disadvantageous. It is even more so if it increases inequalities and labor market disequilibrium.

In the basic strategy underlying this report, however, we are concerned less with wage policy as much as with measures to increase the incomes of Kenya's poor. Thus, much of our analysis and argument is concerned with reorienting growth towards increasing agricultural production as the major means of increasing incomes for the mass of the labor force. We see the agricultural sector as the residual employer, and rural incomes as a function mainly of agricultural productivity. A very real danger which threatens agriculture's capacity to provide employment is the possible extension of minimum wage standards to the small farm sectors. Such a move would create for the rural areas the same kind of open unemployment (but on a much larger scale) as the determination of high wages for the formal sector has in the urban areas. Trade unions have traditionally been more concerned with securing more benefits for the existing members (who are already among the privileged few in the formal sector employment) than with increasing membership through more jobs.[101] Any extension of this approach to the informal sector would be disastrous to future employment in Kenya.

Interest Rate Policy

It is appropriate, also, to review interest rate policy. The arguments we have outlined are basically for much greater flexibility. Flexibility will be our major recommendation. In addition, it should be questioned whether it is desirable to permit foreign firms to borrow money more cheaply in Nairobi than in London or New York.

Some Major Consequences of Policy Reform

Although the policy reform contained in this report will improve the performance of the formal urban sector, and reduce its costs to the rest of the economy, there may still remain conflicts of goals. For instance, although large scale enterprises are likely to do best in exporting and will, through continued access to cheap capital, be at an advantage, small-scale ventures may generate more employment because of lower capital-labor ratios. Small-scale ventures may also be a better way to develop African entrepreneurship. The authorities therefore may wish to penalize large-scale formal activity because of a desire to reduce their dependence on foreign skills and entrepreneurship, while at the same time may consider offering special favors to small scale industry.

---

100. Essentially, permission to workers to benefit from productivity increases in dynamic industries reduces their profitability, which is the major growth signal, and, at the same time, increases the disequilibrium in labor supply.

101. Participation of the trade unions in the series of Tripartite Agreements, where they agreed to suspend wage claims in return for an increase in employment, was a hopeful exception to the unions' normal behavior.

Perhaps the most important area is that of income distribution, which has been only touched upon at various points. If the sole change is in urban formal sector real wages, it can be shown that profit earners in the economy will almost certainly increase their aggregate incomes. Urban informal sector incomes per head will probably rise while individual wages in rural formal employment will fall because of reduced migration, and average consumption in smallholding will also fall if there are decreasing returns to labor. However, *total* labor and smallholder incomes could still rise, depending on the relevant elasticities, since GDP will rise with employment. If a real wage change goes along with a change in trade policy, it is much more likely that rural real wages and smallholders' real incomes would rise, and that profits in urban activities would fall. It would be possible to work out a precise model but, at present, the parameters are unknown. However, it is clear that improvements in real incomes per head of all but urban formal sector workers, and improvements in aggregate labor and smallholders incomes are very likely, if the full reform discussed here is put into effect. There can be no question, however, that successful reform will, in the short run, reduce real incomes per head of people in urban formal sector employment. Such an effect would seem to be in accord with the Government's stated objective of distributing the benefit of development more equitably.

Conclusion

In this lengthy argument, an attempt has been made to show that the price environment of the formal—especially urban—sector reduces its efficiency and imposes considerable and growing costs on the rest of the economy. It is also argued that a major overhaul of trade policy along the lines the Government itself is proposing is the first need for improvement. Government steps taken so far are only the beginning, but they are an earnest of good intentions and deserve the fullest possible support. A reform should, if carefully introduced, also substantially reduce the problems created by a distorted wage structure, although it cannot hope to remove them entirely. Finally, it is argued that a policy reform which includes a reduction in protection to import substituting manufacturing, and a reduction in urban formal sector real wages is likely, in conjunction, to improve income distribution, by raising real incomes of those the ILO calls the "working poor." Reductions in real incomes of the middle class of formal sector employees will have to be set against this. However, it should be remembered that, if improvement in efficiency and growth is considerable, everybody can be made better off in the medium to long run.

CHAPTER 4

CONTROLS ON TRADE AND FOREIGN EXCHANGE

In examining the effect of controls on current balance of payments transactions on the private sector, this chapter excludes discussion of controls on internal prices (a pervasive feature of the Kenyan economy), as well as discussion of controls on capital flows.[1] However, certain of the controls and measures of supervision, which affect current transactions are, in fact, aimed towards control of capital flows. As a result, the discussion will touch upon that area.

The reason for our narrow focus is simple. The annex concentrates on the effect of the private sector's environment on its operation, and price control, and controls on trade affect that operation more than any other. However, almost nothing is known about the effects of price controls; therefore we shall concentrate on trade controls. This focus fits in well with the discussion of trade policy in Chapter 3.

Protection and the Conservation of Foreign Exchange

The issue discussed here is the use of controls for protective reasons. In Kenya, the growth of such controls has been rapid, and they have now made tariffs largely redundant as protective measures. Details of the system will be discussed later, and their effects can be understood in terms of the discussion in Chapter 3. Repetition of the discussion will be largely avoided, since controls have exacerbated the effects of the tariff system, and have not worked against the system to any great extent.

History of Protective Controls

"Prior to 1972 the importation of goods into Kenya was regulated solely according to the objectives of the licensing policy of the government as administered by the Department of Trade and Supplies."[2] The legal foundations of the present system had been laid by the Imports, Exports, and Essential Supplies Act of 1962.[3] This established the Department of Trade and Supplies to supervise the system. Under the legislation, items entered Kenya under Open General License (OGL) or required a Specific Import License (SIL). The scope of such specific import licenses could be determined by the Minister of Commerce and Industry.

From 1964 until 1972, commodities were organized into three schedules. "Items appearing under the first schedule were only to be imported from places other than Uganda and Tanzania under and in accordance with an import license. Those appearing under the second schedule required a license wherever they originated. Those under the third schedule required licenses if imported from Tanzania and Uganda otherwise than by or to the order of the Kenya National Trading Corporation."[4] In 1964, the first substantial increase in items under SIL occurred.

The second substantial increase occurred in November, 1968. As can be seen in Table 25, at least 37 percent of the value of net home consumption was affected by SILs

---

1. This issue will be touched upon subsequently in Chapter 5, *Foreign Private Investment*.
2. V. Vinnai, *The System of Exchange Control in Kenya*, Discussion Paper No. 148 (Nairobi: Institute for Development Studies, September 1972), p. 8.
3. The source for most of this is D. S. McRae, *Import Licensing in Kenya*.
4. KNTC has had a large number of items confined to it. The purpose of this is the Kenyanization of wholesale trade. See in this connection D. S. McRae, *Import Licensing in Kenya*, p. 3.

in that year.[5] This is a jump of about 13 percent over 1967. Subsequently, the proportion fell, partly because of the effect of the controls themselves, and dropped to about 19 percent by 1971.

Over the entire period, the most striking feature is the growth in the number of licensed items in the Standard International Trade Classification (SITC) categories 6 (manufactured goods classified chiefly by material), and 8 (miscellaneous manufactured articles). In 1964, there were only nineteen items at the 6 digit level in the two categories under license, but by 1972 there were 130 items, which was over 40 percent of the 317 items in these categories produced in Kenya.[6] Thus, import licensing has become, within a short period, a pervasive fact in the manufacturing sector. For the economy as a whole, the number of items under SIL increased from 69 in 1964 to 228 by 1972, when the total number of items produced was 688.[7]

The main purpose of the system has been to protect local industries. Because this form of protection is at the disposal of the Kenyan authorities, unlike the tariff, it has been used with increasing frequency. For instance, out of fourteen applications for protection made to the Industrial Protection Committee in 1972, six included requests for import restrictions, and five were granted.

A subsidiary purpose of the licensing system is to assist Kenyanization of wholesale trade. This is done by restricting items to KNTC (at present forty-eight), which permits trade only by African agents.

Applications for protection are sent to the Director of Industry at the Ministry of Commerce and Industry, and his department carries out the initial investigation. Applications are then referred to the Industrial Protection Committee, which includes representatives of the Ministries of Commerce and Industry, Finance and Planning, and Agriculture, as well as advisors. This committee decides on the exact nature of the protection to be granted, which is usually import restriction or duty drawbacks on imported inputs, or both. The Director of Trade and Supplies executes the instructions as far as import licenses are concerned, through his import licensing officers.

Import licenses restrict the freedom to import in five basic ways: price range restrictions, quantitative restrictions, approval by specific bodies, one-channel importing through the KNTC, and total bans. The first method is commonly used for manufactured items, such as soaps or bicycle tires, where imports are permitted only if above a certain unit price; quantitative restrictions are straightforward enough in concept, and are, in fact, frequently superimposed upon price range restrictions; the third method is used for imports of items such as millet, which must be approved by the Ministry of Agriculture, or paints, which require approval of the Association of Manufacturers. In 1971, 9 percent of total net imports were directed through the KNTC whose concentration is in foodstuffs, where it handled 43 percent of imports. Total bans are issued for many foodstuffs and also for items characteristically produced by the Kenya Industrial Estates.

Because of the foreign exchange crisis of late 1971, an entirely new element entered the picture. This was the use of import controls as a means of conserving foreign exchange. Although protection of local import substituting industry has, as part of its purpose, the saving of foreign exchange, this is by no means the main aim, which is to assist rapid industrialization. Thus, the developments of 1972 were genuinely new in spirit, since they were directed entirely at saving foreign exchange.

---

5. Net home consumption equals total value of commercial goods entered at time of importation for consumption *plus* commercial goods exwarehoused for consumption in Kenya *minus* goods transferred from Kenya to Partner States *plus* goods transferred from Partner States to Kenya *minus* goods reexported under drawback.

6. See *Index to Manufacturers and Products* (Nairobi: Ministry of Commerce and Industry, 1972).

7. Ibid. Items on the SIL list have been rarely removed, so the net increase of 159 is virtually the gross increase, too.

The Central Bank Circular Exchange Control 1 of January 1972 detailed the new regulations intended to deal with the crisis. Restrictions were considerably tightened on items already under SIL, and were placed for the first time on many items under OGL. Five schedules were drawn up, of which A, B, and C included all items already under SIL, and D and E items which were previously under OGL. Schedule B and E items were banned; schedule C items could only be authorized by commercial banks when specific prior exchange control approval had been granted; the banks authorize payment for items in schedule A subject to the provisions of administrative notices and instructions; and schedule D items would require a "no objection to foreign exchange" certificate from the Director of Trade and Supplies.

Essentially, the aim of the circular was to ban or restrict all "unnecessary" imports, which were considered to fall into two categories. The first, which included almost all the items under SIL and several under OGL, consisted of goods produced in Kenya. The second category was luxury goods previously imported under OGL, and now placed in schedule D. This desire to exclude all unnecessary imports—thus defined—made it necessary to add the two new schedules of former OGL items and to make the regulations affecting SIL items substantially more restrictive.

One hundred and twenty-seven items in Schedule B were banned, but this was no great change, since most had already been excluded. However, the twenty-three banned items in schedule E had previously been under OGL, so this was a major new restriction. Schedule C items, which numbered 120, were all put under quota. The quotas were allocated to importers on the basis of past performance, and initially ran at 50 percent of 1970-71 levels. Schedule D items, numbering forty-six were also put under quota on the same lines as for Schedule C. Finally, the treatment of the fifty-two Schedule A items was unchanged from the prior position.

As a result of this new system, 369 items, including seventy previously under OGL, were placed under some restriction. One hundred and fifty were banned entirely, and a further 167 were put under quota. It has been estimated that 38 percent of 1971 net home consumption was affected by the circular.[8] Particular areas of concentration were Beverages and Tobacco (where the proportion was 98 percent), Food and Live Animals (69 percent), Miscellaneous Manufactured Articles (51 percent), and Manufactured Goods Classified Chiefly by Material (46 percent). The introduction of this system clearly marked a major change in both the extent and intensity of import restriction and control.

The Government intended to save £25 million in foreign exchange, and believes that it has succeeded. However, although imports have clearly fallen, it is difficult to tell whether the restrictions were responsible, since the late 1971 import boom seems to have been in part the result of stockpiling, exceptional investment, and unique phenomena such as the drought. An analysis of the 1972 trade figures in relation to the restrictions has not yet been undertaken.

Clearly, the extent of import restriction grew considerably after 1964, and a complex system of regulation, mainly for protective purposes, was already in existence by late 1971. Faced with an apparent crisis in the balance of payments in 1971, the authorities reacted by introducing extensive exchange control. Many OGL items were banned or put under quota, and restrictions on items under SIL were tightened. The system had two overlapping purposes, resulting not only in protection for items already produced, but protection for luxury items not yet produced! The effects of the latter incentive soon became apparent.

In the middle of 1973, because of the improving foreign exchange position and the

---

8. D. S. McRae, *Import Licensing in Kenya*, Appendix C. Table II. This table shows what would be the affected percentage of net home consumption if the schedules were applied to 1971 values. (See Table 26.)

problems that the controls had created, the Government substantially reformed the system. Schedules A to E became Schedules I to IV. The OGL items, with the exception of motor cars, were all derestricted. The number of banned items under SIL fell from 127 to 83, and items under quota remained at about 120. Thus, the number for which foreign exchange would be granted automatically rose from 52 to 131. Although the number of items subject to SIL continued to rise (by about 12 percent), the impact of the system was substantially reduced, since the number of items under foreign exchange restriction fell from 316 to 205. Nevertheless, the system remains much more restrictive than prior to January 1972, since, for 205 items, foreign exchange control continues to be superimposed on the basic SIL system.

Consequence of Protective Controls

The general line of policy discussed, together with recent developments, have consequences which have been extensively discussed. Previous work in Kenya, and the mission's own investigations, only provide indicative evidence for most of the material. Indeed, even thorough examination would not provide conclusive evidence on the effects. However, what is known about them can be stated, and can be weighed against the benefits. Since many of the effects parallel what has been said about trade policy (Chapter 3), here we concentrate on aspects peculiar to quantitative restrictions.

The first point is that the system requires a considerable bureaucratic input. Until recently, there was only one licensing officer in Kenya, but the number may increase to six or seven. Since licensing is a difficult job, the requirement is for fairly skilled manpower. If the manpower is not skilled, the job will not be done well; on the other hand, if the manpower is skilled, a very scarce resource is being employed. One of the administrative costs is that of policing. The restrictions do not apply to goods produced in the Community, although they do apply to any good imported *through* either of the other Partner States. It is necessary to establish customs posts to check items for this distinction. In general, smuggling and incorrect identification of consignments has been a constant problem.

Substantial administrative problems arise, too, because six-digit SITC categories contain many disparate items, some of which are produced in Kenya, while others are not. For a manufacturer, this creates special difficulties, since he must give the authorities written confirmation from the manufacturer of the product range that the specific item in question is not produced in Kenya. The mission received specific complaints on these lines about screws, while McRae[9] mentions the case of handbag fasteners.

The economic costs of quantitative and price range restrictions arise both from the original SIL system, and the new exchange controls. It is useful to analyze these economic costs by the type of cost, rather than by the aim of the restriction, since the effects of the varying policies are often similar. Mention will be made of the policies which are likely to create any given effect. In discussing economic costs, the focus is on costs to the economy as a whole and not only to specific groups.

Delay is an important element of cost. Four cases can be distinguished: the first is where an article's international price oscillates considerably, wire rod, for example, where apparently a two- to three-week delay may be associated with a price fluctuation of 5 percent. This is a cost to the importer and to the economy. A second case arises if delays lead to a desire to hold larger stocks. This is now common in Kenya, where firms have been caught twice by the introduction of unanticipated controls—the beginning and end of 1972—and found production increasingly difficult as stocks ran down. Their wish now to secure larger stocks—expensive for them and the economy[10]—will

9. D. S. McRae, *Import Licensing in Kenya*, p. 27.
10. Stock accumulation for this reason is an exceptionally fruitless way of tying up capital, from a social point of view.

create considerable balance of payments problems once controls are lifted. The third problem is the effect of delay on transport costs. One of the side effects of the introduction of the General Superintendence system[11] has been delays in processing necessitating the use of air freight. Air freight imposes a considerable additional cost on importers and the economy. Finally, in the extreme, firms have to close down as raw materials stocks have been used up. This has occurred in a few recent cases.

The SIL system, its recent tightening, and the temporary restrictions on OGL items, some of which were already produced in Kenya, created absolute protection for many manufacturers of consumer goods. On the basis of the mission's interviews, it would not be an exaggeration to suggest that several firms have a license to print money, being subject to no competition, either at home or abroad.

The same effect—but with more serious consequences—occurs with those intermediate goods which are now produced in Kenya under restriction. Important items like packaging—vital to the development of agricultural processing and other industries—are restricted, because they are produced domestically. Complaints of excessive prices are not uncommon, and such high prices imply heavy taxation of exporters. At present, several chemicals, vehicle tires, paper packaging, cement, wire rods, wood screws, and many other goods are subject to import restrictions or bans. Although this offsets to some extent the low effective protection apparently given to intermediates by the tariff, it also implies taxation of users. Some of these taxation rates are very high.[12]

The new measures did, and, to some extent, still do create a class of privileged quota holders. This applied especially to importers of luxury consumer durables, many of which were placed in Schedule D. The effect is essentially to transfer tax revenue from government taxes to quota holders. In addition, the manufacture of such durables is made very attractive. A perfect example is the assembly of motor cars, which is not economically viable, but could, if the quota remains and the components are imported duty free without restriction, be very lucrative. Several interests are now pushing for this development in what is almost certainly a negative value-added industry. Thus, controls on inessential imports make production very attractive, and soon the inputs required will have become, as if miraculously, totally essential.

The fact that quotas are based on importers' past performance has several important consequences. First, it is the established firms who benefit, while smaller African traders have a particularly difficult time. Second, the restrictiveness of the control depends on the rate of growth of demand. Thus, importers just opening new lines have been heavily penalized. Finally, several of the established firms are foreign owned and are therefore able to expatriate profits created by the restrictions. This is a straightforward transfer abroad.

The entire system benefits large and well established firms. Dealing with the bureaucracy requires time and money—both assets of large firms. The more complex the system becomes, the more important are these assets. While several new African firms have been squeezed out by both the allocation of quotas and the costs of dealing with the bureaucracy, others with good connections have obtained licenses for foreign firms. These so-called brief-case importers are an important part of the new African business class. It is obvious that this is not a good test of entrepreneurial ability.

In general, the entire system creates monopoly producers and monopoly traders. Producers are subject to little or no competition at home, and, because they export very little outside the Kenyan or EAC markets, they are subject to little external competition. This has led to stagnation in other countries, and there is little reason to suppose Kenya will avoid similar effects. In addition, because quantitative restrictions, unlike tariffs,

---

11. See the section on "Policy Measures Adopted," below.
12. It would be an interesting piece of research to examine the relative inflation on restricted and unrestricted items during 1972. This has not been done, since the data are not yet available.

impose no price ceilings, it is necessary to introduce whole new mechanisms of price control. It is not surprising that ministers have recently complained about the poor quality and high prices of absolutely protected import substitutes.[13] It is also not surprising it has happened, since that is the direction in which incentives direct the firms. The price control solution is just one aspect of the logic of controls breeding further controls, to which we refer later. Finally, the creation of monopolies makes it exceptionally difficult for the new entrepreneur to break in,[14] outside the protected circle of KNTC.

A very particular twist to Kenyan import licensing is the use of price range restrictions. This system has the effect first, of encouraging overinvoicing, since an importer has no benefit from announcing a lower price than the minimum; secondly, of encouraging the import of more expensive articles, which increases the foreign exchange cost; and finally, of providing complete protection for domestic inefficiency below the specified price.

One particular problem with the use of quotas is that it loses revenue to the Government.[15] This revenue is then earned by import quota holders. In the case of the January 1972 measure, for example, the revenue loss has been estimated at about £7 million. This is quite a significant sum.

One of the major problems created by the habit of tackling foreign exchange crises with import controls is that it becomes progressively more difficult. At each stage there is less "fat" to trim, but, since every bout of restriction tends to tax exports further, there is more need to trim "fat." As Vinnai states, ". . . exchange control at present has little flexibility should the 1971 deficit repeat itself."[16] The recent relaxation has not restored the status quo ante. Thus, in the next drought, tourist scare, or fall in export prices, Kenya will have to cut back investment and start reducing allocations of raw materials to firms. This is why development of exports is vital, but restrictions and delays, superimposed on the tariff system, make it unlikely.

There is, as can be seen, a logic to the development of controls—a process which Kenya is now beginning, but which many countries have followed much further. Controls breed high profits, so price control is introduced. Controls make future management of exchange crises more difficult, and the new restrictions begin to affect the level of output. Controls produce monopoly profits for importers, so quotas are given directly to investors and producers, who must, therefore, themselves be controlled. Meanwhile, desperate attempts are made to encourage exports and new, small businessmen, while every incentive in the economy goes against them.

Kenya is at the start of this process. The recent reduction in controls is an encouraging sign that the Government is aware of the problems. However, this is only one step forward and two steps back. The decision to protect domestic production with extensive import restrictions, and the use in its first exchange crisis of import controls, may indicate its willingness to use further controls. The costs of such a process should be weighed carefully beforehand. Few countries have developed through high cost private monopolies and extensive direct government allocation of resources. In Kenya, where skilled manpower is exceptionally scarce, such an approach seems particularly inappropriate. This early stage may also be the last at which Kenya can draw back

---

13. "Product quality and manufacturing service have all too frequently been secondary considerations in the mind of the manufacturers who tend to squeal every time they are touched by competition from outside and to run to the Government to bail them out every time they run into trouble." Budget Speech, June 14, 1973.

14. See V. Vinnai, "The System of Exchange Control in Kenya," p. 16, ". . . the method used here—the application of reference periods—will close the market to newcomers, which seems contrary to another aim of import licensing, namely the Africanisation of import trade."

15. A ban is similar to a prohibitive tariff; both have the same revenue effect, i.e., they reduce revenue to zero.

16. "The System of Exchange Control in Kenya," p. 19.

easily. Thus, it is to be hoped that decontrol will be taken much further, especially by reducing the scope of the SIL system.

Policy Alternatives

The suggestions on policy follow closely on what has been said in Chapter 3. If possible, the use of quantitative restrictions should be reduced, and they should be replaced by tariffs (which would put a ceiling on prices, ensure some competition, reduce monopoly profits of quota holders, and generate tax revenue). Moreover, the tariff should move towards uniformity, with exceptions for transitional reasons, or infant industries. The transition from controls to tariffs may be more difficult than from high to low tariffs, since the tariff equivalent of the quota may be very high indeed.[17] It may be necessary to put an exceptionally high tariff on during the transition phase or, if this is impossible because of the EAC, to relax the controls very gradually.

Clearly, one of the aims of the 1972 regulations was to inhibit the consumption of luxury items. The Kenya Government's desire not to sacrifice development for the consumption of Mercedes-Benz cars is extremely understandable. However, the Government can employ a method which does not encourage the domestic assembly of such cars. The best way is a heavy tax on the consumption of luxury goods, which would not create the protective effect of tariffs or quotas.

Assuming the authorities will not substantially alter their use of protective controls, methods can be devised to break some of the inhibiting effects of stagnant monopolies. An approach used by some governments is to provide quota protection in the domestic market in return for a given proportion of exports. If these exports are not achieved, the quota protection is reduced. At the same time, the monopoly rent obtained by quota holders in the import trade can be reduced by charging for licenses, as, in effect, the Kenya National Trading Corporation does.

The policy alternatives just suggested are sensible in the long run, but the authorities will still be concerned with crisis management. It is the mission's view that other policy weapons can be used which will not create the distortions of the measures discussed. Reserves can be accumulated to meet short run fluctuations, and various ways can be found to increase the effective price of foreign exchange. In addition, standby credits can be arranged with the IMF. A particular weapon, which has been used successfully in other countries, is the import deposit scheme. Whatever transpires, another crisis can be expected at some time in the future in a country such as Kenya which depends on a few items (coffee, tea, tourism) to earn the bulk of its foreign exchange. Now is the time to prepare policies which will avoid the side effects of a regimen of controls.

The control system which has developed in the recent past is a potentially costly burden. It appears that alternatives can be found to the system and that now, when the balance of payments is in a favorable position, is a good time to go as far as possible to dismantle it.

Overinvoicing, Tax Evasion, and Capital Flight

Kenyan authorities have been concerned, especially recently, with two related problems, overinvoicing and capital flight. The latter is the primary problem. Kenya has a large noncitizen resident community and a large citizen non-African community. Both of these groups have reason to feel insecure, and both may wish to expatriate capital. Together they own a substantial proportion of Kenya's private assets. The mission

---

17. If the desire is for a total ban, there is no reason to replace a control by a prohibitive tariff, but it will be necessary to have a heavy consumption tax, if the protection is not to lead to domestic production.

estimates, for instance, that Asian capital may be as much as £300 million. Measures taken to deal with this problem have created very serious spillover effects onto the rest of the economy.

The Problem of Overinvoicing

Two quite dissimilar problems surface in the phenomenon of overinvoicing of imports (and underinvoicing of exports). The first is the attempt to expatriate capital by groups who are not permitted to do so. Emigrants from Kenya must place most of their assets in a blocked account which entails the enforced holding of approved securities for *at least* five years before capital can be expatriated.[18] Residents cannot expatriate capital at all. The second problem is the attempt to evade taxes on profits by companies who *are* allowed to expatriate dividends and capital (i.e., those companies who have a Certificate of Approved Enterprise). Although both these outlets for possible fraud lead to overinvoicing, each requires a different policy weapon.

Economic analysis of overinvoicing is quite complex[19] and depends, in the first place, on whether companies are engaged in transfer pricing, which permits them to declare profits in the country with the lowest tax rate, or whether they are trying to hide true flows so as to evade tax altogether. The latter requires *different* invoices by exporters and importers, and the consequent salting away of the difference. A transaction of this kind is presumably made much easier if the importer and exporter are both part of the same firm.

If the intent is to avoid all taxes by the latter method, economic analysis is not complex. By raising the apparent price of imports, the firm saves itself corporation tax in Kenya but pays duty on the additional value of imports. Thus, there is a level of duty at which this transaction is unprofitable.[20] In Kenya, the corporation tax on dividends expatriated is 47.5 percent, which makes overinvoicing a more economical way of withdrawing profit when the duty rate is less than 90.5 percent. Since there are few duty rates as high as this in East Africa, there is clearly a general incentive to avoid tax through overinvoicing.

Let us turn to the case of the firm that intends to pay tax, but, through various price adjustments, wishes to minimize the burden. Assume also a double tax agreement between the country in which the central office is situated, and Kenya. If the tax rate in Kenya is less than or equal to that of the host country, the firm has no incentive to withdraw profits through overinvoicing of imports. If, however, there is a higher rate in Kenya, such an incentive exists. In this case, overinvoicing saves the same tax as in the

---

18. The approved securities are in very short supply, so nonresidents have little option to purchase them. The result is that moneys of residents leaving the country are effectively totally blocked (see V. Vinnai, "The System of Exchange Control in Kenya," p. 13).

19. A classic reference on this subject is J. Bhagwati, "Fiscal Policies, the Faking of Foreign Trade Declarations, and the Balance of Payments," *Bulletin of the Oxford University Institute of Economics and Statistics*, February 1967.

20. The condition is that the duty rate should be less than the corporation tax rate over unity minus the corporation tax rate:

$$Pr' > Pr \text{ iff. } M\Delta Pt' + M\Delta Ptt' - M\Delta Pt > 0$$

where
 Pr' = profit after overinvoicing
 Pr = profit without overinvoicing
 M = quantity of imports
 ΔP = change in price of imports
 t = duty rate
 t' = corporate tax rate in Kenya

The first two terms are the tax saved, which is $M\Delta P(1 + t)t'$; the last term is the tax lost, which is: $M\Delta Pt$. Simplifying, the condition is

$$t < \frac{t'}{1-t'}$$

previous example, but there is additional tax burden overseas.[21] Using the formula given in footnote 21, and assuming the overseas tax rate is 40 percent, the critical rate of duty is 14 percent. Since tariff rates of this magnitude are common in Kenya, this sort of overinvoicing is a marginal activity.[22]

In cases like this, the general rule must be that the higher the corporate tax rate and the lower the rate of duty on imported inputs, or rate of subsidy on exports, the greater the likelihood of export underinvoicing or import overinvoicing. Correspondingly, the higher the rate of duty and subsidy, the greater the attraction of export overinvoicing and import underinvoicing. The major problem that concerns the Kenyan is import overinvoicing. It cannot be denied that duty rebates and remissions, and low tariff rates on imported inputs, provide a substantial incentive for this activity.

One additional incentive to overinvoice might be mentioned. If an international firm establishes itself in Kenya on condition that the Kenyan Government or Kenyan citizens take a share in its equity, there can be a great incentive to overinvoice on inputs imported from affiliates overseas, or underinvoice on exports sent to them. The reason is that any losses to the local company brought about by overinvoicing are shared with the Kenyan equity holders, but the direct gains from overinvoicing accrue to the international company alone.[23] This changes the attractiveness dramatically. Thus, a wholly foreign owned enterprise (with a 40 percent overseas corporate tax rate and a 47.5 percent tax rate in Kenya), would find overinvoicing attractive only if the duty were less than 14 percent, but an enterprise with 50 percent Kenyan participation would have an incentive to overinvoice any imports carrying a duty of less than 153 percent. The larger the extent of Kenyan participation, the higher the duty would have to be to discourage overinvoicing: if the Kenyan share was 80 percent of the equity capital, overinvoicing would be attractive at duty levels of over 500 percent! Thus, Kenya's own policy of encouraging local equity participation in foreign companies is a very potent incentive to overinvoicing. This factor needs to be weighed against possible advantages of local participation in determining future policy.[24]

It appears there are substantial incentives to overinvoice imports in the present Kenyan situation. There are many low or zero duty import items, and many foreign controlled firms with substantial Kenyan participation. These incentives to overinvoice to evade tax are clearly the result of government policy.[25]

21. $Pr' > Pr$ iff. $M\Delta Pt' + M\Delta Ptt' - M\Delta Pt - M\Delta Pt'' > 0$
where
t'' = foreign corporate tax rate.
Simplifying; the condition is
$$t < \frac{t' - t''}{1 - t'}$$

22. A similar analysis can be developed for cases of over- and underinvoicing of exports and underinvoicing of imports. The latter, for instance, is attractive if the tariff rate exceeds the black market premium of foreign exchange. Overinvoicing of exports in a multinational company may occur if the firm's tax rate in its base is higher than in Kenya. Underinvoicing of exports may be analyzed in the same way as overinvoicing of imports. If tax can be evaded and export subsidies are low or nonexistent, it will usually be profitable. If tax cannot be avoided (i.e., your cheap exports are someone else's cheap imports), the attractiveness of the operation depends on the difference between the tax rates in Kenya and abroad.

23. It is easy to show that the condition for overinvoicing to be profitable is:
$$t < \frac{1 - t'' - S(1 - t')}{S(1 - t')}$$

Where S = the share in equity of the firm overinvoicing.

24. The ILO/UNDP mission cited other reasons for recommending that investment in foreign international firms is not a sensible use of Kenya's scarce capital. See ILO/UNDP report, p. 191.

25. ILO/UNDP report, p. 455, estimates that if the average overpricing ratio for all intermediates were 5 percent, the total outflow of resources due to transfer pricing would have been 2.9 times as great as actually repatriated profits in 1968.

Overinvoicing to send capital abroad is a different phenomenon. The desire is believed to be particularly strong in the Asian community. It can be analyzed very easily from an economic point of view. Such overinvoicing is profitable whenever the tariff rate is less than the black market premium on foreign exchange. At present, the premium is about 40 percent. Thus, on any goods carrying a duty of less than 40 percent, it is cheaper to expatriate capital through overinvoicing than through the black market. For example, at the present black market premium, £1,000 would purchase only about US$2,000. However, if overinvoicing of an item carrying a 20 percent tariff were the alternative, the same £1,000 could earn US$2,240 in foreign exchange (i.e., $2,800 less the 20 percent duty).

It appears that, under present conditions in Kenya, both types of overinvoicing will continue to be profitable unless tariffs are quite high. Increases in low tariffs, towards a more uniform rating structure, would certainly reduce the incentive to overinvoice somewhat. But the problems of tax evasion and capital flight will continue. For the Kenya Government, the problem is to control them, without strangling trade.

Policy Measures Adopted

It cannot be said that the authorities have approached the issue with any finesse. They simply started a major policing operation. On December 1, 1972, EC 24/72 was released by the Central Bank. The circular stated that all imports into Kenya in excess of an invoice value of £100 were henceforth subject to foreign exchange licensing and had to be cleared by the Department of Trade and Supplies and the Central Bank. The main purpose of this was to use the General Superintendence Co. Ltd. of Switzerland to check on overinvoicing. All imports in excess of an invoice value of £1,000 were, in future, to be subject to preshipment quality and quantity inspection, and price comparison.

> Foreign exchange allocation licenses issued by the Central Bank of Kenya Exchange Control are required for all imports except for certain specified exceptions. Importers were required to apply for foreign exchange allocation licenses before placing firm orders. Sellers were requested to give at least ten days notice before shipment to the Inspection Agency indicating the place where the goods could be inspected and the expected time of shipment. After completion of the inspection, the Inspection Agency would issue a report of findings, which would either be a clear report of the findings, if the inspection yielded a satisfactory result, or a non-negotiable report of findings if the inspection revealed discrepancies.[26]

At the same time, the five schedules discussed above were kept unchanged, although Schedule A items were to be given foreign exchange automatically. All OGL items, excluding those in Schedules D and E, were also to be given foreign exchange automatically.

Under this import licensing system, almost all applications for imports had to pass through the Department of Trade and Supplies, but this requirement had little to do with overinvoicing. The major reason was the "logic of controls." It was believed that commercial banks were not checking properly on whether an item was really outside Schedules A to E. Thus, it was decided that, at the same time as introducing the General Superintendence system, all imports over £100 should be checked by the Department of Trade and Supplies to see whether they were truly outside the five schedules.

Effects of Policy Measures

The measures created chaos. Although delays of up to ten days by General Superintendence were experienced, they were tolerable despite the cost. The major bottleneck

26. D. S. McRae, *Import Licensing in Kenya*, p. 17.

was the Department of Trade and Supplies. Applications increased to 300 a day, and the department fell so far behind that a rush program was made necessary the following April to clear a backlog of about 6,000 applications.[27]

The problem was most acute for small, uninfluential firms, especially those outside Nairobi, some of which had to wait as long as four months for approval. Even well placed firms experienced delays of more than a month before their papers even reached General Superintendence. Few of the firms visited by the mission had not been affected by delays to a greater or lesser extent.

The operation of the system was extremely time consuming and frustrating to almost all firms. Applications forms were delayed for trivial reasons. (One was returned because it did not state that the cargo, originating in Rotterdam, was coming by sea!) Managers had to make many visits to the Department of Trade and Supplies licensing officers—often with little result.

They were costly delays, indeed, and the economic cost had to be added to the direct cost of the inspection service itself of almost £1 million a year. A recent study by McRae indicated that about one-third of fifty firms interviewed were in serious difficulties because of raw materials shortages. The mission's own interviews revealed a similar state of affairs. Some firms had to close down. Others were operating at reduced levels of activity.[28]

Because of the delays, firms were using air freight for items that would otherwise have gone by sea. In addition, firms, especially in construction, were no longer able to air freight major replacements on a twenty-four hour basis, and were holding larger inventories. In general, desired inventories have increased considerably—with serious potential implications for both the balance of payments and economic efficiency.

Yet another problem was that to avoid inspection importers would break down imports into amounts of less than £1,000. This practice merely increases handling and shipping charges, which, like many of the other costs discussed above, result in a loss of foreign exchange.

Reform of the System

It is open to question whether this system will even achieve its immediate objective. International firms can probably conceal overinvoicing from most eyes, and those who wish to expatriate capital will often be traders who can easily import in values of less than £1,000 at a time. Thus, the costs may well have outweighed the benefits so far. Moreover, it is almost impossible to detect variations of up to 5 percent in prices, and such variations must be common.

The first step has been to reform procedures. Since July 2, 1973, applications for imports other than those in Schedules I to IV no longer have to go to the Department of Trade and Supplies, but can instead be sent directly to the Central Bank. (It would be still better if both intermediaries could be bypassed, and invoices were sent directly to General Superintendence.)[29]

Incentives to overinvoice can be further reduced by increasing duties on low tariff imports. This would affect companies engaged in tax evasion, and people trying to get capital out through overinvoicing rather than the currency black market.

In the meantime, the focus of any system of policing should be on low or zero

---

27. "The administrative procedures introduced to implement this inspection-service have been overcumbersome, and delays in the processing of forms have led to a serious shortage of a number of commodities in our economy." Budget speech, June 14, 1973.

28. Details of the cost of delays and allegations of extensive corruption appear in the *Sunday Nation,* April 15, 1973.

29. This suggestion was made by the Executive Officer of the Kenya Association of Manufacturers, in the *Daily Nation,* May 13, 1973.

duty items. Few people are going to tax themselves by overinvoicing on other items, and most people do have a choice, since many imported goods are still subject to low rates of duty.

A Policy for Capital Flight

A relationship no doubt exists between the pressures of Kenyanization on the expatriate business community and the flight of capital. Although there are no hard facts about the extent of capital flight, the Government is convinced that the problem is serious and has, as stated, introduced controls to stem the outflow of capital. These measures, we believe, are costly and not completely effective and we shall suggest an alternative approach to the problem.

First let us restate the vicious circle in the relationship between Kenyanization and the flight of capital. Pressures for Kenyanization naturally lead to new demands for the repatriation of capital. The greatest pressure for the repatriation of capital, it seems, comes from noncitizen traders who have been displaced under the trading licensing regulations, have no plans to remain in Kenya, and have little interest in holding Kenyan assets other than their own businesses. But it must be assumed that the problem is much wider than that involving the Asian traders. Other categories of people, who include expatriate personnel who have finished their contracts, and many Asian and even African citizens, have their own reasons for wanting to convert their savings into foreign exchange.

The fear of a critical drain on foreign exchange reserves has obliged the Kenyan authorities to impose an increasing range of costly controls on the repatriation of capital. The foreigner with capital to export fears (with justification) that even more stringent controls will apply as time goes on and therefore he tries even harder to "get his money out while he can." But controls may also reduce the rate of Kenyanization since, for example, the noncitizen businessman is unlikely to sell his business to a citizen *voluntarily* (or to sell shares in his business), if he heavily discounts the chances of realizing his assets in the currency of his choice. Thus, the circle is closed.

The first step towards an alternative solution is to accept that the capital saved by noncitizens in Kenya is going to flow out of Kenya, in one way or another, at some time or another, whatever controls are imposed.[30] Short of expropriation of capital, capital repatriation is one unavoidable cost of Kenyanizing the economy. Once this fact is faced and accepted, it becomes possible to plan an orderly transfer of capital with the least disruption to the economy.

The first objective is, of course, to prevent rapid and disorderly capital flight. It is clearly not feasible for Kenya to "lift the lid" off the pent-up demand for foreign exchange. There are no reliable estimates of potential capital flight, but the mission has used a figure of £250 million as a rough order of magnitude of the value of assets of the Asian community alone and, of course, Kenya cannot afford capital outflow of such magnitude unless it is spread over a long period of time. The question, then, is how to achieve an orderly transfer of foreign capital.[31] As an alternative to costly controls and regulations which are now employed to slow down capital flight, we suggest that Kenya might use a market mechanism, both to secure a more orderly transfer of capital and to speed up the process of Kenyanization.

One alternative might be to provide noncitizens with an alternative and acceptable

---

30. The exchange control regulations accept this fact in the case of *emigrants* (the critical question being the *rate* of repatriation) but not in the case of residents.

31. In view of the vast amounts involved, it would seem appropriate for Government to consider how to retain a greater proportion of this capital in the country, for example, by persuading noncitizens to invest in alternative fields of enterprise. However, there appears to be no action program of this kind.

medium, such as a foreign exchange bond, in return for their capital assets. There are, of course, various other possibilities for dealing with the problem of capital flight not dealt with here. The mission's purpose is not to argue for any particular solution, but to indicate that there are feasible alternatives to costly controls.

Most important is to find some way of dealing with the basic situation—and we wish to reemphasize its seriousness. The transition from expatriate structure to the Kenyanized economy is vital for Kenya. In this process, techniques of persuasion and incentives are likely to be far more effective than controls and exhortations. It will be very unfortunate if the tail of capital flight is allowed to wag the dog of overall economic management. Finally, the time for decisive policy action is *now* because once controls became entrenched, they will be far more difficult to dismantle in the future.

Worries about capital flight, tax evasion, and overinvoicing have led to a new, chaotic, control system. It is the mission's view that the problem can be tackled on several fronts. First, administrative procedures can be drastically overhauled; second, the incentive to overinvoice can be reduced by raising tariffs on low duty items, and by not taking shares in subsidiaries of major international firms; finally, the pressure of capital flight itself can be reduced by replacing absolute controls with an orderly system of transfer.

Conclusion

It is clear that in the recent past, Kenya moved into an era of controls, which, like mice, bred more of their own kind. Hopes for development, especially exporting, could well be frustrated in this environment, for already many classic problems have arisen, and the psychology of controls is now firmly established in the thinking of both the public and private sectors. The Government, aware of the problem, is slowly drawing back from the worst excesses, but can go much further.

Suggestions made in this chapter are that alternative methods, using incentives, can be employed, and such an approach is consistent with Kenyan attitudes and with the discussion in Chapter 3. The time to try this new direction is now.

Chapter 5

Foreign Private Investment

This topic has been most thoroughly covered in the ILO/UNDP report[1] and, for that reason, this analysis will be brief, will not attempt to be comprehensive, but will focus on a few key issues. Since many of the subjects discussed have already been considered elsewhere, reference to previous parts of the report will be made, where appropriate.

The Role of Foreign Private Investment

The net inflow of long-term private capital has been rather large in the recent past, as can be seen in the following table. From 1969 to 1971, 53 percent of net long term capital inflow was private. Although important, this type of capital inflow is also very volatile, as can be seen by comparing 1970 and 1971 figures.

LONG TERM CAPITAL FLOWS
(in £ million)

	1969			1970			1971		
	Debit	Credit	Net Credit	Debit	Credit	Net Credit	Debit	Credit	Net Credit
Private enterprises	1.9	14.9	13.0	2.1	18.4	16.3	1.7	10.2	'8.5
All public[1]	0.6	7.8	7.2	Cr.4.1	8.8	12.9	Cr.3.1	10.7	13.8
Total	2.5	22.7	20.2	Cr.2.0	27.2	29.2	Cr.1.4	20.9	22.3

[1] Includes government enterprises, local government, and Kenya Government.
Source: *Economic Survey*, 1972.

Another way of evaluating the overall importance of this type of capital inflow is to relate net foreign investment to private capital formation in the monetary economy. Over the same three years, the proportion has been 25, 24, and 11 percent respectively. In the years 1967 and 1968, the proportions were 18 and 19 percent. Thus, foreign investment has been extremely important in financing the balance of payments and, at the same time, private investment.

The two most important sectors of total private activity recently financed by foreign private investment are tourism and manufacturing. Most detailed data are for the latter. An UNCTAD paper[2] estimated that private long term capital inflow accounted for 35 percent of capital expenditure in manufacturing in 1966, 33 percent in 1967, and 42 percent in 1968. An even more significant figure, however, is the ratio of manufacturing investment involving foreign capital to total manufacturing investment. The ILO/UNDP report,[3] using Hermann's[4] data, calculated this ratio to be about 60 percent, which may

1. See pp. 18, 101, 178–9, 184–92, 437–57, and 463–68.
2. L. Needleman, Sanjaya Lall, R. Lacey, and J. Seagrave, *Balance of Payments Effects on Foreign Investment: Case Studies of Jamaica and Kenya*, UNCTAD document TD/B/C.3/79/Add.2/Corr.1, June 30, 1970, mimeo; cited in ILO/UNDP report, p. 441.
3. P. 442.
4. B. Hermann, *Some Basic Data for Analyzing the Political Economy of Foreign Investment in Kenya*, Discussion Paper No. 112 (Nairobi: Institute of Development Studies, 1971). His data derived from the Registrar of Companies, therefore, are legal, not actual figures. Too much faith should not be placed in the details.

be regarded as an indication of the extent of foreign control in manufacturing. (These data are not thought very accurate, so the figures should be seen as indicative only.)

Foreign controlled firms are especially important in tourism, petroleum refining, tobacco, cement, metal products, and textiles. Foreign production plays a major role in many other industries, including miscellaneous foods, footwear, paint, soap, and miscellaneous chemicals.

Government Attitudes and Incentives to Foreign Private Capital

Basic Policy

"The Kenya Government has encouraged foreign investment since the attainment of national independence, although always subject to certain controls."[5] In fact, the Government's attitude has been decidedly ambivalent, desiring on the one hand, the inflow of funds and associated skills and entrepreneurship, but wishing, on the other hand, to secure "an active ... and growing participation of Kenya citizens in management and ownership of industry."[6] The Government's ambivalence also shows in whether or not to secure more control over the activities of foreigners. In general, however, the requirements of growth have come first, as has been stressed in several Plan documents.

However, the Government's policy towards private enterprise is partly explained by its basic attitude, namely its desire to take equity in new enterprises through the Industrial and Commercial Development Corporation (ICDC). It is the Government's belief that this increases its control over foreign firms. Of course, the policy also has a certain incentive effect for foreign investors, especially if the finance provided is in the form of low interest loan capital.

Incentives

The most important incentives[7] are the freedom to expatriate profit and industrial protection—these are, undoubtedly, attractive to foreign firms and both provide opportunities to expatriate foreign exchange which has not been earned. The Foreign Investment Protection Act of 1964 provides the basic guarantees. The Act gives freedom to expatriate profits and "the approved proportion of net proceeds of sale" to companies having an "approved Status Certificate," which is granted by the Minister of Finance at the suggestion of the New Projects Committee. However, each individual transfer of funds requires approval by the Bank of Kenya. In addition, Kenya has been most generous about approving payments of royalties, or contributions to parent company overheads, or research and development.

Profits tax is 40 percent, and a 12.5 percent withholding tax is levied, in addition, on dividends paid by private and public companies, but branches of foreign companies have until recently not paid withholding tax.[8] The most important tax allowance is the 20 percent capital cost allowance in the first year of operation, which is available to all firms.

As already discussed extensively, considerable protection is granted to manufacturing firms. Individual companies are able to negotiate special privileges in the form

---

5. ILO/UNDP report, p. 184.
6. *Development Plan 1970–74*, p. 304.
7. The main sources are the ILO/UNDP report, pp. 437–40 and *A Guide to Industrial Investment in Kenya,* Ministry of Commerce and Industry, 2nd Edition, 1972, especially pp. 76–84.
8. In the 1973/74 Budget, a differential tax on branches was proposed. In any case, the past incentive to organize as a branch has been offset, to some extent, by the fact that ICDC has not dealt with branches, nor provided funds.

of duty refunds and quantitative restrictions. In fact, it appears that foreign firms are lodged securely where protection is highest.[9]

Availability of Credit

The Government has recently restricted the access of foreign firms to cheap finance from the banking system. However, finance can still be fairly easily secured from ICDC (which in some years has been greater than the equity brought in by the enterprises), from other financial institutions, and from the local stock exchange (with the approval of the Capital Issues Committee). In all, some 30 percent of all local private and public capital invested in manufacturing over the 1964–70 period went into foreign controlled companies.[10] Fifty-three percent of the resources, excluding retained earnings, in new investments by foreign owned enterprises were domestically supplied.[11]

This ready supply of domestic funds to foreign enterprises is an important incentive, although there are crucial implications for their evaluation. The return to the project may well exceed the return on the domestic capital invested.

Maximum Advantage from Foreign Private Investment

The issue of how much foreign investment to have is, in the last resort, a political one, and is not discussed here. The more immediate question is how to get the greatest possible benefit from such investment, because of its enormous importance to Kenya, and because of the considerable incentives which are now offered to the overseas investor. Unfortunately, in many respects, the present environment provides an object lesson in how not to get much advantage from it at all.

The potential advantages of foreign investment are essentially twofold: one is the capital inflow, which in Kenya is by no means an insignificant consideration; the second is the supply of skills and technical information which accompany foreign investment. We have no doubt that both these advantages can be enjoyed by Kenya.

Trade Policy

As has been shown in Chapter 3, investors in manufacturing are expatriating unearned foreign exchange through the protection system. Essentially a transfer from agricultural producers to manufacturing is taking place. Thus, the first and most important reform in the incentives to foreign private investment must be in the trade policy system. Without it, what amounts to pure "exploitation" in the classic sense, will continue. Moreover, this exploitation is the direct consequence of government policies.

Failing such reform, the only projects that can be assumed to be economically viable (or at least not to make the country worse off) are those which are overwhelmingly geared to exports. Certain agricultural processing activities come into this category as do many tourist projects. It is, of course, perfectly conceivable that even such export industries are not earning Kenya as much as they could, because of illegal currency activities, overinvoicing of imports, or underinvoicing of exports. But it is most improbable that any export industries, in contrast to many import substitute industries, are resulting in a net loss of foreign exchange.

9. ILO/UNDP report, p. 446.
10. Ibid., p. 453, from B. Hermann, *Analyzing the Political Economy* (for qualification, see footnote 4 above).
11. Ibid., p. 452, from B. Hermann, *Analyzing the Political Economy* (for qualification, see footnote 4 above).

Trade reform would allow—indeed, encourage—foreign firms to concentrate on what they probably know best, namely exporting. Since they are based overseas, they will have ready, first hand information of export markets. A strategy of using foreign firms to supply final processing and marketing of Kenyan produce would take greatest advantage of their true comparative advantage. In the reformed policy system, such activities would no longer be penalized, while import substituting activity would no longer be especially protected.

Trade policy reform would also put an end to the very dubious practice of giving "infant industry" protection to subsidiaries of powerful foreign companies. We have pointed out that Kenya can reap considerable advantages from such investment. But a multi-national corporation, to take an extreme example, is no infant, and if such a wealthy investor is unwilling to bear the cost of setting up a new operation in Kenya, it is not at all clear why the Kenyan consumer should. If Kenya wishes to promote infant industries, she should remember that the most deserving "infants" are her own entrepreneurs and newly established industrialists. The costs of providing protection in the domestic market might be more acceptable if protection were designed mainly to shelter indigenous Kenyan businessmen, as now happens under the Kenya Industrial Estates program.

Trade policy reform would also substantially reduce incentives to overinvoice. As has been shown already, incentives to overinvoice depend usually on the relation between tariffs and the corporation tax. (Additional taxes on management fees and royalties equal to the uniform tariff make sense, since these can be regarded as traded inputs.)[12] Given Kenyan manufacturing's high share of imports in costs, this reform would gain, rather than lose, revenue.

It appears that the grossest defects in the contribution of foreign enterprise to Kenya are the results of trade policy. These defects can be removed, and benefits, such as a greater orientation by foreign firms to exports, can be secured through thorough reform. At the moment, every incentive is provided to foreign firms to expatriate foreign exchange they have neither earned nor saved, to overinvoice imports, and to sit snugly behind protective walls. It is within the power of the Government to change all of this. The results may be smaller investment in total (although this is not necessarily so, as is shown by the high foreign investment for export in countries like Brazil, Israel, and Korea), but the investment would at least be of benefit to Kenya.

Local Participation

If the allocation of functions were made on the basis of comparative advantage, most big businesses would be under foreign ownership, while most Kenyans will be in small business. In due course, the line would become blurred as successful African businessmen move up the economic ladder. However, it is undeniable that progress will be slow if left to natural processes, and, as a result, for obvious and compelling political reasons, the Government has tried to accelerate the process.

So far, Kenya has fostered local participation by encouraging African businessmen and by extending financial participation in foreign companies, either by the state, or to a much lesser degree, by private individuals. In fact, state participation in equity has been the major means of Kenyanizing ownership of the large scale modern sector.

The Kenya Government has followed a cautious and scrupulously fair policy in nationalizing industries or acquiring shares, and its policy has done much to reinforce the confidence of investors. Some degree of state participation in new enterprises has become accepted and even desired by foreign investors. Yet such participation can be

---

12. The Government now imposes a 20 percent withholding tax on royalties and management fees.

costly, for several reasons. First, as already shown, the provision of domestic equity increases the incentive to overinvoice, and thereby to expatriate the return on local capital. Second, the provision of domestic loans at low interest rates also allows foreign firms to expatriate returns on local capital. Third, the more local resources are available, the lower the incentive to the foreign firm to bring in capital. Since capital is scarce overall, funds are thereby taken away from areas where private foreign finance is not readily available, such as agriculture, small scale business, or social services. Moreover, should private firms be forced to borrow more overseas without government guarantee, the risks of project failure are not borne by the Government.[13]

The most direct and obvious cost of state participation in private enterprise is, of course, budgetary and, in the case of acquisition of foreign held shares, this cost reflects on the balance of payments. Quite a different and very serious cost to state participation, however, is the growing management burden imposed on senior government personnel. State participation (however small) usually means a government member being appointed to a board, resulting in yet another demand on the time of senior government officials who are already overburdened. Generally, it is clear that the civil service has a difficult enough job in trying to run the public sector and its complex machinery without intervening in the private sector. This is one of the reasons why the mission has expressed preference for alternatives to direct intervention to influence behavior in the private sector.

What are the economic, as opposed to political, benefits of local participation? First, in some instances, local participation may be a necessary condition for a foreign enterprise to establish itself at all in Kenya, even when the project is economically and financially viable. The firm may be cautious, and if the benefits to the country are sufficiently great, it may be sensible for Government to participate with equity or loan funds to clinch the investment. Second, the Government may think that provision of equity is a useful way to increase Kenyan "control" over the firm's activities, a somewhat dubious argument. Failing direct control over management, it is extremely difficult to check on what a firm is doing. Generally, therefore, it seems economically wise to limit participation by the state, although political reasons for such action must be understood and accepted.

Tax Reform

Apart from the discussion above on trade policy, there is no further question about tax incentives in relation to foreign investment. The refusal to offer tax holidays seems sensible. Because of double taxation agreements, tax holidays are usually no more than a gift of tax to another country.

Investment Appraisals

Recommendations made by the ILO/UNDP mission to improve the system of negotiation with foreign investors are sensible.[14] An important first step is to improve the economic appraisal of all proposed investments. This is essential, while trade policy remains unreformed, since many uneconomic projects are financially very attractive. The

---

13. The one exception to this argument is when Government has access to a perfectly elastic supply of foreign funds at interest rates below those which foreign firms must pay. In this case, it may make sense for the Government itself to borrow (since it foregoes nothing), bear some of the project risk, and charge the foreign firm what it would have had to pay. In this way, the Kenyan authorities can get a little rental surplus from their privileged access to foreign funds. This theoretical possibility is unlikely to occur in practice.

14. ILO/UNDP report, p. 189.

purpose of using a precise and rigorous cost benefit analysis is to ensure rejection of all projects that do not give a return to national resources at least equal to the opportunity cost of capital. Of course, in the event of complete reform, as a result of which economic and financial returns are more nearly equated, improved economic appraisal would be largely unnecessary.

The exact system to be used is not very important, except that it should be complete, and that tradable goods should be evaluated at border prices.[15] It will be important for projects involving Kenyan, as well as foreign capital, to derive a return to national capital. Even viable projects can be nonviable, from the national point of view, if excessive profits are expatriated. A major discrepancy between overall and national economic returns is a warning signal that protection is too high, or that some other aspect of the project, such as the cost of domestic loan funds, should be renegotiated.

Factor Intensity

This seems to be one area where "getting the most out of foreign investment" does not pose any particular problem. The ILO/UNDP report indicates that, if anything, foreign firms in similar lines of activity as domestic firms are more labor intensive.[16] Thus, any problem applies to large scale activity as a whole.

The case remains that the influence of foreign techniques and products on large scale manufacturing, both foreign owned and domestic, must affect the factor intensity of the sector. There is no doubt that informal activity is substantially less capital intensive. However, from a policy point of view, this raises questions not about the role of foreign investment in the formal sector, but the role of the formal sector—influenced by foreign techniques, as it is—in the economy as a whole. The issue, essentially, is whether there is any net benefit in having a formal and therefore relatively capital intensive sector at all in an economy like Kenya's.

Conclusion

It appears that Kenya can reap much greater benefits from foreign investment than at present. The most important changes are in trade policy—failing that, in appraisal technique—and in the willingness to limit foreign firms' access to local resources. Changes in the directions suggested here will provide incentives to foreign firms to act in the best interests of Kenya.

How to Attract Foreign Investment

We have been concerned with the creation of an environment which will get the most out of foreign investment. We will now discuss how to attract the most foreign investment into a favorable environment. What are the policies most annoying to foreign firms who might consider establishment in Kenya? How can they be changed? These are two important questions, since the Kenyan authorities realize the need to attract more investment in order to fulfill their rather ambitious Plan targets.

On the basis of the mission's talks with foreign private firms in Kenya, it is clear that only a few policies—most already discussed in this report—are regarded as very hampering. One major problem has been the exchange controls on imports. These

---

15. Domestic Resource Cost, Social Effective Rate of Protection, Net Present Value, or Internal Rate of Return would all be acceptable. All of these are vastly superior to calculations like value-added generated, or employment per unit of capital employed.

16. ILO/UNDP report, p. 450.

controls have been annoying because they were unforeseen, inconvenient, and have involved firms in extensive bureaucratic tussles. All these factors amount to extra cost and decreased security of operation. Another often mentioned difficulty is that of getting foreign exchange for business travel. Finally, and perhaps the most frequently cited of all, is Kenyanization policy—the bureaucratic way it is carried out, the lack of advance notice, the apparent arbitrariness of many decisions—which has undoubtedly created immense annoyance. Firms do not like fighting with extensive bureaucratic regulation.

All these aspects of Kenyanization policy may be excellently intentioned, and even —although it is dubious—be the best possible in the circumstances. However, there can be little doubt that Kenyanization creates a lack of incentive to new investment by established firms and may even deter would-be investors from "sniffing at the edges."

Trade policy reform will affect the composition and possibly the size of foreign private investment. The question of incentives arises. Although the most important constraints on foreign investment are those just discussed, it may well be that some positive incentives should be developed to offset the reduction in protection in the home market. A duty free zone would be a possibility. However, it will not necessarily be the case that a change in trade policy *will* lead to a reduction in foreign investment, or in industrial investment overall; therefore, further incentives may well be unnecessary, and should be given thought.

In addition, now is an opportune time, as Kenya enters the second decade, to issue new guidelines to the foreign investor. There is already a clearly formulated policy towards the overseas investor in the urban formal sector which could be modified in ways already discussed. But such guidelines need to go further than for manufacturing or mining or tourism, and should be extended to other sectors, particularly agriculture. We believe that agriculture—and especially large scale agro-business integrated with small farm production—is an obvious field for greater foreign investment. Despite the political problems associated with foreign use of land, agriculture is an area of great potential benefit, and there is need for a clear policy statement—a charter for the agricultural investor—to replace the present atmosphere of uncertainty and ad hoc decisionmaking.

Implications of Foreign Investment for Savings

The existence of a large foreign stake in the private sector has important implications for the argument that greater capital intensity entails greater saving, and so growth. As was argued in Chapter 3, greater capital intensity need not mean higher profit shares, since the wage rate is by no means invariant among techniques, firms, or sectors.[17] If movement to a highly capital intensive sector means more foreign investment (and foreign firms do appear to be concentrated in more capital intensive activities), then a substantial portion of extra profits will be expatriated. As the ILO/UNDP mission has shown, an arithmetic average of savings out of profits on foreign equity was only 58 percent from 1967 to 1970.[18] Thus, 42 percent of incremental profits would be expatriated.

This point by no means exhausts the disadvantages of such a strategy, since it will reduce employment in the short run, and may even do so in the long run, if subsequent investment is increasingly capital intensive.[19] Moreover, it is possible to raise savings by other means. However, foreign investment tends to break the logic of the argument at an early stage. Movement from a low profit domestically owned sector to a high profit foreign-owned sector may well not increase investable resources to Kenya. (Movement

17. See also ILO/UNDP report, pp. 135–7.
18. Ibid., p. 136.
19. Ibid., p. 137.

within the foreign-owned subsector from low to high profit activities will increase investable resources if propensities to retain are constant.)

Local Entrepreneurship and Innovation

Two fundamental policy issues stand behind any decision about the acceptability of foreign investment. These issues concern Kenya's basic strategy and the implications of her great dependence on foreign skills and entrepreneurship.

The first point is that foreign investment's domination of the formal sector may have turned many enterprising Kenyans into managers, not entrepreneurs.[20] As we have noted earlier in this report, the greatest deficiency in Kenya is entrepreneurship, and it may be questioned how fast and how successfully local businessmen can be encouraged as long as they operate in the shadow of large and well established foreign firms. Some deliberate restrictions on foreign enterprise might possibly be justified, even at the expense of some growth, if they could lead to faster development of independent Kenyan entrepreneurship. But any policy of restricting noncitizen activity needs to be formulated with great care, and its effects calculated very carefully, lest it should do more harm than good. The mission feels that the foreign investor can continue to make a valuable contribution to Kenya's development, and that this contribution could be much greater than in the past. However, in determining future industrial strategy, it will be necessary to consider how far foreign enterprises can be made more supportive of (or at least not detrimental to) the development of local businesses.

The mission feels that a formula for coexistence can be found. First of all, at the most basic level of investment policy, the foreign firm, like the African businessman, should be encouraged to enter fields in which it appears to have a comparative advantage, especially in providing the technical skills, access to markets and forms of managerial talent which simply do not exist in Kenya. If foreign and Kenyan businessmen are encouraged through suitable policy instruments each to operate in his own field of advantage, the extent of direct competition can be reduced substantially, if not eliminated, and the Kenyan economy can benefit from the contribution which both sectors have to make.[21]

Once the general role of foreign enterprises had been clarified, in the opinion of the mission it would be possible to go further towards making foreign and local businesses more complementary with one another. This can be done in both direct and indirect ways. For example, there is some scope, as the ILO/UNDP report suggests, for large scale business to subcontract to smaller firms directly.[22] But we believe there is much greater scope for ensuring that foreign enterprises fit into the whole strategy for developing small scale African enterprise. For example, foreign investment in agro-

---

20. P. Marris and A. Somerset, *African Businessmen*, p. 4., "The largest concerns in Kenya are mostly European owned or branches of international companies. They recruit and train African managers and may co-opt distinguished Africans onto their boards, but they do not depend on African entrepreneurship. This perhaps is their weakness. They tend to pre-empt only the most obvious opportunities in conditions contrived to favor their chances by a government anxious for their investment. The element of entrepreneurship is diffused among prospective investor, government and supportive agencies, who may manipulate the economy to accommodate a preconceived pattern of organization. Such companies can remain an enclave of sophisticated management, poorly integrated with the rest of society and stultifying as much as encouraging its potential economic vitality."

21. Taking the longer view, a larger foreign owned sector *now* can, of course, mean a larger sector to Kenyanize *later*. There are obvious benefits to be gained if Kenya can induce foreign investors to establish enterprises in Kenya, provide the necessary know-how, eliminate the teething troubles, find the markets, train the labor, and then hand over smoothly operating businesses to Kenyan ownership and control.

22. Chapter 13.

business can provide a market outlet for expanded smallholder production; and in the manufacture of intermediates, foreign firms can reinforce, rather than displace, local technology.[23]

Conclusion

Foreign private enterprise and investment are extremely important to Kenya and the Government wishes to maintain a large flow of overseas investment as part of its overall strategy for continued rapid development. Yet foreign enterprises have not always brought benefits to the country, and the proliferation of controls has diverted the energies of businessmen towards finding new ways to circumvent such controls. An improvement in the policy environment in which the private sector operates could, at the same time, enhance the already considerable attractions of investing in Kenya to increase the benefits which Kenya can derive from foreign private investment. However, underlying these considerations lies a more basic question: whether a major reliance on foreign enterprise may retard the development of domestic entrepreneurship and innovation. If so, it is possible that current policy could prove very shortsighted in the longer run. We believe that formal sector activities, including foreign enterprises, can be made more supportive of Kenyan entrepreneurs and of the general development strategy advocated by the report. The first and most important step is to define what role the foreign private investor in Kenya should play.

---

23. For example, by manufacturing building components which are suitable for the use of small and labor intensive building contractors. This complementarity with local industry should be an important consideration in project appraisal.

CHAPTER 6

CONCLUSIONS

Our analysis of the key issues which we think now faces Kenya's private sector has concentrated on three major themes: incentives versus controls, the costs and benefits of formal urban activity in the present policy environment, and the basic trade-offs which might remain in a reformed environment. In the concluding section, we return to these three basic issues to highlight the fundamental policy choices which Kenya faces in the second decade.

Although the system in Kenya is still one primarily of free enterprise, the degree of government interference in the economy in key matters such as prices, trade, foreign exchange, and manpower has increased substantially over recent years. There is an understandable tendency for governments to believe that direct action and controls can be effectively used to achieve desired changes in production or factor use. There is also a natural tendency to turn towards controls as a quick and easy solution in times of crisis.

However, it appears from our review of the use of controls, in other countries as well as in Kenya, that direct intervention has rarely been fruitful and has often either been counterproductive or had serious side effects which had not been foreseen. In Kenya we see the very real danger that the psychology of control will become entrenched, and that existing controls will inevitably breed more controls. We have pointed out the risks of such a trend, not least of which is that a disproportionate share of Kenya's skilled manpower will be drawn into largely unsuccessful attempts to police the economy. We believe that it is both appropriate and urgent for Kenya—a country with a firm commitment to a private enterprise system—to assess the appropriate extent of intervention and to halt the proliferation of controls before it goes much further.

At various points in our analysis—for example, in discussing imports, overinvoicing, or employment—we have suggested that price incentives will usually be more effective than direct controls as instruments for manipulating the behavior of the private sector. The detailed design of a system of appropriate price incentives will obviously take some time to work out; but the necessary first step is the basic commitment to use the price system, in preference to direct intervention, whenever possible.

Given the right price incentives, the formal sector can look after its own, and Kenya's interests, extremely well without further assistance. The first priority for the use of government manpower and energies are those areas of the economy, for example, small scale agriculture, the informal sector, and social services, which cannot look after themselves. Therefore, the mission's recommendation is not for the Government to withdraw from the development field, but, rather, to focus its scarcest resources on the areas where development assistance is most urgently required. Efforts to control the formal sector in detail waste these scarce resources.

Policy Reform in the Urban Formal Sector

The urban formal sector is operating in a distorted environment, largely because of trade, wage, and credit policies, which reduce the efficiency of its own operation and impose a burden on the rest of the economy. Many of the problems that concern the Government most—unemployment, rural poverty, and the slow growth of nonprimary exports—are a direct consequence of (or are being exacerbated by) the distorted environment. It is almost certainly true that, in present circumstances, formal activity is acting against, rather than in support of, most of Kenya's major development goals.

A reform in trade policy is the most important step towards improving the situation. Through the deflation of urban real wages, and an increase in rural real incomes, such a reform should go some way towards curing the problems created by the "wage gap." At least the urban formal sector itself should be more efficient and its external costs substantially reduced under a reformed trade policy.

Some Basic Trade-Offs

Even if a substantial reform of the policy environment were to take place, however, the Kenya Government would still be left with some basic choices, which have already been alluded to several times.

A strategy of concentration on the formal sector will almost inevitably conflict with the goal of rapid Kenyanization. Formal activity requires, to a great degree, the skills which, at present, only foreigners can supply. Furthermore, any strategy of rapid growth —even one less "formal" in orientation—will require the use of many expatriates in advisory and managerial positions.

Another problem is that the formal urban sector will continue to provide real wages above those in the rest of the economy. Because the informal urban sector is, in this situation, a waiting ground for formal sector jobs, any encouragement given to the informal sector will increase its size but not the incomes of those within it, unless there is also a reduction in the wage gap. Returns (in the urban informal sector) will otherwise be driven down by migration, and attempts at informal sector development may merely serve to increase the scale of urban distress.

Finally, there may be a trade-off between formal foreign dominated activity and the development of Kenyan indigenous entrepreneurship. Undoubtedly, in an appropriate environment, the formal sector can provide considerable growth, especially in tourism and manufacturing. If foreign firms take advantage of profitable opportunities open only to their abilities, growth will be higher than without them. Nevertheless, appropriate relations between large scale foreign formal businesses and Kenyan entrepreneurs must be developed, so that the latter are supported, not stifled.

Appendix A: A Nontechnical Explanation of Effective Protection

In this Appendix we attempt to explain what effective protection is and why it is important. The purpose is to make the discussion of the private sector comprehensible to the lay person.[1]

The most useful explanation of effective protection is an example. Assume the existence of a small country which exports tea and imports a range of manufactured goods. The equilibrium exchange rate between the domestic currency (the Ror) and the US dollar is Ror 2 to $1, and there are no tariffs on any goods. Among the imports are trucks, which cost the country $10,000 in foreign exchange, or Ror 20,000 each. The country would like to produce the trucks domestically, but would have to import the components to make them. These components cost $8,000 (or Ror 16,000) per truck, including freight and handling charges. Local assembly costs Ror 5,000 in labor costs; there are no other variable costs at all, and the local cost of production would be Ror 21,000.

Since all trucks are assumed identical, domestic consumers will not pay more than the price of the freely importable, duty free foreign truck. In free trade therefore there is no profit in constructing trucks domestically, since the margin of Ror 4,000 between the domestic price of trucks and the cost of the imported components does not even cover labor costs, let alone earn any profit.

Nevertheless, the Government is determined to save foreign exchange by proceeding with a strategy of import substitution. It decides to give protection to the industry, so as to give a rate of return of 10 percent on capital which is sufficient to induce domesic production.

To determine the required protection, the Government needs to know more about the capital requirements of the industry. As a matter of fact, the factory, all of which has to be imported, costs $10,000,000 or Ror 20,000,000. Once in full production, the factory will turn out 500 trucks annually. In order to get his 10 percent return, the owner must make Ror 4,000 on each truck or Ror 2,000,000 annually in profit.

Assuming labor is readily available at the going wage, a profit of Ror 4,000 per truck implies a domestic price of Ror 25,000. To achieve this price, the Government imposes a *nominal* rate of tariff on trucks of 25 percent. The situation would then be as follows:

Components of the Price of Trucks to Consumers
(Ror)

	Domestically Produced		Imported
Components	16,000	Truck	20,000
Labor	5,000	Duty	5,000
Profit	4,000		
Total	25,000		25,000

So far everybody appears to be happy—the Government, because it has saved foreign exchange (Ror 4,000 per truck, as a matter of fact), and the owner because he is making 10 percent. Everyone is happy except the consumer, who is paying Ror 5,000 more for his trucks, and the economist.

The economist asks what the true gain to the country is. To do this he estimates effective protection and viability at world prices. What does he mean by these terms and why do they matter?

---

1. A major textbook reference is M. Corden, *The Theory of Protection* (Oxford, 1971).

To explain *effective protection*, one must first consider the concept of value-added. The value-added in a process is the difference between the cost of the materials brought from outside into the factory and the sales value of the product. It is clear enough that the value which the process adds to the basic materials is the difference between these two prices. However, in the case described here, there are two different ways to measure value-added. In domestic prices, the value-added is Ror 9,000, or the difference between the price of the output (Ror 25,000) and of the components (Ror 16,000). In foreign exchange, however, the value-added is $2,000 or Ror 4,000. Effective protection concerns the difference between these two.

The concept of value-added has two important aspects. First, as is clear from the example, the value-added *in domestic prices* is equal to the returns to the two "primary factors of production"—labor and capital (i.e., the factory)—which are engaged directly in the activity. Second, the value-added *in world prices* is equal to the foreign exchange saved by the activity. In this example, the saving is $2,000, the difference between the cost of the truck and the imported components.

Effective protection is defined as measured domestic value-added minus world value-added expressed as a percentage. In the example, this comes to 125 percent,[2] which means that domestic value-added is 25 percent larger than world value-added. The concept is similar to that of nominal protection, except that, instead of assessing protection on the price of the good—25 percent in this example—it assesses protection on the value-added, and this is five times as great.

From an economic point of view effective protection is a more meaningful measure than nominal protection, because it measures protection given to the domestic factors of production, and therefore the attractiveness of the activity. That attractiveness is the motive power leading to reallocation of resources. The example showed a 125 percent effective protection was required to achieve a 10 percent rate of return on capital, the minimum needed to start the factory. (Effective protection can also take account of tariffs on imports. In our example a 10 percent tariff on the components would reduce domestic value-added to Ror 7,400 and effective protection to 85 percent. Thus, the protection to the value-added would be lowered.)

Where does the "additional" value-added come from? The answer is from the consumer. In comparison with the previous situation, when trucks cost Ror 20,000, trucks now cost Ror 25,000. The additional Ror 5,000 is a "tax" on the consumer which is transferred to the producer. This Ror 5,000, in addition to the world value-added of Ror 4,000, provides the domestic factors of production with their Ror 9,000. Alternatively, if the Government had already previously imposed the tariff, the Ror 5,000 is a transfer from government revenue. *In both cases the additional value-added does not imply an increase in GNP but a transfer from one section of the community to the producers of the protected goods.* The other sections are made correspondingly worse off. A corollary is that the domestic value-added at the official exchange rate far overstates the foreign exchange saving of the project—by 125 percent, in fact. The Ror 9,000 of value-added saves exactly $2,000, giving an exchange rate for the project of Ror 4.5 to $1. In other words, Ror 4.5 of domestic resources saves $1.

The last idea leads naturally to a consideration of viability. The Government has arranged a transfer to the produecrs of trucks which makes the project financially profitable. Viability, however, is a measure of the overall benefit of this policy to the community. A simple explanation would run as follows: when the labor is drawn from other activities, production in those activities will fall somewhat. Similarly, when capital is invested in the truck factory, it is withdrawn from another potential use. Let us suppose the labor required to make a truck is five manyears. Let us also suppose that

---

2. $\dfrac{Ror\ 9{,}000 - \$2{,}000}{\$2{,}000} \times 100 = \dfrac{\$2{,}500 - \$2{,}000}{\$2{,}000} \times 100 = 125\%$

one manyear in tea production produces $300 (Ror 600) worth of output. By withdrawing 5 manyears of labor from tea, production will fall by $1,500 (Ror 3,000), which is 60 percent of the wage paid in the truck factory. If the potential rate of return of capital in tea was 10 percent, or the same as in the truck factory, Ror 10 of capital invested in trucks would lose Ror 1 of tea output every year. Thus, for the Ror 20,000,000 ($10,000,000) invested in the factory, the loss would be Ror 2,000,000 ($1,000,000) or Ror 4,000 ($2,000) per truck.

It is now possible to make an overall foreign exchange balance, as shown below.

Value-Added in World Prices:	$2,000
Foreign exchange cost of tea foregone by transferring labor:	$1,500
Foreign exchange cost of tea foregone by transferring capital:	$2,000
Total Foreign Exchange Saving:	−$1,500

Taking into account the value of output foregone through the transfer of factors of production, it appears that this project *loses* $1,500 of foreign exchange over the situation when the labor and capital is occupied in tea. *The project is nonviable.* The 125 percent effective rate of protection permits the establishment of a project which makes the country's foreign exchange balance worse! However, if the labor had been totally unemployed, so that no output was foregone when it was transferred, the project would have been just viable—earning exactly 10 percent on capital.

This result is by no means the only possible one. For example, the project may have been viable. If the components had cost $6,000, the project would have made $500 per truck for the community. The high effective protection would have offset the fact that the financial cost of labor—Ror 5,000 per truck—overstates the economic cost of Ror 3,000 per truck. (The project was viable but unprofitable, and, therefore required protection.)[3] If the components had cost only $5,500, the effective protection would have turned a project already earning 10 percent on capital into one earning 22.5 percent.[4] If the components had cost $11,000 we would have an example of a hopelessly nonviable project—one with negative world value-added. Even if labor and capital were "free," the country would be worse off by having such a project.[5] (Such extreme cases are not rare—they have been found in every study, including those done on Kenya.) Finally, the tariff on inputs might have been 60 percent, which in the example where components cost $5,500 would have made measured domestic value-added Ror 7,400, and effective protection *minus* 18 percent.[6] In this case, a viable project economically would be financially unprofitable, earning only 6 percent on capital. (Such a situation could easily arise if the components were domestically manufactured behind a 60 percent tariff wall.)

The measures of effective protection and viability indicate what Government is doing and analyze the efficiency of policy. In the Kenya study, effective protection is found to be highly negatively correlated with viability. Thus, protection does not simply offset distortions in the labor market, or make more profitable activities which are already viable without protection. Protection makes possible activities which are nonviable, or in other words, which are net losers of foreign exchange. The external benefits of such projects have to be very large indeed to offset this great cost.

3. See following table, lines 2a and 2b.
4. See following table, lines 3a and 3b.
5. See following table, lines 4a and 4b.
6. See following table, line 3c.

Some Combinations of Tariffs and Prices of Components

Cost of Components	Tariff on Output %	Tariff on Input %	Domestic Value-Added Ror	World Value-Added $	Effective Rate of Protection %	Domestic Profitability (Rate of Return on Capital) %	World Price Viability (Overall Foreign Exchange Balance) $
1a) $ 8,000 (Ror 16,000)	0	0	4,000	2,000	0	−2.5	−1,500
1b) $ 8,000 (Ror 16,000)	25	0	9,000	2,000	125.0	10.0	−1,500
2a) $ 6,000 (Ror 12,000)	0	0	8,000	4,000	0	7.5	+500
2b) $ 6,000 (Ror 12,000)	25	0	13,000	4,000	62.5	20.0	+500
3a) $ 5,500 (Ror 11,000)	0	0	9,000	4,500	0	10.0	+1,000
3b) $ 5,500 (Ror 11,000)	25	0	14,000	4,500	55.6	22.5	+1,000
3c) $ 5,500 (Ror 11,000)	25	60	7,400	4,500	−17.8	6.0	+1,000
4a) $11,000 (Ror 22,000)	0	0	−2,000	−1,000	0	−17.5	−4,500
4b) $11,000 (Ror 22,000)	55	0	9,000	−1,000	n.a.[1]	10.0	−4,500

[1] Effective rates cannot be calculated for negative value-added industries.

Note: 1. Financial labor cost per truck is Ror 5,000, and economic labor cost is Ror 3,000 ($1,500).
2. The opportunity cost of capital is 10 percent, both economic and financial.
3. The world price of a truck is $10,000 (Ror 20,000).
4. The total cost of the factory is $10,000,000 (Ror 20,000,000).
5. The factory produces 500 trucks per annum.

Appendix B: Measures of Protection and Viability

The purpose of this note is to review the studies of effective protection used in the Private Sector annex, and to indicate the confidence it is possible to place in their general and specific results. Thus, the first section will deal with questions peculiar to the studies, while the second will be concerned with the usefulness of all studies of this kind.

Studies of Effective Protection and Viability in Kenya

The most important source for the annex was the study carried out by Phelps and Wasow.[1] A subsidiary source, employed in the analysis of the effects of transfer taxes, was a paper by R. Reimer.[2]

The Phelps and Wasow study derived its input-output data from the 1968 survey of industry. Evaluation was done for all individual firms employing more than fifty people. Thus, the study was extremely disaggregated. Domestic prices were derived from inter East African trade statistics, and unit values of firms' inputs and outputs. World prices were derived from East African export prices, Japanese import and export prices (after a transport cost adjustment), or, failing all else, tariff deflators. Capital stock data were derived from the 1968 survey, as were data on the total wage bill. The division between skilled and unskilled labor originated in the 1969 Enumeration of Employment. Skilled workers were defined as those earning more than Sh500 per month. The adjustment for nontraded goods was done by applying the average nominal rate of protection on traded goods to the proportion of the value of intermediate goods in their total value. The basic study was conducted at a level intermediate between the three- and four-digit levels.

Measures of protection are not, in themselves, very useful, since high rates of effective protection can either increase the profitability of an activity which is viable in world prices, or make profitable an otherwise unprofitable activity.[3] Thus, it is desirable to measure the viability of the various activities, as well as the effective protection accorded them, and then to compare the two. The protective system is more "inefficient" the higher the negative correlation between viability and protection.

The Phelps and Wasow study uses several measures of viability. The first, in line with the Heckscher-Ohlin theory, was factor proportions. In fact, two measures were employed, namely a capital-unskilled labor ratio, and a skilled labor-unskilled labor ratio. These performed very badly. The second measure of viability is "world price profitability."[4] The final measure is the "world price rate of return to factor inputs,"

---

1. M. G. Phelps and B. Wasow, *Measuring Protection and its Effects in Kenya*, Working Paper No. 37 (Nairobi: Institute of Development Studies, n.d.).
2. R. Reimer, *Effective Rates of Protection in East Africa*, Staff Paper No. 78 (Nairobi: Institute of Development Studies, July 1970).
3. This is in partial equilibrium. Assuming perfect competition and free factor mobility, all returns are equated, and the effects of protection are mainly on the allocation of resources. Factor returns will be affected in accordance with the Stolper-Samuelson theorem.
4. This is defined as:

$$WPR = \frac{WVA - W_u L_u - W_s L_s - R - D}{K}$$

where:
 WPR = world price profitability
 WVA = world value added
 W_u = wage rate (unskilled)
 W_s = wage rate (skilled)
 R = rent
 D = depreciation
 L_u = employment (unskilled)
 L_s = employment (skilled)
 K = capital stock

KEY ISSUES IN THE PRIVATE SECTOR 323

which measures the ratio of world value-added to the social cost of employing the factors making up value-added.[5]

There are various possible criticisms of these measures. The most important is that, since, in general equilibrium, the return to factors will not exceed their market opportunity costs (i.e., factor returns will be equated throughout the economy), measures of viability must use the correct shadow prices (i.e., market clearing prices of all factors in free trade, assuming perfect factor markets). Since the effect of protection is to change relative factor prices, the shadow prices of some will be higher than the current market price and vice versa. Thus, a general equilibrium model is a necessary condition for deriving shadow prices to be used in evaluating the viability of any given activity. Such a model is not available, of course. In Kenya, derivation of shadow prices is made more difficult by the fact that the factor markets are, in any case, highly imperfect. Thus, estimation of free trade equilibrium factor prices depends on knowing both the effects of the protective system and the independent effect of market distortions.[6]

In measuring protection, or "resource pull," the study also employs various measures. The nominal rate of protection is derived, using the ratio of the domestic price to the world price. Two measures of effective protection are employed, one of which measures the percentage increase in value-added permitted by protection, and the other the proportion of domestic value-added generated by protection.[7] The study relies largely on the latter because its denominator is more stable and usually significantly greater than zero. The world value-added is frequently very close to zero. Both of these measures suffer from the same disadvantage of not being able to cope with negative world value-added. (For instance, if DVA is increased in such an activity, EPU declines!) The final measures are concerned with the effects of protection on factor returns. One measure concentrates on increased profits as the variable determining resource "pull," and the other is concerned with returns to all primary factors.[8]

Some results at the three digit level are reported in Table 15. The overall conclusion is summarized in the following table. Essentially, what is shown is a consistent and highly significant negative correlation between measures of protection and viability. For instance, the correlation between the effective rate of protection and world price profitability is -0.65.

5. This is defined as:

$$WRR = \frac{WVA}{W_u L_u + W_s L_s + Kr}$$

where:
r = shadow rate of return to capital.

This measure is identical to the Domestic Resource Cost Ratio, except that nontradables are removed from the resource cost, an exchange rate is built in, and foreign ownership of capital is ignored.

6. Other standard objections (such as the assumed restrictions on the production function) are elaborated upon in the paper (p. 10).

7. These are:

$$EPZ = \frac{DVA - WVA}{WVA} \cdot 100, \text{ and } EPU = \frac{DVA - WVA}{DVA} \cdot 100$$

where DVA = Domestic Value-Added

8. The first measure is defined as: $CHP = \dfrac{DVA - WVA}{K}$, which assumes all increments in value added accrue to profits. Alternative formulations are:

$$CHP^* = EPZ \cdot WPR \text{ and } CHP^{**} = EPU \cdot DPR$$

both of which assume profits receive only a proportionate share in increments in value-added. The second measure is defined as:

$$CRR = \frac{DVA - WVA}{rK + W_u L_u + W_s L_s}$$

Three Digit Correlation Matrix Between Measures of Viability and Protection
(All entries significant at .99 confidence level)

		Viability	Viability	Protection	Protection	Protection
		World Price Profitability	World Price Rate of Return to Factors	Effective Rate	Change in Profit Rate	Change in Rate of Return to Factors
Protection	Nominal Rate	−0.67	−0.67	+0.78	+0.72	+0.87
	Effective Rate	−0.65	−0.71		+0.68	+0.88
	Change in Profit Rate	−0.65	−0.56			+0.83
	Change in Rate of Return to Factors	−0.70	−0.68			
Viability	World Price Profitability		+0.95			

SOURCE: Phelps and Wasow, *Measuring Protection*, Appendix III.

Before considering overall objections to the use of these measures in analysis of trade policy, certain qualifications have to be made, which, although general in scope, are of great specific importance to the interpretation of this study. First, the figures were derived from firms whose output does not include all outputs under an ISIC code. Thus, the world price profitability of ISIC Code No. 311—basic industrial chemicals—does not mean *all* industrial chemicals are viable, and vice versa for industries found to be nonviable. Second, the data are now five years out-of-date. Third, because of uncertainties about appropriate shadow prices, especially of foreign exchange, individual measures of the level of viability are dubious. This is even more so when the theoretical problem of substitution is taken into account. Fourth, as has been noted, the results for agricultural processing industries are very strange, since a large number are shown to be nonviable. Certain problems with the methodology have surfaced here: where the domestic price has been deflated by the tariff, the world price thus estimated is sometimes an underestimate of the "true" world price, since, in some cases, the tariff is "redundant," and the domestic price is below the world price with the tariff. Moreover, sometimes, when an industry exports part of its output, the entire value of output has been deflated by the tariff, and not merely the part sold domestically. These practices lead to overstatement of protection and understatement of viability. Finally, one cannot infer from the rankings what the effect on resource allocation has actually been. This depends on all relevant elasticities. It is quite possible that the apparent inefficiency of the protective system has led to some inconsiderable misallocation of resources. Such a hypothesis is lent credence by the low correlation between protection and labor intensity. For these various reasons, the study cannot do more than give prima facie justification for the hypotheses that the protective system is inefficient and that this had led to serious misallocation. In particular, although it is at least likely that industries viable in the protected situation will also be viable in free trade, the reverse is not true. Industries that are nonviable, according to the study, could well be viable in free trade, assuming possibilities of substitution between value-added and imported materials. Thus, specific conclusions for individual industries are not to be taken very seriously.

As stated, Reimer's study was used to evaluate the effective protection implicit in the transfer tax system. (He used preliminary information from the input/output table, which was itself based on the 1967 Census of Industrial Production.) Transfer taxes may be imposed by a state if it is in deficit in its trade in manufactured goods with a Partner. This tax may not exceed 50 percent of the common external duty.[9] Table 23 shows that the effects of the tax are considerable. Tanzanian taxes against Kenyan manufactures produce effective rates of protection (EPZ), which rise to 379.3 percent, and eight are over 100 percent. More striking still is the fact that in ten out of twenty industry groups, Kenyan exports to its Partners are taxed relative to the outside world (using the "modified" method).

The Value of the Studies of Effective Protection

For reasons already outlined, both the measures employed and the theoretical justifications for their use are dubious. The assumptions required for measurement of effective protection to be precise and meaningful are rather restrictive—in particular, input-output coefficients must be fixed. Furthermore, the tariff structure can tell one nothing about resource allocation. Among, let us say, fifteen activities ranked by effective protection it is perfectly possible for resources to flow out of the second but into the fifth. Finally, in deriving measures of viability, it is extremely important, and very difficult, to have the "right" prices of primary factors.

For these reasons, interpretation must be cautious. A situation of the type discussed here is only a good prima facie case for inefficiency. However, various country studies indicate the concepts are practically useful when used to explain performance.[10] Furthermore, at least one study of the general equilibrium aspects of protection supports their usefulness.[11] Finally, if measured distortions are extreme—if, for example, it is overwhelmingly likely industries would not exist without protection—some greater confidence can be placed in the results.

Summing up, we would not like to place excessive trust in individual results, especially in the levels (as opposed to rankings) of effective protection and viability, or in the judgment that certain activities are nonviable. However, in spite of many theoretical objections, these measures are extremely useful tools, which can be put to good use in Kenya. No more can be reasonably claimed, but no more needs to be claimed either.[12]

---

9. Details of the system are discussed in "Industrial Development in East Africa: Progress, Policies, Problems, and Prospects," Volume I, p. 5. The economic implications of the transfer tax system are discussed in P. A. Diamond, *Effective Protection in the East African Transfer Taxes,* Institute of Development Studies Discussion Paper No. 68 (Nairobi, n.d.). He shows that a Partner can be penalized in relation to the outside world if:

$$\frac{\Sigma \, aij \, ti}{tj} > k$$

where i is an input, j *is* an output, and k is the ratio of the transfer tax to tj.

10. See, for example, the OECD series on Brazil, India, Mexico, Pakistan, Taiwan, and the Philippines, and I. Little, T. Scitovsky, and M. Scott, *Industry and Trade in Some Developing Countries* (Paris: OECD, 1970), which summarizes them.

11. H. D. Evans, "A General Equilibrium Analysis of Protection: The Effects of Protection in Australia" (Ph.D. diss., Harvard University, 1968).

12. "The qualifications to a theory need not necessarily overwhelm its simple message," M. Corden, *The Theory of Protection* (Oxford, 1971), p. 243.

Appendix C: Promoting Further Kenyanization of the Economy

The Elements of Future Policy

The mission believes that there are several areas to which the Government might give further attention in formulating its future Kenyanization policy. First, as discussed initially, the most effective way of achieving a broader impact in Kenyanizing the economy is by making the necessary structural changes in the pattern of growth, both between and within sectors, to favor those kinds of economic activity in which small businesses can most easily be established. But many Kenyans could not take advantage of new economic opportunities, even if they were created, because they lack the means, and sometimes the inspiration, to do so. Another important element of a future strategy therefore relates to the need to broaden and intensify the direct assistance programs designed to reach the smaller entrepreneur, whether he be the small scale farmer or the small businessman.

This emphasis on small scale enterprises does not, in our view, mean that the formal sector should be ignored or abandoned. On the contrary, as already discussed, the formal sector has a vital role to play in the economy. It does mean, however, that the role of the urban formal sector—and particularly the large foreign controlled segment—needs to be more carefully defined and reconciled with the goals of Kenyanization.

Reaching the Masses

The strategy proposed by this report calls for a relative shift in resource allocation to programs designed to increase production among the mass of small scale enterprises, particularly small scale farmers and African businesses found in the informal sector. We have proposed this strategy because it is the best way, in our opinion, of making the optimum use of Kenya's source resources and bringing accelerated development to the majority of the population. In particular, we feel that this is the *only* practicable method of dealing with Kenya's two most troublesome problems—unemployment and rural poverty—in the foreseeable future. However, we also firmly believe that a deepening of development—reaching down to the majority of the working population—is the most meaningful interpretation of Kenyanization, since it can be expected to bring new opportunities for initiative and growth to the mass of potential businessmen and self-employed people where they now are. We are convinced that in the immediate future, the comparative advantage of African entrepreneurs lies in the smaller management unit—in farming, in trade, and in other sectors of the economy. It follows, therefore, that the development of African economic activity can be fostered most efficiently (i.e., with most benefits and least cost) in those fields in which small management predominates rather than in sectors where the higher demands for capital, experience, and managerial ability make entry very much more difficult.

This report has therefore endorsed the recommendations of other recent Bank reports, as well as ILO/UNDP report, that a larger share of resources be allocated to present and proposed programs to assist small scale African farmers and businessmen. We do not wish to suggest that this can be done easily, and we have referred to some of the severe constraints, particularly the technology base and absorptive capacity of the critical sectors, which will have to be overcome if a reorientation in the pattern of growth is to be achieved. Moreover, we recognize that it will be especially difficult to reach the lower strata of the income scale, and it is neither possible nor desirable to recommend that past emphasis on the formal sector of the economy should be replaced by preoccupation with the informal. We go on to suggest that Kenya's development programs should aim to promote productive activities at all the various levels of the economy.

The Stratified Nature of the Economy

In considering future programs for Kenyanizing the economy, it is first necessary to understand the nature of the economy. We believe that economic activity in Kenya covers a wide continuum of enterprises, ranging from the humblest subsistence farm or informal sector activity at the lowest end of the scale, to large, modern industrial enterprises in the urban formal sector at the other end. In the natural order of things, there is no technological or other line to demarcate "formal sector" activity from "informal sector" activity, only differences in degree between levels of ability, technology, income, and wealth. Nor is there any feeling that one level is better or more desirable than the other, since the continuum allows each potential entrepreneur to establish himself at a level suited to his ability and resources, and each level of activity uniquely provides the goods or services consumed by a particular level of household income.

The dichotomy between formal and informal activity emerges only when an artificial barrier is put up at some arbitrary point in the continuum and discriminating instruments are introduced to impede the development of smaller businesses. The formal sector barrier in Kenya, which was originally based on foreign concepts of standards and development goals and subsequently entrenched in the law, defines the entry point, or threshold, for legal business activity. Thereafter, Kenya experience has shown that the weight of government assistance is then applied to prop up the higher echelons of business activity protected by this artificial barrier, and the rest of the economy is actually penalized by the effects of formal sector protection—and even by legal sanctions and physical harassment.

We believe that priority should be given to assembling a strategy for promoting African small scale business activity. There are several components in such a strategy. First, and probably most important, the legality of all legitimate businesses must be firmly established, and any legal impediments to their operation removed. A start has already been made in legalizing "matatu" taxis, but obviously the process must go further than this. The most characteristic feature of informal sector activities is that they are nonlegal. (Not necessarily illegal, but certainly outside the law.) We cannot see how substantial government assistance programs can reach businesses which are operating entirely outside the law, and legal recognition must therefore be the first step.

Legalization, however, also means recognizing that formal sector standards—particularly those applying to building regulations, labor legislation, and health and safety standards—are simply not relevant to the majority of African businesses or the customers they serve. Therefore, the second need is to confront the whole issue of standards squarely and honestly. The mission does not feel that a formal sector versus informal sector debate is likely to contribute to the determination of better policy in Kenya. Nor will any real purpose be served by tearing down all the barriers which have been erected to define, promote, and protect the formal sector.[1] It has to be recognized that the formal sector has a role to play, and that a significant and powerful segment of the population wishes to maintain a relatively high set of standards for formal sector activity, as a standard of excellence and as a yardstick for the long term goal for the economy as a whole. We have no quarrel with this desire, provided that these standards are not used to impede the development of the country as they have in the past.

1. Although we have suggested changes in policy to induce the formal sector to operate to the greater benefit and lower cost of the economy.

Kenyanization programs, however, must recognize that the economy is stratified and that different standards are appropriate at different levels of the economic spectrum. As a first step, the law in all its forms must reflect the diversity of the economy as it is, rather than trying to provide for an ideal society which does not exist. One suggested approach to the problem, first made in an earlier Bank report[2], is for the law to provide for different grades of business in each sector, to reflect the different capabilities of entrepreneurs and the market they wish to supply. Each grade would carry with it its own licensing regulations, wage legislation, and so on.[3]

Thus, at the top, the formal sector would remain as the pinnacle of achievement. It could offer the highest potential rewards to the more successful businessmen, but it would also demand high standards of service, employment practices, and accounting procedures; and these standards would severely limit entry, as they now do. Lower down the scale, a "Class B" license would be available for the businessman who has climbed several rungs of the ladder, but cannot make the top. He would have a more limited horizon, serve a lower strata of society, and pay lower wages, but because of these less stringent requirements entry would be easier. Similar gradations could go lower down the business ladder, the number depending upon the nature of the sector. The important point is that the further the ladder is lowered into the business sector, the greater the potential impact of any promotional programs. Any businessman who cannot grasp even the lowest rung will continue to be beyond the reach of assistance.

The law should also provide for unrestricted access to all citizens in each category of business. Provided a businessman can satisfy the minimum requirements laid down for a particular class, and pays the prescribed fee, licenses should be readily available. We can see no justification for the general use of licensing, or any other control instrument, to restrict competition among citizens.[4]

Once the legislative impediments had been cleared away, the Government could plan for an extension outreach.[5] The differential licensing system would provide a gradation of entry points (or promotion points) in the continuum of business enterprises. African businessmen would be encouraged to enter the continuum at whatever is their appropriate level, and any particular government extension service could be framed with a specific target community (e.g., Class B traders) in mind. At present, because of the preoccupation with formal sector standards, the best is often the enemy of the good. For example, there is despondency over the urban informal sector because no one can envisage small backyard activities becoming successful businesses. But this misses the point: a little help (in providing sites, for example) can help to increase output and employment significantly at very little cost. Again, in agriculture, there is sometimes a reluctance to identify programs which could bring marginal benefits to the rural population because they fail to attain "target" incomes. Yet most people would accept that it is better to achieve £1 million incremental income by raising the incomes of 100,000 households from £20 to £30 a year than by raising 1,000 families from £1,000 to £2,000 a year.

---

2. See World Bank report no. AE-22, Annex A at para. 52–6.

3. This does not mean we necessarily endorse any particular form of licensing or regulation of private sector activity. But if Kenya is to continue licensing businesses and laying down minimum standards for the conditions in which they operate, then the licensing and the standards should reflect the real world they are trying to regulate.

4. The Government has now accepted the ILO/UNDP report's recommendation that trade licensing should be revised. See "Sessional Paper on Employment," May 1973, para. 165–71.

5. A proposal for a small business development program is given in Annex Five.

STATISTICAL TABLES
Annex Three
Index

Table No.		Page
	Production, Investment, and ICORs	
1.	Share of the Private Sector in the Economy, 1964–72	330
2.	Gross Value-Added in the Private Sector, 1964–72, in Constant 1964 Prices	331
3.	Gross Value-Added in the Private Sector, 1964–72, in Current Prices	332
4.	Private Gross Value-Added as a Percentage of Total Gross Value-Added, 1964–72, by Industry, in Current Prices	333
5.	Fixed Capital Formation by Industry, 1964–72	334
6.	Fixed Capital Formation in the Private Sector, 1967–71	335
7.	Private Sector Capital Formation, by Industry, 1967–71	335
8.	Estimated Sectoral Incremental Capital Output Ratios	336
	Employment, Earnings, and Productivity	
9.	Total Employment, Wage and Nonwage, in 1968, by Sector	337
10.	Total Wage Employment, 1967–71	337
11.	Wage Employment in the Private Modern Sector, 1964–72	338
12.	Private Modern Sector Employment and Gross Value-Added (Output) by Industry, 1965–71, Ordinary Least Squares	339
13.	Modern and Traditional Private Sector Employment and Gross Value-Added (Output), 1967–71, Ordinary Least Squares	340
14.	Average Earnings Per Employee, 1968–72	340
15.	Average Earnings in Modern Sector, 1964–72	341
16.	Average Earnings of Urban Employees, by Occupational Group and Age	342
17.	Average Earnings in the Private Modern Sector by Race, 1964–71	342
18.	Household Income Distribution by Economic Group and Income Size, 1968–70	343
19.	Labor Productivity in the Modern Private Sector, 1964–70	343
	Trade, Protection, and Controls	
20.	The Pattern of Import Substitution, 1970	344
21.	The Structure of Exports	346
22.	The Structure of Exports, 1964 and 1972	348
23.	The Effective Rate of Protection of the East African Transfer Tax	348
24.	Import Implications of Sectoral Increments in Gross Value-Added, 1967	349
25.	Estimated Percentage of Net Home Consumption Affected by Import Licensing	350
26.	Extent of Exchange Control Circular 1/72	350
27.	End Use Analysis of Imports, 1964–72	350

Table 1: Share of the Private Sector in the Economy, 1964–72

	PERCENTAGE SHARE OF PRIVATE SECTOR			
Year	GDP	Value-Added Enterprise Sector[1]	Fixed Capital Formation	Modern Sector Employment
		(percentage)		
1964	76.0	87.3	75.0	68.4
1965	74.7	85.9	74.0	67.7
1966	75.4	86.6	68.4	65.8
1967	75.2	86.6	65.3	64.6
1968	73.5	86.0	63.3	63.4
1969	73.0	85.8	67.3	62.2
1970	72.4	84.8	69.7	61.6
1971	69.1	82.7	64.3	62.3
1972	69.3	83.2	n.a.	61.2

[1] Enterprise Sector = GDP minus General Government.

SOURCE: *Statistical Abstracts* (annual) and *Economic Survey*, 1973.

Table 2: Gross Value-Added in the Private Sector,[1] 1964–72, in Constant 1964 Prices

Sectors	1964	1965	1966	1967	1968	1969	1970	1971	1972[2]	Compound Annual Growth Rates 1964–72
					(£ million)					(percentage)
Outside monetary economy										
Agriculture	73	63	81	84	87	90	93	95	99	3.9
Forestry	2	2	2	2	2	3	3	3	3	4.4
Fishing	0	0	0	0	0	0	0	0	0	3.1
Building and construction	6	6	6	6	7	7	7	7	7	3.0
Water	2	2	2	2	2	3	3	3	3	3.7
Ownership of dwellings	6	6	6	6	7	7	8	8	8	5.2
SUBTOTAL	89	77	98	101	105	109	113	116	120	3.8
Monetary economy										
Enterprises and nonprofit institutions										
Agriculture	52	49	59	58	62	69	72	73	85	6.3
Forestry	1	1	1	1	1	1	2	2	2	9.2
Fishing	1	1	1	1	1	1	1	1	1	3.6
Mining and quarrying	1	1	2	2	2	2	3	3	2	6.2
Manufacturing and repairing	29	30	32	35	38	42	45	48	52	7.6
Building and construction	3	4	5	6	7	7	7	8	8	12.3
Electricity and water	3	3	4	4	4	5	3	0	0	[3]
Transport, storage, and communications	6	7	8	10	11	10	11	11	11	7.2
Wholesale and retail trade	32	34	37	37	40	43	47	51	51	5.8
Banking, insurance, and real estate	7	8	9	9	10	11	11	11	13	6.5
Ownership of dwellings	10	10	10	10	10	11	11	11	11	2.4
Other services	12	13	15	16	17	18	20	22	26	10.2
SUBTOTAL	158	161	182	189	205	219	232	241	262	6.6
Private households (domestic services)	3	3	3	4	4	3	4	4	4	3.3
Total monetary economy	161	164	185	193	208	223	236	245	266	6.5
Private sector value-added at factor cost TOTAL	249	241	283	294	313	332	349	361	386	5.6

[1] At factor cost.
[2] Provisional.
[3] Meaningless because of transfer to Public Sector.

Table 3: Gross Value-Added in the Private Sector, 1964–72[1], in Current Prices

Sectors	1964	1965	1966	1967	1968	1969	1970	1971	1972[2]
					(£ million)				
Outside monetary economy									
Agriculture	73	64	82	85	85	89	92	97	111
Forestry	2	2	2	3	3	3	3	4	4
Fishing	0	0	0	0	0	0	0	0	0
Building and construction	6	6	7	8	9	9	10	10	10
Water	2	2	2	3	3	4	4	4	5
Ownership of dwellings	6	6	7	8	9	10	10	11	12
TOTAL	89	80	102	107	109	115	120	127	143
Monetary economy									
Enterprises and nonprofit institutions									
Agriculture	52	47	56	57	58	63	72	72	90
Forestry	1	1	1	1	1	2	2	3	2
Fishing	1	1	1	1	1	1	1	1	1
Mining and quarrying	1	1	2	2	2	2	2	3	3
Manufacturing and repairing	29	31	35	39	43	49	54	58	64
Building and construction	3	4	5	7	9	9	10	11	13
Electricity and water	3	3	4	4	5	5	3	0	0
Transport, storage, and communications	6	7	8	9	10	10	11	11	12
Wholesale and retail trade	32	34	38	39	42	45	54	59	62
Banking, insurance, and real estate	7	8	8	9	11	11	12	12	14
Ownership of dwellings	10	10	10	11	11	12	13	14	15
Other services	12	13	14	15	16	18	20	21	24
SUBTOTAL	158	160	183	195	210	228	255	266	300
Private households (domestic services)	3	3	4	4	4	4	4	5	5
Total monetary economy	161	164	187	199	214	232	258	271	305
Private sector gross value-added at factor cost									
TOTAL	249	244	288	306	323	347	378	398	448

[1] At factor cost.
[2] Provisional.

SOURCE: *Statistical Abstracts* (annual) and *Economic Survey*, 1973.

Table 4: Private Gross Value-Added as a Percentage of Total Gross Value-Added, 1964–72, by Industry, in Current Prices

Sectors	1964	1965	1966	1967	1968	1969	1970	1971	1972[1]
Nonmonetary economy	100.0	100.0	100.0	100.0	100.0	100.0	100.0	100.0	100.0
Monetary economy									
Enterprises and nonprofit institutions									
Agriculture	100.2	100.4	100.2	100.5	99.7	99.2	98.9	98.7	98.7
Forestry	46.8	43.9	46.1	46.2	42.4	53.1	57.9	62.0	58.1
Fishing	100.0	100.0	100.0	100.0	100.0	100.0	100.0	100.0	100.0
Mining and quarrying	100.0	100.0	100.0	100.0	100.0	100.0	100.0	96.5	96.6
Manufacturing and repairing	84.5	84.0	85.1	86.3	86.2	86.8	86.3	81.6	82.0
Building and construction	47.2	53.2	55.5	59.1	62.8	58.9	59.5	58.2	57.6
Electricity and water	66.9	66.2	68.2	67.1	73.6	74.0	36.0	0.1	0.2
Transport, storage, and communications	26.2	24.9	25.7	28.6	28.7	26.2	26.5	26.0	26.5
Wholesale and retail trade	98.8	98.0	97.2	97.3	95.9	96.8	97.1	96.3	96.1
Banking, insurance, and real estate	71.6	69.1	70.1	68.7	67.8	62.5	57.8	51.3	51.0
Ownership of dwellings	71.5	71.8	72.7	73.5	74.9	76.6	75.4	75.9	76.3
Other services	100.0	100.0	100.0	100.0	99.4	98.9	99.0	98.6	98.0
TOTAL	81.2	79.9	80.4	80.6	80.0	79.9	79.0	76.2	76.9
Private households (domestic services)	100.0	100.0	100.0	100.0	100.0	100.0	100.0	100.0	100.0
Total private value-added as % of GDP at factor cost	76.0	74.7	75.4	75.2	73.5	73.0	72.4	69.1	69.3

[1] Provisional.

SOURCE: *Statistical Abstracts* (annual) and *Economic Survey*, 1973.

Table 5: Fixed Capital Formation by Industry, 1964–72

Sectors	1964	1965	1966	1967	1968	1969	1970	1971	1972[1]
					(percentage)				
Outside monetary economy	11.8	12.5	10.6	9.1	9.3	9.3	8.2	6.9	6.6
Monetary economy									
Enterprises and nonprofit institutions									
Agriculture	15.3	15.2	14.8	11.4	11.9	11.5	11.0	10.4	9.7
Forestry	0.5	0.2	0.5	0.4	0.3	0.2	0.2	0.3	0.2
Mining and quarrying	0.6	0.7	1.1	0.7	0.5	0.7	1.1	0.8	1.4
Manufacturing and repairing	13.1	14.5	13.2	12.1	13.6	10.1	11.5	12.6	17.9
Building and construction	4.3	5.2	4.6	4.9	4.3	4.4	6.2	5.6	4.6
Electricity and water	3.0	4.2	4.2	7.7	4.0	4.1	3.3	6.0	7.1
Transport, storage, and communications	23.1	16.2	21.3	19.9	18.5	17.8	17.6	15.1	13.0
Wholesale and retail trade	6.8	5.3	4.7	4.5	4.8	4.4	3.9	3.8	3.5
Banking, insurance, and real estate	1.6	0.9	0.5	0.9	1.1	0.8	1.6	1.0	1.3
Ownership of dwellings	4.9	4.7	4.9	6.4	7.8	8.4	8.7	9.4	9.3
Other services	5.2	5.1	5.3	6.2	6.6	9.1	7.4	6.7	5.6
SUBTOTAL	78.4	72.2	75.1	75.1	73.4	71.5	72.5	71.7	73.6
Private	63.2	61.5	58.0	56.0	53.9	58.0	61.6	57.3	54.9
Public	15.2	10.7	17.1	19.1	19.5	13.5	10.9	14.4	18.7
General Government									
TOTAL	9.8	15.3	14.5	15.6	17.2	19.2	19.4	21.3	19.8
Total fixed capital formation	100.0	100.0	100.0	100.0	100.0	100.0	100.0	100.0	100.0
Private	75.0	74.0	68.4	65.3	63.3	67.3	69.7	64.3	61.5
Public	25.0	26.0	31.6	34.7	36.7	32.7	30.3	35.7	38.5

[1] Provisional.

SOURCE: *Statistical Abstracts* (annual) and *Economic Survey*, 1973.

Table 6: Fixed Capital Formation in the Private Sector, 1967–71[1]

Sectors	1967	1968	1969	1970	1971
			(£ million)		
Outside monetary economy					
Traditional dwellings	7.52	8.37	8.72	9.24	9.74
Monetary economy					
Enterprises and nonprofit institutions					
Agriculture	9.37	10.36	9.92	11.59	14.13
Forestry	—	—	—	—	—
Mining and quarrying	0.58	0.49	0.64	1.28	1.19
Manufacturing and repairing	7.42	8.64	9.15	12.85	17.62
Building and construction	3.41	2.90	2.98	6.01	7.48
Electricity and water	5.25	2.48	2.87	2.57	3.13
Transport, storage, and communications	9.35	9.01	10.25	11.91	15.53
Wholesale and retail trade	3.70	3.86	3.89	4.17	5.01
Banking, insurance, and real estate	0.76	0.97	0.67	1.72	0.89
Ownership of dwellings	3.32	2.76	4.24	6.39	6.57
Other services	5.07	5.94	8.45	8.13	9.25
TOTAL[2]	48.23	47.41	53.06	66.62	80.80
Private sector capital formation total	55.75	55.78	61.78	75.86	90.54

[1] This table is obtained by subtracting the public sector contribution to capital formation in each industry from the total capital formation in that industry. The former are only published as provisional figures each year whereas the latter series are revised. The latest figures have been used, except for 1971 where both sets of figures used are provisional. This may cause some inconsistencies.
[2] The totals shown here are the sum of the individual industry components and may not necessarily agree with those obtained by subtracting the *total* contribution of the public sector to capital formation from *total* capital formation in Enterprises and Nonprofit Institutions.

SOURCE: *Statistical Abstracts* (annual).

Table 7: Private Sector Capital Formation, by Industry, 1967–71

Sectors	1967	1968	1969	1970	1971
			(percentage)		
Outside Monetary Economy					
Traditional dwellings	13.5	15.0	14.1	12.2	10.8
Monetary economy					
Enterprises and nonprofit institutions	16.8	18.6	16.1	15.3	15.6
Agriculture	16.8	18.6	16.1	15.3	15.6
Forestry	0.0	0.0	0.0	0.0	0.0
Mining and quarrying	1.0	0.9	1.0	1.7	1.3
Manufacturing and repairing	13.3	15.5	14.8	16.9	19.4
Building and construction	6.1	5.2	4.8	7.9	8.3
Electricity and water	9.4	4.4	4.6	3.4	3.5
Transport, storage, and communications	16.8	16.2	16.6	15.7	17.1
Wholesale and retail trade	6.6	6.9	6.3	5.5	5.5
Banking, insurance, and real estate	1.4	1.7	1.1	2.3	1.0
Ownership of dwellings	6.0	5.0	6.9	8.4	7.3
Other services	9.1	10.6	13.7	10.7	10.2
TOTAL	86.5	85.0	85.9	87.8	89.2
Private sector capital formation total	100.0	100.0	100.0	100.0	100.0

SOURCE: Table 6.

Table 8: Estimated Sectoral Incremental Capital Output Ratios[1]

Sectors		Constant	TIME	Rate of Growth	$\bar{R}^2$	DW
		\multicolumn{5}{l}{(ordinary least squares regression)}				
Nonmonetary economy	ICOR =	+0.82 (2.1)[2]	+0.21 (1.7)	+0.0850	0.32	2.9
Monetary economy						
Agriculture and forestry	ICOR =	+1.28 (3.5)	−0.08[3] (−0.7)	+0.0858	0.14	2.6
Mining and quarrying	ICOR =	+0.37[3] (0.6)	+0.45 (2.4)	+0.1116	0.54	3.6
Manufacturing and repairing	ICOR =	+1.56 (19.9)	−0.07 (−3.0)	+0.0994	0.67	2.1
Building and construction	ICOR =	−0.51[3] (−0.50)	+1.27 (4.2)	+0.0520	0.80	1.5
Electricity and water	ICOR =	+8.42 (4.7)	−0.51[3] (−0.9)	+0.0673	0.03	1.4
Transport, storage, and communications	ICOR =	+0.60[3] (1.5)	+0.96 (8.1)	+0.1543	0.94	2.4
Wholesale and retail trade	ICOR =	+0.12[3] (1.0)	+0.04[3] (1.2)	+0.0631	0.09	2.7
Banking, insurance, and real estate	ICOR =	−0.84 (−3.2)	+0.13 (1.7)	—	0.32	2.9
Ownership of dwellings	ICOR =	+41.39 (3.8)	−5.78 (−1.8)	—	0.35	2.1
Other services	ICOR =	+0.35[3] (1.1)	+0.57 (5.8)	+0.0601	0.89	2.1
Government	ICOR =	+1.04 (11.6)	+0.27 (10.1)	+0.0064	0.96	2.7
	ICOR =	+1.16 (7.3)	+0.19 (3.9)	+0.0711	0.78	3.4
TOTAL	ICOR =	+1.05 (5.0)	+0.21 (3.3)	+0.0530	0.71	3.5

[1] ICOR = Incremental Capital Output Ratio
NICOR = Net Incremental Capital Output Ratio
TIME = Time Trend
The coefficients on TIME and the Constant Term were estimated from an equation of the form: NICOR = $a + b$ TIME. This equation was substituted in the identity: ICOR ≡ NICOR + $b'(1/r)$, where b' is the ratio of depreciation to sectoral gross value-added, and r is the sectoral growth rate. b' was estimated from data contained in the 1967 Input/Output Table.
[2] t ratios are shown in parentheses.
[3] Insignificant.

SOURCE: Mission estimates.

Table 9: Total Employment, Wage and Nonwage, in 1968, by Sector

Sectors	Number of Employees	
	(thousands)	(percentage)
Wage employment	1,054.8[1]	24.5
Modern sector	606.4	14.1
Private sector	384.5	8.9
Public sector	221.9	5.2
Small holdings and settlement schemes	366.4	8.5
Rural nonagricultural activities	82.0	1.9
Nonwage employment	3,243.1	75.5
Self-employment	1,035.6	24.1
Family workers	2,207.5	51.4
TOTAL EMPLOYMENT	4,297.9[2]	100.0

[1] This figure in the Plan Document is 1,056.9.
[2] This figure in the Plan Document is 4,300.0.

SOURCE: *Nairobi and National Employment: Structure and Growth, 1964–70*, with data from *Economic Survey*, 1970 and *Development Plan, 1970–74*, compiled by the Nairobi Urban Study Group.

Table 10: Total Wage Employment, 1967–71

Sectors	1967	1968	1969	1970	1971	Average Compound Growth Rate 1967–71
			(thousand)			(percentage)
Modern sector						
Public	212.1	221.9	237.1	247.2	255.7	4.8
Private	385.4	384.5	390.1	397.3	424.0	2.4
TOTAL	597.5	606.4	627.2	644.5	679.7	3.3
Traditional sector						
Small holdings	365.6	366.4	338.7	329.9	342.3	−1.7
Rural nonagricultural activities	61.9	82.0	81.7	90.0	95.0	11.3
SUBTOTAL	427.5	448.4	420.4	419.9	437.3	0.6
Total modern and traditional sectors	1,025.0	1,054.8	1,047.6	1,064.4	1,117.0	2.2
Private sector total	812.9	832.9	810.5	817.2	861.3	1.4

SOURCE: *Economic Surveys*, 1970–72; unpublished data for 1967–69; and *Statistical Abstracts* (annual).

Table 11: Wage Employment in the Private Modern Sector, 1964–72

Sectors	1964	1965	1966	1967	1968	1969	1970	1971	1972[1]
					(percentage)				
Private modern sector									
Agriculture and forestry	51.4	51.4	48.9	44.8	45.0	45.8	46.2	44.7	45.7
Mining and quarrying	0.6	0.6	0.6	0.6	0.8	0.7	0.7	0.7	0.6
Manufacturing and repairing	12.5	13.2	13.6	14.7	15.1	14.8	15.6	17.0	16.8
Building and construction	2.3	2.2	2.7	4.5	4.7	4.2	4.2	5.0	5.4
Electricity and water	0.6	0.6	0.7	0.7	0.7	0.6	[2]	[2]	[2]
Commerce	12.6	11.8	12.0	11.2	10.5	10.7	10.0	10.0	9.2
Transport and communications	2.8	3.0	3.6	3.8	4.1	4.1	4.2	3.8	4.2
Services	17.2	17.1	18.0	19.5	19.1	19.1	19.0	18.7	18.1
TOTAL	100.0	100.0[3]	100.0	100.0	100.0	100.0	100.0	100.0	100.0
Total number employed[4]	393,400	393,800	385,000	385,400	384,500	390,100	397,300	424,000	434,200

[1] Provisional.
[2] Transferred to public sector.
[3] Discrepancies due to rounding.
[4] The average compound growth rate of employment between 1964 and 1972 was 1.2% a year.

SOURCE: *Statistical Abstracts* (annual) and *Economic Survey*, 1973.

Table 12: **Private Modern Sector Employment and Gross Value-Added (Output) by Industry, 1965–71, Ordinary Least Squares**

Equations[1]	COEFFICIENT OF Constant	COEFFICIENT OF TIME	Log Output	$\bar{R}^2$	DW
Agriculture					
$E/O = a + bT$	0.00373 (14.97)[2]	−0.000213 (−3.82)	[3]	0.69	1.29
Mining					
$E/O = a + bT$	0.00194 (6.53)	−0.000152 (−2.29)		0.41	2.02
$\log E = a + b \log O$ (t ratio)	−0.681 (−0.96)		0.215 (2.31)	0.42	2.07
Manufacturing					
$E/O = a + bT$	0.00177 (30.28)	−0.0000618 (−4.72)		0.78	1.68
$\log E = a + b \log O$	−1.617 (−1.51)		0.538 (5.31)	0.82	1.69
Building					
$\log E = a + b \log O$	−8.534 (−5.57)		1.288 (7.34)	0.898	2.57
Commerce					
$E/O = a + bT$	0.00143 (39.10)	−0.0000910 (−11.13)		0.95	2.15
$\log E = a + b \log O$	6.957 (4.63)		−0.301 (−2.13)	0.37	1.54
Transport					
$E/O = a + bT$	0.00175 (20.85)	−0.0000508 (−2.71)		0.51	2.13
$\log E = a + b \log O$	−2.467 (−3.16)		0.563 (6.63)	0.88	2.23
Services					
$E/O = a + bT$	0.00330 (44.33)	−0.000141 (−8.49)		0.92	3.19
$\log E = a + b \log O$	1.138 (1.75)		0.310 (4.86)	0.79	2.44
Electricity					
$E/O = a + bT$	0.000877 (13.29)	−0.0000667 (−3.35)		0.72	2.55
Total					
$E/O = a + bT$	0.00257 (26.14)	−0.000126 (−5.73)		0.84	1.38
$\log E = a + b \log O$	4.411 (4.38)		0.129 (1.55)	0.19	1.14

[1] E = Employment; T = Time Trend; O = Value-Added (£ thousands).
[2] t ratios are shown in parentheses.
[3] Equations with insignificant results have been omitted.

SOURCE. Mission estimates.

Table 13: Modern and Traditional Private Sector Employment and Gross Value-Added (Output), 1967–71, Ordinary Least Squares

Equations[1]	Coefficient of Constant	Coefficient of TIME	Log Output	$\bar{R}^2$	DW
Agriculture					
$E/O = a + bT$	0.00933	−0.000534	n.a.	0.78	1.76
(*t* ratio)	(20.60)	(−3.91)			
Total					
$E/O = a + bT$	0.00469	−0.000225	n.a.	0.87	1.66
(*t* ratio)	(33.28)	(−5.28)			

[1] E = Employment; T = Time Trend; O = Value-Added (£ thousands).

SOURCE: Mission estimates.

Table 14: Average Earnings Per Employee, 1968–72

Sectors	1968	1969	1970	1971	1972[1]
			(£ per year)		
Private sector					
Agriculture	71.1	72.7	74.6	79.9	93.5
Mining and quarrying	241.4	307.7	344.8	355.4	259.3
Manufacturing and repairs	324.7	341.5	367.0	359.4	383.6
Building and construction	254.1	312.9	329.4	323.8	339.6
Electricity and water	518.5	570.3	—	—	—
Commerce	520.0	492.8	572.9	552.2	608.5
Transport, storage, and communications	398.7	375.0	418.2	419.7	459.6
Services	191.6	201.3	221.8	231.7	249.9
Public sector	302.4	302.6	320.2	339.0	349.0
Total private and public sectors	241.1	344.9	261.4	271.2	286.9

[1] Provisional.

SOURCE: *Economic Survey*, 1972 and 1973.

Table 15: Average Earnings in Modern Sector, 1964–72

Sectors	1964	1965	1966	1967	1968	1969	1970	1971	1972[1]
					(index)				
Private Sector									
Agriculture and forestry	100	105.7	112.6	111.0	115.9	119.1	122.1	130.8	153.0
Mining and quarrying	100	92.0	136.7	163.2	139.8	189.2	196.3	202.3	147.6
Manufacturing	100	99.7	119.1	122.9	134.7	140.3	151.1	147.9	157.9
Construction	100	100.6	134.0	119.5	131.0	162.6	171.6	168.7	176.9
Electricity, gas, water, etc.	100	112.6	118.2	132.3	135.1	184.4	—	—	—
Commerce	100	111.6	118.5	133.7	141.3	133.9	155.1	149.5	164.7
Transport, storage, and communications	100	103.8	111.9	118.3	124.9	117.6	131.7	132.2	144.7
Services	100	98.8	102.0	99.9	115.8	121.9	134.1	140.1	151.1
TOTAL	100	104.1	112.7	124.7	134.3	137.0	146.7	150.2	161.5
Public sector total	100	110.4	117.2	119.6	122.4	122.4	129.7	137.3	141.4

[1] Provisional.

SOURCE: *Annual Enumeration of Employees*, 1964–70 (1968–70 data unpublished); *Economic Survey*, 1973.

Table 16: Average Earnings of Urban Employees, by Occupational Group and Age

Occupational Group	15–19	20–24	25–29	30–34	35–39	40–44	45–49	50+
			(Sh. per month)					
Professional, scientific, and technical	—	—	670	775	1,704	4,292	3,500	4,769
Other professional	—	—	650	1,109	1,490	1,924	1,238	1,360
Technicians	—	—	551	769	915	1,485	1,886	1,680
Foremen and supervisors	—	—	335	626	1,176	1,300	2,585	1,288
Administrative, executive, and managerial	—	—	—	1,045	2,445	4,166	4,877	3,442
Clerical and sales	—	263	504	581	802	1,199	1,600	1,348
Skilled	—	360	370	409	477	529	646	754
Semiskilled and unskilled	53	54	156	242	309	324	324	376
Unspecified	—	—	377	425	498	396	393	1,900

SOURCE: World Bank.

Table 17: Average Earnings in the Private Modern Sector by Race, 1964–71

Races	1964	1965	1966	1967	1968	1969	1970	1971
				(£)				
Agriculture and forestry								
African	50	54	57	54	58	60	62	64
Asian	571	714	625	750	857	1,167	1,400	1,600
European	1,583	1,545	1,500	1,500	1,500	1,545	1,700	2,300
TOTAL	62	65	69	68	71	73	75	80
Private industry and commerce								
African	129	133	176	172	201	208	223	226
Asian	516	539	513	621	634	701	816	873
European	1,408	1,489	1,385	1,582	1,591	1,776	1,964	2,167
TOTAL	250	260	285	292	316	326	354	352
Total private modern sector								
African	85	89	111	114	130	135	143	149
Asian	518	543	516	625	640	712	828	890
European	1,427	1,495	1,398	1,573	1,580	1,750	1,935	2,181
TOTAL	154	159	179	192	206	210	225	230

SOURCE: *Statistical Abstract*, 1972.

Table 18: Household Income Distribution by Economic Group and Income Size, 1968–70

Economic Group	Annual Income	Number of Households[1]
	(£)	(thousand)
Owners of medium sized to large nonagricultural enterprises in the formal sector of commerce, industry, and services; renters; big farmers; self-employed professional people; holders of high level jobs in the formal sector.	1,000 and over	30
Intermediate level employees in the formal sector; owners of medium sized nonagricultural enterprises in the formal sector; less prosperous big farmers.	600–1,000	50
Semiskilled employees in the formal sector; prosperous smallholders; better off owners of nonagricultural rural enterprises; a small proportion of owners of enterprises in the formal sector.	200–600	220
Unskilled employees in the formal nonagricultural sector; significant proportion of smallholders; most of the owners of nonagricultural rural enterprises.	120–200	240
Employees in formal sector agriculture; a small proportion of unskilled employees in the formal sector; better off wage earners and self-employed persons in the informal urban sector; a small proportion of owners of nonagricultural rural enterprises.	60–120	330
Workers employed on small holdings and in rural nonagricultural enterprises; a significant proportion of employed and self-employed persons in the informal urban sector; sizeable number of smallholders.	20–60	1,140
Smallholders; pastoralists in semiarid and arid zones; unemployed and landless persons in both rural and urban areas.	20 and less	330
TOTAL		2,340

[1] Very approximate.

SOURCE: *ILO/UNDP Report*, p. 74.

Table 19: Labor Productivity in the Modern Private Sector, 1964–70[1]

Industry	Constant	Log Wages	$\bar{R}^2$	DW
Manufacturing	7.766	0.988	0.93	1.51
(*t* ratio)	(57.17)	(8.90)		
Commerce	8.060	1.627	0.92	1.36
(*t* ratio)	(55.27)	(8.65)		
Other services	6.888	0.905	0.86	1.27
(*t* ratio)	(27.78)	(6.25)		
Total private modern sector	8.286	1.191	0.94	2.82
(*t* ratio)	(38.58)	(9.66)		

[1] The ordinary least square method has been used to estimate the relationship between labor productivity and wages. The equation takes the following form:

$$\log \frac{V}{E} = a + b \log W$$

where: V = Gross value-added (£ thousand); E = Employment; W = Average wages per year.

Table 20: The Pattern of Import Substitution, 1970

ISIC Code	Category[1]	Gross Value-Added (V)	Gross Output (Y')	Excise Duty	Output at Market Prices (Y)	Imports CIF (M')
	Consumer goods			(£ thousand)		
201	Meat products	1,380	7,379	0	7,379	971
202	Dairy products	1,973	10,019	0	10,019	509
203	Canned fruits and vegetables	352	1,722	0	1,722	293
204	Canning and preservation of fish	1	69	0	69	288
205	Grain mill products	2,803	16,526	0	16,526	217
206	Bakery products	899	4,398	26	4,424	45
207	Sugar	1,663	6,229	2,828	9,057	1,735
208	Sugar confectionery	84	344	0	344	569
209	Miscellaneous foods	1,542	6,235	0	6,235	1,759
211	Spirits	47	159	211	370	271
212	Wine	0	0	0	0	157
213/220	Beer and malt, and tobacco manufacturers	6,310	12,008	10,146	22,153	432
214	Mineral waters	1,374	3,626	506	4,132	28
232	Knitting mills	628	1,707	0	1,707	1,435
234	Spinning, weaving, and finishing of textiles	1,065	3,381	297	3,678	10,598
241	Footwear	831	3,115	0	3,115	628
243	Clothing except footwear	2,518	8,804	0	8,804	1,810
260	Furniture and fixtures	1,753	4,099	0	4,099	586
280	Printing and publishing	3,525	7,994	0	7,994	1,274
313	Paints	296	1,201	157	1,358	227
315	Soap	1,397	6,079	436	6,515	423
319	Miscellaneous chemical products	1,696	4,764	157	4,921	6,863
	SUBTOTAL	32,136	109,858	14,764	124,621	31,118
	Intermediate goods					
231/233	Cotton ginning, cordage, rope, and twine	688	3,270	0	3,270	1,112
244	Made-up textiles except clothing	540	2,100	0	2,100	1,408
251	Sawn timber	2,227	5,272	0	5,272	1,049
259	Other wood products	49	378	0	378	169
271/272	Manufacture of pulp paper and paperboard	1,175	4,152	0	4,152	6,575
291	Tanneries and leather finishing plant	322	1,377	0	1,377	331
311	Basic industrial chemicals	634	1,269	0	1,269	7,161
312	Vegetable and animal oils and fats	125	727	0	727	2,702
314	Wattle bark extract	392	1,186	0	1,186	0
316	Pyrethrum extract	170	1,566	0	1,566	29
321	Petroleum products	2,278	14,324	5,146	19,474	2,791
332	Glass and glass products	501	1,122	0	1,122	664
	SUBTOTAL	9,101	36,743	5,146	41,893	23,991
	Capital goods					
300	Rubber products	519	1,994	0	1,994	2,613
331	Clay products	144	220	0	220	485
334	Cement	2,886	7,571	0	7,571	30
339	Other nonmetallic minerals	308	1,390	0	1,390	593
340	Basic metal industries	0	0	0	0	11,850
350	Metal products	4,350	13,131	0	13,131	5,465
360	Nonelectrical machinery	988	2,791	0	2,791	17,077
370	Electrical machinery	3,440	8,260	0	8,260	7,953
381	Shipbuilding and repairs	781	1,262	0	1,262	145
383	Motor vehicle bodies	1,113	4,030	0	4,030	13,570
389	Transport equipment	0	0	0	0	246
	SUBTOTAL	14,529	40,649	0	40,649	60,027
	TOTAL	55,766	187,250	19,910	207,163	115,136

[1] The allocation of categories is arbitrary in some cases. It follows the one used in Dr. S. Guisinger's paper *Tariffs and Trade Policies for the Ethiopian Manufacturing Sector*, Annex Table I.
[2] Figures are meaningless because of negative domestic use.
[3] Excluding petroleum products these ratios become 64.0% and 25.7% respectively.
[4] Excluding Motor Vehicle Bodies this ratio would be 7.2%.

SOURCE: Central Statistical Office unpublished data.

KEY ISSUES IN THE PRIVATE SECTOR

Import Duties (D)	Imports at Market Prices (M)	Community Exports	Non-Community Exports	Total Exports (E)	Total Domestic Supply $Z = Y + M - E$	V/Y'	D/M'	M/Z	E/Z
(£ thousand)						(percentage)			
101	1,070	388	4,481	4,869	3,580	18.7	10.4	29.9	136.0
77	585	2,321	333	2,654	7,950	19.7	15.1	7.4	33.4
131	424	270	1,279	1,548	598	20.4	44.7	70.9	258.9
49	338	0	0	0	406	1.4	17.0	83.3	0.0
43	260	67	1,581	1,648	15,137	17.0	19.8	1.7	10.9
19	63	60	10	70	4,417	20.4	42.2	1.4	1.6
492	2,227	0	125	125	11,160	26.7	28.4	20.0	1.1
165	734	113	2	115	963	24.4	29.0	76.2	11.9
279	2,038	1,430	168	1,598	6,675	24.7	15.9	30.5	23.9
1,001	1,272	25	10	34	1,608	29.6	369.4	79.1	2.1
148	304	0	0	0	304	0.0	94.3	100.0	0.0
344	736	373	38	411	22,478	52.6	87.8	3.3	1.8
4	32	86	6	92	4,071	37.9	14.3	0.8	2.3
655	2,090	365	26	391	3,406	36.8	45.6	61.4	11.5
3,902	14,500	716	75	791	17,387	31.5	36.8	83.4	4.5
87	715	599	335	933	2,897	26.7	13.9	24.7	32.2
899	2,709	289	134	423	11,089	28.6	49.7	24.4	3.8
150	736	740	46	786	4,049	42.8	25.6	18.2	19.4
74	1,348	528	208	736	8,605	44.0	5.8	15.7	8.6
53	280	58	35	93	1,545	24.6	23.3	18.1	6.0
99	522	1,872	26	1,898	5,138	23.0	23.4	10.2	36.9
431	7,293	2,246	374	2,620	9,594	35.6	6.3	76.0	27.3
9,203	40,276	12,546	9,292	21,835	143,057	29.3	29.6	28.2	15.3
109	1,221	190	269	459	4,033	21.0	9.8	30.3	11.4
576	1,985	279	31	311	3,774	25.7	40.9	52.6	8.2
129	1,179	670	294	963	5,487	42.2	12.3	21.5	17.6
9	178	38	301	339	217	13.0	5.3	82.0	156.2
657	7,232	1,319	701	2,020	9,365	28.3	0.0	77.2	1.6
112	444	156	321	477	1,344	23.4	33.8	33.0	35.5
92	7,253	273	165	438	8,085	50.0	1.3	89.7	5.4
208	2,909	403	120	523	3,114	17.2	7.7	93.4	16.8
0	0	4	1,141	1,146	40	33.1	0.0	0.0	2,865.0
9	38	4	2,251	2,256	−652	10.9	31.0	−5.8[2]	−346.0[2]
2,255	5,046	5,816	8,371	14,187	10,329	15.9	80.8	48.9	137.4
159	824	163	237	400	1,546	44.7	23.9	53.3	25.9
4,315	28,309	9,315	14,202	23,519	46,682	24.8	18.0	60.6[3]	50.4[3]
592	3,206	596	21	617	4,583	26.0	22.7	70.0	13.5
82	567	21	0	21	766	65.5	16.9	74.0	2.7
2	32	1,419	1,645	3,064	4,539	38.1	6.7	0.7	67.5
31	624	20	1	21	1,993	22.2	5.2	31.3	1.1
532	12,382	296	31	327	12,055	0.0	4.5	102.7	2.7
532	5,997	1,777	1,045	2,822	16,306	33.1	9.7	36.8	17.3
680	17,756	214	58	272	20,276	35.4	4.0	87.6	1.3
859	8,812	1,073	121	1,194	15,877	41.6	10.8	55.5	7.5
0	145	3	0	3	1,404	61.9	0.0	10.3	0.2
4,266	17,836	50	0	50	21,816	27.6	31.4	81.8	0.2
33	279	7	0	7	272	0.0	13.4	102.6	2.6
7,609	67,636	5,476	2,922	8,398	99,887	35.7	12.7[4]	67.7	8.4
21,127	136,221	27,337	26,416	53,752	289,626	29.8	18.4	47.0	18.6

Table 21: The Structure of Exports[1]

Exports	1964 EAC	1964 Rest of World	1964 Total	1968 EAC	1968 Rest of World	1968 Total	1970 EAC	1970 Rest of World	1970 Total	1972 EAC	1972 Rest of World	1972 Total	Compound Growth Total 1964-72
					(£ thousand and percentage)								
Nonprocessed foodstuffs	2,195	23,478	25,673	3,013	30,757	33,770	3,059	39,253	42,312	3,705	46,635	50,340	8.8
	8.5	49.8	35.2	11.4	53.2	40.1	9.7	54.8	41.1	11.3	51.4	40.8	
Meat[2]	348	820	1,168	326	896	1,222	353	1,035	1,388	234	1,642	1,876	6.1
	1.3	1.7	1.6	1.2	1.6	1.5	1.1	1.4	1.3	0.7	1.8	1.5	
Maize, unmilled	0.0	17	17	23	4,774	4,797	0	4	4	478	1	479	...
	0.0	0.0	0.0	0.1	8.3	5.7	0.0	0.0	0.0	1.5	0.0	0.4	
Wheat and spelt, unmilled[3]	964	0	964	1,579	0	1,579	1,363	0	1,363	1,692	0	1,692	7.3
	3.7	0.0	1.3	6.0	0.0	1.9	4.3	0.0	1.3	5.2	0.0	1.4	
Fruit and vegetables	477	1,189	1,666	722	2,238	2,960	854	3,251	4,105	1,148	3,799	4,947	14.6
	1.8	2.5	2.3	2.7	3.9	3.5	2.7	4.5	4.0	3.5	4.2	4.0	
Coffee	36	15,396	15,432	17	12,808	12,825	11	22,259	22,270	85	24,776	24,861	6.0
	0.1	32.7	21.1	0.1	22.2	15.2	0.0	31.1	21.6	0.3	27.3	20.2	
Tea	370	6,056	6,426	346	10,041	10,387	478	12,704	13,182	68	16,417	16,485	12.5
	1.4	12.9	8.8	1.3	17.4	12.3	1.5	17.7	12.8	0.2	18.1	13.4	
Processed foodstuffs	2,924	2,253	5,177	492	2,595	3,087	432	2,628	3,060	661	4,203	4,864	−1.0
	11.2	4.8	7.1	1.9	4.5	3.7	1.4	3.7	3.0	2.0	4.6	3.9	
Tinned meat[3]	0	1,347	1,347	0	2,130	2,130	0	1,818	1,818	113	3,234	3,347	12.0
	0.0	2.9	1.8	0.0	3.7	2.5	0.0	2.5	1.8	0.3	3.6	2.7	
Pineapples, tinned[4]	0	874	874	0	439	439	0	669	669	3	920	923	0.7
	0.0	1.9	1.2	0.0	0.8	0.5	0.0	0.9	0.6	0.0	1.0	0.7	
Beverages and tobacco	2,924	32	2,956	492	26	518	432	141	573	545	49	594	−18.0
	11.3	0.1	4.0	1.9	0.5	0.6	1.4	0.2	0.6	1.7	0.0	0.5	
Other foodstuffs[5]	3,862	1,570	5,432	2,266	1,559	3,825	4,570	2,671	7,241	5,141	2,503	7,644	4.3
	14.9	3.3	7.4	8.6	2.7	4.5	14.5	3.7	7.0	15.7	2.8	6.2	
Nonprocessed basic materials	0	8,484	8,484	0	4,477	4,477	0	5,117	5,117	8	7,449	7,457	−1.5
	0.0	18.0	11.6	0.0	7.7	5.3	0.0	7.1	5.0	0.0	8.2	6.0	
Hides and skins	0	1,294	1,294	0	1,671	1,671	0	1,653	1,653	0	3,777	3,777	14.3
	0.0	2.7	1.8	0.0	2.9	2.0	0.0	2.3	1.6	0.0	4.2	3.1	
Wool, raw	0	514	514	0	576	576	0	373	373	0	384	384	−4.0
	0.0	1.1	0.7	0.0	1.0	0.7	0.0	0.5	0.5	0.0	0.4	0.3	
Cotton, raw	0	648	648	0	398	398	0	1,226	1,226	4	1,220	1,224	8.3
	0.0	1.4	0.9	0.0	0.7	0.5	0.0	1.7	1.2	0.0	1.3	1.0	
Sisal fibre and tow	0	6,028	6,028	0	1,832	1,832	0	1,865	1,865	4	2,068	2,072	−13.0
	0.0	12.8	8.3	0.0	3.2	2.2	0.0	2.6	1.8	0.0	2.3	1.7	

Processed basic materials, mineral fuels and lubricants	2,512 9.7	4,327 9.2	6,839 9.4	4,409 16.7	8,765 15.2	13,174 15.7	5,600 17.8	9,924 13.9	15,524 15.1	8,184 25.0	15,172 16.7	23,356 18.9	16.5
Pyrethrum extract	0 0.0	2,167 4.6	2,167 3.0	0 0.0	2,504 4.3	2,504 3.0	0 0.0	1,748 2.4	1,748 1.6	12 0.0	3,890 4.3	3,902 3.2	7.6
Petroluem products	2,512 9.7	2,160 4.6	4,672 6.4	4,409 16.7	6,261 10.8	10,670 12.7	5,600 17.8	8,176 11.4	13,776 13.4	8,172 24.9	11,282 12.5	19,454 15.8	19.5
Other basic materials, mineral fuels, and lubricants	396 1.5	2,166 4.6	2,562 3.5	1,230 4.7	2,404 4.2	3,634 4.3	1,307 4.2	2,958 4.1	4,265 4.1	840 2.6	3,265 3.6	4,105 3.3	6.0
Manufactured goods	13,869 53.6	4,591 9.7	18,460 25.3	14,916 56.6	6,835 11.8	21,751 25.9	16,481 52.4	8,926 12.5	25,407 24.7	14,249 43.5	11,174 12.3	25,423 20.6	4.1
Chemicals	3,026 11.7	1,845 3.9	4,871 6.7	3,855 14.6	2,823 4.9	6,678 7.9	4,850 15.4	3,523 4.9	8,373 8.1	5,224 15.9	4,772 5.3	9,996 8.1	9.4
Rubber goods[3]	281 1.1	0 0.0	281 0.4	232 0.9	0 0.0	232 0.3	287 0.9	0 0.0	287 0.3	371 1.1	12 0.0	383 0.3	3.9
Paper, paperboard, and manufactures[3]	866 3.3	0 0.0	866 1.2	1,537 5.8	0 0.0	1,537 1.8	1,485 4.7	0 0.0	1,485 1.4	1,491 4.5	983 1.1	2,474 2.0	14.0
Leather	0 0.0	189 0.4	189 0.3	0 0.0	149 0.3	149 0.2	0 0.0	189 0.3	189 0.2	106 0.3	336 0.4	442 0.4	11.2
Textile[6]	665 2.6	188 0.4	853 1.2	0 0.0	350 0.6	450 0.5	0 0.0	308 0.3	330 0.3	1,231 3.8	426 0.5	1,657 1.3	8.7
Cement	883 3.4	802 1.7	1,685 2.3	999 3.8	1,174 2.0	2,173 2.6	1,419 4.5	1,644 2.3	3,063 3.0	798 2.4	1,964 2.2	2,762 2.2	6.4
Glassware	105 0.4	60 0.1	165 0.2	147 0.6	136 0.2	283 0.3	74 0.2	237 0.3	311 0.3	201 0.6	197 0.2	398 0.3	11.6
Base metals	1,000 3.9	402 0.9	1,402 1.9	88 0.3	0 0.0	88 0.1	298 0.9	0 0.0	298 0.3	233 0.7	46 0.1	279 0.2	−18.0
Metal manufactures	1,616 6.2	377 0.8	1,993 2.7	1,372 5.2	567 1.0	1,939 2.3	1,686 5.4	401 0.6	2,087 2.0	2,235 6.8	795 0.9	3,030 2.5	5.4
Clothing[3]	1,943 7.5	0 0.0	1,943 2.7	975 3.7	0 0.0	975 1.2	615 2.0	0 0.0	615 0.6	336 1.0	201 0.2	537 0.4	−15.0
Footwear	1,398 5.4	77 0.2	1,475 2.0	686 2.6	398 0.7	1,084 1.3	574 1.8	326 0.5	900 0.9	489 1.5	262 0.3	751 0.6	−8.5
Other	2,086 8.1	651 1.4	2,737 3.7	4,925 18.7	1,238 2.1	6,163 7.3	5,171 16.4	2,298 3.2	7,469 7.2	1,534 4.7	1,180 1.3	2,714 2.2	0.0
Miscellaneous	122 0.5	245 0.5	367 0.5	8 0.0	403 0.7	411 0.5	0 0.0	128 0.2	128 0.1	1 0.0	189 0.2	190 0.2	−2.0
TOTAL	25,880 100.0	47,114 100.0	72,994 100.0	26,334 100.0	57,795 100.0	84,129 100.0	31,449 100.0	71,605 100.0	103,054 100.0	32,789 100.0	90,590 100.0	123,379 100.0	6.8

[1] Excludes re-exports.
[2] For EAC exports, meat preparations are included with Meat.
[3] Because of an incomplete breakdown, some domestic exports under these categories may be included under Other.
[4] For EAC exports tinned pineapples are included with Fruit and Vegetables.
[5] All items other than those specifically mentioned.
[6] Includes textile yarns, fabrics, made-up textiles, cotton piece goods, sisal bags and sacks, and blankets.

SOURCE: *Statistical Abstracts* (annual), East African Customs and Excise Department *Annual Trade Report of Tanzania, Uganda, and Kenya, 1972.*

Table 22: The Structure of Exports, 1964 and 1972

	1964			1972		
Export	To EAC	To Rest of World	Total	To EAC	To Rest of World	Total
			(percentage)			
Nonprocessed foodstuffs	8.5	91.5	100.0	7.4	92.6	100.0
Processed foodstuffs	56.4	43.6	100.0	13.6	86.4	100.0
Other foodstuffs	71.1	28.9	100.0	67.2	32.8	100.0
Nonprocessed basic materials	0.0	100.0	100.0	0.1	99.9	100.0
Processed basic materials	36.7	63.3	100.0	35.0	65.0	100.0
Other basic materials	15.5	84.5	100.0	20.5	79.5	100.0
Manufactures	75.1	24.9	100.0	56.1	43.9	100.0
Miscellaneous	33.2	66.8	100.0	1.0	99.0	100.0
TOTAL	35.5	64.5	100.0	26.6	73.4	100.0

SOURCE: Table 22.

Table 23: The Effective Rate of Protection of the East African Transfer Tax

	Transfer Tax Levied by Tanzania on Kenya		Transfer Tax Levied by Uganda on Kenya		Effective Protection Afforded to Kenya	
	Effective Rate	Nominal Rate	Effective Rate	Nominal Rate	"Modified"[1] Method	Balassa Method
Dairy products	6.2	0.8	—	—	92.8	123.6
Canning/preserving fruit and vegetables	18.5	2.8	5.5	0.9	30.9	59.8
Bakery products, cocoa, chocolate, and sugar confectionery	171.1	17.5	—	—	183.8	275.0
Sugar factories and refineries	379.3	24.6	—	—	62.9	104.2
Beer	63.6	25.0	—	—	−24.2	−20.5
Tobacco	309.7	50.0	—	—	−10.6	−9.0
Spinning, weaving, printing, and dyeing	115.6	19.2	—	—	73.6	96.1
Cordage, rope, and twine	—	—	0.8	0.3	28.3	33.1
Blanket manufacturing	—	—	17.3	4.6	−23.5	−22.6
Garment making and knitting	101.2	20.0	40.7	10.6	−32.1	−30.9
Made-up textiles except clothing	69.2	13.8	—	—	−50.3	−49.4
Footwear	115.9	15.0	68.8	11.0	−12.8	−10.1
Pulp, paper, and paperboard and manufactures thereof	34.8	7.3	43.0	8.6	−19.4	−16.9
Rubber products	28.0	7.7	—	—	51.9	61.8
Paints, varnishes, and lacquers	110.7	18.0	45.7	10.0	−4.7	10.0
Soap	140.4	18.1	—	—	0.5	12.2
Other chemicals	39.1	7.2	—	—	−11.5	−8.1
Cement	—	—	12.2	4.7	9.7	23.1
Metal products	29.4	6.7	16.6	4.1	−15.9	−13.5
Miscellaneous manufacturing	0.8	0.3	6.4	2.2	70.9	78.3

[1] The "modified" method assumes prices of nontraded goods are raised in proportion to the average tariff.

SOURCE: R. Reimer, *Effective Rates of Protection in East Africa*, Table 2.

Table 24: Import Implications of Sectoral Increments in Gross Value-Added, 1967[1]

Sector	Amount
	(£ thousand)
Nonmonetary sector	
Agriculture, fishing and forestry	6.2
Building and construction, water collection, and ownership of dwellings	47.8
Monetary sector	
Agriculture, fishing, and forestry	157.5
Prospecting, mining, and quarrying	274.5
Food manufacturing excluding bakeries	213.8
Bakery products, cocoa, and chocolate products	255.9
Beverages and tobacco manufacturing	153.2
Textile raw materials (cotton ginning, cordage, rope, and twine)	288.0
Finishing textiles (spinning, weaving, blanket manufacturing, printing, and dyeing)	807.1
Knitting, garment making, and made-up textiles	969.6
Footwear, leather, and fur products	744.8
Sawmilling	180.1
Wood products, printing, and publishing	683.0
Rubber products	629.5
Paints, varnishes, and soaps	667.4
Petroleum products and other chemicals	840.3
Cement, pottery, and miscellaneous nonmetallic minerals	311.4
Basic metal products, machinery, and miscellaneous manufacturing	796.9
Manufacturing, building, and transport equipment repair	496.2
Electricity and water	189.2
Building and construction	475.7
Distribution	149.0
Transport and communications	258.8
Restaurants and hotels	245.8
Ownership of dwellings	38.0
Financial institutions	62.2
Business services, personal services, recreation, and nonbusiness services	207.8
Education, health, government administration, and defense	120.8
Ownership of business premises	0.0
Unspecified	0.0

[1] Includes direct and indirect import effects.

SOURCE: Extracted from the Input/Output table for Kenya, 1967.

Table 25: Estimated Percentage of Net Home Consumption Affected by Import Licensing

Year	%	Year	%
1962	5.39	1967	22.24
1963	3.61	1968	37.72
1964	15.96	1969	27.90
1965	21.44	1970	29.53
1966	21.60	1971	18.73

SOURCE: David S. MacRae, *Import Licensing in Kenya*, IDS Working Paper No. 90, Appendix B, March 1973.

Table 26: Extent of Exchange Control Circular 1/72[1]

Schedule	0	1	2	3	4	5	6	7	8	9	Total
A	0.59	0.00	5.91	95.98	0.00	4.77	18.63	1.00	4.10	0.00	15.86
B	16.65	0.00	0.00	0.05	0.00	3.00	7.65	0.05	6.53	0.01	4.08
C	41.85	92.67	8.19	0.00	32.00	10.79	16.93	2.75	15.37	8.14	12.22
D	3.86	5.80	3.19	0.00	0.86	2.86	3.01	5.36	23.27	0.00	5.37
E	6.41	0.00	0.58	0.33	0.00	0.00	0.25	0.00	2.22	0.00	0.72
A–E	69.36	98.47	17.87	96.36	32.86	21.42	46.47	9.16	51.49	8.15	38.25

SITC SECTION

[1] The estimates apply the five schedules to the net home consumption figures for 1971. The table includes estimates of the proportions of six digit groups affected for those groupings where only a part of the total is brought under a schedule.

SOURCE: David S. MacRae, *Import Licensing in Kenya*, IDS Working Paper No. 90, Appendix C, March 1973.

Table 27: End Use Analysis of Imports, 1964–72

	1964	1965	1966	1967	1968	1969	1970	1971	1972	Compound Annual Growth Rate
Intermediate goods										
£ million	43.90	54.79	59.96	59.87	64.52	68.28	82.82	104.45	102.20	
%	55.3	58.9	54.2	54.3	55.9	58.0	56.2	56.2	56.1	11.1
Capital goods										
£ million	11.48	11.37	17.15	22.94	19.39	20.22	27.60	36.31	36.25	
%	14.5	12.2	15.5	20.8	16.8	17.2	18.7	19.6	19.9	15.5
Household consumption goods										
£ million	21.64	22.76	26.64	22.29	25.82	24.47	31.35	35.99	35.52	
%	27.3	24.4	24.1	20.2	22.4	20.7	21.2	19.4	19.5	6.4
Government imports										
£ million	2.34	4.23	6.83	5.13	5.68	4.86	5.81	8.95	8.20	
%	2.9	4.5	6.2	4.7	4.9	4.1	3.9	4.8	4.5	17.0
TOTAL										
£ million	79.36	93.15	110.58	110.23	115.40	117.84	147.58	185.70	182.17	
%	100.0	100.0	100.0	100.0	100.0	100.0	100.0	100.0	100.0	10.9

SOURCE: *Economic Survey*, 1970 and 1973.

Annex Four

Domestic Savings and Financial Intermediation

CHAPTER 1

THE ROLE OF SAVING PROPENSITY IN GROWTH

The process of economic growth is often viewed as one of saving, investing, and growing. Actually historical evidence on the process of economic growth suggests that the causal relationships may often have been exactly the opposite. As Kuznets has demonstrated[1] for the United States, the periods of high growth preceded, not followed, increases in saving-income and investment-income ratios. Even in the less developed countries in the postwar period, countries that have attained high growth rates are probably distinguished more by their efficiency of resource use (indicated, say, by incremental capital-output ratios) than by the rate of accumulation. For example, Iran and South Korea which have attained annual GDP growth rates significantly higher than Kenya's (11.3 percent and 11.8 percent,[2] respectively) were characterized by lower ICORs (2.0 and 2.46) and not by higher domestic saving-income ratios (17.3 percent and 17.8 percent).

Even to the extent that investment increases are important, it seems doubtful whether they are always stimulated by higher saving *propensities*; quite often investment increases bring about ex post increases in saving by changes in income or prices.[3] In this process, saving behavior and savings mobilization are important, not because they determine present investment, but because they increase the efficiency of capital formation and determine the process by which ex post equalization of saving and investment is brought about. This, in turn, has implications for future investment possibilities. The financial institutions which mobilize savings help in allocating funds to productive users, thus raising overall efficiency of investment.

Similarly, even though an ex post increase in the saving-income ratio can be brought about by an increased investment financed by credit creation, the ex ante propensity to save determines whether the equalization is brought about by inflation or not. If consumption propensity is high, the equalization is brought about by an increase in consumer prices as well as by an increase in the demand for imported consumer goods, which may reduce resources for investment in future. A high saving propensity, on the other hand, will make any given increase in investment more easily sustainable. Without the stimulus of investment, higher saving propensity may merely result in lower income, as is well known from Keynesian economics.

In light of these observations, we shall study the saving propensity and savings mobilization in Kenya not simply as ex post ratios but in terms of the processes associated with them. We shall conclude that the ex post saving-income ratio in Kenya over the period under study, namely 1964–71, was generally very high. Moreover, the relatively low rate of inflation which prevailed until recently might be an indication that the ex ante propensity to save was also high. The efficiency of investment as indicated by ICORs was also quite good until recently compared with most other less developed countries.

In recent years, however, there are indications that saving propensity may be declining and that the ex post high rate of investment can only be maintained by inflation, balance of payments deficits, and foreign borrowing—all of which could create

---

1. S. Kuznets, "Long-Term Changes in the National Income of the United States of America since 1870," in *Income and Wealth of the U.S.*, ed. S. Kuznets (Cambridge: Bowes and Bowes, 1952).
2. For the five-year period ending in 1970.
3. The effect of inflation on savings is, of course, complex. In general, all relevant factors being equal, an increase in *expected* inflation reduces saving *propensity*, although an actual increase in inflation may bring about an increase in ex post "forced" savings.

problems in the future.[4] Even though it is difficult to be definitive, it seems to us that in spite of the good performance of the past, the time has probably come to increase efforts in the direction of checking the incipient fall in saving propensity. We shall also argue that, from an allocational point of view, it may be necessary to allocate finance to new directions—agriculture and small business—for both efficiency and distributional reasons. The present system of financial institutions is primarily geared to the formal sector and needs some retuning for meeting newly emerging needs.

---

4. In this connection, it is sometimes argued that foreign capital inflows reduce ex ante domestic savings. In the mission's judgment, often it is the reverse, when for extraneous reasons saving propensity declines, and part of the gap may have to be filled by foreign capital inflow. For a more detailed discussion, see Appendix.

Chapter 2

Domestic Savings in Kenya

Movements in Aggregate Saving-Income Ratio

Movements in gross domestic savings and the saving-income ratio in Kenya are presented in Table 1. The ex post saving-income ratio was, except for 1965, around 19-20 percent. This is an excellent savings performance in comparison with most other less developed countries, and seems all the more remarkable in light of the slow rate of price inflation in general and in the consumer price index in particular (Table 2). This implies that ex post saving was by and large a reflection of genuine ex ante saving propensity and not in the nature of forced saving through credit creation.

In Tables 1 and 2, the saving-income ratios do not take into account the effect of international terms of trade. However, to measure the real purchasing power of the goods and services produced in a country, one should adjust the GDP at constant prices by the change in terms of trade. This provides a series of "gross domestic income"[1] from which, after deducting consumption, we obtain a series of gross domestic savings at import prices. This measurement of savings is helpful in computing resource requirements at constant prices.

The estimates of *GDS* and gross national savings (*GNS*)[2] as percentage of gross domestic income for Kenya and a number of other countries are presented in Table 3. In order to take out fluctuations, these are presented as three-year centered moving averages. In the light of these more refined estimates, Kenya's performance again appears to be excellent. Even South Korea, whose success in economic growth is generally regarded as spectacular, did not have a higher saving propensity than Kenya. In Africa, Ivory Coast, which has sustained a remarkable rate of growth (7.5 percent per annum over 1960-70), achieved a savings rate significantly higher than Kenya's. But the expatriate community is even more important in the Ivory Coast than in Kenya and, when allowance is made for factor incomes and transfers, Kenya's performance was comparable to Ivory Coast's. As far as national savings are concerned in recent years, Brazil has come to be regarded as the latest miracle in economic growth. But even there, we find that Brazil's saving-income ratio was lower than Kenya's.

However, while Kenya's long run performance in savings has been very good, there have been some signs of a slackening in savings performance in recent years. As shown

---

1. Gross domestic income (*GDY*), adjusted for changes in terms of trade, is defined as follows:

$$GDY = GDP - (\frac{X}{PX} - \frac{X}{PM})$$

where:
GDY = gross domestic income at constant prices
GDP = gross domestic product at constant prices
$\frac{X}{PX}$ = exports deflated by export price index
$\frac{X}{PM}$ = exports deflated by import price index

2. (*GNS*) defined as:

$$GNS = GDS + FSY + NCT$$

where:
GNS = gross national savings
GDS = gross domestic savings
FSY = net factor service income
NCT = net current transfer received

in Table 4, GDS actually declined in 1971 compared with that in 1970. The decline in GNS was even larger because of increase in net factor service payments and a decline in net current transfers received.

Factors Behind Savings Behavior

It will be interesting to examine the causes behind the good saving performance in Kenya compared with other developing countries. One possible reason could be the high growth rates of income.[3] Regression of domestic saving-income ratio on growth rate of GDP in Kenya over the period under study does show some association.[4] In particular, it "explains" the dips in the saving-income ratio in 1965 and 1971. However, for a cross-country analysis, it is difficult to be sure if high growth rate causes high saving-income ratio, or the other way round.[5] In order to understand the behavioral relationships better, it is desirable to make an analysis of the disaggregated figures on savings. In particular, it is desirable to analyze the saving behavior of households, government, and businesses separately.

As far as business savings are concerned, depreciation allowances accounting for a major part of business savings are determined by past investment pattern and tax laws, and should not be regarded as a function of income. No disaggregated figures on savings are available from published sources of data in Kenya. However, the macro-unit in the Ministry of Finance and Planning has prepared some provisional and as yet unpublished estimates of the components of savings. These figures are presented in Table 5, from which it can be seen that the major source of savings has been the household sector, whose contribution increased very considerably until 1969 (when it was about 54 percent). Since then, however, it has declined rapidly to only 25 percent in 1971. There has been a steady increase in the relative importance of depreciation allowances (in proportion to total capital stock), while the relative share of government savings has increased substantially, especially since 1969.

Does the structure of savings in Kenya throw any light on the factors behind Kenya's good performance compared with other developing countries? Table 6 presents

---

3. For a detailed discussion, see S. K. Singh, "The Determinants of Aggregate Savings," World Bank Economic Staff Working Paper No. 127, March 1972.

4. $S/Y = 0.1706 + 0.22 \frac{Y}{Y}$

   (19.8) (2.1) (t-statistics)
   $R^{-2} = 0.36$; $D.W. = 2.08'$ $SEE = 0.11$

	1965	1966	1967	1968	1969	1970	1971
Saving-Income Ratio							
Actual	0.166	0.202	0.182	0.173	0.194	0.202	0.185
Estimated	0.174	0.204	0.179	0.189	0.188	0.188	0.185

5. Since growth rate of GDP is, by definition,

(1) $G_y = k (\frac{I}{y}) = k \frac{S}{y} + k \frac{F}{y}$

where G_y is GDP growth rate
k inverse of ICOR
$\frac{I}{y}$ investment-income ratio
$\frac{S}{y}$ saving income ratio
$\frac{F}{y}$ foreign capital inflows as a ratio of income

we have

(2) $\frac{S}{y} \equiv \frac{1}{k} \cdot G_y - \frac{F}{y}$

Therefore, causal interpretation on regressions of type (2) could be misleading.

Household Savings

Since household savings has been the major source of savings, its decline in recent years must be a cause of concern. The saving-income ratio of household has fluctuated around 10 percent. The lowest ratio was in 1965, when the growth in personal disposable income was virtually nil. Apart from this drop, the ratio was rising steadily until it reached the level of 14.5 percent in 1969. Since then, however, it has dropped sharply, and was only 7 percent in 1971. Part of the changes in household saving-income ratio could be explained with reference to changes in growth rates of personal disposable income.[6]

Our analysis so far does not indicate any definite conclusions as to why Kenya's household saving performance was good and why it has deteriorated recently. In fact, it is quite possible that the recent decline is only a random fluctuation and the saving-income ratio will improve in the future as it did after 1965 and 1967.[7] However, it is also possible that there is some structural change going on in the economy and some tentative judgment may be made on the basis of what is known of the Kenyan economy.

The progressive Kenyanization of the economy may have operated to depress the propensity to save. The expatriate community has traditionally held much of the wealth in Kenya and could have been expected to contribute disproportionately to national savings. The thriftiness of the expatriate business community may also have been an element in Kenya's good savings performance. Because of the obligations imposed by the extended family system, Kenyans who took over expatriate jobs or businesses may not have been able to save as much as their predecessors, even if they inherited similar incomes.

A similar structural tendency towards a lower propensity to save could be caused by the urbanization process. Urban workers generally tend to save less than rural households, for a number of reasons. For one thing, demonstration effects are much stronger in the urban areas, but agriculturalists also tend to have a higher saving-income ratio because of the greater transient element in their incomes. A farmer can put his savings directly into farm improvement and therefore have better investment opportunities than his urban counterpart who can put his money only in banks;[8] to a farmer a tractor may be as much a status symbol as an automobile is to a city man.[9]

---

6. The regression equation is:

$S = 8.33 + 0.26Y$
   (4.17) (1.1)

where S = saving income ratio (%)
      Y = percentage change in personal disposable income

	1965	1966	1967	1968	1969	1970	1971
Actual	6.5	10.3	10.5	11.1	14.5	11.4	7.0
Estimated	8.4	12.3	9.6	11.3	10.0	10.5	9.6

7. Recent information does suggest, in fact, that savings performance in 1972 returned to the 1970 level.

8. In urban areas, saving to buy a house is an important encouragement to save. Kenya's past housing policy has offered little opportunity to lower income groups in urban areas to own their own houses, and home ownership has been further discouraged by the subsidies injected into

A more recent factor in savings behavior is the possibility that the expatriate business community has repatriated profits, through unofficial means, because of uncertainties about the future. If capital is repatriated by overinvoicing of imports, there is an apparent increase in consumer expenditure. In other words, even when real consumption is not increased, overinvoicing would result in higher recorded consumption in Kenya, even though part of it was actually saved and repatriated abroad.[10]

Another contributing factor to decline in household savings could have been the increased rate of inflation and static interest rates structure. In recent years for the first time since Independence, the real interest rates in Kenya are becoming negative. In 1972, for example, the rate of inflation was about 6 percent, or well above any rate offered by commercial banks (see Table 11).

Government Savings

Even though Kenya is a predominantly private sector economy, the role of the public sector is significant and increasing. The public sector's contribution to saving in the economy is noted in Table 5, and the sources of receipts and the types of expenditure, are given in Table 7. In 1964, tax receipts did not even cover government consumption expenditure. However, there were large international transfer receipts (£20.7 million) which offset this deficit, and gave rise to positive savings. Over the period 1964 to 1969, there was a decline in government savings, partly because of the decline in international transfers and partly because of the rapid rise in government consumption, which increased by about 17 percent in both 1968 and 1969. In 1970 and 1971, however, there was a significant recovery in government savings, a very welcome offset to the decline in private household savings over this period.

Corporate Savings

With economic growth, corporate savings, especially depreciation allowances, normally account for an increasing part of total gross savings.[11] In Kenya, depreciation allowances increased by about 140 percent between 1964 and 1971, an average annual rate of about 14 percent. However, the growth in undistributed profits was disappointing. They actually declined from £13.5 million in 1964 to £3.6 million in 1968. Since then, they have recovered to £13.1 million in 1971, but are still marginally below the 1964 level. Thus, even though the recent recovery in this component of saving is encouraging, the overall stagnation over the period is a cause for some concern.

---

public housing. It is hoped that the increasing emphasis on self-help, low cost urban housing schemes in Kenya will unlock a new source of savings among wage earners.

9. Using the data collected by *Central Province Survey* (1963), M. FG. Scott obtained the following regression:

$$S = -299 + 0.198Y \qquad (R^2 = 0.96)$$

where S = savings as indicated by cash surplus
Y = income

In spite of problems of data and interpretation of cross section equations, the marginal propensity to save of 20 percent indicated by the above equation is impressive. For details, see M. FG. Scott, "Estimates of Shadow Wages in Kenya," February 1973 (Mimeo).

10. In order to reduce the impact of uncertainty, it may be desirable to consider some scheme for smooth transfer of business from expatriate to Kenyan hands. See Annex Three.

11. For example, in the U.S. in 1971, capital consumption allowances were $93.8 billion which was about 9 percent of GNP ($1,050.4 billion). Corporate sector capital consumption allowances ($60.3 billion) and undistributed profits ($20.5 billion) together accounted for 53 percent of *total* private gross investment ($152.0 billion).

Prospects of Savings: Projections in the Macro-Model

Household Savings

The detailed projections on prospects of savings over the Third Plan period and beyond are given in Annex One, in the context of the overall macro-economic scenario. Some relevant figures on savings are reproduced in Table 8. From this table, we note that if the past good performance could be continued the ex ante saving-income ratio would be from 20 to 22 percent. This is a respectable rate although the investment program of the Third Plan, which implies a GDP growth rate of 7½ percent, will require investment-income ratio of about 25 percent. If, however, the average saving propensity of the household sector cannot be maintained at 10 percent, the average over the sample, but remains at the 7 percent reached in 1971, the overall saving-income ratio will be from 19 to 20 percent, which would be insufficient to finance the investment levels required for Plan targets. This would mean inflationary pressure and continuing balance of payments deficits, over the Plan period and beyond. However, the assumption about the saving-income ratio of households is critical and on the basis of statistical evidence available so far, the 1971 behavior could well be random. All that can be said is that there is need for vigilance in this respect, and it may be useful to ponder upon policy alternatives before the problem becomes serious.

Government Savings

In the projections, government savings account for about 24 percent of total savings in 1978, which is the proportion reached in 1971. Thus, if the Government visualizes an increasing relative role for the public sector, it may be necessary to improve government savings performance.[12]

Business Savings

The contribution of depreciation allowances to total savings continues to increase and would amount to 41 percent by 1978 in the projections. The annual growth rate in depreciation allowances of about 14.5 percent (in real terms) is quite reasonable.[13] However, the contribution of undistributed profits registers a decline from 11.8 percent in 1971 to 6 percent in 1978. As already mentioned, the slow growth in undistributed profits over the past and expected future is worrisome, and may deserve more intensive study for discussion of possible reasons and remedial measures.

---

12. For more detailed discussion, see Annex Two.
13. This, however, presupposes that target growth rates and investment rates over the Plan period are feasible, which may be doubtful. See Annex One.

CHAPTER 3

DEVELOPMENT IN FINANCIAL INTERMEDIATION

As discussed in Chapter 1, we believe that institutions for effective mobilization and allocation are important for achieving efficiency of resource use. However, in spite of the importance of the financial institutions, we do not propose to discuss these in this annex because they have been adequately discussed elsewhere.[1] We therefore confine ourselves to a brief reference to the main highlights in the financial sector over recent years.

The banking system in Kenya is fairly advanced in comparison with other developing countries at a similar stage of development. There are eleven commercial banks in Kenya, three of which dominate the banking system and account for 80 percent of total bank deposits. The rate of growth of money supply has shown some wide fluctuations in recent years. As shown in Table 9, the rate of growth of money supply accelerated to 23 percent per annum in 1970. This was due to the rise in deposits, particularly the term deposits, and was due partly to the increase in blocked accounts of emigrants and other nonresidents, and partly to a genuine increase in savings. However, in 1971, there was a decline in the rate of growth of depositors and money supply. In 1972, the money supply expanded by about 14.7 percent.

The loans and advances to the private sector expanded at an accelerating rate up to 1971, when the rate of expansion was 36 percent. This was associated with a serious deficit in balance of payments and, for the first time, the Central Bank used its power of variation in minimum cash balances. The Central Bank announced that from December 16, 1971, commercial banks were to maintain minimum cash balances equivalent to 5 percent of their net deposit liabilities, in addition to the required liquidity ratio of 12½ percent imposed in December 1969 under the Banking Act. However, due to the abruptness of the change, some banks found it difficult to meet the requirement, and the measure had to be withdrawn after six weeks. In 1972, there was a significant slowdown of demand for credit mainly due to the tightening of import controls and the disruption of trade with Uganda. Commercial banks, in general, seemed to have excess liquidity and the monetary authorities were urging them to expand their lending.

As regards allocation of loans, the main problem is to find ways of expanding commercial bank lending to agriculture. As shown in Table 10, the proportion of loans and advances made to agriculture has not been expanding at all—in fact, it has declined from 12.3 percent in 1969 to 10.2 percent in 1971. This is in spite of attempts by the Central Bank and the Government to persuade the banks to expand their loans to agriculture. It seems that unless some way is found by which public institutions can act as intermediaries for channeling funds to agriculture, the share of loans to agriculture is likely to remain inadequate.

Apart from her commercial banks, Kenya has eleven nonbanking financial institutions in the private sector under the category of "specified financial institutions." In the last two years, their role relative to commercial banks has been increasing. At the end of June 1970, the assets of nonbanking financial institutions amounted to only 8 percent of those of the commercial banks; by the end of September 1972, this ratio had risen to 15 percent. This was due partly to the differential impact of credit controls on banking and nonbanking financial institutions; but the ratio rise was also influenced by the more

1. See, for example, G. F. Donaldson and J. D. Von Pischke, *A Survey of Farm Credit in Kenya*, USAID Spring Review of Small Farmer Credit, Vol. VII, February 1973, Washington, D. C.; B. Dillon, *Financial Institutions in Kenya 1964–77: A Preliminary Analysis,* Working Paper No. 61 (Nairobi: Institute for Development Studies, September 1972); *Money and Banking in Kenya,* Bank of Kenya, 1973. The subject has also been covered comprehensively in earlier World Bank reports, including the Agriculture Sector Study (for summary of which see Part III).

flexible and aggressive interest rate policy followed by these institutions in attracting deposits in the face of a rising rate of inflation in contrast to the static interest rates of commercial banks.

There are also a number of specialized lending institutions in the public sector providing development finance for industry and commerce, agriculture, housing, and tourism. In general, these public sector institutions depend on government loans and grants or on foreign capital. They do not mobilize their own resources and are generally undercapitalized. Nor have they succeeded in attracting the long term funds available in other financial institutions (e.g., life insurance companies). If the public financial institutions are to play their proper role in savings mobilizaton for growth, it is desirable to think of ways to broaden their capital base. In particular, some of the public sector institutions (e.g., Agricultural Finance Corporation) might be able to accept deposits from the households they serve. The growth of the cooperative savings movement is especially promising in this respect.

Chapter 4

Some Policy Implications

As suggested in the preceding chapters, the performance of the Kenyan economy in generating and mobilizing domestic savings has been very good and if the trends were likely to continue in the future, policy instruments for improving savings performance would not be of high priority. There are, however, certain indicators which suggest that, left alone, savings performance might deteriorate in the future, and it is therefore necessary to think of policy measures to prevent this deterioration. In fact, as is often found in real life, once a situation starts to deteriorate, destabilizing forces are strengthened and corrective measures become more painful and less effective. It is therefore advisable to anticipate the problems, and discuss and adopt preventive policy measures before the problems get out of hand.

Interest Rate Policy

The first area in which some review of policy is necessary is interest rate policy. As shown in Table 11, the interest rate level and structure have been almost static in Kenya for as long as systematic data are available, which is since 1967. The rate of interest on savings deposits in commercial banks and post offices has been 3 percent per annum. The deposit rates in hire purchase companies and building societies are somewhat higher, but these are restricted in coverage. The minimum rate on loans and advances has been static at 7 percent, but actual rates may have gone up to a certain extent. The Central Bank rates on advances against Kenya Government securities and under crop finance schemes have also been static at 6.5 and 6.0 percent, respectively. The redemption yield rates on locally registered Kenya Government stocks based on government support prices have actually declined since 1965, particularly in the case of long term (over 10 years), and medium-term (5-10 years) stocks. The yield on long term stocks declined from around 8.5 percent in 1965 to around 7 percent in 1972, and that on medium term stocks from around 7.7 percent to around 6.5 percent. The structure and level of interest rates was not a serious problem as long as the rate of inflation was low and the balance of payments strong. However, in 1972, when the rate of inflation reached about 6 percent, the real rate of interest became negative for the first time since Independence. Similarly, the balance of payments position in 1972, though better than in 1971, was still under strain, and it is likely to come under further pressure as the Third Plan programs create new demands for foreign resources.

The rate of inflation is, of course, a worldwide phenomenon at present. However, in many countries, the old orthodoxy about low interest rate policy has been given up and interest rates have moved up along with inflation. For example, as shown in Table 12, in Britain and in Euro dollar markets (the two most important markets for Kenya) interest rates have gone up dramatically and are now much higher than those in Kenya. For an open economy like Kenya's, this could cause serious problems. For example, foreign companies and banks which might under better conditions have borrowed abroad (and thus increased the availability of resources for the economy) are now tempted to borrow domestically. There are, of course, restrictions on domestic borrowing by foreign companies, but the interest differential can still create pressures on domestic resources by tempting foreign companies to borrow to the limit, and even to find ways of bypassing the legal provisions.[1] Similarly, it creates an incentive for foreign companies to repatriate

---

1. See Annex Three.

their profits (on which there is no restriction) which could otherwise have been used domestically. It is true that the rate of inflation in most capital exporting countries is even higher than in Kenya. However, for international financial movement, the relevant consideration is not the domestic inflation rate but the interest rate difference and exchange risk. On both these counts, the dice are loaded against Kenya.

In this connection, it is important to emphasize the mutually destabilizing effects of inflation and balance of payments deficits under a regime of static interest rates and exchange rates. As inflation gathers momentum, it stimulates demand for investment, and by increasing expected rate of inflation, reduces saving propensity. This is associated with, and further stimulates, the rise in imports and the discouragement of exports; the consequent strain on balance of payments and risk of exchange rate depreciation further reduces foreign capital inflow, thus further reducing the total resources available and increasing the rate of inflation. Once this set of forces gets going, it is possible to end up either with a Latin American type of situation, with open inflation and exchange crises, or the Indian type of situation, with repressed inflation and exchange controls. The time for action is before destabilizing expectations get entrenched, and in Kenya's case that time is now.

It is, of course, desirable to make some quantitative estimates of the effects of interest rate variation on savings propensity, on financing of savings, on efficiency of investment (through better allocation and through capital-labor substitution), and on balance of payments (through demand for imported capital goods). In Annex One, we do try to work out the implications of variation in interest on macro projections to 1985, on the basis of some assumptions about elasticity of substitution between capital and labor. However, it has not been possible to make any systematic statistical analysis in Kenya because interest rates have varied so little in the past. In the absence of relevant empirical material in Kenya, it may be of some value to study the experience of other developing countries which have adopted different interest rate policies. It is, of course, possible that the experience of one country does not apply to another. The problem is further complicated by the fact that, even in those countries where interest rates have changed, it is difficult to identify the specific influence of changes in interest rates because of other associated changes going on. All that one can get is a broad feel of the possible association of interest rate policies and the other relevant economic magnitudes.

Among the countries that have made dramatic experiments in interest rate and other financial policies in recent years, the three that are well known are: South Korea (since the mid-sixties), and Indonesia and Brazil (since 1967/1968). The initial characteristics of these three countries were all different. In South Korea, the domestic savings rate (three-year centered moving average) was 5 percent in 1963 and the foreign resource balance was two-and-a-half times the level of exports. But the efficiency of investment as indicated by ICOR was quite good (Table 13). In Indonesia, both domestic savings and ICOR were in bad shape (domestic saving-income ratio about 6 percent and ICOR about five), although the resource balance was only about 25 percent of exports. In Brazil's case, the domestic savings ratio was quite good (about 17 percent) and the resource balance varied between deficit and surplus, but the efficiency of investment was low (ICOR was about four). The financial policies adopted by these three countries also differed markedly.

However, all three countries, although different in circumstance, adopted measures to increase the real rate of interest and, although the mechanism differed, they all accelerated their growth rates by improving the elements in which performance had been weakest. Thus, South Korea improved its domestic savings ratio (which was poor), though not its ICOR (which was good). Brazil accelerated its growth through an improvement in ICOR, but not in its saving-income ratio (which was good). Indonesia had poor performance in both savings and ICORs, and it improved its performance in both respects, though its savings performance still has a long way to go. In all three cases, the financial policies were associated with improvement in the degree of financial intermediation, as indicated by the figures of time and savings deposits shown in Table 14. These figures show that the proportion of money supply held in time and savings deposits increased substantially, particularly in Korea and Indonesia. Obviously, one cannot conclude anything definite about the effects of interest rate policy from this. All one can say is that the three countries which have, in recent years, followed active financial reform policies, have accelerated growth. Their experience may not apply to Kenya; but their experience certainly does not contradict the hypothesis that higher real interest rates may help growth—through stimulating savings, better allocation, or the more intensive use of capital. If Kenya decides to reexamine her interest rate policy, as the mission recommends she should, it will be useful for the Government to examine the experience of these three countries more closely to see what lessons Kenya could learn.

In the context of a brief review of this kind, it is not possible to suggest any detailed policy reforms. However, in the light of the discussion in this chapter, the mission would like to make some tentative recommendations about the direction in which interest rate policy in Kenya might move.

(a) From the point of view of savings mobilization, as well as their allocative efficiency, there is a case for higher interest rates for both deposits and loans.
(b) The increase in rates should be particularly high at the long term end of the interest rate structure. This seems desirable because short term loans are necessary for working capital which is complementary with employment. It is the longer term rate of interest that may be important for reducing capital intensity, which is particularly high in some sectors in Kenya. The longer term interest rate may also be a significant instrument for changing the import intensity of investment goods, because imported investment goods generally tend to be of longer life than similar domestic investment goods. It could be argued that, with fungibility of capital, it is difficult to change the structure of rates by government policy. Actually, both the level and structure of interest rates are now largely determined by administrative fiats and not by market forces. In particular, the low rates that often prevail on long term lending by official institutions can be changed by government policy. Moreover, even though some amount of fungibility is possible, long term capital investment cannot be generally financed by short term loans, due to the costs of rollovers and the risk of illiquidity.
(c) High interest rate policy should not exclude the agricultural sector. It seems to the mission that the real problem is one of *access*, not cost; in other words, it is much better to get credit to small scale farmers at the market rate, than not to get it to them at subsidized rates. In fact, the cost of credit is not a major item in farm budgets, and the mission would not expect a moderate increase in lending rates to have any significant adverse effects on farmers. Quite the reverse, the productivity of credit—particularly on such inputs as fertilizer, improved seed, or grade cattle—should be high enough to make even high cost credit attractive to the progressive farmer.
(d) It is true that many agriculturists in Kenya are at present saddled with heavy debts, partly as a result of the terms of settlement schemes. However, the way to tackle the debt problem on old and new loans is to be liberal in amortization schedule and not in lower interest rates.[2]

2. For example, a settlement farmer with a development loan of £1,000 over ten years at 6½ percent, pays £165 a year (£100 redemption + £65 interest). If the interest rate were halved (to 3¼ percent) he would save £33 in annual costs. But the same result would be

Financial Intermediaries

The second area of suggestions relates to financial intermediaries. In general, our feeling is that the financial institutions are well developed in Kenya and a more active interest rate policy should further stimulate the system and enable it to perform its functions more effectively on savings mobilization and allocation. The main areas in which there is, we feel, a need for strengthening institutions are, first, institutions for channeling financial resources to small African businessmen and farmers, and second, institutions for mobilizing savings from low income groups in both rural and urban areas. In terms of priority, it seems to us that the agencies for channeling of resources are more important than agencies for saving mobilization. At present it seems that financial institutions are net transferers of funds from rural areas to urban areas. Thus, any further development of institutions for mobilization of savings, without a prior (or at least concurrent) development of lending functions, will only accelerate the drainage of funds from rural areas to urban areas.

The development of lending institutions for agriculturists becomes extremely important if the strategy of agriculture oriented growth is accepted. The problems and possibilities in this field have been examined at length in Part III, the Agricultural Sector Survey. Similarly, the institutions for channeling resources to small African businessmen are inadequate and, as discussed in Annex Five, special measures are needed for this purpose, possibly in conjunction with a special Kenyanization Fund. Mobilization of savings from small savers will, however, become more important in the future as policies are adopted for income redistribution. For this purpose, we recommend the following policy measures:

- The strengthening of the Post Office Savings Bank as a savings institution. In many respects the post office network seems most suited as a mobilizer of small savings, but over the period 1963 to 1971, the net balances due to depositors have actually slightly declined. The Government has recently taken some steps to improve the administration of post office savings, which may help to increase its popularity. It may be necessary to introduce more reforms later.
- The mission feels that the rural cooperatives provide an excellent instrument for savings mobilization, as well as for channeling credits to farms. It is hoped that priority will be given to this aspect of cooperative development, rather than unproductive forms, such as consumer cooperatives.
- It would be useful to explore ways in which commercial banks could be encouraged to lower their minimum deposit requirements (as the KCB has already done). More practicable ways than moral suasion will also have to be found to increase commercial bank lending to small farmers and entrepreneurs.

Impact of Restructured Growth Strategy

Apart from these suggestions regarding financial policies, it is important to emphasize that the general policy packages discussed in this report have relevance for savings mobilization also. In particular, it seems worth emphasizing that an agriculture oriented growth strategy, which should help with the balance of payments gap, unemployment, and poverty, may also help to stimulate savings. As already discussed, among people

---

achieved by extending the maturity of the loan from ten to fifteen years. If the maturity were extended to as much as twenty-one years, the farmer could afford to pay 8½ percent on his loan, and still save £33 a year, or 20 percent of his present settlement costs.

with the same level of income, agriculturists tend to save more than urban workers, and the effects of income redistribution on savings will be less serious for growth if the redistribution is from urban rich to rural poor, than from urban rich to urban poor. Because of lack of data on savings in different sectors, it is difficult to be more precise about the effects of restructuring growth. One point worth noting is that, with restructured growth, investment requirements are brought down to a manageable level, and this reduces the savings due to depreciation allowances in the future. This, however, is not a demerit point for restructured growth, because by reducing investment requirements, the gap between investment and saving is actually being reduced, which is what matters from the point of view of internal and external imbalance.

Appendix: Effect of Foreign Capital Inflow on Domestic Savings: A Case Study for Kenya

In recent years, it has been argued that foreign capital inflows reduce domestic savings; it is further argued that because of this substitution effect, the *net* benefits of foreign capital may be significantly less than the inflows suggest. In this appendix, we examine this thesis in the light of the Kenya experience. We begin with a brief review of the stages of development in this thesis and examine its validity from general analytical and statistical points of view. We shall then examine the Kenyan data to test the hypothesis and present some results of our analysis of the problem from a different point of view.

A Brief Survey of the Literature

The literature on this subject has been recently reviewed by Mikesell and Zinser.[1] Without going over the same ground, we would like to summarize the main stages of the debate very briefly:

(i) T. Haarelmo pointed out the general principle that to the extent that foreign capital inflows increase the permanent income of a country, these inflows would be expected to lead to increase in consumption as well as savings.

(ii) Rahman[2] emphasized the importance of "psychological" factors in inducing the government to relax its saving efforts, when foreign funds are available. Rahman and Enos and Griffin,[3] tried to test the hypothesis by estimating cross-country regressions of the following type:

$$\frac{S}{Y} = \alpha + \beta \frac{F}{Y}$$

where S = domestic savings
Y = gross national product
F = foreign capital inflow defined as imports minus exports

They found β to be significantly negative.

(iii) Weisskopf[4] argued that the Rahman and Griffin-Enos results were unsatisfactory because of the econometric problem of identification, and that they are misleading in a trade-constrained situation. Weisskopf developed a technique for identifying savings constraint cases and tested the hypothesis for the cases where savings constraint was binding, and found evidence in support of the hypothesis that foreign capital inflow reduced domestic savings.

(iv) Papanek, in an interesting article,[5] has attacked this thesis from three angles. He argues, first, that the statistical relationship is, in part, the result of an accounting convention, not of a behavioral relationship; second, that estimates

---

1. Raymond F. Mikesell and James E. Zinser, "The Nature of the Savings Function in Developing Countries: A Survey of the Theoretical and Empirical Literature," *The Journal of Economic Literature*, March 1973.
2. M. A. Rahman, "Foreign Capital and Domestic Savings: A Test of Haarelmo's Hypothesis with Cross-Country Data," *Review of Economics and Statistics*, February 1968.
3. K. B. Griffin and J. L. Enos, "Foreign Assistance: Objectives and Consequences," *Economic Development and Cultural Change*, April 1970.
4. T. E. Weisskopf, "An Econometric Test of Alternative Constraints on the Growth of Underdeveloped Countries," *The Review of Economics and Statistics*, February 1972. For a critique of Weisskopf's methodology, see *The Review*, February 1973.
5. G. F. Papanek, "The Effect of Aid and other Resources Transfers on Savings and Growth in Less Developed Countries," *The Economic Journal*, September 1972.

of savings contain wide margins of error. Lumping together different types of capital inflow is wrong. Strikingly different results obtained by different authors cast doubt on their reliability. Third, Papanek contends that these authors mistake association for causality. Exogenous factors may cause both high capital inflow and low saving rates.

(v) Chenery and Carter[6] have shown that even if the substitution hypotheses were correct, the implication drawn about the effects of foreign capital are wrong, because the analysis ignores the interdependence between different variables and their dynamic effects.

Some General Criticisms

The "substitution hypothesis" and the usual statistical analysis to support it seems to us to be defective for a number of reasons. In the first place, it is difficult to imagine a behavioral saving function for the economy as a whole. The saving behavior of the business sector as far as depreciation allowances (which generally account for more than 50 percent of business savings) are concerned, depends mainly on tax laws and the past investment pattern. Similarly, the government saving behavior is influenced by different types of factors, political processes, current expenditure requirements of past capital expenditure, etc., and should be analyzed separately. Thus, it seems difficult to imagine, for purposes of economic analysis, a behavioral entity for the economy as a whole whose "income" is increased as a result of foreign capital inflow and which reacts in such a way as to reduce its domestic savings.

Even if one can imagine a behavioral entity for the economy as a whole, should capital inflow lead, a priori, to lower savings? Possibly, but not necessarily. To the extent that foreign aid increases "permanent income," it can be expected to lead to some increase in "permanent consumption." However, to the extent that the availability of foreign techniques increases the productivity of capital, foreign capital inflow improves the rate at which present goods can be transformed into future goods, and thus may increase the rate of savings. It is difficult to be sure which way the balance will lie.

Even if the a priori thesis has some theoretical validity, its statistical implementation is faulty and fails to test the hypothesis. First of all, the statistical equations use "trade balance" (imports minus exports) as the indicator of foreign aid. Actually, the thesis if correctly tested statistically, would require estimates of grant element of foreign capital by examining terms of lending and sources of finance for the gap; it cannot be approximated by a trade balance which might be financed in any of a number of ways by drawing down of foreign reserves, workers' remittances, profits from foreign investment, suppliers' credits at exorbitant interest rates, or foreign aid on virtual grant terms. Similarly, if the influence of foreign capital inflows on savings is to be estimated, both should be measured independently. Actually, savings are generally estimated by deducting the trade balance from investment so that if there is any error in measurement of the trade balance it is transmitted, one-to-one, to savings estimates, which are then being regressed on the trade balance (thus violating the statistical assumptions underlying regression theory). Moreover, the statistical regressions assume that current income and foreign capital inflows are independent, whereas, in practice, in the absence of foreign capital inflows, current domestic income would have been lower due to lack of raw materials and lacking complementary elements for domestic investment.

Even if the statistical result of negative association between savings and trade balance were correct, the inference of causal relation will be wrong. This is not the usual

---

6. H. Chenery and N. G. Carter, "Internal and External Aspects of Development Plans and Performance, 1960–1970," World Bank Working Paper No. 141, February 1973.

caveat applicable to statistical relation. In the first place, the usual growth rate equation gives definitionally an equation where saving-income ratio is negatively associated with foreign capital *if*, in regression, growth can be assumed to be independent of foreign capital inflow. Thus

$$\frac{S}{Y} = k(G_y) - \frac{F}{Y}$$

$\frac{S}{Y}$ = saving-income ratio

k = ICOR

G_y = growth rate of GDP

$\frac{F}{Y}$ = capital inflow as a ratio of GDP

In this case, the causality is from foreign and domestic savings to growth, not from foreign capital to domestic savings. Second, quite often due to extraneous reasons (for example, a transient decline in income due to bad weather), savings may decline leading to emergency imports and balance of trade deficit. However, here both low savings and high trade deficit are caused by other factors, not one by the other. Some such cases have been pointed out by Papanek. As we suggest later, Kenya's case fits in this category rather well.

Finally, even if the causal inference were correct for ex post relation between savings and foreign capital inflow, the inference about the efficiency of foreign capital will be wrong. As Chenery and Carter argue, "The proper test of the effectiveness of aid, however, is its effect on growth or other social objectives rather than on savings as conventionally measured... In cases where there is constraint other than savings, or where the constraints are mixed over time period, the negative association can be expected as a result of ex post savings falling below ex ante as the system is constrained elsewhere. The association between aid and savings in these case (the vast majority) is not direct and, in fact, were we to reduce F (current trade balance), savings would rise, but *output, investment* and *consumption* would fall."[7] To take a simple example, suppose that food is imported to pay workers on a public works project and workers consume the food instantly. In terms of national accounts, output is increased by the value of public works (investment), consumption and investment are also increased by the same amount, and saving-income ratio is reduced. However, if this food aid had not come in, output, investment, and consumption would have been lower, and the inference from the regression, where output is independent of "food aid," is misleading. The correct way to assess the effects of foreign capital is to work out the alternative scenarios of output, investment, consumption, and so on under alternative assumptions about the levels of capital inflow and examine the difference made by changes in capital inflow to the overall picture. This is what we try in our model in Annex One and the basic results are reported below.

Statistical Analysis with the Kenyan Data

In the light of our comments on the usual statistical analysis of the problem, it is clear that this type of analysis has very limited power of discrimination for testing the hypothesis under discussion, and widely different results could be obtained for different countries and different times and different approximations for "foreign capital inflow." Our analysis of Kenyan data confirms these suspicions. Testing the form used by Rahman and Enos and Griffin, we got

$$\frac{S}{Y} = 0.1707 - 0.1852 \frac{F}{Y}$$
$$(15.2) \quad (-0.57)$$

7. Ibid., pp. 27–28.

$\bar{R}^2 = -0.11$; DW $= 1.2$; SEE $= 0.026$

where $S =$ gross national savings
$Y =$ gross domestic income
$F =$ resource gap
(All figures in constant prices)

However, if the same hypothesis is tested in different form, we get

$$S = -230.5 + 0.36Y - 0.77F$$
$$(-0.37) \quad (7.1) \quad (-3.08)$$
$\bar{R}^2 = 0.89$; DW $= 0.89$; SEE $= 20.0$

It is interesting to note that the coefficient of F is not significantly different from unity which may well be the result of *defining* S as $I - F$. If this were a genuine behavioral response one would expect some lag in response of saving to movements in F. However, if we introduce a lag of one period to F we get

$$S = -114.5 + 0.25Y + 0.422F_{-1}$$
$$(-1.2) \quad (3.3) \quad (0.86)$$
$\bar{R}^2 = 0.72$; DW $= 2.2$; SEE $= 32.8$

Similarly, if we move away from definitional relationship and use long term capital inflows (FC) as the indicator of the foreign capital inflow instead of trade balance, we get

$$S = -139.87 + 0.28Y - 0.24FC$$
$$(1.3) \quad (3.1) \quad (-0.49)$$
$\bar{R}^2 = 0.70$; DW $= 2.74$; SEE $= 33.3$

In order to further examine the hypothesis, we also made a disaggregative analysis. In most cases, foreign capital inflows are not used to finance imports of noncapital goods directly. Therefore, the hypothesis of negative association between F and S implies that due to the fungibility of foreign exchange, the availability of foreign capital either increases imports of consumer goods (MC) or raw materials (MR) or reduces exports (X). In order to test this hypothesis we ran the following regressions:

$$MR = 5.57 + 0.055FC + 0.1399GDP$$
$$(0.1) \quad (0.20) \quad (2.9)$$
$\bar{R}^2 = 0.73$; DW $= 1.2$; SEE $= 19.0$

$$MC = 19.50 - 0.089FC + 0.046GDP$$
$$(0.63) \quad (-0.57) \quad (1.75)$$
$\bar{R}^2 = 0.25$; DW $= 1.54$; SEE $= 10.4$

Government imports (MG)

$$MG = 8.76 + 0.067FC + 0.0031GDP$$
$$(0.83) \quad (1.256) \quad (0.34)$$
$\bar{R}^2 = 0.32$; DW $= 2.0$; SEE $= 3.6$

$$X = 103.09 + 0.144FC + 0.207GDP$$
$$(1.40) \quad (0.39) \quad (3.26)$$
$\bar{R}^2 = 0.79$; DW $= 3.54$; SEE $= 25.1$

Except in the case of government imports (which include import of capital goods), none of the above equations shows any significant evidence in support of the hypothesis under consideration.

Apart from regressions, if we examine the figures, we note that only in the last two years, namely 1970 and 1971, has the current balance (imports minus exports) been significantly positive. As discussed in the text, these were the years when due to extraneous factors, savings propensity probably did decline leading to balance of payments deficit. Thus, the Kenyan experience will fit, rather well, Papanek's examples where causality does not run from trade balance to savings but the other way round. Moreover, the balance of payments deficits were financed largely by drawing down of foreign reserves and this also illustrates the fallacy of equating trade balance with foreign aid.

On the basis of the above results, we conclude that regression equations of ex post aggregate savings on trade balance do not measure the effect of foreign capital inflow on domestic savings propensity. Because of the various conceptual and statistical problems involved, these simple minded regressions give completely misleading (and unstable) results. For more meaningful results, we have to analyze the problem in the framework of a complete model, where the saving functions are treated in a disaggregated fashion and the dynamic effects are studied. This is what we did in our macro-model (Annex One) and some of the main results are reported below.

Result of Analysis with the Macro-Model

Details of the macro-model are presented in Annex One. The model uses slightly modified gap analysis, when the ex post equalization of ex ante and ex post consumption is brought about by changes in relative prices of consumer goods. We note in Annex One that if the target growth rates are to be attained, there is a gap in foreign exchange resources, over and above the past and expected future commitments. If this gap could be filled by commercial borrowing, the macro-economic scenario is as presented in Table 15. If the extra resources are not obtained to fill this gap, and structural and other policy changes are not adopted, the feasible growth rate would be about half of the plan targets. On the other hand, if the additional foreign capital required to fill the gap is provided, domestic savings are, in fact, higher by a substantial amount. However, if we run regressions of savings on income and foreign capital, it does not capture this effect, but shows the usual negative association between savings and trade balance. (See Table 15.)

Our arguments and results should not be interpreted to mean that foreign capital inflow can do no harm. In fact, we argue in Annex One that foreign capital inflows, indiscriminately used, could create debt servicing problems in the future, and we point out at other places that, in the past, foreign private investment and external aid have not always been in Kenya's interest. We also suggest that, when faced with the foreign exchange problem, it is advisable to examine structural and policy changes which may reduce the foreign exchange gap. When foreign capital inflows are available, they may appear to offer an easy solution, and policymakers may ignore the harder alternatives of structural and policy changes and thus harm the long run objectives of a country. All that we argue here is these types of effects cannot be assessed by simple minded regressions, but have to be based on case-by-case country studies. These studies may have to take into account political and institutional factors for analysis of saving behavior in the economy, particularly that of the Government.

STATISTICAL TABLES
Annex Four
Index

Table No.		
1.	Gross Domestic Savings	373
2.	Consumer Price Indices in Various Countries	373
3.	Gross Domestic Savings (GDS) and Gross National Savings (GNS) as a Percentage of Gross Domestic Income (GDY)	374
4.	Domestic Savings Adjusted for Terms of Trade	375
5.	Sources of Savings in Kenya	375
6.	Structure of Savings in Various Countries	376
7.	Government Receipts and Expenditures, 1964–71	377
8.	Projections of Ex Ante Savings, 1974–85	378
9.	Changes in Money Supply and Related Variables	379
10.	Loans and Advances by Commercial Banks	379
11.	Principal Interest Rates, 1967–72	380
12.	Selected Interest Rates in Europe	382
13.	ICORs in Selected Countries	382
14.	Structure of Deposits and Currency in Various Countries	383
15.	Comparison of Systems Dynamics with Different Levels of Foreign Capital Inflow	384

Table 1: Gross Domestic Savings

Year	Gross Domestic Saving	GDP	Saving-Income Ratio
	(£ million)		(percentage)
1964	63.92	355.00	18.0
1965	53.57	356.39	15.0
1966	82.49	415.89	19.8
1967	86.66	437.54	19.8
1968	87.08	479.73	18.2
1969	106.55	519.15	20.5
1970	116.40	577.79	20.1
1971	121.13	630.46	19.2
1972	143.51	711.21	20.2

SOURCE: Ministry of Finance and Planning, Kenya.

Table 2: Consumer Price Indices in Various Countries

Year	Brazil	Colombia	Korea	Philippines	Ivory Coast	Ethiopia	Tanzania	Kenya
				(1963 = 100)				
1960	27	68.0	72.4	88.1	—	—	102.5	93.6
1961	38	74.0	78.3	89.6	101.2	—	103.4	95.4
1962	58	75.8	83.6	94.7	99.8	—	103.4	98.2
1963	100	100.0	100.0	100.0	100.0	100.0	100.0	100.0
1964	187	117.6	127.9	108.2	101.3	—	101.7	99.9
1965	303	121.8	145.3	111.0	102.7	—	108.4	103.5
1966	444	146.0	162.8	117.0	108.4	126.8	113.4	108.4
1967	575	157.9	180.4	124.3	110.9	127.8	116.0	111.1
1968	714	167.1	200.6	127.3	116.7	128.0	120.2	111.9
1969	880	184.0	220.8	129.7	122.0	129.8	121.8	110.8
1970	1,048	196.6	248.9	148.4	133.5	143.0	125.2	113.2
1971	1,269	214.4	279.7	170.0	131.4	143.7	130.3	117.5

SOURCE: *International Financial Statistics*, 1972 Supplement, International Monetary Fund, 1973.

Table 3: Gross Domestic Savings (GDS) and Gross National Savings (GNS) as a Percentage of Gross Domestic Income (GDY)

	Kenya		Tanzania		Ethiopia		Ivory Coast		Colombia		Philippines		Brazil		Indonesia		South Korea	
Per capita income, 1970 in US$	150		100		80		310		340		210		420		80		250	
Population, mid-1970 (thousand)	11,250		13,270		24,625		4,941		21,632		36,850		92,764		115,567		31,793	
Annual GNP, 1960–70 Growth Rate %	6.7		6.1		5.0		7.5		4.9		5.9		5.1		3.0		9.4	
	GDS	GNS	GDS	GNS	GDS	GNS	GDS	GNS	GDS	GNS	GDS	GNS	GDS	GNS	GDS	GNS	GDS	GNS
							(three-year centered moving average)											
1964					10.2	10.5			19.3	17.8	22.4	23.3	18.6	18.0	5.4	4.0	7.6	13.4
1965	18.6	17.8	17.1	15.6	10.1	10.6			19.4	18.0	22.3	23.3	18.4	17.8	6.5	5.4	10.1	15.1
1966	18.3	16.3	17.4	16.0	10.7	11.1	20.8	16.3	19.3	17.8	21.6	22.7	17.3	16.6	5.8	5.0	12.1	16.8
1967	18.5	16.4	17.6	16.7	11.6	11.8	21.1	16.2	19.2	17.7	20.1	21.0	16.1	15.3	6.3	5.6	14.4	18.7
1968	18.4	17.0	17.5	17.6	12.2	12.3	22.2	17.7	19.6	18.1	18.3	19.2	16.6	15.7	5.9	5.0	16.4	20.4
1969	19.1	18.5	17.3	17.9	12.1	12.2	22.7	18.7	20.0	18.4	18.3	18.7	17.4	16.4	7.5	6.4	17.8	20.9
1970	19.5	19.0	18.7	19.2	12.0	12.0			20.0	18.2	18.9	19.3	17.2	16.3	8.5	6.7	17.8	19.9

SOURCE: World Bank *Atlas* and other World Bank estimates.

Table 4: Domestic Savings Adjusted for Terms of Trade

Year	GDP	GDY	Domestic Savings	National Savings
(US$ million, average 1967–69 prices/exchange rates)			
1964	1,024.8	1,033.7	196.3	204.1
1965	1,039.2	1,041.6	172.7	163.6
1966	1,194.6	1,204.3	241.1	214.6
1967	1,241.9	1,246.4	226.4	190.2
1968	1,345.9	1,346.0	233.2	218.7
1969	1,434.1	1,429.3	278.6	274.7
1970	1,544.4	1,536.0	311.8	305.6
1971	1,644.1	1,611.8	304.2	290.7

SOURCE: World Bank estimates.

Table 5: Sources of Savings in Kenya

| | | | BUSINESS ||
Year	Households	Government[1]	Undistributed Profits	Depreciation Allowances
(£ million)				
1964	24.8	12.8	13.5	16.8
1965	17.0	9.8	6.7	17.4
1966	31.7	10.3	12.0	19.2
1967	33.8	10.6	6.9	22.6
1968	39.8	10.7	3.6	26.3
1969	55.4	7.4	10.6	30.1
1970	47.3	20.4	12.0	33.4
1971	30.5	26.2	13.1	41.0
(percentage)				
1964	36.5	18.9	19.9	24.8
1965	33.5	19.2	13.2	34.2
1966	43.2	14.1	16.4	26.3
1967	45.7	14.4	9.3	30.5
1968	49.5	13.3	4.5	32.7
1969	53.5	7.1	10.2	29.1
1970	41.8	18.0	10.6	29.5
1971	27.5	23.7	11.8	37.0

[1] Figures on Government saving given here do not agree with those in Annex Two, due to differences in definition.

SOURCE: Ministry of Finance and Planning, Kenya.

Table 6: Structure of Savings in Various Countries

		% of Total Savings Generated by		
Country	Year	Government	Corporations	Households
Taiwan	1955–59	43.2	56.8	
	1960–64	20.2	79.8	
	1965–68	15.5	84.5	
	1958–59[1]	37.1	6.2	56.7
Philippines	1955–59	24.0	34.2	41.8
	1960–64	13.0	24.0	63.0
	1965–68	8.2	20.7	71.2
	1955–59	12.3	30.9	56.8
Venezuela	1960–64	56.0	10.2	33.6
	1965–68	59.2	13.7	27.0
Brazil	1955–59	24.2	75.8	
	1960–64	10.2	89.8	
	1965–67	22.6	77.3	
South Korea	1955–59	61.0	8.8	30.2
	1960–64	75.2	32.4	−7.6
	1965–67	63.2	23.0	13.5
	1958–59[1]	−51.6	30.6	121.0
Colombia	1955–59	49.6	20.4	29.8
	1960–64	38.2	35.6	26.2
	1965–68	55.2	30.7	14.2

[1] Based on "direct" saving estimates.

SOURCES: U Tun Wai, *Financial Intermediaries and National Savings in Developing Countries* (New York: Praeger, 1972). Based on United Nations *Yearbook of National Income Accounts;* United Nations ECAFE, *Economic Bulletin for Asia and the Far East*, December 1962.

Table 7: Government Receipts and Expenditures, 1964–71

Category	1964	1965	1966	1967	1968	1969	1970	1971	% Increase 1964–71
					(£ million)				
Expenditures									
Government interest paid	4.23	4.57	4.99	5.33	5.69	6.30	7.00	7.70	82
Transfer payments made									
International	5.10	6.20	7.60	6.70	4.40	4.00	3.70	3.90	−24
Households	11.74	9.19	8.12	7.85	9.52	8.49	8.29	8.17	−30
Government consumption	49.35	52.32	57.09	62.23	73.52	85.55	94.25	105.03	113
Business subsidies	0.35	0.53	0.70	1.55	2.64	2.10	1.16	0.97	177
Government saving	12.81	9.75	10.31	10.61	10.65	7.36	20.41	26.24	105
TOTAL	83.58	82.56	88.81	94.27	106.42	113.8	134.81	152.01	82
Receipts									
Tax receipts	48.01	52.17	58.89	66.47	72.78	82.17	95.67	111.17	132
Major areas									
Direct income taxes	10.47	10.70	9.23	14.60	11.96	14.68	16.65	19.90	90
Indirect business taxes	26.91	29.44	35.48	35.97	43.06	46.62	54.55	62.94	136
Personal taxes	10.63	12.03	14.18	15.90	17.76	20.87	24.47	28.33	167
Profits of Government corporations and sales of services	14.87	16.89	19.12	19.40	20.34	20.43	26.74	29.54	99
International transfer receipts	20.70	13.50	10.80	8.40	13.30	11.20	12.40	11.30	−45
TOTAL	83.58	82.56	88.81	94.27	106.42	113.8	134.81	152.01	82

SOURCE: Ministry of Finance and Planning, Kenya.

Table 8: Projections of Ex Ante Savings, 1974–85

	1974	1975	1976	1977	1978	% Increase 1974–78	1980	1985
			(£ million, at constant 1970 prices)					
Basic projections								
GDP at market prices	767.2	827.1	892.1	962.9	1,039.9	36	1,215.2	1,812.7
Gross investment	194.0	210.9	228.5	247.7	268.6	38	316.2	478.2
Investment/income ratio (%)	25.3	25.5	25.6	25.7	25.8		26.0	26.4
Gross savings	161.6	177.1	194.0	212.5	232.3	44	274.1	425.4
Major areas								
Households	51.9(32.1)[1]	55.5(31.3)	59.4(30.6)	63.6(29.9)	68.2(29.4)	31	79.0(28.8)	114.9(27.0)
Corporations								
Undistributed profit	9.3(5.8)	10.2(5.8)	11.2(5.8)	12.3(5.8)	14.0(6.0)	51	21.4(7.8)	43.9(10.3)
Depreciation allowances	61.8(38.2)	69.3(39.1)	77.3(39.8)	86.0(40.5)	94.3(40.6)	53	104.2(38.1)	147.3(34.6)
Government	38.6(23.9)	42.2(23.8)	46.2(23.8)	50.6(23.8)	55.9(24.1)	45	69.5(25.4)	119.3(28.0)
Saving/income ratio (%)	21.0	21.4	21.7	22.0	22.4		22.5	23.5
Projected level of savings (assuming household savings income ratio remains 7%)								
Gross savings	146.1	160.5	176.3	193.5	211.8	45	250.5	391.0
Household	36.3	38.9	41.6	44.5	47.7	31	55.3	80.4
Saving/income ratio (%)	19.0	19.4	19.8	20.1	20.4		20.6	21.5
Projected level of savings (assuming restructured growth)								
GDP at market prices	766.4	827.1	893.1	964.8	1,042.8	36	1,219.9	1,820.3
Gross investment	176.3	191.3	206.9	223.8	242.1	47	283.8	424.4
Gross savings	159.0	173.6	189.6	207.1	226.0	42	265.7	409.1
Households	52.1(32.8)	55.9(32.2)	60.0(31.6)	64.4(31.1)	69.2(30.6)	33	80.5(30.3)	117.5(28.7)
Corporations								
Undistributed profit	10.0(6.3)	11.4(6.6)	12.9(6.8)	14.5(7.0)	16.6(7.3)	66	24.8(9.3)	48.5(11.9)
Depreciation allowances	59.9(37.7)	65.9(38.0)	72.4(38.2)	79.6(38.4)	86.6(38.3)	45	94.1(35.4)	130.6(31.9)
Government	37.0(23.3)	40.4(23.3)	44.3(23.4)	48.6(23.5)	53.6(23.7)	45	66.4(25.0)	112.6(27.5)

[1] Figures in parentheses indicate the percentage distribution of total savings by source.

SOURCE: Mission estimates.

Table 9: Changes in Money Supply and Related Variables

Year[1]	Total Money Supply	Currency Outside Bank	Demand Deposits	Time Deposits
	(annual percentage increase)			
1967	10.9	11.0	6.0	16.8
1968	13.6	8.6	11.7	18.8
1969	15.0	19.0	12.0	15.9
1970	23.3	21.7	15.4	32.3
1971	8.7	5.1	8.8	10.6
1972	14.0	20.5	17.5	7.6

[1] End of December.

SOURCE: Ministry of Finance and Planning, Kenya.

Table 10: Loans and Advances by Commercial Banks

		PERCENTAGE DISTRIBUTION		
	Total	Public	PRIVATE SECTOR	
Year[1]	(£ million)	Sector	Total	Agriculture
1968	66.8	4.6	95.4	11.6
1969	70.0	2.5	97.5	12.3
1970	86.9	5.9	94.1	10.7
1971	120.1	7.3	92.7	10.2
1972	121.4	7.6	92.4	9.9

[1] End of December.

SOURCE: Ministry of Finance and Planning, Kenya.

Table 11: Principal Interest Rates, 1967–72

Investment Category	1967	1968	As of June 30 1969	1970	1971	1972	As of March 31 1973
			(percentage rates)				
Central Bank of Kenya							
Rediscount rate for Treasury Bills	n.a.	n.a.	4.50	4.00[1]	2.00	4.00	3.79
Advances against Treasury Bills	n.a.	n.a.	5.00	4.50[1]	2.50	4.50	4.29
Bills and notes under crop finance scheme							
Discounts	5.00	5.00	5.00	5.00	5.00	5.00	5.00
Advances	6.00	6.00	6.00	6.00	6.00	6.00	6.00
Other bills and notes							
Discounts	5.50	5.50	5.50	5.50	5.50	5.50	5.50
Advances	6.50	6.50	6.50	6.50	6.50	6.50	6.50
Advances against Kenya Government securities	6.50	6.50	6.50	6.50	6.50	6.50	6.50
Kenya commercial banks:[2]							
Deposits							
Time							
Minimum 30 days (7 days' notice)							
Sh 200,000 up to Sh 500,000	3.00	3.00	3.00	3.00	3.00	3.00	3.00
Sh 500,000 and over	3.25	3.25	3.25	3.25	3.25	3.25	3.13
3 to less than 6 months	3.50	3.50	3.50	3.50	3.50	3.50	3.50
6 to less than 9 months	3.75	3.75	3.75	3.75	3.75	3.75	3.75
9 to less than 18 months, w.e.f. 1/9/68	4.00	4.00	4.00	4.00	4.00	4.00	4.00
18 to less than 24 months (minimum Sh 500,000), w.e.f. 1/9/68	...	...	4.50	4.50	4.50	4.50	4.50
Longer periods (minimum Sh 500,000)	...	...	...	...	...	...[3]	...[3]
Savings	3.00	3.00	3.00	3.00	3.00	3.00	3.00
Loans and advances (minimum)	7.00	7.00	7.00	7.00	7.00	7.00	7.00

Other financial institutions:							
Kenya Post Office Savings Bank							
Deposits	2.50	3.00[4]	3.00	3.00	3.00	3.00	3.00
Agricultural Finance Corporation							
Loans	7.50[5]	7.50[5]	7.50	7.50	7.50	7.50	7.50
Hire purchase companies							
Deposits (various periods)	...	3.00– 6.00	3.00– 6.00	3.00– 6.00	3.00– 6.00	3.00– 6.00	3.00– 7.50
Loans	...	10.00–12.00	10.00–12.00	10.00–12.00	10.00–12.00	10.00–12.00	7.00–12.00
Building societies[6]							
Deposits (various periods)	...	4.00– 6.50	4.00– 6.50	4.00– 6.50	4.50– 7.00	4.50– 7.00	5.50– 6.50
Loans	...	7.50–10.00	7.50–10.00	7.50–10.00	7.50–10.00	7.50–10.00	7.50–10.00

... Indicate data not available.
[1] Valid until April, 1970, when the balance of Treasury Bills outstanding was redeemed by the Treasury.
[2] In Kenya, banks collectively agree on the rates they grant or charge on deposits and loans respectively.
[3] Individual banks free to determine rate.
[4] W.e.f. July 1, 1968.
[5] Includes Land and Agricultural Bank of Kenya.
[6] Includes institutions not registered under the Building Societies Act, but whose primary function is to finance the purchase of property.

SOURCE: Central Bank of Kenya annual reports, and *Economic and Financial Review Quarterly*, Vol. V, No. 3, January–March 1973.

Table 12: Selected Interest Rates in Europe

Item	May 11–18 1973	Nov. 16–23 1973
UK		
Long term bond yield	10.24	11.93
Treasury Bill rate	7.15	12.31
Minimum lending rate (former bank rate)	8.75[1]	11.50
Euro-dollar market		
Three-month rate for US$ deposit in London	8.50	10.00
Six-month rate	8.688	9.38

[1] March 1.

SOURCE: *Selected Interest and Exchange Rates for Major Countries and the U.S.*, Board of Governors, Federal Reserve System, May 23, 1973.

Table 13: ICORs in Selected Countries

Five-Year Averages Ending in Year	Kenya	Brazil	South Korea	Indonesia
1965		4.05	2.12	5.09
1966		4.07	2.06	5.82
1967		3.74	2.09	4.56
1968		3.33	2.18	3.24
1969		2.83	2.30	2.41
1970	3.02	2.45	2.46	2.11

SOURCE: World Bank estimates.

Table 14: Structure of Deposits and Currency in Various Countries

	KOREA				INDONESIA				BRAZIL			
Year[1]	Demand Deposits	Time and Savings Deposit	Total Money Supply	Time and Savings Deposits as % of Total Money Supply	Demand Deposits	Time and Savings Deposit	Total Money Supply	Time and Savings Deposits as % of Total Money Supply	Demand Deposits	Time and Savings Deposit	Total Money Supply	Time and Savings Deposits as % of Total Money Supply
	(won billion)				(rupiahs billion)				(cruzeiros million)			
1964	24.5	14.5	63.6	22.8								
1965	34.9	30.6	97.1	31.5	0.7	0.08	2.66	3.0	3,070	130	5,343	2.4
1966	43.5	70.1	157.1	44.6	6.74	0.34	22.55	1.5	5,800	216	9,344	2.3
1967	64.7	128.9	252.9	51.0	15.16	2.25	53.67	4.2	6,193	841	11,415	7.4
1968	73.8	255.5	412.4	62.0	33.98	12.03	125.74	9.6	9,622	1,476	16,602	8.9
1969	118.9	451.5	670.7	67.3	59.98	51.61	233.86	22.1	13,481	2,413	24,051	10.0
1970	182.7	573.3	890.8	64.4	81.04	80.01	321.07	24.9	17,612	2,988	31,823	9.4
1971	218.0	705.1	1,073.6	65.7	108.09	145.28	457.83	31.7	22,429	4,153	40,837	10.1
									29,700	6,554	54,855	11.9

[1] End of December.

SOURCE: *International Financial Statistics*, IMF, 1972.

Table 15: Comparison of Systems Dynamics with Different Levels of Foreign Capital Inflow[1]

Foreign Capital Inflow	GDP (Y)	Growth Rate GDP (%) (GY)	Saving (S)	Foreign Capital Inflow (F)
	(US$ million, constant 1970 prices)			
Low level of foreign capital inflow	2,085	4.6	332.8	27.7
	2,188	4.9	347.4	35.3
	2,297	4.9	361.1	43.2
	2,413	5.1	372.6	54.7
	2,537	5.1	402.9	48.8
	2,664	5.0	464.1	13.5
	2,805	5.3	493.4	11.8
Higher level of foreign capital inflow	2,148	7.5	477.5	65.6
	2,316	7.8	514.5	75.9
	2,498	7.9	553.3	86.6
	2,696	7.9	592.0	101.9
	2,912	8.0	651.3	100.9
	3,147	8.1	699.4	116.6
	3,403	8.1	760.9	124.5

[1] The regression equation obtained from the above data is:

$$\frac{S}{Y} = 0.043 + 0.027\, GY - 0.93\, \frac{F}{Y}$$
$$\quad\ (7.2)\quad\ (17.5)\quad\ (-4.7)$$
$$R^2 = 0.99$$

SOURCE: Mission estimates.

Annex Five

Priorities for Planning and Project Design

CHAPTER 1

PRIORITIES FOR PLANNING

Kenya has devoted much attention to the preparation of her national development plans, which are typically well conceived proposals for the development of the economy. They are based on realistic assessments of the revenues likely to be available, and they incorporate well balanced public expenditure programs for the financial years covered by the plan period. While setting high targets for growth, Kenya's plans have not been over ambitious in macro-economic terms, and the targets of successive plans have generally been attained.

Nevertheless, the emphasis in macro-economic planning has tended to be on the production of the published plan, at the expense of the plan as an implementable program of action. The private sector has been incorporated only peripherally; plans have had little project content; policy proposals are not always previously agreed upon; and plan programs have been frequently disregarded during subsequent preparation of budgets. Commitment to the plans has been weak, from the point of view of the active participation of both the people and the politicians. Even the major operating ministries have not always participated fully in the preparation of plans or monitored the implementation of their own programs.

These kinds of emphases and weaknesses in national planning are by no means unique to Kenya, and Kenya's plans are certainly much better prepared and more realistic than most. Sector planning and investment management has been adequate in some sectors and inadequate in others. Historically, investment has expanded most rapidly in the infrastructure sectors, and in these sectors the public sector has achieved considerable planning and executing efficiency. Projects in these sectors are typically large engineering projects which can usually be implemented by private contractors. Furthermore, Kenya made use of a large international cadre of consulting experts for both project planning and supervision of construction in these sectors. The expenditures on consultants by the Roads Branch of the Ministry of Works, for example, average about 6 to 10 per cent of the investment budgets. For major works in the water supply sector, the budget for consultant services is also substantial. As a result, these ministries now have available to them a local supply of proven expertise to assist in all phases of the investment process. Absorptive capacity is not a problem for these sectors.

Modern large scale industry has also had the benefit of a large input of planning in its investments. The entrepreneurship and technical assistance accompanying foreign private investment in industry have supplemented Kenyan planning and implementation skills in this sector. As a result, large scale industry has expanded rapidly and efficiently within the price framework set by government policy.[1] There is evidence of excess absorptive capacity, for example, in the waiting list for placement in the expanding industrial estates. In the agricultural sector, on the other hand, and in the small scale industrial and commercial sectors, there has been no comparable input of supplemental manpower. Partly for this reason (and partly because project preparation in these sectors is more difficult to begin with), absorptive capacity problems persist in these sectors. In the social sectors, the problem is mainly to constrain investment within the limits of available resources, and to make sure that the highest priority investments are undertaken first. The Harambee movement,[2] and the naturally strong desire for social

---

1. The framework itself is suboptimal, and some of the investments are consequently uneconomic, but this is a weakness of general policy rather than an absorptive capacity problem (Annex Three).

2. To the extent that Harambee projects impose either capital or recurrent costs on the Government, an ideal sector plan for a social sector would allocate Harambee support funds in

services on the part of Kenya's people, require constant discipline from the Central Government to prevent spending in these sectors from getting far beyond what the country can afford.

In the light of the strategy put forward in this report, and the uneven capabilities for sector planning, the mission believes that the priority for future improvement in planning is at the sector level, and that the main concentration of this increased effort should be on all phases of micro-economic planning and development management in the directly productive sectors. Intensive work on sector plans, per se, is needed to establish the main policy parameters for use in evaluating all of the projects and programs in these sectors, and to establish the links between subsector programs and projects. But sector plans must be practical programs of action, not merely statements of philosophy, and very often sector policy will emerge out of the attempt to identify more projects and programs.

Increased management effort is required to mobilize the large government organization, particularly in agriculture, and direct it to systematic and disciplined performance of development functions, both in conjunction with new projects and in the execution of ongoing recurrent programs. This will require, in the first instance, detailed planning, programming and budgeting for the use of staff.

With increased concentration on micro-economic planning within the directly productive sectors, the macro-economic intersectoral planning will acquire more substance because the sectoral investment opportunities will, both in the aggregate and in each sector, exceed the funds allocable to finance them. Only in this situation is it possible, in principle, to maximize social benefit from the investment program by shifting funds, at the margin, between sectors. It seems safe to assume that the other sectors—infrastructure and the social services—will continue to be able to aborb more funds than are available.

The mission believes planning improvement to be particularly important at this juncture in Kenya's development for four main reasons:

(a) As discussed extensively in Part I and in Part II, Annex One, sustaining Kenya's good pace of economic growth will probably require a rapid growth of investment in the directly productive sectors at the expense of slower growth of both infrastructure and social services. Because the micro-economic groundwork for an expanded investment program in the productive sectors is not well developed, this shift cannot be accomplished simply by intersectoral reallocations at the macro-economic planning level; it requires also a concerted planning effort.

(b) As discussed in Part II, Annex Three, resource use in the private industrial sector has not been optimal from the point of view of generating employment or foreign exchange. Within the present policy framework, which is characterized by underpricing of capital relative to labor and of exports relative to production for the local market, it is particularly important to exercise great care in the selection of investments to be stimulated; the price system is not encouraging optimal allocation. Furthermore, local small scale industry, agriculture, and trade are discriminated against by present pricing, exchange rate, and other policies so that additional planning effort is needed to stimulate these subsectors. These are the main employment generating subsectors and probably contain the most important underutilized development potential.

---

order of the priority of projects. In practice, Harambee funds are allocated according to the initiative and the persistence of the local sponsors of projects. The misallocation involved in this selection method is generally regarded as a necessary cost of the Harambee system; it is generally felt that the benefits of Harambee—stimulation of grass roots initiative and cooperation, and mobilization of local savings for social purposes—outweigh these costs.

(c) Because Kenya will become more dependent on external borrowing to finance development expenditures at a time when the performance of donors appears to be shifting to directly productive investments, it is increasingly important that a balanced program of investments be presented for external financing. If, for example, the ability to identify, prepare, and appraise projects for foreign financing is concentrated in the infrastructure sectors, this may reduce the amount of aid available and at the same time bias macro-economic allocation in favor of infrastructure.

(d) The priorities for future development expenditure are the most difficult sectors from the point of view of planning and management. Small scale industry, trade, and agriculture can be expected to respond spontaneously to improvements in policy, but they are presently lagging far behind the urban formal sector in both fixed capital and human capital, and special programs are needed to stimulate them. Many of these programs will be risky, or will involve a preponderance of local cost, or will produce results which are hard to evaluate in financial terms. All of these factors will make it more difficult to identify, appraise, and package projects in a way that will appeal to foreign suppliers of investment funds, or even to Kenya's own project analysts accustomed to dealing with more prestigious projects. Yet it is extremely important that this effort be made, rather than letting these subsectors continue to lag behind the development trend. Programs designed for these subsectors will also require a large management and programming input per shilling invested, and since they will involve very large numbers of firms, the administrative mechanism for executing the programs could become overwhelmingly cumbersome without a substantial improvement in management.

It was the clear impression of the mission that within the whole project cycle, from recognition of a development opportunity to operation of the project, the most glaring lack was at the first stage—project identification.[3] Ideally, identification of development projects should become a major concern of the entire field staff and management of the productive sectors, as well as of their separate planning units. The task of project identification is simply too vast for a few experts, no matter how keen and competent.[4] Furthermore, a "project" most naturally develops as a response to growth, or to overcome a bottleneck in operations, and is first observed by the operators. The more that the eventual operators of the programs contribute to the decision on where to invest and how to design programs, the less are projects liable to fail at the operating stage. But at the lower field levels, the requisite expertise for project preparation is lacking, which throws the burden of project preparation and identification back on the few planners in the central staff of the ministries or even further back to the macro-economic planners.[5] No conceivable expansion of these central staffs is likely to solve the problem of too few identified projects; unless the field staff can be stimulated to do the bulk of the identification work, a shortage of projects will persist.

An important stimulus to field staff to do the initial work of project preparation

---

3. For simplicity, we use the term "project" to refer to any special development effort that is undertaken as a separately managed work. This can, and often should, include broadly based programs identified at the subsector or even sector level of operation. We interpret the term, "project identification," to include the demonstration that a profitable investment opportunity exists and that this opportunity can be implemented (i.e., designed, "constructed," programmed to operate) within the general policy framework of the Ministry.

4. The prevalent misconception in many operating ministries that "planning" is a mysterious, and perhaps even dangerous, activity best left to "planners," is a serious obstacle to development in Kenya.

5. One can observe this process operating in agriculture, and it can be anticipated in small scale business if, as planned, the field staff is greatly expanded.

would be a very quick response by central ministry planning groups to all project ideas emanating from the field. This response would either: reject the project out of hand; accept the possibility of the project on the condition that certain additional information requirements are filled, and then specify the additional information requirements; or accept the proposal as an identified project and commit the Ministry, in principle, to devote resources to the project.[6] Such a quick response would not only serve to reinforce local initiative in cases of government commitment, but would also have a very strong demonstration effect.[7] For this reason, the mission believes that a higher priority within the project planning machinery of the central ministries should be given to this immediate postidentification phase, and that Kenyan planners particularly should be concentrated in this area.[8]

The decision in principle to commit resources to a given project idea, within a clearly identified sectoral strategy, is an essentially Kenyan decision which cannot be taken outside the economic and political decision-making levels of the nation. But the subsequent stages of the project cycle—the phases of detailed project preparation, appraisal and implementation, and the design of a management system for operating the project and coordinating it with other activities—are largely technical and are less concerned with policy decisions. Thus, while Kenya planners should be mainly concerned with the central decisions about policy and the priorities in resource allocation, there is no apparent reason why foreign expertise (in the form of technical assistance or consultant services) could not be employed to do much of the work at these later stages in the cycle.

Once the Government is committed to a reasonably well identified project, there should generally be little difficulty in lining up external assistance, including where necessary, technical assistance in the project's preparation.[9] Most bilateral donors have expressed a preference for concentrating technical assistance more heavily in the project cycle, and we believe that this facility has not been utilized as much as it might have been.

---

6. Initially the commitment need only be to investigate the project in greater depth in the near future with the understanding that further commitment would depend on this investigation.

7. The immense growth of the Harambee movement in the social sectors illustrates how quickly and widely effective local action can be emulated.

8. This suggestion differs greatly from "bottom up" planning, which has been tried unsuccessfully. One of the causes of failure of this planning was that too much work was placed on local authorities of limited planning expertise. The result was a series of generally ill-prepared shopping lists. Our suggestion is that single projects, rather than lists or ill-conceived area plans, be submitted and judged.

9. The common difficulty of donor A refusing to accept the design or the appraisal of donor B is discussed at some length in Annex Six. The mission considers the problem soluble.

Chapter 2

Plan Organization

In past reports, the Bank has given some attention to the planning organization of government, and examined several areas in which planning capacity was deficient or absent. Since Independence, Kenya has made considerable progress in strengthening the planning organization and in achieving more effective coordination. This section will briefly describe some of the more significant developments in planning in Kenya and suggest some areas in which further strengthening is necessary.

Central Government Planning

Central Planning Organization

The Planning Division of the combined Ministry of Finance and Economic Planning is now a fully established Kenyan unit, under its own Deputy Permanent Secretary who, in view of the size and complexity of his task, is of permanent secretary rank. The Planning Division includes sixteen planning posts and six senior planning posts and is overwhelmingly Kenyanized. The Ministry still relies heavily on a high quality team of expatriate advisors, particularly in a few key fields, such as agriculture, rural development, and project planning. In spite of the widening and deepening of indigenous planning capacity, these planning posts will remain a high priority for external technical assistance for the medium term future in view of the requirement for increased absorption of capital in the productive sectors. However, it would be desirable for the Ministry to put less emphasis on the preparation of Plan documents and more on the management of the economy. The Ministry of Finance and Planning's comparative advantage lies in mobilizing the resources for development, in the allocation of national priorities, in resolving conflicts, in coordinating the public sector and the private sector and the various levels of government, and in monitoring the implementation of the plans and ensuring that the resources are provided through the annual budget for their implementation.

A Project Identification and Evaluation Unit was established in 1970, with assistance from Canada, and is the largest single technical assistance project in planning in Kenya. The unit has seven full time expatriate staff working in the central Planning Division and operating ministries, together with a similar number of Kenyans in Nairobi or on overseas training fellowships. The work carried out by the unit provides a systematic method of codifying projects and monitoring plan implementation. The methodology adopted permits more effective coordination between development expenditure budgeting and recurrent expenditure budgeting, including the provision of manpower. The unit is also undertaking a geographical disaggregation of investment expenditure, which is a useful first step in coordination of Central Government investment activity at the local level.

Sectoral Planning Units

One of the more serious problems of planning in Kenya is the inadequate planning capacity of many operating ministries. Despite some progress in establishing and staffing sectoral units, the limited planning capacity of some key ministries remains a constraint to sound policy formulation and project preparation and implementation. Apart from the scarcity of experienced manpower, three factors seem to have been important in restraining the growth of effective planning units in operating ministries. One has been the reluctance of the ministries themselves to accept economic planning, presumably because of the fear that their own technical responsibilities might be eroded. A second and more serious factor has been the tendency to favor the central planning unit at the expense of sectoral units, with the result that most of the senior and more experienced Kenyan economists are located in the Ministry of Finance and Planning. This, in turn, has resulted in a tendency for sectoral development strategy to be evolved by the sectoral specialists in the central Planning Division rather than by planners in the operating ministries. A third related factor has been a reluctance to accept either the *scale* of planning input required in sectors such as agriculture and natural resources, industry and social services, or the *variety* of disciplines required to make up a balanced planning team.

The two ministries with principal responsibility for directly productive investments —Agriculture, and Commerce and Industry—have planning units which, in size and composition, could be classified as sectoral planning units. The largest planning unit— with seven permanent posts and seventeen expatriates attached to the unit under various schemes of technical assistance—is the Ministry of Agriculture. Although large compared with other ministries, this unit has a wide spectrum of responsibilities, including price and general agricultural policy, marketing research and intellgence, project preparation and evaluation, water development programs, the agricultural component of the special rural development program, the development of all crops and livestock, and the provision of general economic support services to the nine technical divisions of the Ministry and to the statutory boards. These numerous functions have allowed little attention to be given to the evolution of a long term strategy for the development of the industry as a whole. The Ministry has also found it difficult to prepare sufficient projects to take advantage of all external aid potentially available for the agricultural sector.

In the Ministry of Commerce and Industry, the unit primarily responsible for the project cycle—identification, evaluation and granting of protection—is the Industry Division. This division has an established strength of eight positions, of which only five were filled at the time of the mission. A UNIDO project provides funds for seven expatriate advisers to the division, but only three of these posts were filled. The Ministry has virtually no project identification capacity, but concentrates on preparing evaluations of private sector proposals for the New Projects Committee, which, in turn, approves projects, and recommends to the Ministry of Finance and Planning whether Certificates of Approved Enterprise should be issued. These evaluations are very short, and, on the basis of the few examples examined, inadequate. Requests for protection are decided upon by the Industrial Protection Committee on the basis of Industry Division recommendations. Evaluation of requests is ad hoc and based on no agreed methodology. These is no apparent limit to the effective protection granted.[1] The Ministry of Commerce and Industry seems to have played very little part in the preparation of the 1974–78 Development Plan.

In the ministries responsible for other productive sectors, planning capability is generally rather weak. Perhaps the most serious deficiency in the past has been the inadequate planning and coordination (both in the Ministry of Tourism and Wildlife and in the Kenya Tourist Development Corporation) given to the development of the tourist industry. There is also inadequate planning staff to give due attention to the development of such sectors or subsectors as wildlife, fisheries, afforestation, and mining, as their potential surely warrants.

The mission has, at several points, referred to the capability of the Ministry of Works, and particularly the Roads Department, to design and implement projects.

---

1. One official, when asked what protection is regarded as reasonable, answered that the reasonable level is that level which ensures "reasonable profitability."

However, it is clear that their capacity to identify projects has run ahead of the evolution of a strategy for the transport sector as a whole. The weakness lies mainly in the Ministry of Power and Communications (since the Ministry of Works is the implementing agency and not the policy-making ministry) and, in a broader context, with the political constraints to exploiting the potential for greater coordination of transport services and policy within the East African Community.

A somewhat similar position exists in the social services, and particularly in the Ministry of Education, where the capacity to use an ever-increasing share of the nation's resources has far outstripped the conception of the contribution which education can make to the nation's welfare. Educational planning was first introduced in Kenya in 1970, when a planning unit was established in the Ministry of Education. But so far, the unit has dealt primarily with immediate problems on a piecemeal basis, and has little influence on policy issues, the definition of objectives, macro-economic planning decisions, or interagency coordination. It is understood that it is now the intention of the Government to make better use of the unit in the future by involving it more closely in the foundation of longer term plans, possibly as part of a much wider national review of education. This would be a most desirable move.

Local Authorities

We have referred elsewhere in this report to the absence of any defined policy towards local government in Kenya. This lack of commitment is clearly reflected in the paucity of planning going into the development of local authorities, both in the administrations of the local authorities themselves and in the Ministry of Local Government. The obvious exception is the Nairobi City Council, which has attempted an ambitious long term development plan for the city. But this kind of autonomous planning must inevitably be constrained by the lack of an overall national policy for local government.[2]

Conclusion

This brief summary of planning organization, while focusing on the major inadequacies, is not intended to leave the impression of a generally deficient planning organization. On the contrary, the mission was impressed by the depth and quality of much of the planning being undertaken in Kenya, and many of the weak points referred to in this chapter are now being strengthened, or are at least recognized as weak points. There is no lack of qualified manpower—both Kenyan and expatriate—in Kenya, although there will quite obviously never be enough experienced planners to do everything. The problem is more a matter of priorities. We see a need for a relative shift in emphasis from macro-planning to sector planning, with an emphasis on the one hand on increasing the absorptive capacity of the productive sectors, and on the other hand, on the development of a more systematic ordering of priorities in social services and infrastructure. We point out some of the implications of these priorities, and suggest some economies of operation in the planning process, in subsequent chapters.

2. The Nairobi Urban Study set out to prepare a master plan for the development of the city during the remainder of the century. However laudable this attempt, it was bound to run far ahead of national policy—even in the short term—in such critical areas as the overall national policy for urbanization, a workable solution to the problem of local government financing, the development of rational low cost housing policies, or a strategy for dealing with urban unemployment.

CHAPTER 3

EXPANDING PLANNING CAPACITY

In the mission's judgment, the Government's capacity to plan for needed changes in investment emphasis and to prepare and execute new programs is severely limited. There is apparently no pool of surplus planning talent beyond that needed for "business as usual." That is to say, that macro-economic planning and the limited sector planning which exist, absorb all available manpower. Indeed, the planning manpower of important ministries—Agriculture, and Commerce and Industry—is already overloaded. To make rapid progress in planning and implementing productive programs therefore will require improvements in planning efficiency and an innovating approach to project preparation and organization. It is particularly important that each trained and capable Kenyan planner has leverage over as wide a range of investment plans as possible. Some possible devices for gaining this leverage are supplementation of Kenyan planning skills, economies of scale in project preparation, and encouraging local initiative in the identification of projects and programs to relieve trained planners of this task.

Supplementation

Two forms of supplementation have been tried with great success but on too limited a scale: first, supplementation of manpower, and second, supplementation of the administrative structure itself through the semiautonomous productive institutions and closer cooperation with the private sector. Both types of supplementation should be expanded, always on the condition that policy formulation remains firmly under Central Government control. We believe that policy control will become more effective as the cadre of experienced Kenyans is relieved of much of the burden of technical work: an overworked administration, attempting to do more work than it can do, is likely to lose control of policy through its inability to give due attention to policy issues.

The Central Government can dispose of part of its burden of detailed project preparation and implementation by making greater use of both the private sector and specialized parastatals. Compared to the ordinary bureaucracy, the private sector and specialized parastatals have obvious potential advantages of flexibility and motivation, for example:

- A much greater flexibility in manpower policies and wage rates.[1]
- A merit system for tenure and advancement of personnel.
- Relatively small (potential) size, avoiding diseconomies of scale.
- Profit (in the case of parastatals, reward to management for financial success) as a discipline and a motive.
- The potential for organizing all supporting services under one administration.

The primary disadvantage of the private sector and the parastatals is the possible divergence between private profit (or institutional financial success) and social benefit. The problem for the Government is how to make maximum use of the flexibility of the private sector and parastatals within a framework giving maximum profit and financial incentives for socially useful activities.

---

[1]. We do not mean to imply that parastatals should raid the bureaucracy by offering high wages for skills in inelastic supply. Rather, the point is that the parastatals can respond to labor markets (e.g., by hiring surplus school leavers at *lower* wages, by hiring only the labor needed for the development task, by doing their own specific training, etc.).

In general, all policies which bring market prices of inputs and outputs closer to their social values will improve the framework for operation of the private sector by making socially useful actions more profitable. These policies—exchange rate adjustment, more uniformity of effective protection, incomes policies, interest rate policies—have been discussed at length elsewhere in this report. The only additional point is that the same types of policies are useful in dealing with the production oriented parastatals; if the prices facing such parastatals conform fairly closely to social values, then the test of profitable operation is sufficient for appraisal of potential parastatal activities and for judging the performance of operating organizations. On the other hand, projects which depend on very high effective protection for their profitability, or which cannot be profitable at all, are dubious uses of funds, either in parastatals or in the private sector. It is becoming increasingly clear that private foreign investment can be very expensive to the economy in the long run if it is channeled into such activities.

In addition to the correction of price signals referred to above (and discussed much more extensively in Part I and Annex Three), the mission recommends that the Government pursue a more active program to directly promote private investment of the right type, both foreign and domestic. In the industrial sector, this would imply expanding the team of experts in the Industry Division of the Ministry of Commerce and Industry for subsectoral planning and project identification. The minimum terms of reference for this unit would be to discover what product lines offer potential for development and to do the necessary preappraisal work to attract foreign or domestic firms into these lines, including a systematic presentation of the infant industry protection available and its duration.[2] Small scale African businessmen in established product lines also have clear capacity for improvement in efficiency and subsequent growth, and the mission endorses the Government's plans for a Small Business Administration, with the reservation that the effort might well be even greater than planned.[3]

Promotion of agricultural production and the associated processing facilities appears to be one area which could benefit greatly from a policy of active encouragement of private investment. Potential investors are likely to be unnecessarily uncertain about questions such as access to land under long term leasehold, estates versus outgrowing arrangements, the willingness of Government to provide infrastructural services and extension, the extent and duration of expatriate management that will be permitted, and so forth. Although the details of some of these questions will have to be negotiated on a case-by-case basis with potential investors, general statements of policy, appropriate to the preidentification stage of investigation, would be helpful for some of them. Such statements are lacking.

The Government should particularly encourage foreign private investment in those subsectors within agriculture where market connections and high specialized skills are prerequisites to success. The current development of the pineapple industry illustrates both a successful application of this principle and a weakness in the Government's approach to such investments. The pineapple industry, a single largely foreign owned and controlled firm, exports about $2.5 million worth of pineapples per year, provides steady employment to about 3,500 Kenyan workers at wage rates ranging from Sh225 per month for unskilled field labor (2,000 workers) to Sh1,500 per month for factory mechanics to Sh2,000 per month for foremen. The total investment in this project was about $7 million. Production of the fruit is heavily concentrated (97 percent) on the company's estate.

---

2. We are assuming that the negative function of this unit, to prevent profitable but uneconomic investments, will be taken care of by policy reform. If not, then it would be necessary to expand the Ministry, just to perform this negative role.

3. A discussion of small business opportunities, the Government's proposed response, and a type of small business project is included in the Appendix to this Annex.

This industry illustrates several important points:

- Given the oligopolistic competition in the product, the entire industry development probably depended upon the foreign firm's market connections and brand name.
- The industry is very productive of wage employment both in agriculture and processing, with a very low investment cost per worker ($2,000) or per dollar of annual exports.
- The industry has done very little to support or encourage Kenyan entrepreneurship. The reason for this is the failure of the outgrower scheme which was intended to produce a high percentage of the fruit. According to most commentators, the outgrower scheme failed because of difficulties in transportation (high cost and too low a reliability to ensure the delivery of high quality fruit) and the low priority that the company assigned to encouraging outgrower production.

It is understandable that a foreign company which invested in agricultural processing would prefer to produce on its own estates in a completely integrated chain from farming to final product, an altogether understandable, risk-minimizing strategy on the part of the private firm. Nonetheless, the operation of such a company can clearly offer great opportunities for real development of African entrepreneurship—in farming, in management for agricultural markets demanding high quality, and in transport. The early identification of these opportunities, the stimulation through credits and extension of the required activities, and the assumption of risk on the part of the Government to guarantee that outgrowers would produce and deliver a certain amount of fruit,[4] could confine the foreign firm to its comparative advantage—the international marketing and organization of processing. It is the mission's opinion that the opportunities to involve foreign private capital in agriculture can be exploited on a much greater scale with proper identification work and that, by careful design of Kenyan participation, the benefits to the economy can be greater.

The parastatal form of organization could be more useful for rapid development of commercially profitable activities, such as high valuable crop cultivation. Some of the existing production oriented parastatals could be strengthened with this aim in mind, and parastatals with surplus administration capacity might be given development responsibility for a wider range of products. We do not advocate the creation of new institutions; rather that better use be made of existing ones. The advantages of small size and specialization, relative to the Ministry of Agriculture, and the potential for efficient organization of supporting services have already been pointed out. These advantages seem to outweigh the difficulties inherent in bureaucratic fragmentation.

Supplementation of the bureaucracy through the addition of production subsidiaries has proven successful, most notably in the tea industry through the Kenya Tea Development Authority (KTDA), but also in the industrial estates program through Kenyan Industrial Estates, and the large scale industrial lending field through the Industrial and Commercial Development Corporation. In the opinion of the mission, delegation of operating responsibility to productive subsidiaries is a sound procedure, subject only to the condition that the policy framework within which these subsidiaries operate is itself sound.[5]

Because the tea program has been particularly successful, it is worthwhile comparing this industry with the situation in other major agricultural programs where

---

4. Although guarantee arrangements could prove costly to the Government in event of default, this mechanism seems the only way to keep risk of nonperformance (a "development" rather than a "business" risk) from being an impediment to development.

5. Elsewhere in the report we have commented unfavorably on some of the policy parameters within which these subsidiaries operate. It is not an adverse reflection on the subsidiaries that by efficient management within that framework, suboptimal results are obtained.

few working projects have emerged. The reasons for the comparative lack of progress in implementing major programs lie partly in the organization of the bureaucracy. The Ministry of Agriculture, with over 14,000 employees, probably suffers from serious diseconomies of scale, compared, for example, to the compact tea authority. Undoubtedly, the Ministry's extension agents have a much more difficult task—general extension and farm management advice, rather than the promotion of a single crop. In addition, the Ministry works under the considerable handicap of the civil service system, supporting a large percentage of inadequately trained extension agents who, in effect, hold tenured positions. KTDA, by contrast, can work on a merit system of tenure and promotion. The Ministry also suffers from fragmentation since, although it probably suffers from diseconomies of scale in extension proper, the logical correlative activities—marketing, stocking of inputs, irrigation, land settlement, cooperative management—are often under the control of more or less autonomous marketing agencies, the private sector, or other ministries.

No single stroke, least of all massive reorganization, is likely to solve all of the problems which impede the planning and implementation of agricultural programs within the Ministry. Rather, the transformation of the Ministry into an effective development institution for small farmers is a process which must be begun now, and which will yield results only after a number of years. Meanwhile, the mission suggests a new concentration on planning and implementation of productive programs which can be split off from slower moving government machinery. This concentration offers prospects for effective implementation of certain progams, even in the short run, and should serve, in general, as a supplement to programs designed to increase ministerial effectiveness, rather than as a substitute for that effort.

The example of the KTDA suggests that it is possible to organize a complicated small farmer production and marketing program quite efficiently when the scale of the overall operation is manageable and the management is able to concentrate, with some autonomy, on a single specialized activity which offers high potential returns to croppers. These organizational features of KTDA, combined with the relatively high return in tea, offer the best explanation of the apparent anomaly of very efficient operation of a complicated production and handling process within a sector which has not succeeded very well in organizing the much simpler and less demanding processes of maize or cotton production by small growers. Therefore, the mission suggests that in other fields of potentially high return to croppers, the basic organizational structure of KTDA might be duplicated.[6] This would require reorganization or expansion of existing parastatals to bring extension, input management, wholesaling, and exporting for a particular crop under the direction of a single agency responsible for its development. The existing Horticultural Crops Development Authority (HCDA) could, for example, provide the nucleus for several specialized crop development efforts.[7] The mission does not have the qualifications to determine which parastatals should be upgraded to first class development institutions. (HCDA was cited only as one possibility.) Rather, our recommendation is that serious attention should be given to upgrading and assigning development

---

6. An obvious objection—that manpower would not be available for duplication of KTDA management and extension teams—is not valid in the opinion of Kenyan specialists in government personnel. Sufficient underutilized talent, particularly in middle management, appears to be available from within the agricultural bureaucracy. The same experts in personnel point out that KTDA has expanded and succeeded under Kenyan manpower, most of it drawn from the agricultural bureaucracy.

7. At present HCDA has neither the staff nor the budget for a major development effort but important preconditions to a development effort—large productive potential, some experience, a wealth of studies—already exist.

responsibility to some of the parastatals which now serve only regulatory or marketing functions or, if necessary, to creating new parastatals for development purposes.[8]

By delegating a large segment of the implementation and operation of required productive investment to the private sector and parastatals, the Government reduces its planning task to setting out the correct guidelines and incentives within which these organizations will operate. Control is not lost in this process; it is, indeed, probable that the private sector and parastatals will perform more efficiently than the Government, since private (institutional) project incentives can be equated to social profit incentives through correct use of policy tools.

A second form of supplementation that is now underutilized is the direct addition of manpower from outside the Government establishment to work in micro-economic planning. Most of this manpower would have to be recruited from outside the country. This could be accomplished through a redirection of bilateral technical assistance. Kenya could also make greater use of resident consulants from the private sector, and groups such as the Institute for Development Studies of the University of Nairobi could be recruited for project work. Local knowledge is, of course, desirable, but except for initially identifying projects, is not indispensable for most of the technical project preparation work. Therefore, in our opinion, the Government should be even-handed in its recruitment of technical experts.[9] It is worth noting again that in just those areas where supplemental manpower has been most heavily utilized for planning, absorptive capacity has ceased to be a problem.

Economies of Scale

It is a cliche among planners and among donors that the planning work going into a one-million-dollar project is very similar in extent and difficulty to that of a twenty-million-dollar project. It follows that the larger the projects are, on the average, the more can be done to increase the rate of growth of investment in the productive sectors with given planning skill. There is no apparent disagreement from Government that large projects should be sought. This section of the annex will not therefore discuss the principle of large projects, but rather will discuss some ways in which larger projects can be identified and implemented.[10]

The most obvious way to achieve economies of scale is to define projects as broadly as possible. A "project," subject only to the condition that it retains sufficient clarity to be managed to the production stage in a unified effort, might, at an extreme, embrace an entire subsector program. The mission has found much support, both in the planning organization and in the external aid community, for very broadly defined projects which aim to affect a great number of people and to concentrate decisions about sectoral and

---

8. Part III, the Agricultural Sector Survey, has made various suggestions for strengthening the Ministry of Agriculture and for the merger or expansion of boards.

9. An exception would be the manpower required at the immediate postidentification stage. Since this initial evaluation is less technical and more a matter of quick judgment of the feasibility of the proposal within the context of the economy and the Government administration, local expertise and judgment is a primary requirement. This is why at the beginning of this annex we have suggested that Kenyan experts, suitably supplemented with technical subordinates on long term contract, be concentrated at this level.

10. The mission found that some people interpret "large" projects to mean "capital intensive" projects or, worse still, that this is the criterion by which a project is judged to be suitable for external aid. Let it be clear, on the contrary, that our concept of "large" projects is typically programs of low unit cost which are large mainly because they are designed to benefit a large number of people.

subsectoral alternatives within a given project preparation.[11] Some of the most urgent planning tasks in agriculture could be approached on this basis. For example, the future development of crops such as sugar, oilseeds, tree crops, or horticultural commodities probably needs to be planned on a nationwide basis, through broadly based programs designed to integrate all aspects of research, production, marketing, and program. On the other hand, other priorities in the agricultuural sector—and particularly the design of a major development strategy for the drier arable areas—seem more suited to broadly conceived regional programs. But the broad approach need not be confined to agriculture. We suggest elsewhere that small business assistance and even road planning would benefit from a broader sector or subsector investment program preparation (Annex Six). This process is virtually automatic in the case of some development oriented parastatals (e.g., the existing organization of the tea industry), where everything from input supply through extension and processing to final marketing is the function of a single management. Elements of a broad program can be organized, however, without necessarily concentrating all power within a single agency. The Government has already had some successful experience along these lines in programs such as livestock development and industrial forest plantations; but in general, the device of unified subsector programs is underutilized.

The preparation of these broad based projects or programs is anything but easy. But they are worth striving for, not only because they can use planning manpower more efficiently, but because they should result in more effective planning and a better allocation of resources. A single nationwide oilseed development program, for example, would be less likely to make allocation errors, or to leave gaps or cause duplication, than a series of smaller and uncoordinated oilseed production projects. Moreover, at a time when Kenya is short on well conceived sector strategies, this subsector or program building can go a long way towards assembling the components of an agriculture sector strategy.[12]

A second scale-increasing device is to expand a production oriented project to include both indirect benefits and indirect costs. This may simply mean undertaking several separate but related investments concurrently and treating them as a unit. For example, a project to improve husbandry methods of subsistence maize producers in a given locality might be combined with the introduction of a high value crop, the provision of required water, transport and processing infrastructure and the provision of basic health and technical education services. Not only would this bring many separate fixed investments under one planning exercise, but it would also bring into the project analysis many indirect benefits and costs. In our example, the latter would include the increases in government overheads and recurrent costs caused by the different services required in going from the minimal government support for subsistence maize farmers to the more complex package required for diverse market production.

There will, of course, be a loss of apparent precision in project evaluation with such broad project definitions. On the plane of pure logic, it is clear that this loss is apparent rather than real; indirect costs and benefits are the same as those required for the success of a much simpler maize project, but they would typically be covered by fairly imprecise assumptions about indirect project effects in a narrowly defined maize project if, indeed, they were considered at all. The accuracy of the micro-economic

---

11. The mission found a great eagerness on the part of donors to support integrated programs of sectoral or subsectoral development, with greater or less stress on their preparation, as identifiable single projects depending on the sector and the donor. It is our impression that the Government underestimates the donors' flexibility in the design of major subsector programs.

12. This is another example where the best can be the enemy of the good. To wait for a full-fledged agricultural development strategy—in which everything is optimized and coordinated—is to wait a long time. In the meantime, four or five soundly conceived subsector or commodity programs, with a heavy emphasis on implementation, could have a marked effect on agricultural production and incomes in a relatively short period.

analysis is thus seen to improve as the project is broadened, although the project itself is more difficult to evaluate. As to the planning and financing problems associated with such complex projects, we can only repeat that donors appear anxious to direct technical assistance effort to this kind of work, and that foreign financing of the indirect project components is clearly more likely if these indirect project components are included in production programs rather than excluded.

Program planning and operation would be more difficult than project work because by its nature a program cannot be managed as a unit up to the operating phase. For example, elements of a major maize production program (if one were launched) already exist; the extension agents to service the program are already effectively tenured, a marketing board is already operating, and various public and private input supply agencies (from fertilizer and hybrid seed to credit) are already in the field. Program design would imply a massive coordination effort of agencies only partially suited to a development effort, rather than the creation of a unit to undertake a specific development task. Each of the existing units which would have to be incorporated in a maize production program has its own bureaucratic inertia and its own set of operating policies. The mission suggests that the Government give strong consideration to preparing one or two major crop development plans, complete with required management systems. If such a program or two could be identified, and obtain Government commitment in principle, the technical work of preparation could be delegated to suitably directed technical assistance teams. We believe that financing for such a major crop program could be arranged with little difficulty (Annex Six).

Another proven method for achieving economies of scale in investment is to design projects which can be replicated with little or no variation. This method is particularly suitable for use when the target activity is carried out by a number of small enterprises all of which need a package of project assistance. This method also overcomes two difficulties in this type of project situation: the ineffectiveness of a single service (e.g., credit) when a number of services are required (e.g., credit, extension, input supply, marketing); and the scarcity of personnel required to plan and implement the package of services.[13]

The planning economies in replicable projects come from spreading a given planning effort over many project units. Given the fact that it will be reused again and again, the plan for a very small project can economically be given the same attention that would be given a project equal in size to the sum of the many replications of the small project. In other words, a serious project identification, financing plan, detailed preparation, and execution can be carried out for a small project.

The mission believes that project replication is applicable to at least the following:

(a) Minimum package programs for small scale agriculture. Under these programs, a representative unit is identified. The required services and other inputs are planned in detail, the representative unit is appraised, and, if economic, the units similar to it are provided with the planned services.

(b) Small business credit and extension services. For each of several activities (each containing a large number of small firms), a detailed operations plan (including plans for investment, production, inventory management, sales, accounting, and control) is designed. This package of information, together with needed technical assistance and credit, are then provided to as many potentially viable firms in the business as can be identified.

---

13. An important side effect of replicability is that it makes it easier to avoid the use of foreign personnel in actual project implementation. Experts, from whatever source, can do the preliminary design and planning work and the model applications of the project while leaving the replication process to local personnel. Moreover, standardization and simplification of design can usually allow personnel of limited academic qualifications and experience to be employed in implementation.

(c) Site and service programs for agriculture. In each of several regions, a small parcel of land is procured and prepared with all necessary services and inputs to produce a high value crop suitable to the region. Farmers from the immediately surrounding region are invited to rent on a share-crop basis a portion of this land (say, half-an-acre to one acre per farmer) to produce the designated crop under the close supervision and guidance of an extension agent whose responsibilities include looking after input supplies and transport/marketing arrangements.

A desirable feature of each of these programs is that they attack directly the problem of the small, usually poor, and usually hard-to-educate Kenyan small businessman and traditional farmer. Once designed, all of the programs can be staffed by relatively junior personnel because the job of project management is very specialized and requires far less skill and training to teach several clients the same thing than to give unique assistance to each client. Each of the projects affects a great number of productive units which otherwise might be too small to be assisted. Some suggestions for replicable projects are examined at greater length in the Appendix to this annex.

Encouraging Local Initiative

There is little scope for local initiative in project planning, implementation, or operation within the present vertically organized ministries. Local governmental units have no development funds of their own and no hope of generating them given their present tax base. This historical pattern has been to increase concentration of revenues, planning, decision-making and administrative control under the Central Government ministries in Nairobi. Although this centralization was probably necessary because of shortages of trained administrative personnel, it has effectively cut off the flow of productive ideas from the local operating units of the ministries. The coordination of interministerial activities at the local level, which would be necessary for all but the simplest projects, is quite difficult in a situation where each local officer is primarily responsible to his ministry in Nairobi. There have been some attempts at investment planning from the bottom up, but these have resulted in impossible shopping lists of inadequately analyzed ideas and their effect on the investment programs of the ministries has been minimal.

As discussed earlier in this annex, we believe that local initiative in project identification is a necessary condition for an adequate investment pipeline in the productive sectors, and that the best way to stimulate this local initiative is by central response to project ideas coming from the field staff of the ministries. To the extent that a project falls within the jurisdiction of a single ministry, this implies nothing more than strengthening the ministry to provide staff for this function. Interministerial projects, which probably constitute the majority of worthwhile ideas, will require a more cumbersome working group approach, but sponsorship of the project by an expanded ministerial staff can speed this process.

The Development Opportunity Team (DOT) is an experiment in its early stages, hardly more than a concept. The idea of the DOT is that a team of project evaluation specialists based in Nairobi, probably in the Ministry of Finance and Planning with channels into ministerial headquarters, would do field work to help in the preparation and appraisal of projects identified at the local level. In our opinion, the DOT could be most useful as an instrument for performing the screening function for projects financed by district development grants.

District development grants, a device for transfering small allocations of government funds to the districts for use in approved investments, have potential to become an important stimulant to local initiative. They have, until now, been quantitatively unimportant and their use has not been tightly controlled. Lacking central control, these grants have often been diverted either to projects of doubtful productivity or to projects in the social service sectors which have little to do with the basic development purpose of the grants. If the transfer of resources to the district were accompanied by a strong screening process, however, the grants could become a useful device for decentralizing investment to some extent, and thus shifting some of the burden of development planning and execution from the central ministries.

A project consisting of funding for an expanded district grant program plus a project evaluation team, such as the DOT, to screen and improve local project proposals, would also introduce some flexibility into the government investment program, which is now too centralized, and would make use of the initiative of the district governmental team in projects of a manageable scale. In expanding this program, by adding a project team and increasing allocations, the control mechanisms would be strengthened automatically, both by the process of economic evaluation and by the increased visibility of the program. This combination of increased visibility and effectiveness might also have a strong educational effect upon local politicians. To the extent that these projects produced noticeable increases in employment, incomes, and standards of living in the local area, they should pay political dividends. In the relatively short run, it might therefore be possible to attract the kind of political attention to the productive sectors that have so far been monopolized by the social services sectors now under strong direct local pressure to expand through the Harambee movement.

The emerging practice of disaggregating national plans and the annual investment budget to the district level will also encourage local initiative, to the extent that district officers contribute to such plans or budgets. Because ministerial plans are prepared independently, there is ample scope for imbalances and inconsistencies in any single district. To bring these to the attention of the Central Government is a useful bureaucratic function as well as a potentialy important learning exercise in planning and coordination. At present, plan disaggregation is concerned only with identified projects. It would probably be useful to expand the exercise to include indicative investment totals that could be financed if well conceived projects were found, disaggregated by district and by economic sector.

Although attempts have been made at district development planning—ranging from solicitation of investment plans from general district level ministerial staffs who are inadequately trained to produce plans, to the preparation of detailed comprehensive plans for some districts by a team of experts—these attempts have not produced a worthwhile increase in workable investment projects. For the present, the mission does not expect district planning to be a stimulus to local initiative: district staffs themselves are too inexperienced in the art, and imported experts have not succeeded in stimulating local input into the fancier plans that have been attempted.[14] In the longer run, with growth in the number and quality of planners available, the district planning idea might profitably be reintroduced. For now, what planning talent can be spared for work on the district level, should probably be channeled into work in project identification.

---

14. There is an additional problem of effective policymaking by foreigners if these development plans are taken seriously. It appears far more advisable to confine the foreigner to a technician's role.

Chapter 4

Implications for Project Design and Appraisal

The Need for New Types of Investment

The need to increase investment in the productive sectors has implications for project design as well as for planning. We have already noted some of them in the previous chapter covering economies of scale in project preparation. Broadly defined projects and programs were shown to be ways to get more investment per unit of planning effort. More broadly, the situation in the Kenyan economy dictates that any large increase in productive investment will imply movement to new types of investment. Sector-by-sector we observe:

(a) In manufacturing, the scope for efficient import substitution—which has been the main engine of industrial growth in the past—is diminishing, and the potential for further export of import substitutes to the EAC market is also limited by the industrialization programs of the other Partner States. The underlying strategy of this report has emphasized the major priorities for industry; to place greater emphasis on resource based manufactures for export, to promote small-scale enterprises, and to reform the incentives system to improve the efficiency of the private manufacturing sector and avoid the more costly, later phases of import substitution. We have indicated in the previous chapter that new directions of this kind will require an increased planning capacity. But there is also a clear need for new and better project ideas if the desired new emphases are to be attained without a slackening in the momentum of industrial growth.

(b) In the agricultural sector, the potential for productive investment and growth is enormous. But the opportunities as well as the priorities are changing. Some of the export crops (such as coffee and tea) on which Kenya has built up her agricultural industry are facing uncertain market prospects. Investment associated with the transfer of the previous Scheduled Areas to Kenyan ownership will dwindle as the remaining foreign farms disappear, and other large programs, such as land registration, are reaching diminishing returns. A great challenge lies ahead in building onto and extending the firm foundation already laid in the agricultural sector. But, like the manufacturing industry, agriculture is another case where new sources of growth must be found. The obvious underexploited resources are the land and labor presently locked up in the agricultural smallholdings, including the subsistence agricultural sector. But, as pointed out in Part III, the techniques for developing this potential are not yet generally available. If a large incremental investment in agriculture is to be achieved, now projects will have to have a new style and a new and greater scope.

(c) In the infrastructure sectors, where there is excess absorptive capacity in the sense of the capability to identify and implement investment projects, our macro-economic strategy calls for a relatively low allocation of resources. In some sectors, this will also entail a lower growth rate, while in others it will hopefully be possible to maintain past rates of growth, despite a lower investment rate, through the more efficient use of resources. In either case there will have to be a careful consideration of priorities within each sector, and a systematic attempt to design projects which can stretch the available resources further.[1]

(d) In the social sectors, Kenya is faced with the need to clear up distortions in incentives and provide a development focus to her investment effort (education sector) or to start virtually from the beginning to design whole programs (national housing policy) or to decide on the very highest priority services in cases where the obviously desirable level of services is beyond budget capabilities (health care, potable water, water supply in general). In none of these sectors are there obvious solutions awaiting only the infusion of large amounts of investment funds, and program preparation will be very tough work. As often as not, there are few relevant lessons to be learned from other countries, and innovative approaches, designed for Kenya's own particular needs, will clearly be necessary.[2]

Even if there were no absorptive capacity problem as such, other goals (in addition to growth of output) would require innovative approaches to project preparation. Kenya is committed to helping her poor to develop, be they subsistence farmers or small scale businessmen and their employees, and this commitment would call for direct investment action in support of these groups, even if ample potential for inducing growth existed in the modern industrial sector, the large farm sector, and large scale business. Trickle-down effects have not been reliable in relieving poverty, either in Kenya or in many more advanced countries. Direct investment action to improve the productivity of poor persons is probably called for, pursuant to the goal of eliminating the worst excesses of want, whether or not this would maximize growth. However, the macro-economic and sector analyses seem to indicate that there is not much of a trade-off between growth and poverty relief; the more prosperous sectors are not the sectors where rapid growth in investment can be anticipated. The maximum underutilized potential appears to lie in the resources—land, labor, and small business ownership—of the poor.

Methodological Problems for Required New Projects

The stress on new types of projects which must characterize any serious effort to increase investment in the productive sectors will bring with it an accentuation of some common methodological problems and some new ones. In the following, we attempt to anticipate some of these problems and suggest solutions.

Evaluation of Outputs and Inputs at Economic Prices

Many of the required projects would produce outputs which until now have been relatively discriminated against by major government policies. Thus, for example, the value of foreign exchange earned by agricultural exports, the correct domestic price of foodstuffs, and the value of the output of informal sector manufacturing as compared to domestic industry, would all have to be calculated. Observation of present prices would be misleading, given the distortions in the pricing system. An internationally agreed system (or rather a set of closely related more or less agreed systems) exists for evaluating project outputs and inputs at economic prices even in the presence of serious distortions in observed prices in the market. The problem is a technical one and

---

1. As pointed out in the main report, we feel that there is considerable scope for lower ICORs (and thus greater output per unit of investment) in the infrastructural sectors, particularly in construction.
2. The rural water supply system of financing and planning is both an exception to the general rule of inadequate program development and an example of the type of innovative approach that Kenya can and must develop in the social sectors.

considerable experience with the solution has been compiled by the Institute for Development Studies and various international consultants to Kenya. The problem reduces to one of calculation of the relevant package of shadow prices within the Kenyan growth program, factor endowment, and policy framework.[3] Using all these sources of expertise, there should be enough manpower to subject at least the more important projects to an adequate evaluation.

Were it not for the fact that price distortions facing the productive sectors are so many and so large, the risk of error inherent in departure from observable market prices would perhaps outweigh the advantages of a calculated economic value approach. The risks are clearly great; for example: the use of shadow prices to reflect no more than prejudice, the "justification" of projects with rigged but superficially plausible shadow prices, and the risk of gross error in observation given the generally weak statistical base. But the solution seems to be to approach shadow prices (particularly those prepared ad hoc for a particular project evaluation) with caution and suspicion, checking to determine that they are firmly based on careful calculations of opportunity cost. The shadow price tool is simply too valuable and necessary to throw out because of its occasional abuse.

Quantification of Benefits and Costs

Quantification of benefits and costs will become more complex and subject to greater apparent error as projects are defined more broadly or as sector programs are introduced. We have argued earlier that the analysis of broadly defined projects would probably be more nearly correct, and that the apparent increase in error is an illusion created by including more of the errors in the project itself rather than omitting them from consideration altogether by defining projects narrowly. Nonetheless, broadly defined projects do introduce serious quantification problems; for example, if health services are included in a rural development project, quantification of health benefits is necessary.

The increased complexity of broadly defined projects or subsector programs implies an irreducible effort in their preparation, and the Government is not yet equipped to prepare and execute many such projects using its own planning and management resources. On the other hand, most donor agencies would be more than willing to undertake a large part of the preparatory work and the execution phase of major programs, either by diverting technical assistance or as part of a project loan or grant, if the Government were committed in principle to the project. The Government's input could thus be reduced to project identification and the crucial commitment in principle to undertake the project. An additional problem in connection with the financing of a major project many arise if the project is too big for the single donor who does the preparation to undertake alone. However, with early commitment to the project on the part of the Government, international sharing of the financing burden can usually be arranged concurrently with the project preparation. It need not necessarily produce an additional long delay.

Definition of the Project

The logical limits to an expanded project or program will generally be far less obvious than those of an infrastructure project. To cite only one example, much of the expense of a successful maize production program would be incurred in further training, management, and employment of extension agents, and more generally, in overhead activities to set up machinery for delivering development services to smallholders. The infrastructure for such a program might be very small, the imported inputs relatively

---

3. See Appendix A to Annex Three.

minor, and the expense spread out over many years, so that the inclusion of import costs or infrastructure costs or even of start-up costs misses much of the expense. Another difficult evaluation problem for Government is caused by the need to allocate shared costs and joint products between the programs in question and the ordinary recurrent budget. A counterpart to the evaluation problems cause by the difficulty of defining a project will be the difficulty of agreeing with donors on the reasonable limits to projects. As projects shade off into ordinary administrative recurrent cost on the one hand, or into parallel investments out of favor with donors, on the other, the Government can anticipate greater trouble in negotiation for support.

To the extent that methodological problems arising from logically indefinable limits to a program are mostly due to the institutional rules of donors, they can be solved by pragmatic compromise on a case-by-case basis. The mission has no solutions to suggest beyond early definition of the Government's view of proper limits of the project so that those difficult, often multilateral, bargains can be struck during the preparation phase thereby reducing delay to a minimum. In addition, it is the mission's clear impression that donors are, with few exceptions, prepared to be more flexible than the Government gives them credit for. We would urge the Kenyans to be less restrictive in their own definition of projects. No time is lost in going to a fallback position, if necessary, provided this is done early.

The more technical problems of project valuation can be relieved, to some extent, by much greater stress during project preparation on the management system and the programming of inputs at the operating stage. This concentration is necessary, in any case, if the transition to operations is to be smooth and quick, and the identification of input costs can be considered a byproduct of good preparation for management. Joint cost and multiple product problems will, however, persist as "judgment areas," where reasonable men can disagree. This puts a premium on early preliminary identification of the program's limits in order to clear up these disagreements as soon as possible.

Risk

Risk is an ordinary problem in project evaluation to be handled by careful analysis of the sensitivity of the social return on investment to reasonable probable variations in the benefit and cost elements. If probabilities can be assigned to various possible costs and outputs, risk can be quantified and the social return on the project expressed as a net-of-risk return. For the innovative projects recommended in this annex, risk will not generally be quantifiable because we have no experience with similar projects. Risk is an important problem if the innovation depends upon the cooperation of the private sector. For many activities, ordinary business risk may be minimized by a less innovative approach having less development impact. In such cases, the Government should probably intervene as risk-taker, isolating the private sector from some of the uncertainties of developmentally motivated processes.

The example of the pineapple canning industry cited in Chapter 3 is a case in point. Had the Government been prepared to assume the risk of guaranteeing a supply of suitable fruit to be produced by outgrowers, this good project might have been made much more productive of small scale entrepreneurial incomes and management experience. As it is, the entire production chain is under the central entrepreneurship of a foreign firm.

Some Difficulties Arising from New Project Designs

Programs that are large, geographically diffuse, and concentrated in software, rather than infrastructure, present special difficulties of project preparation and financing. This section attempts to anticipate some of these, as well as suggest solutions.

Loss of Visibility

Project visibility may become a difficult issue as programs with a larger scope are introduced. National politicians and international donors both prefer to support projects which are discrete and clearly identifiable. But the kind of project to which we have referred will typically not have built-in monuments, such as large infrastructural or fixed-plan requirements, and even where such requirements are present, a range of much less visible software will usually constitute a greater part of project cost. Very heavy local concentrations of software effort are probably not economic, considering the widespread national need, so it is doubtful that visibility problems can be solved by identifying a project with development in an isolated area.

The problems of visibility will eventually be solved, if at all, mainly by a change in the attitudes of policymakers and donors. There is simply no way to make some of the most important projects visible in the sense that infrastructure or fixed capital is visible. However, visibility of a different type can be obtained by skilful packaging and by an unremitting stress on the output of the programs rather than the inputs.[4] If, for example, an investment package could be designed so that donor A can be clearly associated with the increase in sunflower production due to an oilseeds project (or better still, with the value of that output, or the increased income to the rural poor, as a result of that output), a considerably more meaningful visibility could be achieved.

Critical Mass and Political Constraints

In some instances, opportunities for productive investment will be geographically concentrated. For example, the Nairobi area and the areas surrounding the Mumias sugar project or the Broderick Falls pulp and paper project would be logical locations for projects designed to stimulate small scale business, because of the existing or emerging concentration of consumer purchasing power. In other instances, the attempt to bring about any development may require so large a minimum package of government inputs that the areas would be getting a disproportionate share of public help. In still other instances, a larger package of government inputs may be the most efficient way to plan and promote development. In all of these cases, there is strong political opposition to the geographical concentration of expenditures.

To the extent that the services provided are social services more or less loosely related to the productive investments, the mission has no advice other than that the Government attempt to extract payment for services from persons able to pay for them. In the case of directly productive investment, for example, building up consumer oriented industries to serve the 10,000 newly emerging middle-income earners at Mumias, the mission would urge a focus on the income level of the beneficiary of government service rather than the income level of the area. If projects are concentrated on the small entrepreneur and the small farmer, and through them, aid their wage employees, they will be directed to the very lowest income groups. And, in the mission's opinion, the Government should make every effort to overcome the political obstacles to helping these groups in those areas where high concentrations make this aid most efficient.

It goes without saying, that, in cases where a package of services is required (e.g., improving productivity in subsistence crops), the provision of government services at subminimal levels in order to spread the services geographically is wasteful of resources. The question is partly technical (how does the marginal return to a third dose of services to one subsistence farmer compare with the marginal return of a first dose to another?) and partly political (at what level of development should a farmer be left on

---

4. After all, a visible project, such as a road or factory, is still only an intermediate good, even after it has been "completed."

his own so that aid can be diverted to less developed farmers, regardless of comparison of marginal returns?). The mission feels that the technical choices should be made by carefully weighing the alternative economic benefits against the cost. As to the political problem of just how far the relative economic benefits should determine allocation, we have no suggestion except to note that to the extent a program takes the very poor as a subject for development, even a heavy concentration of services would tend to improve the overall equity of the system.

Project and Program Administration

Finally, and perhaps most seriously, the details of project and program administration in broad gauged projects will tend to merge with the ordinary workings of the bureaucracy. This is all to the good if the program is planned well enough so that it continues uninterruptedly from implementation to operation. But the control of processes and procedures very quickly passes out of the hands of the planners and the donors. Project leverage, as such, will not amount to very much, and the emphasis must shift to improving the ordinary institutions of Government to a point where both Kenya's planners and donor agencies can be confident that the program will be well administered within the bureaucracy.

The problem of reduced project leverage and control, and the consequent uneasiness of donors, can probably best be handled by an additional emphasis during project preparation on the management mechanisms for the operating phase of the project. There is no reason in principle (or apparently, in fact) for donors to insist on new and separate institutions being established if they can be assured in advance that the program will be well administered within the ordinary bureaucracy. On the contrary, since the development of an efficient and development oriented bureaucracy is partly a precondition to, and partly a highly desirable result of development, the early and effective merger of a program into the larger body of ongoing government programs, while it continues to produce its development impact, is an ideal solution. To demonstrate that this result can be achieved—first by showing in careful project preparation how it could be achieved, and later by making a success of such a broad gauged program —is a clear challenge to the planners, to the cooperating donors, and to the bureaucracy.

Packaging Projects for Donors

Each of the donors who support Kenya's development effort has special institutional rules and, at least to some extent, unique preferences. The large number of donors involved relieves Kenya of the need to tailor her development effort to the investment preferences of any one of them, and donors who might be extremely ill-equipped, institutionally, to handle some development programs might be ideal for others. Matching these specialized donor availabilities and institutional constraints to the requirements of productive investment programs is a high priority planning task which would pay dividends in increased aid, better terms, and reduced delays. It is the mission's clear impression that Kenya is devoting far too few resources to this matching problem. Only about five professionals (including the supervisor) are employed in the unit in charge of coordination of all technical assistance and international aid—an annual program of commitments in excess of $100 million in total, scattered among a dozen significant donors, and literally hundreds of separate grant, loan, and technical assistance projects.

Cooperation and coordination of several donors may be required for some of the most important projects. Although necessary, this coordination is an additional project task, and has its costs. An important special case of problems of coordination is the reluctance (or refusal) on the part of some donors to accept each other's identification and appraisal work. The least offensive result of this policy is duplication of work and delay. The most serious result is the (often tacit) refusal to consider projects which are being or have been considered by other donors. This will become a still more important problem to the extent that foreign technical assistance is used to assist in project identification and preappraisal.

International cooperation and coordination, on the program or project level, is a very difficult task given the differing institutional limitations of the donors and the varying delegation of responsibility to their Kenya-based representatives. It is the mission's impression that there is a great potential for vastly improved coordination of this kind. At a minimum, it should be possible to decide for each donor the general limits of acceptability, of preliminary project or program work done by other donors.

Residual Problems for Donors

This annex has made several suggestions for improvements and changes in emphasis in Kenya's development planning. Each suggestion was made in the spirit of expanding the development effort, closing the gap between Government investment goals and the volume of well-prepared projects, and easing the problems of international cooperation in Kenya's development effort. At the end of the day, however, it must be recognized that greater concentration of Government effort in productive sectors and among the poorer portions of these sectors is inevitably going to put intense strain on the usual practices of donors. To cite only the most obvious examples, large geographically dispersed programs aimed at aiding the great mass of businesses or farms are inevitably going to entail, among other things: a closer coordination between technical assistance and the project cycle, a higher proportion of local costs, much smaller procurement packages requiring more flexible procurement rules, a frequent need to cooperate with other donors or accept their preliminary evaluation results, and a lower degree of control, over projects or institutions, than donors have been used to. Because we consider the solutions to these problems to be of major importance, we devote a large part of the next annex, "Priorities for External Assistance," to a discussion of possible donor responses to them. In conclusion to this annex, we recommend to the Government of Kenya that they be bold, innovative, and aggressive in preparing and presenting projects for financing, and that they act on the assumption that sound, well-prepared projects will generally find financing (up to a fairly flexible limit to financial availability) in spite of the institutional limitations of the donors. We reiterate that these limitations are, in general, probably flexible enough to achieve this result.

Appendix: Some Examples of Replicable Projects

We have argued in this annex that a shortage of planning, programming, and management skills can be expected to constrain absorptive capacity in the productive sectors for the medium term future. Although this can be relieved, to some extent, by expatriate manpower supplementation and by a greater stress on micro-economic planning and programming, it will still be necessary to get maximum output from each planner. Designing replicable projects is one device for multiplying the effect, not only of planning effort, but of efforts to design management systems and manpower use programs. In addition, project replicability provides a vehicle for learning from past experience; monitoring the operation of an ongoing project is given greater importance because the results can be incorporated into successive similar projects.

In this appendix, the development of the small scale business subsector is examined to show how a replicated project could operate there, and two alternatives are considered for use in the agricultural sector: the minimum package approach, and a type of site and services program. Both of these agricultural efforts would be replicable.

Small Scale Business Development

There can be little doubt that the development of the small scale business sector is extremely important in the overall development of the Kenyan economy. Small scale firms provide a wide variety of cheap goods and services for the poor. They absorb the surplus labor force which does not find an outlet in slow growing formal employment, supplying well over half of the nonfarm, nongovernment employment. They provide an avenue for capital and skill accumulation by new migrants.

At the same time, labor conditions and real wage rates in the small scale business sector are probably lower than most in the Kenyan economy, so that any development here would have maximum distributional benefits. One cannot expect to elevate the small scale sector in isolation, however, because its position as residual employer of migrants will hold down the wage rate, as long as the large gap between formal sector wages and farm earnings induces large migrations in search of formal sector jobs. On the other hand, measures to improve the productivity of labor in the small scale sector can have an impact on the returns to capital in this sector, on the number of laborers employed and, under some conditions, a short run effect on small scale business wages.

Small scale business can be developed, given adequate extension, credit and training, but no one of these services, in isolation, is likely to accomplish much. Hence, the entire literature on small scale business in Kenya has stressed an integrated approach, and some of the programs which have provided a full range of services with such an integrated approach (e.g., industrial estates programs and the Partnership for Productivity program[1]) have so far experienced a relatively low failure rate. A serious problem arises, however, because in small scale business the small investment required for each operating firm and the lack of standardization of these investments combine to make the subsector a very large potential user of extension and training capacity per shilling invested. There can be no thought of an input of expertise, on a firm-by-firm basis, comparable to the input into a large infrastructure or large industrial project. The low failure rate achieved by both the industrial estates and Partnership for Productivity is based on inputs of expertise which simply cannot be duplicated over a significant number of small scale firms using present methods.

The Government's programs of support to small scale business are undergoing a

---

1. This is a program operated by the Society of Friends.

transition. Emphasis is apparently shifting from an excessive reliance on concentrated assistance on a few firms at the upper end of the small business scale to programs with a wide outreach. This past effort directed towards relatively large firms was quite successful in creating new African firms and maintaining them in profitable operations, but the Government has recognized that this action was at high capital cost and high cost to the consumers in terms of protection. The new emphasis in government policy is towards assistance over a much broader spectrum of smaller firms.

The final form that the Government's program of assistance to small business will take is not yet decided. However, it is clear that the emphasis is shifting towards an attempt to reach a much larger number of smaller firms than have been reached under past programs. The principal official assistance programs have been the Kenya Industrial Estates Program, the small business loans of the Industrial and Commercial Development Corporation (designed primarily to transfer existing businesses from noncitizen to citizen control), and the loans scheme operated by the District Joint Loan Boards. More recently, the Government has designed a Rural Industrial Development Centre (RIDC) program designed to foster African entrepreneurship at the local level, and is considering consolidating all small businesses promotional activities under one national agency.

While the mission concurs with the new emphasis on small business and with the proposals that a single agency provide a package of development aids to these businessmen, we feel that there is a serious risk of inefficiency in the new organization. As the Government itself has recognized, it is necessary for services to be closely coordinated and tailored to the needs of the individual entrepreneur. Each small businessman needs credit, training, and advice in proportions which are unique to his enterprise. But the main loci of these services are the RIDCs which will, for the next few years, have a relatively small cadre of experts scattered very thinly. One center per province is recommended as the near term goal. It is fairly obvious that only with a much larger staff could serious advice and extension unique to the individual firm be given. There is little doubt, on the other hand, that the present proposals for establishing a network of RIDCs will place a heavy strain on the supply of manpower of the type required, i.e., highly trained and experienced men with enough general business sense and experience to design unique advice for many firms and enough leadership, ability, and personal presence to command attention of businessmen.

It is because the task is so large and the available cadre so small that the mission believes that radical innovations in program design are necessary, whatever institutional reforms are adopted by the Government. Two features of any efficient design, given the extreme scarcity of experts available, will be that the work of experts will be reusable and that the scheme itself will generate additional expertise. As an illustration of one scheme which might fit within the proposed government framework for small business assistance, the following paragraphs examine a radical project proposal, specifically designed to save expertise, which has received some support from Government during our mission to Kenya.

There are several small manufacturing and service activities in each of which a large number of small firms operate. By specializing part of the cadre of development assistants in the activities containing the greatest number of small firms, or in those activities where demand is obviously great enough to support a large number of small firms, several advantages would be gained. First, market surveys could be conducted, not only to devise marketing procedures for the firms in the activity, but to determine the number and size of firms that the local market can support. This will help to limit market overcrowding, or excessive shortage of firms in the activity. Second, plan design, production planning, simple bookkeeping systems and control mechanisms, inventory plans, and so forth—in other words, overhead knowledge required for technical assistance and the evaluation of the need for and potential productivity of government assistance—could be obtained once for all the firms in a given activity. For each activity selected, much more expertise could be invested in forming up a prototype of an efficient operation, because the prototype will be reused. The cost of a thorough, first rate analysis would be small per firm assisted. Third, because the heavy emphasis on design will permit advice to be much more precise and detailed, a relatively inexperienced man can be trained quickly to undertake the actual extension work in a single activity. In contrast, only a highly competent and experienced expert could be expected to advise many firms in many different fields. Since Kenya is rapidly developing an oversupply of young, well-educated but inexperienced men, the economic cost of the actual technical assistance would be small. Fourth, the extension worker would quickly develop into a first-class expert in his very limited field, able to evaluate, advise, and command respect for his ability. The number of failures due to unwarranted advice or error in evaluating a firm's procedures and development aspects should be relatively small.

To adopt a specialist approach to development of small business would obviously be inadequate in itself because there are many firms that are either truly unique or too large (actually or potentially) relative to the market for replication to be economic. But this approach would fit in very well as a supplement to the Government's industrial estates program and as a subsidiary function of the proposed central agency. We do not suggest that a few specialists can substitute for the staff of the proposed RIDCs. On the other hand, the task of each of the regional centers would be greatly simplified if, for five or six important types of activities covering perhaps half of the small firms in the area, pretrained experts with prepackaged projects were available.

It remains to be investigated how many types of activities have enough firms to make specialization in them worthwhile and how great a percentage of the total of small businesses could be served in this manner, but some indications are available. Industrial and Commercial Development Corporation data, for example, show that 88 percent of their loans to small business have been concentrated in only ten rather narrowly defined activities, with the number of loans in each activity ranging from 14 to 216. ICDC management doubts that they have come close to exhausting the market in more than one of these activities. It would seem from these numbers that the potential for conscious specialization of assistance is reasonably large. Nearly homogeneous groups of firms in the service trades would probably be still more common, for example, retail trade of various types, commercial handling and bulking of agricultural products, small transport firms, or food preparation firms.

Although we are persuaded that a specialist approach, such as just outlined, would produce large savings of skill in planning and operation, compared to other methods of assisting small business, it cannot be denied that, in its initial phases, such a program would require a lumpy investment of planning. A unit to lay the groundwork for assistance to be channeled to a number of specialized activities would have to be highly skilled and liberally financed. For this reason, we suggest that the Government seek foreign expert advice, under technical assistance, for the nucleus of these planning units. This assistance should be available not only for the design and testing of the most suitable prototype businesses, but also to help in the initial implementation period. In this way, the training of Kenyans who would serve as loan officers, the initial field trials of the prototypes, and any amendments to the package of services which initial experience reveals to be necessary, could also be assisted by the expatriate experts.

Minimum Package Programs for Small-Scale Agriculture

The Special Rural Development Program, which is at present the leading effort in small scale agricultural development, suffers from the same lack of replicability as the successful industrial programs. Once again the problem is less that the SRDP areas have not made development strides (although the record has been spotty) than that the development has been purchased at too great a cost in terms of skilled manpower and financial resources. It is clear that Government is seeking an alternative to SRDP type development efforts.[2] A feature of these efforts must be the applicability to a large segment of the rural area, since it is apparently politically unpalatable as well as inefficient to concentrate resources in a few small areas.

An approach that offers some hope for broadly based improvement in a short time is the minimum package approach. The central ideas of this approach are (a) to select one or two key services which can make a noticeable impact on production of an important crop; (b) to design a plan for the use of these one or two services; (c) to design a mechanism and an optional management unit for delivering them; and (d) to replicate the management unit as fast as possible. The minimum package approach proceeds from a recognition that the Government is in no position to launch a "best practices" development effort over any large share of the agricultural sector. The minimum package approach is to settle for some second best combination which will nonetheless be effective, and spread this second best alternative as broadly as possible.

In some countries, a separate administrative unit for minimum package programs has been advocated, partly in response to an absolute shortage of technical personnel doing extension work. In the Kenyan case it would probably be more appropriate to design a minimum package effort to work directly through the Ministry of Agriculture. Even in Kenya, however, some specialization by area and a thorough and deliberate programming of effort of ministerial personnel specializing in minmum package assistance would be necessary.

We believe that there are many applications of the minimum package approach. One kind of project concentrates on an *area* in an attempt to bring a critical mass to bear on the poverty of the people in a particular area. Another variant is to concentrate on one *crop*. A minimum package arrangement for an important subsistence crop, such as maize, is an excellent example of the shadow area between "projects" and "programs." Enough project elements exist, that is, enough work must be done in identification, preparation for financing, detailed planning and programming of staff, so that a minimum package approach to maize development would greatly benefit from a project approach. No doubt any "project" prepared would have very large local cost elements; except for grain handling and importation of recurrent inputs, it is hard to isolate any foreign cost elements. On the basis of discussions with bilateral donors, the mission believes that this type of project would, nonetheless, appeal to several of the important bilateral donors and we strongly recommend that the Government seek assistance for the design and implementation of this type of development effort.

Another example, already tried with some success in the horticultural industry, is the concentration of a minimum package of marketing services (e.g., collection, grading and packing centers) or of stockist services (supply of seed, fertilizers and chemicals, in appropriately sized packs). Often, these two forms of service will be combined into a wider package, combining both the supply of inputs and the provision of marketing.

This approaches what the mission feels is probably the most valuable variant of the minimum package approach—the entrepreneurial package. This concept, which is very similar to our proposals for small scale business, entails the identification of one type of activity—most probably the production of one commodity—and designs a complete, but standardized, management system, covering design of the operation, the flow of inputs, technical production requirements, and the sale of the product. Like the small scale business project, this need be neither costly nor require much manpower. The essential features are that it supplements (or replaces) the small farmer's limited entrepreneurial ability and is replicable many times over.

---

2. The Agricultural Sector Survey included a discussion of SRDP experience, with some of the benefits that have been gained. See Part III for a summary of the discussion.

Much of the national commodity planning should, in our opinion, be designed with a more or less standardized production unit of this kind in mind. This approach has already demonstrated its relevance to special crops, such as tea or pyrethrum; we feel it could be extended more than it has been in commodities such as horticulture, and in pig and poultry production.

One final application of the minimum package approach relates to the particular problem of subsistence farmers who have too little land to break out of their cycle of subsistence production. In outline form the problem can be summarized:

- Subsistence farmers are growing low value crops, primarily cereals.
- Land crowding and poor husbandry practices combine to hold output down to a bare subsistence level, or even below subsistence levels.
- The traditional farmer's desperate response is to concentrate more and more on the subsistence crop. If all his land and labor resources are not sufficient to grow enough food, it is impossible to convince him that he should divert any of his resources to anything else.
- But, given the scarcity of land, many farmers are doomed to subsistence or subsistence levels of income unless they shift into higher value crops. There is just no way to become even modestly well off by supporting several people on a few acres by growing traditional grain crops.
- Hence a dilemma exists. To become reasonably well off, a farmer must change cropping patterns but to change cropping patterns he must feel secure in his basic food supply, which is difficult, given his limited land holding.

We feel that there many be a way out of the dilemma if the Government can only get hold of some land in the area—either by using state land, or by buying or leasing Trust land or registered private land. The requirements for a site and service project are:

- A sizable tract of land, say fifty acres, located in a densely populated subsistence farming area with potential for growing high value crops.
- Market connections (a road and market knowledge) for supplying necessary inputs to this tract of land, and for marketing the high value crops.
- A single extension agent who understands the technology of the crops, and who can organize the supply of inputs and the marketing of crops.

The method of operation of the site and service project is to rent small portions of the land, say one acre per farmer, on a crop year basis to subsistence farmers in the immediate neighborhood, on the condition that they use the land to grow the high value crop under the supervision of the extension agent. Land rental would be on a proportion of sales basis and inputs would be provided without liability except the claim on a proportion of sales. In other words, the growing of the crop is a no-risk venture to the farmer except that he risks his labor time. The project acts as entrepreneur, except that some of the profit accrues to the farmer as a payment for his labor risk.

A project of this kind might increase the income of subsistence farmers very quickly at small cost and introduce them to a cash income without the awful risk which they currently experience of running short of food if they take a chance. The mission does not believe that a site-and-service project has very wide relevance to rural development, but recommends that this approach might be tried on an experimental basis. We also think that the site-and-services approach may also have relevance to more sophisticated farmers who would be willing to pay a site rent for a plot of land, on a block where certain minimum services (perhaps irrigation) are provided and charged for. We even think the concept might be applied to urban areas, if land could be made available, so that families could grow food for consumption and sale.

ANNEX SIX

PRIORITIES FOR EXTERNAL ASSISTANCE

Chapter 1

Aid Requirements and Terms of Aid

Since Independence, Kenya has received a large and growing volume of official aid. The annual level of disbursements has more than doubled during the period (from about £10 million in 1964 to more than £21 million in 1972), and the total value of external debt has also doubled (see below). On a commitment basis, this has meant that Kenya has received about $4 a year per capita, between 1965 and 1971, which is around the median for countries at a similar stage of development.[1]

Loan commitments have increased quite rapidly, particularly in 1972, when they jumped to £37.2 million, compared with £19.7 million in 1971 (see Table 2). This surge in commitments has resulted in a large increase in undisbursed debt (nearly £56 million at the end of 1972), so that disbursements can be expected to rise quite sharply in the near future. Thus, in general, it can be said that there has been a movement towards a substantially higher level of assistance, not yet fully reflected in the disbursement data. Taking into account the existing undisbursed debt, together with the new commitments expected over the 1974–78 plan period,[2] it is projected that annual disbursements might increase to about £50 million by the end of the period.

The amount, source, and terms of external assistance to Kenya over the last five years are given in the tables to this annex.[3] Some of the more noticeable features of these figures are the changes and diversification which have taken place in the sources of external aid to Kenya (see Tables 1 and 2). As recently as the end of 1968, over half of Kenya's external debt was held by the United Kingdom. All other bilateral donors accounted for 20 percent of debt, and international institutions held less than 15 percent. By the end of 1972, the United Kingdom's share had fallen to only 28 percent, other bilateral donors maintained their combined share at about 20 percent, but international institutions had increased their share to over 37 percent. As we shall refer to later, this changing composition of aid—as well as the increasing magnitude of aid flows—has considerable significance for Kenya.

The terms of financial assistance to Kenya have tended to harden somewhat in recent years (see Table 3). Although the average terms are still reasonable, since 1968 the average interest rate on all loans outstanding has increased by about ½ percent (to almost 4 percent in 1972), and average maturity has slightly fallen. As a result, the grant element of all loans outstanding has fallen from 51 percent in 1968 to 48 percent in 1972 (Table 3). The terms of *new* debts contracted during recent years have deteriorated even more significantly. A recent Bank report[4] shows the following comparison between new debts contracted during the periods 1965–68 and 1969–71:

	1965–68	1969–71
Average interest rate	2.2%	4.8%
Average maturity	29.6 years	27.9 years
Average grace period	4.8 years	7.2 years
Grant element of loans (for discount rate of 10%)	60%	40%
Grant element of loans and grants (for discount rate of 10%)	77%	67%

1. See Table 7. Nearly half of the countries in the $100–200 per capita income categories had per capita commitments within the range of $3–5 per year.
2. New commitments are projected by the mission to be about £56 million a year over the plan period.
3. See also Table 4 in Part I for more information about Kenya's external debt.
4. See "World Debt Tables," World Bank Report No. EC-167-72, December 15, 1973.

The primary reason for the deterioration in the average terms of lending to Kenya is the changing pattern of lending just described, and particularly the growing weight of multilateral aid in Kenya's external debt. The blend of aid from multinational agencies has hardened very considerably since 1968, as the proportion of IDA credits has fallen (see Table 1). The composition of the World Bank Group's lending is an especially sensitive variable in the average terms of Kenya's external aid, because of the growing weight of Bank Group assistance in meeting Kenya's resources requirements.

The average terms of loans from bilateral donors have remained virtually constant over the last five years (Table 4). However, the average interest rates charged by individual donors have risen in some important cases, and as a result, the average terms would have hardened if it had not been for the fact that the share of new commitments provided by the soft-term donors (particularly Sweden, the Netherlands, and more recently, Canada) has been rising over the period.

Thus, the experience of the last few years has been for Kenya to face a generally hardening blend of aid. But many bilateral donors have gone a long way towards liberalizing the terms of their lending, and some are providing loans virtually on grant terms. There is also some evidence that the terms of financial assistance from Governments have tended to soften in 1972 and 1973. Interest rates on loans have been lowered: almost all new commitments in 1972, for example, were at interest rates of less than 3 percent, and rates of between 2 and 3 percent were typical for aid planned in 1973. Important portions of the Swedish program (the 1973 small industries loan), the UK program (land transfer), the US program (population control) will be in grant form, in addition to smaller grants available from Norway, Denmark and the Netherlands. As a result, there is some prospect that the grant element of bilateral aid may increase still further in the coming years. However, many bilateral donors have already gone as far as their national policies allow in softening their aid to Kenya, and there is probably only limited scope for a continuing improvement in the average terms of all lending.

Moreover, the supply of concessionary aid is limited and certainly nowhere sufficient to meet Kenya's increasing needs for external capital. In the past, therefore, Kenya has had to rely to an increasing extent on harder term sources of assistance, primarily the World Bank, but more recently on a growing amount of commercial borrowing. As we discuss later, Kenya is presently quite capable of absorbing some further hardening in the average terms of lending, but there is a limit to how far it will be in Kenya's own interests to increase her borrowing, at the margin, on terms which will significantly increase the future burden of debt servicing.

Debt Service and Creditworthiness

Although the marginal cost of borrowing from abroad has been rising, as just indicated, most of Kenya's external debt is still held on generally favorable terms, and her present creditworthiness is not in any dispute. The total debt outstanding at the end of 1972 was just under $510 million (of which $354 million had been disbursed) or about 30 percent of GNP. On a per capita basis, Kenya's total outstanding debt has risen from about $32 in 1968 to about $40 by the end of 1972, which is a high, but not excessive, level for countries at Kenya's stage of development (Table 7).

The cost of servicing debt has not so far been a significant burden on Kenya's foreign exchange earnings. Total service payments due in 1973 amounted to $33 million, of which $17.7 million was for repayment of principal and $15.3 for interest charges. In 1972, the debt service ratio was 4.2 percent, and it has never been higher than 4.5

percent in the previous five years. The repayments schedule on existing debt suggests no servicing problems in the future, except perhaps for one isolated year (1978) when a substantial portion of one loan falls due for repayment. At present, about 30 percent of total outstanding debt is undisbursed. But even so, allowing for the likely schedule of disbursements, the cost of servicing existing debt will not rise appreciably.

Kenya also has obligations under loans made to the East African Community, most of which are jointly and severally guaranteed by the governments of all three Partner States. At the end of 1969,[5] the East African Community had external debts outstanding of some US$216 million and annual service payments which were projected to mount to some $26 million by 1972. Compared with the Partner States' external debt, the Community has borrowed on generally hard terms.

Bank reports have conventionally assigned a one-third share of the outstanding debt contracted by the Community (and of the servicing costs) to each Partner State in the analysis of debt.[6] If this notional one-third share is added, Kenya's total external debt is probably in excess of $600 million in 1973, and her notional debt service ratio about 5.3 percent. Even allowing for the additional cost of Community borrowing, therefore, it is clear that Kenya's external debt position is still basically sound. As we indicate later, the extent to which Kenya's debt becomes more burdensome in the future will depend upon the magnitudes and terms of new capital flows, but particularly upon the availability of concessionary aid.

Future Aid Requirements

It had been anticipated that the mission would look at Kenya's aid requirements during the period of the forthcoming 1974–78 Plan. However, at the time of the mission's visit to Kenya neither the plan investment program nor the financing plan had been finally determined and we shall not therefore address ourselves to Kenya's quantitative aid requirements in this annex. However, the analysis of Kenya's longer term resource availability undertaken by the Mission does allow a number of general conclusions to be drawn about future aid requirements.

The most obvious feature of the Basic Scenario projections, derived from the macro-economic model used by the mission, is the very large residual balance of payments gap. To fill this gap with increasing flows of concessionary financing from official sources would call for a much larger volume of new commitments from bilateral donors than are anticipated in the near future[7] or could reasonably be expected in the longer term, even on the most optimistic assumption about future aid flows. On the other hand, an attempt to finance a residual gap (of the size implied by the Basic Scenario projections) on commercial rates of borrowing would eventually lead to a debt service

---

5. This is the last year for which a full report on the external debt of the Community has been provided. The only information available on new commitments over the last four years (1970–73) is for the Bank Group, which made World Bank loans amounting to some $87 million over the period.

6. This notional allocation of debt is not very satisfactory since it represents neither the legal responsibility for debt nor the economic impact of Community borrowing on the three Partner States. The Community is presently undertaking a study of the national distribution of community services which might subsequently provide the basis for a more useful formula.

7. An improvement in *terms* of bilateral aid cannot help much. As previously discussed, these terms are already relatively soft, and even moving to pure grants of the projected amounts would leave a large residual gap. Only a much larger *volume* of aid on concessionary terms could be sufficient to fill the residual gap.

burden of unmanageable proportions and would, in any case, be self-defeating as a mechanism for securing external capital.[8]

The general conclusion which we draw from the basic projections, therefore, is that it is not feasible for Kenya to continue a rapid rate of growth, along the same development pattern as in the past, without running into an unmanageable balance of payments problem. The first obvious implication of this conclusion is to suggest a lower overall rate of growth. But we have rejected this alternative, primarily because of its undesirable effects on employment and the income level of the poor. We concluded that the fast growth rate envisaged in the Plan (around 7½ percent) could not be supported for long without changes in the historical pattern of investment and macro-economic policy, and a package of such changes were included in the Preferred Scenario set of projections.

The projections under the Preferred Scenario present a much more optimistic outlook for continued growth in Kenya.[9] Under the hypothetical assumptions of the Preferred Scenario, the restructuring and reform of the economy would allow Kenya to become less dependent on external capital for her continued growth, and the projections suggest that the balance of payments position could be held within manageable limits over the next decade, even with a rapid pace of growth. However, even under the hypothetical and rather unrealistic projections of the Preferred Scenario, which assume that a major restructuring and reform of the economy can be implemented immediately, the anticipated level of official aid would still not be sufficient to eliminate the resource gap altogether, and an accelerated growth of commitments would be required. Thus, even under the *most optimistic* assumptions about Kenya's performance, the economy will continue to need a considerable expansion in capital inflow if it is to maintain its present high and desirable rate of growth. And most of this aid will have to be on concessionary terms if debt servicing costs are not to become a serious threat to Kenya's continued creditworthiness.

Since a fast rate of growth is in fact a necessary condition for Kenya to achieve the objectives of the Preferred Scenario, it is particularly important that Kenya should be able to obtain the resources she needs. But at the same time, as discussed at greater length later, the donors can do much to help Kenya, not only in providing the increased resources required, but in supporting the restructuring and reforming process, in the pattern and quality of their aid. In this way, donors could, during the next plan period, help to reduce Kenya's dependence on external aid in the longer term.

8. To illustrate this point, the table below shows the debt service results of financing the Basic Scenario residual gap on World Bank terms. In the first line, residual gap appears as "gap after allowing for new disbursements from foreign capital inflow and debt servicing" in Annex One, Table 19. Debt service calculation excludes interest on interest and amortization on borrowing to cover interest.

Debt Service Projection—Basic Scenario
(Residual Gap financed at 8 percent interest, 5 years grace, 25-year maturity)

	1975	1980	1985
	(£ millions)		
Interest on debt to finance residual gap	6.4	37.0	121.4
Amortization of debt to finance residual gap	—	4.0	23.2
Total service of debt to finance residual gap	6.4	41.0	144.6
	(percentage)		
Debt service on residual gap ÷ exports	2.8	12.8	32.7
Debt service on residual gap ÷ GDP	.03	3.8	9.1

9. The underlying assumptions are the same as those of the Basic Scenario, but the pattern of investment is assumed to shift in favor of the directly productive sectors and some changes are assumed in macro-economic policy. See Annex One for a full discussion of the various sets of projections.

Chapter 2

Sectoral Composition of External Assistance

Overall Priorities

This chapter will examine the historical characteristics of foreign assistance and the declared intentions of the major donors regarding future aid commitments to see whether the pattern of aid flows is likely to match Kenya's development aid requirements in the qualitative sense. In the opinion of the mission, this is the most important question regarding the sectoral composition of foreign assistance. There is little doubt that Kenya's priorities for external aid are changing and will continue to change, and that donors will need to adapt their aid programs accordingly. We have in this report suggested a reorientation in Kenya's investment programs towards productive sectors, and it follows that we would hope to see a similar shift in emphasis in both financial and technical assistance. However, two important qualifications have to be made to this general conclusion.

First, while it is very important that donors should actively encourage and support desirable changes in Kenya's development programs and aid requirements, there is a limit to the extent that donors can or should attempt to influence the country's development philosophy or major allocative decisions. Of course, the flexibility of the Government's financial planning will increase in any case as the country becomes more self-reliant. The donors should probably try to enhance this flexibility as much as possible, limiting their influence over allocative decisions to a purely advisory role. It seems at least futile and perhaps perverse for an individual donor (or for donors as a whole) to try to shape the development allocations through their aid programs.

Second, the fact that there may be a need for external aid as a whole to shift in emphasis towards agriculture or other productive sectors does not mean that every *individual* donor should aim to channel aid along identical lines. Nor is it necessarily desirable for large donors to spread their assistance over all sectors of the economy. Some degree of specialization would seem to be of benefit to both donors and recipient, and, as we point out later, one objective of aid coordination might be to encourage donor agencies to channel their aid into those kinds of activities in which they appear to have a comparative advantage.

Sectors of Aid Concentration

Table 6 shows the average flow of government investment into the main sectors in the last three years and compares this "average structure" of government investment to the sectoral composition of the projected future flow of financial assistance already committed and the disbursements expected from planned commitments. The directly productive sectors appear to be well taken care of in aid commitments. However, future commitments are only unofficial statements of intent. They are, by and large, not yet "projectized," nor have alternatives to project lending been developed to absorb these funds.

Technical assistance has been much more concentrated than financial aid. In 1968, agriculture accounted for about one-quarter of the program and education about one-third. Technical assistance in industry was comparatively slight, reflecting the heavy involvement of private enterprise in industry and the general lack of government attention to detailed work in the sector.

Technical Assistance in Selected Sectors
(at Cost to Donor)

Sector	1968	1973
	(£ thousand)	
Agriculture	1,604	2,199
Education	2,252	2,128
Industry	73	70

SOURCES: *A Proposed Five-Year Program of Technical Assistance to Kenya,* 1968–73, Volume 1, page 9; Mission estimates based on *Development Assistance to Kenya* (Nairobi: UNDP, May 1973).

By 1973, the combined agricultural programs led all sectors of technical assistance, having increased by about one-third in the 1968–73 period. Education programs had declined slightly and industrial technical assistance remained comparatively small.

Future Commitments

The planned commitments of the major donors for both technical assistance and financial aid point to a continuation of the trend towards a greater concentration in the productive sectors. In technical assistance, the slight decline in education which has characterized the 1968–73 period should accelerate, with the rapidly growing cadre of qualified citizens replacing expatriates in most of the actual teaching positions.[1] Meanwhile, the expressed intention of virtually all of the important donors is to look for acceptable technical assistance projects in the agricultural sector. It also appears likely that opportunities for technical assistance in business and industry will increase due to the expected increase in government support to small scale industry and the planned government program for extension services to business and industry. It is probable that these expanded needs will be met, as donors, particularly Britain, attempt to diversify their technical assistance into productive sectors.

On the financial aid side, the sectoral preferences of the donors are so clearly concentrated in agriculture, or in closely related fields of agro-industries and rural water supplies, that the sectoral composition problem is actually reversed. There is, in fact, little chance that absorptive capacity in agriculture can grow fast enough to permit the commitments of all of the aid that would be available for that sector for the next few years, according to the declared sectoral preferences of the donors. Realized commitments may therefore have to differ considerably from donors' plans, with more aid concentrated in infrastructure or social services sectors unless technical assistance to the agricultural sector can be more closely associated with project identification and implementation.

In the industrial sector, the prospects for sufficient aid to finance a rapid growth of government investment are also very good. This growth will require new types of projects to be evolved, as suggested in Annex Five, and this may in turn lead to short run absorption problems. But there is little doubt that the present aid donors in this field are evolving project methods which can be expanded or duplicated. Although confined to the medium-to-large scale industries so far, the industrial aid program of the Federal Republic of Germany can probably continue to expand, and some of the more recent donors, notably Japan, have shown considerable interest in searching out ad hoc

---

1. Kenya may actually face a surplus of teachers, or a fairly general overqualification of teachers, for primary and secondary school posts within the next decade.

investment opportunities. The experience of Norway in helping to promote a single specialized business/industry (local contracting), with a "program" approach, can provide important lessons to donors desiring to innovate in this subsector, and in industry generally. The recent grant of financial aid by Sweden for a large, reasonably balanced, regionally based expansion plan for industry breaks new ground from an institutional point of view, and represents a considerable advance over single project loans. Overall, the bottleneck to absorption in the sector is likely to be the shortage of qualified personnel for the speedy preparation and execution of programs from among the Government's many new initiatives in the sector.

In general, therefore, the mission finds no problem with the anticipated sectoral composition of foreign assistance. The concentration by the donors on the productive sectors is in line with Kenya's requirements and should succeed in supporting increased investment in these sectors if sufficient programs can be prepared for financing. Only two reservations to this optimistic conclusion need to be made. First, is a cautionary note to donors that they should be prepared to shift some of the funds now earmarked for productive sector investment to other sectors, unless they can directly help through technical assistance, in building up the absorptive capacity of the productive sectors. Second, is the reservation that donors may have to be more flexible in the conditions of their aid if they are to realize their sector preferences. This latter point is discussed at greater length in the next chapter.

CHAPTER 3

CONDITIONS OF FINANCIAL ASSISTANCE

As we have seen in the previous chapters of this annex, prospects for gross aid flow and its sectoral composition are quite favorable, both for technical assistance and for financial aid. Donors' plans are clearly consistent with Kenya's needs, but these plans can be realized only if programs can be prepared for financing. The Government faces a large planning and management task to absorb aid as productively as possible. The success of this task will depend partly on how flexible the donors are prepared to be on the conditions of assistance. In the opinion of the mission, there is considerable scope for improvement in the conditions of both financial aid and technical assistance.

Priorities for Reform

Conditions of financial assistance run the gamut. At one extreme are tied loans to finance only part of the foreign exchange costs of a project selected more for its "aid-ability" than for its contributions to Kenyan goals. At the other extreme are free foreign exchange loans for general support of the Government's investment plan, or programs combining liberal local cost financing, untied foreign financing, and technical assistance. Quite clearly, the more that aid resembles free foreign exchange, the more readily the Government can make use of aid in advancing its highest priority programs. Thus, we agree with the spirit of the discussion of aid in the recent ILO/UNDP report; for example, that tying should be lessened, local cost financing increased, program lending increased, procurement conditions made more realistic, and so forth. Because most of the donors have their own administrative limitations, however, determined by their national governments or legislators (on a global basis rather than on a country-by-country basis), the *terms* of lending to Kenya are not likely to show such dramatic improvement in the near future.

In the opinion of the mission, the highest priority for reform in the conditions of lending should be given to the changes required to increase external support for "mass programs" in the productive sectors. This priority corresponds with our analysis of the needed change in Kenya's own investment pattern. These mass programs potentially involve a very large number of separate productive units at the lower end of the efficiency scale, the income scale, the education scale, and the organization scale. There is no use pretending that these programs will be easy, or that they can be prepared to fit the mold of conventional projects. The more broadly based a program becomes and the more it is involved with masses of people rather than a few, the more inextricably will it have to be integrated into the ordinary day-to-day operation of the administrative structure. For example, any program designed to uplift subsistence agriculture would overlap with the general functions of the already very large extension service. Since duplication is clearly undesirable, elements of the extension service would have to be part of the program "package," and its financing integrated into the Ministry of Agriculture's budget. Similar overlaps will arise between any broad based small business project and the proposed small business assistance program. It is conceivable that several conventional projects could, and will, be devised by nibbling at the edges of these two major problem areas. But an effort to develop these sectors at any speed, across the board will require that the special problems associated with these mass programs be faced up to and solved.

The present assistance policies of most donors discriminate against mass programs in the productive sectors in a number of ways. These are probably accidental biases, since it is clearly not the intent of the donors to discriminate in this direction—rather the reverse. But the cumulative effect of these biases may, in some cases, be sufficient to thwart the best intentions of both donor and recipient, to channel aid into the most productive uses. The following paragraphs discuss some common aid practices and their inherent biases.

While the *financing of foreign exchange costs* may be sufficient in hardware type projects (infrastructure, heavy industry, etc.), this type of aid simply does not go far enough in the kind of broadly conceived project which will be required to bring a growing level of income, employment, and services to the mass of the population. Foreign exchange costs, perhaps 90 percent of some infrastructure projects, might constitute only 25 or 30 percent of the best program for small scale agriculture. If the grant element in foreign assistance is very large, as it is in Kenya's bilateral aid, financing for 90 percent of an infrastructure project is equivalent to a grant for about 60 percent of the project, while the "equivalent grant" for a mass project with a large software component might be about 18 to 20 percent. Such a vast distortion in the costs to Kenya, as seen by government planners, is bound to bias their decisions in favor of import intensive projects.

The following numerical example, showing the costs of hypothetical projects which differ in their foreign exchange components, may help to clarify the nature of the bias which is introduced when foreign exchange costs *only* are financed by external donors:

	(1) Project Cost	(2) Foreign Exchange Cost (= External Financing)	(3) Project Benefits	(4) Grant Element (per £ of loan)	(5) Value of Grant Element (Col. 2 × Col. 4)	(6) Effective Cost of Project to Kenya (Col. 1− Col. 5)	(7) Rate of Return to Kenya on Cost to Kenya (Col. 3 × 100) / Col. 6
	(£)	(£)	(£)	(£)	(£)	(£)	(percentage)
Project A	100	90	15	0.7	63	37	40.5
Project B	100	70	15	0.7	49	51	29.4
Project C	100	20	15	0.7	14	86	17.4

In the example, three projects are financed by soft loans to the extent of their (differing) foreign exchange cost. The terms, summarized by the grant element (column 4) are the same for each loan. The benefits to Kenya and the rate of return on total cost are the same for all three projects (column 3). But if aid is provided for only the foreign exchange element of these projects, the effective rate of return as far as Kenya is concerned—that is, the rates of return on the costs to *Kenya*—varies very markedly between projects (column 7). This surely constitutes an undue bias towards projects of the type shown in Project A (infrastructure, heavy industry, import intensive investment in general), compared to projects such as Project C (mass impact projects, and projects which make intensive use of domestic goods and services and software in general).

The obvious, but difficult, solution is to equalize the *value* of the grant elements of programs financed by foreign assistance, by increasing the grant elements of the mass programs. This will necessarily imply financing some portion of local costs. The mission's suggestion is that enough local costs be financed to leave the percentage of Kenya cost (program cost less grant element of financial aid) about the same in these sectors as in the infrastructure sectors. This can be done by financing the same percentage of project cost for all projects, assuming that the terms of assistance are the same. This suggests a simple formula for local cost financing. If the total assistance for each project is to be about the same percentage of project cost, say 70 percent, the required local cost financing can be derived as the difference between 70 percent of project cost and the foreign exchange cost of the project.

It should be stressed that the above local cost financing "formula" merely equalizes the rate of return to Kenya from her own investment (total cost less grant element) in programs having equal rates of economic return.[1] It cannot be viewed as specially favorable treatment for mass programs, but would go some way towards removing the discrimination imposed on these projects in the past.

In addition to the "price signals" argument for financing local costs in mass programs, there are balance of payments arguments for financing local costs in the aggregate external financial assistance program. During the next few years, disbursements of foreign financial assistance to the public sector will probably constitute about 50 percent of total fixed public investment. To finance this percentage of the total investment will require financing a larger percentage of each assisted program, because many government investment programs will not be assisted. Assuming that 75 percent of government fixed investment is assisted, it would be necessary to finance about 66 percent of project costs, on the average, to cover the balance of payments gap. The assisted projects might have foreign exchange costs on an average of about 45 percent of project costs. Thus, about 40 percent of the local costs of those projects receiving foreign assistance would have to be picked up to cover the exchange gap.

The required local cost financing as calculated above (40 percent in the example) is a useful tool in evaluating the lending program of individual donors. If a donor's program consists only of a selection of import intensive projects of which only the foreign exchange portions are financed, then the remaining projects offered to other donors will have a lower average import content and a greater need for local cost financing. Therefore, the mission suggests that a fair distribution of the overall aid program among donors implies that a single donor should attempt to balance his own aid program, so that in financing 66 percent of project costs, he finances around 40 percent of local costs. Of course these figures are used merely to illustrate the principle, but some guidelines along these lines seems to be necessary. This guideline should, of course, be flexibly applied, with liberal exceptions for special cases, but a guideline on this style appears to be necessary. One way of achieving such a balance would be by sharing in some of the local cost intensive mass programs.

The *financing of discrete projects*, through autonomous agencies or with autonomous management, is a practice well adapted to the big hardware project. The ultimate

---

1. Using the same numerical example given above, this formula would give the following results:

(1) Project Cost	(2) Foreign Exchange Cost	(3) Project Benefits	(4) External Financing	(6) Grant Element per £ of Loan	(6) Value of Grant Element (Col. 4 × Col. 5)	(7) Effective Cost of Project to Kenya	(8) Rate of Return to Kenya on Cost to Kenya (Col. 3 × 100) / Col. 7
£	£	£	£	£	£	£	(percentage)
100	90	15	60	0.7	43	58	25.8
100	70	15	60	0.7	42	58	25.8
100	20	15	60	0.7	42	58	25.8

When the external finance provides the same percentage of project cost, irrespective of their foreign exchange component, the rate of return to Kenya (on the cost of Kenya) is the same for all projects having the same economic rate of return.

form of this practice is the so-called turnkey project, usually associated with power projects or heavy industry, but variations on the same theme can be devised through skilful manipulation of requirements for autonomous existence of a project management that can be closely controlled by the donor. The more that a program has a mass character, the more closely integrated will it be with the ordinary makings of the indigenous administration and the less discrete and donor-manageable. For mass programs in the productive sectors, the Ministry of Agriculture itself and the proposed small business assistance agency will inevitably be central to the management of the programs. If the donors are to be of real assistance with these programs, they must necessarily work through these agencies and, in the process, sacrifice a good part of the usual control over project implementation and operation.[2] With this in mind, the most efficient way to "relate technical assistance to the project cycle," a stated aim of many of the donors, is probably to use technical assistance to supplement the capacity for development effort of the ministries and implementing agencies themselves. Although "institution building" is an overworked phrase, it is still true that a far more ambitious effort is needed to strengthen the central institutions, that is, the relevant ministries and agencies, so that broad based, ministerially managed programs can be supported with confidence.

The practice of *unilateral appraisal and single donor financing,* although slowly eroding, still favors the discrete and relatively small project over the mass programs. Shared financing arrangements have been tried on a number of occasions, but the requirement for individual donor appraisal is still a serious impediment to joint developmental effort by the donors. This constraint is most severe for more complicated projects, because the potential for misjudgment is greater and the possibility for honest disagreement is greater. It will probably be necessary for donors to commit themselves to supporting a program earlier on in the project cycle, so that an appropriate preparation and appraisal methodology can be derived for a program that, when completed, will be acceptable to all donors involved. Shared financing is particularly important in mass programs for two reasons. First, the programs are potentially so large that any single donor would have difficulty fitting the disbursements into the assistance budget. Second, and probably of even greater practical importance, the programs contain a disproportionate share of unpopular elements (e.g., local cost financing, management problems, procurement problems, risks of failure, and so forth). There is a clear danger that this combination of problems would be more than any single donor would be willing to put up with, whereas spread over all of the donors, these problems become an unattractive but minor part of a single donor's assistance program. Short of inducing a large donor to specialize in troublesome programs—an unlikely eventuality—shared financing appears to be the best answer.

The *desire to run a self-contained aid program,* on the part of each bilateral and multilateral assistance agency, militates against mass impact programs. Even assuming that a donor would be willing to tolerate considerable departures from standard operating procedure in order to participate in important development programs, donors naturally shrink from the complications inherent in multiparty compromises. Yet the preferences of donors to negotiate with Government on a bilateral basis is an important impediment to getting mass programs started. We therefore feel that serious and continuous multilateral discussions, addressed to the problems involved in mounting large programs designed to benefit the mass of the people, should be a routine tool to improve the efficiency of assistance.[3]

2. This is not to say that *nothing* can be accomplished by programs working parallel to the ministries (see, for example, our suggestions in Annex Five).
3. On this point, see the concluding section of this annex.

Summing up, the necessary improvements in conditions of assistance, if Kenya is to succeed in maintaining growth and accelerating the development of the poor, appear to be the following:

(a) A progressive move towards support of major programs, rather than isolated projects. As many of these programs will have a predominant local cost element, this implies a willingness to finance at least some local costs.

(b) A willingness to participate and cooperate with other donors in all phases of a project's preparation and financing of major programs. This will require a new attitude of mutual effort among donors as well as cooperation in financing. It will also require innovation in the sharing of different types of costs. As it seems unlikely that lenders can be found to specialize in concessionary financing for local costs, for example, it will be necessary to agree on the distribution of local costs financing and foreign exchange financing.[4]

(c) A willingness to compromise, in a multilateral context, on conventional donor requirements (e.g., requirements for autonomous project control and identity, requirements for procurement procedures, tying arrangements), when this compromise is necessary to carry out the project most efficiently, or when compromise arrangements are necessary to line up joint or parallel financing.

Toward Further Improvements in Lending Conditions

Sector and subsector lending is a logical direction for external assistance to take in the future. We have discussed the advantages to be gained in Kenya's planning and project identification activities by a progressive shift from projects to programs, subsectors or even sectors, as the basic unit of planning (in Annex Five). There are, we believe, very considerable economies in scale to be achieved by such a shift in the emphasis of planning. But, perhaps more important, it seems that for some of the more difficult and urgent development tasks facing Kenya (such as programs for assisting the mass of small scale farmers or businessmen), planning in a broad framework is indispensable if all the necessary conditions for the success of the program are to be included and coordinated. There are also several obvious advantages to the donors—both individually and as a group—to be gained from a shift to larger and more broadly defined projects. For example, it is clearly one of the more efficient ways to tailor aid more exactly to Kenya's needs. But such a shift also provides greater scope for donors to coordinate their financial aid and technical assistance within a clearly defined sectoral strategy, and opens up new opportunities for cooperation and coordination among the donors.

We have previously stressed that the advantages of broad based planning project identification and lending are more relevant to the complex challenges which still lie ahead in the agricultural sector,[5] where the capacity to prepare individual projects is a major constraint. But the desirability of sector lending can also be shown in the road transportation sector, even though this sector has a very good capacity to identify and implement individual projects, particularly for external financing. Normal practice is for

---

4. This is the main use we see for local cost financing formula such as that suggested in this annex.

5. Part III stresses the need for improving the delivery system to get services to small farms, with emphasis on increasing maize production. In the context of a subsector loan for maize production, this technical assistance effort would surely be seen as one indispensable component. How many similar components would be missed by a piecemeal, autonomous agency, unique project, approach to development of this subsector?

the Government to submit a package of individual road projects to a donor, who appraises the package on the basis of the justification for each road included in the package. Partly because of this emphasis on the project approach, the Government concentrates a disproportionate share of its road planning staff in project preparation activity and devotes relatively little effort to sector strategy or assignment of priorities among the projects in the road sector. Moreover, since there are a number of donors providing capital assistance to the road sector, each of them independently appraising a different package of projects, there is no strong impetus for sector planning arising from the donor's operations.

Within the strategy recommended in this report—to decrease the relative share of investment in infrastructure—there must be an effective substrategy to choose those infrastructural investments with the highest priority. During the 1974–78 plan period, the total road development program which the Ministry of Works has proposed for implementation amounts to twice the provisional allocation for roads in the plan. While most of the program is suitable for foreign financing, on the basis of individual merits, the Government will have to assign priorities to the various categories of roads, and reduce the total roads program if it is to stay within the overall plan allocation. This will require a much greater emphasis on sector planning, as against project identification and appraisal.

This evolution in planning would be encouraged and accelerated by a corresponding shift in emphasis, on the part of donors, to a sectoral approach. Once the Government had developed a road investment program, which clearly identifies road priorities over the plan period within the resources allocated to the road sector, donors would have a clearly defined framework within which to identify their assistance programs. Donors could then appraise the strategy for the road subsector as a whole, and assess the benefits of the total investment plan to the economy. Such an approach would open up opportunities for much greater coordination among donors, including possibly joint appraisal, financing, and supervision of the complete sector program. But even if each donor wished to continue financing its own package, the sector approach would ensure that his particular package fitted into a broader program, and neither overlapped with nor conflicted with the activities of other donors.

The Government would gain by being able to operate with more flexibility to plan the entire road sector investment program within the overall allocation for the sector; the question of which road segments are easily aid-financed would no longer be an important criterion for road investment. And, perhaps most important, considering the emerging resource constraints, a fixed allocation could be agreed on in advance for road investment with the assignment of priorities to individual road segments being made within that allocation.

The mission found that several major donors favor a sector or subsector approach to lending, particularly in those areas where individual projects compete for the same resources (e.g., land use or water use alternatives), and a number of donors are already providing assistance at the sector or subsector level in such programs as power and rural water supplies.[6] There is also wide support among donors for the principle of cooperation and coordination in sector lending, and some progress has been made in this direction. One of the earlier ventures in donor cooperation in Kenya was the joint Nordic program to support the development of cooperatives. More recently, an ambitious livestock development program has been identified, with the assistance of the World Bank, in which five donors will be participating, and the Government has succeeded in coordinating the participation of seven donors in supporting a five-year population program.

---

6. The World Bank's lending to the EAC corporations (telecommunications, harbors, and railways) is also essentially at the sector or subsector level.

The experience to date in these initial experiments in broad based donor cooperation suggests that this can be a most valuable approach, but that donors still have a long way to go in learning how to cooperate. It has also shown that the complexities of sector wide coordination of aid places a much larger demand upon the rather frail aid coordinating machinery of government. We would suggest, however, that the obvious advantages of such cooperation warrant perseverance on both sides.

Chapter 4

Conditions of Technical Assistance

The discussion of technical assistance is divided into three main classes: manpower supplementation, advisory assistance, and training assistance. The tasks of an expatriate technical assistance officer or the components of a technical assistance project may include elements of all three classes or of only one.

Manpower supplementation has two main forms. The first is usually called consultancy, in which a technical expert, or team of experts, is employed to perform a specific task, with well defined terms of reference and with a short term of office. Consultancy arrangements are straightforward purchases of specific services for which the consulant has the required background of knowledge and experience. In general, the task is so specific, for example, a single project evaluation, that the question of tenure of the consultant or replacement of the consultant does not arise. A single consultant, or a pool of qualified consultants, may undertake many similar tasks in succession, and may, as a result, become more valuable to the permanent bureaucracy, since the consultants acquire experience in applying their particular expertise to local conditions.[1] As Kenyan consultants become competitive in experience and expertise, one would expect them to share in this work.

It will probably never be desirable to incorporate many of the tasks done by consultants into the bureaucracy, however, since the highly specialized tasks and the intermittance of work fit better within the more flexible consultancy form. We have argued (Annex Five) that the Government should make greater use of consultants, particularly in the preparation or supervision of investment projects. The Government is reluctant, in many cases, to purchase this project software, particularly where consultants have a relatively high foreign exchange cost. To finance consultants under technical assistance grants, thereby assuring the availability of the best possible project advice, has been a highly productive form of assistance. But this assistance has generally been tied aid, with the consultant being hired from the bilateral donor's country, and generally it has been confined to assistance for a single project to be financed by the same donor. Any liberalization of the tying arrangement, which would both widen the consultant market and prevent undue bias in favor of the techniques in vogue in the donor's country, would improve the efficiency of consultancy expenditures and encourage their expanded use. If consultancy assistance can be broadened beyond the single project level (e.g., a sum granted for hiring consultants to prepare and execute a series of projects in small scale industry), intelligent programming and use of consultants by the ministries would be greatly facilitated.[2]

The second form of manpower supplementation is the provision of expatriate manpower to do professional work in those areas where the (temporarily) fixed supply of Kenyan manpower is less than the permanent demand. In these cases, to simply ration the available Kenyan manpower would be inefficient; on the other hand, truly competitive bidding for their services would raise their wage rates without increasing the quantity of services, causing distributional problems and complicating the problem of government wage policy. For this reason, importation of talent makes economic sense. If demand is very large or growing very rapidly relative to Kenyan supply, it is probably

---

1. It is no coincidence, as pointed out in Annex Five, that ministries, such as the Ministry of Works, which have established a pool of tested consulting firms in their sectors, have substantially expanded absorptive capacity.

2. Both forms of liberalization strongly imply that donor's cooperate in preparation and use of consultants' reports. It would be of little use to build up multinational, sector specific consultancy experience, if in the event of each loan, a bilateral (or multilateral) donor insisted upon duplicating the consultant's effort.

sensible to hire expatriate supplementary manpower on long term contracts, recognizing that qualified Kenyans will not be available sooner. The planning horizon for supplementation is the length of time required for training a pool of Kenyan manpower equal to the demand and growing at a rate equal to demand growth. It is quite inefficient to hire such supplementary manpower on a short cycle, constantly replacing it with other experts who require considerable running-in time before they are effective in the Kenyan content.

For those professionals with alternative employment opportunities in private industry, in other government agencies, or in other closely related professions, the relevant supply/demand considerations pertain to the entire market. It would be frustrating and shortsighted to expect, for example, that the Ministry of Commerce and Industry could train the number of financial analysts it requires for its own personnel establishment and then dispense with supplemental manpower. The ministry will, in practice, need supplemental manpower until the supply/demand relationships for financial analysts in the labor market, *as a whole*, have achieved equilibrium and the ministry can hire and retain qualified analysts at a reasonable price. It is poor economics to expect any one ministry or industry to Kenyanize any occupation before such a point is reached. To continue the example, the Ministry of Commerce and Industry may have trained several times the number of Kenyan financial analysts it needs, and still require expatriate assistance because the analysts have found employment elsewhere. The manpower policy of the ministry can legitimately be judged on its training rate and on the effectiveness of its trainees, wherever they end up working, but it cannot be criticized (legitimately) for its failure to retain the services of the men it has trained. Donors who insist that a government institution get into a bidding race, in such a situation of inelastic supply, only complicate the maintenance of a reasonable wage policy and shift the problem of manpower shortage to other (perhaps nonaided) government institutions or private firms.

The main implication of this discussion for the donors is that they should be prepared to provide supplementary manpower, of a given type of skill, with a minimum of turnover, for as long as the scarcity of qualified Kenyan manpower is projected to last. Only by coincidence would this period coincide with the disbursement period for any particular project using this skill, or with any period arbitrarily chosen in advance. The result of shorter term time horizons will probably be excessive costs of turnover of expatriate personnel. If a short time horizon leads to frustration and the withdrawal of needed technical assistance, the cost will clearly be much higher, taking the form of inadequate expert inputs into the planning and execution of government programs.[3]

A second kind of technical assistance is advisory assistance. This is temporary assistance designed to provide Kenyan officials, who are themselves in an operational job, with technical or management advice, particularly during the running-in period after the Kenyan officials are first appointed. This type of assistance can be particularly valuable when the newly appointed Kenyan official is well qualified technically, but lacks operational or management experience. This advisory assistance may be combined with manpower supplementation in a single technical assistance project, but if an individual is assigned both supplementary and advisory duties, confusion and poor performance of the advisory function are invited, because the line of job responsibility is easily blurred. The advisor may end up performing the duties of the officer (usually badly because of an unclear job description), at the expense of both the routine tasks and the advisory function. In this case, the advisor would only undermine the confidence of the official and delay the time when he can stand on his own feet.

---

3. A frustration often mentioned by the donors was the disappearance of "counterparts," and the mission got the impression from several donors that the failure to retain counterparts was in their opinion a government failure. Whether any technical assistance was actually terminated or discouraged because of this supposed "failure" was not clear.

A third class of technical assistance is *assistance in training*. Unfortunately, there is a great deal of confusion over the process of training, and the responsibility for training, under the kind of manpower circumstances which face Kenya. All too often, expatriates in operational or advisory positions are expected to "undertake training," in addition to their primary responsibilities, but their job descriptions fail to specify how, or when, this function should be carried out. Moreover, in many cases, their workload leaves no time for any kind of training, formal or informal. In our opinion, it is very desirable to include a training function in the terms of reference of expatriate officers, and consultants, whether they are in operational or advisory positions, whenever this can be done without conflict with their other responsibilities. But their job descriptions must make clear what their training functions are.

In most cases, training will be directed at relatively junior officers or apprentices, preferably in an explicitly designed and budgeted training program. In some cases, technical assistance personnel might be called upon to give training courses for several hours a week in a formal training environment. This would have the additional advantage of exposing students in academic institutions to problems in the real world. More frequently, however, we believe that the most valuable service is to provide on-the-job training, guidance, and encouragement to young and newly qualified Kenyans. This can seldom be accomplished through a process of osmosis; the function has to be explicitly defined, responsibilities allocated, and time budgeted for individual contact. Unless this is done, the result is almost invariably that other pressures prevail, and excellent young Kenyans fail to gain the experience and guidance they need.

It may often be advisable for the training function to be one stage removed from the expatriate personnel. For example, an expatriate may supplement an experienced and senior Kenyan official, who can then devote more time to training his subordinates, because the expatriate is doing some of his more routine work. If the result is that the Kenyan officer, by virtue of his local knowledge as well as his own competence, can do an exceptional job at training junior personnel, such an arrangement should get high marks for training, or even for replacement of expatriates in a broader, longer run sense, in spite of the fact that there is no "trained counterpart" to point to as evidence of success.

In the mission's opinion, a great deal of confusion about training could be avoided if the "counterpart" notion were dispensed with altogether. In most cases, training should probably be directed at junior officers or apprentices, preferably in an explicitly designed and budgeted apprenticeship program. The suggestion that the trainee should replace the trainer is applicable only in the very special case where a local officer is needed to do exactly the same task as the trainer and has the academic qualifications and practical experience necessary to replace the trainer in a fairly short time. And in that special case, it would probably be better to appoint the Kenyan to the job immediately, with the trainer reverting to a role of advisor. There are, in fact, no circumstances we can think of in which the provision of a counterpart seems to be an appropriate instrument of training or Kenyanization. If training can shed the counterpart requirement, technical training assistance will be more flexible and straightforward. Consultancies or long run manpower supplementation will also be relieved of a constant source of friction.

In a developed noncolonial administration, the usual "counterpart" to an official is his subordinate, all the way down the line. It is generally regarded as good management practice to grade officials partly on how well they are training subordinates to replace themselves. Surely such a self-training bureaucracy is desirable for Kenya in the long run. The implication is that a good deal of training might take the form of advice to senior officials on how to train subordinates, plus the supplementation of manpower which would be necessary to allow every competent Kenyan civil servant or manager time to carry out a training function.

Chapter 5

Aid Coordination

The Coordination Problem and Its Real Costs

Both the Government and the donors stand to gain in efficiency of planning and effectiveness of aid from an improvement in aid coordination at all levels. Chapter 3 of this annex argues that an increase in coordinated effort is almost essential to support the sectors of investment concentration recommended in this report. The agricultural and industrial sectors and mass programs would be insupportable if left to a single donor. The integration of technical assistance projects with financial assistance was one of the main themes of Annex Five, and Annex Three showed fairly clearly the need for similar coordination between technical assistance and the administrative arms of the Government dealing with conditions and incentives for private investment. The mission encountered no argument from Government or from the donors against the proposition that coordination should be improved. Surprisingly, there do not seem to be even the usual bureaucratic reservations about loss of flexibility or freedom of maneuver.

Immediately below this "coordination is a good thing" plane of generalization, however, some real impediments are quickly obvious. First and most obvious are the institutional weaknesses of both the Government and the donors. The Government is simply not using enough manpower to do a thorough job. The donors are, by and large, represented by field staff with very little negotiating power, except as delegated on a *case-by-case* basis, from their national headquarters.[1] Thus, the usual procedure is for a small government staff to conduct a good deal of the actual business of assistance negotiations outside the country, thereby spreading government resources even more thinly and isolating each bilateral negotiation. Coordination, based on quick response to detailed proposal and counterproposal, is clearly impossible in this context.

A second obvious impediment to coordination is competition among the donors for the "best" projects. Operational limitations on the donors are remarkably similar. Almost all of the donors finance foreign exchange costs more easily than local costs. They all favor easily managed projects because of the common shortage of management personnel. They all prefer to be associated with visible projects which have a high probability of success. Although there is some diversity in stated goals of individual aid programs, it remains true that from a given list of government development programs, readily available donors would cluster around a very few. This competition for the few projects that fit well with donor preferences is surely unfortunate, but it is hard to imagine changing it in the short run.

A third impediment to coordination grows out of the first two. This is the (often expressed) impression of the donors that the Government is purposefully vague and uncommunicative in coordination matters in order to play one donor off against the other. An apparent result is that donors sometimes set up counterstrategies of vagueness with both the Government and one another, in order to compete for the best projects at the greatest advantage. For the donors as a group, the competition is useless and, for

---

1. The Economic Division of the British High Commission in Kenya has recently been given considerable freedom of operations. Loans up to £0.25 million can be approved by the field staff subject to the overall limit on aid from the Overseas Development Administration and within the guidelines of an annually revised policy paper. This recent innovation is a hopeful contrast to past British aid practices and the usual practices of other donors.

the Government, the only possible gain is better matching of investments and donors. Meanwhile, the attitude of secrecy (most often expressed as the statement that everyone else is secretive), has real costs to the Government:

- Uncertainty over who is to finance which project leads to delays in project preparation and appraisal since donors are, by and large, unwilling to accept one another's appraisals;
- Switching of (usually implied) project commitments from one donor to another wastes technical assistance or aid management because of duplication of preparation effort;
- Uncertainty biases donors against the more complex project, with a longer preparation period, in favor of the project that can quickly be negotiated, committed, and disbursed.[2]

Some Suggestions for Improvement in Coordination

Any attempt at improving the machinery and coordination should probably take as given, at least in the short term, the manpower shortages in government staff and the limited authority of the donors' field staffs.[3] But even working within these constraints, there is, in our opinion, considerable room for improvement. Some suggestions are:

(a) Early commitment in principle, on the part of the Government, to undertake a given project or program, should be given wide publicity among the donors, and this publicity should include an approximation of the financial aid and the technical assistance that will be required. Technical assistance requests should make clear when it is the intention to relate technical assistance to project aid.

(b) The donors should, in their own interests, attempt to establish their own assistance programs on a long term basis; a rolling four-year operations program for each of the donors would probably suffice, for practical purposes. Such a program would allow both Government and donor to plan manpower and financial budgets, establish the critical path for individual projects, line up necessary joint donors, and so forth. In order that these programs should have real operational content, they should be based as much as possible on the Government's investment commitments. The four-year operations programs of the lenders should be the basis for (perhaps yearly) discussions with the Government, and a statement of intent by the Government and the donor should be issued as a result of that meeting. Clearly, these statements of intent would only be morally binding, and even this depends upon the program or projects being judged to be sound in a final appraisal.[4]

(c) Wherever necessary, the Government should attempt to confront donors with the necessity for cooperation at the project level. For example, if apparently

2. The area or country desks in aid agencies are naturally inclined to grasp any "bird in the hand" project in the country for which they are responsible, if the alternative is to see their financial provision run out at the end of the fiscal year by default, or reallocation to another project. It is by no means unusual for a country's allocation to be influenced, if not determined, by the speed with which the previous tranche was disbursed.

3. This is not to go back on our former recommendation (Annex Five) that the Government increase its aid coordination staff. Rather, it is a recognition that, even with every effort to build up that staff, the scarcity will remain for quite some time.

4. Several donors have now introduced this form of aid programming, and it is to be hoped that others will follow suit. Some donor agencies carry out elaborate internal programming exercises, but do not have a procedure for discussing their programs with the Government. But to form operations programs without discussions with Government is no more sensible that it would be for a commercial bank to decide on its plans for lending to Mr. Jones without consulting Mr. Jones.

available technical assistance from one source would fit efficiently with financial aid apparently available from another, the two donors should be given adequate opportunities to confront and, where possible, compromise their institutional limitations at the earliest possible time.
(d) The Government should seek very wide joint involvement in the major programs, particularly in the productive sectors. Risk of failure is a legitimate cost of vigorous development efforts, but this risk is best shared as much as possible. Similarly, projects with a high local cost or imprecise borderlines should be presented to all donors on the understanding that they are asked to take only a part of the burden of the hard project. Donors should respond in a generous spirit to this government request for support in administratively difficult projects.
(e) The earliest agreement on all joint projects and programs should be the agreement over technical assistance (joint, multilateral, or bilateral) and the agreement in principle to accept the results of the analysis of the program, with ample provision for participation in staffing or supervision of work in progress.
(f) The Government should be seen to be cooperative and evenhanded in dispensing information to other donors concerning its commitments and agreements on bilaterally aided projects. This appears to be perfectly compatible with shopping for the best terms, attempting to match donor limitations with the requirements of the overall investment program, and so forth. This would require increased government manpower to present data and descriptions systematically and periodically; indeed, much of the criticism on the part of the donors of government "secrecy" may be due to a failure of the donors to understand the extremely tight limits on government staff. Systematic tabulations of "the state of play" of various assistance negotiations simply do not exist.

Although improvements in coordination at the project level seem to be the most necessary and the most probable, coordination attempts at the level of the overall investment program and its financing should be continued and, if possible, upgraded. For example, preparation of the project list for meetings of the Consultative Group (see below) appears to have been useful and should be continued with whatever refinements in the project descriptions that are practicable. The UNDP effort to present a periodic overview of technical assistance is also useful. If it could be supplemented with a forward view of government technical assistance, it would be still more helpful in general program planning by the donors. It is the firm impression of the mission, however, that additional effort to increase coordination at the level of the individual development undertaking (discrete project or major program), would have the highest rate of return of all marginal coordination efforts.

Aid Coordination Machinery

The major formal mechanism for coordinating external aid to Kenya is the Consultative Group for East Africa which meets separately in the three East African countries under the chairmanship of the World Bank. There appears to be agreement from both donors and the Government of Kenya that the Consultative Group is performing a useful function, particularly in providing a periodic opportunity for reviewing the overall priorities for external assistance to Kenya. However, the Consultative Group meets only every second year and has little or no function between times. There have been several suggestions from members of the Group that the World Bank, in its capacity as secretariat to the Group, might undertake a more continuous function in coordinating aid, particularly at the project level and in Kenya.

There is also scope, in our opinion, for much closer cooperation among donors in country economic work and sector analysis. As things stand, each donor country, as well as the World Bank and the International Monetary Fund, feels obliged to mount its own economic missions from time to time. While each agency obviously has special interests to follow up in such missions, there is much common ground, and much of the time of each mission is spent in asking the same questions of the same hard pressed Government officials as the last mission. This is not only an unfortunate duplication of effort on the part of the donors but, much more serious, preempts a great deal of the time of senior Government officers.

We are not overly optimistic about a dramatic change in these procedures; there is certainly no immediate prospect of achieving, for example, a unified annual review mission, however sensible that might seem in principle. But some closer coordination is clearly both possible and necessary, if only to relieve the burden on government. It is possible that the World Bank might provide some leadership in coordinating the activities of donors, not only because of its central role in the Consultative Group, but because it is the only donor which regularly makes available its economic reports to other donors. As a start, it might be useful for all donors to assess the extent to which Bank reports can be relied upon to provide the information and analysis they want in planning their own program. The biannual meetings of the Consultative Group provide an obvious (but seldom used) opportunity for donors to suggest any improvements or addition to the Bank's economic work which would make it more widely useful. In addition, there is no reason why bilateral donors should not participate in joint economic missions with the Bank, and this might be of particular value to some of the smaller donors operating in Kenya.

STATISTICAL TABLES
Annex Six
Index

Table
No.

1.	Debt Outstanding and Loan Disbursements, 1968–72	439
2.	New Commitments of External Loans by Source, 1968–72	440
3.	Average Terms of Lending, 1968–72	441
4.	Terms of Lending on Loans from Governments, 1968–72	442
5.	Technical Assistance and Financial Aid on Grant Terms, 1969–71	443
6.	Expected Disbursements of Financial Assistance, 1973–76	443
7.	Indicators of Debt in Kenya and Other Countries	444

Table 1: Debt Outstanding and Loan Disbursements, 1968–72

	\multicolumn{5}{c}{Total Debt Outstanding at Year-End (Including Undisbursed)}	\multicolumn{5}{c}{Annual Disbursements}
Lender	1968	1969	1970	1971	1972	1968	1969	1970	1971	1972
	\multicolumn{10}{c}{(US$ million)}
International Organizations *Major areas*	51.2	74.6	102.0	128.8	187.4	8.5	10.5	10.0	9.7	26.5
World Bank	6.3	29.7	36.9	59.8	88.6	0.1	0.6	2.9	6.6	19.5
IDA	42.6	42.6	61.3	61.8	91.8	8.2	9.7	6.6	3.1	5.9
African Development Bank	2.3	2.3	3.8	6.8	6.8	0.1	0.2	0.4	—	1.0
Governments *Major areas*	226.2	227.8	234.5	232.3	245.3	21.2	16.1	18.8	21.7	16.6
United Kingdom	181.1	177.7	175.3	152.5	144.3	15.0	13.8	15.1	4.5	1.9
United States	16.5	15.9	18.8	26.1	27.6	2.1	1.2	0.7	11.1	0.6
Germany	12.2	15.6	16.6	19.3	18.2	1.9	0.5	1.5	2.7	1.5
Sweden	3.7	3.7	6.3	15.5	26.1	—	—	0.1	0.8	4.7
Italy	7.5	7.5	7.5	8.1	8.1	—	—	—	—	5.5
Netherlands	—	—	—	1.8	8.6	—	—	—	—	1.2
Others	5.2	7.4	8.0	9.0	12.4	2.2	6.0	1.4	2.6	1.2
Private sources[1]	65.9	62.6	57.1	69.7	77.3	7.3	0.1	1.5	11.5	16.1
Total	343.3	365.0	393.6	430.8	510.0	37.0	26.7	30.3	42.9	59.2

[1] Including small amounts of unidentified debt.

Source: Table 21, Part I.

Table 2: New Commitments of External Loans by Source, 1968–72

Sources	1968	1969	1970	1971	1972	Undisbursed at End 1972
			(US$ million)			
International organizations						
World Bank	—	26.1	8.3	23.0	29.0	56.0
IDA	16.4	—	18.7	—	28.0	48.0
Others	—	—	1.5	3.5	—	5.2
TOTAL	16.4	26.1	28.5	26.5	57.0	109.2
Governments						
Canada	—	0.5	—	—	3.7	4.0
Denmark	2.7	—	—	—	—	0.7
Germany	1.1	3.1	1.8	1.2	—	2.5
Israel	1.5	—	—	—	—	—
Italy	—	—	—	—	—	2.6
Japan	—	—	—	0.7	—	0.2
Netherlands	—	—	—	1.7	6.8	7.4
Norway	—	1.4	—	—	—	—
Sweden	3.6	—	4.6	6.2	17.1	20.3
United Kingdom	0.5	0.5	—	0.1	—	4.1
United States	—	—	3.5	7.8	2.3	2.7
TOTAL	9.4	5.5	9.9	17.7	29.9	44.5
Private						
Private banks	—	—	—	3.5	17.3	2.4
Suppliers' credits	—	—	1.1	7.3	—	—
Unclassified	—	—	2.1	—	—	0.1
TOTAL	—	—	3.2	10.8	17.3	2.5
Total annual commitments	25.8	31.6	41.6	55.0	104.3	
Cumulative undisbursed commitments at year-end	96.1	97.7	109.9	124.5	156.3	156.3

SOURCE: Economic Analysis and Projections Department, World Bank.

Table 3: Average Terms of Lending, 1968-72

Terms/Lenders	\multicolumn{5}{c}{LENDING TERMS ON DEBT OUTSTANDING AT YEAR'S END}
	1968	1969	1970	1971	1972
Average interest rates (%)	3.4	3.6	3.5	3.9	3.9
Average original grace period (years)	4.6	5.0	5.6	5.2	5.7
Average original maturity (years)	29.4	29.2	30.2	29.4	29.4
Average grant element of loans (%)[1]	51.0	50.0	51.0	47.0	48.0
Grant equivalent of loans, 10% discount ratio (US$ million)	174.0	181.0	199.0	203.0	244.0
	\multicolumn{5}{c}{AVERAGE INTEREST RATES ON DEBT OUTSTANDING AT END OF YEAR (percentage)}
International organizations					
World Bank	5.82	6.86	6.97	7.08	7.14
IDA	0.75	0.75	0.75	0.75	0.75
African Development Bank	5.00	5.00	5.39	5.66	5.66
International Coffee Organization	0.00	0.00	0.00	0.00	0.00
Governments	3.44	3.41	3.41	3.61	3.43
Suppliers	6.87	6.87	6.89	5.86	6.11
Privately placed bonds	8.00	8.00	8.00	8.00	8.00
Publicly issued bonds	4.02	4.03	4.21	4.21	4.23
Banks	5.99	6.04	6.08	5.82	5.88
Average interest rates on total debt	3.38	3.59	3.54	3.90	3.87

[1] At rate of discount of 10%.

SOURCE: Economic Analysis and Projections Department, World Bank.

Table 4: Terms of Lending on Loans from Governments, 1968–72

Terms/Donors	1968	1969	1970	1971	1972
Terms of government loans (outstanding at year's end) to Kenya					
Average interest rate (%)	3.44	3.41	3.41	3.62	3.42
Average grace period (years)	4.5	4.6	4.9	4.6	5.0
Average original maturity (years)	27.7	27.7	27.9	28.1	28.0
Grant element of loans (%)[1]	49	50	50	48	50
Grant equivalent of loans (US$ million)[1]	111	113	118	112	123
	(US$ million)				
Outstanding loans, by interest rate					
0 to 3%	109	113	120	112	130
Over 3 to 6%	48	47	46	54	52
Over 6 to 9%	69	67	66	63	61
Over 9%	0.2	0.2	1.9	2.1	2.1
Average interest rates on government loans (by donor) outstanding at year's end					
Canada	—	—	—	—	—
Denmark	—	—	—	—	—
Germany	3.32	3.26	3.17	3.10	3.08
Israel	6.00	6.00	6.00	6.00	6.00
Italy	4.50	4.50	4.50	4.50	4.50
Japan	—	5.75	5.75	5.75	5.75
Netherlands	—	—	—	2.50	2.50
Norway	—	0.75	0.75	0.75	0.75
Sweden	0.75	0.75	1.48	0.85	1.01
United Kingdom	3.61	3.60	3.66	4.04	4.13
United States	2.07	2.06	2.10	3.27	3.03
USSR	2.50	2.50	2.50	2.50	1.47
Percentage of outstanding loans (by donor)					
Canada	—	—	—	—	1.7
Denmark	1.2	—	—	—	1.2
Germany	5.4	—	—	—	7.4
Israel	0.8	—	—	—	0.5
Italy	3.3	—	—	—	3.7
Japan	—	—	—	—	0.9
Netherlands	—	—	—	—	3.5
Norway	—	—	—	—	0.6
Sweden	1.6	—	—	—	10.6
United Kingdom	80.1	—	—	—	58.8
United States	7.3	—	—	—	11.2
USSR	0.2	—	—	—	0.2

[1] At rate of discount of 10%.

SOURCE: Economic Analysis and Projections Department, World Bank.

Table 5: Technical Assistance and Financial Aid on Grant Terms, 1969–71

Donor	Technical Assistance	Financial Grants	Total Grants
	(annual average, US$ million)		
Austria	0.2	0.0	0.2
Australia	0.1	0.0	0.1
Canada	1.9	0.1	2.0
Denmark	1.3	0.2	1.5
Germany	2.6	0.1	2.7
Italy	0.2	0.0	0.2
Japan	0.6	0.0	0.6
Netherlands	1.5	0.0	1.5
Norway	1.4	1.1	2.5
Sweden	2.5	0.4	2.9
Switzerland	0.1	0.1	0.2
United Kingdom	7.2	0.7	7.9
United States	4.3	1.0	5.3
TOTAL	23.9	3.7	27.6

SOURCE: Economic Analysis and Projections Department, World Bank (Data Retrieval System).

Table 6: Expected Disbursements of Financial Assistance, 1973–76

Sector	1973	1974	1975	1976	Government Investments[2] 1970/71–1972/73
	Expected Disbursements[1]				
	(US$ million)				(annual average)
Agriculture, veterinary, and forestry	8	14	22	32	23.2
Industry and commerce	4	8	15	18	10.3
Infrastructure	46	60	65	65	59.6
Social sectors	3	5	7	8	29.7
Other (including general purpose)	6	6	8	8	36.1
TOTAL	67	93	117	131	158.9

[1] Mission estimate 1973 sectoral disbursements proportional to estimates of sector distribution of undisbursed debt outstanding, January 1, 1973. Thereafter, sectoral composition shifts according to sectoral plans of donors for commitments, 1973–74.
[2] Annex Two.

Table 7: Indicators of Debt in Kenya and Other Countries[1]

Country	Loan Commitments per Capita 1965–68 Average	Loan Commitments per Capita 1969–71 Average	Debt Service per Capita 1965–68 Average	Debt Service per Capita 1969–71 Average	Debt Outstanding per Capita End 1968	Debt Outstanding per Capita End 1971
Bolivia	6.66	18.89	1.51	4.08	81.21	120.17
Botswana	1.49	27.03	1.09	1.15	16.98	93.72
Mauritania	4.98	16.33	1.77	2.53	33.38	76.31
Swaziland	4.75	3.62	5.22	4.94	72.16	71.96
Tanzania	2.41	10.41	0.59	1.27	17.97	44.40
Cameroon	4.85	5.68	1.00	1.62	26.14	38.88
Kenya	4.33	3.96	1.77	1.73	32.05	36.68
Pakistan[2]	4.02	4.20	0.88	1.30	26.58	34.49
Sudan	3.30	3.57	1.09	2.02	21.25	26.83
Togo	1.66	1.60	0.83	1.11	22.15	24.67
Dahomey	1.44	3.66	0.68	0.95	15.89	24.08
Central African Republic	1.41	4.51	0.76	1.22	14.21	22.45
Uganda	2.45	1.98	0.76	1.19	17.80	20.03
Malagasy Republic	2.20	1.78	0.83	1.03	17.46	19.26
India	2.12	1.57	0.75	0.92	15.53	17.91
Lesotho	1.77	0.34	0.31	0.39	8.31	8.70
Nigeria	1.29	1.79	0.73	1.01	12.00	1.34

[1] For selected countries with an average per capita income of US$101–200.
[2] Includes Bangladesh.

SOURCE: *World Debt Tables*, World Bank Report No. EC-167-72, December 15, 1973.

Part III

Agricultural Sector Survey

Preface

A recurring theme of the first two parts of this report has been the need for Kenya to direct a larger proportion of the resources available for development into productive sectors which will directly benefit the mass of her population. In particular, we have emphasized the unique importance of agriculture, and agriculture-related industry, as being the only means by which Kenya can hope to provide employment opportunities for her rapidly expanding population or to make a substantial impact on poverty in the rural areas, where most of the population lives. Yet available good land is scarce, population pressures on the land are already intense in some areas, and the potential for further development in the rural areas is constrained by a number of complex factors. It therefore becomes of paramount importance in national planning to assess the resource base in agriculture; to identify the ecological, political and institutional constraints; to evolve a strategy for development, and, finally, to translate this broad strategy into detailed investment programs and projects for implementation.

In an attempt to help this planning process, the World Bank mounted an agricultural sector survey mission to Kenya in 1972, which transmitted its report to the Government during 1973.[1] The main findings of the mission have been summarized as Part III of this report. The material presented is selective in coverage and judgmental in nature, and is intended only to outline the broad background and major findings and recommendations. Needless to say, the detailed technical analysis and statistical data, which were included in the technical annexes and which provided the basis for much of our argument, have had to be omitted in the interests of brevity.[2]

The core of rural development policy has to be growth in agricultural output and productivity; the agricultural report concentrated on this area. The task of integrating this component of rural development policy with other aspects, such as rural industry and health and education services, is not discussed. Not much is known about the appropriate list of components, nor their interactions; and, for the moment at least, little help can be given to the political process in deciding on the optimum relative emphasis to be given to each component in an investment package aimed at rural development.

Among the other gaps in the report were the longer run employment implications of population growth and the agricultural land constraint. Not everybody can have land even today in Kenya, but better land distribution and use can provide income improvement opportunities for many people for the decade or two ahead, although it will not be easy to accomplish even this objective. Before the turn of the century, however, this outlet for labor will become saturated. From the point of view of perspective planners, steps taken now on the land front should be considered as interim measures to provide time for designing an economy able to offer nonagricultural employment opportunities sufficient to absorb much of the future growth in the labor force. This same point has been stressed in Part II of this report.

---

1. The mission members were: L. T. Sonley, C. H. Chung, J. R. Burrows, G. F. Donaldson, R. Egli, W. S. Greig, C. Kiefer, J. C. D. Lawrance, H. K. Lindgren, R. W. Longhurst, K. Meyn, D. C. Pickering, R. D. Shaw, V. Sorenson, J. Spears, L. M. Sprague, and F. Thornley.
2. A list of the annexes is given at the end of Part III.

Chapter 1

The Role of Agriculture in the Kenya Economy

The take-off position for a bigger and better effort for the development of agriculture is encouraging. Much of the technological, infrastructure and administrative base has been laid, the agriculture industry has gained considerable momentum, and the Government is making strenuous efforts to raise output and improve living conditions in rural areas. Many successful agricultural programs are under way and there is both a firm determination and a national capacity to find and implement effective ways of promoting rural development. Most important, the task is recognized to be both urgent and difficult.

The 1974–78 Development Plan, which was being prepared during the mission's visit, puts great stress on a more rapid development of the rural areas and proposes a considerable expansion in agricultural momentum. The Plan states: "The attainment of the fundamental goal of this Plan of an improvement in the distribution of national income, with faster rural development and faster growth in employment opportunities, will be dependent in very large measure on the attainment of the particular goals that have been set for the agriculture sector, since it is from agriculture that more than 80 percent of the population will be primarily dependent for their livelihood during the period of this Plan."[1] The agricultural goals of the Plan were to achieve a 6.7 percent target rate of growth of marketed production and increase exports; to improve income distribution in rural areas by increasing commercial farming and promoting more even regional development; to increase employment in agriculture; to improve rural nutrition, and to continue the program of Kenyanization of large scale farms and ranches. To promote these goals, the Government intends to double development expenditure in agriculture, giving the highest priority to programs aimed at developing the smallholder farming areas. If this can be achieved it will imply a considerable increase in the flow of resources into agriculture, compared with the previous plan periods (see below).

The Growth of Agriculture Production

Since Independence, the agriculture sector has accounted for some 35 to 40 percent of GDP in Kenya, compared with 10 to 12 percent from manufacturing, 10 percent from commerce, and 13 to 15 percent from the government sector. Slightly less than half of value-added in agriculture is in the monetary sector; the remaining is production for home consumption. The monetary sector of agriculture showed an average real growth rate over the period 1964–72 of 6.5 percent. While significantly less than the rate of growth of other sectors such as manufacturing (8.1 percent), building (9.5 percent), or government services (9.9 percent), the rate of growth of monetary agriculture in Kenya since Independence must be considered very satisfactory in comparison to most countries. Value-added in the nonmonetary agriculture sector, which is assumed to increase a little faster than the rate of population growth, is estimated to have increased by 3.7 percent a year since 1964. Thus, the whole agriculture sector, both monetary and nonmonetary, has grown at an average rate of about 5 percent a year in real terms.

In line with the growth of agriculture, the gross marketed production of agriculture has tended to increase, but with significant interyear variations and official data suggest that annual growth rates for selected crops in the 1962–71 period have been as follows:

1. Republic of Kenya, *Development Plan, 1974–78*, p. 197.

	Percentage		Percentage
Coffee	3.3	Cashew nuts	4.3
Tea	11.5	Pulses	−2.1
Sisal	−4.9	Maize	7.6
Wattle bark	−6.9	Rice (paddy)	10.5
Seed cotton	9.0	Wheat	9.9
Sugarcane	18.5	Pineapples	34.0

Agricultural exports, making up some 70 percent of total exports and the leading foreign exchange earner, increased from £37 million in 1965 to almost £50 million in 1971. Coffee and tea are by far the most important, accounting for some 64 percent of the agricultural export total. With sisal, pyrethrum, and wattle extract, they make up about 76 percent of agricultural exports and more than 50 percent of total exports. Other exports include meat, fruits and vegetables, dairy products, cotton, wool, nuts, and animal feed. Export growth has been most marked in coffee and tea. Coffee exports were close to 57,000 tons in 1971, worth £19.5 million, some 49 percent above the volume and 52 percent above the value for 1968. Tea exports doubled between 1965 and 1971, from about 16,900 tons to some 34,300 tons, worth £6.5 million and almost £12.2 million, respectively.

Kenya produces about 70 percent of the world's pyrethrum. Exports increased by 47 percent, from about £2.2 million in 1965 to £3.3 million in 1971. Wattle bark extract, cotton, cashew nuts, and animal feeds have also shown some export growth. Sisal exports declined from 58,000 tons worth £3.8 million in 1965, to 35,000 tons worth £1.5 million in 1971.

Exports of fresh fruits and vegetables, such as pineapples, mangoes, capsicums and french beans, increased from about 1,500 tons in 1968 to more than 8,000 tons in 1972. The value of air freighted fruits and vegetables was almost £0.9 million in 1972.

The livestock industry accounts for a small part of exports, some 9 percent in 1971, of which about half was meat and meat products. The export volume of meat products and hides and skins was roughly constant over the period 1965–71; however, rising world prices resulted in increases in the value of exports of some 50 percent and 100 percent, respectively, over the period. Marketed livestock production made up about 30 percent of the total marketings of agriculture in 1971, a proportion which has changed little in recent years. Most of the industry is outside the money economy; 75 percent of dairy production, 80 percent of beef, and well over 90 percent of goat and sheep output are consumed on the farms and ranches where produced. Wildlife (which competes with domestic livestock for resources) is the basis of the rapidly growing tourist industry. In 1971, tourist receipts reached £24 million, a 30 percent increase over 1970. This is the first time that tourism receipts have been larger that those from coffee. It is reasonable to attribute some £8 to 12 million of tourism returns to the wildlife resource.

In the period 1962–71, the area in export crops in the large scale farm sector declined from about 187,000 hectares to 154,000 hectares, whereas smallholder acreage of export crops expanded from 69,000 to 189,000 hectares.

Agricultural imports, including farm machinery and tractors, selected chemicals and fertilizer, totaled £31.6 million in 1971. The main food imports are edible fats and oils, and oilseeds. Animal feeds, manufactured tobacco, and sugar also are important import items.

The forestry sector is now on a significant net import basis, mainly because of paper and paperboard imports. Imports of main forest products in 1971 were valued at more than £9 million, which created an adverse trade balance in the forestry account in excess of £5 million. Forestry and forest industries taken together account for approximately 2 percent of GDP, and about the same proportion of public sector expenditure. The forest sector employs some 20,000 persons (about 2 percent of wage earning labor) and forest-based industries employ a further 10,000 persons. The gazetted forest areas cover 1.7 million hectares (about 3 percent of the total land area), more than 90 percent of which consists of indigenous forests of slow growing species.

Estimated output of fish and fish products in 1971 was about 30,000 tons. Lakes Victoria and Rudolf are the most important fresh water fisheries, with estimated catches of 15,000 and 3,500 tons, respectively. Most of the balance was made up from marine fisheries, largely from inshore waters, which produced some 9,000 tons, 3 percent of which were high value shrimp and lobster. Kenya is a net importer of fish and fish products, mainly salted and smoked from Tanzania and Uganda in recent years.

Employment and Income

Up to 90 percent of the total population is directly dependent on agriculture for a livelihood, and this mainly in a self-employment status. Rough data are:

	Wage employment	Self-employment and family labor[1]	Total	Distribution
	(millions of people)			(percentage)
Urban	0.3	0.2	0.5	10
Rural				
Agriculture	0.6	3.7	4.3	84
Other	0.2	0.1	0.3	6
TOTAL	1.1	4.0	5.1	100

[1] It is assumed that all women aged 15 to 59 in rural areas are in the labor force.

Earnings from wage employment in agriculture are much less than in other sectors, even though agriculture employs more than twice as many people. This reflects the relatively low wage rate in agriculture and the seasonal nature of the demand for labor. Distribution of earnings from wage employment in 1969 was roughly as follows:

	£ million	Percent
Urban Areas		
Nonagricultural activity	113.2	80.8
Agricultural activity	0.8	0.6
Rural Areas		
Large farms	13.0	9.3
Small farms and settlements		
Regular workers	4.7	3.4
Casual workers	4.4	3.1
Other	3.9	2.8
TOTAL	140.0	100.0

Earnings from self-employment and family labor in agriculture are more difficult to gauge. The ILO study suggests that some 80 percent of rural households have access to land, and hence the opportunity for self-employment. The number aproximates 1.2 million smallholders and 200,000 pastoralists. Of the total, the study estimates the number of progressive commercial smallholders at about 225,000; the less progressive, partly commercial smallholders at about 225,000; and somewhat more than 600,000 households at the subsistence level. In addition, there are the large farms, some of which are in fact densely settled as cooperatives or companies. Taking this presumed distribution into account, and the fact that households may get income from several sources, the ILO study estimates 1969 average income per rural household at about £134, the equivalent of £24 per head. The severity of the rural income problem becomes still more striking when the income distribution is taken into account; the ILO judgment on this is as follows:

	Approximate Annual Household Income (£)
Large scale farmers	1,000 or more
Medium scale farmers	
Less prosperous large farms	600–1,000
Prosperous smallholders	200–600
Less prosperous smallholders	120–200
Employees in formal sector agriculture	60–120
Sizeable proportion of smallholdings and workers employed on smallholdings	20–60
(Most) smallholders, pastoralists, in semiarid and arid zones, unemployed and landless persons	20 or less

It appears that prosperous smallholders are probably at least ten times as well off as the least privileged. Many of the latter have little or no land, and extract a meager and precarious livelihood under exceedingly harsh conditions.

Public Outlays for Agriculture

Total public expenditures have more than doubled since Independence. However, outlays for agriculture have fallen, totaling about £13 million in 1970/71 as compared with more than £14 million in 1963/64. Relative to total public outlays, the fall has been very sharp, from 21 percent in 1963/64 to 8.4 percent in 1970/71. The data are:

	All Purposes	Agriculture	Agriculture
	(£ million)		Percent of total
1963/64	68.1	14.4	21.1
1967/68	94.6	13.3	14.1
1968/69	105.0	15.0	14.3
1969/70	121.4	12.6	10.4
1970/71	156.8	13.1	8.4

Public development outlays for agriculture are about equally divided between the Ministry of Agriculture and the other ministries directly concerned with the sector. Recent data follow:

	Ministry of agriculture		Other[1] ministries		Total	
	Estimates	Actual	Estimates	Actual	Estimates	Actual
			(£ million)			
1966/67	5.6	4.3	5.7	4.9	11.3	9.2
1968/69	5.7	4.7	5.1	5.0	10.8	9.7
1969/70	5.3	4.0	4.7	4.5	10.0	8.5
1970/71	6.8	4.3	6.1	5.2	12.9	9.5
1971/72	9.6	7.7	8.9	7.4	18.5	15.1

[1] Lands and Surveys, Natural Resources, Wildlife and Tourism, and Settlement.

Expenditure estimates are typically in excess of the actuals; the latter have been virtually static over the last few years, both in the Ministry of Agriculture and in the other major ministries concerned. Much of the sharp increase in the expenditure estimate for 1970/71 and 1971/72 is due to the provision of funds for the purchase of shares in sugar companies and for loans for a new sugar scheme at Mumias in Western Province. If these items are excluded for 1971/72, the estimate for the Ministry of Agriculture becomes £7.5 million, rather than the £9.6 million shown in the above tabulation.

In contrast to the allocation of domestic public resources, there has been considerable emphasis on agriculture in the distribution of external assistance. Over the past seven years, over 20 percent of external capital aid has been for the Ministry of Agriculture, and it has financed almost half of that ministry's development expenditure. The data are:

	Development Expenditure			External Aid	
	Total Ministry of Agriculture	From External Aid	External as percent of Total	Total	Agriculture as percent of Total
	(£ million)			(£ million)	
1966/67	4.3	1.3	30	6.2	21
1968/69	4.7	2.3	49	6.8	34
1969/70	4.7	1.0	21	7.4	14
1970/71	4.0	2.6	65	11.5	23
1971/72	4.3	1.8	42	11.1	16
Total	22.0	9.0	41	43.0	21

Other agriculture-related ministries (for example, Cooperatives, Education, and Works) also receive assistance. Some aid is also given directly by private and charitable organizations for rural development.

Chapter 2

The Land and Its People

The Ecological Potential

Kenya is a country of enormous contrasts in topography, climate, and soils. Within the country's 575,000 sq.km. of land and 8,000 sq.km. of open water, conditions range from a limited Afro Alpine Zone in the center south to the tropical coastal strip, and from near desert in the north to high rainfall forest in the southwestern highlands.

Mapping on the basis of ecological land units derived from combinations of climate, soil, and topography equated with vegetation types began only recently, and coverage is limited. For lack of detailed data, a classification based on six broad ecological zones was devised in 1966. As shown on the Ecological Potential and Catchment Areas map (page 246), these are:

Zone I. This extends some 800 sq.km. and is found at high altitude above the tree line. Vegetation is moorland or grassland, but barren land is common. Land use is limited to water catchment and tourism.

Zone II. This covers about 53,000 sq.km. and embraces the bulk of Kenya's indigenous and planted forests. The agricultural potential is high, particularly in the highlands. Tea, coffee, and pyrethrum are important cash crops at higher altitudes; there is good potential for development of macadamia production, and, at lower elevations, cotton yields well. Livestock can be kept intensively on leys with carrying capacity up to one stock unit per half hectare. Well managed natural grassland will support one stock unit per 1 to 1.5 hectare.

Zone III. This covers some 53,000 sq.km. and has medium agricultural potential. The zone contains most of the large scale mixed farming areas in which hybrid maize, wheat, and barley are important crops. In smallholder areas, maize is the dominant crop. Cotton, groundnuts, pulses, and oilseeds are also grown, and have considerable potential for expansion and improved productivity. Cashew and coconut are important crops at the coast, where the former has considerable expansion potential. Livestock can be kept intensively on leys with carrying capacities similar to Zone II. Natural grassland can carry one stock unit for every two hectares.

Zone IV. Covering about 53,000 sq.km., this zone at present has only marginal agricultural potential. Commercial ranching on well managed natural pasture can support one stock unit on four hectares or less. Subsistence crop farming and livestock are important in smallholder areas. Drought-escaping Katumani maize has been developed for this area, but, like cotton, pulses, and oilseeds which are grown in the area, the considerable expansion potential requires increased research. Important concentrations of game occur in this zone.

Zone V. This covers just over 300,000 sq.km. and has moderate rangeland development potential. The zone is the focus of many of the present and proposed livestock development programs, with wildlife important in many areas. Increasing subsistence oriented shifting cultivation reflects population pressure on better lands, and the risk of crop failure is great.

Zone VI. This zone includes about 112,000 sq.km. in northern Kenya. Sparse and erratic rainfall, giving flush growth of predominantly annual grass species, leads to the nomadism of the pastoral peoples of the zone.

Thus, of the total land area in Kenya, some 800 sq.km. in Zone I has no agricultural potential. No more than about 106,000 sq.km. (18 percent are classified as having high to medium potential (Zones II and III); 53,000 in Zone IV (9 percent) has marginal potential; and some 300,000 (52 percent) in Zone V has moderate rangeland potential but in parts is being forced into shifting cultivation. The remainder, or 20 percent of total land area, in Zone VI can only sustain nomadic pastoralists. If these data are combined with estimates on population for the decades ahead, it is seen that the amount of good land per capita may fall from the 1970 figure of around 0.88 hectare to some 0.36 hectare by the year 2,000, as shown in the chart. This decline of some 60 percent is startling, and makes clear the urgent need for an effective agricultural and population strategy, and improved perspective planning.

Population and Land Tenure

The problem of getting productive farming systems into this extremely complex range of ecological conditions is made more difficult by the rapid rate of growth of population and by tribal influences on the distribution of land among people. Population was estimated at 11.2 million in 1970 and 12.1 million in 1972. The current population growth rate is probably about 3.5 percent per year, a high figure by any standard. Children under 15 years of age make up almost 50 percent of the population; with a dependency ratio of about one, the productive age groups are heavily burdened. About 10 percent of the population lives in urban centers of 2,000 or more in size; of this group, 70 percent are in the two main cities, Nairobi and Mombasa. Urban centers are growing at about 7 percent per year and if the current mortality and fertility rates continue, the population will reach some 34 million by the year 2,000. In fact, this figure could be exceeded if the accepted family size norm, now high, persists, and if the mortality rate continues to decline, as is expected.[1]

Population pressure is greatest in ecological Zones II and III. However, pressure is building up in all areas through natural growth and, in Zones IV and V, as a result of migration. On medium and high potential land available for small scale farming in Western, Nyanza and Central Provinces, overall densities approximate 150 to 200 persons per sq.km. on holdings averaging three hectares. There are localities, such as the Vihiga Division of Kakamega District in Western Province, with densities of about 500 per sq.km. on holdings of no more than one hectare. On the other hand, there are areas with much lower densities, even in localities of high and medium potential.

There are two main reasons for the extreme variations in population densities. One is that most land is regarded as the exclusive domain of a particular tribe; the other stems from the colonial period, when some land was alienated for large scale expatriate farms or set aside as Government land. Thus, Trans Nzoia District, with medium to high potential land, has large scale mixed farming enterprises, now mainly in African hands with a population density near 50 persons per sq.km. Narok District, which has land of medium to good production potential, is occupied and strongly defended by the pastoral Masai tribe, and supports only 7 persons per sq.km. This compares with a density of about 54 per sq.km. in Machakos District, which has a markedly lower production potential, but which is occupied by a different tribe, the Kamba.

---

1. The Government has drafted a five-year family planning program with the objective of reducing the annual population growth rate to about 3 percent by 1980. The Ministry of Health operates some 600 rural health facilities, including 414 dispensaries and 185 health centers. About 63 percent of the health centers and 5 percent of the dispensaries offer family planning services on a part-time basis through their Maternal and Child Health units. Clients, mainly urban, totaled some 180,000 in 1971.

The upshot of the present land holding situation is that in many densely settled districts able-bodied men are migrating in search of work in other rural areas or in urban centers, and whole families are moving into the lower potential areas of Zones IV and V where rights to land are not so zealously guarded. These movements underline the need to develop technologies and farming systems to increase land productivity. An equally important and perhaps more difficult problem is how to improve access to land now underutilized because of the production systems employed by the tribes having exclusive rights of occupancy.

The problem is basic because the greater part of the nation's land is regarded as the exclusive domain of particular tribes. In late 1970, *Trust Land* amounted to about 420,000 sq.km. (73 percent of the total land area); this was held under traditional tribal systems of allocation and rights. In contrast *Private Land*, i.e., registered land in private ownership (including some 18,000 sq.km. in Trust Land areas) or held on lease from the Government, amounted to some 51,500 sq.km. *Government Land* for forest reserves and national parks (including land set apart for reserves in Trust Land areas) totaled some 50,000 sq.km. plus a further 46,500 sq.km. available for disposition, mainly in Coast Province.

Tribalism also slows the ongoing adjudication and registration program designed to provide individual rights in land and enable the development of a land market. Apart from the sheer physical immensity of the registration task, a major impediment is tribal exclusiveness—the unwillingness of one community, such as a tribe or clan, to allow members of another community to establish rights in lands which they regard as their exclusive domain. This unwillingness can and does lead to violence. Such activities deny access to good agricultural land to persons who could develop and use it with their own initiative and resources. In turn, this means that local land pressures intensify, settlement schemes become more difficult to design and manage, and the farming population is unable to make the best use of the nation's critically short land resource. The probability of dispute over land rights and usage is ever present, threatening social stability. Thus, despite its fundamental political implications, the issue of tribal exclusiveness must be faced squarely now, before it reaches unmanageable proportions. Ways must be found to redress the imbalance in land holding so that production from all areas can be expanded.[2]

In the period before and just after Independence in 1963, the tenure problem centered on the occupation of high quality land by Europeans in the "Scheduled Areas." The "Scheduled Areas" cut across several tribal boundaries. Policy in the sixties was to transfer such land back to Kenyan proprietorship and when this was done, the displaced tribes sought to reestablish traditional boundaries, and even to expand them. The two elements of the ongoing land transfer program (settlement schemes and direct transfers of large farms) must be seen in this context. The settlement schemes were an effort to meet the demands for land with a planned program, including careful attention to tribal balance. Competition for ownership of the large farms reflected the concerns with maintaining or expanding traditional boundaries.

Outside the "Scheduled Areas," there has been an active program of land adjudication and registration, as just noted. There have also been changes in farm size and ownership in response to land pressures, and often this has taken the form of subdivision, or amalgamations through purchase or marriage. Some farmers have also

---

2. It is true, of course, that small scale farmers in some localities have developed farming systems and asset positions which give good returns, despite heavy national population pressure and the impact of tribalism. Examples are Kisii District in Nyanza Province, the bulk of the five districts of Central Province, and the high potential areas of Meru and Embu Districts in Eastern Province. This is partly because past development efforts have stressed these areas; perhaps equally important is the willingness of the people to take advantage of available opportunity. But these encouraging situations are exceptional.

established "satellite" farms in other areas using family members as managers, while other farmers have migrated to new farms or to the towns.

Overall, the complex influences of the past on land ownership have resulted in a wide range in size of holding, forms of ownership, and patterns of production. In turn, these have created difficult policy issues concerning employment opportunities, income and wealth distribution, and the design of development programs.

The present evidence on the size distribution of farms (taking twenty hectares as the minimum size of a large farm) is as follows:

- some 2,750 residual "large farms" within the former "Scheduled Areas," as defined in the official Statistical Abstract;
- some 400 individually held large farms plus forty cooperative units that exist within the formal settlement schemes;
- a number of large farms in Trust Land areas; plus
- ranches held on lease in Government Lands and group and individual ranches in Trust Lands.

Omitting this last category, it is estimated that there are in the high and medium potential (arable) areas about 3,000 to 3,200 farms larger than twenty hectares in size. The "small farm" category would then include (a) all farms, except a few large units, in the arable zone lying outside the former "Scheduled Areas," and (b) all the smallholder units in the "conventional" and "haraka" (squatter) settlement schemes, with a few exceptions in the low density conventional schemes where settlers were allocated more than one plot, making in all about 35,000 units. An indicative estimate of the total number of smallholdings is then approximately 1.2 million, based on extrapolation from the data for farms adjudicated and registered to 1969.

On this same basis, it is estimated that about 25 percent of smallholdings are less than one hectare, probably less than enough to provide subsistence, and roughly 50 percent are less than two hectares. This bottom 50 percent of smallholdings may occupy less than 4 percent of the total arable land in Kenya. The picture is rounded out by the landless. Taking the census estimate of 1.7 million rural households, and allowing for some 200,000 households living as pastoralists in semiarid areas, there are probably some 300,000 rural households (or 16 percent of the rural population) without direct access to land.

Two additional features of the tenure situation should be noted. First, smallholdings are farmed mainly by owner-operators, often by the women of the household. Second, in areas outside the traditional smallholder areas and settlement schemes, there are two groups of small farmers: (a) squatters on Government land and some private estates; and (b) residents of "group owned" large farms who either have a separate subsistence plot or farm part of the unit as a smallholding. There is a further group in traditional smallholder areas: (c) "acceptees" who farm the land of neighboring tribes to which they do not belong. Groups (a) and (b) seldom have access to extension, credit facilities, or other public services, and their tenure is not guaranteed.

Nutrition

Many rural families have diets deficient in calories, protein, and vitamins A, B_2 and C. Although most pronounced in Nyanza Province and parts of the eastern plateau, and variable by season, the deficiencies are nationwide. In the preharvest period, 25 percent to 30 percent of rural families consume less than 60 percent of estimated calorie requirements. Probably more than 25 percent of the children suffer from some form of malnutrition. Overall, the position may by worsening. Pressure on land is increasing, people are moving into marginal areas, maize has largely taken over from the more protein rich millets and sorghums, and there is no reason to believe that pulse production is going up at a faster rate than population.

One of the reasons for the unsatisfactory nutritional and related health conditions is the lack of household water supplies. Rural people probably rank water for household use near the top of the list of "felt" needs. Over the years, several ministries have had many projects of varying kinds to help ease the problem. However, many of these schemes are poorly operated and maintained. A stepped-up effort on rural water supplies is now under way, and the Government target is to provide piped water to the entire population by the year 2,000. The task ahead is immense, as, in 1972, only an estimated 9 percent of the rural population had an adequate water supply.

Chapter 3

A Proposed Development Strategy

This review of the present position of agriculture makes it clear that the rate and pattern of development of the sector will determine in large measure the welfare of Kenya for many years to come.[1] Improvement in agricultural performance is urgently needed. Production and export expansion must be stressed simultaneously with increasing income earning and nutritional improvement opportunities for the rural poor. The total public resources assigned to this job should increase at the fastest rate permitted by personnel, administrative, and project preparation and management capacity. What is called for is an adjustment in the terms of trade, which now fail to recognize the role of agriculture in expanding national output and employment opportunities. Production expansion measures must be of a type which will absorb labor, reduce seasonal variations in labor demand, increase labor productivity, conserve soil and water, and upgrade the commodity mix. Farm size will inevitably become smaller, intensifying an already urgent need for a reorientation of public services to agriculture.

In many respects, the smallholder is the key to the future. Although small farmers already occupy most of the productive land, and produce more and more of the total marketed output, they must be helped to expand production at a faster pace if the nation is to grow. Increments and improvements in public programs should therefore center on the smallholder sector. This does not mean, however, that the large farm sector should be neglected, but rather that the historic imbalance in the emphasis of development programs should be redressed more rapidly. Indeed, the deteriorating large farm sector must be urgently rehabilitated, both in the interest of getting more output and employment in the short term, and assuring adequate supplies of improved seed and breeding stock for the longer run. Of course, outlays for rehabilitation should generally avoid forms of investment which will become redundant if and when the large farms are subdivided.

It is equally important that the Government help the parastatals, private entrepreneurs, and cooperatives to contribute more to smallholder development. These agencies handle much of the credit, inputs, and marketing services for agriculture, but so far they have not been effectively integrated into smallholder development programs (perhaps partly because they are outside the civil service). Integration of these agencies together with their full involvement are urgently needed. A strategy designed to bring a substantially larger number of smallholders into the market economy over the next few years will also require additional outlays for infrastructure, trained manpower (including farmers), and public services. This means both financial and organizational change. The finance side may be relatively easy to solve. Agricultural agencies have not been able to use all available domestic funds, even though the share of public expenditures going to agriculture has been small in comparison with its role in the economy and its importance for the future. But more finance is unlikely to be very helpful without organizational improvements to increase the Government's capacity to give effective support to agriculture, particularly to small farmers. Increasing this capacity is difficult, because it is as much or more a matter of men and motivation as it is method and mechanism. Without discipline, penalty and reward, no organizational system will work.

The Ministry of Agriculture must monitor performance and equip itself to define clearcut goals and guidelines for the many agencies under its jurisdiction, which places a special premium on strengthening the Ministry's planning unit. This unit must determine agency objectives, priorities, and responsibilities; identify and prepare programs and

1. Republic of Kenya, *Report of the Working Party on Agriculture Inputs* (The Havelock Report), 1971.

projects in a professional way; and sustain effective information flows on progress and emerging problems. To do this, the planners must recognize the special conditions facing smallholders: (a) wide diversity in climate, soils, degree of commercialization, culture, and infrastructure; (b) the inability to accept risk, and the high priority necessarily given to subsistence; (c) seasonal labor peaks and shortages as determinants of enterprise combinations; (d) nutritional and health deficiencies. These conditions sharply limit returns to public effort if only a part of the required smallholder service system is provided, and emphasize the need for well timed complementary access to technical knowledge, the financial system, inputs, and markets. The fact is that not much is known about traditional farming systems and their whys and wherefores. This is a priority area for research so that fully useful recommendations can be offered to smallholders. However, this knowledge will take time to acquire, and in the meantime, action must be taken on what is known.

A special effort needs to be made to improve the performance of field staff in setting objectives, assigning resources to achieve these objectives, reporting problems and progress, and integrating and coordinating the delivery of services. Staff must be more rigorously disciplined if performance is to be improved.

Agricultural planners face a difficult task in deciding on the distribution of the development effort among areas, agencies, functions, and commodities. Fortunately, there is no dearth of high return farm commodities awaiting expansion; in some cases, this of itself provides an important determinant of area and functional emphasis. In the better lands, areas emphasis should reflect the current relative levels of economic activity, potential, and population density. In marginal areas, the priority task is to develop technologies which can raise productivity, and then follow with the integrated area-based type of program discussed below, including selected components, such as household water supplies.

Research has been very heavily concentrated on export crops and maize. To help smallholders (and hence the nation), a broadening of geographic and commodity coverage is needed, with special attention to the drier marginal areas. At the same time there should be emphasis on the place of each crop and livestock enterprise in farming systems, taking account of typical cropping patterns, seasonal labor demands and the priority of food crops. To be adequate, technologies must also be capable of providing the farmer with a return sufficient to encourage adoption. The peak season labor constraint merits particular attention through research on shorter yielding varieties, and on mechanization designed specifically for smallholders.

Once potential growth points and technologies have been identified, planners must design projects and programs. This involves setting targets, identifying minimum essential components of programs aimed at meeting targets, and arranging for the integrated delivery of components. In this task, the Ministry of Agriculture must provide much more and better guidance to the parastatal bodies and the other ministries supplying services to agriculture, such as Cooperatives and Social Services, Lands and Settlement, Natural Resources, Tourism and Wildlife, and Works. Close liaison with the private sector and cooperatives is essential in handling this job.

The problem of interagency coordination must be tackled if integrated services are to be delivered to a much greater number of smallholders. To organize and manage a successful coordination mechanism is one of the most difficult tasks facing the Government today. It is an urgent one because the provision of a complete smallholder service system—extension, credit, inputs, and marketing—at the *right* time is critical if smallholder programs are to succeed.

In some cases, multipurpose cooperatives (including the Kenya Farmers' Association and its network of agents) might do the job, perhaps under a subsidy system in the initial stages. In other situations, an area-based project, with a manager responsible for and empowered to bring together the various components, would be the most practical design. In yet other cases, an extension of the functions of some of the parastatal bodies (such as KTDA and the Coffee and Pyrethrum Boards) to include other crops appropriate for the relevant farming system needs consideration. Another possibility is to use the Ministry of Agriculture extension service as the coordinating agent (indeed, this is the primary way to get more value for money from the extension service). In each case, the Government in Nairobi must design coordinated management systems which can be effectively implemented by participating agencies at the field level.

The general economic environment of farmers also needs attention. The relative prices in the beef-dairy-pork-poultry-maize complex need to be rationalized to provide incentives for a higher value product mix. To help improve the efficiency of the product and input markets, more competition should be permitted under appropriate Government rules and regulations. In some cases, the direct control of marketing by parastatal agencies should be reduced and the capacity of the public and private sectors to stabilize prices of staple crops should be expanded. Farm commodity taxes need adjustment. Household water supplies and rural health and family planning services are probably the strongest claimants for subsidies. These income transfers can be directed to specific target groups, and their yield, through labor productivity improvement, should quickly create the possibility of subsidy withdrawal.

Measures must be taken to reduce the population-land imbalance among regions, and the associated underuse of land and labor. The situation is complicated by migration, especially to squatter settlements, and by the variety of forms of occupation of the large formerly European farms. The development of a land market by speeding up registration and other measures can help solve this problem, providing the accumulation of underutilized holdings by wealthier farmers is prevented. The broader question of intersectoral competition for land (such as forestry, agriculture, irrigation, power, wildlife, and grazing livestock) should be handled by an activated Land Use Committee supported by a permanent technical staff and working under an unequivocal mandate to conserve soil and water, and to optimize land use.[2]

The credit service must be adapted in a way which permits it to become an integral part of smallholder service systems and its coverage must be extended. For this it needs more resources. One way to acquire some of the needed funds is to raise interest rates, and tap rural savings more effectively. As soon as the credit system demonstrates its capacity to use more funds effectively, the Treasury will be strongly inclined to make them available.

The overriding objective must be more intensive land use and upgrading of product mix. Maize must be strongly emphasized as the key, both to help move the smallholder into the commercial economy and to support the expansion of beef exports. Area-based package programs stressing subsistence crop production, and including other crops and livestock appropriate for the specific area and market conditions, offer the best prospects for improving small scale agriculture. Commodity and area selection is discussed in Chapter 3, and specific project proposals are made in the Appendix. The large farm strategy should center on safeguarding seed supplies and pedigree breeding stock, and give weight to wheat production.

This strategy is consistent with a large number of measures which are already under way, and with many others for which plans are afoot. The problem is implementation.

---

2. The exact status of the Land Use Committee at this time is not clear. If actually set up, it appears not to have been operational. The purpose of a body of this type was described in the 1970–74 Development Plan as follows: "to advise on the rational allocation of land between alternative uses such as agriculture, forestry and wildlife. Limits will be imposed on the amount of individual land ownership to facilitate efficient management and maximum utilization." It is understood that the proposed composition of the committee was the Ministers for Lands and Settlement, Agriculture, Natural Resources, Tourism and Wildlife, and Finance and Planning, with the Finance and Planning minister serving as chairman, and the Permanent Secretary of the Ministry of Finance and Planning as secretary.

Chapter 4

Policy and Program Improvement

The Government must make several basic decisions in tooling up to implement the proposed strategy. These concern the distribution of the incremental development effort among areas, functions, and commodities; its organization; and improvement in the economic environment of farmers.

Product Emphasis

In deciding on the product mix to be targeted for the years ahead, the demand outlook and the relative difficulties in expanding output are important considerations. In general, the prospects for demand are strong, and the future rate of output growth in agriculture must be much higher than in the recent past if significant upward trends in prices and imports of farm products are to be avoided.

Maize is Kenya's staple grain, and the most important crop in terms of acreage and output value. Small scale farmers with holdings of less than 5 hectares produce over 90 percent of the output and sell whatever is not needed for family consumption. Almost all farmers in high and medium potential areas grow maize, usually interplanted with beans or other pulses on subsistence farms. Mainly because of climate, production fluctuates widely from year to year, contributing to a similar foreign trade pattern—for example, a net export position of some 281,000 tons in 1968 and a net import position of 29,000 tons in 1971. Yields vary, probably averaging about 1,600 kg. per hectare.

Research workers have developed hybrids and synthetic varieties with a yield potential at least two to three times that of unimproved types, and a good seed multiplication and distribution system is in operation. With good husbandry practices, improved varieties at present prices typically produce value/cost ratios for fertilizers of well over 2, and on occasion up to 4. Area planted with improved maize increased from 13,600 hectares in 1964 to over 300,000 hectares (or about 30 percent of total area) in 1972. Of this latter figure, some 270,000 hectares were planted with hybrids and the smallholder area was about 210,000 hectares.

The agricultural development effort should place top priority on maize expansion. The technology is available. Demand for human consumption will grow. More maize is needed to develop the pig and poultry industries, thereby helping free beef for export. Maize is the main crop through which the smallholder can enter the commercial economy and higher yields will enable subsistence needs to be met on a smaller area, and free land for cash earning enterprises. The key to higher yields is smallholder service systems which include improved seed, other modern inputs, credit, technical guidance, marketing facilities, and support prices. As efficiency increases, exports may become possible.

Wheat is grown on high and medium potential land, mainly at elevations of between 1,850 and 3,000 meters, by large scale farmers using modern powered equipment. Planted area declined from 172,000 hectares in 1968 to 101,000 hectares in 1972 (output fell from about 225,000 tons to 159,000 tons over the same period). This decline coincided with the transfer of European owned farms and with a period of increasing competition from maize in the high potential areas. However, yields increased significantly in this period, and averaged about 1,575 kg. per hectare in 1972, largely due to improved varieties resistant to stem rust and because producers with lower yields gave up the crop. Exports peaked at 53,000 tons in 1968; in 1971 some 6,500 tons were imported (plus

13,000 tons imported for re-export). Domestic consumption is trending upward strongly. Production and marketing of wheat are tightly controlled by the Wheat Board. In mid-1972 the purchase price was changed to Sh50 per 90 kg. bag from the 1970/71 figure of Sh45.55 plus a Sh5 bonus.

To avoid large import bills for wheat, production must be expanded. This means devising ways of opening up Narok District where some 400,000 hectares are probably suitable for wheat. The area is Trust Land held by the pastoral Masai people, who are not generally familiar with crop farming. Their present wheat area is about 7,000 hectares, farmed by contractors. The land has not yet been adjudicated. The contractor system of production is already resulting in severe erosion, both on area cropped and on surrounding grazing areas, due to the resulting localized overstocking. These have to be recognized as major practical problems in developing wheat in Narok, as is the ethnic constraint.

Barley is grown on contract for commercial breweries and output is increasing, mainly in Narok. Production is centered in wheat areas on large farms, with yields believed to be around 1,300 kg. per hectare. Malting capacities are being increased, and barley output will probably continue to grow under the sponsorship of the brewery industry.

An estimated 235,000 hectares of *sorghum, bulrush millet,* and *finger millet* are planted annually. Yields may average no more than 500 kg. per hectare and almost all production is consumed on the farm. Although grown in many areas, the heaviest concentrations are in Nyanza Province and in areas marginal or too dry for maize. Kenyan researchers have given little attention to these crops, although they are important in the diet in many areas. The East Africa Agriculture and Forestry Research Organization has produced improved planting materials, but there is no effective distribution. Little is known about appropriate agronomic practices for the major production areas. However, the importance of these crops is growing rapidly as more people move into marginal areas, and research is urgently needed to find suitable varieties and improved husbandry practices applicable to the farming systems.

Rice is a minor crop grown under supplementary irrigation; output (28,500 tons paddy in 1971) is sufficient to meet domestic demand. A policy of self-sufficiency is being followed. Expansion beyond that point depends on the supply of irrigated land and on how profitable rice is relative to such crops as cotton and sugar.

The *pulses* are probably second only to maize in terms of planted area. Small scale farmers produce most of the output, frequently interplanting with maize and other crops, mainly for consumption on the farm. Surplus production is marketed, usually locally, and in consequence the bulk of marketed production is not recorded. Annual production is thought to be on the order of 200,000 tons. Estimates of crop areas on small farms and settlement schemes in 1969/70 show a total pulse area of 542,000 hectares; of this, about 59 percent was under beans (*Phaseolus spp*), 23 percent pigeon peas, 12 percent cowpeas, and the balance divided equally between field peas and grams. Little research has been done on pulses, and they are largely neglected by extension staff, even though pulses are good protein sources and therefore particularly important to smallholders, many of whom cannot afford much animal protein.

Today *oilseeds* are minor crops. Cottonseed, the most important, is a byproduct of the fiber industry and comes mainly from Nyanza, Eastern and Central provinces. The crop is grown entirely by small scale farmers who rarely plant more than one hectare. Yields are low, averaging about 250 kg. of seed cotton (about 80 kg. of fiber) per hectare, largely because of late planting and poor pest control. At these yields, the crop nets less than maize or beans. Farmers dislike cotton because it requires a lot of labor at the same time as food crops. Copra is produced in Coast Province, mainly by smallholders, and production averages some 3,000 tons per year. Yields are low. Sunflower is grown mainly in Western Province on medium to high potential land, by smallholders and large farms, and production is about 2,700 tons per year, mainly from low oil content types (29 percent oil), with yields averaging 850 kg. per hectare. Varieties with 40 percent oil content can be grown, but only limited research information is available. Groundnuts are grown mainly by smallholders in Nyanza. Varieties are mainly large seeded, best suited to the confectionery trade, with yields not more than 600-800 kg. of shelled nuts per hectare. Costs of production are high because of the need to use a high seeding rate and because of the heavy input of labor, particularly at harvest. Groundnuts compete with subsistence crops for labor, and producer prices are low (£65 per ton in 1971). Sesame is the only other oilseed which farmers sell in any quantity; an average of 650 tons was marketed annually between 1969 and 1971. Planted area is not known and yields are thought to be in the 300-500 kg. per hectare range.

Net imports of edible oils and fats almost doubled over the past ten years, and were in excess of £4.4 million in 1971. Over 11,000 tons of oilseeds were imported (net) per year in the 1969–71 period, which is equivalent to about 58 percent of domestic oilseeds production. Existing crushing plants operate at 50 to 60 percent of rated capacity.

Oilseeds should get urgent research attention. In the short run, potential supplies of maize germ oil recoverable from the byproducts of the milling industry should be realized if the return to processing is reasonable. In the medium term, an increase in production of sunflower appears feasible on small farms and rapeseed on large farms, in association with wheat and livestock. Groundnut expansion should be concentrated in new localities. If ongoing research results in high yielding hybrid coconut trees, an intensive breeding and planting program should be undertaken. In the meantime, efforts should be concentrated on improving existing stands, mainly to cover the demand for fresh nuts. Consideration might be given to freeing oilseeds from import duty and putting a duty on imported edible oils and fats.

Kenya increased semirefined *sugar* production steadily in the last few years, from 29,000 tons in 1965 to 125,000 in 1971. Imports vary from year to year, and totaled 72,000 tons in 1971 (valued at almost £4 million). Consumption grew at an annual rate of about 7 percent in this period, and demand will probably be strong in the decade ahead. Sugarcane yields are low, partly because the crop is being grown in unsuitable areas. For example, the Kano Plains production area has an average annual rainfall of only 1,200 mm., and even this is subject to annual and seasonal fluctuations which make the area marginal for cane. The poorly drained black cotton soils make it necessary to use cambered beds, ditches, or furrows to handle the surplus water during heavy rainfall periods; at such times it is also difficult to get cane out of the fields. The area in cane has an elevation of 1,200 to 1,400 m. The planted crop matures in twenty to twenty-two months, and each of the two ratoon crops in eighteen months. The coastal production conditions are also unsuitable; annual rainfall averages about 1,000 mm. with a well defined dry season of five to seven months when monthly rainfall is consistently below 50 mm. The soils are coastal sands on an impervious layer. These soils become waterlogged in April and May; over 300 mm. of rain in each of these months is not unusual. However, Mumias, the new area not yet in production, is likely to be able to produce acceptable cane yields.

Both the factory nucleus estates and smallholders tend to have low yields, on the order of thirty tons per hectare, but some large farms have higher yields, about sixty tons per hectare, because of better field management. The crop is not attractive for smallholders at its present price (Sh40 per ton in the field).

The Government plan is to expand cane area around existing plants, but this should be reconsidered. Little is known about appropriate husbandry practices, yields are low, and field management is poor. All need to be improved to make production economic and competitive with alternative crops before area expansion is pursued on a large scale. However, because natural conditions for cane in the Mumias area are much better than elsewhere, this zone offers possibilities for area expansion after its initial development phase is completed (say, in the mid-seventies). Another yield improvement possibility for the longer term is to irrigate part of the cane in the Kano Plains. Preliminary trials at Ahero show a good response; the task now is to determine economic feasibility. Varietal improvement is also possible, and cane transport costs can probably be reduced.

Even under the most optimistic assumptions on the growth of domestic production through area expansion and yield improvement on existing schemes, Kenya is likely to face a sugar deficit of some 60,000 to 70,000 tons as 1980 approaches.[1] Possible longer term solutions which should be explored through an inclusive study (see *Project 19: Studies*, pages 502–03) include:

- expanding the Mumias cane area to supply a second factory, if agronomic results in the next year or two are as favorable as now appears probable;
- developing the Yala swamps to grow cane under irrigation, and
- growing cane in the lower Tana River irrigation project, now under investigation.

The export of *fresh fruits, vegetables, and flowers* by air has expanded spectacularly in recent years, increasing almost sixfold in volume and value between 1968 and 1972, to an estimated 8,250 tons worth nearly £1 million in the latter year. Exports are to Western Europe, and have been severely limited by availability of air freight space, due partly to insistence by the East African community that its airline should be the sole carrier. Pineapples make up 32 percent and french beans 8 percent of the total volume. Shipping is heaviest from November through May, with exports in the remaining months averaging 55 percent of this level. Promotion is in the hands of the Horticultural Crops Development Authority, a statutory body.

Prospects for further expansion depend on increased air freight space, transport charges, cost-quality relationships between Kenya and competitors, improved market intelligence, and the future attitude of the European Economic Community towards Kenyan exports. If these issues can be solved in Kenya's favor, continued rapid growth can be predicted, since the European market for fresh out-of-season and exotic horticultural produce is very large in relation to Kenya's output and is projected to expand rapidly. The outlook for the production and processing of pineapple, passion fruit, and other fruits and vegetables is encouraging. Steps are being taken to improve the marketing of fresh fruits and vegetables for domestic use; however, ways of expanding domestic demand and the growth in production to meet it need more attention.

Attempts to promote *cotton* have a sad history. The crop was introduced in 1904 and, despite expenditure of large sums of money and staff resources, total production reached no more than about 32,600 bales in the 1970 season, roughly double that of 1960/61. With the exception of one irrigated, 400-hectare project on the Lower Tana, the crop is all rainfed and produced on small farms. Yields approximate 250 kg. of seed cotton per hectare on average, very low by any standard. Producer prices approximate Sh1.10 per kg. for first grade (AR) and Sh0.50 per kg. for second grade (BR) seed cotton; thus, average gross returns per hectare are in the range of Sh130 to Sh300, depending on quality. Cotton production is not attractive relative to competitive crops, such as maize and beans. However, the technical problems of cotton production are, to a large extent, solved and varieties capable of yielding over 1,000 kg. of seed cotton are available. The problem is to design cropping systems which permit labor to be available for adequate land preparation, timely planting, weeding, and spraying. Until these systems are available, farmers will continue to shy away from the crop because of its high labor requirement at times when subsistence crops need attention.

---

1. This figure is based on the MOA demand estimate of about 290,000 tons in 1978, and the estimate appears reasonable.

Cotton has a place in integrated smallholder production projects in selected areas. The first step in project preparation is to analyze cropping patterns and labor profiles to help determine input packages. These should be accompanied by staff selection and training, the formulation of delivery systems for inputs (especially the relatively expensive chemicals and equipment for controlling insect pests), and substantial strengthening of the Cotton Lint and Seed Marketing Board (the most logical body to handle inputs). The Board should consider ways to reduce ginning costs, increase producer prices, and put buyers with funds at buying points.

Coffee is produced by estates and smallholders. The estate sector is old, whereas smallholder plantings started only in 1955/56. There has been little or no planting in the estate sector over the past ten years, thus all the trees are mature. There has been a decrease in area, from 32,000 to 28,000 hectares, due mainly to the transfer of European-owned estates. In the smallholder sector, consisting of about 270,000 growers with an average coffee area of 0.2 hectare, the area planted to coffee increased in the early sixties from 28,000 to 54,000 hectares.

During the last few years, the smallholder coffee area has dropped slightly because of coffee berry disease. This reduced profitability, in particular making the return to labor relatively less attractive, and some planters changed to alternative enterprises, such as tea, vegetables, and milk production. It is estimated that between 500 and 1,000 hectares of coffee were uprooted in the past three years, but this is not a well-defined trend, and if the planting ban were lifted, the smallholder coffee area would certainly increase.

Yields in the early sixties were of the order of 800 to 1,000 kg. per hectare, with yields on smallholdings consistently higher than on estates. When coffee berry disease became virulent in 1966, yields fell generally to not much more than 400 kg. per hectare. Since then, however, estate yields have recovered to pre-1966 levels, but smallholder yields have remained about 400 to 500 kg. per hectare. The reason for this is that disease control is expensive and, unless carried out systematically, ineffective. In general, the estates have the means to carry out efficient control, but smallholders are unable or unwilling to incur the necessary expenses. To overcome the difficulties of disease control in the smallholder sector, so-called intensive coffee production methods are being developed.

Production has recently fallen short of targets, and the Coffee Board is reviewing coffee policy. The recent removal of International Coffee Organization quotas introduces a new dimension into the review. The first task is to phase an output expansion program. Target magnitudes should be determined by an independent assessment of the market outlook for mild coffees, keeping in mind the role that Kenya wishes to play in such supply control programs as the coffee producing countries may eventually develop, along with the fact that larger Kenyan sales would not of themselves have a marked effect on prices. Coffee is a labor intensive crop well suited to smallholder production. Suitable areas for expansion are available, and the technical, marketing, processing, and promotional infrastructure already at hand would permit a rapid take-off.

The Government's *tea* policy is to keep the estate tea sector at its present level of about 23,000 hectares and to concentrate all efforts to increase production on the smallholder sector. With the completion of the 14,800-hectare scheme now in hand, the area planted to tea by smallholders will reach well over 40,000 hectares by 1978/79. When these plantings mature, annual tea production will be in excess of 100,000 tons, and the crop will be a major source of smallholder income. Field production has no major problems and it appears quite feasible, technically, to attain the set goals. As planting progresses in the years just ahead, however, world demand and price outlook must be kept under continuous scrutiny to assure that plans for the longer term are consistent with optimum resource use. With an estimated tea potential of 600,000 hectares, it is clear that even a 20 percent exploitation would lead to a considerable expansion of plantings. In the face of inelastic demand and declining tea prices, other crops can become more attractive.

Two crops which need sharply greater emphasis are *cashew* and *macadamia*. Exports of raw cashew nuts doubled in the period from 1965 to 1971, to 14,000 tons. Average yields are about 200 kg. from random plantings among other crops, the typical production method. With correct spacing and selected seed, yields of 600 kg. per hectare are possible at maturity, and food crop interplanting and grazing are possible for many years after the trees are established. Demand outlook is strong. Expanded output, in combination with improved marketing and local processing, would greatly increase the crop's contribution to the smallholder economy. Growth targets of the Ministry of Agriculture for cashew are much too low.

Production and market prospects for macadamia are also promising, although much more work remains to be done on planting materials. Macadamia can be intercropped for many years after planting, and smallholders are rapidly taking up the crop on their own initiative. A major public effort to expand macadamia is called for, particularly in densely populated smallholder areas. Meanwhile, research on planting materials should be greatly strengthened.

Both domestic and foreign demand for *beef* is strong and is expected to grow rapidly. With over nine million head of cattle and an impressive array of ongoing development programs, Kenya is in a good position to exploit this market. Only 4 percent of Kenya's land area is used for crop farming, and area expansion possibilities for crops are limited. Much of the remaining 96 percent of the land area will therefore continue to be used for grazing livestock and wildlife. The task ahead is to improve husbandry practices and to raise offtake.

Programs to make better use of the low rainfall pastoral areas through the provision of water points and controlled grazing are well underway.[2] Systems for moving cattle from low rainfall pastoral areas to higher potential zones for pasture or feedlot backgrounding and fattening are being developed. Along with disease control programs, these measures over time should significantly improve the pastoral-based cattle economy. The next task is to improve the livestock enterprise in the medium and high potential areas, which account for well over half of the livestock population, and where average carrying capacity of unimproved grazing land is above one livestock unit per hectare, roughly ten times higher than in pastoral areas. In these better areas, some 80 percent of even the smallholder acreage is in unimproved grazing.

Cattle development programs today concentrate mainly on the range areas. While implementation of the latest range project will still not result in full exploitation of the rangeland potential, it must be recognized that the majority of cattle are in the medium and high potential areas, and that the potential in these areas has scarcely been tapped. Slaughter cattle originating in high and medium potential smallholder districts are generally underfinished and are seldom fed up to their maximum slaughter value. Most bull calves from dairy herds are slaughtered a few days after birth because rearing is uneconomical, especially on smallholdings. An estimated 60 percent of the dairy bull calves would be suitable for beef production, if the problem of the high cost of feeding to six months of age could be solved (the remaining 40 percent are not fully suitable, because of breed type). By rearing these animals on good pasture and fattening them intensively during the last phase, carcasses of 220 kg. could be produced at an age of two years. By 1978, the number of bull calves suitable for fattening may approximate 130,000 per year, which would contribute an additional 29,000 tons of beef annually. In short, the high and medium potential areas merit a vastly increased effort to develop livestock.

---

2. Some 35 percent of the nation's domestic livestock units are on land which gets less than 600 mm. of rain per year.

The preservation of appropriate areas for water catchment is the most urgent issue in the *forestry* subsector. With this in mind, the Government should: (a) give the activated Land Use Committee (see Chapter 3) the necessary capacity and power to adjudicate forest land use issues; (b) prevent further illegal and uncontrolled settlement and other abuses in the forest catchment areas, and (c) mount further studies of the cropping possibilities (including charcoal) and of the soil conservation measures and storage dam capacity needed to ensure adequate protection of forest catchment areas now coming under heavy population pressure. The needed changes in forest legislation are before Parliament.

Fuelwood and building pole plantations in marginal areas (established under the Rural Afforestation Scheme) are viable and should be continued. Plantations in alpine zones present serious technical problems which are far from being resolved. Accordingly, acceptable rates of growth and financial return to afforestation are only likely to be achieved between the 1,500 m. and 3,000 m. contours in areas with at least 1,000 mm. rainfall. Some of this land may have profitable alternative uses in agriculture. Careful and continuing analyses of the rates of return to alternative uses of land are needed, bearing in mind the world timber demand outlook, and the economic costs of labor and foreign exchange.

Measures to improve lumber quality are needed, particularly in the case of smaller sawmills. The few remaining larger sawmills should be expanded to assure a marketing capability and a regular supply of low cost, high quality lumber needed in opening new export markets. The Government, in its forest concession decisions, should continue to guarantee these few large enterprises the long term security of tenure required to justify the heavy investment in processing and seasoning plant. Integration between sawmilling and pulpmill operations in the Broderick Falls area is needed to make use of sawmill waste residues and reduce sawn lumber production costs. It is particularly important that technical and business management training of smaller sawmill operators be stepped up. Charcoal needs attention and it may be possible to develop exports through systematic exploitation of the indigenous forests, preferably coupled with a program of planting. The most obvious potential for doing this lies in the Arabuko Sokoke forest area, north of Mombasa.

In *fisheries*, the work under way to improve the knowledge base should be expanded so that appropriate regulations and development programs can be established. Utilization of existing staff and equipment in the Fisheries Department needs to be improved, and a management system to help define field staff functions, improve reporting, and enable better supervision of junior staff is essential. For Lake Victoria, a long term development program is needed to provide for an orderly transition from current traditional fishing methods to a modern fishing industry, taking account of the supply of alternative employment opportunities and the sustainable catch level. If the resource is found to be in jeopardy, a full management plan should be instituted; this could embrace limited entry through licensing, and a habitat improvement program for Tilapia, the most valuable species. Credit might be issued through cooperative societies, in conjunction with the licensing system, for the improvement of gear to exploit the potential in the mid-depth zone. The exploitation of the large resources of Haplochromis in deeper waters requires international agreement and cooperation and the proposed Joint Fisheries Commission for Lake Victoria, now being discussed, is a prerequisite.

For Lake Rudolf, more resource data must be assembled before a reasonable management plan can be designed. Existing evidence suggests that a very cautious approach is needed.

The roughly 30,000 fish ponds in Kenya represent an underutilized resource. The first task in development is to assess systematically the Kenya experience on pond culture. A small research staff should be assembled, with the work emphasizing local varieties of fish.

As river systems are modified, particularly the Tana, environmental conditions at river mouths may change. At that time, it may be feasible to explore the economics of using a large tract to grow shrimp under controlled conditions. Despite considerable local interest, the evidence suggests that Kenya should not invest in tuna longline vessels at this time. Consideration could be given to investment in a cannery at the Mombasa freezing facility; however, many other countries have found tuna canning a precarious venture, so a thorough feasibility study is essential.

There may be scope for the gradual expansion of crustacean fisheries by modern methods, particularly in water deeper than 10 m. Enforcement of a minimum size limit would be desirable to improve the lobster fishery.

Sport fishing offers possibilities for development as a lucrative adjunct to the tourist industry. This requires greater coordination between the Fisheries and Tourism Departments, more promotion, improved facilities in some areas (most notably on the coast), and antipoaching patrols on trout rivers. A preinvestment study is necessary.

Development Areas and Program Orientation

A striking feature of Kenyan agriculture is the marked imbalance in both the distribution of land among the people and the intensity of land use. This causes wide differentials in labor productivity, production, and incomes. To lessen disparities, improve the lot of the poor, and raise the national agricultural output, two courses of action are possible in principle. One is to move people from areas of high population density into areas of lower density, taking inherent land productivity into account. The second is to increase employment and income potential *in situ*. Concerning the first course, a rough indication of the rural population which could be supported in each province at a modest living level is shown in the following data, along with the apparent opportunities for interprovincial population redistribution:[3]

Province	Present Rural Population	Estimated Population Which Could Obtain £70 Annual Income	Difference
	(millions)	(millions)	(millions)
Western	1.44	1.34	−0.10
Nyanza	2.40	1.56	−0.84
Rift Valley	2.30	5.0–6.0	2.7–3.7
Central	1.80	1.80	0
Eastern	2.00	1.70	−0.30
Coast	0.75	2.00	1.25
Total	10.70	13.4–14.4	2.7–3.7

These indicative data suggest a relative underuse of land in Rift Valley and Coast provinces, and tremendous population pressure elsewhere. But the figures in the "difference" column of the table do not mean that large numbers of people can relocate. Most of the underused land in the Rift Valley and Coast is in Trust status. Unfortunately, it is not readily available for redistribution because of the tribal exclusiveness already

---

3. Calculation is based on the application of available technology under reasonable small farmer management practices. Implicit are assumptions on yield, prices, cost, and labor requirements. Note also that (a) modern technology has had a very limited impact on small farmers, hence the imbalances are greater than the data suggest, and (b) North Eastern Province is omitted because of lack of data; however, few would argue that it can support more people than it now has.

discussed; this will persist as a major constraint on economic development and aid to the rural poor.

Over the longer term, the market in land will grow, enabling more people to move and helping ease the population-land imbalance. The development of this market can be promoted by speeding up adjudication, providing mortgage finance, completing the land transfer program, and strengthening pressures on the owners of underused land (through foreclosure, management orders, and the like).

But these measures will not help much today. Thus, it becomes imperative to seek *in situ* employment and income improvement by intensifying land use in heavily populated localities, mainly through area-based programs.[4] Three kinds of areas should be distinguished in designing the attack, with each being defined relative to the other rather than in any absolute sense. The Nandi District illustrates the characteristics of the first kind of area, which we may call Category A. The land is in ecological zones II and III. Population density is less than 90 per sq.km. It has few cash crops other than tea, which has been less successful than elsewhere. Nandi is an area of low population pressure and low economic activity, with the latter being defined as the average value of output per hectare relative to land of similar production potential elsewhere.[5]

Category B areas are typified by Kakamega District. Like Nandi, the land is in ecological zones II and III. However, the population density is about 250 per sq.km. Few cash crops are produced, and the tea program has had poor results. It is in an area of low economic activity and high population density. Kisii District illustrates Category C. In ecological zones II and III, its population density is over 300 per sq.km., and it is the nation's biggest producer of tea and pyrethrum. Coffee and passion fruit are also grown, and grade cattle enterprises are common. It is an area of high economic activity and high population density.[6]

Using these concepts and the available district data (mainly the distribution of the cultivated area by crop, and per capita income from crop sales), it is possible to group the nation's districts into the described categories, as follows:

Category A	Category B	Category C
Keiyo Marakwet	Baringo	Embu (upper areas)
Kericho	Bungoma	Kiambu
Kilifi	Busia	Kirinyaga
Kwale	Embu (lower areas)	Kisii
Lamu	Kakamega	Meru (upper areas)
Nakuru	Kiambu (small lower area)	Muranga
Nandi		Nyandarua
Narok	Kirinyaga (small lower area)	Nyeri
Trans Nzoia		
West Pokot	Kisumu	
Uasin Gishu	Kitui	
Isiolo (rangeland)	Machakos	
Kajiado (rangeland)	Meru (lower areas)	[table continued on next page]

---

4. The use of area-based programs and some concentration of resources are inevitable in any development effort which goes beyond measures (such as pricing) which improve the general economic environment of farmers. Such programs need not be inequitable if the total development effort is carefully distributed in geographical and other relevant terms.

5. The underlying notion here is the production function, or the relationship between output per hectare (vertical scale) and inputs of capital and labor. Such a relationship can be drawn for each land class. Areas with low economic activity (or intensity) are applying resources to land at the left portions of the curve, relative to high activity areas.

6. A fourth category, low population density and high economic activity, is omitted because this is not of great interest when trying to design programs to relieve poverty. The market will induce the maximum acceptable inflow of population into such areas, and the level of development already attained should be sufficient, relative to other areas, to permit expansion to continue.

Category A	Category B	Category C
Laikipia (rangeland)	Muranga (small lower area)	
Marsabit (rangeland)	Nyeri (small lower area)	
Narok (rangeland)	Siaya	
Samburu (rangeland)	South Nyanza	
Tana River (rangeland)	Taita	
	Baringo (rangeland)	
	Garissa (rangeland)	
	Kitui (rangeland)	
	Mandera (rangeland)	
	Turkana (rangeland)	
	Wajir (rangeland)	

This indicative grouping would probably change somewhat with further study, which should be undertaken.[7] However, the exercise suggests a way of distributing emphasis in agricultural problems. If Government concern is with the rate of return to rural programs in terms of income distribution, it will center incremental effort in Category B areas, which have both the population problem and a considerable unexploited production potential. Category B areas are mainly composed of smallholders and are in two main blocks. One comprises Nyanza and Western Provinces, the other the medium to low potential areas of Eastern Province and the adjacent lower ends of Central Province. Also in this category are the range areas (which are more difficult to classify) of Turkana, Wajir and Mandera and probably Baringo.

Category C embraces only smallholder areas; the main ones cover most of the five districts of Central Province, the high potential parts of Meru and Embu Districts, and Kisii District. These areas have benefited most from past public effort. Despite their high population densities and small farm size, they lead in average incomes. They have built up a development momentum and can continue to progress with the present level of government assistance. In these areas, however, a greater effort should be made to help the poorest smallholders by shifting more of the existing development effort to them; the total effort in these areas need not be increased at this time.

Category A areas are located primarily in Rift Valley and Coast Provinces, and include districts with obvious cropping potential such as Narok, Kericho, Nandi, and Trans Nzoia in the Rift; and Kilifi, Kwale, and Lamu in the Coast. The range areas of Narok, Kajiado, Samburu, Marsabit, and Tana River are also in this category.

Category A Areas

For reasons already noted, in Category A areas land use can be intensified, for the most part, only by the present occupants. The main case is Narok, an area well suited to wheat, rapeseed, and livestock. Both acreage in effective use and yields can be sharply increased, but efforts to do so have had little success so far. The problem, once again, is imbalance of land distribution. The Masai occupy almost all of Narok, but they are relatively few in number, whereas elsewhere large numbers of people of different tribes are short of land. If the Government does nothing, infiltration will continue until there is more intense tribal conflict (fighting already occurs). Alienation for official settlement of non-Masai in significant numbers would produce the same result, and tend to undermine the whole concept of land rights. The only feasible course is to adjudicate

---

7. For example, Keiyo Marakwet might shift to Category B. More categories would be better. But a considerable production, evaluation, and manipulation of data would be necessary to delineate more classes and get more homogeneity within each. The present construction is admittedly somewhat arbitrary and subjective, although sound in principle and adequate in practice to lead to useful judgments. (The Town Planning Department has worked along these same lines, but with regional physical planning as its main objective.)

the area, using the "setting apart" procedure described later in this chapter, where possible, to try to improve intratribal distribution, at least somewhat; develop it in the long run national interest; and, in the course of time, promote land redistribution by legal and orderly transfer through the market. The Government should proceed with adjudication in Narok and resume preparation of a mixed farming project.[8] Adjudication should first cover the areas suitable for this project, almost totally Masai-held; thereafter it should be done in the smallholder areas occupied by non-Masai, with development programs to follow at a later stage. The land should be adjudicated to the present occupants, and the Government should not allow the Masai or the county council, as custodians of the Trust Land, to interfere. Legislation may be needed. The mixed farming project should include mapping, land use, and farm planning; technical services; credit for farm development and input supplies; and infrastructure, mainly roads and storage facilities. Livestock development should also be included, as the areas are not covered adequately by the current or planned livestock programs. The cost of a first phase project of this sort of four years' duration would approximate £2½ million, of which some 50 percent would probably be in foreign exchange.[9]

As already mentioned, a part of the large farm sector is doing badly, and the Government is already preparing a project to rehabilitate these farms. As a second project for Category A areas, this should be widened to include subdivision of group farms where owners so desire.[10] It should provide for a farm management advisory service, and credit for farm development and inputs. (See later section on large farms.)

Third, the cashew industry should be expanded, first as a component in the proposed integrated rural development project in Kwale and Kilifi Districts, and later as a part of the farming system for the suggested Lamu settlement project. Processing and marketing must be included in the projects.

In Category A areas the other major development effort should center on the beef industry in the highlands, particularly in Kericho and Nandi Districts. Aside from dairying, livestock programs so far have focused on range areas. The highlands contain large numbers of stock on high potential land, and efforts to improve the industry are overdue.

Category B Areas

While the A area projects just discussed are important, the Government should concentrate its incremental development effort in Category B areas. Here, there is development potential, not always as great as in the other two categories, but still significant. The overriding consideration is that the B areas contain dense populations at totally unsatisfactory income levels, often at bare subsistence. The land available to these people is now no more than would provide a modest income if developed to the level of that of the most advanced areas of Category C; yet population grows apace. No major impact on these areas is to be expected from land redistribution. The only solution is *in situ* development to intensify land use.

---

8. Project preparation was suspended a few months ago, pending policy decisions on land ownership.

9. Quite aside from getting production, an effort of this sort is essential for resource conservation. The present development in Narok is entirely exploitative, and the largest remaining untapped land potential in Kenya is being degraded. Only under the guidance of an officially sponsored development program will conservation, which is vital to the future of the nation, be given proper attention.

10. The term "group farm" is used here not in the usual sense of a farm held by a recognized *social* group, but rather to denote a farm operated by a number of persons, each farming his own small plot, and in some cases participating in joint exploitation of parts of the farm. Members have tended to concentrate their efforts on their individual holdings, and the remaining acreage often produces relatively little.

The priority task is to realign and expand technical research. Work on oilseeds and pulses and the drought resisting grains, sorghum, and millets, should be stepped up. Farming systems research is required as the medium and low potential areas grow only annual crops and thus suffer from seasonal labor shortages and low labor productivity. Attempts must be made to overcome this constraint. Husbandry techniques which would improve both soil and moisture conservation are required for the drier areas. Investigations should be made into ways of improving the drainage of the badly drained soils in Nyanza Province and other areas. Improving the productivity of rainfed agriculture in such areas would probably be more rewarding than irrigation, as evidenced by costs and results to date on the Ahero scheme. Another research priority is macadamia which has considerable potential and should be introduced as a new cash crop in the high potential areas of Western Province, even on the basis of existing knowledge.

Research takes time, and lack of research data will constrain short term achievements. Nevertheless, an early start must be made to prepare and launch development programs, based on present knowledge, even though the results will not be spectacular. The income problem in Category B areas is too severe to permit delay, and it is worsening rapidly with population growth. Furthermore, first phase programs will test new ways of reaching the poorer and smaller farmers. Some type of integrated area-based program is the best approach, as proposed later. Such programs form the backbone of the development effort in many countries, as for example, the Lilongwe Project in Malawi and the package programs in Ethiopia. Of course, these and similar efforts elsewhere cannot provide a blueprint for Kenya because of the differing relative development levels and circumstances of today, but they merit study as possible sources of ideas which may be adapted to fit Kenyan needs.

Kenya has adequate resources and a considerable potential for this type of effort. The extension service is large, although admittedly not very productive. There is some competence in cooperatives, credit, marketing, and input distribution. The need is not to create institutions, but rather to make better use of those which exist and to integrate their activities. The farmer must have simultaneous access to advice, credit, inputs, and marketing channels; lack of one can nullify the value of the others. Simultaneous provision of closely integrated services should be the core of the development programs. One way to do this is through "development centers." These could be under the control of the extension service, with each being the operational headquarters for its locality. Drawing upon other agencies, these centers could improve markets, provide credit and input supplies, help service local cooperatives, and perhaps monitor the operation of other related service agencies working in the locality. All this would require change in the functions and responsibilities of existing institutions, particularly the extension service.

Preparation of the first phase of two area–based programs should begin now: one to serve Western and Nyanza Provinces, the other to serve the medium to low potential areas of Eastern and lower Central Provinces. Only an outline of the proposed programs can be given here. Two separate centers seem desirable for each region, both to spread impact and to gain experience in different areas. In keeping with Government's contemplated planning approach, each focal point could be a district and later phases would expand the program to all districts. In Western Province appropriate starting points would be Kakamega and South Nyanza Districts. It would then be possible to apply the lessons learned in the Vihiga and Migori Special Rural Development Programs (SRDPs).[11] In Kakamega, tea and macadamia would be important cash crops, passion

---

11. The SRDPs have been less experimental and innovative than was intended. With a few exceptions, their principal emphasis has been on coordinating and integrating existing programs rather than trying new methods. They have been developed in the context of national policies which generally give little attention to the needs of small farmers concerning such matters as agricultural research, pricing and marketing and smallholder delivery systems for exten-

fruit could be promoted, and increased attention given to dairying, milking goats, poultry, and pigs. This cash enterprise package must be part of a more inclusive program which attacks the "whole farm," and includes intensification of subsistence output. This will help assure the food supply and hence release land for cash crops. In densely settled areas with very small farms, this is the only way for the poorer farmer to break into the cash economy. From this it follows that expansion of hybrid maize production must be a cornerstone of these programs.

The potential of South Nyanza is lower than that of Kakamega, and cash crop possibilities are more limited. However, the output of cotton, groundnuts and, to a lesser extent, fire-cured tobacco could be expanded jointly with intensified food crop production. Also, in South Nyanza, output from the large livestock population could be increased. The technical component of the program should be complemented by development of the necessary infrastructure.

East of the Rift Valley, the starting points should probably be Machakos District and the Mbere Division of Embu District. The Government has been trying to prepare a development project for this region. In addition, Mbere is the location of an SRDP receiving bilateral assistance. These foundations can be built on. Intensification of food crop production would be the major thrust in these medium to low potential areas, but there is potential for expanding cotton, and, with more research, oilseeds and pulses. Livestock also merits attention, especially in the drier areas as insurance against the ever-present risk of crop failure. In these areas the use of work oxen should be promoted. Domestic water supplies should be developed, and the possibilities for minor supplementary irrigation should be explored. There is some potential for irrigation around the Machakos Hills, for example.

Large Farms and State Land

The development program mix must also include large farms and State Land if all possible ways of improving man-land ratios and land use intensity are to be exploited. Since Independence, much has been done to redress imbalances arising from the earlier policy of alienating land for large-scale expatriate farms. Much remains to be done, however. In the medium term, population pressure will mean that land ownership in the large farm areas must become less concentrated. Today, it may not be politically feasible to tackle this problem directly, although all public forces should be mobilized to help prepare the way and to design a pattern of shift which will avoid interruptions in production when the time comes to take action. Meanwhile, large farm rehabilitation, now under study, should be supported; as noted previously, many of the large farms transferred in recent years are in difficulties. Rehabilitation should stress investment of a type which will not become redundant when redistribution occurs. Another measure is to require holders of underutilized land to do a better farming job if they wish to continue as owners. Foreclosure action should be taken at once against those with loans in default and hopefully the Government could buy the properties at the resulting public auctions, with the land then being distributed more equitably. Much more land should be brought under management orders to increase labor absorption capacity, and production—provided, of course, that measures are taken to assure that the orders are effectively administered in the interests of better resource use.

Some large farms in the hands of individuals or small groups can be subdivided,

---

sion marketing services, inputs, and credit. The SRDP undertakings are of doubtful replicability, partly because of heavy pressure on project managers for quick, tangible results, and because of the considerable financial and technical resources contributed by foreign donors. Detailed assessments of the SRDPs are given in: (a) "An Overall Evaluation of the Special Rural Development Programme" (Nairobi: Institute for Development Studies, 1972); (b) R. Rasmusson, "Kenyan Rural Development and Aid" (Stockholm: SIDA, 1972).

particularly in the Trans Nzoia. The constraint is the Government's present attitude toward subdivision. Present policy aims at group ownership and large scale operation (the "Shirika" schemes). Groups with privately purchased land which they wish to subdivide are not now allowed to do so. A reversal of policy is called for. Those wishing to subdivide their jointly owned large farms should be allowed and assisted to do so. The assistance should form a component of the large scale rehabilitation program mentioned previously, since many of the problem farms are in group ownership. Later, if the Shirika schemes prove unproductive—as well they may because of lack of member participation in management decisions and other reasons—the Government should accept that these farms, too, should be subdivided where technically feasible.

Of course, there will continue to be a place for some land to be operated on a large scale, both because it is technically unsound to subdivide some areas and because large farms can best produce the quality seed and breeding stock required for an improved agriculture. Large areas of Nakuru and Uasin Gishu Districts should not be subdivided, but rather should be used to produce breeding stock and seed for small grains and many of the grasses. Other areas must be reserved for seed maize production, probably in the Trans Nzoia. This must be a large scale operation because of the isolation zone required around seed maize. The Government should examine this issue carefully before embarking on further subdivision. Some 11,000 tons of hybrid seed, requiring about 5,500 hectares of land, may be needed by the early nineteen eighties. Maize seed should probably not occupy more than 10 percent of the gross area of a farm when allowance is made for nonarable land, rotation requirements, and the isolation required. This would imply that in the Trans Nzoia some 55,000 hectares of large farms should be retained. However, maize seed requirements will expand during the nineteen eighties, and a total of some 75,000 hectares of large farms should probably be reserved now for maize seed production. These farms could also supplement production of grass and minor crop seeds as required. Similarly, large farms are needed to participate in the national dairy and beef cattle breeding program to improve stock for smallholders. The crucial point concerning seed and breeding farms is the scale of operation; ownership does not need to be individual in all cases, but a high level of management is essential.

When the larger settlement farms can be subdivided through foreclosure or on a willing-seller basis, the process should be assisted rather than resisted. Many settlers would probably be glad of an opportunity to improve their liquidity by selling part of their land at its market value. This would require development of the land market, including credit facilities for land purchase.

A final way of easing the marked land imbalance is by moving people on to underutilized State Land. Unfortunately, there is little State Land with a cropping potential; the only area of significance is Lamu District. Building upon a rather inconclusive pilot cotton production scheme, the Government is now preparing a proposal to settle about 12,000 hectares, the potential of which has been determined. This project should be brought to fruition rapidly, bringing in needy people from overpopulated areas, particularly, if possible, Category B areas, where landless laborers and very small farmers are seeking employment. However, before large scale development can start in Lamu, a land use plan is required to assure a good distribution among game, livestock, and crop farming uses. The Government recognizes the need for such a plan, and it is understood that a bilateral aid agency is interested in doing the study.

Land Tenure

The Government should legalize and regularize the process of spontaneous settlement except where resource conservation is endangered. One method would be to select suitable areas for settlement, to construct rudimentary infrastructures (initially roads and water supplies which would direct settlement activity), and to allow settlers to develop land on the basis of a temporary occupation license. In cases where squatters are already on government land chosen for assisted settlement, they might properly become participants in the scheme on the same basis as other settlers.

The Government should take whatever steps are necessary to institute "setting apart" procedures for unused Trust Land and open it to minimally assisted settlement. The adjudication criteria should be adjusted to require proof of occupation and use, thereby helping prevent the allocation to individuals of large parcels of unused "clan land," as for example, in Narok.

The land adjudication and registration program requires reexamination by the Government to decide on its appropriate scale and priority areas for action. The targets of the 1970–74 Development Plan will not be attained, and the tentative targets for the forthcoming plan look equally ambitious. Costs per hectare for the program are rising and it is now moving into areas which are less easy to adjudicate, or in which the economic benefits from adjudication may be lower than has been the case to date. A formally constituted board (with political representation and an independent chairman) might be helpful in this task.

To expedite adjudication, the Government should consider requiring officers to adjudicate with the advice of the associated committee, rather than leaving the decision to the committee. Appeal against first registrations might well be directed to the established courts, rather than to the Minister of Lands and Settlement. Disputes over group ranch boundaries are an important cause of delays and a land court might be set up to resolve such disputes before adjudication. This might require changes in the governing legislation. In cases of prolonged dispute, the adjudication staff should be withdrawn until local attitudes change.

If the Government decides that leasehold tenure in settlement areas is desirable, it must recognize that a ten to fifteen year term is much too short. It would deny leaseholders access to longer term credit on the security of land. Moreover, leasehold and freehold systems can readily be adjusted to equivalency in terms of farmer payments. For example, proposals now exist to grant ninety-nine-year leasehold titles to farmers in settlement areas with an annual rent at 5 percent of the land value and subject to revision every thirty-three years. If the leaseholds are marketable, they can stimulate investment in land development in the same way as freeholds, given appropriate land use and tax policy. Under either system, if desired, payments can be deferred to permit more expenditures for capital items and improved production practices.

All possible steps need to be taken to improve the land market. This offers the best possibility of overcoming tribal exclusiveness and bringing land into optimum use. To this end, the registration program must be improved and the register must be properly operated. The Survey of Kenya should reexamine the decision to produce new maps for settlement areas. If map discrepancies are not serious, the allocation maps might be used for registration without further survey. If resurvey is believed essential, the job should be done in not more than three years, using foreign aid as necessary. Titles should be registered at once on authorized schemes on government land, particularly "Haraka" schemes; for this, new registry maps are needed. There is a need for more subdivisional surveys, which are already in arrears, and the Survey of Kenya may need more capacity to handle the task. The service should not be subsidized. The register provides a service to the public and the cost of keeping it current should be met by those who use it. The Survey should staff itself at the level required to keep fully abreast of subdivisional dealings, and it should price the service at cost. Another problem is that four different systems of registration are now in use. The Registered Land Act of 1963 was intended to apply to all registered land; existing titles under various other Acts should be converted accordingly. This is not an expensive exercise.

Landowners should be kept under constant pressure to improve land use. Among the possible ways of bringing vacant or underused land into production are prompt repossession of land for which payments are in arrears to the Agricultural Finance Corporation and Agricultural Development Corporation, and the use of properly administered management orders. In the longer term, introduction of a suitably drafted national tax on agricultural land could also help promote improved land use. The Government may have to seek wider powers to acquire underused land.

It must be recognized that the unofficial subdivision of land on inheritance cannot be stopped. This means that subdivisions should be recorded in the register, permitting the register to function as a correct land record in the interests of land market development. As the market develops, ceilings on land holdings may become necessary, even though they may be difficult to enforce.

The implications of population pressures for farm size were pointed out previously, and it is not clear for how long the people will see the large farm as being in the national interest. The Government should anticipate the inevitability of a downward trend in farm size, reserve a sufficient number of large farms to produce seed and breeding stock, as already noted, and forestall subdivision when technical conditions are unsuitable for smaller farms.

The settlement program needs attention. A subcommittee of the Land Use Committee should be set up to examine key issues, such as the possibility of subdividing larger holdings. Since many are underutilized, the "family exclusion" clause could be dropped to permit subdivision inheritance on all holdings.[12] Absentee ownership needs to be investigated, especially where this is leading to poor land use or defaults on repayments. Registration of individual holdings is urgently needed, if only to permit settlers who have paid off their debt to get short term credit from commercial banks. The regulatory and debt collection activities in settlement schemes should be wholly separated from technical services by passing responsibility for all production programs to the Ministry of Agriculture, as the first step in integrating the schemes into the sector as a whole. More credit should be provided, but higher interest rates will be necessary on development credit. Debt on land purchase could be rescheduled to stretch out repayments over a longer period. After this has been done, foreclosure action should be taken against people whose payments are in arrears—including prominent citizens.

A program of registration and development is required for existing "Haraka" settlements. The "Shirika" approach should be regarded as an interim or trial approach only. It may not be viable.

Consideration should be given to reorganizing the Department of Settlement to divest it of all functions for which parallel authorities exist outside of the Settlement Schemes (see Chapter 5). This includes cooperatives, extension, technical and veterinary services, and all production programs, as well as roads and water supplies. The Department would retain responsibility for planning, coordination, and regulatory functions associated with land transfer. The longer run aim should be to reduce the special attention given to settlement schemes and to integrate them into the national development programs.

The Government should give priority to a management assistance and credit project to increase production on the many transferred large farms which are deteriorating. Appropriate measures would include: formalizing de facto subdivisions by adjudicating and registering residents; purchasing farms for subdivision on a willing-seller basis; foreclosing on rundown farms in financial difficulties, also with a view to subdivision;

---

12. Under the law, subdivision of land among heirs is not permitted when nonviable units are likely to result. Instead the law permits up to five persons to be registered as proprietors in common of the entire property. In practice, however, the land then is often unofficially subdivided among heirs and farmed individually; this produces a different pattern of actual ownership than is shown on official records. But this will make dealings increasingly difficult, to the detriment of development of the market in land.

and restructuring cooperative farms by improving membership arrangements and providing experienced managers. As noted, it is in the national interest to retain some large farms as breeding stations and seed farms although ownership of these need not be private. While some of the better run units might usefully remain in private ownership and benefit from the proposed management and credit program, all farms not held "in the national interest" must be considered as candidates for redistribution and ceilings on size.

Irrigation

Although irrigation potential is limited, its development can provide income improvement possibilities for a considerable number of the rural poor. It is in this context that plans should be made. About 7,000 hectares are now irrigated on five major schemes ranging in size from 200 to 4,700 hectares. Some 85 percent of the irrigated area produces rice, about 9 percent cotton, and the balance is used for onions. Current plans are to expand annual development capacity for major schemes from its present level of 800 hectares to about 2,000 hectares by 1978, by which time irrigated areas on major schemes would approximate 13,000 hectares. Simultaneously with the expansion of two existing schemes and construction of five new ones, further feasibility studies are to be carried out, and staff training intensified. Provisional outlay estimates are £7 million for the period 1974–78.

Minor irrigation is also given weight in the 1974–78 Development Plan. These propose the construction of thirteen schemes in four provinces totaling some 4,200 hectares, which would range in size from 100 to 500 hectares. Preliminary cost estimates are incomplete but are at least £350 per hectare. Schemes would be located in areas marginal for rainfed crops and would seek to reduce the need for famine relief. More detailed consideration may lead to a scaling down of the number of projects and a simplification of design, which would be wholly desirable in the light of present and likely future staff shortages.

The most important irrigation possibility is the Tana River Basin, for which detailed studies are available. A Tana River Development Authority was recently created, and a chairman appointed. Its main tasks are to monitor the design and execution of planned projects, to gather and store resource data, to monitor abstractions, and to carry out the needed additional studies.

Three organizations are now involved with irrigation: the Water Department (WD), the National Irrigation Board (NIB) and the Land and Farm Management Division (LFMD) of the Ministry of Agriculture. All major schemes are constructed and operated by the NIB, a semiautonomous organization answerable to the Ministry of Agriculture. Minor irrigation schemes, on the other hand, are designed and operated by three units of the LFMD. The expansion of minor schemes proposed in the 1974–78 plan would require a substantial increase and diversification in the work of the LFMD, and would result in competition with the Division's other tasks, particularly soil and water conservation, the importance of which cannot be overstressed.

It would be more efficient to allocate the sole responsibility for irrigation to the NIB, which is now the only organization with irrigation expertise. This change would allow the Water Department to concentrate on planning the overall development of the national water resource[13] and handle domestic water supply programs, and allow LFMD to expand its soil and water conservation and farm management activities.

---

13. The Government has accepted the recommendation of a second UNDP financed study for the preparation of a national water use plan. A strengthened WD should become the executing agency for this planning project.

NIB would certainly be fully extended in promoting large scale irrigation development, and would have to be expanded to handle small scale schemes. In the expansion, it should be recognized that large and small scale schemes call for different design, evaluation, and operational criteria. Both the civil and on-farm works are costly in large scale projects; technical and economic criteria need careful application in their design and appraisal, as well as in getting the maximum possible acreage of high value enterprises into the farming pattern. In small scale schemes, there may be more leeway in weighting social benefits. NIB must be equipped to do this work. Design of low cost schemes must be simple so that they do not require a level of management which costs more than they can support.

Target income is one of the major issues in large scale irrigation schemes, which are costly both in gross terms and on a per family basis. There is as yet no evidence that widespread irrigation development is an appealing proposition in economic terms. The main objective of such development must be to help combat the problem of increasing population pressure in rainfed areas. Policy should aim at the greatest possible number of beneficiaries, thereby making the maximum impact on low income groups. The present target income (£150 a year per family) exceeds average rural incomes by much more than is needed to compensate for the loss of managerial freedom and limited land rights which tenants of irrigation schemes must accept. For this reason, policy on target income and the associated plot size should be reviewed, taking account of average rural incomes and the management problems which may arise if the planned size of irrigated holdings were reduced. Reduction of target income to about £100 might be appropriate.

A further, all-pervasive issue is the need to build up staff capacity. Irrigation development is now overly dependent on non-Kenyans. This applies at all levels, including planners, engineers, surveyors, mechanics, and accountants. Irrigation development planning must take account of staff needs well in advance of construction of new projects, and construction should be phased so that Kenyan staff can be recruited, trained and, perhaps most important, given field experience under competent supervision before being called on to accept major responsibility.

Soil and Water Conservation

Soil conservation is a vital necessity in a land short country such as Kenya. Unless a better job is done, deterioration in per capita living levels is more probable than improvement in the decades ahead. A much more effective effort to conserve the agro-ecosystem is essential, and resources must be set aside for this purpose in all relevant development programs.

Despite a well established Soil Conservation Service and considerable past effort in this field, recent performance has been poor. The medium to low potential and range areas are most vulnerable and in need of protection, as they are under severe population pressure. Parts of Ukambani and Baringo districts are tragically eroded, and erosion and ecological deterioration is a common feature throughout the range areas, particularly around permanent water. But the problem is not confined to these areas. For example, the high potential land in Narok is threatened by exploitative use, as is much of Central Province, especially parts of Nyeri and Muranga districts.

Local leaders must be educated to the need for soil and water conservation. Field extension staff should be assigned full responsibility for promoting and policing conservation measures. This staff needs more in-service training on conservation techniques, and day-to-day technical guidance by the district officers of the Land and Farm Management Division whose responsibility it is to take care of conservation activity in the field. Extension staff should not spend time on litigation arising from enforcement. There is a cadre of staff in Government versed in litigation and employed in a related field, namely

Water Bailiffs. It is suggested that Water Bailiffs take on the legal aspects of enforcement, with their numbers being increased as necessary to do the job.

At a recent meeting of senior Government agricultural and administrative staff, the urgent need to improve soil and water conservation measures was acknowledged. The administrators promised their backing to technical staff in bringing to book farmers who fail to observe adequate conservation procedures. The problem is not the lack of legislative power to enforce conservation, but the will to use it. Nonetheless, there is a need to make existing legislation less cumbersome in application.

Less than 10 percent of Kenya's land area receives high rainfall, supports forests as natural vegetation and gives rise to permanent streams; this explains why water conservation is of paramount national importance. As explained in Chapter 1, a considerable part of the high potential land is occupied by forest. The bulk of this is indigenous forest which has been preserved for catchment protection. Many now believe that a part of this forest area should be diverted to agricultural use. Such a change from forest to agriculture would be irreversible. The matter must therefore be intensively studied before any action is taken, using the findings of the research already being carried out by East African Agriculture and Forestry Research Organization. Because the step is irreversible and adequate investigation will take time, change of use from forest to farming should be seen as a last resort. All other measures for expanding the supply of farmland and improving its distribution should be exhausted first.

Technical Services to Agriculture

Five ministries and eighteen statutory boards are the main sources of public services to farmers. As noted earlier, many services are successful, but in spite of continuing and often innovative efforts basic shortcomings persist.

The *research* effort is dispersed among a large number of organizations, including four units in the Ministry of Agriculture (MOA) and several statutory boards, but coordination is lacking, with the result that some urgent problems are neglected and work on others is duplicated. The research program neglects most food crops, with the notable exception of maize. Concentration on high potential areas, while of great importance, has resulted in a failure to examine production problems in localities less favorably endowed but increasingly used. A rigid, technically oriented commodity approach has produced only partial solutions to farmers' problems. This is because researchers have failed to grasp the merits of traditional farming systems and the limitations to change which are imposed by such factors as the seasonal labor constraint. The research program is not designed to meet the needs of smallholders.

The Department of Technical Services of the MOA administers *extension* work. Provincial directors of agriculture and their district agricultural officers carry out local programs, which are formulated by provincial and district agricultural committees on the basis of MOA guidelines. Staffing is generous (some 6,300 people). This work has had limited results, partly because extension advice is not integrated with a delivery system for inputs, credit, and marketing facilities. Due to the narrow focus of the underlying research, as already noted, the recommendations offered by the extension worker are often impractical and of little use. Workers often tend to "preach" down to farmers, rather than to "communicate" with them. Several of the parastatal bodies also carry out extension work, including those concerned with tea, coffee, and pyrethrum. These agencies are generally effective since their efforts are concentrated on a single commodity about which a great deal is known and for which complete service systems are available.

As the foregoing illustrates, expanding and improving research is a top priority task in agriculture. The Government should set up a working group of senior civil servants and agricultural scientists to recommend the best way to reorganize technical research. Several months might be allowed for this work. The aim would be to propose a detailed and time phased reorganization plan, including a personnel policy which ensures the recruitment and retention of good staff; long term funding to allow implementation of the appropriate research strategy, and an improved link between research and extension. Future research projects should center on solving practical problems in crop and animal husbandry, with a strong emphasis on small scale farming. The work should be designed so that results can be interpreted in terms of practical economic and farm management problems, including labor requirements of proposed innovations. The research staff itself should propose and design the specific programs and projects needed for the implementation of research policy. A research advisory board is needed, partly to help the Ministry of Finance and Planning assess priorities, progress, problems, and financial requirements. Despite their probable scarcity, each research project should have at least the parttime services of a farm management specialist and statistician.

The narrow commodity and geographic spread of research must be corrected, with more attention to pulses, millet, sorghum, oilseeds, horticultural crops, and sheep and goats. On wheat, work on stem rust, tillage methods, and production systems for wheat-rapeseed-leys should be stepped up. New cotton projects should contain a research component focusing on the constraints faced by small producers, including pest control, agronomic practices, and seasonal labor supplies. Bilateral technical assistance might be sought, possibly from an institution such as the Cotton Research Corporation of the United Kingdom. The existing staff of ten professionals in horticultural research is not enough, and economic and nutritional criteria should be added to the appraisal of results in this field. Opportunities for smallholder production need special attention. Researchers on coffee, tea, and pyrethrum should broaden coverage to include substitute and complementary crops, such as macadamia and essential oils and spices.

Research on East Coast fever will continue to need emphasis, with help from the FAO. Assistance from international research organizations should be sought to strengthen ongoing research on trypanosomiasis. Less costly control methods for contagious bovine pleuropneumonia merit investigation, while research on liver fluke parasites is needed to establish economic control measures. Efforts to develop a serological test for cysticercosis should be continued and more research on the control of internal parasites of sheep is needed, along with a survey of goat diseases followed by research projects to help find ways to control them. The UNDP/FAO wildlife disease research work should be fully supported. A great deal remains to be done in range management research, and pasture research needs to be expanded to include semi-arid and coastal areas. Much more work is also required on fodder crops, particularly in Zone IV and the coastal belt, and in small scale farming systems. The stratification of the beef cattle industry needs more attention and husbandry systems for dairy goats need to be developed for the tiny smallholdings.

Research is the priority claimant for foreign technical assistance and for resources to train Kenyan staff and foreign assistance should be designed with emphasis on training. Although there is a sufficient amount of research information available now to permit development programs to go ahead, at least a decade of lead time is typically necessary to produce practicable recommendations useful to farmers. The lengthy period between the initiation of research and the production of practical findings needs more recognition by policy makers.

The present extension research linkage is wholly inadequate. A unit of subject matter specialists within the Ministry of Agriculture would be helpful if made responsible for a two-way information flow between research and extension staff. The unit would evaluate research recommendations, translate them into a form usable by field extension staff, and brief research workers on farming problems encountered by extension staff. The Agricultural Information Center would draw on the linkage unit for the raw material needed to prepare extension aids, such as handbooks, pamphlets, posters, and film strips. With this in mind, the staff of the Center should be strengthened.

Extension work would benefit from improved supervision of the provincial directors of agriculture by headquarters. There is an urgent need to incorporate farm management advice into extension programs and to assure that inputs, credit, and marketing facilities are available. Extension agents need to recognize the constraints faced by the farmer and special attention should be paid to the need for female extension workers.

Farmer training centers are underused and require more staff and funds. Courses need review to make sure they are providing farm families with information they can use. Current proposals to merge training and extension are not acceptable; the training task is specialized and requires separate administration.

Mechanization

Tractors and combines are used on large farms, and public and private tractor hire services are available to both large and small farms. Seven major international firms deal in farm machinery, with two handling some 70 percent of the total volume. These firms have exclusive franchises, or operate as a direct branch of the manufacturer. Low turnover makes necessary a considerable markup to cover the cost of a national distribution network and a reliable service system. Machinery imports are free of customs duties. Customs and direct taxes are paid on tractor fuel. In 1971, there were an estimated 5,000 to 5,500 tractors on large scale farms, another 500 in local and central government hands, and some 1,000 to 1,500 in private use on small scale farms and in construction and transport. Ox power is used on smallholdings in certain localities.

Most smallholders depend entirely on hand tools (mainly the *jembe* and *panga*). Little can be done to improve these tools, although there is room for more and better hand operated equipment, such as shellers and pumps. In contrast, ox-drawn equipment, used in conjunction with trained oxen, could contribute to smallholder development in areas with sufficient land to produce a feed supply. Oxen are now used in several districts, including Nyanza, Kakamega, Nandi, Machakos, and Kitui, but very inefficiently. Performance could readily be improved if the impressive development work done at Egerton, Arusha, and Serere during the last fifteen years or so were drawn upon.

A wide range of proven ox-drawn equipment has been developed, including plows and tool frames with numerous fittings, all suitable for local manufacture and repair. The need now is to make this equipment readily available, and, most important, to teach farmers how to train and manage oxen. The mere training of animals in pairs would quickly increase the efficiency of use of the available power, and open up new demands for improved equipment. Any effort to expand and improve the use of ox power is believed by many to be a regressive step. In fact, it would be a great step forward, and in some areas a better use of oxen is the only way at this time to use power to increase the demand for labor and labor productivity. To this end, selected farmer training centers should offer courses in oxen training and the breeding, selection, and management of work animals.

Mechanized cultivators and two-wheel tractors have not proven to be very satisfactory so far, partly because it is difficult to produce a power unit at prices which can compete with larger conventional tractors. Nevertheless, there is a real need for power in some of the highly populated areas where it is costly to produce feed for oxen. Research and development of mechanized power sources for these areas should be intensified.

The Government's Tractor Hire Service, using some fifty tractors for soil preparation work, is heavily subsidized and it is unlikely that the service could be redesigned to make expansion recommendable. It would probably be better to phase out the service and use the equivalent of the amount of money it now loses, or more, to stimulate development of private contractor services. Private services are said to be shrinking, because of problems in getting purchase credit and spare parts, and the cumbersome procedures of the Guaranteed Minimum Return credit scheme. This is a problem which can and should be solved without delay.

Supply of Inputs

The Ministry of Agriculture's *seed* inspection service enforces legislation and certifies that seed offered for sale meets legally prescribed purity and germination standards. A commercial organization, the Kenya Seed Company (KSC), organizes the multiplication of maize, sunflower, and pasture seed.[14] The Wheat Board handles wheat seed. Improvements in the seed system for wheat were being considered in late 1972. Under the proposal, the KSC would take over responsibility for wheat seed multiplication, as the Wheat Board has had difficulty in managing an effective scheme. Distribution of KSC and imported seed is largely handled by the Kenya Farmers' Association (KFA) through a network of depots and agents, mainly in the high potential areas. Planting materials for commodities such as tea, pyrethrum, and coffee are handled by the respective development agencies (such as the Coffee Board), through nurseries located in main production areas. Cotton seed supplies are handled by the Cotton Lint and Seed Marketing Board (CLSMB) through the ginnery network. Production and distribution of sugarcane planting material is loosely organized by the Ministry of Agriculture and by private growers on estates and sugar settlements.

Improvements are needed in distribution of maize seed to small farmers and to producers in medium potential and marginal maize areas located considerable distances from the point of distribution. The seed market is limited to a short period of the year, but plentiful supplies must be available within easy reach of farmers. Positioning of stocks is difficult under these circumstances. Distribution outlets are probably too few, with retailers being reluctant to stock maize seed, partly because of the seasonality of demand and partly because they feel that Kenya Farmers Association commissions are too low. These problems will become increasingly acute as more small farmers become interested in using better seed. Possible solutions include higher agent commissions, improved credit facilities to agents, and closer coordination among Ministry of Agriculture extension staff, the Kenya Farmers Association, and the Kenya Seed Company to improve demand estimates.

For other major smallholder crops, the research stations have not yet produced much basic material suitable for multiplication. As material becomes available, there will be a need to establish additional multiplication facilities. Whether these should be part of the Kenya Seed Company organization is a matter for study. On the one hand, the Company has proven itself capable of responding to a massive demand for a crop needing relatively sophisticated multiplication techniques. On the other hand, it is a monopoly supplier, a position which has potential dangers; and it already has a big job to meet the expected substantial increases in demand for maize seed. Fostering private seed production would probably promote efficiency, but because of demand constraints it may be difficult to generate much private interest for other than maize seed. A quasi-governmental organization, such as the Agricultural Development Corporation, with appropriate specialized expertise and facilities, may be a suitable alternative.

14. The remarkable rise in the uptake of improved maize seed from a quantity sufficient for an estimated 13,600 hectares in 1964 to over 300,000 hectares in 1972 is largely due to the efforts of KSC working in close collaboration with the Ministry of Agriculture and its maize breeding staff. For other smallholder crops, the research stations have not yet produced much material suitable for multiplication.

Pricing and Marketing

Consumer and producer prices for milk and beef are controlled by the Government. In relation to production costs, producer prices for milk are too high relative to beef and other types of meat. This causes the medium and high potential areas to overallot resources to dairying, creates costly milk surpluses, and inhibits beef exports. Both the milk price and the method of pricing require adjustment. As the first step, the producer price of milk should be lowered from the present figure of Sh0.745 per liter by, say, 15 percent to 20 percent, perhaps in two stages a few months apart. This would help the Kenya Cooperative Creameries meet operating costs, accumulate some funds for use in developing the industry and servicing its capital charges, and, most important, improve fluid milk quality and packaging, an urgent necessity. (This experimental price reduction may not be sufficient for the medium term.)

The second needed step is to introduce a seasonal price differential to even out fluctuation in deliveries, which now peak sharply in the wet season when production costs are low. This fluctuation can result in excessive factory capacity and low use rates, or simply dumping excess milk or milk by-products at peak seasons, and endangers supplies for the fresh milk market in the dry season. Additionally, as soon as possible, a blended price system for milk should be introduced, based on actual end-use realization, and taking full account of the capital costs in processing and marketing. This system would include farmer quotas based on dry-season delivery levels, to assure that in the wet season at least this quota amount receives the price earned by fluid milk sales rather than the lower price payable for milk used in manufacturing. This would also permit the Government to pursue its policy of favoring smallholders in agricultural development programs (the price adjustment proposed here would still leave dairying an attractive enterprise for smallholders). A progressive reduction in the maximum farmer quota might be undertaken on a preannounced schedule to permit larger farms to adjust their enterprise mix and smaller farmers to plan to take up dairying or expand output.

This proposal is not intended to restrict the supply of milk and dairy products to the domestic market. Rather, its purpose is to bring market supply and demand into balance at prices which fully reflect costs, and to promote an output pattern which forestalls losses on exports. Domestic demand will continue to grow, but requirements can be met at a greatly lower resource cost than at present. Indeed, the supply response to the present milk price has not yet had time to fully appear; it may well be such that the resumption of the export of dairy cattle will merit early consideration.

The proposed adjustment in the milk price level and pricing system would help shift resources into beef, a highly desirable move to enable exploitation of the strong world beef market. But a much greater inducement is needed, i.e., the freeing of beef prices to let them rise to export parity levels. The increase would probably be in the 20 percent to 30 percent range, over present levels.[15] This would help open up expansion possibilities for alternative sources of meat (pork, mutton, goat, poultry) and for pulses; shift resources out of dairying into beef; improve cattle offtake rates, especially for the lower grades; and lessen the rural subsidy to urban consumers.

A rapid expansion of the market for poultry and pork can be expected only if beef prices are permitted to rise. With higher beef prices, the considerable potential in pigs and poultry can be exploited, particularly if a reliable feed supply is assured by means of a large scale development program for maize by means of development projects of the type suggested for Western and Eastern Kenya in Chapter 6, and through maize price stabilization. As the most efficient converters of maize, these two enterprises can

15. These figures are indicative only, as the Kenya Meat Commission, the monopoly exporter, does not make export price data available to the public, and has not published an annual report since 1970.

probably absorb a considerable tonnage of maize at prices higher than may be realizable on the export market over the longer term. In any event, pig and poultry expansion can contribute significantly to national development by enabling more beef exports.

The price of maize is basic in promoting a better use of resources. The tendency has been to adjust the price payable by the Maize and Produce Board (MPB) rather sharply upwards or downwards in response to essentially weather-induced variations in annual output. This results in overreaction by producers, along with costly emergency measures of disposition or procurement abroad. Maize now appears to be fully priced relative to other crops. What should be done is to gradually decrease the support price until it more nearly matches the crop's increasing value as feed. If this action is combined with getting modern production methods to smallholders through recommended intensive programs and effective price stabilization, adequate supplies should become available at lower prices relative to other products than is the case today. Once these programs are proven and more is known about the livestock industry's capacity to use maize at export competitive prices, a longer range goal on maize output can be established.

The future of the parastatal organizations in marketing is a key issue to which there is no general answer. Each board must be judged in terms of the specific task to which it is assigned, its actual performance, and the experience or expectations concerning alternatives—mainly direct government operations and the private sector. Perhaps the most important indicator is the degree to which a board has exclusive rights in its regulatory–commercial activity. It is clear that boards oriented primarily to the export market cannot become monopolists in the traditional sense. These boards must compete on international markets, which means that prices must be designed to draw forth production; a measure of operational efficiency must be maintained; quality controls must be enforced, and programs should be designed which help farmers reduce costs. For the three major export crops, coffee, tea, and pyrethrum, the boards are doing a good job in providing farmers with inputs, credit, technical know-how, and a workable system for marketing the product. Of course, these organizations can be improved, and the Government has a role in monitoring their internal activities.[16]

The position is less satisfactory for products marketed internally, and domestic marketing would probably be more efficient and developmental if boards shared the task with the private sector. The Government should consider withdrawing statutory monopolies in livestock, and making investment and operating credit available to parastatal bodies and private enterprise on an equal basis for the marketing task. In livestock products, a mixed system supported by information, grades, and standards provided by Government would likely do a better job than the present system. For poultry, private enterprise can readily handle processing and market development, with Government providing sanitary and grading standards and inspection services. For pigs, the trend should be towards small farm production, and local slaughter. The task of moving the industry in this direction would be easier if the powers of the Pig Board and the Uplands Bacon Factory were redefined, making them elements in a competitive system. In dairying, neither a near monopoly nor a national marketing organization can serve a useful purpose. The monopoly attributes of the Kenya Cooperative Creameries concerning sales rights should be terminated, giving regional cooperatives and private entities a better chance to undertake the task if they so desire. If this type of marketing redesign were accepted, the job of the Livestock Marketing Division of the Ministry of

16. Returns to small coffee growers in 1972, for example, were about 32 percent of the world coffee price f.o.b. Mombasa. Although this was due mainly to heavy charges by local cooperatives, which retained 37 percent of the value received f.o.b. Mombasa, both the Coffee Board and the Government should be vitally concerned about the effects on production and income of this arrangement.

Agriculture would be to formulate and enforce rules and regulations to promote the growth of an efficient marketing system for all livestock products.

Grain marketing is more complex, as many more small farmers are involved. The system must not only be physically efficient, but must also provide facilities which will permit stock and price management. A lessening of direct controls and an opening up of opportunities for more private initiative would be helpful in doing this job. Moving maize from local surplus areas to places where it is needed for stock feed or human consumption does not require a national organization with a monopoly on grain movements. There is no need to gather all grain at central points from which it must be redistributed, at a substantial cost of movement in each direction. Parastatal activity in grain markets should be limited to implementing government price and stock management programs. Commercial operations by parastatals should rest on the ability to compete with private and cooperative enterprise, and not on exclusive rights.

In taking action along these lines, the first step would be to establish a close working relationship between the Wheat Board and the Maize and Produce Board, and to remove monopoly powers from each. The resulting gains could include lower handling costs because of joint use of facilities, and an increased trader activity which, in turn, could lead to construction of private facilities to reduce costs of collection, distribution, and storage. A closer working relationship should also be able to produce better planning information at lower cost. Judgments on import needs, export possibilities, and price policy must be developed jointly for wheat and maize, as they are substitutes to some degree on both the production and consumption sides. Closer cooperation should also be able to reduce administrative costs, and might allow a smaller field staff to do the marketing and carry on such development work as may be assigned, such as working with stockists and local cooperatives to improve marketing.

Certain principles should be given weight in deciding how to redesign the Government's effort to improve agricultural marketing. Marketing is an integral part of the development problem for any commodity, and needs to be seen jointly with the farm production side. An effort by Government to improve marketing and pricing may or may not involve direct market intervention through actual purchase and sales of commodities. If market intervention is undertaken, the parastatal agency charged with the task should work under a specific set of instructions from Government which make clear its discretionary powers on terms of purchase and sale, and establish criteria of performance. Provision for testing performance needs to be a part of the system and this can be done by permitting competitive institutions to operate in the market. If the parastatal body is asked to undertake activities which are not commercially oriented, such as famine relief or an export transaction at a loss, provision should be made for an appropriate accounting system and for reimbursement from public funds of the costs. Similarly, if any agency is asked to undertake developmental activities, such as advising stockists on storage shed design, it should be reimbursed. Parastatal bodies should be seen as a part of a coordinated system for the development of production and marketing activity, entering the market where necessary, but without monopoly powers.

It is doubtful if the present degree of price intervention is productive. At the very least, the price determination system should be reviewed with the thought of turning over much of the task to the market under a set of rules and regulations aimed at sustaining a competitive process. The removal of the monopoly position of government sponsored agencies in handling staple farm products, as just proposed, would open the door to an improved price stabilization performance by permitting the market to operate. The task of the appropriate boards would then be to stand ready to buy nonperishable staples at support prices announced before planting season, and to implement a stocks policy which would hold seasonal and interyear price variations at their economic level. Both imports and exports may be used to complement domestic storage for this purpose, if cheaper. The system should operate on a no-profit, no-loss basis over any period of, say, five years. Costs of direct commodity developmental (promotional) activities carried out by the relevant boards should not be charged to the price stabilization program. The determination of optimum carryover levels (and hence storage capacity) and management procedures requires a great deal of study. Market prices significantly above support prices are no cause for alarm; rather they are a datum for use in establishing stock release schedules, and the support price for the coming year. The fact that it is not uncommon for the maize price at different locations at the same time to be both lower than the Maize Board's purchase price and sharply higher (often double) suggests both the nature of the problem and the scope for improvement.[17]

The minimum support prices announced before planting time should be determined by the planning and management unit of the Ministry of Agriculture (discussed later), taking full account of the evidence and judgments of the boards concerned. The role of the Ministry in price determination is critical because, as amply demonstrated by the recent sharp expansion in milk production,[18] intercommodity relationships must be given much more weight than in the past. However, the boards must have complete authority and responsibility for implementation, including selling schedules and carryover levels.

Determining appropriate support prices is difficult and acreage and supply response information is limited. Many smallholders have little leeway in resource use, and the availability of inputs is probably a major determinant, which suggests that price adjustments will have to be largely experimental at the outset. Brusque changes should be avoided, and prices which appear likely to lead to an accumulation of supplies in excess of stabilization requirements should be lowered, taking into account the probability of occurrence of poor crop years.

Credit and Cooperatives

Many institutions and programs provide *credit* to farmers. The oldest are those which served European settlers, including commercial banks; merchant suppliers, mainly the Kenya Farmers Association and similar firms; the Land and Agricultural Bank, now amalgamated with the Agricultural Finance Corporation; and the Guaranteed Minimum Return program.[19] The more recent institutions provide credit to smallholders, including the cash crop agencies, such as the Kenya Tea Development Authority, the Pyrethrum Marketing Board, the Cotton Lint and Seed Marketing Board, and the Horticultural Crop Development Authority; the cooperative societies, especially those associated with coffee production, and the more recent Cooperative Production Credit Scheme; the major commercial banks and merchant suppliers; the FAO input supply projects; and the smallholder credit schemes of the Agricultural Finance Corporation.

There are also credit programs to help the transition from the formerly European commercial agriculture to one based on African ownership, notably in connection with the British-supported land transfer program and its related Agricultural Settlement Fund. Outside the institutional sources, there is also a traditional supply of rural credit, and this includes transactions at the village level and between members of families and clans. Village headmen and local merchants also provide credit in various forms. There are no studies of this informal credit market, but rural indebtedness of this type is thought to be small.

Of some 1.2 million smallholders, probably fewer than 200,000 have access to

---

17. For example, during several months in 1973, the market price of a 90-kg bag of maize in Kitale was somewhat below the Maize Board's purchase price of Sh35, and over Sh70 in Kisumu.

18. The intake of whole milk by the Kenya Cooperative Creameries was increased from 214 million liters in 1971 to 265 million liters in 1972, in terms of whole milk equivalent.

19. This program provides seasonal production credit for growers with more than fifteen acres under wheat or hybrid maize.

formal credit; most of these are believed to be in the top 20 percent in terms of farm size. This figure includes cooperative society members who obtain credit mainly for the coffee crop. Most of the crop agencies provide credit in kind for planting materials and fertilizer, but little or no credit is available from any source for subsistence crops. The three smallholder medium-term credit programs of the Agricultural Finance Corporation amount to less than 15 percent of the corporation loan portfolio and reach only some 15,000 farmers, mostly those who are better off.

It is estimated that loans outstanding to smallholders at the end of 1972 totaled about £18.3 million. Of this amount, some 66 percent came from the land transfer program. Loans to large scale farmers amounted to some £29 million. Overall, it is estimated that the 3,000-odd large farms receive more than 60 percent of all farm credit, and over 80 percent of the short and medium term credit available from organized sources. These farms produce about 50 percent of the marketed output from agriculture. By comparison, the 1.2 million smallholders get about 20 percent of the short and medium term credit, and produce not only half of the marketed output but also subsistence for some 90 percent of the nation's total population. Thus the adjustment of the credit institutions to foster the smallholder agriculture is far from complete. The institutional structure is fragmented and there is little coordination of sources or flows of credit to farmers. There are few operative special policies or regulations affecting the provision of farm credit by financial institutions, and the agricultural credit system is effectively isolated from the wider financial system of the country. Consequently, the various categories of farms and types of production are not served on a uniform or integrated basis and this is reflected in the imbalance in lending between the subsectors, and, most importantly, in the lack of coordination between credit provision, input supplies, and extension advice.

The farm *cooperatives* are the major channels for the processing and marketing of certain smallholder cash crops, especially coffee, pyrethrum, and dairy produce. Increasingly, they also provide farm requisites, such as seed, fertilizers, and pesticides; and short term credit, cattle dipping facilities, and tractor hire services. There are some 1,500 active societies, with an estimated membership of 500,000, as well as a small number of production cooperatives, including farming, fishing, ranching, charcoal production, and native crafts. Most of the 1,500 "primary societies" are grouped into forty cooperative unions on a regional and functional basis. The societies and unions are members of the Kenya National Federation of Cooperatives, the apex organization, as is the Cooperative Bank of Kenya. The Cooperative College of Kenya provides training services.

In addition, there are the formerly European farmer cooperatives: the Kenya Planters Cooperative Union, Ltd., Kenya Cooperative Creameries, Ltd., Kenya Farmers' Association, Ltd., and the Horticultural Cooperative Union. Their main concern is the processing and marketing of coffee, dairy products, cereals and fruits, respectively, though the KFA is also the largest farm supply merchant.

The Department of Cooperative Development of the Ministry of Cooperatives and Social Services has broad regulatory and development functions, and participates at all levels and in all activities of the movement. Its operations have reduced the overall responsibility of the National Federation. Although a large part of the Department's energies over the last eight years has been taken up with auditing, supervision, and control, a concerted development planning effort has been initiated.

The agricultural credit program is unbalanced in favor of the land transfer program and larger farmers; it largely ignores the traditional small scale sector. The first remedial step is to set up central machinery to guide and regulate the credit institutions. There is great scope for better links between lenders to coordinate programs, and for lending institutions to establish closer links with outside bodies whose activities affect the use of credit, including the marketing boards and the Ministry of Agriculture. Less complicated records and accounts are needed, and institutions should coordinate to enable checks on creditworthiness and permit reciprocal repayments by deductions from crop sale proceeds. There is also a need for training programs; both in-house courses and broader based programs in the educational institutions.[20]

Rigid adherence to the use of land as collateral and related creditworthiness requirements obstruct the efficient use of credit. A larger field staff of education oriented "collectors" would help improve repayment performance. Interest rates should be raised to provide a return which enables greater credit coverage. Known yields to investment on smallholdings indicate that a much higher rate could be charged without greatly reducing the profitability of borrowing. Rates on deposits should also be raised to increase savings for use by credit agencies. Once an effective credit system is established, the Treasury will undoubtedly find it possible to provide funds for farm credit expansion.

A concerted program to expand credit use is needed. Credit is required for land purchase; to permit capital reconstruction, particularly for livestock after drought periods; to improve subsistence crops, especially where farm size restricts cash cropping unless land can be released from its subsistence use; for special purposes, such as school fees (school "dropouts" of a year or more due to poor crops or prices are quite commonplace); and for the entire range of outlets open to the many farmers who are "technically uncreditworthy" because of existing charges against their assets. But the greatest scope for credit use is in lubricating the adoption of improved husbandry practices, especially where fairly radical changes are being promoted. In this sense, the use of credit should be strongly fostered, rather than seen as a need which merits no more than a passive response by credit agencies.

The expansion of credit use can only be achieved if the capacity to deliver and absorb it can be developed. All this adds up to the need for service systems of which credit is a part. To be an effective participant, the Agricultural Finance Corporation (AFC) probably needs some reorganization, and the Ministry of Agriculture needs to do a better planning and coordinating job.

The complexity of the credit improvement task has been recognized, and the Government is making arrangements for an inclusive study. This will investigate needed institutional changes, including policy machinery, delivery mechanisms (and their integration with complete smallholder service systems), and evaluation of the needs and scope for more credit. The study should also design credit projects suitable for foreign support.

Cooperatives show promise of becoming an important commercial institution in marketing, processing, input retailing, field services, and credit for smallholders. To further this promise, it would be useful to:

- Improve election procedures for officers;
- Expand the management program of the Cooperative College, drawing on more foreign finance where possible and using the University of Nairobi for advanced courses;
- Standardize conditions of service for personnel nationwide and improve the possibilities for an attractive career in the cooperative field;
- Strengthen central control and audit procedures;
- Develop the Department of Cooperative Development (DCD) planning and implementation capability;
- Strengthen coordination between the Department and the Ministry of Agriculture;
- Expand the area coverage of cooperative production credit and saving schemes;
- Provide members with farmgate transportation services, and make cooperative services more widely available in hitherto neglected areas.

---

20. The innovations of the Cooperative Production Credit Scheme deserve close study as an example of what might be done.

Rural Services

Complete operational responsibility and authority for rural domestic *water supplies* should be given to the Water Department to avoid further failures in design, construction, operation, and maintenance. The Ministry of Health has largely accomplished its goal of demonstrating the benefits of piped water, and should now work only in remote areas. Although county councils seem interested in expanding their water supply activities, perhaps for revenue purposes, there is little in the record which suggests they are able to do the job well. Ongoing self-help schemes which are now in the hands of county councils should be turned over to the Water Department, and permission to collect funds for new schemes should not be given until the Department has approved the technical feasibility of such proposals. The Water Department could train staff to operate the larger self-help schemes and take them over on a phased basis as circumstances permit.[21] The Department should also take over the responsibility for water supplies in settlement areas from the Department of Settlement.

These changes would result in a sharp increase in the Water Department's workload, and more resources and better organization would be needed. More mobile district water teams should be created as soon as practicable to handle operation, maintenance, and construction. The size of the total national water supply program will have to be keyed to careful projections of the supply of qualified staff and criteria to determine geographical distribution of the program should be developed. The answer to the difficult question of water charges depends in part on the weight which is to be given to income redistribution, and on judgments as to the effect of a convenient water supply on health, nutrition, and productivity. At the very least, operation and maintenance costs of systems delivering to individual outlets should be paid by the beneficiaries. But a total recovery of outlays is unlikely, and subsidies on communal supplies may be desirable.

In designing the attack on *nutrition* problems, it must be recognized that there is no short term answer and that a higher yielding agriculture is a fundamental part of the solution. The groups requiring priority attention are smallholders in marginal areas and families with very small farms in high and medium potential areas, including those with female heads of household. The basic need is to develop and extend more drought-resistant varieties of maize and higher yielding millet and sorghum varieties. More research on legumes and high-lysine maize can also be helpful in the medium term. Increased production of fruit and vegetables is required, along with the expansion of small stock. Increased livestock productivity will help pastoralists, but famine relief will continue to be necessary. The urban poor require an increase in the marketed supply of crops with a high nutrient value, complemented by institutional feeding programs and food fortification (for example, sugar and vitamin A). The nutrition education effort should be focused on pregnant and lactating women, many of whom suffer from intra-family food distribution customs.

Kenyatta and Karen Colleges, along with the Institute for Development Studies and the Department of Community Health of the University of Nairobi, should be given major responsibility for nutrition program evaluation and staff training. A select group from these agencies might provide the secretariat for a government working party on nutrition, to be chaired by the Office of the President.

The responsibility for rural *roads* policy, planning, construction, and maintenance should be concentrated in the Ministry of Works (MOW). No other agency has the staff, experience, or equipment to undertake these tasks; the one exception is forest roads, which should continue in the hands of the Ministry of Natural Resources. To improve interministry coordination, the Government should place the Roads Department

---

21. These proposals do not rule out the possibility of subsequently returning the responsibility for rural water supplies to local authorities, if and when they are able to do the job.

of MOW in the same relationship to its client ministries as the Building Department of the MOW now has. The client ministries would then have the task of justifying their road proposals to the MOW; for example, the Ministry of Lands and Settlement, for settlement roads; the Ministry of Agriculture, for special purpose roads (tea, sugar, etc.), and general feeder roads; and the Ministry of Tourism and Wildlife, for tourist roads. The MOW would study proposals in terms of relative returns and the relationship to the national road network, and the Ministry of Finance would continue to control the distribution of the development budget among the various classes of roads, and the size and distribution of the maintenance budget.

In deciding upon local road priorities, ways will have to be found to make the District and Provincial Development Committees effective in expressing local views. The Committees should assess local needs and priorities on an annual basis and within a five-year perspective for the consideration of the MOW.

The MOW will need to consider setting up special decentralized units to handle local roads. These should be able to construct, upgrade, and maintain unclassified roads, using labor intensive methods where appropriate. Each unit might report to a senior executive officer in the MOW, and work under a vote covering its core staff and equipment along with a block sum for payment of seasonal labor. Experiments along these lines should begin as soon as practicable, perhaps initially with the assistance of a consulting firm experienced in labor intensive methods of road construction.

The rural roads program should be carefully integrated with agricultural development projects. An increase in expenditures on rural roads is needed in the years just ahead, and the Government should consider mobilizing local sources of finance to help meet the costs.

Taxation

Agricultural taxes account for a small and falling proportion of total tax revenues. The appropriate basis for taxing agriculture, along with the tax level, must be assessed as part of a wider review of national fiscal policy. This assessment should take into account the future role of local authorities in the governmental system and the set of production expansion incentives to be given to the agricultural sector. In the meantime, the overall burden of taxation on agriculture should not be increased.

The scale of allowances provided in the income tax legislation should be reviewed with the aim of making allowances more development oriented. Abatements and allowances might be made more favorable for entrepreneurs who take special measures to increase employment, and new incentives might be offered for firms undertaking projects in the national interest.

If imposed at all, commodity taxes should be levied by the Central Government; if necessary, local authorities should be provided with alternative revenue instruments or a form of revenue sharing.

The justification for export taxes (or subsidies) needs to be made in the context of Kenya's overall trade policies. If imposed, export taxes should be on an ad valorem basis, or, if specific, the rates should vary with world prices. Consideration might be given to a scale of levies designed to bear least heavily on the small producer.

A land tax might be a powerful tool for influencing land use and providing public revenue and needs to be seriously considered when an inclusive review of fiscal policy and administration is undertaken.

Information for Planning

Jointly with data-using agencies, the Central Bureau of Statistics (CBS) should reexamine the objectives of its agricultural surveys, and try to produce better smallholder data on: acreages of major crops, both planted and harvested; yields; farming systems; use of modern inputs and farming practices by enterprise; and labor inputs and wage rates by season and crops. Where feasible, this information should be by district and ecological zone.

Survey results need to be checked against other sources of information. For example, statistics for tea, coffee, and cotton could be compared with corresponding data produced by the statutory agencies.[22] At the enumerator level, data should be checked against alternative sources, such as the Special Rural Development Programs. Agricultural technicians in the survey areas could check findings. A formal link is required between the CBS and the Ministry of Agriculture at the field level. One possibility is district Statistics Review Committees, each consisting of the District Farm Management Officer, the District Extension Officer, the District Representative of the CBS, and, where available, a representative of the Department of Urban and Regional Physical Planning. These Committees would need to be in close touch with District Development Committees charged with district planning.

The Ministry of Agriculture is the main client for farm management data and its Farm Management Section should provide supervisors for farm management surveys, or take over the entire task. Extension officers in the survey areas could assist in the enumerations. Provision for transport of survey staff is necessary. Enumerators should be trained, perhaps at Farmers Training Centers.

A stronger central staff is needed, both in the CBS and the Farm Management Section of the Ministry of Agriculture. Senior staff doing field supervision should be freed from administrative duties. Crop cutting would be useful, and could be started in priority areas, such as those selected for district planning. Data should be released to users more quickly; the proposed Statistics Review Sub-Committees could help cut delays, as revalidations would be less necessary. Use of a uniform format for recording and collation would also save processing time. Particular efforts need to be made to install and adequate data production system in new project areas and funds for this purpose should be included in the project.

The network of meteorological observation stations throughout East Africa requires expansion, and the agro-meteorological section of the East African Meteorological Department should be developed. This is necessary to improve agricultural forecasting services and their use in commodity management, and to provide planning information for the marginal areas into which increasing numbers of people are having to migrate. The Government should propose to the East African Community that foreign aid be sought for this purpose.

The recently launched soil survey project needs to be redesigned to stress those areas of primary concern for the development effort, particularly the densely settled parts of Nyanza and Western Provinces and selected parts of Lamu District. Large farm areas should be deemphasized.

---

22. This type of validation would help forestall errors such as the recent finding that the tea area in Kakamega is larger than acreage under tea in Kisii, a fairly obvious mistake.

Chapter 5

Public Services Organization

It is fully recognized by the Government that the organization and administration of the public services to agriculture need improvement so that resources can be concentrated on attaining development goals. For example, technical research should have higher status and priority; there is an urgent need to improve the organization of support for smallholders, and water resource management needs more attention than it is likely to get if the Ministry of Agriculture continues to carry major responsibilities. Change should be based on thorough study, however, as shifts in agency responsibilities and in administrative procedures can waste scarce manpower and disrupt ongoing programs.

Of the ministries concerned with agriculture, only the Ministry of Agriculture has a significant planning division. However, much of the time of this planning division goes into short horizon work and little time is left to consider long term strategy. The division has even found it difficult to prepare enough projects to absorb the available external aid. The Government has acknowledged the need to strengthen planning in the Ministry of Agriculture, and we have suggested that three units be set up, each responsible to a deputy permanent secretary for development planning and management. These units would be:

(a) Programming and Budgeting Division. Following the Ndegwa Report's recommendations, this unit should prepare the annual financial and manpower budgets; design management systems, including work program outlines for divisions and field offices; oversee disbursement of funds, including external aid; and monitor program and project progress.

(b) Development Planning Division, in three sections:
  (i) Sector Planning Section, to do overall sector planning, guide regional and district planning, and develop land use policy and long term strategies for the annual and five-year plans. The section should give emphasis to most pressing planning problems, such as the rural poor, the lower rainfall areas, and the most densely populated rural areas.
  (ii) Commodity Planning Section, to design national commodity programs, including production, marketing, and pricing; set up policy guidelines for the statutory boards; and coordinate policy with other ministries.
  (iii) Market Development Section, to assemble and analyze information on supply, demand, stocks, and prices of products and inputs; and study market trends and develop outlets for raw and processed products in domestic and foreign markets.

(c) Project Preparation Division, to identify projects and prepare them for appraisal and implementation. The division should have technical specialists, economists, and financial analysts, and should work closely with the Development Planning Division, the Planning and Budgeting Division, and the various technical departments. The division should translate the strategies and programs of the Development Planning Division and technical departments into implementable national projects, and help the provincial and district staff to design local projects. It should not be assigned any other type of duty.

Strengthening the planning and management capacity of the Ministry of Agriculture in this way merits high priority. Much of the manpower for the new structure can be found in the existing Planning Division. But more middle level and senior professional staff are needed. Experienced expatriate personnel should probably continue to be used for key advisory tasks but eventual phasing out should be anticipated and carefully planned. With this is mind, a prime function of the proposed Development Planning and Management Department would be on-the-job training of sector planning and project evaluation personnel.

Sector planning in other ministries associated with agriculture also needs attention. As sectoral planning units are built up, the Ministry of Finance and Planning can be relieved of sectoral work and concentrate on macro-economic planning, the allocation of resources between competing claims, coordination of policy, and the monitoring of plan implementation.

The *Ndegwa Report* noted that the relationship between the statutory boards and their parent ministries ran all the way from too much board autonomy to cases in which civil servants interfered in day-to-day operations. The Government should limit ministerial control to policy matters, and arrange that a great deal more ministry effort go into developing coherent policies for the Boards—so that their activities reinforce each other and direct government development work. This staff work for agriculture should be done by the office of the deputy permanent secretary for development planning and management of the Ministry of Agriculture. No need is foreseen for new specialized commercial and regulatory boards. Instead, the longer term goal should be amalgamation and a phasing of indispensable functions into the ministries as circumstances permit. However, Government supervision and control of the parastatals needs strengthening, and the professional staff of the Inspectorate of Statutory Boards should be reinforced. The accounting system and financial procedures of the Statutory Boards should be improved and standardized and the prompt publication of audited accounts is indispensable. The boards should be made subject to the provisions of Treasury Circular No. 11 of September 1972, and be required to review budget proposals and policy statements with the Programming and Budgeting Division of the Ministry of Agriculture.[1] As previously noted, steps need to be taken to remove monopoly powers from some of the statutory boards.

It is essential that the Government pay more attention to interministerial coordination on land use matters. The Land Use Committee should be activated and meet regularly and should have a senior officer, located in the Office of the President, to prepare the agenda for meetings, to develop action strategies from policy decisions made in the Committee (in conjunction with staff in the operating ministries), and to follow up on implementation.

---

1. Treasury Circular No. 11 requires that budget requests submitted to the Ministry of Finance include a defense of all proposed outlays for ongoing programs. Hitherto, the requirement has been limited to proposed incremental expenditure.

Appendix A. Annexes in the Agricultural Sector Survey[†]

Annex No.	Title
1	The Land Resource and Its Development Potential
2	The Outlook for Demand for Agricultural Products
3	Land Tenure and Settlement
4	Expansion Possibilities in Crop Production and Processing
5	Grazing Livestock and Wildlife: Production and Marketing
6	Improving Agricultural Research and Extension
7	Agricultural Credit
8	Local Planning and Participation in Rural Development
9	Nutrition
10	Forestry
11	Fisheries
12	Irrigation
13	Agriculture: General Summary and Recommendations of Recent ILO/UNDP Study
14	Pigs and Poultry
15	Wildlife and Tourism in Rural Development
16	Rural Cooperatives
17	Rural Roads, Water Supplies, and Electrification
18	Agricultural Taxes and Subsidies
19	Selected Farm Inputs and Agro-Industries
20	Statistical Annex

[†] Agricultural Sector Survey—Kenya. World Bank Report No. 254a-KE, December 20, 1973, unpublished with restricted circulation.

Appendix B. Project Possibilities for Foreign Lenders

The judgments and recommendations on strategy and policy outlined in this appendix should be expressed partly through a set of agricultural development projects, including some which are designed to utilize assistance from abroad. As has been noted, Kenya has been unable to prepare enough projects to absorb all of the funds available from foreign lenders, and the Ministry of Agriculture and agriculture-related ministries have been unable to spend all of the funds allotted to them in recent years. Part of the problem arises from the great range of ecological conditions, the complex bureaucratic structure, the dispersion of decisionmaking power and capacity in matters affecting the rural community, and the fact that agriculture is still in transition from the colonial days. Another reason for the lack of projects is the inherent difficulty in defining a clear-cut development strategy and mobilizing political and civil service support for what must be agriculture's central focus—the relatively underprivileged smallholder with reasonable production expansion potential. Another very important obstacle is the political need to assure an equitable geographical and tribal distribution of effort, a fact which conditions suitable project designs. Still another difficulty is the limited amount of technical and socioeconomic evidence which is available and a good deal of fairly speculative judgment must be used in identifying optimum investment opportunities. Implementation problems also must be given weight; particularly difficult is the core task of designing workable smallholder service systems, and assuring that expenditure patterns fully reflect the need to make production expansion the paramount objective in integrated agricultural development projects.

Project possibilities for foreign donors listed in the following pages for the consideration of the Government try to take the constraints hitherto mentioned into account. Priorities are indicated in the proposed disbursement table which follows the project descriptions. Loan amounts for the projects shown in the table are indicative only, particularly for second phase activities. They total close to US$100 million in the first five-year period, including funds set aside for storage and marketing, credit, and rural water supplies and roads. When the project-associated net increase in local outlays for agriculture is added, the increment to investment in the sector during the five-year span would be significant in absolute terms and in relation to historical outlay levels; in fact, the rate of expansion is probably close to the maximum which is administratively feasible. The proposed foreign-supported expenditures for the second half of the ten-year period are still higher, although it is obvious that these need to be evaluated in the light of experience with the first five-year period, taking changing circumstances fully into account. (As noted in the Preface to Part III, the contribution of the proposed projects to the attainment of government goals for production, employment, and income, while undoubtedly significant, cannot be estimated in a meaningful way until preliminary work on project preparation is completed.) The proposed projects are:

Project 1: Integrated Agricultural Development, Eastern Kenya

Purpose:	To expand smallholder output and raise living levels in the lower, medium-potential parts of Central and Eastern Provinces which have low economic activity but reasonable production expansion potential.
Location:	Because of work already under way, the project should be started at two locations, in Machakos District and the Mbere Division of Embu District.
Nature:	Smallholder service system integrating credit, inputs, marketing, and extension. Infrastructure, particularly water supplies, would be improved. The first phase would have a research component

to investigate the potentials of oilseeds and pulses, of crop diversification, and of drought-resistant cereals, to ensure food supplies.

Commodities: Initial emphasis would be on maize, cotton, and livestock. As research findings become available, effort would be diversified to include oilseeds and pulses.

Loan Amount: US$5 million for the first four-year phase.

Project 2: Commercial Farms Rehabilitation

Purpose: To restore and expand output levels on transferred large farms, mainly mixed farms and coffee estates.

Location: Throughout former scheduled areas, mainly Rift Valley and Central Provinces.

Nature: The most important element would be the creation of a management advisory service and improvement of management at farm level where necessary. Debts would be rescheduled and credit made available. A component to subdivide farms, where this is desired by present group owners, should be included, preferably in a first phase, and certainly in a second phase.

Commodities: The project would increase output, mainly of coffee, wheat, maize, and beef.

Loan Amount: US$5 million for a first three-year phase.

Project 3: Large Scale Irrigation

Purpose: To develop the land and water resource of the Lower Tana Basin, create outlets for smallholders, increase the demand for labor, and expand cash crop output.

Location: The Bure area of the Lower Tana Basin.

Nature: A smallholder project extending to perhaps 8,000 hectares and capable of absorbing 8,000 to 10,000 families. Building up the National Irrigation Board's capacity and assessing the costs and benefits of a meaningful scale of development in the Lower Tana would be important side objectives.

Commodities: The first phase would probably be geared to cotton production with maize, groundnuts and beans grown in the offseason. Sugarcane might well feature in later phases.

Loan Amount: US$15 million for a first five-year phase.

Project 4: Agro-meteorological Stations

Purpose: To improve the climatic data base, and help enable the development of a weather forecasting service, hence improved agricultural planning (including marginal areas) and commodity management.

Nature: Jointly with the East African Community, expand the network of agro-meteorological stations in Kenya, Tanzania, and Uganda.

Loan Amount: US$1.0 million.

APPENDIX

Project 5: Integrated Agricultural Development, Western Kenya

Purpose: To expand smallholder output and raise living levels in the densely populated and underdeveloped Western and Nyanza Provinces.

Location: To capitalize on the lessons learned in the Vihiga and Migori Special Rural Development Programs, the project should be started at two locations, Kakamega and South Nyanza Districts. Thereafter, the project should be spread through the two provinces as rapidly as possible.

Nature: Similar to Project 1 for Eastern Kenya. A particular feature in these densely settled areas would be the intensification of subsistence crop production, thereby permitting cash crops to be taken up. Introduction of macadamia and, taking market considerations into account, inducing acceptance of more tea planting would be important. The project would include a research component to develop improved planting material and husbandry practices for macadamia, and to investigate drainage techniques for the poorly drained areas.

Commodities: Intensification of maize production would be the foundation of the project. Important cash crops would include cotton, tea, macadamia, and groundnuts. Livestock would also be covered, but only is a supporting role to the high potential areas livestock project (No. 7) described later.

Loan Amount: US$5 million for the first four-year phase.

Project 6: Small-Scale Irrigation

The project should be designed to embrace two types of small scale irrigation: the first would seek to increase food production in the arid areas; the second would be geared more to high value crops, centering on Naivasha, Yatta, and the Athi River. More study is necessary.

Loan Amount: A national US$2.5 million is included for a five-year first-phase program.

Project 7: Livestock Development, High Potential Areas

The three proposed components of livestock development in the high potential areas (dairy, feedlots, and dairy bull calves) could form one integrated project. They are here discussed separately for convenience.

7a. Dairy

Purpose: Over 70 percent of the land in high potential smallholder areas is occupied by poor quality pasture which supports, for the most part, unimproved Zebu cattle of low productivity. This is an intolerable resource wastage. It is most extreme in districts west of the Rift Valley, particularly Kericho and Nandi with low population densities, but also acute in Western and Nyanza Provinces which have lagged in the move to upgrade Zebu stock. The proposed project would aim to improve resource use and, by so doing, rural income.

Location:	The project should have three or four foci in Kericho and Nandi Districts and Western and Nyanza Provinces, and be designed to progressively expand its impact.
Nature:	The project would provide more and better extension; veterinary and artificial insemination services; credit for farmers, stockists, and cooperatives, additional milk collection and cooling centers; and measures to ensure a flow of grade stock to the project area from surplus areas east of Rift.
Loan Amount:	US$15 million for a first five-year phase.

7b. Beef

Purpose:	To develop the relatively unexploited beef potential of the large Zebu herd in the high potential areas west of Rift Valley through increasing offtake and finishing.
Nature:	The main element of the project would be the development of feedlots and allied backgrounding facilities. Probably three units would be appropriate in a first phase. They should be operated by the Agricultural Development Corporation either on its own behalf or on a contract basis for cattle owners. Some investment might also be needed to improve market infrastructure.
Location:	The project would tap the Zebu herd in the high potential areas west of Rift Valley. Market infrastructure should be located as required, with feedlots and backgrounding facilities in a first phase being provided in or near Kericho and Nandi Districts.
Loan Amount:	US$3 million for a first five-year phase.

7c. Dairy Bull Calves

Purpose:	To produce beef from bull calves from the grade dairy herd. Most such calves are presently slaughtered just after birth; an estimated 60 percent would be suitable for beef production if the costs of rearing to six months of age could be reduced. By 1978, the number of calves suitable for fattening may approximate 130,000 per year, sufficient to produce 29,000 tons of beef.
Nature:	The project would be of a pilot nature. It should be designed along the lines of the UNDP/FAO Beef Project, the aim being to test, in a practical way, the feasibility of collecting and rearing bull calves. Low cost feeding and housing systems need to be developed. A suitable unit might extend to 100 hectares, with an annual rearing capacity of 1,000 calves to six months of age. If a viable system can be developed, rearing units would be built throughout the high potential areas in the second phase. Feedlots would also then be required, to carry calves from the six-month stage through slaughter.
Location:	The pilot unit could be located anywhere in the high potential areas, taking account of the need for good communications and proximity to a concentration of grade cattle. If the pilot effort were successful, second phase activity would need to be widely dispersed in the high potential areas.
Loan Amount:	US$0.5 million for a first five-year phase.

Project 8: Pigs and Poultry

Pig and poultry development could be combined into one project for its first phase. Each component is discussed separately here for convenience. Alternatively, each could form a minor element of the Livestock Project for High Potential Areas—No. 7.

8a. Pigs

Purpose: To expand low cost pig meat production as a substitute for beef in the domestic market. (This is an essential complement to a policy of increasing the domestic price of beef with the aim of increasing beef supplies for the export market.)

Nature: Present pig policy is geared to production of high quality pigs and pig products, and costs are high. The proposed project would aim to promote smallholder production of a lower cost product for the domestic market. The project would improve extension, credit, input supply, and marketing services to producers. It would also provide for the construction of slaughter and cooling facilities in the smaller urban centers to facilitate marketing of pig products, which are highly perishable. A first phase project might aim to reach 1,000 farms; produce some 30,000 pigs annually, and construct ten to twelve slaughter and cooling facilities.

Location: First phase activity should center on Central and Eastern Provinces where there is already some smallholder production. Slaughter and cooling facilities are needed at selected locations, probably including Thika, Kiambu, Fort Hall, Nyeri, Thompsons Falls, Embu, Meru. Later phases would expand effort to Western Kenya.

Loan Amount: US$0.8 million for a first four-year phase.

8b. Poultry

Purpose: As with pig production, to provide a cheaper meat to substitute for beef.

Nature: A package of extension, credit and input supplies for the small "farmyard" poultry farmer. Also a pilot component to assist perhaps fifty farmers develop smallholder broiler units.

Location: As for the pig project. The poultry effort should be a component of an integrated pig-poultry project, as previously noted.

Loan Amount: US$0.2 million for a first four-year phase.

Project 9: Forestry Plantation Development

Purpose: To continue the present IDA-supported planting program.

Nature: As ongoing, adjusted to include a rural afforestation component, a county council afforestation component, and extension service support. A charcoal production element might be included, depending on the outcome of studies (see later).

Loan Amount: US$5 million.

Project 10: Wildlife and Tourism

Purpose: To further the controlled exploitation of the wildlife resource, and in particular to develop data and a planning capacity to prepare programs which will permit the exploitation of game as a complement to domestic stock in game dispersal areas. (Failure to do this and to ensure that reasonable returns accrue to the pastoral peoples would condemn game to extermination, and destroy the potential contribution of wildlife to rural development.)

Nature: The project would develop infrastructure in existing and new Game Parks and Reserves, training and research, and planning units.

Loan Amount: US$10.0 million for a five-year first phase.

Project 11: Integrated Agricultural Development, Coast

Purpose: To expand smallholder output and raise living levels in the medium potential areas of the coastal strip.

Nature: Similar to Projects 1 and 5 previously described. The common denominator would be expanded production of maize and other subsistence crops. A specific feature would be expansion of cashew production and improvements in cashew processing and marketing. Other important cash crops would be cotton, groundnuts, and sesame. A dairy component would be included to integrate with tree crop production and to expand milk supplies for the coast which currently are supplemented from up-country areas.

Location: First phase activity would focus on Kwale and Kilifi Districts, later extending northwards.

Loan Amount: US$3 million for a four-year first phase.

Project 12: Narok Mixed Farming

Purpose: Taking tribal considerations into account, to begin to tap the impressive production potential of the area in a manner which ensures adequate soil and water conservation. (The project is particularly important in view of the foreign exchange implications of the recent downward trend in wheat production, and for the intermediate term, to help reduce the already large outlays for vegetable oils from abroad.)

Nature: Accelerated land adjudication, basic infrastructure such as roads and grain storage facilities, and on-farm development. The longer term objective would be to develop intensive conservation oriented mixed farming—wheat, barley, and oilseed rape in rotation with leys of exotic species supporting high grade livestock. The initial effort would have to be modest, centering on adjudication and road construction, followed by a credit program for equipment, stock water, fencing, and current financing.

Loan Amount: US$5 million for the first four-year phase.

APPENDIX 501

Project 13: Forest Industries

Purpose:	To develop an advisory service and a credit system to help improve the technical and managerial capacity of small scale business in sawn lumber, furniture, joinery, and prefabricated housing.
Loan Amount:	US$1 million.

Project 14: Lamu Settlement

Purpose:	Lamu District contains most of the unutilized government land of good potential. The proposed project would pioneer development through settlement of this valuable resource. Settlers would be drawn from among the landless and unemployed, as feasible.
Location:	Near Mkununga in the Lamu District hinterland.
Nature:	Settlement of some 3,000 low-income families on about 14,500 hectares, and provision of infrastructure (roads, water supplies, markets, social services) and land clearing. Other elements would be similar to the integrated projects previously discussed, including the development of farming systems. Initial emphasis would be given to securing subsistence. Thereafter, cash crops would be promoted, with emphasis on cashew, cotton, groundnuts, and sesame. Livestock would be introduced, initially goats, giving way to dairy cattle as the area is cleared and developed.
Loan Amount:	US$4 million for a four-year first phase.

Project 15: Range Livestock

Purpose:	Similar to IDA Phase II, with emphasis on integration with the high potential areas.
Loan Amount:	US$25 million.

Project 16: Cereal Storage and Handling and Processing Facilities for Livestock and Livestock Products

Purpose:	To promote price stabilization of staple cereals, reduce handling costs, permit rationalization of the dairy processing industry, and expand livestock processing facilities as necessary.
Loan Amount:	US$10 million, subject to the findings of the study mentioned below, and specifically including funds for on-lending to the private sector.

Project 17: Smallholder Farm Credit

Purpose:	To improve the credit component of smallholder service systems, as supplements to Projects 1, 5, and 11, if the credit study about to be undertaken indicates such a course to be feasible.
Loan Amount:	US$5 million.

Project 18: Rural Water Supplies and Roads

Purpose:	To improve rural health and save labor through provision of household water supplies, and to increase the rate of com-

mercialization of subsistence agriculture through improving accessibility and lowering transportation costs. (Project formulation would require close interministerial coordination.)

Loan Amount: US$4 million.

Project 19: Studies

The proposed phasing of these project possibilities is shown in Table 18. In some cases, as already noted, additional basic study is necessary before project preparation can be undertaken. In other cases, studies need to be done to produce new project proposals, revise development programs, and to design ways of improving the general economic environment of farmers. The studies listed below meet these objectives, and are believed appropriate for technical assistance donors. Where appropriate, these studies should be designed to include project preparation, as this latter task is likely to continue to be a major problem. But however done, the Government should arrange for an ample flow of finance for project preparation. In terms of purpose, the studies are:

(a) To design a long term sugar development plan; and analyze management of the sugar factories, and propose improvement measures.

(b) To investigate the amount, type, and location of storage facilities required to stabilize staple grain prices; and of appropriate handling facilities inland and at the port — taking into account the relative economy of domestic storage versus use of the foreign market as stabilization devices, the probabilities of a bad crop year or succession of bad years, and the need for jobs. (This is a complex study and should be done carefully.)

(c) To determine the extent to which forest catchment areas, if any, can be used for agricultural production, bearing in mind the vital function of such catchments in preventing erosion and preserving stream flows.

(d) To determine the irrigation potential of the Naivasha area with a view to developing high value horticultural crop production on smallholdings, and processing.

(e) To prepare proposals for full development of the irrigable land commanded by the Yatta furrow, including an investigation of appropriate subsistence and horticultural crops.

(f) To determine the feasibility of irrigating a narrow belt along the middle reaches of the Athi River, including its suitability for horticultural crops. (Poverty is widespread in this area.)

(g) To investigate the charcoal market prospects in the Middle East, production prospects in the Arubuko Sokoke and coast mangrove forests, and ways of organizing the swamp charcoal industry in the Lamu area.

(h) To design a Lamu District Development Plan—centering on the very large area of land suitable for agriculture, and including the approximately equal amount usable for ranching; the control of tsetses; the wildlife resource; and the tourism potential. (The investment requirements ultimately will be substantial; for example, a first phase project for wildlife and ranch development would probably cost around US$8 million.)

(i) To determine the best organization of technical and farming systems research in agriculture, the distribution of commodity emphasis and the design and management of specific problem oriented teams. The requirements for finance, training, and staffing should be included in this fundamental study, along with ways of drawing more effectively on the services of international research agencies. This study is vital to the future of Kenyan agriculture.

(j) To design and test smallholder service systems. Working with the proposed Programming and Budgeting Division of the Ministry of Agriculture, a technical assistance group from abroad might include specialists in administration, manpower, credit, marketing, agronomy, livestock, and farm management. Cost might approximate US$300,000. Any such team should be financed and recruited by a single bilateral source, or a multilateral agency should serve as executing agency responsible for recruiting and leading the team. Finance is likely to be readily available. Improved service systems for smallholders are fundamental to progress in the rural society.

STATISTICAL TABLES
PART III—Agricultural Sector Survey

Table
No.

Land and its Potential

1.	Rainfall by Months, Main Recording Stations, 1970–71, and Long Term Average	506
2.	Distribution of Agricultural Land by Class	508
3.	Distribution of Land by Legal Status and Province, December 31, 1970	509
4.	Size Distribution of Large Farms in Former Scheduled Areas, 1970	510
5.	Size Distribution of Registered Smallholdings, 1969	510

Production and Price

6.	Estimated Marketed Output of Principal Crops and Growth Rates, 1962, 1966–71	511
7.	Acreage of Major Crops on Large Farms, by Province, 1965 and 1970	512
8.	Acreage of Major Crops on Small Farms, by Province, 1969–70	513
9.	Livestock Numbers by Province and Type of Farm, 1970	514
10.	Average On-Farm Prices for Crops, 1961–72	515

External Trade in Agricultural Commodities

11.	Agricultural Imports, Main Products, Tonnage, 1966–71	516
12.	Agricultural Imports, Main Products, Value, 1966–71	517
13.	Imports of Agricultural Inputs, Physical Quantities, 1966–71	518
14.	Imports of Agricultural Inputs, Value, 1966–71	519
15.	Agricultural Exports, Major Products, Tonnage, 1965, 1968–71	520
16.	Agricultural Exports, Main Products, Prices f.o.b. Port, 1966–71	521
17.	Agricultural Exports, Major Products, Value, by Destination, 1965, 1968–71	522

Project Phasing

18.	Project Possibilities for Foreign Donors: Loan Amounts and Disbursements for the Coming Decade	525

CHART:

Present Organization of Public Services to Agriculture	526

Table 1: Rainfall by Months, Main Recording Stations, 1970–71, and Long Term Average

Month	Kiambu	Nyeri	Nanyuki	Njoro	Kitale	Kakamega	Kisumu	Kisii	Embu	Machakos	Kilifi
						(millimeters)					
January											
1970	98	130	37	136	106	148	186	138	73	87	0
1971	110	71	2	44	9	42	12	271	3	117	0
Average[1]	47	48	21	30	24	57	63	83	22	52	18
February											
1970	6	45	16	14	9	152	70	54	0	0	54
1971	2	23	0	0	1	6	11	15	0	0	0
Average	51	46	25	35	42	99	87	143	24	53	16
March											
1970	109	138	66	131	226	258	204	430	140	205	58
1971	36	32	28	22	21	26	74	63	45	27	56
Average	114	71	62	71	88	155	162	329	98	128	37
April											
1970	358	191	106	154	144	317	216	392	138	188	85
1971	297	142	159	141	148	227	383	379	491	276	16
Average	233	185	127	134	151	241	206	287	378	208	142
May											
1970	155	165	64	155	136	259	115	216	94	66	311
1971	316	126	143	136	118	361	289	1,027	332	102	198
Average	167	167	85	118	157	261	171	223	261	75	270
June											
1970	61	58	58	65	89	158	68	175	16	0	51
1971	20	30	63	147	218	238	45	140	31	23	169
Average	52	32	43	78	108	186	95	155	25	12	116

STATISTICAL TABLES

July											
1970	0	46	43	76	177	219	23	97	51	0	50
1971	62	30	36	55	181	151	59	588	63	0	76
Average	23	36	56	106	139	167	63	109	48	4	76
August											
1970	11	27	45	128	205	345	61	195	57	3	30
1971	18	51	160	174	167	313	97	143	31	2	32
Average	27	38	66	117	165	237	88	90	68	4	57
September											
1970	0	14	83	68	86	217	54	114	150	0	30
1971	9	3	63	78	75	203	48	135	12	0	46
Average	32	30	49	66	97	182	79	144	47	4	71
October											
1970	46	44	76	60	83	82	73	90	56	0	17
1971	25	42	40	14	171	108	170	458	126	5	10
Average	67	94	85	54	102	132	72	177	189	47	72
November											
1970	110	63	54	109	32	113	69	140	203	95	17
1971	84	72	63	55	60	104	92	182	169	134	3
Average	148	116	95	80	73	116	116	165	272	194	74
December											
1970	19	60	24	25	14	52	125	487	39	121	5
1971	213	77	61	61	57	89	153	130	78	181	88
Average	82	77	45	49	45	86	104	122	84	121	42

[1] Average for the number of years the station has been in operation.

SOURCE: East African Meteorological Department.

Table 2: Distribution of Agricultural Land by Class

| | POTENTIAL ||||| High and Medium as % of Total |
Province	High	Medium	Low	Other Land	Total	
	(thousand hectares)					
Central	909	15	41	437	1,402	65.9
Coast	373	796	5,663	1,480	8,312	14.1
Eastern	503	2,189	11,452	1,311	15,455	17.4
Northeastern	—	—	12,690	—	12,690	—
Nyanza	1,218	34	—	—	1,252	100.0
Rift Valley	3,025	123	12,353	1,519	17,020	18.5
Western	741	—	—	82	823	90.0
Nairobi	16	—	38	14	68	23.5
TOTAL	6,785	3,157	42,237	4,843	57,022	17.4

SOURCE: *Statistical Abstract*, 1971.

Table 3: Distribution of Land by Legal Status and Province, December 31, 1970

Category	Western	Nyanza	Rift Valley	Central	Eastern	Northeastern	Coast	Nairobi
				(square kilometers)				
Government land								
Forest reserves	549	—	4,408	2,865	1,308	—	600	23
Other reserves	3	23	332	45	163	—	356	236
Townships	—	21	228	31	36	—	545	93
Alienated	257	329	19,767	2,033	2,823	—	1,251	238
Unalienated	—	5	404	35	9,868	—	36,169	31
National parks	—	—	21	708	7,232	—	13,997	114
Open water	137	3,610	290	3	5	—	558	—
SUBTOTAL	946	3,988	25,450	5,720	21,435	—	53,476	735
Freehold land								
Smallholder schemes	663	332	1,075	1,816	602	—	—	—
Other	3	—	425	1,181	21	—	451	135
SUBTOTAL	666	332	1,500	2,997	623	—	451	135
Trust land								
Not available for smallholders								
Forest	264	9	5,965	13	865	—	63	—
Government reserves	7	5	21	165	242	—	3	—
Townships	11	12	116	16	78	254	30	—
Alienated land	—	1	15	102	323	—	7	—
Game reserves	—	—	4,800	—	3,706	—	—	—
Open water	—	26	3,416	—	5,346	—	5	—
Available for smallholders								
Already registered	3,850	2,392	5,507	4,095	2,139	—	83	—
Not yet registered	2,617	9,396	127,081	25	125,134	126,648	29,300	—
SUBTOTAL	6,749	11,841	146,921	4,416	137,833	126,902	29,491	—
TOTAL	8,361	16,161	173,871	13,133	159,891	126,902	83,418	870

SOURCE: *Statistical Abstract*, 1971.

Table 4: Size Distribution of Large Farms in Former Scheduled Areas, 1970

Size of Farms in Hectares	Large Farms Number	%	Estimated Total Area Hectares (thousand)[1]	%
0–19	417	13.1	4	0.2
20–49	324	10.2	11	0.4
50–99	304	9.6	23	0.8
100–199	364	11.5	54	2.0
200–299	321	10.1	80	3.0
300–399	253	8.0	88	3.3
400–499	218	6.9	98	3.6
500–999	498	15.7	373	13.9
1,000–1,999	243	7.6	364	13.5
2,000–3,999	107	3.4	321	11.9
4,000–19,999	111	3.5	} 1,273	} 47.3
20,000 and over	15	0.5		
Total	3,175	100.0	2,690	100.0

[1] Estimated from the number of farms in each group by the midpoint of the size group. The residual land was attributed to farms with 4,000 and more hectares.

Source: *Statistical Abstract*, 1971.

Table 5: Size Distribution of Registered Smallholdings, 1969

Size of Farm in Hectares	Smallholdings Number (thousand)	%	Total Area Hectares (thousand)	%
Less than 0.5	91	11.7	28	1.1
0.5–0.99	121	15.5	89	3.4
1.0–1.9	192	24.6	274	10.3
2.0–2.9	128	16.4	303	11.4
3.0–4.9	104	13.3	404	15.1
5.0–9.9	88	11.3	629	23.8
10 and over	54	7.0	923	34.9
Total	777	100.0	2,646	100.0

Source: *Statistical Abstract*, 1970.

Table 6: Estimated Marketed Output of Principal Crops and Growth Rates, 1962, 1966–71

Crop	1962	1966	1967	1968	1969	1970	1971	% Annual Growth Rate (1962–71)
				(thousand tons)				
Clean coffee	50.0	56.9	48.0	39.6	52.4	58.3	59.5	3.3
Tea	16.5	21.4	22.8	29.8	36.1	41.1	36.3	11.5
Sisal	59.6	64.0	51.3	50.7	50.0	44.0	44.8	−4.9
Pyrethrum extract	1.3	1.3	0.1	0.2	0.1	0.1	0.1	−22.5
Wattle bark[1]	62.0	50.0	54.9	37.3	33.8	29.2	28.2	−6.9
Seed cotton	5.4	14.4	12.7	14.3	17.1	14.0	16.8	9.0
Sugar cane[3]		514.6	706.4	947.2	1,375.7	1,551.2	1,528.0	18.5[2]
Raw cashew nuts	6.6	9.9	11.8	8.5	8.1	9.9	12.0	4.3
Pulses	12.0	19.5	14.6	4.6	8.1	11.5	12.5	−2.1
Maize[4]	152.5	134.3	248.8	352.6	280.3	205.7	256.6	7.6
Rice paddy	15.2	16.6	15.9	18.7	22.7	28.5	30.0	10.5
Wheat	84.2	128.4	162.2	216.3	241.6	221.5	205.7	9.9[5]
Pineapples			12.0	14.9	17.1	32.0	35.0	34.0[6]

[1] Green and stick bark purchased by Kenya Wattle Manufacturers Association.
[2] 1963–71.
[3] Delivered to sugar factories for production of white sugar.
[4] Delivered to Maize and Produce Board.
[5] The comparable figure for 1968–72 is −6.45 percent.
[6] 1967–71.

SOURCE: *Statistical Abstract*, 1971.

Table 7: Acreage of Major Crops on Large Farms, by Province, 1965 and 1970

(thousand hectares)

Crop	Nyanza 1965	Nyanza 1970	Rift Valley 1965	Rift Valley 1970	Western 1965	Western 1970	Central 1965	Central 1970	Eastern 1965	Eastern 1970	Coast 1965	Coast 1970	Nairobi 1965	Nairobi 1970
Maize	—	—	36.1	58.0	1.9	0.1	0.6	0.9	0.2	0.1	0.1	—	0.1	0.1
Wheat	—	14.1	94.9	101.2	0.4	—	11.5	14.9	2.1	5.1	—	—	—	—
Sugar cane	11.0	—	1.7	7.1	—	—	—	—	—	0.2	5.5	4.9	—	0.1
Pyrethrum	—	—	4.1	2.7	—	—	0.6	0.6	0.1	—	—	—	—	—
Sisal	—	—	29.2	27.2	—	—	27.1	18.7	13.5	9.4	32.1	26.0	5.3	3.8
Tea	0.6	0.9	16.8	19.2	—	0.1	1.9	3.6	—	—	—	—	—	—
Coffee	—	—	7.7	6.1	0.1	—	18.5	19.8	1.7	2.2	—	—	1.6	1.6
Wattle	1.0	—	18.3	15.9	3.1	—	1.3	1.3	—	—	—	—	0.1	—
Fruit	—	—	0.4	0.4	—	—	0.8	2.2	0.1	0.1	1.4	1.0	—	—
Fodder crops	—	—	6.3	9.1	—	—	0.5	1.2	0.4	1.2	—	—	0.2	0.1
Employees' cultivation	0.1	0.5	19.4	26.2	0.4	0.1	4.8	17.4	1.0	3.0	0.4	0.4	0.2	0.7
Grass leys	—	—	12.3		—		13.7		4.9				0.1	
Other	—	—	15.3	25.6	—	0.1	1.7	5.5	0.9	1.3	2.9	1.8	0.1	0.1
TOTAL	12.7	15.5	262.5	298.7	5.9	0.4	83.0	86.1	24.9	22.6	42.4	34.1	7.7	6.5

SOURCE: Statistics Division, Ministry of Finance and Planning.

Table 8: Acreage of Major Crops on Small Farms, by Province, 1969–70

	Nyanza	Western	Rift Valley	Central	Coast	Eastern
	\multicolumn{6}{c}{(thousand hectares)}					
Cereals						
Improved maize	28.2	64.7	30.0	8.9	0.1	14.9
Unimproved maize	162.3	69.4	42.6	164.2	129.4	280.6
Bulrush millet	—	0.9	—	3.6	0.2	40.0
Finger millet	11.9	14.7	5.6	*[1]	0.8	3.1
Other millet	2.8	2.1	—	1.7	0.7	5.3
Sorghum	77.1	21.8	0.6	1.4	4.0	36.3
Wheat	—	—	1.7	2.5	—	1.3
Other cereals	0.1	0.5	—	0.4	2.0	0.6
Pulses						
Beans	40.0	24.6	9.3	113.7	8.3	125.9
Pigeon peas	—	—	*	0.6	0.4	121.0
Cow peas	4.4	0.9	0.2	0.2	5.2	55.7
Field peas	3.5	—	0.8	6.1	*	2.4
Yellow, green, and black gram	0.8	0.2	*	3.0	*	10.4
Other pulses	—	—	—	1.1	—	0.9
Temporary Industrial Crops						
Cotton	17.9	14.2	—	6.1	3.2	25.1
Sugar cane	10.6	4.6	8.8	9.7	4.8	18.1
Pyrethrum	6.9	—	0.4	16.3	—	4.5
Ground nuts	13.0	3.4	—	0.3	0.7	3.8
Oil seeds	2.5	2.5	0.2	0.3	5.9	13.4
Other temporary industrial crops	*	—	*	0.2	5.1	4.6
Other Temporary Crops						
Cassava	33.9	33.7	1.1	1.9	61.2	21.8
English potatoes	0.8	*	1.7	20.6	0.7	13.9
Sweet potatoes	10.9	6.0	0.8	12.3	1.9	13.6
Yams	—	—	0.1	2.1	0.9	13.2
Cabbages	0.2	2.2	0.2	6.0	3.1	0.8
Other vegetables	0.3	—	—	0.8	0.1	—
Other temporary crops	4.2	0.5	*	6.8	4.7	12.2
Permanent Crops						
Coffee	10.4	4.2	0.3	27.0	1.6	19.1
Tea	3.8	4.2	3.9	6.6	—	1.1
Coconuts	—	—	—	—	79.9	—
Cashew nuts	—	—	—	—	66.3	2.4
Pawpaws	*	—	—	—	9.0	2.3
Bananas	13.6	19.3	0.4	50.6	26.5	40.0
Other fruits	0.6	0.3	*	2.6	29.0	3.0
Other permanent crops	1.5	—	*	2.2	0.6	5.0
Total Land Use						
Aggregate area of crops[2]	461.3	294.9	108.7	479.8	456.3	916.3
All farm land	1,214.2	751.1	752.6	630.4	1,479.2	3,428.1
Total cultivation	284.2	212.2	91.5	267.2	214.1	476.4
Paddocked grazing	4.7	0.6	0.4	33.1	—	13.5
Other farm land[3]	925.3	538.3	660.7	330.1	1,265.1	2,938.2

[1] Asterisk indicates less than 0.05 but not zero.
[2] Crops grown in mixtures are double counted.
[3] Includes communal grazing.
SOURCE: Statistics Division, Ministry of Finance and Planning.

Table 9: Livestock Numbers by Province and Type of Farm, 1970

(thousand)

Livestock	Nyanza	Western	Rift Valley	Central	Coast	Eastern	North-eastern	Nairobi	Total
Cattle									
Large farms	1.9	1.6	599.4	101.5	6.8	58.7	—	12.0	781.9
Small farms	1,241.4	725.5	1,426.3	505.2	259.6	1,550.4	—	—	5,708.4
Pastoral areas	—	—	1,894.0	—	n.a.	440.0	597.0	—	2,931.0
TOTAL	1,243.3	727.1	4,279.7[1]	606.7	414.4	2,049.1	597.0	12.0	9,929.3
Sheep and goats									
Large farms	—	—	272.7	83.9	1.7	71.5	—	2.7	432.5
Small farms	575.5	213.7	1,003.2	610.1	435.2	1,473.3	—	—	4,311.0
Pastoral areas	—	—	1,798.0	—	—	542.0	291.0	—	2,631.0
TOTAL	575.5	213.7	3,923.9	694.0	529.9	2,086.8	291.0	2.7	8,317.5
Pigs	—	8.9	24.0	25.1	1.4	0.8	—	1.1	61.3
Chickens	4,269.0	2,294.0	1,160.0	1,260.0	1,051.0	3,230.0	—	54.0	13,318.0
Donkeys	9.3	—	129.7	2.2	2.7	35.1	2.7	—	181.7
Camels	—	—	181.0	—	—	159.0	176.0	—	516.0

Within-province breakdowns are incomplete; item totals may therefore not add to the indicated figures.

SOURCE: Statistics Division, Ministry of Finance and Planning.

Table 10: Average On-Farm Prices for Crops, 1961–72

Year	Coffee	Tea	Sisal	Pyrethrum Extract Equivalent	Seed Cotton	Rice Paddy	Wheat	Sugar Cane
				(Sh. per hundred kilogram)				
1961	660.22	784.14	—	34,270.92	113.29	—	52.16	—
1962	669.91	845.81	—	27,903.08	109.30	—	52.16	—
1963	571.80	776.00	—	28,446.00	108.00	—	53.25	—
1964	700.00	721.00	—	31,936.00	108.00	—	52.27	—
1965	667.00	741.00	—	37,968.00	104.00	—	51.99	—
1966	654.60	780.00	122.40	41,578.00	95.00	44.08	54.48	—
1967	583.00	783.00	107.80	39,684.00	95.00	45.51	56.78	4.22
1968	640.40	585.00	92.60	34,440.00	98.00	45.75	56.26	4.52
1969	617.10	618.91	90.02	32,518.51	97.48	54.87	54.51	4.52
1970	747.84	673.78	78.09	31,024.78	99.18	50.73	45.10	4.52
1971	626.54	650.47	67.78	33,946.06	104.77	50.73	50.61	4.52
1972[1]	746.00	651.24	119.37	35,200.00	99.12	59.55	50.61	5.18

[1] Second quarter.

SOURCE: *Statistical Abstract* and *Kenya Statistical Digest*.

Table 11: Agricultural Imports, Main Products, Tonnage, 1966–71

Product	1966	1967	1968	1969	1970	1971
			(tons)			
Meat and meat preparations	556	878	334	364	339	254
Dairy products	918	2,206	1,696	1,886	2,585	1,720
Fish and fish preparations	2,061	2,787	4,813	3,577	3,295	1,596
Cereal and cereal preparations	160,581	17,871	17,375	8,633	32,521	65,474
Fuits and nuts	2,213	2,140	1,845	1,770	1,759	2,300
Fresh	905	1,009	898	882	766	929
Dried and prepared	1,308	1,131	947	888	993	1,371
Vegetables	15,904	23,974	12,313	10,547	20,463	33,989
Beans and peas	13,106	22,093	10,203	7,866	14,293	21,464
Other	2,798	1,881	2,110	2,681	6,170	12,525
Sugar and sugar preparations	111,116	46,945	61,339	32,841	44,343	76,508
Coffee, tea, cocoa, and spices	1,089	1,622	1,502	1,973	2,034	2,139
Animal feed	9,865	10,797	6,008	7,618	8,365	15,985
Fish meal	405	874	916	1,332	1,390	2,345
Other	9,460	9,923	5,092	6,286	6,975	13,640
Margarine and shortenings	3,160	4,892	3,923	3,453	4,426	3,913
Beverages[1]	2,754	2,472	2,710	1,624	2,816	2,228
Tobacco	2,454	3,052	1,805	838	2,819	2,947
Unmanufactured	2,365	2,986	1,750	798	2,782	2,892
Manufactured	89	66	55	40	37	55
Hides and skins	185	328	707	445	472	223
Oilseeds, oilnuts, and oil kernels	7,251	7,462	8,925	6,597	10,877	13,193
Linseed	126	126	74	25	—	85
Copra	1,967	1,013	192	306	534	3,102
Other	5,158	6,323	8,659	6,266	10,343	10,006
Crude rubber	1,397	925	1,294	1,271	1,599	2,526
Pulp and waste paper	2,901	830	3,144	2,197	2,933	6,139
Textile fibers	4,315	4,570	5,607	5,458	6,709	15,110
Animal oils	4,950	3,769	5,663	8,612	8,078	13,119
Vegetable oils	16,549	14,216	16,114	21,430	17,621	23,896
Soybean oil	282	6	537	3,578	604	624
Olive oil	34	28	41	32	22	40
Linseed oil	186	180	357	342	236	262
Palm oil	4,434	2,202	6,274	12,102	6,866	15,460
Coconut oil	3,624	1,718	954	1,555	1,241	1,871
Palm kernel oil	72	348	92	83	85	39
Castor oil	49	43	51	62	51	60
Cottonseed oil	7,805	9,517	7,616	3,540	8,406	5,441
Fixed vegetable oils	54	47	55	59	98	99
Other	9	127	137	77	12	—
Animal and vegetable oils, processed	1,275	2,230	2,580	2,592	2,737	4,110

[1] Thousand liters.

SOURCE: Annual trade reports, 1966–71.

Table 12: Agricultural Imports, Main Products, Value, 1966–71

Product	1966	1967	1968	1969	1970	1971
			(£ thousand)			
Live animals	68	122	218	96	129	97
Meat and meat preparations	150	272	96	107	113	77
Dairy products	227	331	196	196	513	413
Fish and fish preparations	296	474	678	663	708	235
Cereals and cereal preparations	4,779	895	1,180	626	1,405	2,926
Fuits and nuts	382	353	402	451	478	478
Fresh	209	220	258	316	329	290
Dried and prepared	173	133	144	135	149	188
Vegetables	763	944	546	568	982	1,470
Beans and peas	484	724	329	306	609	1,046
Other	279	220	217	262	373	424
Sugar and sugar preparations	3,479	1,957	2,391	1,480	2,081	4,302
Coffee, tea, cocoa, and spices	482	524	316	652	732	787
Animal feed	190	261	206	250	337	528
Fish meal	33	55	55	88	122	186
Other	157	206	151	162	215	342
Margarine and shortenings	591	910	736	617	858	802
Other food	244	244	384	392	557	691
Beverages	407	531	714	569	838	841
Tobacco	1,012	1,361	765	476	1,403	1,391
Unmanufactured	864	1,278	686	346	1,346	1,324
Manufactured	148	83	79	130	57	67
Hides and skins	102	117	169	229	262	178
Oilseeds, oilnuts, and oil kernels	280	283	266	209	321	526
Linseed	7	6	4	1	—	4
Copra	132	62	13	19	29	219
Other	141	215	249	189	292	303
Crude rubber	236	140	181	231	254	347
Wood, lumber, and cork	124	221	422	176	329	338
Pulp and waste paper	60	15	82	58	86	190
Textile fibers	320	341	411	545	760	1,672
Crude vegetable materials	163	154	229	332	288	462
Animal oils	420	249	359	568	756	1,229
Vegetable oils	1,882	1,579	1,869	1,998	2,169	2,911
Soybean oil	43	1	65	316	97	118
Olive oil	13	11	16	12	9	16
Linseed oil	23	22	46	43	31	36
Palm oil	417	192	419	823	654	1,497
Coconut oil	384	177	119	170	152	244
Palm kernel oil	9	35	11	11	12	9
Castor oil	8	8	9	8	8	13
Cottonseed oil	969	1,106	1,149	588	1,179	946
Fixed vegetable oils	14	13	14	14	26	32
Other oils	2	14	21	13	1	—
Animal and vegetable oils, processed	119	185	187	214	267	468
TOTAL	16,776	12,463	13,003	11,703	16,626	23,359

SOURCE: Annual trade reports, 1966–71.

Table 13: Imports of Agricultural Inputs, Physical Quantities, 1966–71

Category	1966	1967	1968	1969	1970	1971
From all sources:						
Chemicals (tons)	4,329.6	3,942.6	5,268.8	5,241.8	6,444.0	6,979.9
Disinfectants	n.a.	n.a.	394.5	47.1	103.9	149.0
Fungicides	n.a.	n.a.	1,234.0	931.7	1,365.6	821.0
Insecticides	n.a.	n.a.	1,951.4	2,139.0	2,084.5	2,692.8
Weed killers	n.a.	n.a.	130.3	310.3	327.5	345.7
Other	1,332.0	1,407.0	1,558.6	1,813.7	2,562.5	2,971.4
Fertilizers (tons)	94,213.6	80,735.3	76,875.0	93,827.0	141,215.0	130,139.0
Tractors (number)	1,028	773	1,185	760	1,100	896
Crawler and truck	50	32	36	31	51	62
Other wheeled	978	741	1,088	718	1,049	830
Other	—	—	61	11	—	4
Bags and sacks (thousand)	6,634.1	6,796.3	2,675.0	4,136.4	332.1	122.1
Hoes and matchetes (thousand)	598.1	333.5	592.6	568.5	400.2	564.4
From Tanzania:						
Chemicals (tons)	45	36	89	185	161	244
Disinfectants	n.a.	n.a.	3	10	1	—
Fungicides	n.a.	n.a.	—	—	—	—
Insecticides	n.a.	n.a.	46	125	125	105
Weed killers	n.a.	n.a.	—	—	—	—
Other	2	10	40	50	35	139
Fertilizers (tons)	—	—	208	980	370	297
Bags and sacks (thousand)	17	—	—	25	—	10
Hoes and matchetes (thousand)	—	—	—	—	—	—
From Uganda:						
Chemicals (tons)	26.0	26.0	33.0	49.1	11.7	7.1
Disinfectants	n.a.	n.a.	—	0.1	2.8	—
Fungicides	n.a.	n.a.	—	—	—	—
Insecticides	n.a.	n.a.	15.0	12.4	6.0	4.9
Weed killers	n.a.	n.a.	1.0	—	—	—
Other	24.0	17.0	17.0	36.6	2.9	2.2
Fertilizers (tons)	24,853	16,515	11,994	18,881	22,487	18,565
Bags and sacks (thousand)	14	—	1	1	—	—
Hoes and matchetes (thousand)	106	59	58	15	30	86

SOURCE: Annual trade reports, 1966–71.

Table 14: Imports of Agricultural Inputs, Value, 1966–71

Category	1966	1967	1968	1969	1970	1971
			(£ thousand)			
From all sources:						
Chemicals	1,292.7	1,032.3	1,585.4	1,556.0	2,310.3	2,199.9
Disinfectants	n.a.	n.a.	72.0	20.7	29.6	49.4
Fungicides	n.a.	n.a.	578.2	433.2	762.6	342.1
Insecticides	n.a.	n.a.	670.2	638.8	806.9	1,026.3
Weed killers	n.a.	n.a.	9.0	133.7	193.5	265.6
Other	200.7	164.1	256.0	329.6	517.7	516.5
Fertilizers	2,406.0	1,845.0	2,067.0	2,602.0	3,405.5	3,362.5
Agricultural machinery	659.5	1,013.2	826.9	679.7	654.7	814.8
Soil preparation	293.7	361.3	358.5	408.4	380.1	393.5
Harvesting	255.7	430.6	364.4	215.1	200.7	319.4
Dairy farm equipment	63.0	112.5	93.4	56.2	53.2	58.2
Other	47.1	108.8	10.6	—	20.7	43.7
Tractors	1,194.9	1,105.2	1,446.7	1,150.3	1,763.9	1,709.3
Crawler and truck	326.7	362.7	442.1	407.1	673.9	645.7
Other wheeled	868.2	742.5	914.6	715.3	1,090.0	1,057.7
Other	—	—	90.0	27.9	—	5.9
Bags and sacks	864.6	684.2	251.0	444.2	78.6	34.2
Hoes and matchetes	90.0	57.6	85.0	75.9	224.1	86.8
TOTAL (ALL SOURCES)	6,507.7	5,737.5	6,262.0	6,508.1	8,437.1	8,207.5
From Tanzania:						
Chemicals	14	13	13	22	42	87
Insecticides	n.a.	n.a.	8	20	34	53
Other	1	1	5	2	8	34
Fertilizers	—	—	3	14	6	3
Agricultural machinery	—	—	1	1	1	1
Soil preparation	—	—	—	1	1	—
Dairy farm equipment	—	—	1	—	—	—
Other	—	—	—	—	—	1
Bags and sacks	3	—	—	1	—	—
TOTAL (TANZANIA)	17	13	17	38	49	91
From Uganda:						
Chemicals	13	14	14	4	3	1
Disinfectants	n.a.	n.a.	—	—	1	—
Insecticides	n.a.	n.a.	2	2	2	1
Weed killers	n.a.	n.a.	1	—	—	—
Other	12	12	11	2	—	—
Fertilizers	362	244	189	316	359	297
Agricultural harvesting machinery	—	—	1	—	—	—
Bags and sacks	2	—	—	5	—	—
Hoes and matchetes	30	19	15	4	8	24
TOTAL (UGANDA)	407	277	219	329	370	322

SOURCE: Annual trade reports, 1965, 1968–71.

Table 15: Agricultural Exports, Major Products, Tonnage, 1965, 1968–71

Product	1965	1968	1969	1970	1971
	(thousand tons)				
Coffee	38.4	37.6	51.1	53.8	56.2
Tea	16.9	28.4	33.8	36.1	34.3
	(0.9)[1]	(0.9)	(1.0)	(1.0)	(0.8)
Sisal	58.5	42.0	35.9	44.6	34.7
	(0.3)	(0.2)	(0.1)	(0.3)	
Pyrethrum products	1.1	2.2	2.4	1.8	2.3
Meat products	8.1	8.1	7.1	7.7	8.0
	(1.2)	(1.0)	(1.1)	(1.0)	(0.9)
Hides and skins	7.4	7.0	6.6	6.0	7.7
		(0.1)			
Maize, unmilled	0.2	281.4	190.3	4.7	0.1
		(3.7)	(49.4)	(4.6)	(0.1)
Wheat	57.2	53.5	24.7	44.0	19.5
	(57.2)	(52.9)	(24.7)	(44.0)	(19.5)
Canned pineapples	9.1	5.4	8.1	7.6	10.9
		(0.1)	(0.1)	(0.1)	(0.1)
Butter and ghee	2.3	2.1	2.3	2.1	1.0
	(1.5)	(1.1)	(1.5)	(1.4)	(0.8)
Beans and peas	11.5	21.8	14.5	14.4	12.7
	(2.1)	(4.1)	(3.6)	(4.9)	(4.6)
Cotton, raw	3.3	1.7	2.8	5.1	4.6
Wool	1.4	1.8	1.8	1.7	1.3
Animal feeds	18.4	31.6	34.3	42.1	94.9
	(7.4)	(3.1)	(4.4)	(10.3)	(6.9)
Cashew nuts	6.7	8.6	9.1	23.2	10.6
Wattle extract	0.7	1.6	1.4	1.1	1.4
	(0.1)	(0.1)		(0.1)	
Wattle bark	3.9	3.6	1.3	0.9	0.8
Oil seeds	8.6	10.7	7.3	14.5	6.5
		(0.7)	(0.4)	(0.3)	

[1] Number in parentheses indicates exports to Uganda and Tanzania.

SOURCE: *Economic Survey*, 1970 and 1972; *Annual Trade Reports*.

Table 16: Agricultural Exports, Main Products, Prices f.o.b. Port, 1966–71

Product	Unit	1966	1967	1968	1969	1970	1971[1]
		(sh. per unit)					
Coffee, unroasted	kg	6.90	6.17	6.81	6.61	8.29	7.03
Tea	kg	7.71	8.00	7.30	6.87	7.25	7.10
Maize	100 kg	—	35.21	34.41	39.36	—	—
Meat products	kg	6.89	6.90	8.53	8.74	8.53	9.77
Pyrethrum extract	kg	149.25	148.17	136.77	121.14	132.15	149.80
Sisal	100 kg	119.82	99.62	87.46	96.05	84.20	87.76
Hides and skins	kg	6.77	5.08	4.78	5.71	5.52	5.77
Wattle extract	kg	1.11	1.07	1.09	1.38	1.52	1.58
Beans and peas	kg	0.93	1.16	0.94	0.97	1.07	1.13
Cashew nuts, raw	kg	1.52	1.39	1.46	1.49	1.37	1.44
Wool	kg	7.84	6.90	6.40	6.05	5.45	3.93
Animal feed	100 kg	42.13	36.55	35.64	34.88	41.07	35.54
Cotton, raw	kg	4.15	4.04	4.72	5.47	4.82	5.02
Pineapples, canned	kg	1.75	1.77	1.67	1.82	1.79	1.77
Butter and ghee	kg	7.59	6.80	6.66	6.66	7.14	8.00
Wattle bark	100 kg	55.91	54.91	54.79	63.06	64.79	58.68

[1] Provisional.

SOURCE: *Economic Survey*, 1970 and 1972.

Table 17: Agricultural Exports, Major Products, Value, by Destination, 1965, 1968–71

	1965	1968	1969	1970	1971	% Distribution 1971
			(£ thousand)			
Coffee, not roasted	14,096	12,820	16,858	22,273	19,530	100.0
F. R. Germany	6,036	4,972	6,865	5,848	5,939	30.4
Sweden	1,444	1,511	1,975	3,226	2,744	14.1
United Kingdom	1,387	1,205	1,312	1,163	1,648	8.4
United States	805	1,472	1,848	3,788	1,495	7.7
Netherlands	662	763	1,388	2,369	1,306	6.7
Japan	27	9	117	54	1,285	6.6
Other	3,735	2,888	3,353	5,825	5,113	26.1
Tea	6,476	10,387	11,705	13,182	12,174	100.0
United Kingdom	3,762	6,632	7,892	9,369	7,997	65.7
United States	648	1,175	1,514	1,238	1,467	12.1
Netherlands	481	449	384	692	919	7.5
Canada	492	694	703	688	552	4.5
Other	1,093	1,437	1,212	1,195	1,239	10.2
Sisal fiber and tow	3,870	1,839	1,721	1,878	1,515	100.0
India	84	117	186	199	239	15.8
Australia	269	159	137	143	152	10.0
Japan	351	185	138	165	148	9.8
United Kingdom	441	197	168	238	144	9.5
France	337	240	187	151	140	9.2
Other	2,388	941	905	982	692	45.7
Pyrethrum extract	1,965	2,510	2,228	1,752	2,766	100.0
Australia	165	203	242	219	429	15.5
United Kingdom	362	528	338	202	397	14.4
Italy	157	380	234	254	277	10.0
United States	768	691	820	537	106	3.8
Other	513	708	594	540	1,557	56.3
Pyrethrum flowers	266	536	570	414	571	100.0
Thailand	62	104	87	88	92	16.1
Malaysia	2	67	118	48	77	13.5
Japan	63	111	95	26	70	12.3
Argentina	6	47	44	65	68	11.9
Italy	12	19	24	27	55	9.6
Hong Kong	18	38	43	37	55	9.6
Other	103	150	159	123	154	27.0
Meat and meat preparations	2,829	3,533	2,960	3,206	3,980	100.0
United Kingdom	1,282	1,751	1,612	1,633	2,105	52.9
Libya	23	—	170	190	432	10.9
Hong Kong	113	160	87	257	261	6.5
Zambia	14	59	107	142	219	5.5
Other	1,397	1,563	984	984	963	24.2
Hides and skins, undressed	1,760	1,684	1,873	1,658	2,442	100.0
United Kingdom	320	276	301	335	613	25.1
Italy	448	273	406	255	442	18.1
Spain	223	190	228	212	430	17.6
Netherlands	143	73	79	137	184	7.5
F. R. Germany	104	51	28	66	65	2.7
Sweden	17	47	72	81	61	2.5
Other	505	774	759	572	647	26.5

Table 17: (Continued)

	1965	1968	1969	1970	1971	% Distribution 1971
			(£ thousand)			
Wattle bark extract	715	1,138	1,148	1,145	1,207	100.0
India	373	550	517	692	618	51.2
Pakistan	101	174	250	203	241	20.0
Poland	—	50	—	22	88	7.3
Other	241	364	381	228	260	21.5
Wattle bark	118	104	40	28	22	100.0
India	113	104	40	28	22	100.0
Other	5	—	—	—	—	—
Pineapple, tinned	776	450	732	679	970	100.0
United Kingdom	582	274	464	380	388	40.0
F. R. Germany	22	30	21	84	167	17.2
Sweden	18	16	35	8	97	10.0
Spain	13	14	23	22	84	8.7
Netherlands	6	7	48	44	70	7.2
Italy	26	24	39	37	58	6.0
Other	109	85	102	104	106	10.9
Butter and ghee	879	759	856	779	425	100.0
Uganda	374	146	321	299	219	51.5
Tanzania	212	294	261	246	113	26.6
Ethiopia	14	16	18	14	16	3.8
Burundi	14	17	17	26	15	3.5
P. D. R. Yemen	55	7	11	19	10	2.4
Other	210	279	228	175	52	12.2
Cotton, raw	747	398	761	1,228	1,182	100.0
China (Mainland)	427	179	292	450	706	59.7
Netherlands	—	—	32	—	212	17.9
F. R. Germany	164	142	78	53	83	7.0
India	21	—	10	181	51	4.3
Other	135	77	349	544	130	11.1
Beans, peas, and lentils	576	1,010	683	788	760	100.0
Tanzania	76	128	120	170	240	31.6
United Kingdom	56	186	120	65	90	11.8
Uganda	25	48	34	106	64	8.4
Malawi	7	32	6	35	45	5.9
Netherlands	5	23	31	15	44	5.8
Italy	20	12	45	44	43	5.7
Belgium	16	16	4	41	36	4.7
United States	14	42	13	20	29	3.8
Other	357	523	310	292	169	22.3
Wool, raw	560	576	551	374	264	100.0
F. R. Germany	30	55	267	147	181	68.6
Czechoslovakia	108	283	114	106	60	22.7
Other	422	238	170	121	23	8.7
Oilseeds, nuts, and kernels	452	692	365	565	464	100.0
Netherlands	—	42	31	38	161	34.7
P. D. R. Yemen	1	40	18	73	102	22.0
United Kingdom	184	293	104	132	63	13.6
Other	267	317	212	322	138	29.7

Table 17: (Continued)

	1965	1968	1969	1970	1971	% Distribution 1971
	(£ thousand)					
Cashew nuts, raw	480	627	680	1,588	747	100.0
India	480	622	679	1,587	746	99.9
Other	—	5	1	1	1	0.1
Animal feed	448	666	764	1,078	792	100.0
Uganda	168	94	146	283	197	24.9
Tanzania	56	66	97	141	168	21.2
Belgium	28	189	269	200	123	15.5
United Kingdom	30	84	65	82	82	10.4
Japan	39	111	36	145	50	6.3
Denmark	47	32	29	56	43	5.4
Other	80	90	122	171	129	16.3
Total major agricultural exports	37,013	39,729	44,495	52,615	49,811	
All other exports	10,160	18,066	18,837	18,991	23,374	
TOTAL EXPORTS	47,173	57,795	63,332	71,606	73,185	

SOURCE: *Annual Trade Reports*, 1965, 1968–71.

STATISTICAL TABLES 525

Table 18: Project Possibilities for Foreign Donors: Loan Amounts and Disbursements for the Coming Decade

Project[1]		1	2	3	4	5	6	7	8	9	10
						(US$ Million)					
	Integrated crop development										
No. 5	Western Kenya	1.2	1.2	1.3	1.3	4.0	4.0	4.0	4.0	4.0	4.0
No. 1	Eastern Kenya	—	1.2	1.2	1.3	1.3	4.0	4.0	4.0	4.0	4.0
No. 11	Coast	—	—	0.7	0.7	0.8	0.8	2.5	2.5	2.5	2.5
No. 12	Narok mixed farming	—	—	1.2	1.2	1.3	1.3	2.5	2.5	2.5	2.5
No. 14	Lamu settlement	—	—	—	1.0	1.0	1.0	1.0	—	—	—
No. 2	Commercial farms rehabilitation	1.6	1.7	1.7	2.0	2.0	2.0	2.0	2.0	2.0	2.0
	Irrigation										
No. 3	Large-scale	3.0	3.0	3.0	3.0	3.0	5.0	5.0	5.0	5.0	5.0
No. 6	Small-scale	—	0.5	0.5	0.5	0.5	0.5	1.0	1.0	1.0	1.0
	Livestock development										
No. 7	High-potential areas	—	3.7	3.7	3.7	3.7	3.7	6.0	6.0	6.0	6.0
No. 15	Range area	—	—	—	—	—	5.0	5.0	5.0	5.0	5.0
No. 8	Pigs and poultry	—	0.25	0.25	0.25	0.25	0.4	0.4	0.4	0.4	0.4
	Forestry										
No. 9	Plantation development	—	0.8	0.8	0.8	0.8	0.8	0.8	1.0	1.0	1.0
No. 13	Forest industries	—	—	0.2	0.2	0.2	0.2	0.2	—	—	—
No. 10	Wildlife and tourism	—	2.0	2.0	2.0	2.0	2.0	—	—	—	—
No. 4	Agro-meteorology	0.2	0.2	0.2	0.2	0.2	—	—	—	—	—
	SUBTOTAL	6.0	14.55	16.75	18.15	21.05	30.70	34.40			
No. 16	Storage, handling, and processing	(Tentatively 10.0 for first phase)									
No. 17	Smallholder farm credit	(Tentatively 5.0 for first phase)									
No. 18	Rural water supplies and roads	(Tentatively 4.0 for first phase)									
No. 19	Studies	(Not costed)									

[1] Priorities are indicated by the disbursement schedules. However, if Project 1 could be prepared at an earlier date than Project 5, Project 1 might be given priority.

SOURCE: Mission estimates.

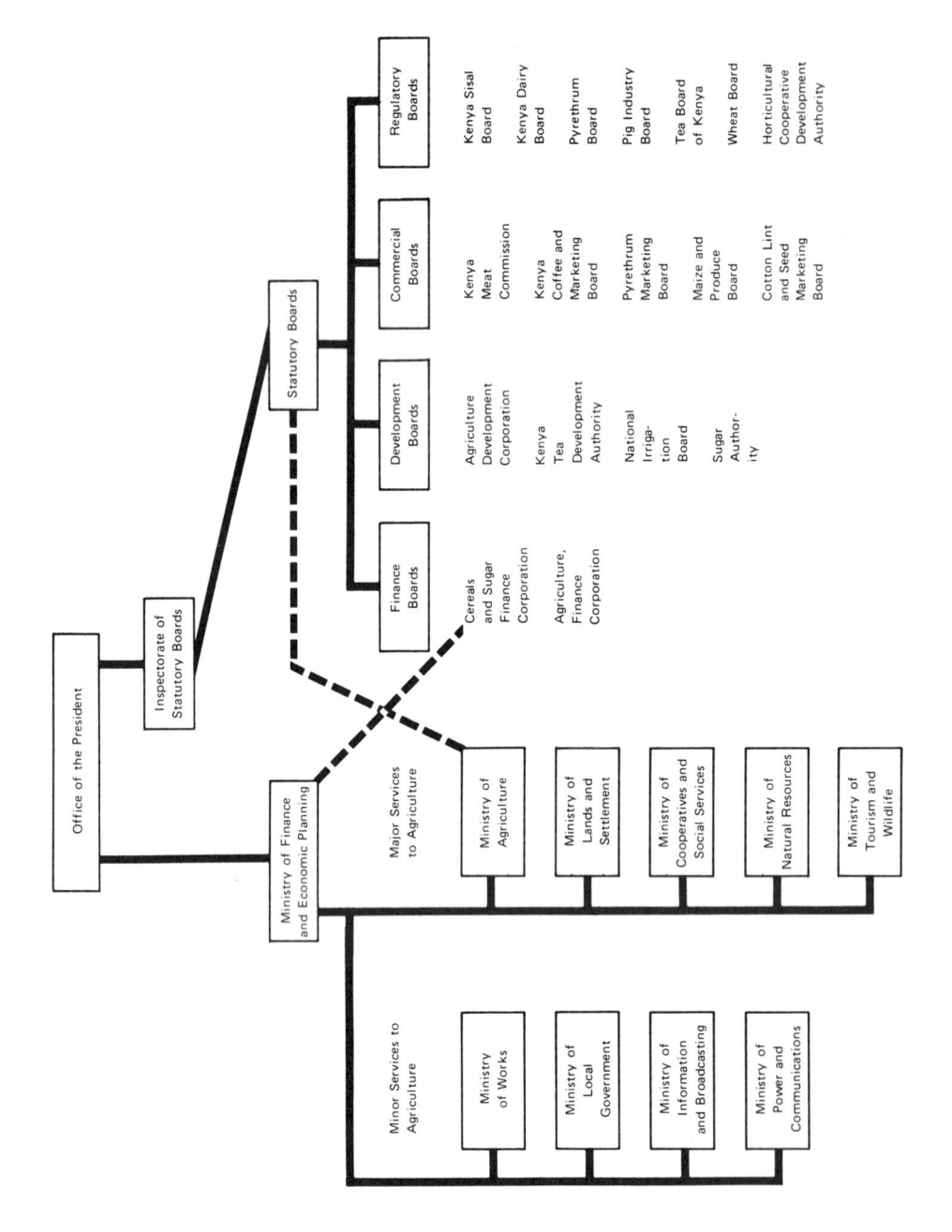

AGRICULTURAL SECTOR SURVEY

CHART: Present Organization of Public Services to Agriculture

- Office of the President
  - Inspectorate of Statutory Boards
    - Statutory Boards
      - Finance Boards
        - Cereals and Sugar Finance Corporation
        - Agriculture, Finance Corporation
      - Development Boards
        - Agriculture Development Corporation
        - Kenya Tea Development Authority
        - National Irrigation Board
        - Sugar Authority
      - Commercial Boards
        - Kenya Meat Commission
        - Kenya Coffee and Marketing Board
        - Pyrethrum Marketing Board
        - Maize and Produce Board
        - Cotton Lint and Seed Marketing Board
      - Regulatory Boards
        - Kenya Sisal Board
        - Kenya Dairy Board
        - Pyrethrum Board
        - Pig Industry Board
        - Tea Board of Kenya
        - Wheat Board
        - Horticultural Cooperative Development Authority
  - Ministry of Finance and Economic Planning
    - Major Services to Agriculture
      - Ministry of Agriculture
      - Ministry of Lands and Settlement
      - Ministry of Cooperatives and Social Services
      - Ministry of Natural Resources
      - Ministry of Tourism and Wildlife
    - Minor Services to Agriculture
      - Ministry of Works
      - Ministry of Local Government
      - Ministry of Information and Broadcasting
      - Ministry of Power and Communications

INDEX

Agricultural Development Corporation, 178, 476, 482, 498
Agricultural Finance Corporation, 361, 476, 486–88
Agricultural Information Center, 480
Agricultural Settlement Fund, 486
Agriculture: capital formation in, 34n, 188; constraints on, 35, 447, 464; and credit availability, 286, 364, 460, 471–72, 476, 482, 486–88, 501; development of, 20, 46, 49, 167, 193, 399–401, 403, 412–14, 447–48, 451–52, 458–61, 468–74, 477, 492–93, 495, 497, 500; employment in, 96–97, 106, 197–99, 292, 447, 450, 458; expenditures on, 451–52; and exports, 102–03, 395–97, 403, 449, 461, 464, 467, 484; foreign investment in, 44, 313, 395–96, 406, 413, 452, 473, 495–503; government expenditure on, 198–200, 395, 399, 414, 447, 458, 467, 485; growth of, 33–35, 365, 403, 448–50, 461; imports 95, 449, 463; income in, 25–26, 95, 105, 112, 184, 193, 197–98, 450–51, 468, 478; investment in, 29, 31, 34, 44, 200, 395–96, 398, 403, 413, 495–503; loans to, 360, 387, 495–503; and the macro-economic model, 90, 92, 94–96, 102, 106, 109, 112; marketing in, 483–86, 492; marketing boards, 163, 167, 460, 462, 465, 485–86; mechanization in, 481–82; planning in, 395–97, 399–401, 447–48, 458–60, 492–93, 495; and pricing, 39–40, 197, 200, 483–86; in private sector, 20–21, 395–96; processing in, 395–97, 465–66; productivity in, 15, 33–34, 97, 395, 397, 414, 458, 468, 472, 476; research in, 459, 461, 472, 479–81, 502–03; residual employment in, 96, 133; taxation of, 39, 188–89, 198, 281–83, 290, 460, 490; technical aid to, 421–22, 479–82, 502–03. *See also* Cooperatives; Farmers; Land; Livestock; Ministry of Agriculture; specific crops
Agro-business, 313–15
Agro-meteorological stations, 491, 496
Asian merchants, 3, 15, 184, 303, 305
Association of Manufacturers, 295
Assumptions, model. *See* Model, macro-economic

Balance of payments: deficits, 353, 360, 363, 371; deterioration in, 13, 27; gap, 25, 104, 106, 420; and the macro-economic model, 92, 99, 104, 106, 114; position, 9–10, 92, 288, 362; pressure, 6, 181; and trade, 104, 106, 279–81
Banking system, 20, 42, 168, 181–83, 274–75, 286, 309, 360
Barley, 462
Basic scenario: strategy projections in, 24, 28–30, 105–06, 108, 419, 420n
Beef, 466, 483
Borrowing: bank, 42, 181–82, 286, 360; commercial, 106–07; cost of, 42, 183, 274–75; domestic, 8, 42, 179–82, 309; government, 179–82. *See also* Debt, external
Bruton, H., 127
Budget, 203, 490; deficit, 8, 97, 173, 181; and fiscal reforms, 182–83; performance, 42, 165–68, 170–71, 173; and wage bill, 164, 172
Business, small, 403, 410–12

Capacity utilization, 94, 104n, 278–79
Capital expenditures, 100, 171–73, 181, 287
Capital flight, 300–01, 303–06
Capital formation, 43–44, 163, 306–09, 353
Capital-labor ratio, 97, 99–101, 127, 197

Carter, N. G., 368, 369
Cashew nuts, 449, 453, 466, 471
CBS. *See* Central Bureau of Statistics
Central Bank, 5, 8, 98, 103, 165–66, 168, 179, 181, 183, 296, 303–04, 308, 360, 362, 365
Central Bank of Kenya Act, 166n, 360
Central Bureau of Statistics, 490–91
Certificates of Approved Enterprise, 301, 392
Chenery, H. B., 117, 118, 368, 369
Civil service, 3, 11–12, 164n, 311, 397, 493, 495; and expatriate officers, 15, 492; salaries, 22, 171
Coffee, 20, 34, 102–03, 158, 197, 403, 449, 453, 465, 479–80, 484
Coffee Board, 460, 465
Common service corporations, 163
Consultants, 431, 433
Consultative Group for East Africa, 436–37
Controls, 285, 315; administration of, 297–98, 316; direct, 264; import, 9–10, 19, 27, 91, 107, 117, 267, 294–300, 303–06, 312; price, 297–300, 316; reduction in, 299–300, 306, 316
Cooperative Production Credit Scheme, 486
Cooperative savings movement, 361, 365
Cooperatives, agricultural, 458–60, 472, 476, 483–84, 486–88
Cotton, 449, 453, 464–65, 473, 480
Cotton Lint and Seed Marketing Board, 465, 486
County councils, 174–75, 192
Credit, 103, 418–20; to agricultural sector, 20, 42, 286, 364, 460, 482, 486–88, 501; commercial, 48, 106–07, 286, 360–61, 418; and the macro-economic model, 115; policy, 41–44, 274–75, 360; restrictions, 10, 309

527

Debt, external, 5, 32, 48, 106–07, 117, 165–66, 168, 182, 353, 389, 418
Debt servicing, 87, 89, 91–92, 102–04, 107, 132, 182, 371, 418–20
Deficit financing, 181
Department of Trade and Supplies, 294–96, 303–04
Depreciation allowances, 7, 93, 109, 129, 356, 358–59, 366
Development: constraints, 7, 43–44, 427–28; distribution of benefits of, 5, 22–23; goals, 24; mobilization of resources for, 5, 7–9, 13, 24, 41–44, 165, 182–83, 391; and the macro-economic model, 108–13, 420; philosophy, 17, 260; plans, 4, 264, 387, 389, 392, 402, 407–09; potential, 6, 408; of private sector, 260; of public sector, 21–23, 40–41; rate of, 10, 408; strategy, 24–32, 45, 49, 197, 315, 326–27, 495. *See also* Agriculture (development of)
Development Finance Company of Kenya, 178
Development Opportunity Team, 401–02
District Joint Loan Boards, 411
Donors, international, 44, 405–07, 420; availabilities of, 408, 502; bilateral, 413, 417–19, 425; cooperation of, 427, 429–30, 436–37; and domestic policy, 421; and financing, 424–29, 435; planned commitments, 422–23, 435; policies of, 424; problems for, 409, 434–37; project possibilities for, 495–503; requirements of, 428
DOT, 401–02
Duties. *See* Tariff, Taxes

EAC. *See* East African Community
East Africa Agriculture and Forestry Research Organization, 462, 479
East African Common Market, 4, 265
East African Community, 21, 102, 163–64, 179, 266–67, 269, 298, 300, 393, 403, 419, 491, 496

East African Development Bank, 265
East coast fever, 480
Eckstein, P., 117, 118
Ecology, 453–54
Economy: management of, 5–6, 104, 111, 387, 420; past performance, 5–6, 93–98; redirection of, 24, 420. *See also* Growth, economic; specific sectors
Education, 284; deficiencies in, 11–12; expenditures on, 37–38, 170–71, 175, 177, 201; planning for, 393, 404; relation to wages, 271–73; technical aid to, 422
Effective protection, 318–20, 322–25; Phelps–Wasow measurement of, 267–69, 273, 277, 279, 322
Elasticities: output-labor, 101; of substitution, 101, 127–28
Employment, 16, 96–97, 167; government strategy, 89, 195–97, 204; and the macro-economic model, 89–92, 96–97, 103–06, 110–12, 115–16, 127–29, 132–33; in private sector, 18, 196–97, 261–63; problems of, 96–97, 105, 284; programs to increase, 27, 194–96, 204–06, 447; in public sector, 22–23, 164, 195–96, 199, 201. *See also* Agriculture (employment in)
Enos, J. L., 367, 369–70
Entrepreneurship, 3, 11–12, 18–20, 39–40, 43, 45, 196, 260, 264, 286, 292, 314–15, 326, 387, 396, 411, 413
Estate duty. *See* Taxes
Ethiopia, 4
"European Areas." *See* "Scheduled Areas"
European Economic Community, 464
European managers, 3, 15
Exchange rate, 108, 128–29, 287; changes in, 28, 30, 87n, 98–100, 108, 288; devaluation of, 48, 88n, 99–100, 288; and the macro-economic model, 87n, 94, 98–100; overvalued, 14, 100, 197–98, 275, 290; as policy instrument, 26, 31–32, 94, 98, 283
Excise duty. *See* Taxes

Expatriate personnel, 3, 11–12, 15, 18, 39, 47, 105, 357–58, 431–33
Expenditures. *See* Government (expenditures)
Exports: agricultural, 102–03, 395–97, 403, 449, 461, 464, 467, 484; duties, 198; of industries, 35, 266; market for, 3, 265; and the macro-economic model, 91, 99, 101–05, 108, 114; structure of, 265–66, 267n; subsidy, 36, 196, 288–91; tariff, 15, 287–91
Extension service, 401, 414, 460, 462, 472, 476, 478–81, 491

Factor intensities, 275–78
Factor prices, 14, 26, 28–30, 39, 194–95, 200, 279; and the macro-economic model, 87n, 90, 94, 102, 108–13, 117, 127–29
Family planning, 454n, 460
Farmers, 20, 326, 357, 461; large-scale, 451, 473, 496; small-scale, 20, 412–13, 451, 462, 480; subsistence, 407, 414, 456, 480, 487, 502. *See also* Smallholders
Fiscal policy. *See* Government (fiscal policy)
Fisheries, 450, 467–68
Food and Agriculture Organization of the United Nations, 480, 486, 498
Foreign aid, 5, 10, 44, 49, 89, 110, 130, 132, 201, 313, 390, 395–96, 406, 413, 452, 473, 495–503; coordination of, 427, 429–30, 434–37; future requirements for, 419–20, 422–23, 495–503; increase in, 103, 417; multilateral, 418; requirements for, 417, 420; sectoral composition of, 421–23; sources of, 417; technical, 12, 43–44, 195, 387, 390, 398, 409, 412, 421–24, 427, 431–33, 435–36, 480, 502; terms of, 417, 419n, 424–27
Foreign capital inflow, 10, 27, 43–44, 89, 91, 101, 103–04, 108, 111, 132, 165–66, 168, 194, 306, 308–09, 354n, 367–71, 420
Foreign exchange, 128–29, 279; conservation of, 31, 295–97,

INDEX

305; constraint, 7, 9–10, 24, 48, 98, 112, 424; costs of, 101, 424–25; crises, 295, 299; expatriation of, 308, 310, 313; licensing of, 303; price of, 28, 32, 108, 280, 300, 424
Foreign Investment Protection Act of 1964, 308
Forestry, 449, 467, 479, 499, 501–02
Formal sector, urban, 3, 18–19, 46–47, 49, 257–59, 270, 283, 313; and policy reform, 316–17; standard, 326–28
Fuelwood, 467

Gap: analysis of, 89–92, 96–97, 104–13, 116–17, 371; residual, 48, 89–90, 102, 132. *See also* Balance of payments (gap); Resource (gap); Savings (gap); Trade (gap); Wages (gap)
GDI. *See* Gross domestic income
GDP. *See* Gross domestic product
GDS. *See* Gross domestic savings
Ghai, D. P., 270
GNS. *See* Gross national savings
General Superintendence Co., Ltd. (Switzerland), 303
Government: budgetary performance, 42, 165–68, 170–71, 173; consumption, 96; expenditures, 9–10, 16, 22–23, 37–38, 164, 168, 171–73, 175, 177, 191–93, 201–02, 206, 448, 451–52; fiscal policy, 7, 16, 42–43, 48, 168, 194, 201, 316–17, 421, 490; incentives to private investment, 308–09, 406–09; loans program, 177–78, 411–12; participation in private enterprise, 310–11; revenues, 7–9, 21, 92, 164, 168–69; salaries, 164, 172, 195–96, 201, 206; savings, 9, 91, 125–26, 168, 172–73, 182, 358–59, 368; securities, 181–82. *See also* Agriculture; Civil service; Local governments; Planning; Plans; individual Ministries
GPT. *See* Taxes (graduated personal)
Griffin, K. B., 367, 369–70
Gross domestic income, 355, 370

Gross domestic product, 5, 16, 90, 92, 94–97, 104–05, 107–08, 111, 120–22, 355
Gross domestic savings, 355–56
Gross national savings, 355–56, 370
Groundnuts, 453, 463, 473
Growth, economic, 5–6, 109–11, 113, 259, 353, 355, 365–66; and employment, 45–46; pattern of, 10, 25–38, 47, 89–90, 94, 108–09, 207, 353, 420; reform of process, 31–32, 38–41, 326–27; target of, 48, 89–91, 96, 105, 107, 371
— rate, 5–6, 89, 96, 101, 104–05, 194, 202, 355, 365, 371; and the macro-economic model, 117, 127; sectoral, 10, 92, 102, 388
Guaranteed Minimum Return program, 486

Haarelmo, T., 367
Harambee movement, 205, 387, 388n, 390n, 402
Harris, J. R., 19, 276, 283, 285n
HCDA, 397, 464, 486
Health services, 37, 175, 177, 192, 404, 457, 460
Horticultural Crops Development Authority, 397, 464, 486
Household consumption, 130–31. *See also* Savings (household)

ICDC, 308, 396, 410–11
ICOR. *See* Incremental capital-output ratio
Imbalances, internal and external, 116
Imports: control of, 9–10, 19, 27, 91, 107, 117, 267, 294–300, 303–06, 312; dependency on, 280, 449; duties, 18, 169, 190, 203; licensing of, 303–04; and the macro-economic model, 25, 89–92, 94–96, 99, 101–02, 104–05, 107–08, 114, 117, 120–22; of nonfactor services, 90, 95–96; overinvoicing of, 102, 300–06; of raw materials, 90, 95, 463; substitution, 6, 18, 35, 40–41, 94–95, 264–65, 267–69, 279–80, 299, 403; tariff, 18, 35, 39, 42, 203, 205, 267, 281, 287, 294, 298, 300, 306, 321

Income, 3, 110, 111; in agricultural sector, 25–26, 95, 105, 112, 184, 193, 197–98, 270, 450–51, 468, 478; distribution, 15–17, 22, 24, 28, 45–46, 95, 97, 99–100, 106, 108, 110, 167, 184–85, 191, 282, 284–85, 366, 448, 468, 470; ratio to investment, 353, 359; ratio to savings, 106, 108, 353, 355–57, 359, 369; taxes, 42–43, 90–91, 95, 169, 173, 185–89, 191, 203–04, 490
Incremental capital-output ratio, 29, 31, 90, 97, 277, 363; level of, 23, 90, 93–94, 102, 353; and the macro-economic model, 25–26, 90, 92–94, 101–02, 118–19; movements in, 13–14, 93–94, 101–02, 404n; sectoral, 21, 36, 94
Industrial capacity, 196, 267–69
Industrial and Commercial Development Corporation, 308, 396, 410–11
Industrial estates, 396, 410, 412
Industrial Protection Committee, 195
Industry: and consumer goods, 265; and import substitution, 264–67, 269, 403; infant, 290–91, 310, 395; planning for, 387, 403; protection of, 308–10; technical aid to, 421–23; viable, 268; and wages, 273–74, 277–78. *See also* Manufacturing
Inflation, 5; and the macro-economic model, 116–17; problems of, 6, 9, 27, 183; rate of, 97–98, 100, 103, 353, 358, 362–63
Informal sector, 19–20, 40, 257–58, 285–86, 327
Infrastructure, 22, 30, 33, 36–37, 92, 204, 387, 403, 429
Input/Output Table for Kenya, 90, 95, 104n
Insurance companies, 180–83
Interest: on government securities, 181–82; rates, 26, 28, 32, 41–42, 100, 109, 183, 275, 292–93, 358, 362–65, 488
International Coffee Organization, 465
International Labour Organisation/United Nations Development Programme report: and capacity utilization, 278; and

International Labour Organisation/United Nations Development Programme report (*Continued*)
employment growth, 16; and expatriate labor, 39; and external aid, 424; and foreign investment, 282n, 307–08, 311, 312, 313; and import substitution, 269; and informal sector, 18n, 20, 257, 285–86; and overinvoicing, 302; and role of urban wage rates, 14; and rural income, 26n, 450–51; and working poor, 5, 100
Investment, 353; in agriculture, 29, 31, 34, 44, 200, 395–96, 398, 403, 413, 495–503; allowance, 32, 87, 94, 196, 205; appraisals, 311–12; efficiency of, 24, 29, 363; foreign private, 10, 43–44, 194, 307–15; government program of, 8–9, 31, 36, 111, 165–67, 173, 182, 201, 204, 388–89, 402, 409, 421; incentive, 196, 311–12, 315; management of, 41–43, 387, 424; and the macro-economic model, 87, 90, 93–95, 103, 114; need for new types of, 403–09, 495–503; in private sector, 5, 36, 262, 313, 395, 398; ratio to income, 353, 359
Irrigation, 462, 464, 472–73, 477–78, 496–97, 502

Johnson, G. E., 272–73

Kenya African National Union, 4
Kenya Commercial Bank, 42
Kenya Farmers' Association, 459, 482, 486–87
Kenya Industrial Estates program, 310, 411
Kenya National Federation of Cooperatives, 487
Kenya National Trading Corporation, 294–95, 299–300
Kenya Seed Company, 482
Kenya Tea Development Authority, 178, 396–97, 460, 486
Kenya Tourist Development Corporation, 178–79
Kenyanization, 3, 6, 11–12, 15, 17, 39, 45, 47, 111, 113, 295, 305–06, 310–11, 313, 317, 326–28, 357, 432–33, 448
Kuznets, S., 353

Labor, 127–28; constraints, 11–12; force, 105–06, 410, 447; and the macro-economic model, 91–92, 97, 105, 113; productivity change, 92, 96–97, 103, 106, 108, 197; shortages, 11, 113, 435, 492–93; skilled, 5, 7, 10–12, 14, 16, 31, 38n, 41, 47, 97, 276–77, 314, 398, 401–02, 405, 408, 411–12, 432–33; supplementation, 431–33; unions, 195–96, 272–74, 292
Labor-capital ratio. *See* Capital-labor ratio
Labor-output ratio, 197, 275–78
Land, 414; availability, 447; distribution, 447, 471, 473–77; government, 454–56; potential of, 454; reform, 34–35; state, 473–74; tenure, 454–56, 474–77; transfer program, 455, 476, 486; trust, 454–56, 462, 475; use, 453, 460, 468–71, 473–77, 493, 500–01
Land and Farm Management Division (Ministry of Agriculture), 477–78
Land Use Committee, 460, 467, 476, 493
Livestock, 34, 449, 453, 460, 466, 471, 473, 484, 497–99, 501
Loans: agricultural, 360, 387, 495–503; allocation of, 360; 425; commitments, 417; government, 182, 411–12; improved conditions for, 428–30; short-term, 364; terms of, 418; tied, 424
Local Government Loans Authority, 177
Local governments, 163, 166–67; central government loans to, 177–78; expenditure pattern, 192; financial viability of, 176–78, 205; and planning, 393; as savers, 173–74

Macadamia, 466, 472, 497
Maize, 34, 449, 453, 459–61, 474, 479, 482, 484–85, 497
Maize and Produce Board, 484–85
Management, 47–48, 388, 406; manpower, 397n, 398, 401–02, 408; skills, 10–12, 308, 311, 314, 476–77
Manpower. *See* Labor
Manufacturing, 33, 94–95; and foreign investment, 306–10; growth of, 35–36, 102, 266–67, 317; priorities for, 403; protection of, 266–67, 269; small-scale, 36, 403, 410–12.
Mechanization in agriculture, 481–82
Migration, 283–84
Milk, 483
Millet, 462, 472
Mining, 33, 93, 95
Ministry of Agriculture, 295, 392, 394, 397, 413, 427, 451–52, 458–59, 476–77, 479–80, 482, 484–88, 490–93, 495, 503; Land and Farm Management Division, 477–78
Ministry of Commerce and Industry, 295, 392, 394–95
Ministry of Cooperatives and Social Services, 487
Ministry of Education, 393
Ministry of Finance and Planning, 37n, 44, 96, 101, 170, 185, 201n, 287n, 308, 356, 391–92, 401, 480, 493
Ministry of Health, 489
Ministry of Lands and Settlement, 475
Ministry of Power and Communications, 393
Ministry of Works, 37, 392, 429, 489–90
MOA. *See* Ministry of Agriculture
Model, macro-economic, 26, 30, 103, 105, 359, 369–71, 419; and agriculture, 90, 92, 94–96, 102, 106, 109, 112; algebraic description, 114–33; and analysis of the past, 93–103; assumptions, 26, 87–88, 90, 96, 101, 103, 105–06; and balance of payments, 92, 99, 104, 106, 114; data limitations in, 88; employment and, 89–92, 96–97, 103–06, 110–12, 115–16, 127–29, 132–33; and exports, 91, 99, 101–05, 108, 114; factor price and, 87n, 90, 94, 102, 108–13, 117, 127–29; flow diagram of, 157; foreign capital and, 89, 91, 101, 103–04, 111, 369–71; gap analysis,

INDEX

89–92, 96–97, 104–13, 116–17, 371; hypotheses, 87–88, 93–103; ICOR in, 25–26, 90, 92–94, 101–02, 118–19; and imports, 25, 89–92, 94–96, 99, 101–02, 104–05, 107–08, 114, 117, 120–22; and investment, 87, 90, 93–95, 103, 114; and manpower, 91–92, 97, 105, 113; nature of, 87–88; objectives of, 89–90, 359; operation of, 116–17; and policy alternatives, 89, 94, 104–10, 359; policy variables in, 98–104; and prices, 108, 110, 112–13, 115, 117, 127–29, 130–31; projections, 24–30, 87, 93, 97, 101, 104–10, 359; residual gap in, 419, 420n; and savings, 91, 96, 111, 123–26, 130–31, 359; structure, 26, 89–92; two-gap, 88n, 89, 97, 130–31; uses of, 24, 87–89, 371

Money supply, 92, 97–98, 115, 130, 360, 364

MOW. *See* Ministry of Works

MPB, 484–85

Municipal councils, 175–76, 203

National Commission on Education Objectives and Policies, 38

National Housing Corporation, 177

National Irrigation Board, 477–78, 496

National Social Security Fund, 180, 182, 183

Ndegwa Commission, 11, 22, 492–93

New Projects Committee, 308

NIB, 277–78, 496

NSSF, 180, 182, 183

Nutrition, 456–57, 489

Oilseeds, 34, 453, 462–63, 472

Open General License, 294, 296, 298, 303

Organization of African Unity, 4

Overinvoicing, 300–06, 310–11, 358

Pack, H., 276–77

Papanek, G. F., 367, 371

Parastatal bodies, 164–65, 167, 178–79, 183, 394–96, 398, 458–60, 479, 484, 493

Partnership for Productivity program, 410

Petroleum exports, 265–66

Phelps, M. G., 267–69, 273, 277, 279, 322

Pineapples, 395–96, 449, 464

Planning: capacity, 394, 403; central government, 391–93, 398, 401–02, 405–09, 424, 428–29; district development, 402; and economies of scale, 398–401; information for, 490–91; macro-economic, 387–88, 393–94; micro-economic, 388, 398, 410; priorities, 393, 408, 459; program, 400, 412; sectoral, 387–88, 391–94, 399, 428–29. *See also* Agriculture; Development

Plans, government, 24–26, 49, 89–90, 101, 104, 167, 198, 312, 359, 362, 392, 429, 448, 475, 477

Population: growth, 5, 194n, 454, 471; pressure, 34, 49–50, 447, 454, 469–70, 473, 476, 478

Post Office Savings Bank, 42, 180–81, 365

Poverty, 3, 5, 104; attack on, 46, 90, 193; index, 25–27, 30, 105, 108–09; and the macro-economic model, 115–16; problems of, 16–17, 100, 108–12, 326, 404; rural, 3, 33, 451, 458. *See also* Working poor

Power, J. H., 289

Power facilities, 36

Preferred scenario: strategy projections in, 30, 34, 92, 420. *See also* Preferred strategy

Preferred strategy, 29–30, 38, 45, 47–49, 110

Prices: agricultural, 39–40, 197, 200, 483–86; of consumer goods, 89, 371; controls on, 297–300, 316; distortions in, 14–15, 111, 196, 199, 293; export, 91, 99; factor, 14, 26, 28–30, 39, 87n, 90, 94, 102, 108–13, 117, 127–29, 194–95, 200, 279; future rises of, 206; import, 91, 102; and incentives, 316; and the macroeconomic model, 108, 110, 112–13, 115, 117, 127–29, 130–31; product, 14; shadow, 40, 405; signals in, 19, 31, 39–40, 395; stability of, 97–98, 484–86; system of, 18, 39, 44, 404–05

Private sector, 257–59; in agriculture, 20–21, 395–96; and development, 260; as employment source, 18, 196–97, 261–63; government influence on, 18–19, 259–60; and investment, 5, 36, 262, 313, 395, 398; manipulating behavior of, 38–40, 44, 258–59; performance of, 260–63; planning in, 394–95, 398; resource use by, 17–21, 388; urban formal, 3, 18–19, 46–47, 49, 257–59, 270, 283, 313; urban informal, 19–20, 40, 257–58, 285–86, 327

Productivity, 5, 15, 33–34; in agriculture, 15, 33–34, 97, 395, 397, 414, 458, 468, 472, 476; of investment, 93–94; labor, 92, 96–97, 103, 106, 108, 197

Project Identification and Evaluation Unit, 391

Projects: administration, 408; costs, 424–29, 435; definition of, 405–06; design, 403, 406–08, 495; evaluation, 399, 406, 493; financing, 424–30; identification, 389–90, 398, 401–02, 409, 428–29; management, 401, 408; methodological problems with, 404–06; possibilities, 495–503; preparation, 389–90, 394, 399, 408, 492, 495, 502; replication, 400, 410–14; visibility, 407. *See also* Donors, international

Public corporations, 179

Public sector: capacity of, 38; and development, 21–23, 40–41; employment by, 22–23, 164, 195–96, 199, 201; expenditure program, 22–23, 36, 164, 191–93; financial indicators, 164–65; macro-economic indicators, 163–64; resource use by, 21–23, 165

Public services, 167, 191–93, 195, 526; and minimum package programs, 412–14

Pulses, 34, 449, 453, 462, 472

Pyrethrum, 20, 266, 449, 453, 479–80, 484

Pyrethrum Board, 460, 486

Quota system, 298–300

Racial inequalities, 184
Rahman, M. A., 367
Rating Act, 177
Registered Land Act of 1963, 475
Reimer, R., 322, 325
Remple, H., 284
Resources, 96; allocation of, 390, 403; available, 7–12, 89, 96, 447; constraint on, 6, 13, 24–25, 28, 30–31, 33, 48–49, 94, 326, 353, 360, 403; gap between GDP and GNP, 10, 26–28, 48, 91, 92, 102–03, 106–10, 112–13, 182, 370–71; inefficient use of, 19, 32; mobilization of, 5, 7–9, 13, 24, 41–44, 165, 182–83, 391; in private sector, 17–21, 388; in public sector, 21–23, 165; residual gap in, 48, 89–90, 102, 132
Revenues. *See* Government (revenues)
Rice, 449, 462
RIDC, 411–12
Roads, 36–37, 429, 489–90, 501
Rural Afforestation Scheme, 467
Rural development, 198–99, 412–13, 472–73, 491
Rural Industrial Development Centre, 411–12

Savings: business, 91, 124–25, 356, 359, 368; corporate, 7, 358; domestic, 7–8, 21, 41–42, 104, 165, 354n, 355–59, 368–69; and foreign investment, 111, 313–14; gap, 89, 97; government, 9, 91, 125–26, 168, 172–73, 182, 358–59, 368; household, 7, 26, 41–42, 91, 96, 104, 106, 108, 123–24, 130–31, 356–59; mobilization, 5, 353, 361, 364–65; and the macro-economic model, 91, 96, 111, 123–26, 130–31, 359; performance, 8, 32, 96, 355–56, 362; propensities, 353–55, 357, 363, 371; ratio to income, 106, 108, 353, 355–57, 359, 369
Sawmills, 467
Scenario. *See* Basic scenario; Preferred scenario

"Scheduled Areas," 403, 455–56
Scott, M. FG., 133, 269, 281, 284, 358n
Seed program, 482
Self-help movement. *See* Harambee movement
Services. *See* Public Services
SIL, 294–98
Sisal, 102, 197, 449
Small Business Administration, 395
Smallholders, 34–35, 198, 403, 414, 449–51, 456, 458–60, 463, 465, 470–71, 480–84, 486–90, 492, 495, 497, 500–03
Social security, 180, 196n
Social services, 22–23, 31, 33, 37–38, 172, 192, 201, 387–88, 393, 404
Soil conservation, 478, 491
Soil Conservation Service, 478
Somalia, 4
Sorghum, 462, 472
Special Rural Development Program, 198–99, 412–13, 472–73, 491
Specific Import License, 294–98
SRDP. *See* Special Rural Development Program
Standard International Trade Classification, 295, 297
Sugar, 34, 449, 452, 463–64, 502
Survey of Kenya, 475

Tanganyika, 4
Tanzania, 9, 265–66, 294
Tariff, 15, 35, 321; EAC, 267; export, 198; external, 39; import, 18, 169, 190, 203; protective, 42, 294, 298; reform, 203, 205, 300, 306; revenue from, 281; uniform, 42, 287–91, 300
Taxes: agricultural, 39, 188–89, 198, 281–83, 290, 460, 490; buoyancy of, 170; and capital gains, 185, 191, 204; common external, 289n; consumption, 169, 185–86, 189–92, 202; direct, 43, 203; East African transfer system of, 268; equity in, 184–91; estate, 185–86; evasions of, 176, 188–89, 300–03, 306; excise, 189–91, 202–03; exemptions to, 173, 186–87, 191; on exports, 279, 490; and foreign investment, 308–13; government effort to increase, 168–70; graduated personal, 166, 169, 175–76, 203, 205; income, 42–43, 90–91, 95, 169, 173, 185–89, 191, 203–04, 490; indirect, 42–43, 169, 189–90, 202–03; and investment allowances, 18, 308; land, 43, 178, 198, 490; on personal services, 189–90; property, 43, 177, 185–86, 191, 204; rates of, 16, 177, 186–87, 301–02; reform of, 167, 169, 173, 182, 191, 202–04, 287, 311–13; sales, 9, 42, 169, 173, 189–90, 202–04, 289–90; structure of, 9, 167, 173, 178, 184–85, 188, 191, 193, 196, 204; value-added, 289; on wealth, 43, 185–86, 191
Tea, 20, 34, 102–03, 159, 396–97, 403, 449, 453, 465–66, 479–80, 484
Tobacco, 473
Todaro, M. P., 19, 276, 283, 284, 285n
Tourism, 9, 48, 266, 290, 307, 317, 392, 449, 468, 500, 502
Tractors, 481
Trade: and balance of payments, 279–81, 294; controls, 9–10, 19, 27, 91, 107, 117, 267, 294–300, 303–06, 312; deficit, 3, 9; gap, 89, 97, 101, 104–05; and the macro-economic model, 89, 91, 101, 104–05; policy, 6, 39, 104, 264, 267–69, 275, 277–79, 287–88, 293, 306, 309–10, 317, 490; protective system, 18–20, 267–69, 294–300, 306; structure, 265; 306, 309–10; terms of, 102, 458. *See also* Exports; Imports
Trade unions, 195–96, 272–74, 292
Training: assistance in, 432–33, 480–81, 491, 493
Transfer payments, 206–07
Treaty for East African Cooperation, 4
Tribalism, 455, 468, 470, 475

Uganda, 4, 9, 265–66, 294, 360
Unemployment, 5–6, 15, 167, 285; and the macro-economic

INDEX

model, 89, 96–97, 100, 108; problem, 96, 171, 194–95, 326; remedies, 89, 199, 284; and wage gap, 283. *See also* Employment (problems of)

United Nations Development Programme, 436, 498. *See also* International Labour Organisation/United Nations Development Programme report

United Nations Industrial Development Organization, 392

Wages, 109, 128; in agriculture, 450; and education, 271–73; freeze on, 195; gap, 22, 271, 273–74, 283–86, 317; government expenditures on, 22, 164, 171–72, 201, 206; growth of real, 28, 46, 171, 271, 292, 317; legislation, 14, 17n, 272; policy, 291–92; and productivity, 275–78; rates of, 14, 17–18, 32, 100–01, 171, 201, 206, 271–74, 277–78, 292–93, 394; reduction of, 195, 290; in small-scale business, 410; structure of, 16, 195, 269–74, 293

Wasow, D., 267–69, 273, 277, 279, 322

Water conservation, 478–79, 492

Water Department, 477, 489

Water supply, 404, 457, 459–60, 489, 501
Wattle bark, 449
Wealth: concentration of, 16–17, 46
Weather forecasting, 491, 496
Weisskopf, T. E., 367
Wheat, 34, 449, 460–62, 480
Wheat Board, 462, 482, 485
Wildlife, 466, 500, 502
Winston, G. C., 127
Working poor, 96–97, 105, 109–10, 194, 293
World Bank: lending to Kenya, 418, 419n, 429n

Zarembka, P., 127